TREASURE ACT 1996
The Treasure Annual Report is presented to Parliament pursuant to Section 12 to the Treasure Act 1996

Treasure Annual Report 2007

and

Portable Antiquities Scheme Annual Report 2007

November 2009

PORTABLE ANTIQUITIES AND TREASURE

ANNUAL REPORT 2007

Published by the Department of Portable Antiquities and Treasure, British Museum
ISBN 978-0-9563795-0-4 paperback
ISBN 978-0-9563795-1-1 download

CONTENTS

Foreword	4
Preface	6
Key points	8
Introduction	11
Learning and outreach	14
Research and publication	25

Catalogue

Artefacts

Stone Age	35
Bronze Age	39
Iron Age	58
Roman	70
Early Medieval	92
Medieval	118
Post-Medieval	141

Coins

Iron Age	166
Roman	173
Early Medieval	192
Medieval	196
Post-Medieval	209

References	215

Indexes

Table of Treasure cases 2007	227
Update on 2005 and 2006 Treasure cases	256
Index by findspot	257
Index by acquiring museum	263

Recording finds	265
Contacts and organisations	285
Illustrations	291

I am very pleased to introduce the first joint Portable Antiquities Scheme and Treasure Annual Report. This combined report will provide a single reference for all the most important archaeological finds in England, Wales and Northern Ireland.

The discovery of archaeological objects is always enormously exciting and interesting for all those involved as the objects offer an invaluable and irreplaceable way of understanding our past. The Treasure Act 1996 enables treasure objects to be acquired by museums so that everyone can benefit from being able to see them and learn about our history. There are many people involved in the discovery of these objects but I would like to start by thanking those who have voluntarily recorded their finds through the Portable Antiquities Scheme or reported them under the Treasure Act. This has resulted in many new archaeological sites being discovered and has allowed important new research to be conducted which should add to our understanding of our past. The role of the Portable Antiquities Scheme Finds Liaison Officers who advise people on their legal obligations, inform them about the Treasure process, couriering finds and writing reports on them, should also be commended.

In 2007, 747 treasure finds were reported and a further 66,311 archaeological finds were recorded by the Portable Antiquities Scheme. 41 (18%) finders or landowners donated their treasure finds to museums and waived their rights to a reward and I would like to thank all those people who have made such donations. Museums often have to make difficult decisions about which finds to obtain for their collections and these generous donations are extremely welcome to the museum community. Many other archaeological items are acquired with financial help from the various funding bodies – in particular, the Art Fund, the V&A/ MLA Purchase Grant Fund, the Headley Museums Treasure Acquisition Scheme, the National Memorial Fund, and the Heritage Lottery Fund. Their help contributes to the wonderful variety of objects in our museums and has enabled over 1,700 events, including talks and exhibitions attended by many people.

An important part of the treasure process is the valuation of the items of treasure which is necessary before a museum is able to acquire them. I am always grateful for the independent advice provided to me by the Treasure Valuation Committee (TVC) and would like to pay tribute to all the Committee members and their chairman, Norman Palmer. The Committee is expertly supported in this work by a panel of valuers and the Treasure Valuation Committee Secretariat.

From recent media coverage it is clear that the discovery of archaeology, and in particular treasure, captures the interest of the nation in a positive way. The recent discovery of the Staffordshire Hoard is an outstanding example and offers an incredible and unique insight into Anglo-Saxon times. Finds like this tell us about our past and help to define our sense of identity. The quality and quantity of the Hoard is exceptional and, as scholars study it, we look forward to discovering more about this treasure and how it came to be left in Staffordshire soil.

The changes to the Treasure Act proposed in the Coroners and Justice Bill offer a unique opportunity for the system to be improved and for cases to be dealt with quickly. My Department will continue to work with all those involved with the Portable Antiquities Scheme and the Treasure Act to make sure that the system is as efficient and effective as possible, and to ensure that the archaeological objects themselves and information about how and where they were found is available to as many people as possible.

Margaret Hodge

Margaret Hodge
Minister for Culture and Tourism
November 2009

The Museums, Libraries & Archives Council (MLA) and the British Museum have been key supporters of the Portable Antiquities Scheme and the Treasure Act (1996) since their inception, and therefore very much welcome the Minister's kind words in her foreword.

The MLA and the British Museum jointly chair the Portable Antiquities Advisory Group, a consortium of bodies that helps take the project forward, and we are extremely grateful to the members of that group who have worked hard to ensure the continuing success of the PAS, especially following the uncertainty after the last Spending Review settlement. This success was highlighted by the 2008 *Review of the Portable Antiquities Scheme*, which, as the Minister has said, shows that the PAS makes a valuable contribution to museums, as well as to the historic environment sector. It is in recognition of the overarching potential of the Scheme to impact on the work of museums and their audiences, that following the 2008 Review it was agreed to support the regional elements of the Scheme through the MLA's Renaissance programme, and to form the Portable Antiquities Management Group. This aims to complement the work of the Advisory Group, and explore synergies between the work of the Scheme and museums more generally, and in particular with other projects being delivered through MLA's Renaissance programme.

Since the PAS was established in 1997, the standards it sets itself, and those that record with it, have risen. It is now common practice for finders of archaeological objects to have them properly recorded with the PAS or reported under the Treasure Act; the *Code of Practice for Responsible Metal Detecting*, which was endorsed by the main archaeological bodies and metal-detecting and landowner organisations, provides an agreed statement on best practice. In the first year of the Scheme (1997/8), 3,125 finds were recorded on its database; the total in 2007 was 66,311. Likewise, in the first full year of the Treasure Act (1998), 201 finds were reported as Treasure, while the total in 2007 is 747. Similarly, in 1997/8 the proportion of PAS finds recorded to at least a 6-figure National Grid Reference (100m^2) was 56%; in 2007 it was 90%. These are significant increases, which also demonstrate the Scheme's educational benefits.

It is very welcome that in 2007 the PAS organised 1,761 outreach events that were attended by at least 33,298 people, including 11,089 children, and this work complements that of both the MLA's Renaissance programme and British Museum's Partnership UK programme. In 2011–2013, the British Museum is planning an exhibition about the PAS – *Our nation's history told* – that will tour Exeter, Lincoln, Norwich, Newcastle and Wales.

PREFACE

Besides educating people about archaeology and finds, and giving people the opportunity to get involved, the data generated by the PAS has great research potential, and indeed it is the case that many researchers are making use of it. 460 people currently have full access to PAS data for research purposes and five students are undertaking collaborative Arts and Humanities Research Board-funded PhDs analysing PAS data. The results of this work are transforming our understanding of the past, highlighting new sites and the relationships between peoples over time. All this data is made publicly available on the PAS website – wwww.finds. org.uk – which is currently being redeveloped to increase functionality and improve the user experience.

The Minister has already highlighted the mutually beneficial relationship between the PAS and the Treasure Act, and it is very welcome that museums are increasingly able to acquire Treasure finds, thanks to the generosity of the various funding bodies, and also due to increasing numbers of finders and landowners who donate their share of a reward. The fact that museums are able to acquire such finds not only enables the public to enjoy them, but it ensures the objects are available for future research. The PAS is currently working with English Heritage to explore options for cataloguing collections of finds found before the PAS was established that finders are willing to donate to museums. This highlights the need for finders to make appropriate provision for their finds in the future, if they wish them to have maximum public benefit.

Museums are increasingly acquiring non-Treasure finds recorded by the PAS. Notable examples (all Roman) acquired over the past few years include the Staffordshire Moorlands pan (WMID-3FE965), a horse and rider figurine from Cambridgeshire (SF-99E3E4) and the Winterton pan (NLM-F50443). It is therefore welcome that the Headley Fund has extended its acquisition scheme to include non-Treasure finds, and this will almost certainly benefit many regional and local museums.

We would also like to thank the Headley Trust for £148,000 over three years to fund interns to work with the PAS. The aim of these posts is to give people who want to develop a career in museums and/or archaeology the opportunity to acquire new skills and expertise, and also make a valuable contribution to the recording work of the PAS. The first interns are being appointed in Cambridgeshire & Essex, Hampshire & Wiltshire, London & Sussex, the North West, Suffolk, the West Midlands and Yorkshire.

Looking to the future, both the MLA and the British Museum are committed to ensuring the PAS continues to be a success and agreeing a way how best it can be best supported and delivered, and in this respect we very much value the Government's support to date.

Roy Clare, Chief Executive Officer, Museums, Libraries & Archives Council

Neil MacGregor, Director, British Museum

The main achievements of the Portable Antiquities Scheme (PAS) and the Treasure Act 1996 in 2007 can be summarised as follows:

The extent of the PAS and the Department of Portable Antiquities and Treasure: A network of 37 Finds Liaison Officers (FLOs) covers the whole of England and Wales. Their work is co-ordinated and supported by a central unit of a Head and Deputy Head, Resources Manager, Education Co-ordinator, ICT Adviser (all based in the Department of Portable Antiquities and Treasure, British Museum) and six Finds Advisers. A Treasure Registrar and four Assistant Treasure Registrars are also employed as part of the Department of Portable Antiquities and Treasure. In 2007, at least 101 people volunteered with the PAS.

Spending Review 2007: Following an unfavourable settlement for the MLA in the Comprehensive Spending Review 2007, the PAS budget for 2008–9 was frozen at the current level (£1.3 million). In November 2008, the MLA announced that as a result of a Review of the PAS, it would restore funding for 2009–11. Currently, the Scheme is funded until the end of March 2011.

Recognition of success: In November 2008 *A Review of the Portable Antiquities Scheme* was published. Its author, Kate Clark, found that the PAS was efficient and cost effective. Among a series of recommendations made, it was suggested there were synergies between the PAS and the MLA's Renaissance programme that could be explored further, and more could be done to develop recording capacity by using volunteers and promoting self recording among finders.

Finds recorded through the PAS: A further 66,311 archaeological objects have been recorded on the PAS finds database during 2007, some of which are illustrated in this report. Of these, at least 84% have been discovered by people while out metal-detecting; the rest have been found by other means.

Finds reported Treasure: There were a further 747 cases of Treasure in 2007 (some of these cases include multiple numbers of finds), which is an 11% increase on 2006, and there has been a continuing increase since the Act became law. However, this report also shows that the increase has been most notable since 2003, when the PAS was expanded to cover the whole of England and Wales, and there has been an average increase of almost 194% in the reporting of potential Treasure finds. Most cases (92.4%) have been discovered while metal-detecting.

Acquisition of Treasure: 303 new Treasure finds have been, or are being, acquired by museums, 301 have been disclaimed, 125 were deemed not to be Treasure and 18 cases are still to be determined. Table of

Treasure Cases 2007 (p.227–255) gives the outcomes of all 2007 Treasure cases.

As in previous years, museums have received help to enable them to acquire Treasure from the Art Fund (case numbers), V&A/MLA Purchase Grant Fund (case numbers), the Headley Museums Treasure Acquisition Fund (case numbers), the National Heritage Memorial Fund (case numbers) and the Heritage Lottery Fund (case numbers), without which many finds would not have been acquired.

Donations: In 2006, the DCMS launched a new initiative to encourage finders and landowners to consider waiving their rights to rewards to enable museums to acquire Treasure finds, giving certificates signed by the Minister to those who did so. In 2007 there were 53 (7%) cases where one or both parties waived their rewards.

Findspot information: Almost 92% of PAS finds have been recovered from cultivated land, where they are susceptible to plough damage and artificial and natural corrosion processes. 90% of finds are now being recorded to the nearest 100m^2 (a six-figure National Grid Reference) or better, and almost 50% of all finds are being recorded to the nearest 10m^2 (an eight-figure National Grid Reference).

Finds data: The finds data generated by the PAS is made available to Historic Environment Records (HERs) – the key record holders for information about the historic environment – and is published on the Scheme's website: www.finds.org.uk. A protocol has been agreed on the transfer of PAS data to HERs, which 54 HERs (more than two-thirds) have now signed.

New sites discovered: Many important new archaeological sites have been discovered as a result of the finds recorded by the FLOs or reported Treasure. Research undertaken by Adam Daubney (Lincolnshire FLO) shows that since the PAS was established, its data has added knowledge to 328 'sites' in Lincolnshire, of which 53% were previously unknown.

Research: New research is showing that PAS data has the potential to radically alter our understanding of the historic environment and further archaeological knowledge. At time of publication, 460 people, including academics and professionals, have full access to PAS data for research purposes. Five students are currently undertaking collaborative Arts and Humanities Research Board-funded PhDs analysing PAS data (see the Research and publication section for further details). Besides these, it is known that 14 other PhDs, 26 MA dissertations and 12 undergraduate research projects have used PAS data in 2007.

Publications: Several publications associated with the work of the PAS have appeared in the period of this report, including the Portable Antiquities sections of Britannia volume 38, Medieval Archaeology volume 51, and Post Medieval Archaeology volume 41.

Outreach: 1,761 outreach events, including talks, finds days and exhibitions, were organised in 2007; these were attended by at least 33,298 people, including 11,089 children. At least 258 articles about the work of the PAS were published or broadcast, including academic publications, articles in the popular press, and reports on television and radio. As part of National Archaeology Week 2007, the PAS was involved in 68 events, attended by at least 4,193 adults and 3,040 children, and its Finds Liaison Officers (FLOs) examined more than 2,331 finds.

Liaison: During 2007 the FLOs maintained regular contact with 161 metal-detecting clubs, attending 728 club meetings, and also liaised with local archaeological and history groups. Members of the PAS attended at least 831 other meetings to promote the Scheme and its aims.

Social inclusion: In 2006, a socio-economic analysis of postcode data showed that 47% of people recording finds with the PAS (since 1997) were from groups C2, D and E, which compares favourably to visitors to museums (31 per cent). [1]

Website: There were 295,567 visits by 165,118 unique visitors to the PAS website – www.finds.org.uk – during the period of this report. At the time of publication, the online database allows public access to 404,706 objects within 269,474 records, and 216,826 images.

Heritage protection: In 2007, the Department of Portable Antiquities and Treasure at the British Museum continued to monitor eBay for finds of unreported Treasure; intelligence on 144 cases was passed to the police.

Since September 2007, the Department has been an expert advisor on the Export Licencing of metal-detected finds, and in the period of this report approved 312 licences, of which more that 85% were exported outside the European Union.

The Department has been working with the Association of Chief Police Officers (ACPO) in the hope of developing guidance for local police forces on how to tackle heritage crime, such as illicit metal-detecting. The PAS works closely with relevant colleagues in HM Customs & Revenue and the MLA Exporting Unit, and since February 2007 Michael Lewis (Deputy Head) has been seconded (part-time) as a Special Police Constable with the Metropolitan Police Service's Art and Antiques Unit.

[1] 10.5 million people visited museums in 2005, of which 30.6% were C2, D and Es (Great Britain Target Group Index, Spring 2006).

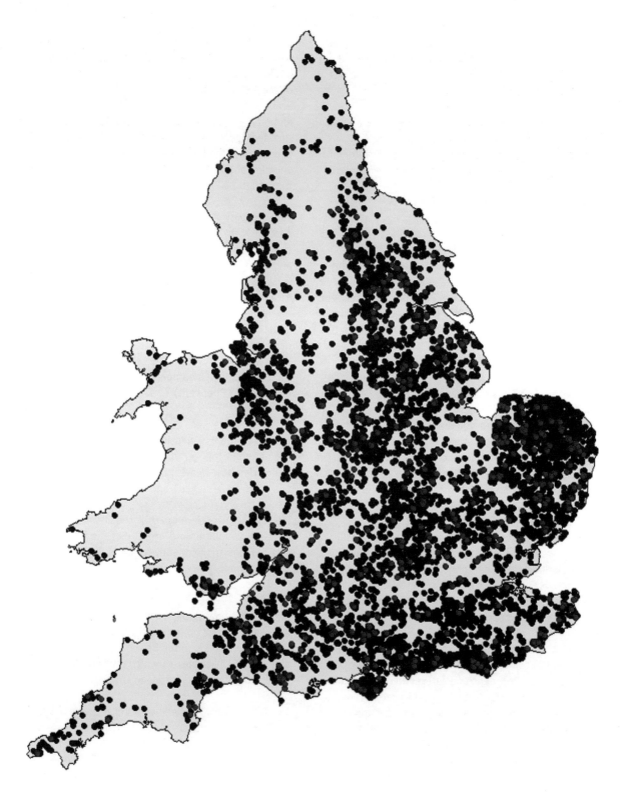

● 2007 PAS records
● 2007 Treasure cases

The Portable Antiquities Scheme (PAS)

The PAS is a voluntary scheme to record archaeological objects found by members of the public. It also has an important educational role, enabling children and adults alike to learn about archaeology, get involved and bring the past to life.

Every year, many thousands of archaeological objects are discovered, most of these by metal-detector users, but also by people while out walking, gardening, or going about their daily work. These objects offer an important and irreplaceable way of understanding our past. The PAS offers the only proactive and comprehensive mechanism for systematically recording such finds for public benefit. This data is made available to Historic Environment Records (HERs) and is published on the PAS website: www.finds.org.uk. This data is an important educational resource that can be used and enjoyed by anyone (not just archaeologists) interested in learning more about the past.

Organisation

In the period of this report, 37 Finds Liaison Officers (FLOs) covering the whole of England and Wales were employed in the work of the PAS. FLOs are based with local 'host' partner organisations who manage them on a day-to-day basis. Their work is co-ordinated and supported by a Central Unit of a Head and Deputy Head, Resources Manager, Education Co-ordinator, ICT Adviser, all based in the Department of Portable Antiquities and Treasure at the British Museum, and six Finds Advisers, of which all but one are based elsewhere. In 2007, 101 volunteers also provided an invaluable contribution to the work of the PAS.

Since 1 April 2006, the PAS has been managed by the British Museum on behalf of the Museums, Libraries & Archives Council (MLA), and funded by the Department of Culture, Media and Sport (DCMS) and local partners.[2]

The work of the Scheme is guided by the Portable Antiquities Advisory Group, which meets biannually. Members of the group are the Association of Local Government Archaeological Officers, the British Museum, the Council for British Archaeology, the Country Business and Landowners Association, the Department for Culture, Media and Sport, English Heritage, the Federation of Independent Detectorists, the Institute of Archaeology (University College, London), the MLA, the National Council for Metal Detecting, the National Farmers Union, National Amgueddfa Cymru – National Museum Wales, Natural England, the Society of Museum Archaeologists and the Royal Commission on the Ancient and Historical Monuments of Wales.

[2] Before this date (since April 2003) the PAS was funded by the HLF, through the MLA.

As a result of the Review of the PAS (published September 2008), a Portable Antiquities Management Group was formed to provide a clear distinction between the management of the PAS and policy relating to portable antiquities-related issues, such as environmental stewardship schemes, metal-detecting rallies, and illicit metal-detecting. The first meeting of this group, chaired by the MLA with representatives from the British Museum, the PAS and Renaissance, took place in March 2009.

Terms of reference
Portable Antiquities Management Group
The Portable Antiquities Scheme is run by the British Museum on behalf of the MLA. The British Museum has ownership of the Scheme and the role of the Management Group is to assist the British Museum to ensure the effective and efficient delivery of the Portable Antiquities Scheme in accordance with its aims. Management Group will oversee the long-term planning and funding of the Scheme and advocate its value to stakeholders. The Management Group will have an overview of budgets and management in line with the Renaissance performance framework; it is for the British Museum to manage the budget. The Management Group will not be concerned with policy issues relating to portable antiquities matters which are matters for the Advisory Group. The Management Group will be chaired by the MLA and will consist of representatives from the MLA, the British Museum and the Renaissance programme.

Portable Antiquities Advisory Group
The Advisory Group will consist of representatives from national stakeholders (listed above) with an interest in portable antiquities and will discuss and provide advice and guidance on portable antiquities matters, including offering advice to the Management Group. It will develop policy and best practice in relation to the discovery and recording of finds made by the public and to foster co-operation between archaeologists, museum professionals and finders.

Aims of the Portable Antiquities Scheme
The Portable Antiquities Scheme is a partnership project which records archaeological objects found by the public in order to advance our understanding of the past.

In order to do this, the Scheme:
- promotes the maximum public interest and benefit from the recovery, recording and research of portable antiquities
- promotes best practice by finders/landowners and archaeologists/museums in the discovery, recording and conservation of finds made by the public

- in partnership with museums and others, raises awareness among the public, including young people, of the educational value of recording archaeological finds in their context and facilitate research in them
- creates partnerships between finders and museums/archaeologists to increase participation in archaeology and advance our understanding of the past
- supports the Treasure Act, and increase opportunities for museums to acquire archaeological finds for public benefit

The PAS is run by the British Museum on behalf of the Museums, Libraries & Archives Council and works through 33 principal partners which employ staff, and many more local partners which contribute to each of the posts. There is a network of 37 Finds Liaison Officer posts, based in museums and county councils throughout England and Wales, six National Finds Advisers and a team of four at the British Museum. The data gathered by the Scheme is published on an online database – www.finds.org.uk

In order to fulfil the aims of the Scheme, staff:
- maintain an online database and promote it as a resource for education and research
- hold outreach events such as finds days, attend metal-detecting club meetings, and give talks to national and local groups and societies
- facilitate displays of finds recorded by the Scheme in museums and elsewhere
- help finders to fulfil their obligations under the Treasure Act
- publish an annual report and other publications in print and online

Treasure

Under the Treasure Act 1996, finders have a legal obligation to report all finds of potential Treasure; for a summary see www.finds.org.uk/treasure or the leaflet *Advice for Finders of Archaeological Objects, Including Treasure*. The process allows a national or local museum to acquire such finds for public benefit. If this happens a reward is paid, which is normally shared equally between the finder and landowner. The reward is fixed at the full market value of the find, determined by the Secretary of State on the advice of an independent panel of experts – the Treasure Valuation Committee. Although Treasure finds account for a relatively small proportion of archaeological finds found in England and Wales by the public, the FLOs play an increasingly important role in the effective operation of the Act, advising finders of their legal obligations, providing advice on the process, and writing reports on Treasure finds.

Organisation

Much of the administration of the Treasure process is undertaken via the Department of Portable Antiquities and Treasure, British Museum, which employs a Treasure Registrar and four Assistant Treasure Registrars, one of whom is part-time. This work involves the preparation of Treasure cases for inquest (at a Coroner's Court), the handing of disclaimed cases, the secretariat of the Treasure Valuation Committee, and the payment of rewards to finders/landowners.

Pre-inquest procedures for Treasure cases in Wales are carried out by Amgueddfa Cymru – National Museum Wales.

Learning and outreach is fundamental to the work of the Portable Antiquities Scheme (PAS), as this is the principal mechanism by which the Finds Liaison Officers (FLOs) meet finders and educate people about the value of recording finds and best practice. The data collated by the Scheme, and published on its online database – www.finds.org.uk – is also a valuable learning resource for both academics and the general public alike.

CHILDREN: FORMAL LEARNING

Object-based learning is an excellent way of engaging with children and developing their interest in archaeology and the past. This also overlaps with other key subjects, such as ICT, Citizenship, Science and Maths. Often there are opportunities to work outside of the classroom, which the children particularly enjoy. The FLOs value the opportunity to work with children in both a formal and informal learning environment, which can be extremely rewarding.

In the classroom
Queen Victoria School, Dudley, West Midlands
In June 2007, Caroline Johnson (Staffordshire & West Midlands FLO) was invited to Queen Victoria Primary School to talk to two nursery classes and one reception class (65 children in total, aged between 3 and 6 years) to talk about archaeology. Prior to Caroline's visit, the children had dug a sandpit (mimicking an archaeological site) to excavate bones and other objects that had been placed there. The teachers wanted a 'real archaeologist' to come and talk to the children about what they had found and what artefacts can tell us about how people lived in the past. Although the children were very young, they appeared to grasp a basic level of understanding of archaeology.

Tatham Fells Primary School, Lancashire
Dot Boughton (Lancashire & Cumbria FLO) was invited to talk to the children of Tatham Fells Primary School, which only has about 20 students, aged between 7 and 11, most of them children of local farmers and landowners. The children had found many finds on their parents' land, and wanted to learn more about archaeology and the finds they had found. Instead of identifying their objects for them, Dot helped the children to identify their own finds – including coins, bones and pottery. They learnt about the different materials that objects can be made from – such as metal, pottery, bone, glass or wood – and which material survives well in the ground and which does not. They also looked at what happens to different materials when they are in the ground for a long time.

Outdoor classroom

'Hands on archaeology' at Yaxham Primary School, Norfolk

Nellie Bales (Norfolk FLA) ran a 'hands on archaeology' session for Class 1 at Yaxham Primary School in Norfolk. The class was mixed, with a total of 21 children (Reception, Years 1 and 2) aged between 5 and 7, so it was important that the activities were engaging and accessible to even the youngest students. The children were divided into three groups of seven, and rotated between three short activities. The first was to 'excavate' a sandpit outside, where pieces of pottery, tile, brick, animal bone and shell had been hidden, which the children were asked to excavate, sort into find types and discuss. In the second exercise the children had a chance to put a sheep skeleton together, talking about the bones as they did so. Finally, they analysed a selection of genuine and replica Roman finds, and discussed Roman tableware and eating habits, comparing different pottery types, and handling Roman objects and coins. The activities were a great success, and even the youngest children derived a great deal of satisfaction from making deductions about the objects they were able to handle.

Michael Faraday Primary School community excavation

The Aylesbury Estate in Southwark, London, is one of the largest estates in Europe with extremely challenging socio-economic conditions. It was here, in the playground of Michael Faraday Primary School, that Kate Sumnall (London FLO) and colleagues from the Museum of London's London Archaeological Archive & Resource Centre (LAARC) organised the annual community excavation. For two weeks the archaeologists worked closely with all the pupils at Michael Faraday Primary School and those in other local schools, the Young Archaeologists Club (YAC), community groups and other interested individuals. Everyone was encouraged to actively participate in exploring the local history of the area through studying the old maps, learning how to dig and process and identify maps, and then piecing together how their discoveries contributed to the bigger picture. Kate identified finds that were found within the wider local area and gave all the groups the details of the PAS educational website for children (PASt Explorers), local YAC groups and the museum's events programme so that the local residents were able to pursue their interest in the past. The evaluation revealed that out of the 500 people who took part, 99% of the children enjoyed the experience and 95% learnt something

Top: finds recording in Lancaster.
Bottom: finds handling in West Yorkshire.

new and interesting about archaeology. One secondary school teacher mentioned that 50% of her class was now considering a career in archaeology!

CHILDREN: INFORMAL LEARNING

It is often the case that informal learning works best for many children, where there are opportunities for active learning and they can express themselves in a way not appropriate in the classroom environment. There are many examples of this type of work in 2007, of which the examples below are a selection.

Roman villa at Coberly, Gloucestershire

In September 2007, Time Team excavated a Roman Villa at Coberly in Gloucestershire, where Kurt Adams (Gloucestershire & Avon FLO) had organised a small group of metal-detectorists to work on the site. One of the days saw a number of children who had won an Ordnance Survey competition visit the excavation. As part of the day, Kurt organised an artefact identification workshop, which involved showing and discussing some of the Roman artefacts that had been found on the site. This continued with a more practical session where they were given the opportunity to handle real artefacts in order to identify, draw and record them. The children then presented their findings to the rest of the group, who discussed what these artefacts were able to tell us about the past.

Experimental archaeology week at Lackford Lakes, Suffolk

In 2007 Suffolk County Council Archaeological Service (SCCAS) launched an experimental archaeological project designed to excite and enthuse young people about the past. Between 31 July and 4 August experimental activities were held at Lackford Lakes in Suffolk, including the building and firing of a replica Roman kiln, the construction of an Iron Age roundhouse, and the designing and building of bread ovens and cooking pits in which to experiment with Iron Age cooking. 25 children a day (aged between 7 and 15 years) attended, of whom all were members of Young Archaeologists Club (YAC) or the Suffolk WildBunch (volunteers from the Suffolk Wildlife Trust).

The week involved collaboration between SCCAS, the Suffolk Wildlife Trust education team, West Stow Anglo-Saxon Village and Jane Carr and Faye Minter (Suffolk FLOs), who arranged the attendance of the YAC members. Funding was approved by English Heritage and made available through the Aggregates Levy Sustainability Fund, a scheme which in part aims to address the environmental impacts of past aggregates extraction through local education, outreach and community involvement.

'This was a different way of learning... We are not inspired to learn [at school] and we don't get to do anything like this.'
Student (who worked on the project at Lackford Lakes)

Experimental archaeology at Lackford Lakes.

Events at Uttoxeter and Burton-upon-Trent libraries

Caroline Johnson (Staffordshire & West Midlands FLO) conducted a number of activities and workshops in collaboration with libraries in north and east Staffordshire, including an archaeology and artefact identification workshop at Uttoxeter Library with 38 children aged between 9 and 10 years old. This workshop involved Caroline using the Birmingham City Museums' Learning and Outreach Early Romans loan box, which contains various artefacts for the children to study including Samian ware, a roof tile, a brooch, a bone hair pin, an oil lamp and a small selection of coins. After a short talk on archaeology and the work of the PAS, the children were separated into small groups, and each group was given an artefact to study. They studied its material, size, texture, colour and technology in order to reach a conclusion about each artefact's purpose. These workshops were very successful and the children were very enthusiastic. They also enabled the children to work as part of a team. Additionally, these workshops incorporated different disciplines valid within the National Curriculum, including Science, Art, Geography and Citizenship.

HIGHER AND FURTHER EDUCATION

Students in higher and further education are the archaeologists of the future, so it is crucial that the PAS informs them, and their lecturers(!), of the potential benefits of liaising with metal-detectorists and recording archaeological finds found by the public. It is also fundamental that they understand the research potential of the data collated by the PAS, and are encouraged to undertake research using it.

Newcastle University

Rob Collins' (North East FLO) outreach programme, is typical of many FLOs. In 2007 he met with more than 120 students at Newcastle University to talk about the work of the PAS and the benefits of recording finds found by the public. The university's Department of Archaeology has now invited Rob to provide introductory and in-depth teaching on the subject of the PAS and Treasure for all relevant undergraduate and Masters' students.

'The Portable Antiquities Scheme is a great way of learning about a wide range of artefacts with a hands-on approach. I have accumulated beneficial and constructive knowledge that has been related to my course and I believe I can use these skills to aid my future career.'
Wendy Woodiwis (undergraduate student, Newcastle University)

Amgueddfa Cymru – National Museum Wales and University of Cardiff

The PAS in Wales, in collaboration with Amgueddfa Cymru – National Museum Wales, has been working with Cardiff University to develop the skills of students. Through this partnership students are trained in archaeological fieldwork through excavations resulting from PAS finds and research; the students' work is assessed as part of their degree.

Besides work in the field, undergraduate classes are also held at the museum. Here, with the support of the PAS, they are trained in the identification and recording of finds; students also benefit from access to the museum's collections. The PAS is able to provide a dataset of complementary records to illustrate the scale of recovery and character of regional artefact types. These workshops also illustrate the academic importance of finds recording and material culture studies.

Geophysical and topographical training programme at Bacton Roman site, Suffolk

In August 2007 a third Roman site was investigated as part of an ongoing collaboration between Faye Minter (Suffolk FLO), Professor Martin Millett and Helen Woodhouse (Cambridge University), and Jude Plouviez (Suffolk County Council Archaeological Service) to facilitate geophysics and topography training for Cambridge University Archaeology students on Roman sites discovered by local metal-detector users in Suffolk. The survey work was funded jointly by the Council for British Archaeology (CBA) East Anglia and the Suffolk Institute of Archaeology and History.

The site at Bacton was initially discovered in 2006 by local metal-detectorists, who reported their finds to the PAS. The distribution of Roman tile and other building material on the surface suggested that the site was a Romano-British settlement. The survey revealed twelve roundhouse structures within an enclosure; these are probably Iron Age with continued occupation and maybe construction into the Roman period. Outside the enclosure there is a probable trackway providing access from the north and a Roman structure with a furnace area (most likely to be a bath house), which appears to sit in a second smaller enclosure. These results exceeded expectations, providing information on the transition between the Iron Age and Roman periods and demonstrating the value of implementing this type of non-intrusive survey in conjunction with analysis of surface finds.

Archaeological fieldwalking course at Ludlow Resource Centre

During autumn 2007, an eight-week archaeological fieldwalking course was run by Peter Reavill (Herefordshire & Shropshire FLO) and Bob Milner (archaeologist and fieldwalker) at Ludlow Museum Resource Centre. The course was designed to take the interested amateur to a level where they were able to recognise commonly found archaeological finds and recover, record, understand and analyse them within a landscape setting. The course was taught through a series of sessions in the museum where artefacts were studied and students were introduced to various archaeological methods used to interpret sites. These lessons were then reinforced by active fieldwork on a farm near Richards Castle, Herefordshire, where a series of cropmarks was investigated. The finds were then processed by the group and analysed. The site revealed a broad range of finds from the Mesolithic to the modern. However, the main material recovered was from the late Iron Age and Roman period. The work of this group has led the site to be interpreted as a Romano-British farmstead.

One of the strengths of this course was that it combined interested members of the public with metal-detectorists, fieldwalkers and landowners. Feedback from the course has been extremely positive with everyone rating the course as excellent in a survey by the museum staff. 94% of the participants on the course have asked if something similar could be run again by the museum. It is hoped that many of the students will continue fieldwalking by forming a small fieldwalking/archaeological survey group to study the archaeology and fields in South Shropshire and North Herefordshire.

'I loved the fieldwalking... it was totally absorbing and it amazed me how much stuff we walk over.'
Martin (student)

'Fascinating course – it has given me the confidence in identifying field finds and appreciating the methods of fieldwalking and archaeological survey.'
Sue (student)

FINDERS AND THE PUBLIC

It is essential that the PAS reaches out to as many potential finders as possible. Besides visiting metal-detecting clubs, the FLOs organise a number of outreach events, including finds identification and recording days, community archaeology projects, exhibitions and displays. They also give talks to schools, universities, colleges and other groups. In 2007, 33,298 people (including 11,089 children) attended learning and outreach events organised by the PAS.

Finds days

Finds days are a good way of reaching out to finders who might not otherwise proactively record with the PAS, such as members of the public and independent detectorists. In 2007 the PAS organised 477 finds days, which attracted at least 8,383 people. Many of these events took place in local museums, as the examples below show:

National Archaeology Week 2007

The PAS was involved in 68 events to support National Archaeology Week 2007 – a nationwide celebration of archaeology run by the Council for British Archaeology (CBA) – which were attended by 4,193 adults and 3,040 children, and 2,331 finds were identified.

Making laurel wreaths in Cornwall.

The activities run by the PAS varied tremendously. Anna Tyacke (Cornwall FLO), for example, helped organise an event at the Royal Cornwall Museum exploring 'Greek Myths and Roman Soldiers'. The workshop involved looking at the depictions of emperors on Roman coins to inspire children to create laurel wreaths out of brass wire and foil, and then to decorate them using metalworking tools. The children then wore these, along with other items, such as Medusa masks, togas, shields and swords that they had made in other activities, and marched with 'real' Roman soldiers (the *Gladiators* of *Agrippa*), listened to Greek plays, and sampled Greek and Roman food.

'We've been doing a project on the Romans at school and it's brilliant to see what they really looked like. The costumes are really cool.'
Alex Humphreys (aged 12)

The Romans were also in Dorchester. Ciorstaidh Hayward Trevarthen (Dorset FLO) and the Dorset County Council's Historic Environment Team co-ordinated a range of activities and displays in and around the site of a Roman townhouse at County Hall, including an opportunity for people to view several fine mosaics and other features revealed during archaeological excavations. Finds identification and recording sessions were complimented by finds displays organised by local metal-detecting clubs. *Legio II Augusta* re-enacted Roman military and domestic life. Mini-excavations and colouring competitions were organised for children.

Dot Boughton (Lancashire & Cumbria FLO) prepared games and activities for children and families at Lancaster City Museum to coincide with the launch of the Lancaster Young Archaeologists' Club, for which she is a leader. Children were encouraged to try out coin jigsaws, make Roman brooches and learn more about the Roman cavalry tombstone found in Lancaster in 2005. Dot also organised a 'timeline' of objects using a handling collection of various Prehistoric, Roman, Medieval and post-Medieval items, which the children were encouraged to look at, date (if they could!) and put in the right spot on the timeline.

Local children were invited to choose a real archaeological object and have a go at doing the job of a FLO as part of an event at Jewry Wall Museum organised by Wendy Scott (Leicestershire & Rutland FLO). The children proved expert at describing and measured finds following simple questions as prompts. They then illustrated the object using coloured pencils, with some very artistic results.

COMMUNITY ARCHAEOLOGY PROJECTS

It is one of the main aim of the PAS to get people involved, so they can learn about archaeology, understand the educational value of archaeological finds in their context, and appreciate how finds recording advances our understanding of the past. Below are a few examples of community archaeological projects involving the PAS.

Fieldwalking project at Boden

In December 2007, Anna Tyacke (Cornwall FLO) helped to organise a fieldwalking project, adjacent to the Iron Age *fogou* (Cornish earth-house) site at Boden, along with colleagues from the Historic Environment Service

Finds recording in Surrey.

and the Cornwall Archaeological Society. Members of the Society, the local community, archaeology students and detectorists were invited to help. Many interesting finds, including Iron Age pottery, were discovered. The success of this venture and the interest and support of the local community has led to setting up the Meneage Archaeological Group (MAG) which has since organised events including finds days, talks, walks and training sessions such as cleaning, sorting and identifying the fieldwalking finds. MAG has gone on to be awarded a grant from the Cornwall Archaeological Society for future excavation work at this site, particularly focusing on the Bronze Age houses found while excavating the Iron Age *fogou* in 2003.

Community excavation at Leasowe Lighthouse
In September and October 2007, a community excavation was carried out around the lighthouse at Leasowe in Merseyside by the National Museums Liverpool archaeological field unit. Frances McIntosh (Cheshire, Greater Manchester & Merseyside FLO) was involved in various aspects of this outreach event and facilitated the involvement of the West Kirby Metal Detecting Club, which was invited to detect the spoil and also land surrounding the excavation site. Although not many finds were discovered (it was hoped to find more evidence for the ancient port at Meols close by), the club members enjoyed being involved and benefiting from experiencing an archaeological project first hand. The other volunteers were able to see how responsible metal-detecting can help in our understanding of a site. Frances also helped with eight school sessions which allowed about 150 children to come to site and handle finds. The event was immensely popular and a great chance to bring local history to life for the children.

BEST PRACTICE

The PAS strives to promote best practice, including the importance of recording finds, making a precise record of where finds are found, and offers advice on storage and conservation. Below are a few examples of where finders have followed best practice, and/or have been rewarded for following archaeological principles.

Dorset Archaeological Awards
Three amateur archaeologists, including a metal-detectorist, have come second in the Dorset Archaeological Awards, made by the Dorset Archaeological Committee to give recognition to a wide range of projects and individuals in the county. John and Verena Harper, together with Denise Parsons, have been searching land at Compton Abbas for many years. Through metal-detecting and surface collection they have retrieved flint, pottery, coins and metalwork dating from the Mesolithic through virtually all periods and into to the 20th century, which have been recorded with Naomi Payne and Ciorstaidh Hayward Trevarthen (Somerset & Dorset FLOs). All three finders have a keen desire to discover more about their local area, to record what they unearth and to share the information with others. The awards were presented by HRH the Duke of Gloucester in a ceremony held at Sherborne Castle. The Duke was impressed by the range of projects represented in the eight nominations.

'We are delighted with the recognition our efforts have received from the Dorset Archaeological Committee. We feel it is very important that we get all our finds recorded through the PAS as this gives many people access to the information through the database.'
John and Verena Harper

Policing the past
The Department of Portable Antiquities and Treasure at the British Museum is involved in several initiatives to ensure better protection of the UK's cultural assets. Since 2006, the Department has been monitoring eBay for items of unreported potential Treasure, with some success. In 2007 the Department followed up 144 cases of unreported items, and the intelligence received was passed to the police.

Since September 2007, the Department has been an expert adviser on the Export Licensing of detector finds, in the hope of encouraging people who export such finds to have them recorded before they leave the country. Unfortunately most finds are exported by dealers who have no knowledge of the object's provenance, and therefore – since the export regime does not require exports to give precise findspot information or finds to be recorded first – hundreds of finds are being exported with great detriment to the archaeology of the country. To date the Department

Recording finds at a metal-detecting rally.

has approved 557 Export Licences, of which 82% are for exports outside the EU; only a fraction of these have been recorded by PAS.

The Department has also been working with the Association of Chief Police Officers (ACPO) in the hope of drawing up guidance for local police forces on how to tackle heritage crime, including the non-reporting of Treasure and illicit detecting. The PAS has also been a partner in English Heritage's Nighthawking Project (run by Oxford Archaeology), which has attempted to access the extent of illicit detecting in the UK and its dependencies.

Since February 2007, Michael Lewis (Deputy Head of the PAS) has been seconded one day a fortnight as a Special Police Constable to the Metropolitan Police Services Art & Antiques Unit. He has joined the Unit on several searches and investigations related to heritage crime, and has also arrested people for antiquities related offences.

EXHIBITIONS AND DISPLAYS

Exhibitions and displays are a good way of highlighting the work of PAS, important local finds and the contribution finds can add to archaeological knowledge. Through such finds people are able to learn more about the history of their local area.

Permanent display case set up at Salt Museum, Northwich

In 2007 Frances McIntosh (Cheshire, Greater Manchester & Merseyside FLO) organised a case at

the Salt Museum which has been made permanently available for the display of local metal-detected finds. This has proved popular with the local detecting club as a way to show local people what finds have been discovered. The Huxley Hoard, a hoard of Viking Silver

arm bracelets found in Cheshire, was loaned to the Salt Museum in February and March, so this display case was changed to include Early Medieval finds to stay in keeping with activities on the Anglo-Saxons and Vikings.

'The PAS case is a very welcome addition to our coffee shop – it is a way of making visitors aware of the variety of interesting finds from the area and shows the detectorists that we value the material that they are bringing to the Finds Liaison Officer.'
Emma Chaplin (Heritage and Museums Officer, Cheshire County Council)

CONFERENCE AND TALKS

Part of the PAS's outreach work involves talking to people about archaeology, the work of the PAS and the value of recording finds. In 2007 more than 556 talks were given to 31,351 people, including groups such as metal-detecting clubs, archaeological and historical societies, and other groups and societies. The major event of the year was the PAS's tenth anniversary conference – A Decade of Discovery.

A Decade of Discovery

On 17–18 April 2007 the British Museum hosted a conference to celebrate the tenth anniversary of the PAS. The main purpose of the conference was to highlight patterns emerging from the data collated by the PAS, and demonstrate how this is beginning to change our ideas about the past. Subjects of the papers varied from the contribution of lithics to insights into pilgrim's trinkets – but all demonstrated the great potential of PAS data. Speakers included Mark Blackburn (Fitzwilliam Museum), Richard Bradley (University of Reading), Duncan Garrow (Oxford University), Fraser Hunter (National Museums of Scotland), Jude Plouviez (Suffolk County Council), Tim Schadla-Hall (Institute of Archaeology, University College London), Gabor Thomas (University of Kent), Martin Welch and Sue Harrington (Institute of Archaeology, University College London), as well as staff from the PAS. The conference proceedings are to be published by British Archaeological Reports.

Medieval Lincolnshire Conference

Lisa Staves, (North Lincolnshire FLO) took part in a Medieval Lincolnshire Conference at The Collection, Lincoln, sponsored by Heritage Trust for Lincolnshire and Archaeological Project Services. She gave a paper on 'Norman Finds from Lincolnshire', an area she is currently researching. The paper looked at the large amount of Romanesque style metal work found in Lincolnshire and recorded by the PAS.

Detectors and Collectors

During the first half of 2007, Anna Tyacke (Cornwall FLO) offered a talk on 'Detectors and Collectors' to Cornish groups and societies through the Cornwall Arts Centre Trust's performing arts touring scheme called 'Carn to Cove'. They organise and advertise their talks and entertainment through a county-wide brochure, held in the local Tourist Information Centres, and online. Various societies, such as the Old Cornwall Societies, took up the offer and booked the talk, which focused on recent finds from their parish, and also brought along their artefacts on the evening for Anna to identify. One of the most interesting of these was a brass *sestertius* of Faustina II, (CORN-D75CB0), wife of Marcus Aurelius (c. AD 145–175), but issued after her death in memoriam, found by Antony Gardiner in Perranzabuloe. As a result of being advertised in the 'Carn to Cove' brochure, Anna was asked by several other societies, including Women's Institutes, local antique clubs and church-based groups, to give talks and finds sessions over the rest of the year. It is hoped now that more landowners and finders are aware of the PAS and what to do if they find something, and how these finds add to the archaeological knowledge of their local area.

'I found it very interesting to hear Anna Tyacke speak about recent finds from my area, and I also brought along a Roman coin that I found to show her. I was grateful to her for recommending that I join the Kernow Search and Recovery Club, as now I can show my finds to Anna every month.'
Antony Gardiner (metal-detectorist and Perranzabuloe Old Cornwall Society)

Suffolk farmers seminar

In November 2007 Faye Minter (Suffolk FLO) participated in a seminar on archaeology and soil management for local farmers. The seminar was funded by DEFRA (Department for the Environment, Food and Rural Affairs) and organised by Christine Stevens (Catchment Sensitive Farming Officer). Faye spoke at the seminar about metal-detecting and archaeology in Suffolk and offered advice for farmers concerning many aspects of metal-detecting. She also organised a finds identification and handling session as part of the seminar.

Talks in the USA

In June 2007, Roger Bland (Head of the PAS) was invited to give talks on the PAS in New York and Washington DC, through the generosity of the American Numismatic Society. The talk in Washington, which was organised by the American Coin Collectors Guild, was hosted by Congressman Culberson and included staff from the US State Department and several foreign embassies who wished to learn about the approach adopted in England and Wales for protecting portable antiquities.

'I have so admired the PAS that I was pleased to host Dr Bland for a recent lecture about the PAS at the US Capitol. I was particularly impressed to learn how the PAS has successfully brought ordinary…citizens together with members of the archaeological community in a joint effort to record the past. I hope this success can be replicated here in the United States.'
Congressman Culberson (Texas)

MEDIA

The FLOs regularly talk to the media about interesting finds and sites discovered though the work of the PAS. This helps more people learn about the work of the PAS and come forward with new finds to record. In 2007, 117 articles about the PAS appeared in the media and printed press.

BBC Countryfile

In February 2007, a film crew from BBC television's Countryfile team recorded a day's metal-detecting with the Historical Search Society (Mold) presented by Juliet Morris. Peter Reavill (Herefordshire & Shropshire FLO) was invited to discuss the work of the PAS and the Treasure Act 1996. He also provided information and recorded the finds discovered on the day. This provided an excellent opportunity to promote the PAS to a wide audience of people interested in the countryside and rural affairs, as well as reinforcing the importance of recording finds discovered by metal-detectorists, fieldwalkers, farmers and landowners. The programme was aired in late Spring 2007 on BBC1.

REACHING OUT TO NEW GROUPS

The FLOs are always keen to make contact with new groups of people, in the hope of recording their finds or advising people what to do if they make a find. The examples below highlight the varied nature of this outreach work.

Mobile Library Service

The PAS and Warwickshire Mobile Library Service collaborated to provide a finds identification session on the mobile library on a route that travelled to a number of different rural communities, including Radway and Pillerton Priors.

In rural Warwickshire, many people use their local mobile library for a variety of reasons, including the lack of public or personal transport to the larger towns/cities, or personal mobility problems. During August 2007, Angie Bolton (Warwickshire & Worcestershire FLO) travelled with the Mobile Library, meeting people, talking about local archaeology, promoting research resources such as the PAS database, the Museums Service, Historic Environment Records and archives.

The event was enhanced by a display and the use of ceramic and worked flint handling collections. One library user, who was partially sighted, particularly welcomed the opportunity to touch the pottery to her face so that she could feel the different textures as Angie talked through what she was holding. She said that she would be too shy to go to a museum and ask all the questions she would like, but this was possible in the familiar environment of the Warwickshire Mobile Library Service.

The Mobile Library driver, Keith Bennett, who has a personal interest in archaeology and history and is well liked on the route, had generated a lot of enthusiasm in its users so the event was lively and well attended. The Mobile Library Service is in the process of acquiring a fleet of more up-to-date vans shortly in which there will be a computer with internet access. Once the new fleet is in place, it is planned to repeat the collaboration, making use of this computer and the PAS website, database and the Past Explorers education microsite.

Recording finds on board Warwickshire Mobile Library Service.

Somerset Carers' Conference
Naomi Payne (Somerset FLO) was asked to present two workshops at the 2007 Somerset Carers' Conference. This is an annual event which takes place in June each year, during National Carers' Week. It is an opportunity for carers to do something completely different for a day and meet others who have caring responsibilities. Participants attended one morning and one afternoon workshop and this year sessions included first aid in the home, relaxation and belly dancing. Naomi's workshop, entitled 'Unearthing Somerset History', was an overview of the archaeology of Somerset, including examples of recent finds recorded by the PAS. A variety of objects from the PAS teaching collection was taken along for the workshop participants to handle. The interactive sessions were based around a PowerPoint presentation, with questions from the audience throughout. The workshop's attendees were fascinated

by the variety of finds that are reported to the PAS and really enjoyed handling real artefacts. Feedback was very positive with one person commenting that the workshop had actually been her second choice, but as it turned out she was very glad that the belly dancing session had been full! Each participant took home a pack of information about getting involved in archaeology and history in Somerset, including information on the PAS, museums, the online Somerset Historic Environment Record, the Record Office and National Archaeology Week.

Kenny Wright Project
On 3 September 2007, Rob Collins (North East FLO) met with members of the Kenny Wright Project, an initiative started by local metal-detectorists Kenny Wright and Tony Beck, also a social worker for South Tyneside District Council, with the aim of helping recovering drug addicts stay off of drugs by learning new hobbies – in this case metal-detecting. Rob met with the members of the project and provided a talk about the types of artefacts the new detectorists might hope to find in the North East, and how to properly record these finds and look after them.

WORKING WITH HERITAGE PROFESSIONALS

The FLOs benefit greatly from other heritage professionals who help them in their work, such as county archaeologists, Historic Environment Record Officers, museum curators and education officers, but learning is a two-way process. Often it is the FLO's expertise that is invaluable to other heritage professionals, as the examples below demonstrate.

Wiltshire Heritage Museum
In June 2007, Katie Hinds (Wiltshire FLO) ran a workshop for volunteers currently working on the documentation of the collections at Wiltshire Heritage Museum, Devizes. The aim was to become more familiar and confident with identifying and recognising the types of objects they would come across in their work at the museum. Each attendee brought with them a find that intrigued them and that they wanted to find out more about – either something they had found themselves or something they had been working on from the museum collections. Perhaps the most interesting (and surprising) find was a Medieval glazed roof finial found in a volunteer's back garden.

'It was a great success, covered a lot of ground, and we would like to hold another workshop and more like it in the future!'
Heather Ault (Assistant Curator and Volunteer Co-ordinator, Wiltshire Heritage Museum)

South Western Federation of Museums & Art Galleries

Kurt Adams (Gloucestershire & Avon FLO) was asked to organise a day of lectures by the South Western Federation of Museums & Art Galleries. The purpose of the workshop was to help curators of smaller museums and organisations know how to deal better with archaeological public enquires, how to start identifying artefacts, where to go to further research them, who to contact with difficult questions, and who to contact with potentially recordable items.

During the morning, talks were given by Gail Boyle (Bristol City Museum) and Jane Hill (North Somerset Museum) who drew on their own experiences of object handling and discussed how to deal with difficult and sometimes amusing enquires. The second half of the day was more practical and concentrated on artefact handling. The session was run by Kurt and Peter Twinn (local metal-detectorist and archaeology student) using many of the finds that Peter had found. The attendees were very happy with the day and felt that a helpful balance between artefact handling and public enquiry techniques meant that even the experienced found the day very useful.

Hadrian's Wall Heritage Ltd.

Rob Collins (North East FLO) has continued to work with Hadrian's Wall Heritage Ltd. to provide basic training for Hadrian's Wall Country volunteers in the recognition of objects of archaeological interest and illegal searching on the Hadrian's Wall World Heritage Site. Training has consisted of practical seminars and the completion of a small 'pocket guide' that trail volunteers can keep with them in the field. It is hoped that this training will bring to light more casual finds of objects from Hadrian's Wall, but also further protect the important archaeological resource of the World Heritage Site by increasing awareness of both the potential and dangers of illegal searching.

VOLUNTEERS

Volunteers make a valuable contribution to the work of PAS, especially as most FLOs are overworked, with increasing numbers of finds to deal with. In 2007, 101 people from all sorts of backgrounds, with varying expertise and experiences, volunteered their services with the PAS.

- After undertaking a university placement with Liz Andrews-Wilson (North & East Yorkshire FLO), Anna Booth is continued to volunteer for the PAS weighing, measuring and identifying finds and recording them on the PAS finds database, whilst completing an MA at the University of York; Anna was subsequently employed as Somerset FLO.

Volunteer Cliff Reeves.

- Brian Hawe is retired but is also a metal-detectorist. He was keen to learn more about finds and assist with the recording work, so helps Liz Andrews-Wilson (North & East Yorkshire FLO) identify and record finds on the PAS finds database.
- Jim Halliday, who is well known to most in the metal-detecting community, helps Liz Andrews-Wilson (North & East Yorkshire FLO) at Yorkshire Museum Finds Days, talking to finders and helping collect and return finds.
- Kate Roe, a trained graphic designer, spends time at home and in the museum helping Lisa Staves (North Lincolnshire FLO) editing photographs for the PAS database. Kate also draws objects for publication.
- Cliff Reeves is retired and volunteers with Lisa Staves (North Lincolnshire FLO) each week identifying large collections of Roman coins. His expertise on Roman coins has been invaluable and he doesn't complain too much about the grots!
- Martha Loader from Holbrook High School undertook a work experience placement with the PAS in Suffolk. She was interested in archaeological illustration and worked with Donna Wreathall (Suffolk County Council Archaeology Service's illustrator), to learn how to illustrate objects of different materials and types.
- Tom Lucking from Orwell High School and Charlotte New from Thurston Community College both worked with Colin Pendleton (Suffolk Historic Environment Record Officer) and Faye Minter (Suffolk FLO) learning about object identification and recording. Tom was especially interested in finding out about finds recording as he is a metal-detectorist and now regularly records his finds with Faye. Charlotte was pleasantly surprised about how interesting archaeology could be and encouraged her friends and family to bring in pottery they had found on local fields, which helped to increase information about a local Romano-British settlement site.

- Chris Hall volunteers with Amy Cooper (South & West Yorkshire FLO) and is working from home, entering his extensive musket ball collection onto the PAS database. Chris and his detecting partner Frank Andrusyk became interested in musket balls after detecting on several Civil War sites and were keen to record their finds in detail. They have also been learning about rigorous survey techniques and they are undertaking a long-term detailed survey of one of their sites.
- Molly Harrison volunteers for the PAS by trawling past publications of metal-detecting magazines for objects that are relevant research projects undertaken by various FLOs. These include all the late Iron Age and Roman ox head bucket mounts for Angie Bolton (Warwickshire & Worcestershire FLO), Roman finger rings marked 'TOT' for Adam Daubney (Lincolnshire FLO) and Viking Age material for Wendy Scott (Leicestershire & Rutland FLO) Finds Liaison Officer.
- MA students Beth Echtenacher, Yvonne Brownlee and Beth McNestrie volunteered with Rob Collins (North East FLO), learning the basics of finds identification and recording on the PAS database. Beth went onto become an FLA for the PAS in North & East Yorkshire. Likewise, undergraduates Wendy Woodiwis and Verity Anthony also identified and recorded objects for the PAS. All the volunteers have found that first-hand experience of artefacts was beneficial to their degrees.

'I've been interested in archaeology from my childhood and frequently visited the local museums wherever I lived. In 2007 I volunteered my skills at the North Lincolnshire Museum and was promptly snapped up by the FLO Lisa Staves who needed a photography assistant. Since then I've also started to produce archaeological illustrations of some of the more interesting finds for publication and I'm quite proud of that! The work is fascinating and I feel privileged to be able to get a really get a close look at artefacts that normally one only sees in photos or under glass. It's given me a much better understanding of where I live as even a selection of Roman grots, pot sherds or tiny Anglo Saxon brooch fragments found in a field can tell a story. I've learnt so much already working with Lisa and I'm proud to be involved with the PAS, I believe it's an invaluable resource not only for the finders, but for everyone from armchair archaeologists and historians like me to serious researchers.'
Kate Roe (volunteer with PAS at North Lincolnshire Museum)

'It gives me great pleasure assisting Liz Andrews-Wilson and meeting fellow detectorists on finds days at the Yorkshire Museum, at the same time sharing our knowledge to help create this massive database for

future generations. This also gives the metal detecting hobby some credibility and the freedom to detect without too many restrictions as those imposed in other parts of Europe.'
Jim Halliday (volunteer with the Yorkshire Museum)

'I began volunteering with the PAS as part of a MA work placement, but decided to continue volunteering after this had ended as I found I was gaining much valuable work experience. My course was looking at the management of our cultural heritage, so it was fantastic to gain first-hand, practical experience of some ways in which this may be achieved, and this really complemented the course content. My time with the PAS has also really reinforced my recognition of the need for greater community involvement in archaeology, as the Scheme appears to have had great success in this regard, and this is something I will take with me into my future career within the sector.'
Anna Booth (volunteer with the Yorkshire Museum, now Somerset FLO)

'I have been collecting information regarding musket shot for the last 18 months. In that time I have learnt a tremendous amount of information about them, including types, sizes and markings. The PAS has helped me identify them and photograph and record my findings as it is very important that they do not go unrecognised. The English Civil War is a very important part of our history, and this musket ball survey could help build a better picture of the battle at Marston Moor in 1644.'
Chris Hall (volunteer for PAS in South and West Yorkshire)

INTRODUCTION

Portable antiquities (archaeological small finds) provide vital clues about the past, including how the historic landscape was used, and how people once lived and worked. For many periods of history, particularly those with no or little written record, archaeological finds are the main or only evidence for understanding the past. While controlled archaeological survey, excavation, and/or evaluation provide the ideal circumstances for investigating the past, many finds come to light by chance or are found by people proactively searching while field-walking or metal-detecting. These finds are typical of those recorded by the Portable Antiquities Scheme (PAS).

In most cases such finds will be found unstratified, without a precise archaeological context; indeed, 92% of finds recorded with the PAS in 2007 were recovered from cultivated land. These finds are generally susceptible to plough damage and artificial and natural corrosion processes, and therefore it could be argued that their recovery has saved them from further damage or destruction.

In the past archaeologists generally dismissed unstratified finds as having limited archaeological value, but this view is changing. While it is true more can be learnt about a find that is found in a stratified archaeological context, and such finds are of most value to the interpretation of a particular site, the finds recorded through the PAS do have an archaeological value, and are in fact changing the archaeological map of England and Wales by helping to identify and interpret new sites. These objects are adding to the overall picture of the distribution and use of particular finds, and are helping to understand the meaning and significance of specific object types.

With over 400,000 objects recorded to date, the PAS dataset is a significant resource for future research. It is important to note that this resource is not only available to academics and specialists but everyone, as the examples below illustrate.

ACADEMIC RESEARCH

Increasing numbers of academics in UK universities (and abroad) are using PAS data in their own research. The extent of this was highlighted at the 2007 PAS Conference (17–18 April) – *A Decade of Discovery* – at which 21 papers were given involving 24 speakers. Papers varied from 'The Technology of Enchantment and the Enchantment of Technology? Iron Age Celtic Art, GIS analysis and the PAS' (Duncan Garrow, University of Oxford) through to 'Winchester and the

Anglo-Saxon Settlement of the Itchen Valley: a PAS Perspective' (Martin Biddle, University of Oxford) and 'Personal and Impersonal Impressions: identity revealed though seals' (John Cherry, formerly British Museum). The conference proceedings are to be published in 2010 as a *British Archaeological Report*.

The case studies below highlight examples of how PAS data is being used by academics to better understand particular artefact types and the wider historic environment.

Bracteates
Charlotte Behr, Roehampton University
Bracteates from the early Anglo-Saxon period are round pendants made out of gold or (sometimes) silver or bronze foil that was stamped with figurative images. They show either stylised animals or anthropomorphic figures. A loop was attached and they were worn on necklaces, often together with beads and other pendants. Bracteates were first made in southern Scandinavia in the 5th century and more than 900 of them have been found in Scandinavia and neighbouring countries. In recent years, the small number of finds known from England increased substantially, mainly thanks to metal-detector finds and their systematic recording with the PAS and through the Treasure Act 1996. These new finds allow a reassessment of their distribution, connections with Continental and Scandinavian bracteates, range of iconography and modes of deposition.

With the new finds, the known area of their distribution in Britain is extended. Outside eastern Kent from where most Anglo-Saxon bracteates originate they have been found along the east coast as far north as East Yorkshire and as far west as Oxfordshire and Warwickshire and the Isle of Wight.

The close links between bracteates from England and from Scandinavia and northern Germany have always been recognised. However, how, when and from where bracteates arrived in England has been debated. The new finds point to the possibility that bracteates were not introduced to England over some time, randomly in a series of unrelated events, but may have been conveyed through one central place in northern Germany only.

Bracteates were not just precious jewellery that conferred status but also objects with sophisticated images that were perceived as powerful amulets. The iconography of bracteates is characterised by their long series of thematically and stylistically related images. It is therefore notable that among the new finds several images are – so far – unique even if they are clearly related to the known iconography. They may point to specific local Anglo-Saxon developments in bracteate

iconography, an observation that adds to the discussion about religious specialists in the pre-Christian period, who had the knowledge and ability to conceptualise and design these images.

In southern Scandinavia, the 5th and 6th centuries are renowned for their wealth of sacrificial hoard finds, including many bracteate hoards, whereas in contemporary Anglo-Saxon England it has remained very difficult to identify any sacrificial depositions in the archaeological record. The find circumstances of several of the new bracteate finds suggest that they were not always buried in graves as previously observed, but also buried as single depositions comparable to Scandinavian depositions. Thus, they contribute to the debate about the occurrence of sacrificial or ritual hoarding in pre-Christian Anglo-Saxon England.

Results from this research will be published in *Medieval Archaeology*.

Winchester: from *Venta* to *Winancaestir*
Martin Biddle and Birthe Kjølbye-Biddle
In a recent paper, Martin Biddle and Birthe Kjølbye-Biddle (2007, 189–214) examine how Winchester Old Minster came to be built in the ruins of the Roman city of Winchester, *Venta Belgarum*. In seeking to explain why this church was built in this unconventional location, they argue that Winchester remained a dominant centre in Hampshire even after the Roman period ended. Afterwards, in the Anglo-Saxon period, it remained an important centre of authority and lordship over the surrounding area, reflected in the clustering of cemeteries and settlements of the later 5th, 6th and 7th centuries in and around the (Roman) walled area, and soon after became a centre for the West Saxon royal house. This explains the reason why the Minster was founded, and why it was founded within the Roman city.

Besides looking at the evidence from archaeological sites, Biddle and Kjølbye-Biddle also makes use of PAS data. Of 275 Early Medieval finds recorded by the PAS since 1990, 55 dated between AD 400 and 700 were found in 14 parishes. Through mapping techniques, it was evident there were some discrete concentrations of Anglo-Saxon activity, and significant evidence for the occupation of Winchester, though, interestingly, a notable absence of finds between Winchester and Southampton raises important questions itself. The finds recorded (and analysed) included complete Anglo-Saxon brooches, probably indicative of burials, though in one cluster the topography makes it an unusual cemetery site. As more finds are discovered and reported, our understanding of Early Medieval Winchester increases.

It is also the case that many academics, based in universities, museums and elsewhere, offer their expertise to the Finds Liaison Officers (FLOs) and National Finds Advisers (NFAs), enhancing the quality of the PAS data and its value as a research tool.

In 2007, academics contributing to the work of the PAS included: Lindsay Allason-Jones (University of Newcastle), Jens Andersen (Camborne School of Mines), Claude Ardouin (British Museum), Steven Ashley (Norfolk Museum and Archaeology Service), Richard Bailey (University of Newcastle), Luke Barker (Sussex Archaeological Society), Charlotte Behr (University of Roehampton), Edward Besly (National Museum of Wales), Ian Betts (Museum of London), Mark Blackburn (Fitzwilliam Museum), John Blair (University of Oxford), Richard Brewer (National Museum Wales), Serena Cant (English Heritage), Andrew Chamberlain (University of Sheffield), Evan Chapman (National Museum Wales), Henry Chapman (University of Birmingham), John Cherry, John Clark (Museum of London), Barrie Cook (British Museum), Jon Cotton (Museum of London), Trevor Cowie (National Museums of Scotland), Mary Davis (National Museum Wales), Tania Dickinson (University of York), Ben Edwards, Hazel Forsyth (Museum of London), Adam Gwilt (National Museum of Wales), Jenny Hall (Museum of London), Martin Henig (University of Oxford), David Higgins (clay pipe specialist), Fraser Hunter (National Museum of Scotland), Ralph Jackson (British Museum), Meriel Jeater (Museum of London), Jennifer Jones (University of Durham), Malcolm Jones (University of Sheffield), Jackie Keily (Museum of London), Gerald Legg (Booth Museum), Rory Naismith (Fitzwilliam Museum), Stuart Needham, Peter Northover (Oxford Materials), Tim Pestell (Norwich Castle Museum), John Prag (University of Manchester), Henrietta Quinnell (University of Exeter), Mark Redknap (National Museum Wales), Julian Richards (University of York), Peter Robbins (Norfolk Museum and Archaeology Service), Ben Roberts (British Museum), Andrew Rogerson (Norfolk Museum and Archaeology Service), Ian Rowlandson (Lindsay Archaeological Services), Judith Rudoe (British Museum), Fiona Seeley (Museum of London), John Schofield (Museum of London), David Shotter (University of Lancaster), Roy Stephenson (Museum of London), Keith Sugden (Manchester Museum), Dave Symons (Birmingham Museum & Art Gallery), Rob Symonds (Sussex Archaeological Society), Irene Szymanski, Roger Taylor (University of Exeter), Roger Tomlin (University of Oxford), Elizabeth Walker (National Museum Wales), Helen Wang (British Museum), Andrew White (Lancaster City Museum), Christopher Whittick (East Sussex Records Office), Rev David Williams (Wales).

RESEARCH BY MEMBERS OF THE PAS

Besides researching finds for the purpose of recording them onto the PAS database, many of the FLOs and other members of the Scheme undertake further research. Often, as might be expected, it is the FLOs and NFAs who first notice trends in artefact recovery that identify new sites or peculiarities of particular find types. Hence, they also develop their own research interests, as the examples below illustrate.

Roman ToT rings
Adam Daubney, Lincolnshire FLO
Each year, a number of Roman finger-rings that bear the inscription TOT or variations thereof are recorded with the PAS or reported Treasure.

TOT rings date to the 2nd and 3rd centuries AD and are distinctively Romano-British. To date, 50 rings are known; two are gold, 44 are silver and four are copper alloy. The letters 'T-O-T' are known in a number of formats; the Ts usually have serifs and the Os can be upper case, lower case or even a single dot.

The identity of 'ToT' was suggested as Toutatis as far back as the 1980s, and this was confirmed recently by a silver ring from Battlesden, Bedfordshire, that bears the inscription DEO TOTA (to the god Toutatis). Toutatis was one of the principal Celtic deities, and is often paired with the Roman god Mars. The Proto-Celtic word *teutá* means 'people' or 'tribe', and so Teutates is usually thought of as the 'tribal protector' or the 'father of the tribe'. The name is fitting when related to the distribution of the rings; nearly every example falls within the suggested boundaries of the Corieltauvi.

The rings are found on both rural and military sites in the East Midlands, which may suggest that they are associated with retired soldiers attached to the *Colonia*. This idea is supported by the distribution of Continental inscriptions to Toutatis on stone. The eight inscriptions known mark out the eastern extent of the Roman Empire, showing the deity was popular with soldiers serving on the frontiers. Toutatis is known from Rome, Bulgaria, Hungary, Austria and Germany, and so it is likely that the cult of the deity was brought over by soldiers who served in Britain and retired to Lincoln. These rings were worn as a very specific material expression of group or personal religious identity, perhaps even indicating soldiers from a specific unit.

The PAS and the Roman Frontier
Rob Collins, North East FLO
The recording of artefacts with the PAS has benefited many specialisms in archaeology, and the Roman frontier is no exception. Late Iron Age, Roman, and Early Medieval finds from throughout the north of England

continue to expand knowledge of the establishment, maintenance, and eventual transformation of the Roman Empire's northernmost frontier.

A survey of the Roman artefacts recorded from the recording areas of Cumberland and Lancashire and the North East provide a number of interesting conclusions. Overall, it can be confidently claimed that patterns from PAS data are consistent with those determined through archaeological research. For example, there is a contrast between higher numbers of artefacts dated to the early Roman period and higher numbers of coins dated to the 4th century; objects (coins and artefacts) dated to the 4th century seem to have a less geographically extensive distribution in the frontier than objects from the previous centuries.
The distribution of different types of personal objects, notably brooches, suggests an east-west difference in terms of dress and personal appearance, in that brooches have a more extensive distribution east of the Pennines. Despite the highly militarised occupation of the frontier, military objects are not frequently found, and when they are found, it is almost always in proximity to military installations. The date of recorded coins generally concurs with the regional pattern of coin loss, though not the national pattern. Few high value coins (of silver or gold) have been found, and those that have been recorded all date to the early empire; less than half the coins could be attributed to an issue period – a figure that is significantly higher than the percentage from excavated sites. This is probably due to the fact that most PAS data is from land in agricultural use where ploughing regularly destabilises the depositional environment; most Roman military installations in the north are Scheduled Monuments and, consequently, are rarely ploughed.

While these conclusions are rather general, they do offer an important validation of the patterns established through archaeological research in the frontier, in contrast to other regions of Britain. PAS data can be used for more focused investigation, and research in progress by Rob Collins has been examining late Roman and Early Medieval brooch use in the frontier.

Future research along Hadrian's Wall, particularly finds-based studies or that focusing on economic activity, must take account of PAS data, as this represents a valuable and constantly growing database for areas that are lacking in archaeological investigation.

RESEARCH UNDERTAKEN BY FINDERS

Many finders (both field-walkers and metal-detectorists) undertake research to learn more about the finds they discover and better understand the sites they search. The publication and wider dissemination of information about these discoveries is currently (in the most part) left to archaeologists and academics, but finders who plot their own finds – preferably using handheld GPS (Global Positioning Systems) devices – and do much of the primary research, are making a valuable contribution to archaeological knowledge.

Roman Leicestershire
Phil Harding, metal-detectorist
Phil Harding has been metal-detecting several Roman sites in Leicestershire, meticulously recording all his finds using GPS to plot findspots, and recording them on a database. All of this data is made available to Wendy Scott (Leicestershire & Rutland FLO) so it can be recorded on the PAS database. Dr Harding uses Reece-period analysis (which allocates a 'period' to each coin) allowing this data to build patterns of coin distribution. By studying this data, and Dr Harding's distribution maps, Sam Moorhead (National Finds Advisor) has been able to identify some interesting patterns in rural Leicestershire, including a possibly Late Roman pagan temple site. Particularly interesting is that most of the sites in Leicestershire show a decline after AD 350, but the evidence at the temple site investigated by Dr Harding shows there was activity there (and probably other parts of the county) until the early 5th century.

Research into a Bronze Age Midden
Andrew Gardner, field-walker and metal-detectorist
A number of individuals who record their finds with the PAS have undertaken metal-detecting as part of larger landscape surveys. For example, at Brailes, Warwickshire, Andrew Gardner's work – combining systematic metal-detecting, intensive field-walking and geophysical survey – has led to the discovery of an important Late Bronze Age or early Iron Age midden.

Since 1999, Andrew Gardner has been metal-detecting and field-walking in the parish of Brailes and recording all his finds with the PAS with meticulous attention to detail. Everything retrieved, whether it is a piece of metalwork or pottery fragment, has a 10-figure National Grid Reference (NGR), plotted using a handheld GPS device.

In the course of these investigations, a Late Bronze Age or early Iron Age midden site was located, and was subsequently investigated in collaboration with the PAS, Warwickshire Museum Field Services and ArchaeoPhysica.

The midden site covers two fields, one of which is called the 'Long Barrow' field. Because of this place name evidence Peter Foster (Warwickshire Museum Field Services) visited the site to see if any trace of a long barrow could be discovered. Although nothing was visible on the ground or on aerial photographs, nor identified on the Historic Environment Record, Mr Gardner had recovered numerous Late Bronze Age and early Iron Age finds from the site, including about 500 pottery sherds, animal bones, a quern stone, a spindle whorl, lots of fire-cracked stone, a Bronze Age razor, and a possible palstave axe butt. Thereafter, volunteers from the Warwickshire Field Services and the PAS field-walked 'Long Barrow' field. Mr Gardner himself also highlighted a large spread of dark soil across 'Long Barrow' and the neighbouring 'Pond Field'.

Stuart Palmer (Warwickshire Museum Field Services) first suggested the site may be a midden site based on the recorded material and highlighted a similar site 10 miles west of Brailes, at Whitchurch, which Kate Waddington and Niall Sharples (Cardiff University) are investigating. On a site visit to Brailes, Dr Sharples agreed that Brailes is probably another midden site and is keen to incorporate it into further research of these site types.

Subsequently, Cardiff University recently held a seminar – 'Unquiet Residues' – where Dr Sharples suggested a possible definition of Late Bronze Age and early Iron Age midden sites as having high artefact densities, in particular ceramic material, and a thick layer of organic soil. During the seminar a midden site at East Chisenbury, Wiltshire, was described as looking like a long barrow from a distance. Brailes has a relatively high artefact density of ceramic material, a large spread of organic material and its field name of 'Long Barrow' suggests there was at one time a mound here similar to that at East Chisenbury.

The place name evidence, the finds, and on-site observations allowed Angie Bolton (Warwickshire & Worcestershire FLO) to make a successful application to the 'Auction of Survey Time' by ArchaeoPhysica to undertake a magnetic survey of the site. This identified an unenclosed Bronze Age settlement reached by a track, which was then replaced by an early Iron Age enclosed settlement, with evidence for burning in its north-east portion.

The ceramic material recorded by Mr Gardner through the PAS, when overlaid on the survey results, reveals two hot-spots, one of which corresponds to an enclosure, and the other overlays a ditch and therefore may be unrelated to the structure beneath; instead it could represent the overlaying midden on a disused part of the earlier settlement.

Mr Gardner's work at Brailes considerably advances archaeological knowledge of midden sites. The distribution of midden sites tends to fall south of a line from the Wash to Llanmaes, south Wales. The Brailes site, along with sites at Whitchurch and Welland Bank, falls along this line. Brailes also adds to the discussion on whether these sites tend to be a single phenomenon within the landscape or whether clusters occur, such as in Wessex.

The recording of the Brailes site has also provided a springboard for further research. Warwickshire Museum Field Services are keen to research the prehistoric landscape in south Warwickshire. Likewise, ArchaeoPhysica are enthusiastic to survey more of the site, and it is hoped this will be carried out in due course. Mr Gardner is continuing his field-walking and detecting survey and maintains his high quality of recording with the PAS. Similarly, the landowner is excited at what has been discovered and has agreed not to deep plough the site and to explore ways of protecting it. Subsequently, this project was 'Highly Commended' at the British Archaeological Awards 2008.

Landscape Survey in the Trent Valley, Lincolnshire
Thomas Jolliffe, field-walker and metal-detectorist
In the Trent Valley, south of Lincoln, what began as a Saturday morning search for Victorian pennies turned into a study that has revealed a large area of dispersed Romano-British settlement, including a previously unrecorded Roman villa. Intensive field-walking by Thomas Jolliffe, followed by a large-scale geophysical survey, has gone on to show faint traces of Bronze Age land use and to suggest that the landscape was first settled in the mid to late Iron Age. The PAS has been involved since the start of the project and has been assisting in the identification of the finds, both metallic and stone. Dr Jolliffe has also been able to involve a number of specialists working in the region, in what is an important analysis of the development of the historic landscape. Metal-detecting formed a vital part of this project, as small metal objects can often be dated which, when looking at the changing pattern of land use over the millennia, provides vital anchor points.

'Without the help, encouragement and guidance of Kevin Leahy (NFA Medieval Objects) the project would never have been completed.'
Thomas Jolliffe

MAJOR RESEARCH PROJECTS

Several major research projects have made use of PAS data in 2007. These include the following which are funded by the Arts and Humanities Research Council (AHRC): *The Viking and Anglo-Saxon Landscape and*

Economy (VASLE) project (Julian Richards, University of York), *The Context of Bronze Age Hoards and Single Finds* (Richard Bradley, University of Reading), and *Technologies of Enchantment: Celtic Art in Southern Britain* (Chris Gosden, University of Oxford). A major project exploring *Anglo-Saxon Kingdoms in Southern England AD 400–750* (Martin Welch, University College, London) is funded by the Leverhulme Trust.

Viking and Anglo-Saxon Landscape and Economy (VASLE) project, York
Led by Professor Julian D Richards, University of York (John Naylor)
The VASLE project, funded by the AHRC, ran at the University of York from October 2004 until December 2007. The first major project to utilise PAS data, VASLE also used portable coinage data (provided by the Early Medieval Corpus of Early Medieval coins) to investigate rural settlement and economy during the period from c. AD 700–1050. The project had several objectives, relating both to the Early Medieval period and more general research into portable antiquities. Firstly, VASLE explored the nature of PAS data, analysing the constraints on data collection and what effects this has on how archaeologists should approach the material. With this in mind, the research then focused on the broad trends in the data from England and Wales in the study period, before looking in depth at the interpretation of individual 'productive sites'. Alongside a number of publications in edited volumes and journals, the full results of the project are published in *Internet Archaeology* 25.

Contexts of Bronze Age Hoards and Single Finds
Led by Professor Richard Bradley (David Yates)
During 2008, the AHRC funded a one-year pilot study to explore the context of Later Bronze Age metalwork finds. Richard Bradley and David Yates (University of Reading) have investigated a hundred findspots in parts of Hampshire, Sussex and Kent. The priority has been to look at well-provenanced findspots, and in this respect PAS data has been invaluable. Working with FLOs and with the co-operation of detectorists and landowners, visits have been made throughout the study area to look at the setting and to consider the significance of placement in those locations.

During the European Bronze Age (2500–750 BC), widely spaced parts of the continent were drawn together by an expanding communications network resulting in the rapid spread of new ideas, material wealth and the movement of people. The range of prestige bronze work found in southern England is the legacy of this first golden or international age. Those finds have much to tell us about territorial control, political power and prevalent belief systems. Throughout Europe, social organisation was based on a close relationship between prestige goods exchange and a complex ritual system

which perpetuated an elite ideology. It was a social network which collapsed in the Iron Age transition. The investigation of the nature of this dynamic extended economy, and its eventual demise, is of considerable interest to both British and European archaeologists. The international delegates at the conferences noted with envy the quality of the archaeological records available in England. Such invaluable research databases (particularly the PAS) enable us to explore the Bronze Age power bases of southern England within the wider setting of an English Channel-North Sea economic region.

The provisional results were presented to two recent conferences: the Bronze Age Forum (Sheffield University) and the Theoretical Archaeological Group (Southampton University). The results are now being written up ready for publication. The intention is to take this research further, concentrating initially on the Thames Valley, the Fenlands and the North Sea coastal regions, again in co-operation with FLOs and metal-detectorists.

UNDERGRADUATE AND POSTGRADUATE RESEARCH

The PAS, in partnership with several major academic institutions, has been successful in bids to the AHRC for collaborative PhD studentships. These include Tom Brindle (with King's College, London) analysing Roman rural landuse in Britain – comparing PAS and Historic Environment Records data, Ian Leins (with the University of Newcastle) examining Iron Age coinage based on PAS and Celtic Coin Index data, and Philippa Walton (with University College, London) exploring coin use and loss in Roman Britain based on PAS data. In 2008, Richard Kelleher (with the University of Durham) began researching patterns of coin use and loss in England between 1180 and 1560, and in 2009, Katherine Robbins (with the University of Southampton) started investigating how representative the PAS data is for understanding the spatial distribution of artefact types and human activities in the past. These studentships demonstrate the value of the data collated, and also very welcome that the AHRC is funding such research in the advancement of archaeological knowledge.

Besides these it is known that 14 other PhDs, 26 MA dissertations and 12 undergraduate research projects have used PAS data in 2007.

The PAS and Roman Britain: an assessment of the potential for using amateur metal-detector data to enhance understanding of the Roman period
Tom Brindle, formerly Northamptonshire FLO
Tom Brindle is undertaking a PhD exploring the potential for PAS data to add to our understanding of Romano-British landscapes. His research is based on a series of regional case studies, covering Wiltshire, Worcestershire and Warwickshire, Northamptonshire, North Lincolnshire and Cumbria. In each of these regions, Tom is exploring methodologies for defining Romano-British sites based upon their artefact assemblages, and comparing the distribution of sites represented by metal-detector finds with those recorded by more traditional archaeological techniques.

Research so far has shown that finds reported by metal-detectorists are leading to the recognition of a number of previously unknown Romano-British sites, and that the landscape in much of Britain during the Roman period was even more intensively populated than previously recognised. For example, in Wiltshire, it has been possible to identify at least 42 new Romano-British sites, known solely from material recorded on the PAS database. One of these sites may even be the location of a previously unknown Romano-Celtic temple. Where metal-detector finds are reported from sites that are already known, they have the potential to provide new information about those sites. Finds from near the Roman town of *Bannaventa* in Northamptonshire, for example, are providing useful chronological information about the development of this area over time, perhaps suggesting that the focus for settlement at the town shifted between the early and late Roman period.

An Applied Numismatic Analysis of the PAS Roman Coin Data
Philippa Walton, Institute of Archaeology, University College, London
Philippa Walton has been studying 56,339 Roman coins recorded on the PAS database as part of an AHRC collaborative project at University College, London and the British Museum. By using this resource, her project aims to transform knowledge of the Romano-British rural landscape. She intends to explore regional and chronological differences in the use and loss of coin, assess site functions through coin profiles and investigate in more detail sites which have been preliminarily identified as rural temples and shrines.

This project will complement and build upon existing applied numismatic research, particularly that of Richard Reece, which analysed excavated material from 140 sites in Britain including forts, temples, urban centres and villas. As the PAS data is both a rural and a national dataset, it will be possible to create a more balanced picture for the province. For the first time,

there will be potential to study regional patterns and differences across 400 years of Roman rule and these results will have wide appeal to academics, professional archaeologists and members of the public.

The first year of the project concentrated on data cleaning and identifying individual coin assemblages on the PAS database. Organising the data by modern county, Philippa has shown that Roman coins have been recorded by the PAS in nearly a third of all English parishes and identified 470 parishes where 20 or more have been found. This means that the picture for areas such as Lincolnshire, Suffolk and Northamptonshire has been vastly improved with several assemblages comprising more than 1,000 coins.

The next stage of Philippa's research will be to identify geographical and chronological patterns in the PAS data. She will also try and establish potential function for some of the sites with large assemblages by comparing their coin profiles with those from nearly 400 excavated sites throughout Britain.

SIXTH-FORM RESEARCH PROJECTS

Besides study at university, some A-Level students are also making use of PAS data. Unlike universities with archaeological departments, the PAS does not have a proactive outreach programme with sixth-form schools and colleges, and it is therefore somewhat accidental if students in secondary education use PAS data in a research topic.

Understanding Taunton Deane in the Roman Period
Virginia Spencer
As part of her A-Level archaeology coursework, Virginia Spencer (Richard Huish College, Taunton) examined the extent to which metal-detecting and PAS data impact upon our understanding of occupation in the Roman period around the Taunton Deane area of Somerset. Using the PAS website and database, Virginia was able to study the types of Roman coins discovered locally as well as their date and method of discovery. From the data, she was able to draw up a map of Somerset, which showed the majority of finds were made by metal-detecting after 1975. Consequently, she contacted a local metal-detecting club and sent its members a short questionnaire enquiring about any Roman artefacts they had found. Although she only received one reply, it did reveal the wealth of artefacts being discovered, though not all of it was apparently reported, and therefore of no research benefit.

From the data collated, Virginia was able to conclude that the information from the PAS database does advance our knowledge of Romanisation in Somerset. However, one limitation was that the finds were mainly stray ones, indicating accidental dropping instead of hoarding. A study into the impact of the PAS also revealed that between 1999 and 2005, the number of user hits on the PAS website had increased 105%. The number of reported Treasure cases had also shot up dramatically after being level for nearly 10 years. These increases were attributed to the ease of service and a greater public understanding of how to deal with finds (again, brought about by the PAS).

'My main conclusion was that the PAS is fundamental in helping us understand our history. It certainly helped me!'
Virginia Spencer

DESK-BASED ARCHAEOLOGICAL RESEARCH AND ASSESSMENT

The data generated by the PAS is made available to Historic Environment Records (HERs), the key record holders of information about the historic environment. A protocol has been agreed on the transfer of PAS data to HERs, which 54 HERs (more than two-thirds) have now signed. This enables PAS data to be migrated with information about sites on the HER and also helps identify new sites that were previously unknown. This data is made available to local archaeologists and other researchers, and also helps inform the development control process. Examples of how this data is being used and enhance our understanding of the past are given below.

Historic Landscape Characterisation Project on the Isle of Wight

The Isle of Wight Council has recently completed a programme of Historic Landscape Characterisation (HLC) and is now using this information to prepare a Historic Environment Action Plan (HEAP). PAS data has been used to create a digital map for the HEAP in which PAS finds were displayed in relation to HLC areas. Inclusion of the PAS data has added an extra dimension to the analysis and understanding of Isle of Wight HLC areas and may suggest new priorities for future fieldwork or research. However, it will also have a practical impact on the future management of the island's historic environment as the HEAP is being used to inform the 'Island Plan', one of the first Local Development Plans to be prepared under recent Government legislation.

Lincolnshire PAS-HER Survey

Adam Daubney (Lincolnshire FLO) has recently carried out a comparison of finds recorded on the PAS and sites recorded on the Lincolnshire Historic Environment Record (HER). As of October 2008, the PAS dataset for Lincolnshire stood at 21,169 finds contained in 15,992 records. The aim of the survey was to examine how many finds recorded on the PAS for Lincolnshire came from new sites, and how many were from sites already recorded on the HER, including undated crop marks. An artefact scatter was interpreted as 'five or more associated finds'. If there were no related archaeological sites within a 300-metre radius, the group of finds was classed as a 'new site'. Similarly, if a known related site fell within this radius, the group of finds was noted as coming from an existing site. A fuller explanation of the methodology and results is hoped to be published in due course.

The survey revealed that within the 21,169 finds recorded for Lincolnshire on the PAS, there are 328 'sites' (an area containing five or more related finds). Of these 328 sites, 175 (53%) were previously unknown; 141 (43%) embellished sites were already recorded on the HER. 12 sites (4%) recorded on the PAS came from undated crop marks recorded on the HER, thus providing tentative dating evidence.

This equates to 1.34 new sites being recorded every month between 1997 and 2007. It might be expected that the majority of these sites was recorded during the first few years of the PAS expanding to the whole of England and Wales in 2003. However this is not the case. An analysis of data recorded between 1 January 2008 and 30 September 2008 showed that finds were recorded from a further 32 sites, of which 14 were previously unknown. This equates to 1.55 sites being recorded each month during the first 9 months of 2008, making this one of the largest and fastest growing archaeological datasets in England.

The most significant contribution to new sites in Lincolnshire is for the Roman period, followed by 6th-century Anglo-Saxon cemetery sites. The division between districts is shown in Table 1.

	West Lindsey		
	New sites	Existing sites	Crop marks
Prehistoric	0	1	0
Roman	23	14	2
Early Medieval	11	1	0
Medieval	4	17	1
Post-Medieval	0	3	0
	East Lindsey		
	New sites	Existing sites	Crop marks
Prehistoric	0	0	1
Roman	24	4	2
Early Medieval	5	2	0
Medieval	13	27	0
Post-Medieval	0	2	0
	South Kesteven		
	New sites	Existing sites	Crop marks
Prehistoric	3	0	0
Roman	22	10	0
Early Medieval	5	1	0
Medieval	2	13	0
Post-Medieval	0	1	0
	Boston & South Holland		
	New sites	Existing sites	Crop marks
Prehistoric	0	0	0
Roman	0	3	0
Early Medieval	0	0	0
Medieval	3	4	1
Post-Medieval	2	3	0
	North Kesteven		
	New sites	Existing sites	Crop marks
Prehistoric	5	1	1
Roman	30	21	4
Early Medieval	11	3	0
Medieval	12	9	0
Post-Medieval	0	1	0

Table 1: sites recorded in Lincolnshire, by district.

PUBLICATIONS

Augustus Pitt-Rivers once said that an archaeological site has not been discovered until it has been recorded, researched and published, and his words are just as relevant today as they were in the Victorian period. Portable antiquities, though many upon first sight seem to lack aesthetic appeal or appear insignificant, are no different. Until they have been recorded and published, they are unknown and therefore their potential cannot be realised. While the PAS encourages finders to make their own records of their finds, it is essential all these discoveries are recorded and published to high archaeological standards. All finds recorded by the PAS

are published on its online database, and full data is made available to HERs and researchers.

Important finds recorded by the PAS are also published in this annual report, and in the period journals *Britannia* (Roman), *Medieval Archaeology* and *Post-Medieval Archaeology*. In addition, the FLOs regularly contribute to local journals. A few of the notable articles and publications published in 2007 include:

Worrell (2007): Of particular interest are the local and regional variations in Iron Age material culture use and deposition through space and time. This paper examines the Iron Age artefact data recorded by the PAS between 1997 and October 2004. It represents a broad-brush preliminary analysis which aims to highlight the real potential of this data by investigating some important general trends through quantitative and distribution analyses. It includes studies examining the Late Iron Age brooch and horse-and-vehicle equipment recorded by the PAS, highlighting strong regional variation. In addition, it features a study comparing the Iron Age metallic artefacts from Hampshire recorded by the PAS against those discovered during archaeological fieldwork or as earlier chance finds. The study of material culture is key to understanding regional variations among Iron Age societies. In addition, the national coverage of the PAS makes a major contribution to the 'regionality' debate.

Sutton and Worrell (2007): This paper gives an overview of the 695 Roman objects interpreted as relating to the sphere of 'religion' recorded by the PAS between 1997 and April 2006. Within this group, the 199 copper-alloy, lead, stone and ceramic figurines represent a very significant addition to the known corpus of objects of this type. A wide range of deities is represented and while the classical deities or their attributes frequently occur, some representations of gods of Romano-Celtic type also occur. The figurines and miniature objects are widely distributed across central and southern Britain, but particular concentrations are seen in East Anglia and Lincolnshire. The final section of the paper publishes a selection of the nine objects of religious character recorded in Oxfordshire.

Naylor (2007): This paper employs quantitative and distributional analyses to finds of Early Medieval coinage in an area of north-east England. The results show that observed patterns of coin loss on individual sites do represent the overall coin loss for the study area, and sites can be confidently compared to each other and the region as a whole. It appears that the role and function of coinage changed dramatically over the period from a medium of long-distance trade in the early 8th century to a cash currency by the

Viking takeover of York. A review of 'productive sites' in the region suggests that they can only be adequately interpreted through analysis of their assemblages against the background of the regional circulation of coinage and artefacts.

Lewis (2007): This paper considers William's Class A, Type 11a stirrup-strap mounts which are traditionally attributed as late Anglo-Saxon, and argues that they are in fact Romanesque – dating to between about 1070 and 1140, based on parallels in art. The paper also discusses the spatial distribution of Class A, Type 11a mounts. Here it is suggested that the concentration of these mounts and artistic models in Kent might indicate they were manufactured locally.

Editor: Michael Lewis

Some interesting stone objects have been recorded in 2007; it is particularly good to see finds of Lower Palaeolithic handaxes from areas where they were previously unknown, as at Newport, Isle of Wight (1). These are starting to fill out the ancient landscape. Both Mesolithic flaked axes and Neolithic polished axes continue to be found. The unpolished, rough-cut, axe from Aspatria, Cumbria (11) was made from stone extracted at Great Langdale, Cumbria, and reflects the way in which axes were transported, unfinished and presumably ground by the user. Perforated pebble 'mace-heads' are interesting, if enigmatic, finds and it is useful to see further examples, such as those from Weethley, Warwickshire (3), and Camberley, Surrey (4).

The Stone Age section of this report is small and does not reflect how common worked flint and stone is in Britain. The recording of lithic materials has great potential but it also offers challenges. The groups of flints from Ridge, Hertfordshire (5), and Tatworth and Forton, Somerset (6), are small, but flintworking sites can be prolific and present a formidable problem for Finds Liaison Officers (FLOs) who record these finds. That said, many of the fieldwalkers who are collecting worked flint are now using handheld Global Position Systems (GPS) devices which can record findspots to within a metre. This not only helps the FLOs who record the finds, but also has enormous potential for understanding the Prehistoric landscape.

STONE AGE

1. Newport, Isle of Wight: flint handaxe (PAS: IOW-A0FB18)

Date: Lower Palaeolithic (c. 500,000–c. 100,000 BC).
Discovery: Found by Brian Masterton while metal-detecting in 2007, and recorded by Frank Basford (Isle of Wight FLO).
Description: An almost complete 'sub-cordate' flint handaxe. Symmetrical and worked on both faces, the implement has a pointed tip and a rounded butt. Its great age is shown by its slightly 'rolled' surfaces. This implement, a surface find on cultivated land, is in a remarkably good condition. Dimensions: 148.5 x 79.2 x 37.1mm.
Discussion: This is an important find locally as it came from an area where Palaeolithic implements would not have been expected to be found. It is one of the increasing number of Lower Palaeolithic implements recorded by the PAS.
Disposition: Returned to finder.

F BASFORD

2. Wrabness, Essex: flint tranchet adze (PAS: ESS-43E6D6)

Date: Mesolithic (c. 9000–c. 6000 BC).
Discovery: Found by Sarah Whitcombe while walking the beach in May 2007, and recorded by Laura McLean (Essex FLO) via Colchester Museum.

Description: Axe or adze roughly knapped from a flint nodule, its butt end retaining traces of cortext representing the nodule's original surface. Both faces of the tool have been worked to give it a lentoid section. Its cutting edge was formed by the removal of a single large flake from the end of the axe. Dimensions: 138.7 x 49.7 x 29.4mm.

Discussion: Tranchet axes are a characteristic of the early Mesolithic period, although there have been suggestions that the type may have also been used at a later date. These tools get their name from the way in which they were sharpened: oblique 'tranchet' flakes being removed to form a sharp cutting edge with one or two blows.

Disposition: Returned to finder.

L MCLEAN

---

3. Weethley, Warwickshire: perforated stone pebble (PAS: WAW-BA8194)

Date: Mesolithic (c. 8300–c. 4500 BC).

Discovery: Found by Liam Maude while gardening in 2007, and recorded by Angie Bolton (Warwickshire & Worcestershire FLO).

Description: This tool was made from a hard quartzite pebble through which a hole had been chipped. The hole has a biconical 'hourglass' shape due to it being made by working from both sides of the stone, the two holes narrowing as they neared the centre. The pebble probably came from river gravels, becoming rounded by being tumbled with other stones on the river bed. However, further shaping may have been done by the maker of the tool. Dimensions: 107.9 x 101.3 x 40.53mm. Diameter of hole: 28.3mm (at its narrowest).

Discussion: It is not easy to either date pebble tools or to say for what they were used. Many date from the Mesolithic period but it appears that they were also made at a later date. Suggested uses for them include mace-heads, digging stick or bolas weights.

Disposition: Returned to finder.

A BOLTON

---

4. Camberley, Surrey: perforated stone implement (PAS: SUR-425AB0)

Date: Mesolithic to Neolithic (c. 8000–c. 2000 BC).

Discovery: Found by the father of Mr A G Seale in the garden of his house in Camberley in 1945, and brought to a Finds Day at Frimley Green Library, where it was identified by David Williams (Surrey FLO).

Description: A perforated stone implement made from a fine-grained, oval river pebble, buff coloured with closely spaced lighter streaks. The hole has an hourglass shape, its diameter tapering from 11.6 to 12.2mm. There is no sign of further working to form an implement. Dimensions: 90.7 x 65.8 x 29.7mm.

Discussion: This fine object belongs to the same class as No. 3 and the same points can be made about it. It

is curious that the makers of these objects should have chosen to make holes through some of the hardest and most intractable stones found in Britain. However, it may be wrong to see perforated stones just in terms of practicality, as they also may have had some ritual function.

Disposition: Returned to finder.

D WILLIAMS

---

5. Ridge, Hertfordshire: collection of five flint blade cores (PAS: BH-2C8256)

Date: Late Mesolithic to Early Neolithic (c. 6500–c. 3000 BC).

Discovery: Found by Michael Lidington while field-walking in 2007, and recorded with Julian Watters (Hertfordshire & Bedfordshire FLO).

Description: Five flint 'cores' representing waste products from the manufacture of flint tools. The parallel-sided scars down the sides of the cores show where flakes have been detached before being 'retouched' to make tools (see 14).

Dimensions: The largest core measures 57.9 x 40.9mm and the smallest 43.4 x 40.8mm.

Discussion: A further 60 worked flints were found in the same area as the cores, and this provides good evidence for Prehistoric flint working on the site. Two types of core were found and it is possible that they are of different periods.

Disposition: Returned to finder.

J WATTERS

---

6. Tatworth and Forton, Somerset: flint implement (PAS: SOM-F73913)

Date: Neolithic or Early Bronze Age (c. 3800–c. 1500 BC).

Discovery: Found by Douglas W Long while metal-detecting in 2007, and recorded with Naomi Payne (Somerset FLO).

Description: A notched flint flake with an integral awl. The implement has been made on a primary flake; the original surface of the flint cobble covers most of one side. On the worked faces the knapping scars, with their typically rippled faces, can be clearly seen. One edge of the flake has been retouched to form a pointed awl. Dimensions: 72.0 x 42.6 x 10.6mm.

Discussion: This find is only one of a group of around 30 worked flints found in the same area which may represent a flintworking site.

Disposition: Returned to finder.

N PAYNE

7. City of London: polished stone axehead (PAS: LON-E1FFD6)

Date: Neolithic (c. 3500–c. 2200 BC).

Discovery: Found by Andy Johanessen and Steve Brooker while searching the Thames foreshore in 2007, and recorded with Kate Sumnall (London FLO).

Description: Polished stone axehead made from an attractive, mottled green stone. An asymmetrical cutting edge suggests either damage or wear. Dimensions: 96 x 48.9 x 30.2mm.

Discussion: This axe is made from a stone which is clearly not from the London area and must have been imported from an axe production site in the west of Britain. It is possible that it was, like many other Prehistoric objects, deliberately deposited in the river.

Disposition: Returned to finder.

K SUMNALL

8. Breamore, Hampshire: polished flint axehead (PAS: WILT-E544F7)

Date: Neolithic (c. 3500–c. 2000 BC).

Discovery: Found by L Haston while gardening in 2007, and recorded by Katie Hinds (Wiltshire FLO).

Description: Polished flint axe. Its cutting edge has been broken in antiquity and resharpened by removing flakes from both sides. Dimensions: 106 x 53.2 x 28mm.

Discussion: This axe was probably made from flint extracted from a mine and roughly shaped by knapping. Once shaped it was polished using sandstone and water to grind away all trace of the flake scars. This produced a fine axe but, following damage, a new cutting edge was produced by knapping. However, this re-working was not polished and the flake scars were left. A difference in colour between the original and reworked surfaces suggests that some time must have elapsed between these events. Sharpened in this way, the axe would not have worked so well, tending to stick when cutting wood.

Disposition: Returned to finder.

K HINDS

9. Weaverham, Cheshire: flint adze (PAS: LVPL-0E5426)

Date: Neolithic (c. 3500–c. 2100 BC).

Discovery: Found by Joy Beresford on a ploughed field while metal-detecting in March 2007, and identified by Sally Worrell (National Finds Advisor) and recorded with Frances McIntosh (Cheshire, Greater Manchester & Merseyside FLO).

Description: Neolithic adze with an elegant, waisted, shape. It was made using a toffee-coloured flint, ground to produce a highly polished surface. Dimensions: 136 x 51 x 16mm.

Discussion: This adze belongs to the 'Seamer type' which are marked by their characteristic incurved sides, high quality of the polishing and the use of coloured stone.

Disposition: Returned to finder.

F MCINTOSH

10. Welwyn, Hertfordshire: puddingstone grain rubber or hammerstone (PAS: BH-7431C5)

Date: Probably Prehistoric (Neolithic to Iron Age) but could extend into Roman period (c. 3500 BC–c. AD 43).

Discovery: Found by Nick Tracken while field-walking in 2007, and recorded by Julian Watters (Hertfordshire & Bedfordshire FLO).

Description: This hand-sized puddingstone implement is spherical with flattened top and bottom surfaces. Its outer faces are pitted, showing that it was shaped through repeated blows from another stone. The underside has a smoother appearance, suggesting that it was used to grind grain over a longer period. Dimensions: 65 (diameter) x 44.7mm.

Discussion: Puddingstone is a concretion of rounded flint pebbles set in matrix of fine sand and silica. Recent work in east Hertfordshire (the main source of puddingstone) may have revealed evidence for quarry sites, probably used from as early as the Neolithic period. By Roman times puddingstone was well regarded as a material for the production of querns. It is not certain what this object was used for, although it is likely to have been either as a grain rubber or for shaping the quernstones themselves.

Disposition: Returned to finder.

J WATTERS

11. Aspatria, Cumbria: rough-out for a stone axe (PAS: LANCUM-B5A373)

Date: Neolithic (c. 3000–c. 2000 BC).

Discovery: Found by Malcolm Dunn while field-walking in the 1970s, and recorded by Dot Boughton in 2007 (Lancashire & Cumbria FLO).

Description: Unfinished stone axe made from the dark green volcanic stone which, during the Neolithic period, was quarried at Great Langdale, Cumbria. Dimensions: 359 x 87.8 x 54.9mm.

Discussion: Axes made from this lithified volcanic tuff were in use all over northern Britain and Great Langdale must have been a major production centre. Although knapped to shape, the Aspatria axe had not been polished, suggesting that, in the Neolithic period, people polished their own axes. Prior to being shown to the FLO this axe had been serving as a doorstop!

Disposition: Returned to finder.

D BOUGHTON

12. Mildenhall, Suffolk: flint axehead (PAS: SF-60C586)

Date: Neolithic (c. 3500–c. 2100 BC).
Discovery: Found by Jamie Thompson while metal-detecting in 2007, and recorded by Faye Minter (Suffolk FLO) and identified by Colin Pendleton (Suffolk County Council Archaeology Service).
Description: Flint axe that is partly polished. The central portion has notable areas of gloss within the flake scars. These are possibly the residues of an adhesive used to fix the axe to its handle, if this is the case this is a rare occurence on axeheads.
Dimensions: 133 x 42 x 21mm.
Discussion: Neolithic axeheads are generally more common finds than Mesolithic examples in Suffolk; there are 821 Neolithic axeheads recorded to date on the Suffolk Historic Environment Record to 185 Mesolithic examples.
Disposition: Returned to finder.

F MINTER & C PENDLETON

13. Paul, Cornwall: flint knife (PAS: CORN-DB49D2)

Date: Late Neolithic to Early Bronze Age (Beaker Period) (c. 2700–c. 1700 BC).
Discovery: Found by David Edwards while field-walking in May 2007, and recorded by Anna Tyacke (Cornwall FLO).
Description: Flint 'plano-convex' knife shaped by pressure flaking. Traces of gloss on one of the knife's edges suggest that that it was used to cut organic material. The flint used is a mottled, light grey to translucent brown colour and could have been made from local flint sources. Dimensions: 83 x 25 x 11mm.
Discussion: Flint knives of this type have been found in Beaker Period and Early Bronze Age graves, which enables them to be dated.
Disposition: Returned to finder.

A TYACKE

14. Birkin, North Yorkshire: flint arrowhead (PAS: SWYOR-C19C04)

Date: Late Neolithic (c. 2500–c. 2000 BC).
Discovery: Found by Andrew Diamond while metal-detecting in 2007, and recorded with Amy Cooper (South & West Yorkshire FLO).
Description: Arrowhead made from a fine, translucent flint; both faces are plain, retouch being restricted to the edges. The arrowhead is asymmetric with a single barb on one side of the blade. Dimensions: 38.2 x 22.3 x 3.6mm.
Discussion: With its single, asymmetrical barb, this flint has the shape of a Late Neolithic 'oblique' arrowhead but, unusually, the retouch extends almost all around its edges leaving them blunt. The arrowhead exhibits the features that mark it as a humanly worked flint: on its faces are the curving ripples of the characteristic 'conchoidal' fracture and around its edges can be seen the marks left when small flakes were removed during 'retouching'.
Disposition: Returned to finder.

A COOPER

Section editor and further research: Kevin Leahy.
Editor: Michael Lewis.

As in previous years, an extremely diverse range of Bronze Age metalwork, including weapons, tools and ornaments, has been recorded. Particularly unusual and noteworthy finds include the Early Bronze Age flat axe decorated with a 'rain-pattern', found in the Shrewsbury area, Shropshire (17); the incomplete Middle Bronze Age looped palstave mould from Hempnall, Norfolk (33); the two Middle Bronze Age 'Ornament Horizon' artefacts represented by the incised penannular arm-ring from Binsted, Hampshire (34), and the quoit-headed pin from Ranby, Lincolnshire (28); and – dating from the Late Bronze Age – the unusual indented socketed axehead of Type Ulleskelf found at Ilam, Staffordshire (48), and the decorated spearhead of Alpine Type found at Appledram, West Sussex (59).

Apart from lithic objects dating to the Bronze Age, there were other unusual and noteworthy non-metallic finds from this period. These include the wooden weaving paddle from Heptonstall (16) and the bone artefacts in the funerary deposit from Stanbury (19), both in West Yorkshire. Although Bronze Age pottery sherds are not generally common finds, a very significant quantity of 184 pieces of Late Bronze Age to Iron Age handmade, shell-tempered pottery was recorded accurately using a GPS (Global Position Systems) device, from the probable midden site at Brailes, Warwickshire (see Research section).

During 2007, 27 Bronze Age Treasure cases were reported, of which 16 are base-metal hoards or groups; there are 12 single gold finds. The Treasure case that particularly stands out is the exceptional group of four hoards of Late Bronze Age to Early Iron Age socketed axes from Langton Matravers, Dorset (60), which contain 276 complete socketed axes, 107 halves of socketed axes and 117 fragments of socketed axes. This represents one of the largest hoards ever discovered in Britain and the largest-ever socketed axe hoard. Other unusual Treasure cases are represented by the find from Stanbury, West Yorkshire (19), deposited with the cremated remains of a young male, which consisted of two bronze basket-shaped earrings, an accessory vessel, a bone pin, a bone belt hook and a battle-axe.

In comparison with previous years, the chronology of the base-metal hoards is more evenly divided between the Middle and Late Bronze Age with six and ten cases respectively; the only Early Bronze Age Treasure case was from Stanbury, West Yorkshire (19). The Late Bronze Age base-metal hoards are distributed with three cases in Kent (54, 55 and 2007 T144) and single cases from Suffolk (2007 T206), Essex (52), Norfolk (53), Warwickshire (2007 T615), Hampshire (51) and Dorset (60). The distribution of the Middle Bronze Age base-metal hoards is more widespread with single cases from East Sussex (31), Wiltshire (41), Suffolk (2007 T526), Hampshire (32), Cornwall (24) and East Yorkshire (2007 T518).

BRONZE AGE

The gold ornaments reported this year include three bracelet fragments, from Seagry, Wiltshire (36), West Wight, Isle of Wight (58), and near Shorwell, Isle of Wight (2007 T429), one bead from Burton, Wrexham (35), one sheet strip fragment from West Acre, Norfolk (39), one ribbon ornament fragment from Ansley, Warwickshire (38), and one composite ring from Stone, Buckinghamshire (37). In all but one instance (58) the objects date to the Middle Bronze Age. There were five penannular rings (40 & 44–47), all consisting of a single gold ring, representing an artefact type which mostly dates to the Late Bronze Age and may be either plain or decorated with stripes of yellow and paler gold stripes.

Excluding examples of Middle Bronze Age composite gold penannular rings with multiple (but usually two or three) gold rings, and finds of penannular gold rings found in groups or in hoards which combine gold and base-metal objects, a total of 49 penannular rings have been recorded between 1996 and 2007 as single finds. A 1997 corpus of penannular rings, edited by George Eogan (1997: 308–320), maps the distribution of 19 finds known mainly from the Sussex-Wessex region. Largely as a result of the introduction of the Treasure Act 1996, in just 10 years not only has there been a very significant increase in the quantity of gold penannular rings known, but the distribution (see Figure 1) can now be shown to extend across much of central Britain, with a definite focus in Hampshire, where 10 examples have now been recorded (O'Connor, Cowie and Worrell 2008: 12–13).

Figure 1
Penannular rings recorded by PAS

▲ 1996 to 2006
★ 2007

15. Ringland, Norfolk: flint arrowhead (PAS: NMS-27F534)

Date: Late Neolithic/Early Bronze Age (c. 2500–c. 1500 BC).
Discovery: Found by Lavinia Leanard in 1918–1920 on ground disturbed by horses and reported to Norfolk Museums and Archaeology Service by Beverley and Eunice Hutchin in April 2007, where it was identified by Peter Robins.
Description: A small barbed and tanged arrowhead of 'Sutton Type b' (Green 1980: 50–51; Butler 2005: 162–165, fig. 69). It has pointed barbs, a rounded tang and an intact tip. Both lateral edges are flaked bifacially and a large area on each face is retouched. Thickness: 4mm.
Discussion: It is probable that this arrowhead represents a hunting loss as this object was intended for use rather than for ceremonial purposes. Barbed and tanged arrowheads date to the Beaker Period at the end of the Neolithic and the start of the Bronze Age. Although this arrowhead was discovered some time between 1918 and 1920, the object and a precise findspot were passed down in the family, allowing a full record to be made.
Disposition: Returned to owner.

E B DARCH

16. Heptonstall, West Yorkshire: wooden weaving paddle (PAS: SWYOR-93A570)

Date: Probably Bronze Age (c. 2500–c. 800 BC).
Discovery: Found by Brian Howcroft while fieldwalking in 2005, reported to Anna Marshall (South & West Yorkshire FLO) and recorded by Amy Cooper (South & West Yorkshire FLO) in 2007.
Description: A paddle, tangentially aligned, and consisting of a flat-faced blade, slightly thicker at the top (11mm) than at the bottom (8mm), and a handle with a sub-rectangular cross section extending back from the rear of the blade. The tip and bottom of the blade appear damaged and are probably broken. Dimensions (total): 470 x 72 x 11mm. Dimensions (handle): 205 x 22 x 11mm.
Discussion: The paddle has been examined by Henry Chapman (Birmingham Archaeo-Environmental) and Michael Bamforth (L-P: Archaeology) and it is believed that it may have been used as a flax beater. The wood is certainly worked, though the species has not yet been identified. Similar sized objects have been assigned as possible weaving swords during the operation of looms. Weaving swords date back to the Early Bronze Age and have been used through to the Medieval period. However, without contextual or other dating evidence it is not possible to positively assign a function to this artefact. A probable Bronze Age date is suggested since Bronze Age flints have been found at the same place.
Deposition: Returned to finder.

A COOPER

17. Shrewsbury area, Shropshire: copper-alloy flat axe (PAS: HESH-299826)

Date: Early Bronze Age (c. 2250–c. 1900 BC).

Discovery: Found by Ian Collins while metal-detecting in 2007, and reported to Peter Reavill (Herefordshire & Shropshire FLO).

Description: An incomplete, decorated flat axe with approximately 75% now surviving. The axe is broadly sub-rectangular in plan and has a splayed, crescentic edge which displays a distinctive curve. The opposite edge is relatively flat, a feature which is likely to have been caused by the axe having been cast in an open stone mould. The edges of the axe have not been raised to form flanges; however, a slight median bevel (proto stop-ridge) is present on both faces. This feature has been formed from hammering and small oval (dished) scars can be seen on both faces where the metal has been worked. Below the bevel the sides continue to expand. The area between the median ridge and junction with the blade facet is decorated on both faces with a series of parallel linear lentoid lozenges. This form of decoration is known as 'rain-pattern' and is common on the later decorated axes of the Migdale metalworking tradition. In addition, both sides of the axe are decorated with a series of cabled motifs formed by hammering and which survive better on one side where three distinct facets of the cabling can be seen. The break, close to the butt of the axe, is relatively jagged and uneven; its patina suggests that damage occurred in antiquity. Dimensions: 110.4 x 89.3 x 12.7mm. Weight: 417g.

Discussion: This axehead forms part of the corpus of the earliest bronze axes of Britain and dates to the same period as Beaker pottery, barbed and tanged flint arrowheads, copper halberds and gold *lunulae*. It is best described as coming from the later phases of the Migdale tradition of metalworking (stage IV-VI) corresponding to Needham's (1996: 127–132) Period 2–3, dating to c. 2250–c. 1900 BC, calibrated. However, this axe also bears some similarities in blade shape to the Developed Early Bronze Age Axes, specifically variants Falkland and Scrabo Hill. This would suggest that this example is dated to the very final phases of the Migdale tradition. A good comparison to the style of decoration is known from Cuminstone, Aberdeenshire (Schmidt and Burgess 1981: 46, no. 205, pl. 17).

Disposition: Returned to finder.

P REAVILL

18. Collingham, Nottinghamshire: copper-alloy miniature flat axe (PAS: LIN-A8A8A1)

Date: Early Bronze Age (c. 2150–c. 1600 BC).

Discovery: Found by Brian Hillier while searching with a metal-detector in 2007, and recorded with Adam Daubney (Lincolnshire FLO).

Description: A miniature copper-alloy flat axe or axe-chisel. The narrow butt is slightly rounded at the end, the body is straight sided with a lenticular cross-section, and the blade end gently expands at the cutting edge. The surface of the axe is covered with a mid-brown surface patina, but where the core is exposed, such as along the cutting edge, the copper-alloy is light green, indicating active corrosion. Dimensions: 43 x 15 x 5mm.

Discussion: Miniature flat axes are rare finds, and only three other examples are recorded on the PAS database: from Misterton, Somerset (SOMDOR-8A1F53), Burnham Market, Norfolk (NMS592), and Westerfield, Suffolk (SF6514). In addition, a flat axe with narrow butt and a central bevel which was expanded through re-sharpening was found at Danebury, Hampshire (Cunliffe and O'Connor 1979: 236, no. 1, fig. 12.1). It is believed that, due to their diminutive size, such axes were probably the blades of light woodworking tools such as chisels (Britton 1963: 271) although they could also have been used as votive flat axes.

Disposition: Returned to finder.

A DAUBNEY

19. Stanbury, West Yorkshire: funerary deposit with two copper-alloy basket-shaped earrings (PAS: SWYOR-C4F166; Treasure: 2007 T388)

Date: Early Bronze Age (c. 2020–c. 1770 BC, confirmed by radiocarbon dating (SUERC-16360).

Discovery: Found by Mr Holmes while digging garden features in March 2007, and reported to Amy Cooper (South & West Yorkshire FLO). Excavation completed by Archaeological Services, West Yorkshire Archaeological Service.

Description: The cremated remains of a young middle adult male were contained in a large collared ceramic urn and accompanied in the urn by an accessory cup of Contracted-mouth class (Longworth 1967), a pair of bronze basket-shaped earrings, a bone pin of Atkinson's (1951: 142–143) skewer-pin type, a bone 'belt-hook', and a stone 'battle-axe' of Herd Howe type, Roe (1966: 207) Stage III, all burnt in the funeral pyre. The cremation urn had been placed, inverted, in a pit together with two small collared urns.

Discussion: The two collared urns deposited in the pit with the cremation urn show no signs of having been associated with the cremation process, nor did they contain additional cremated bone, thus they can be regarded as grave goods. It is likely that most of the objects were personal possessions, while the burnt accessory cup may be regarded as a deposition to the pyre. As it is pierced by a pair of perforations, it suggests that it may have been used for burning substances, such as incense, as part of this funerary act (Allen and Hopkins 2000: 313; Woodward 2000: 113–114). It has been suggested that the 'belt-hook' might have been a fastening for a burial shroud as all known examples derive from funerary contexts (Sheridan 2007: 112). The function of the bronze items as earrings has been reviewed in a discussion of two pairs of gold earrings accompanying a male cremation burial from Chilbolton, Hampshire (Russel 1990: 166). The occurrence of two or more collared urns is a feature of Early Bronze Age funerary assemblages in the Pennines and occurs occasionally elsewhere in northern England and southern Scotland (Varley 1938). This assemblage is of considerable interest, including as it does some items which are relatively common, both nationally and also within the region, as well as others which are unusual, while confirming some characteristics which are regionally significant. Thus collared urns and 'battle-axes' are not uncommon either regionally or nationally, but the bronze earrings and bone items are more unusual finds, tending to be more frequent in Yorkshire than elsewhere, while the accessory cup belongs to a regionally specific ceramic group.

It is clear from the cremated bones that only one person was included in the burial, thus all the grave goods relate to his personal possessions or the esteem in which he was held. A number of factors suggest that the Stanbury burial is that of a significant person. The assemblage is exceptionally rich for the earlier Bronze Age in Britain as a whole, and especially for the eastern Pennines area, containing as it does a number of items which are relatively unusual even as individual grave goods. The association of bronze earrings with a collared urn burial appears to be unique.

Disposition: Bradford Museums hopes to acquire

J RICHARDSON

---

20. Bardney, Lincolnshire: copper-alloy flat axe (PAS: LIN-D527F1)

Date: Early Bronze Age (c. 2000–c. 1800 BC).
Discovery: Found by Colin Warwicker while searching with a metal-detector in 2007, and recorded by Adam Daubney (Lincolnshire FLO).
Description: Incomplete cast copper-alloy flat axe of Class 3F (Needham et al. 1988: 386, fig. 1). It has a narrow butt with a rounded end, a narrow blade with slight flanges, and a broad and extended blade. The sides gently flare outwards to the crescentic cutting edge which is very abraded and damaged with both blade tips missing. The axe is so worn that the crest is nearly at the same level as the main body. There are no visible edge bevels. The entire surface of the axe is mid-green with a light brown patina. Length: 75mm.
Discussion: Although there is a good record of Late Bronze Age activity in the Witham Valley, where a number of barrow cemeteries are located, as well as numerous finds over the years of axes, spears and hoards, less is known of the Early to Middle Bronze Age. Therefore, this flat axe adds significantly to the evidence for settlement and ritual activity in the area

in the Early Bronze Age.
Disposition: Returned to finder.

A DAUBNEY

---

21. Mildenhall, Suffolk: copper-alloy axe-chisel (PAS: SF-618EF2)

Date: Early Bronze Age (c. 2000–c. 1600 BC).
Discovery: Found by Jamie Thompson while metal detecting, identified by Colin Pendleton (Suffolk County Council Archaeological Service) and recorded by Faye Minter (Suffolk FLO).
Description: A small copper-alloy narrow-butted flat 'axe-chisel' with slight cross 'stop' bevel. It is complete except for slight recent losses from the two ends of the convex blade and two small chips from the blade edge. The body is a thin sub-trapezoidal form with straight sides on the butt-half broadening to the expanded blade. The long profile is lenticular or slightly angled at the central, thickest part where the slight 'stop' cross bevel occurs. The blade also has a slight crescentic sharpening facet parallel to and c. 8mm from the edge. There is no 'flanging' to the sides of the axe. There are three linear recent abrasions (perhaps caused by a plough) on one face. There is some visible green invasive corrosion, especially along the blade facets, causing slight pitting in places, but elsewhere the surfaces are good with a mid to dark brown patination. Length: 87mm. Width (across blade): 34mm. Width (across butt): 19mm. Thickness: 8.9mm. Weight: 87g.
Discussion: The size and form of the 'axe-chisel', although having slight 'stop' bevels, is very similar to that excavated from a dated context at Worlingham, Suffolk (Find: WGM 007) in 2001 found in association with Beaker pottery and dated to c. 2100 BC. The stop-bevels on this suggest a slightly later date, probably c. 2000 BC, for this specimen.
Disposition: Returned to finders.

F MINTER & C PENDLETON

---

22. Newark area, Nottinghamshire: copper-alloy spearhead (PAS: DENO-1DCEB3)

Date: Middle Bronze Age (c. 1680–c. 1400 BC).
Discovery: Found by Stuart Boden while metal-detecting in early 2007, and recorded by Anja Rohde (Derbyshire & Nottinghamshire FLO).
Description: A copper-alloy side-looped spearhead with a wide, flame-shaped blade with flat wings, a prominent lozenge-sectioned midrib and a conical, socketed shaft with a flattened loop on either side. There are defined blade edge bevels on both sides of the blade demonstrating that the blade was extensively re-sharpened. Dimensions: 104.8 x 31 x 1.9mm. Diameter (socket): 19.4mm. Weight: 54.2g.
Discussion: Various forms of side-looped spears are known during this period when the bronze spear can be considered as the predominant weapon (Rowlands

1976; Ehrenberg 1977). Side-looped spearheads have a pair of loops which are lozenge-shaped in plan and which are usually placed halfway down the socket. On the basis of radiocarbon dates, spearheads of this type date to the Acton Park 2, Taunton and Penard metalworking Phases, corresponding to Needham's (1996: 133–134) Period 5, dated to c. 1500–c. 1100 BC. However, the recent radiocarbon dating of a side-looped spearhead from the Thames at Mortlake (Finds Ref: DoB 31) produced a date (Ref: OxA-5948) of 3225+/- 65BP (c. 1680–c. 1400 BC), with a 95% confidence rating (Needham *et al.* 1997).

The site where this spearhead was found also yielded an Early Bronze Age flat axe, which suggests that the site was inhabited for a long period throughout the Bronze Age.

Deposition: Returned to finder.

A ROHDE

---

23. Garveston, Norfolk: copper-alloy chisel (PAS: NMS-894E92)

Date: Early to Middle Bronze Age (c. 1600–c. 1400 BC).
Discovery: Found by Richard Girling while metal-detecting in March 2007, and recorded by Andrew Rogerson (Norfolk Museums & Archaeology Service).
Description: A narrow chisel of palstave form in quite fresh condition with a small part of one end of the cutting edge and patches of the patinated surface missing. There is no stop-ridge but the broad faces of the haft slope up quite abruptly to meet the full thickness of the blade. The flanges run from this point to the butt. One face of the blade is bevelled above the cutting edge. Dimensions: 111 x 21 x 14mm. Weight: 98.77g.
Discussion: This chisel dates to the transitional period from the end of the Early Bronze Age and the beginning of the Middle Bronze Age. The distribution of this form of flanged chisel is concentrated in East Anglia with similar examples known from Burwell Fen, Cambridgeshire, and West Row, Suffolk (Rowlands 1976: 350, 353, nos. 1097, 1099 & 1129, pl. 34). An example from Great Witchingham, Norfolk (HER Ref: 28968), is slightly smaller and another, similar in length but with a more widely flaring blade, was found at Swaffham, Norfolk (HER Ref: 2664), during the 19th century.
Disposition: Returned to finder.

E B DARCH

---

24. Wadebridge, Cornwall: base-metal deposit of two palstave axes (PAS: CORN-9155C2 & 90A647); Treasure: 2007 T630)

Date: Middle Bronze Age (c. 1500–c. 1400 BC).
Discovery: Found by Yvonne Parker while metal-detecting in October 2007, 20cm apart, and reported to Anna Tyacke (Cornwall FLO).

Description:
1. Shield pattern palstave, Crediton Type. Broken blade and butt ends with worn down flanges, one missing. The remains of a raised edge in the form of a shield can be seen below the stop-ridge. Length: 156mm. Weight: 450.3g.
2. Shield pattern palstave, Crediton Type. Broken blade and butt ends with worn down flanges. The remains of a raised edge in the form of a shield can be seen below the stop-ridge. Length: 162mm. Weight: 525.15g.
Discussion: The two shield pattern palstaves are not identical, with no. 2 having a rounded and shorter shield indicating that they were cast in different moulds. Nonetheless, they are both Crediton Type dating to the Acton Park metalwork Phase and have been found in Cornwall in hoards such as Perranzabuloe, Truro and Veryan (Pearce 1983: 577–581, pl.16, 18–20).
Disposition: Royal Cornwall Museum hopes to acquire.

A TYACKE & B ROBERTS

---

25. Kendal, Cumbria: copper-alloy rapier fragment (PAS: LANCUM-81DDE1)

Date: Middle Bronze Age (c. 1500–c. 1150 BC).
Discovery: Found by Robert Wilson while metal-detecting in 2007, and recorded with Dot Boughton (Lancashire & Cumbria FLO).
Description: An incomplete cast copper-alloy rapier blade which is likely to belong to the Acton Park 2, Taunton (Cemmaes) or Penard metalwork Phases of the later Middle Bronze Age and corresponding to Period 5 (Needham *et al.* 1997: 133–134). The hilt (which was made from perishable material such as antler, wood or bone) is missing and so are the rivets with which it was attached to the blade. The flat blade was very thinly cast and the edges are chipped. Dimensions: 142.43 x 31.8 x 2.32mm.
Discussion: Towards the end of the Middle Bronze Age there was a decline in the quality and design of rapiers and a move from those with a trapezoidal hilt to notch hilted rapiers characterised by a flat midrib blade and with rivets placed at the hilt sides (Rowlands 1976: 71), as is the case with the rapier from Kendal. A similar rapier fragment was found at Alrewas and Fradley, Staffordshire, and recorded by the PAS (WMID-A78747).
The finder was very pleased to have discovered this object and wanted to share the find with others. He generously donated the rapier to the FLO's handling and teaching collection.
Disposition: Lancashire & Cumbria FLO handling collection.

D BOUGHTON

26. Eaton Bray, Bedfordshire: copper-alloy knife (PAS: BH-C79921)

Date: Middle/Late Bronze Age (c. 1500–c. 800 BC).
Discovery: Found by Andrew Hancox while metal-detecting in 2007, and recorded by Julian Watters (Hertfordshire & Bedfordshire FLO).
Description: An unusually small tanged knife with a thin and flat blade. This implement is slightly shouldered, and at the centre of the upper edge of the incomplete short, flat tang there is a trace of a single rivet hole which would originally have been used to secure a bone or wooden handle. The blade is sub-triangular in plan and has a shallow, central midrib extending from approximately one third the way down the blade to just above the rounded tip. The blade tapers towards the rounded point and the cutting edges on both sides are slightly convex and show no signs of having been sharpened. Dimensions: 46.8 x 16.5 x 2.2mm. Weight: 6.19g.
Discussion: Tanged knives occurred from the late Middle to the Late Bronze Age. Similar, but larger, examples of this type of knife are known from the River Thames, near Runnymede, Surrey (Rowlands 1976: 355, no. 1143, pl. 35), and from a Late Bronze Age hoard from Yattendon, Berkshire (Coghlan 1970: 17 Y. 15, pl. III). It is suggested that knives cut from larger pieces are relatively common in this period (Macgregor 1987: 110, no. 11.72), although in this case, there is no evidence to suggest that the implement was formed from a larger object.
Disposition: On temporary display at Stockwood Park Museum, Luton.

J WATTERS

27. Hampton Lovett, Worcestershire: copper-alloy tanged chisel (PAS: WAW-F5FF52)

Date: Middle/Late Bronze Age (c. 1450–c. 500 BC).
Discovery: Found by Ivor Wills while metal-detecting in 2007, and recorded by Angie Bolton (Warwickshire & Worcestershire FLO).
Description: An incomplete cast copper-alloy tanged chisel dating to the Ewart Park to Llyn Fawr metalworking Phases. The blade is widely splayed and there is a projecting collar at the junction with the incomplete rectangular-sectioned tang to prevent the handle slipping down the blade, which expands in width towards the collar. The blade is sub-triangular in plan with slightly concave sides and the lower blade expanded, convex and abraded. The surface of the chisel has an incomplete dark brown patina, which is pitted, particularly on one surface. Dimensions: 38.98 x 18.74 x 5.38mm. Weight: 11.5g.
Discussion: Tanged chisels occur from the end of the Bronze Age and remain in use until Llyn Fawr metalwork (c. 1450–c. 500 BC). They are characterised

by the collar at the junction of the tang and blade and probably functioned as leather knives as they are not suited to work on metal. Up to 22 of these type of chisels are recorded on the PAS database, of which three are from the West Midlands region. This is the first example recorded by the PAS from Worcestershire.
Disposition: Returned to finder.

A BOLTON

28. Ranby, Lincolnshire: quoit-headed pin (PAS: NLM-15CFB4)

Date: Middle Bronze Age (c. 1400–c. 1300 BC).
Discovery: Found by Garry Mills while metal-detecting in 2007, and recorded by Lisa Staves (North Lincolnshire FLO).
Description: Complete cast copper-alloy quoit-headed pin of the Taunton metalworking Phase dating to the late Middle Bronze Age. The pin's head is oval and is slightly pointed where it joins the circular-sectioned shaft. The head has an H-section which appears to have been formed by hammering the edges of the ring to raise them into the flanges. The head is decorated with nicks on the edges of both sides of the ring. Length: 144mm. Diameter (head): 60–66.1mm. Weight: 29.11g.
Discussion: The pin dates to the Middle Bronze Age and is a native British 'Ornament Horizon' product. Quoit-headed pins probably represent the first use and manufacture of pins for dress fastening and adornment. Many of the shanks are slightly bent, and this suggests that they were damaged in use (Rowlands 1976: 86; Lawson 1979: 120–124). Most of the quoit-headed pins found come from the southern half of Britain and therefore, since this pin found in Lincolnshire, it is an unusual find.
Disposition: Returned to finder.

L STAVES

29. Loggerheads, Staffordshire: copper-alloy palstave axe (PAS: WMID-835786)

Date: Middle Bronze Age (c. 1400–c. 1300 BC).
Discovery: Found by Ian Wild while metal-detecting in June 2007, and recorded with Duncan Slarke (Staffordshire & West Midlands FLO).
Description: A copper-alloy low-flanged looped palstave from the Taunton Phase. Below the thick butt, and running approximately halfway down the blade, there is a ribbed decoration representing a version of the trident pattern, with converging rib motifs forming a V design pointing towards the cutting edge with a ribbed sub-triangular design nested within. The blade has a distinctive expanded edge and protruding tips as well as a heavily curved faceted cutting edge and a well-developed edge bevel. The palstave survives in exceptionally good condition, with only minor damage visible, and has a dark brown patina. Length: 138.5mm. Width (blade edge): 66.6mm. Width (butt): 34.9mm.

Discussion: This axe is an example of an early palstave with a low flange and broad blade of Group III (Schmidt and Burgess 1981: 128–141, nos. 825–830, pl. 60). Within Group III, this palstave fits most closely within the South-Western Palstave group characterised by the high angled flange which continues to rise above the stop and then is angled sharply downwards after the highest point. In addition, the distinctive expanded blade edge and protruding blade tips and decoration (usually in the form of a version of the trident pattern of this group of palstaves) is similar to that of low-flanged palstaves. A palstave from the south of Scotland, with decoration in the form of a ribbed triangle, is similar to the palstave from Loggerheads (Schmidt and Burgess 1981: 142, no. 840, pl. 61).

Disposition: Returned to finder.

D SLARKE

---

30. Blisland, Cornwall: copper-alloy palstave axe blade fragment (PAS: CORN-CA0B11)

Date: Middle Bronze Age (c. 1400–c. 1300 BC).
Discovery: Found by Brian Parker while metal-detecting in February 2007, and recorded by Anna Tyacke (Cornwall FLO).
Description: Cast copper-alloy blade fragment from a palstave. When complete, the palstave would have had a stop-ridge where the broken end is now, to stop the wooden haft or handle from slipping down the blade. The casting seams still remain on both sides of the blade. The axe seems to have been poorly cast as it looks quite porous at the broken end of the blade, and the stop-ridge end has also been hammered in antiquity. On the basis of the style and thickness of this palstave fragment, it probably dates from the Taunton Phase. Length: 82mm. Width: 59mm. Thickness (cutting edge): 3mm & 22mm wide; Thickness (at stop): 19mm. Weight: 192.38g.
Discussion: Peter Northover (University of Oxford) analysed the metallic composition of the palstave and comments: 'The palstave may be unused, having been broken during the late stages of manufacture or perhaps when someone first tried to use it. When you cast a palstave there is a tendency for the septum to freeze before the much thicker centre section. Hot metal can no longer feed into that area which then suffers a lot of shrinkage; as it is the last area to freeze any dross and other debris ends up in that area too. The analysis gave a high tin bronze content (15.7% tin) which is much to be expected either side of the Channel at that time. The blade is as cast and it is rather more usual to find whole or broken imported palstaves in that state than more locally produced ones. It probably came from the north coasts of the Armorican peninsula, to as far east as the Cotentin in France.'
Disposition: Returned to finder.

A TYACKE & P NORTHOVER

---

31. Pett, East Sussex: base-metal deposit of three palstaves (PAS: SUSS-15B261, 15DD86 & 15E741; Treasure: 2007 T125)

Date: Middle Bronze Age (c. 1400–c. 1250 BC).
Discovery: Found by Jeff Forrow while metal-detecting in February and March 2007, in a straight line no more than 15 feet apart, and reported to Liz Andrews-Wilson (Sussex FLO).
Description:
1. Palstave, very heavily corroded; the blade, flanges and the butt are severely worn. The blade appears fairly expanded and the flanges of medium height. It is possible to detect three small ribs at the base of the septum. Length: 153mm. Weight: 291g.
2. Palstave, Norman type; the blade, flanges and the butt are severely worn and heavily corroded. The blade is relatively unexpanded, the flanges are low and these merge into a broken butt. There is an elongated triangular indentation below the stop-ridge. Length: 123mm. Weight: 291g.
3. Palstave, Norman type; the blade, flanges and the butt are severely worn and very heavily corroded. The blade is relatively unexpanded, the flanges are low and these merge into a damaged butt. There is an elongated triangular indentation below the stop-ridge on one side. Length: 119mm. Weight: 247g.
Discussion: The finds retrieved represent a dispersed hoard. One palstave is of undefined type though appears to be of the broad-bladed and unlooped form. The other two palstaves are Norman type which is characteristic of Normandy, although examples have been found in concentrations in east Hampshire and West Sussex (O' Connor 1980: 47–49) which is indicative of the connections between the southern British coast and north-west France. The evidence for the cross-channel traffic of bronze objects at shipwreck sites and the absence of any large-scale mining in Ireland or Britain during this period would appear to indicate extensive procurement and recycling of metal objects, such as the Norman palstaves, that originated on the Continent. The explanations for the discovery of palstaves in the landscape remain orientated towards ritual deposition in specific places (Bradley 1998).
Disposition: Hastings Museum hopes to acquire.

B ROBERTS

---

32. Hambledon area, Hampshire: base-metal group of a palstave axe and a socketed hammer (PAS: HAMP-3056F8 & 2CB8E2; Treasure: 2007 T662)

Date: Middle Bronze Age (c. 1400–c. 1150 BC).
Discovery: Found by Lawrence Hall while metal-detecting in November 2007, and reported to Rob Webley (Hampshire FLO).
Description:
1. Palstave with a narrow square butt, low tapering flanges, slight lip on the stop-ridge with a complete

loop adjoining. This leads down to narrow body divided by single midrib finishing with a slightly flared blade. Length: 148mm. Weight: 418.7g.

2. Socketed hammer. Sub-rectangular mouth with single collar moulding leading to a square section and a slightly curved, smooth and worn terminal with flared edges, presumably due to repeated impacts rather than design. Length: 63mm. Weight: 134.9g.

Discussion: The palstave can be classified according to Rowlands' (1976: 34–36) scheme as Class 5 Group 1 and dates the group to the Taunton and potentially the subsequent Penard Phase metalworking assemblages. It is during these centuries that the earliest socketed hammers are evidenced (O' Connor 1980: 61).

Disposition: Acquired by Winchester Museums Service.

B ROBERTS & N DOSHI

---

33. Hempnall, Norfolk: copper-alloy palstave mould (PAS: SF-3C3B46)

Date: Middle Bronze Age (c. 1400–c. 1100 BC).

Discovery: Found by Terry Read while metal-detecting in 2007, identified by Colin Pendleton (Suffolk County Council Archaeological Service), and recorded by Faye Minter (Suffolk FLO).

Description: An incomplete single bronze valve from a two-piece looped palstave mould. The blade end and 'corner' are missing due to an ancient patinated break. The interior of the mould has an impression of a single looped palstave. The length of the cast palstave produced in the mould would have been 140mm. The flanges on the edge of the mould have four small concave sockets to fit matching knobs on the now missing second half of the two-piece mould, allowing accurate assembly of the two parts for the casting process. There is also a casting sprue for excess molten metal at the top of the mould. The exterior edges of the mould are very irregular (much as cast). The form of the palstave is clearly visible on the exterior though the blade is decorated with a cast design in the form of ribs, defining a raised triangle with a dividing central line. The design on this mould is very similar to one of the pair of palstave moulds from Harling, Norfolk (Wymer 1987). Although similar to the Harling mould, the exterior finish of this example is somewhat cruder. Dimensions: 170 x 60mm. Weight: 288g.

Discussion: According to Rowlands (1976) looped palstaves do not occur until the Taunton Phase of the Middle Bronze Age. Bronze palstave moulds are extremely rare; this is only the tenth example known from mainland Britain. The only other examples from East Anglia are a complete example from Harling, Norfolk, and a fragment from the Late Bronze Age hoard from Isleham, Cambridgeshire (O' Connor 1980: 366).

Disposition: Returned to finder.

F MINTER & C PENDLETON

---

34. Binsted, Hampshire: copper-alloy penannular arm-ring (PAS: HAMP-C73581)

Date: Middle Bronze Age (c. 1400–c. 1100 BC).

Discovery: Found by Peter Wonson while metal-detecting before 2006, and recorded by Rob Webley (Hampshire FLO) in 2007.

Description: Complete cast copper-alloy penannular arm-ring dating to the Taunton metalworking tradition. It has a slightly oval shape with the terminals flattened by hammering. Decorated panels of geometric patterning consisting of pairs of incised, surmounted lozenges alternately with chevrons in a herringbone pattern, separated by columns of five or six vertical grooves. Diameter (external): 63mm. Width: 54mm. Thickness: 8mm.

Discussion: Gold and bronze objects associated with the 'Ornament horizon' form part of a North European tradition. This has led to the suggestion that the examples from southern England may have been imported or at least inspired by ornaments derived from overseas, initially among the earliest ornaments. However, it is also likely that bronze ornament production occurred in southern England (Roberts 2007: 141–143).

Penannular and annular arm-rings with incised decoration are uncommon and have a distribution concentrated in the southern counties of Hampshire, Wiltshire, Dorset and West Sussex with examples also known from Suffolk and Norfolk. Great variety exists in the incised decorative motifs used on Liss Type arm-rings and on other Middle Bronze Age 'Ornament horizon' artefacts, such as Picardy pins. Decorated arm-rings were frequently found in association with other 'native' ornament forms in hoards and are often also associated with palstaves (Rowlands 1971: 185). It is interesting that a very large proportion of the known 'Ornament horizon' incised bronze penannular and annular arm-rings have been found in Hampshire (Roberts 2007: 159–160), which include the two arm-rings from Liss and the annular arm-ring from Stroud (FASW-DA4387; Worrell 2002: 89).

Disposition: Returned to finder.

R WEBLEY

---

35. Burton, Wrexham (addenda): gold bead and gold wire (PAS: NMGW-99FED6; Treasure: Wales 07.13)

Date: Middle Bronze Age (c. 1400–c. 1100 BC).

Discovery: Found by Joseph Perry, Peter Skelly and William May while metal-detecting in August 2007, reported to Mark Lodwick (Finds Co-ordinator, Wales) and identified by Adam Gwilt (National Museum Wales).

Description:

1. A biconical bead made of sheet gold with a central perforation for suspension. The bead is damaged and misshapen, with a snag and a tear evident. Diameter: 13.5mm. Height/width: 8mm. Thickness (sheet): <0.1mm. Weight: 0.84g.

2. Gold wire, sub-rectangular in cross-section, with curving meanders, suggesting it was once coiled. One terminal has a globular-shaped head; the other has a flattened and folded back hook terminal. Length: 40.7mm. Diameter (wire): 0.7–1mm. Weight: 1.13g.
Discussion: These two artefacts were found in exactly the same location as the Burton Hoard (*TAR* 2004, no. 485), and are therefore additions to the original hoard. The biconical bead is of identical form and similar dimensions to three other examples within the hoard. In Britain and France, good parallels may be found in Middle Bronze Age contexts (c. 1400–c. 1100 BC). The gold wire was found attached to the biconical bead, the flattened hook terminal being held inside the interior of the bead. This object is hard to parallel, however its terminals resemble hook and clasp terminals on cuff armlets and ribbon torcs of gold, which date to between c. 1600–c. 1300 BC. The wire may once have been a finger-ring joined with 'bulb and clasp' terminals. Semi-quantitative metallurgical analysis of both the bead and the wire indicated a very high gold composition, with a small percentage of silver and 1–1.5% copper.
Disposition: To be acquired by the National Museum of Wales.

A GWILT

---

36. Seagry, Wiltshire: gold penannular bracelet fragment (PAS: NMGW-A93765; Treasure: 2007 T510)

Date: Middle Bronze Age (c. 1300–c. 1100 BC).
Discovery: Found by Pat Good while metal-detecting in May 2007, and reported to Mark Lodwick (Finds Co-ordinator, Wales).
Description: A twisted penannular bracelet fragment. It is made on a rectangular-sectioned bar with a plain, unexpanded terminal, the edges and corners of which are sub-rounded. The bracelet has a comparatively loose twist (of 180° on the fragment) and approximately one-third of the original length is represented. The break would appear to have been cut through a little over half the thickness and bent or twisted through the remainder. The curvature on the bracelet fragment is likely to be similar to the original. Length: 40mm (straightened: approximately 58mm). Weight: 10.2g. Surface analysis: gold and silver contents of approximately 86% and 12% respectively; this composition is broadly consistent with Middle Bronze Age goldworking.
Discussion: The penannular bracelet is of bar-twisted type which is characteristic of the Middle Bronze Age with examples known in Ireland and Britain. Eogan (1994: 50) classifies the form of bar bracelet as Type 3. This bracelet fragment can be closely paralleled with two complete examples found at Saintjohns, County Kildare (Eogan 1994: 63, fig. 27B 2–3, pl. XII; Taylor 1980: ref. CoKd 9–10). Twisted gold bracelets and torcs have been found in Wiltshire and throughout south-

west England, though they have tended to be deposited with accompanying gold objects (Roberts 2007).
Disposition: Wiltshire Heritage Museum hopes to acquire.

M LODWICK, M DAVIES & B ROBERTS

---

37. Stone, Buckinghamshire: gold composite ring (PAS: BUC-9754C7; Treasure: 2007 T118)

Date: Middle Bronze Age (c. 1300–c. 1100 BC).
Discovery: Found by Richard Baier while metal-detecting in March 2007, and reported to Ros Tyrrell (Buckinghamshire FLO).
Description: A small, tripartite composite gold ring comprising three sections of oval-sectioned gold rod, probably soldered together. Diameter: 10.35 x 10.25mm. Weight: 7.21g. Surface analysis: gold and silver contents of 76–80% and 16–19% respectively.
Discussion: A well-known type, decorative in nature.
Disposition: Acquired by Buckinghamshire County Museum.

G VARNDELL

---

38. Ansley, Warwickshire: gold ribbon ornament (PAS: WAW-C0C0B3; Treasure: 2007 T672)

Date: Middle/Late Bronze Age (c. 1300–c. 800 BC).
Discovery: Found by Simon Hall while metal-detecting in August 1999, and reported to Angie Bolton (Warwickshire FLO).
Description: A gold fragment of a parallel-sided strip or ribbon. One end is neatly broken forming a straight edge while on the other the corners have been rounded, perhaps implying the original finish. The back is undecorated, while the front carries eleven very finely executed grooves aligned longitudinally.
Length: 22.5mm. Thickness: 0.2mm. Weight: 2.4g.
Discussion: This object cannot be identified with total certainty, but similar multi-grooved ribbon ornaments of Bronze Age date and of varied sizes are known from north-west Europe; this provides the most likely cultural background. Narrow-ribbon ornaments from the Saint-Marc-le-Blanc Hoard, Brittany, have fewer and correspondingly broader ribs/grooves (Eluère 1982: 91, fig. 107). There are finer grooves on an earring from Saint-Père-en-Retz, Loire-Atlantique (Eluère 1982: 53, fig. 63), and finer still on some Irish Bronze Age ornaments. Among the latter are examples in two important associations, from Saintjohns, County Kildare, and Derrinboy, County Offaly. The Derrinboy pieces have enhanced ribs along the long edges not present on the Ansley fragment (Eogan 1994: 63, fig. 27B, pl. XII). See also *TAR* 2003, nos. 1–2 for comparable British fragments.
Disposition: Acquired by Warwickshire Museum.

B ROBERTS

39. West Acre, Norfolk: gold sheet strip fragment (PAS: NMS-BE02A4; Treasure: 2007 T8)

Date: Possibly Middle/Late Bronze Age
(c. 1300–c. 800 BC).

Discovery: Found by Stephen Brown while metal-detecting in December 2006, and reported to Erica Darch (Norfolk FLO) in 2007.

Description: Fragment of gold sheet strip with one straight end complete and the other missing. Throughout its length one long edge is folded over. Eight longitudinal grooves cover the remainder of the object apart from a narrow strip along the other edge, which was probably once also folded over. Length (minimum): 32mm. Weight: 1.12g. Surface analysis indicated a gold content of approximately 89–91%.

Discussion: Though the object cannot be identified with total certainty, it is very comparable to multi-grooved ribbon ornaments dating to the Bronze Age in Britain and north-west Europe. Parallels in mainland Britain include The Hamel, Oxfordshire (Palmer 1980), and recent finds at Fontwell Magna, Dorset (*TAR* 2003, no. 1), and Flixton, North Yorkshire (*TAR* 2003, no. 2). The compositional evidence is admittedly lower in copper than might be expected for this period, but this is not always reliable in assigning date. Although it is not possible to be certain that the fragment is Bronze Age, it is almost certainly ancient.

Disposition: Norwich Castle Museum hopes to acquire.

B ROBERTS

40. Trearddur, Isle of Anglesey: gold penannular ring (PAS: NMGW-9AC224; Treasure: Wales 07.23)

Date: Middle/Late Bronze Age (c. 1300–c. 800 BC).

Discovery: Found in the course of an archaeological excavation by the Gwynedd Archaeological Trust during October 2007; the developer-funded project was being undertaken in advance of an industrial estate development. Reported to Mark Lodwick (Finds Co-ordinator, Wales) and identified by Adam Gwilt (National Museum Wales).

Description: A small penannular ring of sheet gold construction, with simple terminals separated by a narrow gap. The sheet strip has been carefully folded over, to give an oval shaped cross-section, the internal edges around the interior diameter being separated by a gap of 1–1.5mm. The ring has been dinted, with a compression crimp in one place causing a small tear. Diameter (external): 14.8mm. Thickness (ring): 2.3–3.7mm. Thickness (sheet): <0.5mm. Weight 1.41g.

Discussion: This ring finds parallel with both penannular gold rings and 'hair-rings' of the Middle and Late Bronze Age (c. 1400–c. 800 BC), which are now generally thought to be either hair or ear adornments. Rings of twisted bar or circular rod construction tend to date to the Middle Bronze Age, while 'hair rings' covered with gold foil, electrum wire or plating are most common during the Late Bronze Age. This example may represent the transition between solid gold and foil construction, therefore as a potentially early example of a 'hair-ring', could date to as early as the end of the Middle Bronze Age (c. 1300–c. 1150 BC). Semi-quantitative analysis of the ring indicates a very high gold composition, with a small percentage of silver and 1% copper. The ring was found in the lower fill of a ditch at the periphery of a settlement, providing important dating evidence for its occupation during the Later Bronze Age.

Disposition: Acquired by Oriel Ynys Môn, Llangefni, with the rest of the site archive; the landowner donated their share.

A GWILT

41. East Knoyle, Wiltshire: base-metal hoard of 11 palstave axes (PAS: YORYM-954174; Treasure: 2007 T295)

Date: Middle Bronze Age (c. 1275–c. 1150 BC).

Discovery: Found by Neal Blatherwick while metal-detecting in May 2007, all together (except one recovered 3m away), and reported to Beth Echtenacher (North & East Yorkshire FLA).

Description:
1. Palstave, with heavy corrosion and chipping. It has a damaged butt, worn flanges and potentially the remains of a broken loop. There is no decoration evident. The narrow blade and apparent shape of the flanges indicate a Transitional Type. Length: 117mm. Weight: 230g.
2. Palstave, with heavy corrosion and chipping. It has a damaged butt, broken loop and worn flanges. The narrow blade and apparent shape of the flanges indicate a Transitional Type. Length: 131mm. Weight: 215.7g.
3. Palstave, with heavy corrosion and chipping. It has a damaged butt and blade, broken loop and worn flanges. The triangular flanges create a relatively deep stop-ridge that leads down to a gently flaring blade. It can be classified as a Transitional Type. Length: 151mm. Weight: 345.4g.
4. Palstave, with heavy corrosion and chipping. It has a damaged blade and worn broken flanges. The narrow blade and apparent shape of the flanges indicates a Transitional Type. Length: 149mm. Weight: 235.7g.
5. Palstave, with heavy corrosion and chipping. It has a heavily damaged butt and blade and worn flanges. The loop is intact. The flanges are triangular-shaped leading down to the gently flaring blade with visible trident decoration. It can be classified as a Transitional Type. Length: 146mm. Weight: 374.1g.
6. Palstave, with heavy corrosion and chipping. It has a heavily damaged butt, broken loop and worn flanges. A casting seam is visible on either side. It can be classified as a Transitional Type. Length: 144mm. Weight: 348.8g.

7a. Palstave blade fragment with a narrow blade that is heavily corroded. Length: 58mm. Weight: 99.8g.
7b. Palstave butt fragment. The flanges and stop-ridge are heavily worn and corroded. The break does not look fresh, yet this piece fits the above fragment. This can be classified as a Transitional Type. Length: 61mm. Weight: 96.2g.
8. Palstave, with heavy corrosion and chipping. It has a damaged butt, broken loop and worn flanges. The form of the flanges appears to be triangular running down to a gently flaring blade. It can be classified as a Transitional Type. Length: 146mm. Weight: 330.2g.
9. Palstave, with heavy corrosion and chipping. It has a heavily damaged butt, broken loop and worn flanges. There are visible trident markings on the narrow blade. It can be classified as a Transitional Type. Length: 131mm. Weight: 300.7g.
10. Palstave, with heavy corrosion and chipping. It has a heavily damaged butt, broken loop and worn flanges. The base of the stop-ridge is decorated with three straight raised lines. The blade is gently flaring and is a Transitional Type. Length: 143mm. Weight: 314.5g.
11. Palstave, with heavy corrosion and chipping. Broken at the stop-ridge leaving only a narrow blade and the remnants of very worn flanges. The narrow blade indicates a Transitional Type. Length: 149mm. Weight: 235.7g.
Discussion: The palstaves are of the Transitional Type typical of the Penard Phase metalworking assemblages. While it is hard to define much more typological detail, there is substantial variation in the sizes and overall forms of the palstaves. The deliberate placing of the palstaves in a pit concurs with broader patterns of metalwork deposition in the landscape.
Disposition: Acquired by Salisbury & South Wiltshire Museum.

B ROBERTS

---

42. Heytesbury, Wiltshire: copper-alloy palstave axe (PAS: WILT-D1AD62)

Date: Middle Bronze Age (c. 1250–c. 1100 BC).
Discovery: Found by George Bates while metal-detecting in 2007, and recorded by Katie Hinds (Wiltshire FLO).
Description: Middle Bronze Age transitional looped palstave of Type Roundhay, Midribbed Variant (Schmidt and Burgess 1981: 149–150, pls. 64–65). The butt end is slightly damaged but this is a result of the casting process rather than through use or plough damage. Further casting errors can be seen just below the butt end and on the stop. The stop is c. 75mm from the butt end and the flanges are highest here (c. 13–14mm). In profile, the stop is not obtrusive, as on late palstaves. Below the stop the sides, which are 23.3mm wide below the stop, are parallel and narrow before gradually expanding at the cutting edge to a width of 40.3mm. At the centre there is a prominent rounded midrib extending from below the stop and which tapers towards the cutting edge. Visually the midrib creates two strips with rounded ends either side of the midrib on both sides. The cutting edge has been worked a little so it is only slightly splayed. The edge itself is damaged and on one side heavily pitted. The sides of the axehead have been smoothed down so the casting flashes are only just detectable. Much of the original patina survives as dark green and black, between the flanges and either side of the midrib particularly, although it is missing from the more prominent areas. Length: 153mm. Thickness (blade edge): 40.3mm. Thickness (at stop): 32.4mm. Weight: c. 400g.
Discussion: Transitional palstaves are narrow-bladed and with a chronology and form which is positioned between Middle Bronze Age broad-blade palstaves and the Late Bronze Age narrow-bladed palstaves (Schmidt and Burgess 1981: 145). Type Roundhay is associated with the Penard Phase which represents the latest of the Middle Bronze Age phases.
Disposition: Returned to finder.

K HINDS

---

43. Trotton with Chithurst, West Sussex: copper-alloy hammer (PAS: SUSS-2D5992)

Date: Middle/Late Bronze Age (c. 1150–c. 800 BC).
Discovery: Found by Tim Claydon while metal-detecting in 2007, and reported to Liz Andrews-Wilson (Sussex FLO).
Description: An incomplete copper-alloy socketed hammer surviving in two joining fragments. The hammer has a rectangular section and a socket which is 36mm deep. The sub-rectangular mouth has a single, wide undecorated mouth moulding and below this there is a series of narrow mouldings. The edges of the hammer are slightly curved. The object has broken about two-thirds of the way down its length. The break is badly worn and corroded but appears to have been a relatively recent, rather than an ancient break. The metal has a silver patina which is likely to be a result of the casting process. No casting sprues lines are evident but some miscast marks are visible indicating that this hammer was never finished to a high level. Length (combined): 96.6mm. Diameter (socket, internal): 15.6–15.9mm. Thickness: 19.9–29.2mm. Depth (socket): 36mm. Weight: 235g.
Discussion: Socketed hammers are relatively rare finds in late Middle Bronze Age contexts but are known from Late Bronze Age contexts, more commonly occurring in Ewart Park Phase hoards, dating to c. 1000–c. 800 BC. Hammers are likely to have been metalworkers' tools and similar examples are recorded by the PAS from Bedingfield, Suffolk (SF-B89096), and Basingstoke, Hampshire (HAMP-1F3730).
Disposition: Returned to finder.

L ANDREWS-WILSON

44. Fawley, Hampshire: gold penannular ring (PAS: HAMP-4AA958; Treasure: 2007 T59)

Date: Late Bronze Age (c. 1150–c. 750 BC).
Discovery: Found while metal-detecting in November 2006, and reported to Rob Webley (Hampshire FLO) in 2007.
Description: A penannular ring with a plump oval cross-section. Some lifting at the terminals indicates that the piece comprises a gold covering over a base-metal core. The ring bears decorative stripes of yellow and paler gold, but the decoration is extremely worn, except where protected in the centre. Diameter: 16.5 x 16mm. Weight: 7.71g. Surface analysis: gold and silver contents for the yellow stripes of approximately 78% and 19% respectively.
Discussion: A well-known type, decorative in character.
Disposition: Hampshire Museums Service hopes to acquire.

G VARNDELL

45. Witchingham area, Norfolk: gold penannular ring (PAS: NMS-EA2C32; Treasure: 2007 T475)

Date: Late Bronze Age (c. 1150–c. 750 BC).
Discovery: Found by Marilee Doucet while metal-detecting in August 2007, and reported to Erica Darch (Norfolk FLO).
Description: Penannular gold ring of flattened oval cross section. A tear at one terminal has exposed the base-metal (bronze) core. There is no evidence of decorative bands of differing colours of gold. Diameter: 15–16mm. Weight: 7.21g. Surface analysis: gold and silver contents of 75–78% and 15–18% respectively.
Disposition: Acquired by Norwich Castle Museum; the finder donated her share.

A ROGERSON & G VARNDELL

46. Theydon Mount, Essex: gold penannular ring (PAS: ESS-45C591; Treasure: 2007 T259)

Date: Late Bronze Age (c. 1150–c. 750 BC).
Discovery: Found by Mike Steele while metal-detecting in May 2007, and reported to Laura McLean (Essex FLO).
Description: A penannular ring of oval cross-section. The piece originally had alternate stripes of yellow and paler gold although this is now barely visible, except internally where the surface is less worn. Measurement of specific gravity indicated that it comprises a gold covering over a base-metal core. Diameter: 16–18mm. Weight: 9.21g. Surface analysis: gold and silver contents for the yellow stripes of 79–83% and 13–17% respectively.
Disposition: Acquired by Epping Forest District Museum.

G VARNDELL

47. Kettering area, Northamptonshire: gold penannular ring (PAS: NARC-773944; Treasure: 2007 T74)

Date: Late Bronze Age (c. 1150–c. 750 BC).
Discovery: Found by Ian Wray while metal-detecting in January 2007, and reported to Steven Ashby (Northamptonshire FLO).
Description: A plain penannular ring of near-circular cross-section. Some lifting at the terminals shows the piece to comprise a gold covering over a base-metal core. Diameter (external): 16.5 x 17.5mm. Weight: 7.46g. Surface analysis: gold and silver contents of 70–74% and 22–24% respectively.
Discussion: A well-known type, decorative in character.
Disposition: Acquired by Northampton Museum.

G VARNDELL

48. Ilam, Staffordshire: copper-alloy socketed axehead (PAS: WMID- DE6E34)

Date: Late Bronze Age (c. 1100–c. 1000 BC).
Discovery: Found by Julian Lee while metal-detecting in 2007, and recorded with Caroline Johnson (Staffordshire & West Midlands FLO).
Description: An almost complete copper-alloy indented socketed axehead of Type Ulleskelf of the Wilburton metalwork tradition. The mouth is square and has three narrow, horizontal-mouth mouldings and a single loop. The axe is sub-rectangular in plan with a slender, straight-sided body with a semicircular indentation on each side of the body accentuated by a raised plate. The axehead is slightly worn but generally in a good condition with an even green/grey patina. Length: 102.5mm. Width (socket): 30mm. Thickness: 22.5mm. Width (cutting edge): 40mm. Weight: 163.24g.
Discussion: Indented axes are an uncommon form of socketed axe which follows the earlier tradition of Taunton Type and Variant Bishopsland axes which also have similar long, slender bodies, but differ in having the pair of indentations on the sides. Similar examples are known from Ulleskelf, West Yorkshire, Newbald, East Yorkshire, and two examples from the River Ribble, Lancashire (Schmidt and Burgess 1981: 178–179, nos. 1010–1013, pl. 71). Schmidt and Burgess state that this form 'of indented socketed axe is clearly in the tradition derived from Type Taunton and Variant Bishopland' and that 'they are similar to other socketed axes of the Wilburton/Wallington Type, with a similar long, slender, square-mouthed body, with straight or slightly curved sides.'
Disposition: Returned to finder.

D SLARKE

49. Lavenham, Suffolk: copper-alloy harness fitting (PAS: ESS-B46EE5)

Date: Late Bronze Age (c. 1100–c. 1000 BC).
Discovery: Found by Mr P Sexton while metal-detecting in 2007, and recorded by Laura McLean (Essex FLO). Adam Gwilt (National Museum of Wales) and Mark Lodwick (Finds Co-ordinator, Wales) also commented on this object.
Description: A bugle-shaped fitting which is part of a composite strap distributor in the form of a toggle. The D-shaped ring is hollow with a central hole (diameter: 5.8mm). A staple-like loop with a sub-triangular section is appended to the flatter upper edge (dimensions: 3.31 x 13.81 x 6.87mm). There are some sandy inclusions on the upper surface of the fitting, and these may be the remnants from the casting. The artefact has a dark grey-black patina, with small patches of copper corrosion. Dimensions: 30.29 x 24.65 x 13–9.94mm.
Discussion: This fitting can be closely paralleled by examples in the Parc y Meirch (Abergele), Conwy, Hoard of harness fittings (Savory 1980: 119, no. 269, fig. 39) in the National Museum of Wales. Other examples of bugle-shaped fittings are known from Late Bronze Age hoards at Ramsgate, Kent (*TAR* 2005/6, no. 61, fig. 61.2), and Berwick-upon-Tweed area, Northumberland (*TAR* 2005/6, no. 20, fig. 64.1).
Disposition: Returned to finder.

L MCLEAN

50. Mildenhall, Wiltshire: copper-alloy model for socketed axehead (PAS: WILT-12C795)

Date: Late Bronze Age (c. 1000–c. 800 BC).
Discovery: Found by Mark Gillett while metal-detecting in 2007, and recorded by Katie Hinds (Wiltshire FLO).
Description: Copper-alloy model of a socketed axehead in miniature form. The mouth has a slight moulding which is emphasised by a groove beneath. The loop is cast integrally with the axe rather than being set well into the side; it is 8.7mm long with a circular perforation and shows no sign of wear. The socket is shallow and there are traces of iron within it (dimensions: 9.2 x 5.6 x 3mm). The surface of the axe has lost some of its original patina, although it is mostly smooth and shiny. Length: 38.5mm. Width: 16.8–24.8mm. Depth (mouth): 12.7mm. Depth (blade edge): 1.1mm. Weight: 31.28g.
Discussion: Socketed axeheads of diminutive size or models are most likely to have been used as amulets or votive objects, although well-made examples such as this, may have been used as a tool in a similar manner to very small flat axeheads of the Early Bronze Age (see above). The lack of datable archaeological contexts associated with the majority of miniature axeheads has meant that their date range is very wide, spanning from the Late Bronze Age to the end of the Roman period. The majority of miniature axeheads come from

south-west England with the largest concentration in Wiltshire (Robinson 1995: 60). Although most have been considered to date to the Roman period, it is interesting that a number of examples have recently been discovered during the metal-detector survey of a large occupation and 'midden' complex dating to the Late Bronze Age and Earliest Iron Age at Whitchurch, Warwickshire (Waddington 2007).
Disposition: Returned to finder.

K HINDS

51. Amport area, Hampshire: base-metal deposit of three palstave axes and three socketed axes (PAS: HAMP-4F38A4, 4F1980, 4EB8B3, 4EA817, 4DE734 & 4F78E6; Treasure: 2007 T704)

Date: Late Bronze Age (c. 1000–c. 800 BC).
Discovery: Found by Giles Woodhouse and Vivienne Brett while metal-detecting in April and October 2007, and reported to Rob Webley (Hampshire FLO).
Description:
1. Palstave, Transitional Type with a narrow body with slightly flared blade, three midribs, a side loop, deep flanges and a broken butt. There is some post-depositional scratching and impact damage. Length: 145mm. Weight: 399.9g.
2. Palstave, Transitional Type with a narrow body with slightly flared blade, two midribs, a pronounced stop-ridge, a large side loop, deep flanges and a slightly broken butt. There is some post-depositional scratching and impact damage. Length: 146mm. Weight: 479g.
3. Palstave, Transitional Type with a narrow-bodied palstave with flared blade, with four midribs, a side loop, a pronounced stop-ridge, deep flanges and a straight butt. There is some post-depositional scratching and impact damage. Length: 126mm. Weight: 391g.
4. Socketed axe, South Eastern Type, with double-mouth moulding, sub-rectangular body section, and a rectangular cross-sectioned socket with body running parallel along its length. It has a slightly flaring collar and two internal ribs. There is slight post-depositional damage to the collar. Length: 80mm. Weight: 174g.
5. Socketed axe, South Eastern Type, with double-mouth moulding, sub-rectangular body section, and a rectangular cross-sectioned socket with body running parallel along its length. There is slight post-depositional damage to the blade. Length: 75mm. Weight: 164g.
6. Socketed axe, South Welsh Type, with flared blade, straight-sided body diverging slightly, three midribs, loop coming directly from the collar and pronounced casting seam. Length: 96mm. Weight: 277g.
Discussion: The South Eastern socketed axes can be further classified as Type A1 Plain (Needham 1990: 28, fig. 2) and Type B4 ribbed- and double-mouthed (Needham 1990: 36, fig. 6), broadly dating the hoard to the Ewart Park metal Phase as above. However,

the transitional palstaves may be slightly earlier in date (Schmidt and Burgess 1981) and thus kept in circulation through time before being deposited. The deliberate placing of bronze objects in the Hampshire landscape is well documented (Lawson 1999).
Disposition: Hampshire Museums Service hopes to acquire.

B ROBERTS

---

52. Uttlesford District, Essex: base-metal hoard of ten socketed axes or fragments and 22 metalworking fragments (PAS: ESS-259C45; Treasure: 2007 T497)

Date: Late Bronze Age (c. 1000–c. 800 BC).
Discovery: Found by Barry Knee while metal-detecting in September 2007, all within 50cm of each other, and reported to Laura McLean (Essex FLO).
Description:
1. Incomplete looped socketed axe, Bilton (Worthing) Type, a variant of the ubiquitous South Eastern Type axe (Schmidt and Burgess 1981: 214, pl. 85, nos. 1275–1280). The sides are gently concave and terminate in an unexpanded blade; the upper half of the loop is missing. The entire circuit of the mouth is absent, along with part of the upper ends of the four sides. Length: 97.5mm. Weight: 198g.
2. Complete looped socketed axe, Bilton (Worthing) Type. The sides are gently concave and terminate in an unexpanded blade; the loop is present. There is an unobtrusive horizontal moulding immediately below the rim and another further down at the level of the upper end of the loop. Each broad face has a rib inside the socket that runs from the mouth to a quarter of the way down. Ribs of this kind are Ehrenberg (1981: 215–216) Type 5a. Length: 79mm. Weight: 166g.
3. Two fragments of an incomplete looped socketed axe, South Eastern Type. The sides are gently concave and terminate in an expanded blade; the loop is present. There is a horizontal moulding immediately below the rim and another further down at the level of the upper end of the loop. On the narrow side that survives in its entirety, the casting seam is particularly prominent, especially on the loop where no attempt had been made to remove or file it down. Most of two of the adjacent sides are missing from the rim to a point just over halfway towards the blade. The blade edge is still sharp. Length: 96mm. Weight: 142g.
4. Incomplete looped socketed axe, Bilton (Worthing) Type, heavily corroded. The sides are gently concave and terminate in an unexpanded blade; the loop is present. There is an unobtrusive horizontal moulding immediately below the rim and another further down at the level of the upper end of the loop. Length: 89.6mm. Weight: 116g.
5. Socketed axe blade. The cutting edge is gently curved and still sharp; both casting seams had been removed with care. One face had been gently bent

inwards when the axe was broken up for scrap in antiquity. Length: 48.5mm. Weight: 101g.
6. Socketed axe blade, deeply corroded; both broad sides have been bent inwards when the axe was broken up for scrap in antiquity. Length: 56.9mm. Weight: 93g.
7. Socketed axe fragment from the mouth of an artefact with a prominent casting seam. Length: 28.9mm. Weight: 24g.
8. Socketed axe fragment from the mouth of the artefact; a casting seam is present. The mouth had been bent out of true when the axe was broken up for scrap in antiquity. Length: 47.5mm. Weight: 18g.
9. Socketed axe fragment from the mouth of the artefact; all that survives of the loop are two stumps. Length: 30.2mm. Weight: 16g.
10. Socketed axe fragment from the mouth of the artefact; the stump of the upper loop is present below the rim. Length: 21.6mm. Weight: 8g.
11–32. 22 copper-alloy ingot fragments. Weights: 42–786g. Weight (total): 5,314g.
Discussion: The finds represent a hoard of Late Bronze Age scrap metalwork. The South Eastern Type axes in the hoard anchor the find securely in the Ewart Park Phase of the Late Bronze Age. 32 items were recovered with a total weight of 6,196g.

The association of ingot material with scrap metalwork destined for recycling lends the hoard a distinctly industrial character. Many hoards of this kind have been reported from East Anglia and the home counties; their links with industrial production have led to them being described as founders' hoards.

A consensus has emerged over the last thirty years that these Ewart Park Phase hoards are caches of bronze and copper that were buried over a relatively short period of time when ironworking became widespread towards the end of the Ewart Park Phase, c. 800 BC. However, there is still debate as to whether or not the bronze in these hoards was recovered from the ground because the demand fell when iron replaced bronze as the staple metal for weaponry and tools (Burgess 1979: 275–276; Needham 1990: 130–140; Needham *et al.* 1998: 93).
Disposition: Saffron Walden Museum hopes to acquire.

P SEALEY & B ROBERTS

---

53. Attleborough area, Norfolk: base-metal deposit of a socketed axe and 26 metalworking fragments (PAS: NMS-1E6A46; Treasure: 2007 T555)

Date: Late Bronze Age (c. 1000–c. 800 BC).
Discovery: Found by Mark Dover while metal-detecting in September 2007, and reported to Erica Darch (Norfolk FLO).
Description:
1. Socketed axe, South Eastern Type. It has sub-rectangular double-mouth moulding of which the upper moulding is prominent while the lower gives rise to the loop on the side of the body. The body is plain

and undecorated with relatively few pits running down to a flared blade. One blade corner has broken and corroded away. Length: 99mm. Weight: 331.1g (with earth remaining in the socket).

2–9. Eight planoconvex bronze ingot fragments with curving cast surfaces. Lengths: 117–41mm. Weight (total): 3,368g.

10–11. Two bronze fragments with flat cast curved surfaces. Lengths: 28 & 57mm. Weights: 69.1 & 201.3g.

12–27. Sixteen bronze fragments with broken edges. Lengths: 31–86mm. Weight (total): 3,760g.

Discussion: The South Eastern Type socketed axe can be further classified as Type A1 Plain (Needham 1990: 28, fig. 2) and broadly dates the hoard to the Ewart Park metal Phase. The remaining objects are bronze fragments of varying size, several appearing to have been part of planoconvex ingots, the forms, patinas and dimensions suggesting that certain fragments may have been part of the same ingot.

The placing of apparently scrap metal in the landscape is well documented during this period and has been well researched in Norfolk and Suffolk during this period (Pendleton 1999). Traditional interpretations see these hoards as metalworkers' reserves stored for later use. However, the failure to recover so many stored metal objects implies that recovery may not always have been the aim.

Disposition: Acquired by Norwich Castle Museum.

B ROBERTS

---

54. Offham, Kent: base-metal deposit of 14 socketed axes or axe fragments, two possible sickle fragments and ten ingot fragments, (PAS: KENT-C2ABB7; Treasure: 2007 T579)

Date: Late Bronze Age (c. 1000–c. 800 BC).

Discovery: Found by Ron Bowman while metal-detecting in October 2007, across an area 5 x 5m, and reported to Andrew Richardson (Kent FLO).

Description:

1–2. Two complete socketed axes, South English ribbed Types. Both are trumpet-mouthed, with single collars from which loops protrude. They have three equally spaced ribs on the straight-sided bodies and slightly flaring blades. The larger axe possibly has two extra ribs, although it is fairly worn so difficult to assess. The axes have visible casting seams. Lengths: 71.5 & 87.5mm Weights: 159.9 & 223g.

3. Complete socketed axe, South Eastern Type with drapery wing decoration. It has double-mouth moulding with a more prominent upper moulding and the loop protruding from the lower moulding. It has a sub-rectangular body with angular corners leading down to fairly sharply flaring blade. The blade appears to have been broken. Length: 97.5mm. Weight: 197.5g.

4–6. Three complete socketed axes, South Eastern Type Plain A1. All have double-mouth moulding with a more prominent upper moulding and the loop

protruding from the lower moulding. They have sub-rectangular bodies with angular corners leading down to flaring blades. The blades chipped and worn, and on the smallest axe the blade appears to have been completely broken off. Lengths: 81.5–93.5mm. Weights: 162.4–179.9g.

7. Socketed axe, South Eastern Type Plain A1. It has double-mouth moulding with a more prominent upper moulding and the loop protruding from the lower moulding, and a sub-rectangular body with angular corners. The body and blade have been broken off around halfway down. Length: 52.5mm. Weight: 114.4g.

8. Socketed axe fragment. It has a broken collar and curved body fragment. Length: 40mm. Weight: 23.8g.

9. Socketed axe blade. Part of its body is flaring sharply to a complete, but chipped and worn, blade. Length: 60mm. Weight: 130.7g.

10. Socketed axe body fragment. It is heavily broken, bent and corroded. Length: 44.5mm. Weight: 65.1g.

11. Socketed axe blade. It is part of the body, flaring sharply to fairly unworn blade. Length: 46mm. Weight: 88.9g.

12–13. Two socketed axe blades. Both are broken parts of the body, flaring to chipped and worn blades. Lengths: 38.5 & 44mm. Weights: 52.4 & 86g.

14. Socketed axe mouth and body part. It has a heavily worn collar, two sets of three ribs and an angular body. Length: 46mm. Weight: 36.7g.

15. Possible sickle fragment, with a pronounced stop-ridge with low tapering flanges leading towards a curving broken section that appears to have been a blade structure. There is one hole in the body of the stop-ridge together with a faint triangular imprinted decoration. Length: 69mm. Weight: 48g.

16. Possible sickle fragment, representing the terminal of the stop-ridge of no. 15 with tapering flanges and broken ends. Length: 28mm. Weight: 9.5g.

17–19. Three planoconvex ingot fragments, with curving cast surfaces. Lengths: 88–104.9mm. Weight (total): 2,140.4g.

20–26. Seven bronze fragments, one with a cast edge. Lengths: 26–78mm. Weight (total): 1,095.7g.

Discussion: The socketed axes broadly date the hoard to the Ewart Park metal Phase. With the exception of the potential riveted sickle (Fox 1939: 137–139, possibly Group A), the remaining objects are bronze fragments of varying size. The drapery decoration on the South Eastern socketed axe no. 7 is relatively rare in this country, though recent parallels are known from Pencoyd, Herefordshire, (TAR 2005–6: no. 59), Bognor Regis (Maraszek 2006: 606, fig. XVII), as well as several older hoards (O' Connor 1980: 521, List 122), which include Wateringbury and Stourmouth, Kent.

The placing of apparently scrap metal in the landscape is well documented during this period in Kent, though Offham lies beyond the traditional concentrations of hoards in east Kent.

Disposition: Acquired by Maidstone Museum.

B ROBERTS & N DOSHI

55. Hoaden, Kent: base-metal group of 13 socketed axes or fragments, a palstave axe fragment, a socketed gouge fragment, a sword blade fragment, a blade fragment and 16 metal-working fragments (PAS: KENT-C93982; Treasure: 2007 T580)

Date: Late Bronze Age (c. 1000–c. 800 BC).
Discovery: Found by Daren Bishopp while metal-detecting in October 2007, in an area of about 7m², and reported to Andrew Richardson (Kent FLO).
Description:
1. Socketed axe, complete South Eastern Type Plain A1. This has a double-mouth moulding with a more prominent upper moulding and the loop protruding from the lower moulding. It has a sub-rectangular body with angular corners leading down to fairly sharply flaring blade. The collar and part of the body is broken off. Length: 106mm. Weight: 223.7g.
2. Socketed axe, complete Plainseau Type with drapery wing decoration interspersed with a single pellet decoration. It has double-mouth moulding with a more prominent upper moulding and the broken loop protruding from the lower moulding. It has a long and slender body with angular corners leading down to slightly flaring blade. Each body side has drapery wing decoration. The blade is fairly worn and chipped. Length: 116mm. Weight: 277.1g.
3. Socketed axe, complete Continental variant on South Eastern Type with long drapery wings extending down the body. It has a single-mouth moulding with a broken loop protruding from below the collar. The slender body leads down to a slightly flaring blade. The blade is fairly worn and chipped. Length: 98mm. Weight: 171.1g.
4. Socketed axe blade. Part of its body is flaring slightly to a fairly worn and chipped blade. Length: 59mm. Weight: 101.1g.
5. Socketed axe blade, its body leading down to a fairly worn and chipped sharply flared blade. There are possible rib terminals. Length: 53mm. Weight: 95.2g.
6. Socketed axe loop and collar fragment, with double moulded collar and complete loop. Length: 28mm. Weight: 16.4g.
7–9. Three socketed axe blades with fairly worn and chipped blades. Lengths: 46–34mm. Weights: 71–61.4g.
10–13. Four socket fragments, three sub-angular, one curved. Lengths: 29–20mm. Weights: 18.8–6.3g.
14. Palstave stop-ridge fragment, with low worn flanges with a partially bent flange top. Loop is intact. Length: 84mm. Weight: 190.2g.
15. Socketed gouge fragment, with plain semicircular gouge terminal tapering towards the beginning of a semicircular socket terminal. Length: 48mm. Weight: 27.5g.
16. Sword blade fragment, with rounded midrib leading to substantial edge bevels divided by a singular incised line. Length: 40.5mm. Weight: 38g.
17. Blade fragment, with rounded midrib and heavily worn edge bevels. Length: 21mm. Weight: 6.1g.
18. Curved sheet fragment, with semicircular curved section. Length: 38mm. Weight: 11.3g.
19–20. Two bronze ingot fragments, with curving cast surfaces and broken edges. Lengths: 91 & 45.5mm. Weights: 666.4 & 168.8g.
21–34. Fourteen bronze fragments. Lengths: 67–22.5mm. Weight (total): 1,057.1g.
Discussion: The socketed axes broadly date the hoard to the Ewart Park metal Phase; see 54 for discussion of parallels for the drapery decoration. The gouge fragment is comparable to that found at Egham, Surrey (Needham 1990: 40, fig. 10, no. 74), and is relatively common throughout the Late Bronze Age.
The placing of apparently scrap metal in the landscape is well documented during this period in Kent, with this group located close to other concentrations of hoards in east Kent.
Disposition: Acquired by Dover Museum; finder and landowner donated their share.

B ROBERTS & N DOSHI

---

56. Tywardreath, Cornwall: copper-alloy socketed axehead (PAS: CORN-B2A682)

Date: Late Bronze Age (c. 1000–c. 800 BC).
Discovery: Found by Jamie Holland while metal-detecting in May 2007, and recorded by Anna Tyacke (Cornwall FLO).
Description: Incomplete copper-alloy socketed axehead of South Welsh Type dating to the Ewart Park metalwork tradition. The sides are straight sided and the cutting edge is expanded with the blade tips intact, if somewhat abraded. Its loop, mouth and moulding are missing and the surface is worn and pitted, especially along the casting seams. A layer of the original patina remains on one face with three ribs still visible. The ribs extend down about three-quarters of the length of the body and the central rib is more pronounced and appears to be the longest. Dimensions: 83 x 30 x 20mm. Thickness: 3mm. Weight: 94.27g.
Discussion: South Welsh axes are three-ribbed socketed axeheads with distinctive features including that the loop usually extends from the collar at the mouth and the ribs which extend halfway down the face before converging sharply, although parallel ribs are not uncommon (Schmidt and Burgess 1981: 239). South Welsh socketed axeheads are also referred to as Stogursey Type following the discovery in 1870 of a large hoard of 27 socketed axeheads and 40 fragments of South Welsh axes, two palstaves, two socketed gouges, two socketed knives, one chape, 22 sword fragments, 18 spearheads, 15 casting jets and 15 ingot fragments in Stogursey, Somerset (McNeil 1973: figs. 1–2, nos. 1–30). Pearce (1983: 565, no. 43a, pl. 4) illustrates a similar example from St Erth, Cornwall, which is now in Penzance Museum.
Disposition: Royal Institution of Cornwall hopes to acquire.

A TYACKE

57. Thurlestone, Devon: copper-alloy spearhead (PAS: DEV- 2B4697)

Date: Late Bronze Age (c. 1000–c. 800 BC)

Discovery: Found by Justin Dalton while out walking in 2007, and recorded by Danielle Wootton (Devon FLO).

Description: An incomplete, copper-alloy barbed spearhead of Type IV (Burgess, Coombs and Davies 1972: 219–222, fig. 2) of the Ewart Park metalworking tradition. The spearhead has a hollow, fillet-defined and narrow leaf-shaped blade with a lozenge-shaped section and two short rudimentary barbs at the base. The upper blade is missing. The socket has opposed peg holes which are characteristically set high up and located just below the blade.

Discussion: Four main forms of barbed spearheads are classified on the basis of the shape and size of the blade and tangs (Greenwell and Brewis 1909: 454; Smith 1909–1911; Burgess et al. 1972: 219–222). The vestigial barbs on the Thurlestone spearhead identify it as an example of the rare Donington Type after the example from Donington on Bain, Lincolnshire, which is characterised by its narrow blade of elliptical section and rudimentary barbs (Thompson 1954: 238). This spearhead is very similar to examples from the Hatfield Broad Oak Hoard, Essex (Davies 1979: 156, no. 36, fig. 8.5), and Staines, Berkshire (Needham et al. 1997: 90, fig. 19.2, DOB 39).

This spearhead is an important find as it was found in the same general area as the famous Bloody Pool Hoard of 1854 from South Brent, Devon, which contained fragments of Type I and Type II barbed spearheads and tubular ferrules (Burgess et al. 1972: 237).

Disposition: Returned to finder.

D WOOTTON & S WORRELL

58. West Wight, Isle of Wight: gold penannular bracelet (PAS: IOW-FA17F8; Treasure: 2007 T490)

Date: Late Bronze Age (c. 1000–c. 750 BC).

Discovery: Found by Colin Saunders while diving in June 2007, and, in agreement with the Receiver of Wreck, reported to Frank Basford (Isle of Wight FLO).

Description: A complete gold penannular C-section bracelet with expanded terminals. The width of the C-shaped body varies slightly throughout its length due to its misshapen state. The terminals are D-shaped with flat faces. Dimensions: 96.6 x 14mm. Weight: 70.61g.

Discussion: This type of penannular bracelet has been found throughout southern England. Eogan (1994) has noted nine different varieties in the British group and this bracelet, with its C-shaped body and expanded terminals, coincides with Eogan's Type 3. Two bracelets from the Tisbury Hoard, Wiltshire, are similar to this example from West Wight (Eogan 1994: 85, fig. 38, pl. 11, nos. 4 & 5). A Late Bronze Age gold bracelet (Eogan 1994: Type 1) was found about 2km from the location

of this bracelet in July 2000 (TAR 2000, no. 4).

Disposition: Isle of Wight Heritage Service hoped to acquire but withdrew; to be returned to finder.

F BASFORD & B ROBERTS

59. Appledram, West Sussex: copper-alloy spearhead (PAS: SUSS-2F7D75)

Date: Late Bronze Age or Early Iron Age (c. 900–c. 700 BC).

Discovery: Found by Tim Claydon while metal-detecting in 2007, and recorded by Liz Andrews-Wilson (Sussex FLO).

Description: An incomplete copper-alloy pegged socketed spearhead. The socket of the spearhead is possibly incomplete and very little of the badly damaged blade survives. The blade would have been leaf-shaped with a lozenge-shaped section. Where the socket joins the blade there is a sharp midrib of lozenge section which is decorated with three incised chevrons on each side. On the apex of one of the chevrons there are four small incised grooves on one side. The base of the socket is decorated with three closely set narrow mouldings, with two further mouldings 21.7mm up the socket and another moulding close to the junction of the socket and blade. The socket mouth contains two copper rivets, one of which extends through the whole width of the socket, while the other extends inwards from the side of the mouth and meets the other one in the middle; this appears to be broken and would once have extended to form a cross with the other rivet. Four rivet holes can be seen on the external rim of the mouth of the socket. From this point the socket tapers inwards towards the blade. Length: 89.2mm. Width (blade): 33.3mm. Width (socket): 19.4mm. Diameter (socket): 3.7mm (internal), 20.5mm (external). Weight: 74g.

Discussion: The spearhead is a rare example of an elaborately decorated Alpine Type. Several other copper-alloy examples of this Type are known and also one iron example was found with the Melksham Hoard, Wiltshire (Gingell 1979: 246–7, no. 5, fig. 13), now in Devizes Museum (DZSWS:1972.11.1).

Disposition: Returned to finder.

L ANDREWS-WILSON & S WORRELL

60. Langton Matravers, Dorset: base-metal hoard (PAS: HAMP-2865F1 & 893364; Treasure: 2007 T629 & 640)

Date: Late Bronze Age or Early Iron Age (c. 800–c. 600 BC).

Discovery: Found by Tom Pierce, Leslie Keith and Brian Thomas (2007 T640 only) while metal-detecting in late October and early November 2007 (Spencer 2008). Subsequent excavations by Wessex Archaeology confirmed that the hoards had been placed in three adjacent pits and a single pit 19m south-west. The bases of the four pits were found in the excavation, but the sides of the pits had been destroyed during the removal of the axeheads. Two postholes, one containing pottery fragments of later Prehistoric date and possibly, but not necessarily, contemporary with the hoards, were also found. The charred plant remains from the postholes suggest that a settlement stood nearby.

The hoards were deposited on the north-facing slope of the Purbeck limestone, above a re-entrant to the west with wide views across the Purbeck Ridge and Swanage Bay, and from just above the site are wider views east to the sea and the Isle of Wight. From interviewing the finders and looking at their photographs, the axes appear to have been tightly packed in each pit in no particular arrangement, potentially suggesting that they had been placed in a bag. The exact composition of each pit cannot be confirmed for the three adjacent pits (2007 T629) though they collectively contained 161 socketed axes, 72 halves of socketed axes and 69 fragments of socketed axes. The finders report that there were around 30 socketed axes in the two outer pits with the remainder in the larger central pit where they were located under a stone slab. From the single pit to the south-west (2007 T640), 115 socketed axes, 35 halves of socketed axes and 48 fragments of socketed axes were found.

Description: There are 276 complete socketed axes, 107 halves of socketed axes and 117 fragments of socketed axes in the four hoards of Langton Matravers. All but one of the socketed axes in these four hoards is of Type Portland which dates to the Llyn Fawr Stage of the Bronze Age (Pearce 1983: 616, pl. 55; Needham *et al.* 1997; O'Connor 2007). This type is distributed in Dorset, particularly on the coast.

The axes display a single-mouth moulding, beneath which a loop protrudes. The socket mouth of these axes is 'back-to-front', referring to the long axis being at right angles to the blade of the axe; the collar is thicker at the ends of the long axis (O' Connor 1980: 232). The upper body is slender, leading down to a sharply trapezoidal lower body and a straight, broad edged blade. 257 axes in this hoard have fillet-defined facets. Most axes have a bright silver patina with patches of green/white encrusted corrosion. This type of axe is shaped from thin metal and there are prominent casting seams. Almost all socketed axes and half those from the Langton Matravers Hoard have three ribs ending in single pellet decoration; however, four ribs are present on 10 axes, and five ribs on eight axes. The casting core is still present in 370 of the 382 Type Portland socketed axes and half-axes.

The other socketed axe type represented in this hoard is Type Blandford (2007 T629, axe no. 297), which is far rarer and found with high tin bronze gouges as at the Blandford Forum Hoard (Pearce 1983: 465). It is comparable in form, albeit the axe is half broken, but has no casting core and no facets. The main difference

lies in the four ribs which, rather than running straight down the body, curve in two pairs towards each side of the axe and do not finish in pellets.

The sample of 15 socketed axes compositionally analysed revealed a high-tin bronze content which can probably be assumed to be representative of the four hoards. The high-tin bronze composition of the axes gave them their silvery patina but also left them highly brittle and unsuitable for functional tasks such as woodworking. The thinness of the axes and the frequently poor quality of casting would suggest that the intention was that they would never be used. Furthermore, the remains of the clay casting core appear to have been left inside the vast majority of the axes, many socketed axes have their casting flashes intact, and very few show any signs of sharpening on the blade. The microscopic examination of a small sample of the axes revealed vertical striations (parallel to the ribs), which suggest that the axes may have been polished. The dimensions and style of the axes in the Langton Matravers Hoard are very similar, although not identical, indicating that they were not mass-produced in identical moulds as might have been expected for this quantity.

Discussion: The Langton Matravers Hoard represents one of the largest hoards ever discovered in Britain and the largest ever socketed axe hoard. However, aside from its size, the deposition is not out of the ordinary for the Llyn Fawr metalwork Phase. There are variations of decorated linear faceted socketed axes found in hoards nearby such as Blandford, Eggardon, Portland, and near Weymouth in Dorset, as well as at Netherhampton and Thorney Down in Wiltshire, and in East Anglia such as at Rudham, Norfolk (O'Connor 2007: 68). There are further concentrations of similar rib and pellet decorated socketed axes in northern and south-east France, western Iberia, the eastern Netherlands, north-west Germany and Belgium (Butler 1963; O'Connor 1980: 227, Map 76; Huth 1997; Huth 2000; Butler and Steegstra 2005–2006).

The unusable condition of the socketed axes at Langton Matravers is also reflected in broader patterns of socketed axe deposition in south-central and south-east England, north-west and south-east France, north-west Iberia and northern Albania during this period (Huth 1997; Huth 2000). Those socketed axes found in England typically have a high tin composition and small quantities of lead (Northover 1982: 67). While this is different from the typically high lead composition of the thousands of contemporary socketed axes of Amorican type in north-west France (Briard 1965; Briard 1987), the idea of creating a vast number of distinctly shaped and coloured socketed axes for apparently placing in the ground remains the same. Debate continues regarding the purpose of this activity and whether the objects were intended for later retrieval. However, the frequency with which such 'scrap' or 'founders' hoards' are discovered points towards an interpretation beyond the simple storage of metal. Indeed, it would appear in this case that a vast number of axes were produced to a specific type, removed from their moulds, polished and subsequently discarded with no apparent functional use. While it is currently impossible to establish a fine chronological resolution on the date of deposition, it occurred at the very end of the Bronze Age, perhaps within a generational timespan, where bronze apparently ceased to be circulated or hoarded but when iron was still relatively rare (Thomas 1989; Needham 2007). Contemporary activity to the socketed axes in the locale of the hoard on the Isle of Purbeck (Calkin 1949) is seen in settlement and midden evidence at sites such as nearby Langton Matravers (Calkin and Piggott 1939), Compact Farm (Graham *et al.* 2002), Eldon's Seat, Kimmeridge (Cunliffe and Phillipson 1968), and Rope Lake Hole (Woodward 1987). While this indicates that there were communities present who may have been responsible for the production and deposition of the hoard, there is no indication as to why they were responsible for such a vast undertaking.

Disposition: Acquired by Dorset County Museum.

B ROBERTS

Section editor and further research: Sally Worrell.
Editor: Michael Lewis.

Particularly unusual Iron Age discoveries recorded in 2007 include two bronze bowls, a wine strainer and a wooden tankard found in close proximity to one another at Langstone, Newport (88); the possible drinking horn terminal depicting a finely modelled bovine head found in Needham, Norfolk (78); the copper-alloy baldric ring or sword belt fitting from Constantine, Cornwall (71); and the polychrome enameled mount from Burton Fleming, East Yorkshire (86). The large quantity of 16 Iron Age toggles recorded this year includes an unparalleled toggle with lipped decoration found in Charlton Mackrell, Somerset (79), and demonstrates the contribution to artefact research that data collected through the PAS can offer.

During the later Iron Age there was a very noticeable increase in the volume of material culture in circulation, especially coinage, brooches and items of harness equipment. This phenomenon is evident in data from both archaeological excavations and through metal-detection as seen by the quantity of finds recorded by the PAS.

A very significant quantity and interesting range of harness equipment was recorded in 2007, including 35 terrets (rein guides) and ten linchpins. Particularly interesting terrets reported include the unusual example from Kendal, Cumbria (67), which is undecorated but has a flat saddle attachment at the centre, and the terret with ring-and-dot motifs in red enamel from Kirby Hill, North Yorkshire (76). Wheels on horse-drawn vehicles in the Iron Age were secured by linchpins which were predominantly composite in structure, having an iron shank and copper-alloy terminals. Of the seven incomplete linchpins recorded by the PAS and three linchpin terminals recorded as Treasure (from the Attleborough area, Norfolk (80)), seven have been identified as vase-headed linchpins and one (from Clipstone, Nottinghamshire (74)) as a ring-headed type. Four linchpins were reported from the West Midlands (WAW-FCDA60, D82ED6, CEE943 & WMID-947693) – a pattern noted in the PAS Annual Report 2006. The polychrome enameled copper-alloy and iron vase-headed linchpin from Hatherton, Staffordshire (85), is a particularly fine example. Other horse-gear also recorded in the same area includes the harness mount from Stoneleigh, Warwickshire (84).

Besides coins, brooches are the most numerous Iron Age artefact type recorded by the PAS; this is also the case in the Roman period. Brooches were manufactured in Britain from the late 6th century BC onwards, although individual examples may have been imported from the Continent at an earlier period. As well as offering dating information, brooches and other small personal objects may also indicate the status or identity of the wearer. Some of these may not represent accidental losses but instead deliberate

IRON AGE

deposits in rituals on both settlement sites and at 'special places' (Haselgrove 1997).

164 Iron Age (or possibly Iron Age) brooches were recorded by the PAS in 2007. Of the 24 Early to Middle Iron Age brooches (i.e. dated from the 6th to 3rd centuries BC), there are four Late Hallstatt brooches, including one from Madley, Herefordshire (63), 17 La Tène I and three La Tène II brooches. More than half these were found in south-east England (Figure 2). Like other Middle Iron Age La Tène II brooches recorded in previous years, those reported this year are frequently elaborate in form and close parallels for them are difficult to find. Their distribution differs markedly from that of the more numerous early Iron Age brooches and lies predominantly in northern counties. Examples this year were found in Barmby Moor, East Yorkshire (NCL-091917), Roxby cum Risby, North Lincolnshire (65), and Swinfen and Packington, Staffordshire (WMID-C836644).

Early to Middle Iron Age brooches are significantly outnumbered by the 140 Late Iron Age to early Roman period brooches (i.e. those dated to the late 1st century BC and 1st century AD). This phenomenon is sometimes referred to as the 'fibula event horizon' and describes a massive increase in the quantity of brooches being worn and deposited. It is particularly evident in the brooches from excavated contexts as well as those metal-detected in southern and eastern Britain (Figure 3). During 2007, significant quantities were recorded in Suffolk (24 brooches), Lincolnshire (14), Kent (11) and Hampshire (9).

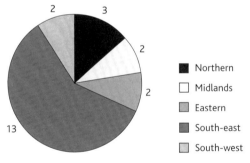

Figure 2: Early to Middle Iron Age brooches recorded 2007

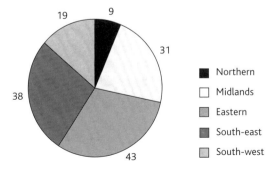

Figure 3: Late Iron Age to Roman brooches recorded 2007

An exceptional quantity of miniature objects dating from the Late Iron Age to the Roman period were also recorded during the period covered by this report. This includes the possible miniature shield from Sleaford, Lincolnshire (70), and a large assemblage consisting of 23 shields, five spears, four swords and one axe, all found during the 1980s at the same site in Nettleton, North Lincolnshire. It is plausible that this material derives from a shrine, perhaps dedicated to Mars. The quantity of shields in the Nettleton group is reminiscent of the Salisbury Hoard (Stead 1998).

---

61. Swindon area, Wiltshire: incomplete copper-alloy 'moustache-like' object (PAS: WILT-616785)

Date: Iron Age (c. 800–c. 300 BC).
Discovery: Found by Amanda Last while metal-detecting in 2007, and recorded by Katie Hinds (Wiltshire FLO).
Description: An incomplete object, referred to as a 'moustache-like' object, with one damaged pointed end and the other end now missing. Cast in one piece, the three-dimensional object has a swollen body with a pointed drop-shaped part on either side of a central vertical constriction with a square perforation on the underside. The drop-shaped parts are decorated with slanting grooves on both faces and the terminals taper and curve upwards and the intact and tapering pointed end is plain. The underside is slightly flattened. Length: 32mm. Dimensions: 58.5 x 12.3 x 11.7mm. Perforation dimensions: 4.4 x 3 x 3.8mm. Weight: 24.31g.
Discussion: It is difficult to identify the function and date of objects of this type. Although originally thought to be Medieval, an example in the Salisbury Hoard (Stead 1998: no. 117) suggests an Iron Age or earlier date. As none have yet been found in an excavated datable context their date remains uncertain. In total, twelve examples have been recorded by the PAS; some of these are single examples, while most are 'double' and perforated, as this example. In the opinion of J D Hill, British Museum, these objects date to the Iron Age rather than the Bronze Age.
Disposition: Returned to finder.

K HINDS

---

62. Leyburn, North Yorkshire: copper-alloy pin (PAS: LANCUM-5ECCE3)

Date: Early Iron Age (c. 800–c. 100 BC).
Discovery: Found by Ken Hurst while metal-detecting in 2007, and recorded with Dot Boughton (Lancashire & Cumbria FLO).
Description: A complete copper-alloy ring-headed pin of Becker's (2000) Variant 1.2. The head is circular, and the shaft is straight with a bend at the shoulder (Becker 2000: Variant 1). The end of the head touches, but is not joined to the shoulder. The outer circumference of the head is decorated with moulded

notching. Dimensions: 115.2 x 2.9mm. Diameter (head): 17.7mm. Weight: 7.25g.

Discussion: Ring-headed pins are characteristic of the Iron Age in Britain and Ireland. At this time items of personal adornment were not common and pins may have been used to secure garments or to style the hair. Although the form of this pin is relatively simplistic, such pins are rare and examples are most often found on settlement sites or as stray finds and rarely in graves. Most English pins are found in south and central England, with concentrations in Wessex and the East Anglian counties of Cambridgeshire, Suffolk and Norfolk. A very similar pin to the example from Leyburn was found in the Thames at Hammersmith along with two other forms of ring-headed pin (Dunning 1934: 274, no. 5, fig. 3; Smith 1925: 97, fig. 104).

Disposition: Returned to finder.

D BOUGHTON

63. Madley, Herefordshire: copper-alloy brooch (PAS: NMGW-8809A8)

Date: Early Iron Age (c. 650–c. 450 BC).

Discovery: Found by Maxine Jones while metal-detecting in 2007, and recorded by Mark Lodwick (Finds Co-ordinator, Wales).

Description: An almost complete copper-alloy bow brooch of unusual form, probably of Late Hallstatt or early La Tène Type. At the rear of the head is a small perforation aligned with the catch-plate by which it is possible that the brooch was secured with a separate pin, which was connected behind the head. At each side of the head there is an integral spherical knob. The high arched bow is straight sided with a faceted section. At the centre of the bow there are two integral spherical side knobs. The leg is of the characteristic U-shaped form, incorporating the catch-plate on the side of the lower bow. The foot has a single, central and integral spherical knob with a recessed circular cell probably intended to hold a decorative substance, possibly glass. The surface of the brooch is well preserved with a green-brown patina. Evidence of finishing and file marks are evident on the rear of the bow. Dimensions: 52.2 x 18.1mm. Weight: 14.2g. Metallurgical analysis was conducted using a scanning electron microscope (SEM) to assess the composition of the metal in the hope of clarifying the age of the brooch. A very small area of exposed metal from the damaged area at the terminal was analysed and proved to be a pure copper-tin alloy composition (89% copper, 11% tin) with no other elements detected. This result strengthens the case for a pre-Roman date for the brooch.

Discussion: The brooch is very unusual in its proposed method of attachment by utilising a separate pin, which presumably would have had a spherical head, in keeping with the decoration on the brooch. Wear on the interior of the perforation would seem to strengthen the case for a separate pin, although it is possible that a separate head was riveted through the perforation or a pin wound around the loop. The head arrangement makes the brooch difficult to closely parallel, although knobbed decoration with a short arched bow can be paralleled on two Atlantic Type brooches with a crossbar head, and upturned foot with a disc of Hull and Hawkes Group K found at Mount Batten, Cornwall (Boudet 1988: 64, nos. 66–67).

Disposition: Returned to finder.

M LODWICK

64. Lane End area, Buckinghamshire: copper-alloy brooch (PAS: BUC-E0D317)

Date: Early to Middle Iron Age (c. 400–c. 250 BC).

Discovery: Found by Robert Piercy while metal-detecting in 2007, and recorded by Ros Tyrrell (Buckinghamshire FLO).

Description: An incomplete copper-alloy insular La Tène IBc Type brooch. The flattened, leaf-shaped bow has a low arch and is ornamented with a pair of grooves forming a pointed oval close to the centre. The incomplete spring consists of two coils and the pin is missing. Iron corrosion at the spring suggests that an iron rod passed through the coils. The incomplete foot is short, its stem reverted and the catch-plate survives. Dimensions: 67.9 x 10.6mm. Weight: 19.02g.

Discussion: It is a little unusual for brooches of this type to have only a pair of grooves ornamenting the bow, although a parallel for this decoration is known from Ewell, Surrey (Hull and Hawkes 1987: 109, no. 7376, pl. 32). Other brooches of this type have decoration on the bow which can consist of four, six or eight grooves to fill the space. Brooches are known with copper-alloy rods passing through the spring, but the use of an iron rod is rather unusual and suggests that this was a 'mock spring' rather than a repair using a replacement iron pin. A similar feature is noted on La Tène I brooches from southern England and specifically Wessex.

Deposition: Returned to finder.

R TYRRELL & S WORRELL

65. Roxby cum Risby, North Lincolnshire: copper-alloy brooch (PAS: NLM-A01FB1)

Date: Middle Iron Age (c. 300–c. 200 BC).

Discovery: Found by Harry Jeffries while metal-detecting in 2007, and recorded by Lisa Staves (North Lincolnshire FLO).

Description: A copper-alloy La Tene 2Bb brooch dating to the 3rd century BC. The brooch is truncated with the upper part of the bow and the attachment mechanism missing. In profile, the bow is gently curved and is formed from an opposing pair of conjoined loops, each of which curves in to form a heart terminating at the internal edge with a pair of circular cup sockets; these retain traces of a white paste, although no trace of the form of the internal setting. The integral rectangular-sectioned foot tapers from the bow and is cast in a loop to join the front of the bow at the base of the openwork heart. The foot also terminates with the same circular setting that can be seen on the bow. At the back of the foot are the remains of catch-plate. Dimensions: 29.8 x 15.4 x 12.1mm. Weight: 5.61g.

Discussion: La Tène 2B brooches form a small but diverse and inventive type. Iron Age brooches with openwork bows are very unusual. The bow of a brooch of Type 2Bc in the form of an opposed pair of omega figures but with the outward ends up-curved to form cast-on knobs is known from Cold Kitchen Hill, Wiltshire (Hull and Hawkes 1987: 153, no. 7139, pl. 43); an example from Newnham Croft, Cambridge, has a wheel-shaped openwork bow decorated with five knobs of white shell and a further two inlaid knobs on the returned foot. Although it has not been possible to identify the substance within the three circular settings of the brooch from Roxby cum Risby, La Tène 2Bb brooches ornamented with glass or amber are known. The brooch from Datchet, Buckinghamshire (Hull and Hawkes 1987: 148–149, no. 2249, pl. 43), has nine sockets for ornamental beads, some of which contain amber, resin or calcitic material; the example from Danes Graves, Kilham, East Yorkshire (Hull and Hawkes 1987: 151, no. 151, pl. 42), has three groups of eleven cup sockets, some of which contain small bosses rather than beads, probably of amber which were retained by adhesive.

Disposition: Returned to finder.

L STAVES & S WORRELL

---

66. Penllyn, Vale of Glamorgan: copper-alloy terret (PAS: NMGW-6E2371)

Date: Late Iron Age (c. 300 BC–c. AD 100).

Discovery: Found by Malcolm Jones while metal-detecting in 2007, and recorded by Mark Lodwick (Finds Co-ordinator, Wales).

Description: A complete terret of simple type with a number of interesting features. The bar is slightly curved and has a sub-triangular section which expands at the centre to a lozenge. The prominent circular collar mouldings at either end of the bar are worn, but a V-shaped decorative groove and rib are still evident on the underside of the mouldings. The oval hoop narrows towards the top and is decorated with a central double rib. One side of the hoop displays evidence of pounding or hammering which is likely to have occurred in antiquity and file marks from the finishing of the terret are evident on the bar. The inside of the hoop has subtle wear-facets resulting from straps rubbing against the surface through time. Dimensions: 63.4 x 77.1mm. Diameter: 10.1mm. Weight: 65g.

Discussion: The terret corresponds to Spratling's (1972) Group I, dated to the 4th century BC to 2nd

century AD. This example may be suggested as having a date within the mid-range, perhaps c. 3rd century BC to 1st century AD. It is believed that Iron Age vehicles had a set of four terrets set along the yoke, one to guide each rein of a pair of horses, and another larger terret, the function of which is not understood. The comparatively large size of this terret would suggest that it was employed as the central larger terret of a group consisting of five terrets. The form and style of the double-rib decoration can be closely paralleled on terrets found at Glastonbury, Somerset (Bulleid and St George Grey 1911: 229, no. E8), and terret moulds from Cadbury Castle, Somerset (Barrett, Freeman and Woodward 2000: 298). These parallels may suggest a distribution concentrated around south-western Britain.

Disposition: Donated to the National Museum Wales.

M LODWICK

---

67. Kendal, Cumbria: copper-alloy terret (PAS: LANCUM-C133A7)

Date: Late Iron Age to early Roman (c. 300 BC–c. AD 100).

Discovery: Found by Eric Bryers while metal-detecting in the 1990s, and recorded by Dot Boughton (Lancashire & Cumbria FLO) in 2007.

Description: An undecorated large terret of simple type. The hoop is oval and has a circular section. The bar has a splayed, prominent collar moulding at each end and has an integrally cast, flat saddle attachment at the centre, with a protrusion with rounded ends. Dimensions: 80 x 72mm. Diameter: 61mm. Weight: 80.1g.

Discussion: The form of the bar is an unusual feature of this terret. Only two other terrets with a similar flat, saddle attachment are known, both found in the hoard of metalwork from Stanwick, North Yorkshire (MacGregor 1962: 43 & 46, nos. 61 & 65, fig. 10). It is of interest that the terret from Kendal and those from Stanwick (dimensions: 90 x 77mm & 120 x 110mm respectively) are all large examples.

After suffering a bad stroke last year, Eric and a friend gathered together all of his unreported finds and brought them to his detector club meeting to be recorded with the PAS.

Disposition: Returned to finder.

D BOUGHTON & S WORRELL

---

68. King's Lynn area, Norfolk: electrum torc terminal (PAS: NMS-D38F38; Treasure: 2007 T104)

Date: Iron Age (c. 200–c. 1 BC).

Discovery: Found by Terrance Norman while metal-detecting in February 2007, and reported to Erica Darch (Norfolk FLO).

Description: A buffer terminal of a multi-strand torc, paired with one found in December 2005 (TAR 2005/6: no. 81). The decoration on both terminals is the same and consists of a band of cable decoration around the edge. The flat surface of the terminal is decorated with an engraved, curvilinear La Tène 'mirror-style' design with pecked dots on the face, although this second example lacks a curlicue on the front face. It is also pockmarked with larger casting flaws. Again, stubs of wire line the periphery of the reverse. Diameter: 21.5mm. Weight: 15.79g. Surface analysis: gold and silver contents of approximately 33–36% and 58–61% respectively.

Discussion: Torc terminals of this type are not as common as the ring-shaped terminals, but examples of similar buffer terminals with engraved or raised cast decoration are known from Bawsey (Jope 2000: 255, pl, 120 l) and Snettisham (Hoards F and H), Norfolk (Stead 1991a: 449–451, fig. 10, pl. II).

Disposition: Acquired by Norwich Castle Museum.

A ROGERSON

---

69. Norwich area, Norfolk: gold torc fitting (PAS: NMS-C6DFC1; Treasure: 2007 T119)

Date: Iron Age to early Roman (c. 200 BC–c. AD 100).
Discovery: Found by Alan Matthewson while metal-detecting in January 2007, and reported to Erica Darch (Norfolk FLO).
Description: A rotating dorsal muff from a torc made from an alloy of gold and silver. It is formed of a composite ring with six components comprising two broad semicircular-sectioned concentric hollow ribs (or tubes) between three narrow twisted wires (probably square-sectioned) soldered to a sheet inner part. The twisted wires appear very worn. The surface of the inner sheet has concentric wear and scratches where the separate parts of the torc were twisted together. Diameter: 24mm. Weight: 10.94g.
Surface analysis: gold and silver contents of 84–87% and 10–12% respectively.

Discussion: It is likely that torcs with a rotating dorsal muff were probably easy to wear and to put on and take off. One end of the light loop is engaged in the lateral opening of a buffer and the other end terminates in a detachable ring or muff (Elùere 1987: 30–31). Examples of tubular torcs with ornamental muffs are also known from Snettisham, Norfolk (Jope 2000: 253, 112 a–g, pl. 112). Alternatively, it may possibly have formed part of the terminal of a twisted torc, as the diameter of the muff is particularly small. The relatively high gold content of the muff and the unusual twisted wire decoration suggest that the object may extend into the early Roman period.
Disposition: Acquired by Norwich Castle Museum.

S J ASHLEY

---

70. Sleaford, Lincolnshire: copper-alloy possible miniature shield (PAS: LIN-BC5A95)

Date: Late Iron Age to early Roman (c. 200 BC–c. AD 100).
Discovery: Found by Charles Raphael while metal-detecting in 2007, and recorded by Adam Daubney (Lincolnshire FLO).
Description: Two non-joining fragments of an oval, miniature shield made from a flat sheet of copper-alloy. It is decorated with six stamped pellet-in-ring motifs closely spaced around the perimeter. Dimensions: 48 x 28.7 x 1mm.
Discussion: Miniature shields can be strikingly similar in form to full-sized examples and, as such, can provide an important source of information on a rare object type. The decoration on miniature shields is variable and includes repoussé, incised and stamped motifs. The PAS has currently recorded a total of 25 miniature shields, 22 of which were found at Nettleton, Lincolnshire, where the quantity of shields is reminiscent of the Salisbury Hoard (Stead 1998: 1–35; Stead 1991). Other examples have been found at Dragonby and Kirmington, North Lincolnshire (Knowles and May 1996: 271, nos. 1–2, fig. 11.17; Henig and Leahy 1986: 388–391).
Disposition: Returned to finder.

A DAUBNEY

---

71. Constantine, Cornwall: copper-alloy baldric ring (PAS: CORN-B177A3)

Date: Late Iron Age (c. 120 BC–c. AD 50).
Discovery: Found by Harry Manson while metal-detecting in March 2007, and recorded by Anna Tyacke (Cornwall FLO).
Description: An incomplete cast copper-alloy baldric ring or sword belt fitting dating to the La Tène III/D Phase of the Late Iron Age. The fitting would have been used in conjunction with a strap that went over the shoulder onto which a scabbard or sword was suspended (Collis 1973: 130). The object takes the form of a short cylinder with the stub of a tapering projection extending from the base, which, when complete, may have extended to a stud at right angles as a means of attachment to a leather strap. The ring is decorated with two rows of repeated inward-pointing triangles infilled with 'sealing wax' glass, so-called because of its opaque, deep red colour. Although technically known as enamel, it is in fact small lumps of glass which were pressed into the cavity after being heated to soften (Hughes 1972: 98).
Analysis of the glass using a Scanning Electron Microscope (SEM) by Mary Davis (National Museum & Gallery Wales) identified a leaded glass with copper as a colouring agent, with the bedding metal as a tin rich solder containing lead; this is unusual for bedding glass. Dimensions: 24.4 x 8.6 x 3mm. Length (extension): 7mm. Diameter: 17mm. Weight: 5.25g.

Discussion: Baldric rings are generally formed from a copper-alloy narrow loop, with or without wings, and with an extending neck from which a stud projects at 90°. The elaborately decorated example from Constantine represents an unusual variant. J D Hill (British Museum) commented that he had 'not seen a fitting with decoration around the ring, but on some 1st-century AD variants there is decoration on the end of the stud.'

Baldric rings are not common finds although six have been recorded by the PAS. Four are recorded from West Sussex: Coldwaltham (SUSS-D82452), Houghton (SUSS-4C9825), Sullington (SUSS-4C8491) and Storrington (SUSS-913C68), and another from Wickham Bishop, Essex (ESS-1D1BC2) (Andrews-Wilson: forthcoming).

Disposition: Acquired by the Royal Institution of Cornwall (Acc. no. 2007.42).

A TYACKE

72. Driffield, East Yorkshire: copper-alloy amulet (PAS: YORYM-8826A5)

Date: Iron Age (c. 100 BC–c. AD 100).

Discovery: Found by Malcolm Brown while metal-detecting in 2007, and recorded by Liz Andrews-Wilson (North & East Yorkshire FLO).

Description: A copper-alloy amulet in the form of a miniature socketed axe. The axe has a defined single-mouth moulding, an integral loop and straight sides which expand suddenly at the lower blade forming a crescentic blade edge with rounded terminal knobs instead of blade tips. Length: 39.05mm. Width (blade edge): 45.15mm. Diameter (socket): 6.6mm. Weight: 17.4g.

Discussion: No direct parallel for this object is known, but stylistically it is most similar to objects dating from the Late Iron Age to early Roman period such as the miniature axe discovered during the excavation of the Late La Tène cemetery at Arras, East Yorkshire. This object was found with the pin connecting it to a glass bead, and was identified as a pendant (Stead 1979: 84, no. 3, fig. 34). Another miniature socketed axehead of broadly similar size to that from Driffield, but with a straight, expanded blade edge has recently been recorded from Whittington, Northumberland (NCL-346DE5).

Disposition: Returned to finder.

L ANDREWS-WILSON

73. Wychavon, Worcestershire: copper-alloy possible miniature wheel (PAS: WAW-360062)

Date: Iron Age (c. 100 BC–c. AD 100).

Discovery: Found by Mr H Sterry while metal-detecting in 2007, and recorded with Angie Bolton (Warwickshire & Worcestershire FLO).

Description: A cast copper-alloy possible miniature wheel. It has a concentric frame, an openwork triangle forming a tricorne (concave-sided triangle) motif within and joining the frame, and has a large, integral solid circular pellet at the centre. The outer edge is decorated with two horizontal grooves with fine, narrow oblique ribbing either side of the grooves. Where the triangular moulding meets the concentric frame there are signs of damage. The surface of the wheel is slightly pitted with an incomplete mid-green patina. Diameter: 43.8mm. Thickness: 7.1mm. Weight: 3.93g.

Discussion: Wheel models are generally thought to be votive in nature. They are numerous in Gaul and the Rhine and Danube regions but are less abundant in Britain, where examples are focused on the south and east and also along Hadrian's Wall (Green 1996: 116). Four wheel models were found in the small hoard of metalwork from Wavendon Gate, Buckinghamshire (Williams *et al.* 1996: 113–116), and another was found at Hounslow (Jope 2000: fig. 161, o). The Hounslow and Wavendon Gate examples are very similar to the other miniature wheel recorded by the PAS from Thimbleby, Lincolnshire (DENO-0BBA52). Alternatively, this object may be a particularly elaborate belt loop, although no close parallel is known.

Disposition: Returned to finder.

A BOLTON

74. Clipstone, Nottinghamshire: copper-alloy and iron linchpin (PAS: DENO-7ED404)

Date: Late Iron Age (c. 100 BC–c. AD 100).

Discovery: Found by Alan Chambers while metal-detecting in February 2007, and recorded by Anja Rohde (Derbyshire & Nottinghamshire FLO).

Description: An incomplete ring-headed linchpin with a broad, oval looped head. The terminals expand slightly where they meet the broad, domed central boss. The boss is perforated horizontally by a large circular hole. The corroded remains of the incomplete iron shaft extend from the base of the boss. Length: 100.5mm. Dimensions (head): 36.4 x 7.1mm. Dimensions (shank): 16.4 x 15.1mm. Diameter (hole): 6.8mm. Weight: 99.3g.

Discussion: It is interesting that of the 40 linchpin fragments recorded by the PAS, this is the only ring-headed linchpin type represented, compared to a minimum of 15 vase-headed examples. Similarly, linchpins of composite ring-headed type in copper-alloy and iron are not well represented among the earlier and published finds, but examples are known from Stanwick and Melsonby, North Yorkshire, and Middleton-on-the-

Wold, East Yorkshire (MacGregor 1962: 25, 46, nos. 70–71, 79, figs. 10–11; Stead 1979: 45, no. 2, fig. 14). These linchpins are closely related to the more numerous vase-headed type and the examples from Stanwick and Melsonby have been classified as the so-called vase-ring combination type with a 'terret-like' loop above the inverted vase-shaped element (MacGregor 1976: 73; Macdonald 2007: 38–39).
Deposition: Returned to finder.

A ROHDE & S WORRELL

---

75. Wilstead, Bedfordshire: silver brooch fragment (PAS: BH-B96102; Treasure: 2007 T491)

Date: Late Iron Age to early Roman (c. 50 BC–c. AD 50).
Discovery: Found by Albion Archaeology during excavation in July 2007, and reported to Julian Watters (Bedfordshire & Hertfordshire FLO).
Description: A fragment of a silver *knotenfibeln* or boss-on-bow brooch consisting of part of the bow and the start of the spring only. The bow has a diamond cross-section or lozenge-shaped section with a defining 'button' between two neat mouldings. The lower bow is broken and twisted out of alignment. The bow is shallow with a gentle curve approaching the head, rather than with a sharp and distinct 'knee' with the spring directly below it. Dimensions: 44.3 x 3.7mm.
Discussion: This type of brooch is sometimes referred to as *knotenfibeln*, because of the 'knot' or boss on the bow; the type is also described as a Feugère Type 8b or an Almgren Type 65. Examples of brooches of this type are known across southern Britain, France, western Germany and the Low Countries. A small number of boss on bow brooches are silver, such as the two pairs, each joined by a silver chain found in cremation burials at Great Chesterford, Essex, in 1856 (Jope 2000: 298, nos. 266–267 j–m) and from the Horncastle area, Lincolnshire (*TAR* 2003: no. 29), but the majority of examples were made in bronze or iron.
Disposition: Disclaimed; to remain with the main archive at Bedford Museum.

H DUNCAN & S WORRELL

---

76. Kirby Hill, North Yorkshire: copper-alloy enamelled terret (PAS: SWYOR-3B8107)

Date: Late Iron Age to early Roman (c. 50 BC–c. AD 100).
Discovery: Found by Andy Riley while metal-detecting in 2007, and recorded by Amy Cooper (South & West Yorkshire FLO).
Description: A complete terret of simple form with an oval hoop with an oval section. There is a splayed, prominent collar with two grooves at each end of the strap bar, which also has a rudimentary tang. The front and back surfaces of the hoop are decorated with five ring-and-dot motifs inlaid with deep red glass. The dots are more evenly spaced on one side than on the other.

There is an area at the top right-hand side with greater wear on the inside of the terret, which may indicate the angle formed by the reins as they passed through the hoop. The terret is a little pitted, but has a smooth, mid-green patina and survives in a very good condition. Dimensions: 60.1 x 57.6 x 16.8mm. Weight: 75.2g.
Discussion: Examples of simple terrets with similar enamelled ring-and-dot decoration are unusual, although others recorded by the PAS include a terret with red glass from Climpstone, Nottinghamshire (DENO-7EF2B4). Platform terrets with the platforms and hoop decorated with red enamel dots and ring-and-dot motifs in red glass are known from Fremington Hagg, North Yorkshire (Macgregor 1976: no. 68), and Whitchurch Rural, Shropshire (LVPL2442).
Deposition: Returned to finder.

A COOPER

---

77. Wibtoft, Warwickshire: enamelled copper-alloy and iron linchpin terminal (PAS: WAW-CEE943)

Date: Late Iron Age (c. 50 BC–c. AD 100).
Discovery: Found by Mr R Partridge while metal-detecting in 2007, and recorded by Angie Bolton (Warwickshire & Worcestershire FLO).
Description: The cast, copper-alloy foot from a Late Iron Age linchpin of vase-headed type. The modelled foot appears as the upturned hoof and fetlock of a horse, giving rise to linchpins of this type being previously classed as the 'hoof type'. The shank is sub-triangular in profile and narrows to the tip before expanding and terminating with a flat, circular base which is set in the vertical plane. The back of the disc is convex and has an integral, triangular tip which tapers at the back of the socket. The circular base is decorated with a moulded four-petal ornament made up of curving petals with traces of red glass in the surrounding recesses. On the cylindrical shank there is an inverted triangular cell above the base and a pelta or cusp cell on one side which contains slight traces of red glass. Extending down the centre there is a sub-rectangular cell which would have held the missing iron shaft of which traces of corroded iron survive. Dimensions: 35.37 x 19.03 x 16.74mm. Weight: 32.7g.
Discussion: There are very marked differences in the incidence of Middle to Late Iron Age horse and vehicle equipment within the PAS data (Worrell 2007: 376–380). For example, of the 40 Iron Age linchpins recorded by the PAS, a very significant total of 13 examples have been recorded in the West Midlands, with four from Staffordshire, two from Worcestershire and seven from Warwickshire. In comparison, on the basis of earlier chance finds and excavations in this region, only four linchpins were known. Normally the number of Late Iron Age brooches recorded from a county exceeds that of horse and harness fittings. Interestingly, in Warwickshire and Staffordshire the opposite is the case and it is possible that although the dataset is

comparatively small, this feature may highlight an unexpected regional trend. The previous view of the West Midlands as being less socially complex and peripheral to the core areas of south-east England has been reassessed on the basis of data recorded by the PAS.

Disposition: Returned to finder.

A BOLTON & S WORRELL

---

78. Needham, Norfolk: copper-alloy possible drinking horn terminal (PAS: SF-882904)

Date: Iron Age (c. 50 BC–c. AD 100).
Discovery: Found by John Halles while metal-detecting in 2007, and recorded by Faye Minter (Suffolk FLO).
Description: An incomplete terminal of what is probably a drinking horn. It consists of a curving, hollow socket with a flaring, open terminal at one end, which tapers to a bovine head at the other. The animal's head has moulded, oval protruding eyes and pronounced brows. The large curving horns project from the side of the head at 45°, and then curve upwards and outwards slightly. One horn has a surviving terminal knob, but the other is missing. Behind the head, the shaft curves abruptly and the head is set parallel to it, looking down it. The short snout is rounded and terminates with flared, upward curving nostrils which have a horizontal circular hole through their centre. The underside of the snout touches a transverse moulding on the shaft. Dimensions: 78.24 x 26.3mm. Diameter (socket): 14.84–18.45mm. Weight: 74.65g.
Discussion: There is very little evidence for drinking horns in Iron Age Britain and this is the only example known with a bovine-headed terminal. A pair of curved tubular terminals of a drinking horn, decorated with an asymmetric tendril pattern, is known on the Torrs Chamfrein (horned helmet) from Kelton, Kirkcudbright, one of which has a terminal in the form of a stylised bird head (Atkinson and Piggott 1955; Jope 2000: 246, 58–59). Foreign parallels with a similar hollow and curvilinear form include a bronze mount in the form of a dragon from a drinking horn from Hungary and a series of drinking horn terminals from Scandinavia where they take the form of cattle heads (Atkinson and Piggott 1955: 227).
With its protruding oval eyes, large curving horns and flaring nostrils, this terminal is very similar in style to some bovine-headed vessel mounts such as the 1st century AD bucket mount from Ham Hill, Somerset (Jope 2000: 266, pl. 166i–j), and the strainer spout from Kirmington, Lincolnshire (May 1971: 253–259).
Disposition: Returned to finder.

F MINTER & S WORRELL

---

79. Charlton Mackrell, Somerset: copper-alloy toggle (PAS: SOM-946D43)

Date: Late Iron Age to early Roman (c. 50 BC–c. AD 100).
Discovery: Found by Paul Burton while using a metal-detector in 2007, and recorded with Naomi Payne (Somerset FLO).
Description: A cylindrical copper-alloy toggle with a sub-rectangular attachment loop on one side (Payne 2008: 202, fig. 2). The loop has a broader curving central section which narrows slightly on each side before flaring out again at the point where it meets the main body of the toggle. At each end of the cylinder there is a slightly expanded terminal which contains a deep and wide groove on the side opposite the loop. There is a further similar feature in the centre of the bar. Dimensions: 30.4 x 16.6 x 10.5mm. Diameter: 5.5mm. Weight: 14.9g.
Discussion: The toggle could have been attached to clothing or horse harness and currently no close parallel is known. Lipped decoration such as this is more commonly seen on Late Iron Age lipped terret rings and currently no close parallel is known.
Disposition: Returned to finder.

N PAYNE

---

80. Attleborough area, Norfolk: copper-alloy and iron group of linchpin elements (PAS: NMS-248F38; Treasure: 2007 T589)

Date: Late Iron Age to early Roman (c. 50 BC–c. AD 100).
Discovery: Found by Brian Anderson while metal-detecting in September 2007, and reported to Erica Darch (Norfolk FLO).
Description: A group consisting of a minimum of two linchpins with one head and two feet:
1. An incomplete copper-alloy head and iron shank of a vase-headed linchpin. The inverted vase-shaped head is waisted and has a prominent, wide and rounded moulding at the base and a similar moulding forming a large, flat circular top. The head is perforated by a horizontal hole, the ends of which are defined by rounded mouldings. There are two circular recessed cells inlaid with red glass between the perforations on one side only. The upper surface of the flat head has a wide border at the edge and a circle formed by short, very closely spaced radiating ridges around a central, circled tricorne (concave-sided triangle) motif in reserved metal, with traces of red glass in the recessed pointed oval cells. A stub of the corroded, rectangular-sectioned iron shank protrudes from the rectangular socket at the base of the head. Part of the edge of the flat top has been worn at the edge creating one straight side on the same plane as one edge of the shank. Much of the original surface is damaged and parts are covered with iron corrosion. Length: 35mm. Diameter (external): 42mm.

2. A copper-alloy linchpin foot. The curved, tapering lower terminal has a circular moulding above the globular body and ends in a flat, circular base set in the vertical plane, the rim of which touches the body forming an aperture behind and giving the lower terminal the appearance of an animal's hoof. The body is decorated with two circular cells inlaid with red glass, one on the same plane as the flat terminal, the other at right angles to it, with engraved or stamped lines forming chevrons between the two cells. The flat, disc terminal is recessed and the form of its decoration exactly matches that on the top of the linchpin head, also retaining traces of red glass. One side of the disc terminal is worn creating a flat edge. The rectangular socket for the missing shank is surrounded by iron corrosion. The moulding around the socket may also be worn but the surface is too corroded to be sure if this is wear or later damage. Much of the original surface is damaged and parts are covered with iron corrosion. Length: 51mm. Diameter: 23mm.

3. A copper-alloy linchpin foot, identical in form and decoration to no. 2. The rectangular socket for the missing shank is completely covered with iron corrosion. Most of outer edge of the flat base is now missing or damaged; much of the original surface is damaged and parts are covered with iron corrosion. Length: 47mm. Diameter: 22mm.

Discussion: Single finds and hoards of equipment from Late Iron Age horse-drawn vehicles are well known from Norfolk, although single linchpins are not frequently found with contemporary material (Hutcheson 2004). The importance of the pair of linchpins represented here is clear, but increases when previous discoveries of harness fittings from the area are considered. These include two vase-headed linchpins with ring-and-dot decoration on the head (Hutcheson 2004: 110, nos. 48–49) and more recently the hoard consisting of a platform terret decorated with polychrome (blue and yellow) enamel, a lipped terret and harness mount with red enamel cells (TAR 2004: no. 32).

Disposition: Acquired by Norwich Castle Museum.

E B DARCH & S WORRELL

---

81. South Perrott, Dorset: copper-alloy Birdlip brooch (PAS: SOM-CC69D6)

Date: Late Iron Age or early Roman (c. 30 BC–c. AD 60).
Discovery: Found by Christopher Adams while metal-detecting in 2007, and recorded by Naomi Payne (Somerset FLO).
Description: An incomplete brooch of Birdlip or Beaked Bow Type. The head consists of a domed 'trumpet' where the missing spring and pin would have been attached. There is a moulded transverse projection or 'beak' which curves upwards and narrows to bluntly pointed terminal with a projecting flange-like moulding above it and which continues around the back of the bow. The triangular-sectioned lower bow tapers

gradually and there is a small, slightly rounded foot-knob. On the back of the lower part of the bow is the incomplete flat catch-plate which has two rectilinear perforations separated by narrow bridgework. Length: 54.2mm. Weight: 12.4g.

Discussion: Birdlip Type brooches, thought to be a British variant of the Continental Flügelfibeln brooch, are found in small numbers across central England. Examples made of precious metal are very unusual and include the two brooches in gold found at Market Rasen and Normanby le Wold, Lincolnshire (TAR 2003: no. 24). Of the 42 Birdlip Type brooches made of copper-alloy recorded by the PAS, 16 were found in the East Midlands counties of Lincolnshire (11), Leicestershire (3), Rutland (1) and Northamptonshire (1).

Disposition: Returned to finder.

N PAYNE & S WORRELL

---

82. Cowbridge, Vale of Glamorgan: bronze terret and rein-ring (PAS: NMGW-9B2D52 &-9BEE04; Treasure: Wales 07.06)

Date: Late Iron Age (c. AD 1–c. 75).
Discovery: Found by John Pugh while metal-detecting in February 2007, reported to Mark Lodwick (Finds Co-ordinator, Wales) and identified by Adam Gwilt (National Museum Wales).
Description:
1. A large cast bronze terret with an oval shaped ring and an attachment bar defined by moulded collars. The terret has a wear facet and a hairline crack on the apex of the ring. Width: 83.6mm. Height: 75.6mm. Weight: 72.6g.
2. A cast bronze ring with a circular cross-section. Diameter (external): 61.9–63.1mm. Diameter (ring): 6.5–6.9mm. Weight: 47.6g.

Discussion: This Group I simple terret was found 6–7m from the rein-ring, but was deemed, on a balance of probability, to be associated when buried. Semi-quantitative metallurgical analysis of both indicated a similar tin bronze composition, with no lead or zinc present. Simple terrets were rein guides for chariots or wagons and examples have elsewhere been found in contexts dating between the Middle Iron Age and early Romano-British periods (c. 400 BC–c. AD 150). However, many have been found in contexts spanning the Late Iron Age and the time of the Campaigning Period of the Roman army (c. 150 BC–c. AD 75). The rein-ring has a similar diameter and form as the rings on two-link bridle bits of the Polden Hills sub-type, which date to the 1st century AD. These associated artefacts are therefore considered to be of Late Iron Age manufacture, though probably buried during the Campaigning Period of the Roman army in Wales (c. AD 50–75).

Disposition: Acquired by the National Museum of Wales; the landowner donated his share.

A GWILT

83. Marbury, Cheshire: copper-alloy fob (PAS: LVPL-F98596)

Date: (c. AD 1–c. 150).

Discovery: Found by Ray Lander while metal-detecting in 2007, and recorded by Frances McIntosh (Cheshire, Greater Manchester & Merseyside FLO).

Description: An incomplete copper-alloy fob or dangler. The disc head is decorated with an openwork, threefold whirligig, triskele motif, which extends to the circular rim. There are four stamped ring-and-dots with one at the centre and one on each arm. The circular-sectioned shank projects from the rear of the disc and terminates in a broken suspension loop. Dimensions: 42 x 4mm. Diameter: 39mm. Weight: 31g.

Discussion: The function of fobs or danglers is not fully understood, but it is likely that they could have hung from items of equipment, personal apparel or harness decoration (Jope 2000: 285). Nine examples of fobs decorated with the triskele from the British Isles were recorded by MacGregor (1976: 37) and a fob with a simple openwork triskele is recorded by the PAS from St Nicolas and Bonvilston, Vale of Glamorgan (NMGW-43E1D4).

Deposition: Returned to finder.

F MCINTOSH

84. Stoneleigh, Warwickshire: copper-alloy harness mount (PAS: WMID-9460B5)

Date: Late Iron Age to early Roman (c. AD 40–c. 80).

Discovery: Found by Stephen Quinn while metal-detecting in September 2007, and recorded with Duncan Slarke (Staffordshire & West Midlands FLO).

Description: A fragment of a decorated copper-alloy fitting, which can probably be identified as a horse harness mount. The fragment includes two adjoining curved edges and the front is decorated with wavy and zigzag lines, and incised comma-shaped and triangular cells with straight and curved sides, some of which are infilled with opaque red glass. The reverse is undecorated but has a large number of shallow, linear indentations. It has a well-developed green patina. Dimensions: 54.4 x 33.3 x 3.2–3.8mm. Weight: 25.92g.

Discussion: Two similar fragments found at the same location over the past 10 years are held at the Market Hall Museum, Warwick. One of these fragments adjoins the object described in this record. Adam Gwilt (National Museum of Wales) comments that this fragment is likely to be from a quadrilobed harness mount, possibly of a type with two larger lobes rather than a four-eared one. The use of geometric elements (triangles), incised swags and zigzag borders suggest that the fragment may date to c. AD 40–c. 80. Similar decorative motifs, also using opaque red glass can be seen on examples of harness equipment from the Polden Hill Hoard which has been dated to AD 50–80 (Brailsford 1975: 222–234).

Disposition: To be donated to Warwickshire Museum.

D SLARKE

85. Hatherton, Staffordshire: enamelled copper-alloy and iron linchpin (PAS: WMID-947693)

Date: Late Iron Age or early Roman (c. AD 40–c. 80).

Discovery: Found by Colin Pearson while metal-detecting in October 2007, and recorded by Duncan Slarke (Staffordshire & West Midlands FLO).

Description: An incomplete copper-alloy vase-headed linchpin with a polychrome enamelled head and corroded iron, square-sectioned shank. The head has a D-shaped section and is decorated with alternate red and yellow champlevé enamelled cells in a geometric chequerboard within a copper-alloy grid. The cells are square apart from at the perimeter where they are rectangular. There are also alternating red and orange enamel square cells round the lower part of the head on the front surface only. A broadly circular perforation, approximately 5mm in diameter, runs transversely through the base of the head. The copper-alloy head has a well-developed green patina. Length: 61.7mm. Dimensions (head): 18.2 x 26.4 x 18.9mm. Length (shank): 43.5mm. Diameter (shank): 14.5mm. Weight: 72.5g.

Discussion: The linchpin's asymmetrical head is particularly unusual and the example held in the Saffron Walden Museum, which is similar in both form and decoration, provides the only published parallel (Major 1988). Similar geometric chequerboard ornament in red and yellow enamel is also known on the linchpin foot from Kingsholm, Gloucestershire (Webster 1990). The use of orange enamel is unusual. The geometric polychrome enamelling technique is found on a range of metalwork, including items of harness equipment, mounts, belt fittings and fasteners, and is recognised as a regional expression of a widespread trend in Britain (Davis and Gwilt 2008: 167–171). Although vase-headed linchpins span the 4th century BC to the late 1st century AD, the geometric design in polychrome enamel does not start until the campaigning/conquest period and consequently a date c. AD 40–c. 80 is suggested for this artefact (Adam Gwilt, personal communication).

Disposition: Returned to finder.

D SLARKE

86. Burton Fleming, East Yorkshire: copper-alloy enamelled mount (PAS: NCL-04C774)

Date: Late Iron Age to Roman (c. AD 40–c. 80).

Discovery: Found by Derick Sirett while metal-detecting in June 2007, and reported to Rob Collins (North East FLO).

Description: A copper-alloy mount with an enamelled polychrome surface. In plan, the mount is roughly kidney-shaped, with two moulded circles positioned above a pelta-shaped panel which contains a circle with a horizontal leaf-shaped motif at either side. The circles have prominent, moulded borders in high relief and all three circles are decorated identically with the outer borders enclosing a chequerboard grid in reserved metal with three rows of alternate red and yellow rectangles. Below this, the pelta-shaped panel has a third circle at its centre and a leaf-shaped motif in yellow enamel at both sides and triangles of red enamel in the areas close to the circle on each side. On the back there are traces of two circular-sectioned pegs or other form of attachment. Dimensions: 45.7 x 32.4 x 8.2mm. Weight: 45.2g.

Discussion: The combination of red and yellow glass in 'curvilinear' style found upon La Tène objects continued with the 'geometric' style which gave a jewelled effect, as is seen with this mount, and on other contemporary objects, including harness equipment, such as linchpins and terrets, and button and loop fasteners. Jody Joy (British Museum) commented, 'in form, this object is Megaw's (1970) 'Cheshire cat' style, but with Roman-style colouring.'

Disposition: Returned to finder.

R COLLINS & S WORRELL

---

87. Redbourn, Hertfordshire: copper-alloy horse harness strap-mount with enamel inlay (PAS: BH-74D076)

Date: Late Iron Age to early Roman (c. AD 40–c. 100).
Discovery: Found by Graham Batt in 2007 while metal-detecting, and recorded by Julian Watters (Hertfordshire & Bedfordshire FLO).
Description: A strap-mount with a rectangular loop on the reverse which would have served to secure the mount to the harness strap. The central part of the elliptical mount is a pointed oval with a boss in the centre and a rectangular 'wing' plate extends at either side concealing a single strap bar. At its centre, the boss has a blue enamel-filled circular cell surrounded by a concentric circle in red enamel and then flanked by a deep groove; each 'wing' contains a setting similar to that on the central boss, while the top and bottom ends of the mount each have a pair of similar, but smaller, circular motifs. Dimensions: 55.2 x 45.9 x 16.6mm. Weight: 43.14g.

Discussion: No exact parallel could be found for this object, but its elliptical form is similar to a cruciform strap-junction comprising linked petal boss units flanked by two rectangular plates but with two strap bars on the reverse from Newstead, Roxburghshire (MacGregor 1976: no. 24). The use of blue and red enamel fits into the widespread trend in Britain of polychrome enamelling as seen on the quadrilobed strap unions from Hambleden, Buckinghamshire (Feacham 1991).

Deposition: Returned to finder.

J WATTERS

---

88. Langstone, Newport: two bronze bowls, a wine strainer and a tankard (PAS: NMGW-9C0216; Treasure: Wales 07.24)

Date: Bowls and wine strainer: Late Iron Age (c. AD 25–c. 75). Tankard: Romano-British (c. AD 50–c. 350).
Discovery: Found by Craig Mills while metal-detecting in December 2007, and reported to Mark Lewis (National Roman Legion Museum, Caerleon) on behalf of the PAS for Wales, who with Adam Gwilt (National Museum of Wales) identified the objects.
Description:
1. A virtually complete copper-alloy bowl of shallow squat form with a rounded base. It has a low girth, upright neck and everted rim, which is decorated with incised circular grooves and wavy lines, set in low relief. The bowl was lathe finished with incised circular grooves visible on the interior base. A copper-alloy cast escutcheon is attached by a shank perforating the vertical rim and has an attached ring for hanging and storage. The decorative escutcheon is lobed and winged with insets containing a red 'sealing wax' glass of Iron Age tradition. Some damage is evident, caused by differential erosion in the ground and minor denting during retrieval. Diameter (internal rim): 174mm. Diameter (girth): 215–220mm. Height: 99.5mm. Weight: 56.5g.
2. A near-complete and lathe-finished copper-alloy bowl of shallow squat form with a rounded base. It has a low girth, upright neck and an everted rim, which is decorated with incised circular grooves and infilling 'ladder' work. A copper-alloy escutcheon is attached by a shank perforating the vertical rim and secured with an internal washer. An attached ring provided the means for hanging and storage. The decorated escutcheon is lobed and lipped, with a central biconcave 'toggle' motif defined by lateral incised margins. The bowl is damaged through differential erosion and recent denting: there is a long gash around the girth and a dint, which has caused a small tear between rim and body. Diameter (internal rim): 164mm. Height: 86.5mm. Diameter (girth): 200–205mm. Weight: 243.1g.
3. A complete copper-alloy wine strainer with a round-bottomed bowl or body, with a wide circular flange. The flange (23.5–25mm wide) has an upturned external margin, with an interior 'rollover' margin and ledge. The base of the bowl is decorated with a perforation pattern occupying a circle approximately 100mm in diameter. A triskele design with circular flourishes at the end of each limb is defined by the absence of perforations, while the surrounding perforated spaces are made up of three arched trumpet motifs, each occupying 120° of the circular design. The strainer has a simple looped escutcheon with a suspension ring, attached to the underside of the flange. The flange is slightly nicked, dented and scratched. Diameter (external flange): 178–179mm. Diameter (internal rim): 130–131mm. Height: 113mm. Weight: 223.3g.

4. A virtually complete wooden and stave-built tankard with sheet copper-alloy fittings and a cast copper-alloy handle. The vessel has a near vertical profile with a simple rim and a flat raised base, which has been slotted into grooves in the six stave walls. Two wide and continuous circular bands of sheet copper-alloy surround the outer circumference of the tankard and an overturned narrow strip of copper-alloy forms a rim lip. The cast handle is plain with a continuous C-shaped back and T-shaped lateral attachment plates attached to the body by two pairs of bronze rivets with widened and slightly domed heads. The tankard has suffered some cracking damage and shrinkage during the drying out process. One stave has been damaged with a break near the rim, the fragment still surviving. Height: 149–150mm. Diameter (internal rim): 150mm. Diameter (base): 166mm. Thickness (stave): 11.2–11.5mm. Length (handle): 77–78mm.

Discussion: The two bowls may be identified as of the southern British Rose Ash Type, Late Iron Age and Native forms, which have been dated to between c. 50 BC–c. AD 50. The escutcheons are of the late La Tène art style, the lip and wing mouldings echoing a wider mid-1st-century AD development also viewed on horse and chariot equipment. The red 'sealing wax' glass is of Iron Age tradition. However, the lathe finishing and circular grooves on these vessels suggest manufacture late within this range, between c. AD 25–c. 60. The wine strainer is one of a small known group with broad flanges and without handles (Tomalin 1989). By virtue of their association elsewhere with trullei (dippers, oar-handled strainers and shallow bowls of Roman form), they have previously been dated to the late 1st and early 2nd centuries AD. However, this example has been decorated with a Native or 'Celtic' triskele design and fitted with a suspension ring to work as a set with, and fitting into, the directly associated Iron Age bowls. A date of manufacture of the strainer between c. AD 40–c. 60 is proposed, while the hoard of bowls and strainer is thought to have been deposited between c. AD 50–c. 75. The tankard is a Native form of drinking vessel used for communal drinking of beer or cider and especially prevalent across western Britain. It is one of only six known complete surviving tankards from Britain and Ireland. Its plain handle and form ally it with examples of Class V tankards (Corcoran 1952: 93). The existing parallels are thought to span in date between the mid 1st to 4th centuries AD. A close tankard-handle parallel has been identified, having been discovered in a well at the Roman fort of Loughor, Swansea. This burial context is thought to date to the early to mid 2nd century AD, suggesting this form of tankard was made and in circulation between c. AD 50–c. 150.

Follow-up archaeological investigation of the findspot was undertaken during January 2008 by Mark Lewis, Mark Lodwick (Finds Co-ordinator, Wales), Evan Chapman and Adam Gwilt (National Museum Wales),

with the help of the finder. This established that all four artefacts were deposited into the same bog or lake edge context, probably with votive intent. It was established that the tankard was buried 12.8m distant from the hoard of bowls and wine strainer, possibly, though not demonstrably, at a similar time. Since it was not a directly associated object, it was deemed not to be Treasure. Further research into the landscape and environmental context of the hoard and tankard is planned.

Disposition: Tankard (not Treasure) acquired by the National Museum of Wales. The National Museum of Wales also hopes to acquire the bowls and strainer.
A Gwilt & M Lewis

Section editor and further research: Sally Worrell.
Editor: Michael Lewis.

The Roman artefacts recorded in 2007 represent another very significant dataset, both quantitatively and qualitatively, and include some particularly unusual and unique finds as well as an extensive range of everyday objects. There is substantial regional variation in the quantity of Roman artefacts recorded this year, from single figures in north and west Wales and several northern English counties to 2,322 in Suffolk. In general, much higher quantities are recorded in the eastern counties (Norfolk, Suffolk and Lincolnshire) than elsewhere.

2007 saw the recording of many more religious objects and 1st- to 3rd-century military equipment, although fewer items of toilet and medical equipment and harness pieces were recorded. Of the religious objects featured in this report, the figurine representing Cautopates (an attendant of the god Mithras) from Newton Kyme cum Toulson, North Yorkshire (101), is exceptional and without known parallel. The cult of Mithras was popular with soldiers and it is very likely that this figurine was associated with the army. In addition, the crocodile figurine from Wherwell, Hampshire (98), which suggests an interest in the cult of Isis, and the bust depicting Antinous (the emperor Hadrian's favourite) from Capel St Mary, Suffolk (112), are noteworthy finds.

A significant number of artefacts with inscriptions or associated with literacy were recorded this year. Inscribed objects are frequently linked to the military and within this category the most significant individual find is the diploma found at Brompton, North Yorkshire (113), the issue of which can be dated to 17 July AD 118. This example, now acquired by Yorkshire Museum, represents an important addition to the small group of documents of this type known from Britain. The possibility of providing such a precise date for a non-coin object occurs very infrequently. The fragmentary tombstone from Cherington, Gloucestershire (133), is also an unusual find and is likely to commemorate the death of a legionary soldier whose name is now lost. Other inscribed objects of everyday types, more commonly referred to as *instrumentum domesticum*, include brooches, finger-rings, buckles and military fittings. Of the 13 finger-rings of precious metal three are inscribed with 'TOT' or variations thereof and dedicated to the God Toutatis (Daubney: forthcoming). The finger-ring from Hockcliffe, Bedfordshire (120), is an extremely important addition to this dataset since its inscription 'DEO TOT' represents the first reference to Toutatis specifically as a deity. In addition, two very interesting objects inscribed in Greek were recorded; the gold foil amulet with magical 'characters' in Greek cursive from south Oxfordshire (135), which represents a charm to ensure safe childbirth, and a gold finger-ring from the Bures area, Essex (128), bearing an inscription wishing good fortune.

ROMAN

Although lacking an inscription, the wax spatula handle depicting the bust of Minerva, found at Llanharry, Rhondda Cynon Taff (100), is closely linked with Roman literacy as it is likely to have been used for applying wax to writing tablets. In recent years the quantity of similar finds recorded by the PAS has risen very significantly and this adds weight to the suggestion that the spread of Roman literacy in the countryside was perhaps more developed than previously thought.

An extremely interesting range of unusual copper-alloy knives was recorded this year and include the knife handle depicting the myth surrounding Hercules and Antaeus from Irnham, Lincolnshire (124), the double-headed knife terminal from Trowbridge area, Wiltshire (95), and the folding knife handle representing a three-dimensional panther from Wickham Skeith, Suffolk (140).

Studies in the archaeology of Roman Britain have identified regional variation in the quantities and styles of everyday artefacts such as hairpins, cosmetic sets, nail cleaners, brooches and other objects relating to dress. These have the potential to enable a fuller understanding of the mixture of indigenous and imported traditions in the life of the province, and PAS data continues to make a significant contribution to this picture. As seen in previous years, brooches are the most abundant Roman artefact type recorded after coins. The 1,831 brooches and 430 other items of personal adornment (finger-rings, bracelets, hairpins, beads and earrings) account for 12.3% and 2.9% respectively of all Roman finds recorded in 2007. The volume of brooches and other forms of personal adornment is particularly high in Lincolnshire and Suffolk.

Some very unusual individual brooches were recorded in 2007, including a silver zoomorphic brooch depicting a hound and hare from Hale, Cheshire (106). Although no close parallel for this brooch is known from Britain, similar examples are known from Hungary. The two other Roman brooches found in north-west England and discussed in this report – the Kräftig-profilierte brooch from Atherton, Greater Manchester (90), and the swastika brooch from Northwich, Cheshire (130) – are both of types which originated in Pannonia on the Danube frontier (modern Hungary). It is likely that they came to Britain with troops raised or stationed in that province.

Some of the other brooches discussed in this report, such as the Polden Hill Type from Highnam, Gloucestershire (110), and the dragonesque brooch from Gisburn, Lancashire (105), are examples of types with a strongly regional distribution pattern. Polden Hill brooches are most commonly found in west and south-west England. Dragonesque brooches are not particularly common and although they have been found across much of Britain, with a spread from south-east Scotland to East Anglia, there is a very marked concentration in Yorkshire.

Button-and-loop fasteners, another dress-related item, are likely to have served as multi-purpose fasteners for clothing and harness. Between October 1997 and April 2008, 177 examples have been recorded by the PAS. The significance of this number can be gauged by comparison with Wild's (1970) fundamental discussion, based on a catalogue of 165 items, which includes examples from outside Britain. Previous studies suggested that their main distribution was in lowland Scotland and the north of England, with significant numbers also documented in Yorkshire, the Welsh Marches and south Wales. Analysis of fasteners recorded by the PAS reveals a much wider distribution, showing finds in significant quantities not only in Durham, North Yorkshire, East Yorkshire and South Yorkshire, but also in the East and West Midlands, the eastern region (especially Suffolk) and a small scatter in the south-eastern counties (see Figure 4 for the distribution of button and loop fasteners recorded by the PAS by type). One subtype, the double-headed fastener, was previously known only in very small quantities – the five examples recorded by the PAS (including that from South Cave, East Yorkshire (115)), all from northern counties, are therefore of particular interest.

A particularly interesting range of late Roman artefacts recorded in 2007 include a silver finger-ring with shoulders, in the form of a water bird, from Godmanchester, Cambridgeshire (136), a gold finger-ring with its bezel ornamented with a stylised bunch of grapes from Aldborough, North Yorkshire (137), and a copper-alloy seal-ring engraved with the chi-rho motif from Narborough, Leicestershire (145). Finally, the very rare gold crossbow brooch found in Gunthorpe, Norfolk (148), is an exceptional object and one which must have signified high status.

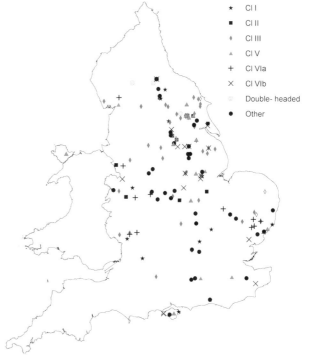

Figure 4. Button and loop fasteners recorded by PAS October 1997–April 2008

89. Eynsford, Kent: copper-alloy pan-handle (PAS: LON-B47821)

Date: Roman (c. AD 43–100).
Discovery: Found by Bill Robson some years ago while searching on the spoil heaps from the building of the M25, and recorded by Kate Sumnall (London FLO) in 2007.
Description: A copper-alloy handle, with a ram's head terminal, from a shallow handled pan or skillet. The shaft of the handle is tubular and hollow and is decorated with grooves extending along much of its length leading to a collar at the junction with the ram's head. The solid head is moulded three-dimensionally with curling horns with three circular perforations on each side and incised details of the eyes, nostrils and mouth. Beneath the jaw, the fleece is represented by moulded pellets. There are traces of iron corrosion on the surface. Length: 101.58mm. Diameter: 22.25mm. Weight: 199.6g.
Discussion: Pan-handles terminating with an animal's head occur in two forms: either with the zoomorphic terminal and shaft cast as a single component (such as this example), or with the handle's terminal and shaft cast as separate components and later soldered together. The earlier form, classified as Nuber's Type D, was in use in the Augustan period (31 BC–AD 14) until around AD 50 and the later form continued in use until the end of the 1st century. A pan-handle terminating in a ram's head of similar form to the example from Eynsford is known from Hod Hill, Dorset (Brailsford 1962: 4, no. A132, fig. 5, pl. X), and St Albans, Hertfordshire (Waugh and Goodburn 1972). Although no other examples of this later form with a ram's head terminal have been recorded by the PAS, an example with the handle terminal in the form of a dog's head was recently recorded from Newstead, Nottinghamshire (LVPL-F535A7).
Bill Robson keeps accurate records of his finds, noting the findspot, date found and providing further details about the object when reporting them. He has also recently started looking through his older finds not previously recorded by the PAS in order to identify the most important items for recording. He found the current find on the spoil heap from the building of the M25 during the late 1970s. Close by he found other Roman finds including a knife handle in the form of a dog, and figurines of Mercury and a panther. It is likely that these finds might indicate the site of a temple or shrine that was destroyed during the building works.
Disposition: Returned to finder.

K SUMNALL & S WORRELL

90. Atherton, Greater Manchester: copper-alloy brooch (PAS: LVPL-1B0623)

Date: Roman (c. AD 43–c. 100).
Discovery: Found by Thomas Jackson while metal-detecting in 2007, and recorded by Frances McIntosh (Cheshire, Greater Manchester & Merseyside FLO).
Description: An incomplete copper-alloy bow brooch of Kraftig-profilierte Type. The wide head narrows to a neck before widening into its side wings. The head does not cover the incomplete spring which has 6-coils and is held in place by a short forward hook; the pin is missing. The upper bow is arched and has a pronounced knop at its centre which is made up of two mouldings, the lower one being prominent. The lower bow is narrow and tapers to a foot-knob which extends below the complete catch-plate. Dimensions: 40 x 17mm. Weight: 7.6g.
Discussion: Kraftig-profilierte Type brooches, also known as the Pannonian Type, originated from Pannonia, an area on the Danube-Rhine frontier, and it is very likely that they were associated with troops raised or stationed in that province. Small numbers of brooches of this Type were introduced to Britain at the Conquest, probably with the 9th Legion who were drafted from Pannonia, and they remained in use throughout the 1st century. The distribution of this type of brooch is largely confined to the south-east of England and so it is particularly interesting that this example was found in the north-west.
Disposition: Donated for use in the FLO's handling collection.

F MCINTOSH

91. St Buryan, Cornwall: gold jewellery fragment (PAS: CORN-929E07; Treasure: 2007 T140)

Date: Roman (c. AD 43–c. 200).
Discovery: Found by David Edwards while metal-detecting in March 2007, and reported to Anna Tyacke (Cornwall FLO).
Description: A broken and distorted component of Roman gold jewellery, probably a necklace link. The fragment comprises a parallel-sided band, made from thin gold sheet, fractured at one end and with a double-eyed fastening loop at the complete end. The band has a front (outer) face and a back (inner) face. The latter displays working marks but no finishing marks and was evidently not intended to be seen. The front face is ornamented with a restrained and finely applied decoration; ribbed and channelled mouldings divide the band into two equal panels each occupied by a plain zone balanced by a line of five embossed ring-and-dot mouldings. Soldered to the complete end is a lyre-shaped twin loop of filigree wire. Width: 12mm. Predicted original length: 41mm approx. Weight: 3g.

Discussion: The function of this object, while almost certainly part of a piece of jewellery, cannot be unequivocally identified. However, assuming a symmetrical design, it seems probable that the band was broken just short of its end which would have terminated with a second soldered lyre-shaped fastening loop (or possibly a double hook). As such it can be conceived as one link from a necklace or bracelet.

Disposition: Acquired by Royal Cornwall Museum.

R JACKSON

---

92. Snape with Thorpe, North Yorkshire: gold jewellery component (PAS: YORYM-CBED34; Treasure: 2007 T443)

Date: Roman (c. AD 43–c. 200).
Discovery: Found by Jim Coon while metal-detecting in August 2007, and reported to Beth Echtenacher (North & East Yorkshire FLA).
Description: A small, hollow, sub-rectangular sheet-gold object with two undecorated planar faces. A ribbed moulding (four ribs defined by three channels) runs around one long and two short sides and a slender tubular perforation, formed by the addition of a strip of gold sheet, occupies the fourth side. The object, which resembles a bulla-type pendant, is identifiable as a component of Roman jewellery, probably a bead-like pendant from a composite ear-ring or necklace. Dimensions: 10.9 x 8.5 x 3.7mm. Weight: 1.3g.
Disposition: Acquired by the British Museum.

R JACKSON

---

93. Ely, Cambridgeshire: silver finger-ring (PAS: CAMHER-9B2FA5; Treasure: 2007 T535)

Date: Roman (c. AD 43– c. 200).
Discovery: Found by Dinah Northfield while metal-detecting in August 2007, and reported to Philippa Walton (Cambridgeshire FLO).
Description: A penannular snake-headed finger-ring, with opposed flattened snake-head terminals and a solid, circular-sectioned hoop. The ring is badly crushed, which may have been done deliberately. The ring is classified as Johns (1996) Type Bi/Bii. Length: 25mm. Weight: 7g.
Disposition: Acquired by Ely Museum.

R HOBBS

---

94. Pocklington, East Yorkshire: copper-alloy tripod mount (PAS: YORYM-EC06D2)

Date: Roman (c. AD 43 –c. 200).
Discovery: Found by Bernard Ross while metal-detecting in 2007, and recorded with Beth Echtenacher (North & East Yorkshire FLA).
Description: A tripod mount depicting the bust of a young male figure, portraying Bacchus or a priest of Bacchus. The bust is naked and no musculature is defined on the chest. The facial features are worn and the probable wreath on the wavy, mid-length hair meets above the forehead in a top-knot which may have been intended to represent a flower. The bust is positioned above an incomplete, hollow and rectangular base which has three transverse mouldings. An integral, copper-alloy square-sectioned shank extends horizontally from the centre of the figure's back then turns upwards at right angles to end in a square terminal. 77.94 x 32.36 x 38mm. Weight: 130g.
Discussion: This is the eighth tripod mount to have been found in Britain. Other mounts also representing Bacchus were found at Birrens, Dumfries and Galloway (Robertson 1975: 120, no. 96, fig. 35), Lincoln (Thompson 1971: 101–102, pl. xxv), Harlow, Essex (Bartlett 1985), and London (Henig 1976), and two examples recorded by the PAS were found at Greetwell, Lincolnshire (LIN-1632D1), and Pickhill with Roxby, North Yorkshire (LVPL-CB8BO4). It is likely that tripods were used as stands for vessels used for the mixing of wine and therefore the choice of figures of Bacchus (the god of wine) or of followers of Bacchus as tripod stands was particularly appropriate.
Disposition: Returned to finder.

B ECHTERNACHER & S WORRELL

---

95. Trowbridge area, Wiltshire: copper-alloy double-headed knife terminal (PAS: WILT-251A24)

Date: Roman (c. AD 43–c. 200).
Discovery: Found by Steve Booth while metal-detecting in 2007, and recorded by Katie Hinds (Wiltshire FLO).
Description: Copper-alloy terminal from a toilet knife in the form of a double-headed bust with a circular-sectioned iron projection visible on the underside of the neck (Worrell 2008: 364–365, no. 14, fig. 18). The two faces are separated by a deep horizontal groove dividing the two tops of heads. The facial features are moulded: the mouths are depicted by two short horizontal grooves, above which is a punched dot below a prominent, triangular nose. The eyes are pointed ovals with dots at the centre representing the pupils and have curved eyebrows. The hair is combed forward and is depicted using deep, vertical grooves. Both faces are clean-shaven with pointed chins, expanding to the ears then curving over the top of the head. The base of the terminal is circular and

there is a trace of a circular-sectioned iron projection extending from its centre. The nose-to-chin area is a slightly upstanding triangular shape. The head sits on a circular terminal 13–14mm in diameter, with the iron projection extending from the middle of the underside; the 'shoulder area' is 5mm high. The silvery/grey sheen of the patina suggests a high tin content. Dimensions: 25.6 x 15.2 x 17.4mm. Weight: 22.85g.

Discussion: Two similar terminals have been discovered and recorded by the PAS, from Hartest (SF-6944) and Bures St Mary (SF-D0D636), both in Suffolk. Ralph Jackson (British Museum; *personal communication*) compares terminals of this type to an example with an integral copper-alloy handle from Richborough (Bushe Fox 1949: Pl. XLV). This example is one of a series of distinctive knives published by Kaufmann-Heinimann (1998: 32–35, figs. 9–11). Where iron blades survive they are of Manning's (1985) Type 1. The knife series dates to the 1st or 2nd century, so it seems likely this knife is of a similar date.

Disposition: Returned to finder.

K HINDS

---

96. Carlisle, Cumbria: silver hair-pin fragment (PAS: NCL-0061D8; Treasure: 2007 T258)

Date: Roman (c. AD 50–c. 150).

Discovery: Found by Derek Jones while metal-detecting in April 2007, and reported to Rob Collins (North East FLO).

Description: A hair-pin fragment in form of a human hand. The tips of the fingers are broken, leaving only the lower part of the fingers, defined by a series of rather crude incised grooves. The curved thumb is intact, as is the flat disc which separated the pin-head from the shaft. Only a small part of the iron shaft survives. Dimensions: 22.1 x 12mm. Weight: 7.6g.

Discussion: Roman hair-pins with a terminal in the form of a human hand are a well-known type. They belong to Cool's (1990: 157–158) Type 7, which usually have a fruit or egg grasped between the thumb and forefinger. This example seems slightly larger than normal for the type, and is also unusual because most seem to have been discovered in the south of Britain.

Disposition: Acquired by Tullie House Museum & Art Gallery, Carlisle.

R HOBBS

---

97. Scawby, North Lincolnshire: copper-alloy pan-handle (PAS: NLM-B0A171)

Date: Roman (c. AD 65–c.85).

Discovery: Found by John Lockwood while metal-detecting in 2007, and recorded by Lisa Staves (North Lincolnshire FLO).

Description: A terminal fragment from a cast copper-alloy handle from a saucepan (*trulla*). The flat handle tapers towards the break and has a disc-shaped terminal with a central hole for suspending the vessel. There is a moulded cord design bordering both edges of the handle and surrounding the circular perforation although the border is incomplete on the circular terminal. On the inside of the border is a further concentric row of punched dots, which is clearer near the handle end of the terminal but fades away midway around with punched dots in between. Part of the maker's stamp, reading 'CI. PI----', survives on the handle just before the terminal. The broken end also has at least two incomplete rivet holes, suggesting that the vessel may have been repaired. Diameter (external): 47.1mm. Length: 60.7mm. Thickness: 3.4mm. Weight: 39.04g.

Discussion: 'CI. PI' identifies this pan as a product of the workshop of C. Cipius Polybius, a major producer of the Campanian copper-alloy industry and member of a Capuan family of bronze-smiths. Cipius Polybius produced a wide range of vessel forms but is well known for the handled saucepans or skillets which have been found widely in the Western Roman Empire as well as outside its borders. The earliest products date from the Tiberian or Claudian period (AD 14–54) while the main period of production appears to be the Neronian (AD 54–68) and possibly Flavian period (AD 69–96) (McPeake and Moore 1978; Bennett and Young 1981). Products of this workshop are unusual finds outside the northern frontier region, although a hoard of copper-alloy vessels consisting of three pans, two of which were the products of Cipius Polybius, and two strainer-bowls was recently found in Kingston Deverill, Wiltshire, and recorded by the PAS (WILT-92B052). The PAS has recorded a total of 18 copper-alloy pans or skillets, most of which are represented by handle fragments. On the seven handles where the makers' stamps survive, five are products of C. CIPI. POLYBIVS.

Disposition: Returned to finder.

L STAVES & S WORRELL

98. Wherwell, Hampshire: copper-alloy figurine in the form of a crocodile (PAS: HAMP-453C46)

Date: Roman (c. AD 43–c. 200).
Discovery: Found by Martin Hams while metal-detecting in about 2000, identified by Martin Henig and recorded by Rob Webley (Hampshire FLO) in 2007.
Description: A cast copper-alloy Roman zoomorphic figurine in the form of a crocodile (Worrell 2007: 338–339, no. 36, fig. 37). The animal is well modelled with its neck, head and raised and curving tail rising from a flat underbelly. The legs are bent back on themselves and each foot terminates in three toes. The raised snout tapers, and the open jaws reveal its teeth. The eyes are raised mouldings coated with traces of a while metal (John Philpotts, *personal communication*). The upper surface is decorated with punched and engraved linear decoration to render the animal's leathery skin. Down the length of its back are two longitudinal grooves crossed by numerous transverse lines to create three rows of irregular squares and rectangles. The flanks and legs have been decorated using punched circular stamps. The greyer colour of the underside of the body suggests that the figurine might have been soldered to another surface, although it could also have stood alone. Dimensions: 56.6 x 21.5 x 27.7mm. Weight: 25.5g.
Discussion: This figurine is presumably part of an imported Nilotic group and suggests a local interest in the Cult of Isis. It lacks parallels in Britain and the few Continental examples are unprovenanced. Romans are known to have worshipped the Egyptian crocodile god Sobek. Elsewhere, Roman representations of a crocodile with its tail raised over its back are depicted on the Augustan coins struck at Nîmes and in statue form at Hadrian's villa at Tivoli.
Disposition: Returned to finder.

R WEBLEY

99. York area: silver finger-ring with inscribed motif (PAS: SWYOR-6B2484; Treasure: 2007 T438)

Date: Roman (c. AD 43–c. 300).
Discovery: Found while metal-detecting in August 2007, and reported to Amy Cooper (South & West Yorkshire FLO).
Description: A small finger-ring, complete and undamaged, with slender ovoid hoop, convex shoulders and broad, flat oval bezel simply incised with a stylised palm-branch motif flanked at the base by a pair of crosses. Dimensions (external): 20.5 x 16.9mm. Bezel: 12.5 x 9.2mm. Weight: 4.3g.
Discussion: An example of a standard Roman ring type made variously in gold, silver or copper-alloy. The palm-branch motif was a ubiquitous symbol of victory believed to offer protection against malign forces and to help a deceased wearer reach the afterlife. For comparative examples see *TAR* 2005/6, nos. 107, 108 & 114.

Disposition: Acquired by the British Museum.

R JACKSON

100. Llanharry, Rhondda Cynon Taff: copper-alloy wax spatula handle (PAS: NMGW-89FC33)

Date: Roman (c. AD 43– c. 300).
Discovery: Found by Alan Jenkins while metal-detecting in 2007, and recorded by Mark Lodwick (Finds Co-ordinator, Wales).
Description: A near complete wax spatula handle depicting Minerva, the Roman goddess of crafts, poetry and wisdom. Although the detail is slightly eroded, the form of the handle differs from other recorded examples, with Minerva shown wearing a three-dimensional helmet with concave sides and a wide central groove at the rear. The tops of the garments are discernible below the neck and the figure thins near the base to produce an ergonomic handle. The missing iron blade was secured within a damaged V-shaped opening at the base of the handle. Dimensions: 67.2 x 18.6 (across the shoulders) x 15.4mm. Weight: 43.4g.
Discussion: Wax spatulas were used for smoothing wax writing tablets and applying the wax. This handle is an example of Feugère (1995: 321–338) Type A5 and its discovery brings the total number of known A5 spatula handles from Britain to 25, 16 of which have been recorded by the PAS. The wax spatula handle from Llanharry represents the most westerly of the recorded examples and is the first recorded from Wales. In addition to this example, others are known from Helmsley, North Yorkshire (YORYMM404), Scawby, North Lincolnshire (NLM-DB0143), Bourne, Lincolnshire (LIN-F37090), Reepham, Lincolnshire (LIN-69A207), Britwell Salome, Oxfordshire (BH-6D69E7), Stonham Earl, Suffolk (SF8530), Wenhaston with Mells Hamlet, Suffolk (SF-9AAE10), Middleton, Essex (SF-3292E6), Popham, Hampshire (HAMP2607), Micheldever, Hampshire (HAMP3507), Hook, Hampshire (HAMP-4EB6C5), Alfriston, East Sussex (SUSS-AF5905), Kington, Wiltshire (NMGW-DED9D2), Heytesbury, Wiltshire (WILT-9F0F01), and Hucclecote, Gloucestershire (BUC-270D12). The rural context of these findspots comprises significant evidence for literacy, if these artefacts were being used for their primary function.
Disposition: Returned to finder.

M LODWICK & S WORRELL

101. Newton Kyme cum Toulson, North Yorkshire: copper-alloy figurine of Cautopates (PAS: SWYOR-9FCBB3)

Date: Roman (c. AD 43–c. 410).

Discovery: Found by Chris Hall while metal-detecting in 2007, and reported to Amy Cooper (South & West Yorkshire FLO).

Description: A copper-alloy figurine depicting Cautopates, one of Mithras's two attendants, who symbolises darkness (Worrell 2008: 352–353, no. 1 fig. 5). Cautopates is standing facing forwards with his head turned slightly to the right. His legs are crossed at the calves, his right hand holds his torch pointing downwards, and his left hand is placed on the left hip. He wears trousers and a short-sleeved tunic, both of which have grooved, curved lines representing the folds of the cloth, a cloak ornamented with V-shaped motifs and grooved, and a Phrygian cap; he has mid-length tousled hair. There is no evidence for attachment to a larger object, but the figurine is not free-standing and despite the lack of evidence for an attachment it must have been fixed to a base. The back of the figurine is almost flat but the decoration on the cloak indicates that it was made to be seen. Dimensions: 81.5 x 34 x 11mm. Weight: 91g.

Discussion: The Cult of Mithras was popular with soldiers who were stationed in Britain, as demonstrated by the concentration of *mithraea* (places of worship for the followers of Mithraism) on Hadrian's Wall, although it excluded women. Mithras and his companions are usually depicted in Persian dress, normally consisting of trousers and Phrygian caps. The companions, Cautes and Cautopates, represent the opposing attributes of light and dark, or life and death, symbolised by the position of the torch they hold. Cautes holds his torch up, allowing it to burn, while Cautopates holds his down, extinguishing it. Mithraic temples had to be near water for purification purposes (Henig 1984), and it is interesting that this figurine was found near both a Roman fort and a river. Despite the popularity of Mithraism, very few metallic votive items are known and it has not been possible to find a parallel for this figurine. The Cult of Mithras was popular until the advent of Roman Christianity under Constantine I (r. AD 306–337) although it is unlikely that Mithras ceased being worshipped by all.

Deposition: Returned to finder.

A COOPER

102. North Yorkshire area: silver *ligula* (PAS: YORYM-F9FB75; Treasure: 2007 T187)

Date: Roman (c. AD 43–c. 410).

Discovery: Found while metal-detecting before April 2007, and reported to Simon Holmes (North & East Yorkshire FLO).

Description: A silver *ligula* of normal Roman form, with a small angled disc, a quite rudimentarily finished multiple disc-and-baluster moulding and a slender, tapered, circular-sectioned stem, its pointed tip broken. Length: 93.7mm. Weight: 4.3g.

Discussion: This type of object, most commonly found in copper alloy, was a multi-purpose implement principally with toilet and cosmetic applications, which included the removal of wax from the outer ear and the extraction of unguents from slender containers.

Disposition: Disclaimed; returned to finder.

R JACKSON

103. Middleton, Warwickshire: copper-alloy bust (PAS: WMID-01FA06)

Date: Roman (c. AD 43–c. 410).

Discovery: Found by Andy Robinson while metal-detecting in December 2007, and recorded with Duncan Slarke (Staffordshire & West Midlands FLO).

Description: A cast copper-alloy mount in the form of a draped bust, presumably female. The mount consists of the head, neck and upper torso at the front and on the reverse the bust terminates below the head at about the neck and is then recessed; the torso is hollow. Details of the hairstyle are unclear due to wear, but the hair appears to be waved and loose with a narrow band of uncertain function around the head. There is no surviving detail on the back of the head. The facial features are particularly robust and rounded, and the head joins the broad neck at an angle of around 45°. The bust has a well-developed green patina, but the surface has suffered some chipping around the edges of the torso, around the chin and at the top of the back of the head. Dimensions: 54 x 39 x 27.7mm. Weight: 73.82g.

Discussion: The lack of iron on this bust suggests that it was soldered onto a vessel or box. It is broadly similar in form and style to two female busts thought to be of local workmanship from Cockfield, Suffolk, and Adderbury, north Oxfordshire (Brown 1973: 264–265). Both have well-defined, presumably provincial hairstyles suggestive of Romano-British workmanship rather than imports. It is possible that this bust is Bacchic in style and could represent a maenad, a female devotee of the god Bacchus. The provincial style of the facial features, particularly the triangular nose, is shared by that on the copper-alloy mount from the Bedford area, Bedfordshire (BH-22D0A3), and the bound captive figurine from Andover, Hampshire (HAMP-378231, below).

Disposition: Returned to finder.

D SLARKE & S WORRELL

104. St Minver, Cornwall: copper-alloy brooch (PAS: CORN-24EB51)

Date: Roman (c. AD 50–c. 75).

Discovery: Found by Yvonne Parker while metal-detecting in July 2007, and recorded by Anna Tyacke (Cornwall FLO).

Description: An incomplete copper-alloy example of the Applied Hook Type of T-shaped brooch, now in two parts. The pin is hinged and the axis bar was seated in the pierced ends of the wings in the Polden Hill manner. Each side of the pin is grooved to form a fake spring with the external 'chord' held by a rearward hook, below the upper mouldings at the head which is now broken. The cord is in fact a wire tucked between the wing and fake spring. The elaborate 'hook' is a metal plate with six bosses, with the third and six bosses riveted to the head and body of the bow. The bow tapers to a point and the catch-plate is intact. Dimensions: 54 x 39mm. Weight: 20.96g.

Discussion: The distribution of brooches of this type is concentrated in the south-west with a small number of outliers elsewhere. The consistent feature of these brooches is the applied plate simulating a hook, rather than the manner in which the pin was fixed or the attempt to give the appearance of a spring, as in this case (Mackreth 1991: 232). Examples of brooches from Camerton, Somerset, in particular, demonstrate the elaboration and inventiveness of the decoration on the plate of brooches of this type (Wedlake 1958: 225, fig. 51).

Disposition: Loaned to Royal Institution of Cornwall (Loan 311).

A TYACKE & S WORRELL

105. Gisburn, Lancashire: copper-alloy brooch (LANCUM-411DE2)

Date: Roman (c. AD 50–c. 175).

Discovery: Found by Steve and Matthew Jones while metal-detecting in 2007, and recorded by Dot Boughton (Lancashire & Cumbria FLO).

Description: An incomplete copper-alloy dragonesque brooch missing one terminal and its pin. The head has a marked eye and backward sloping ear with the nose ending in a scroll. The body has elegant boss-and-trumpet decoration moulded in relief and also has a cell at each end which is likely to have originally held enamel, although no traces now survive. On the surviving terminal there is a stamped ring-and-dot motif representing the creature's eye and a small, single dot for the nostril. No enamel now survives in the facial features. The back is flat and there are many parallel scratch marks which possibly derive from the movement of the pin. Dimensions: 41.56 x 23 x 6.65mm. Weight: 10.89g.

Discussion: This brooch can be identified as a decorated version of the 'boss style' dragonesque brooch with characteristic relief trumpets, but also represents a hybrid form since the relief decoration was also intended to be augmented with enamelling. Fraser Hunter's (National Museum, Edinburgh) forthcoming study of dragonesque brooches and beaded torcs discusses the survival and adaptation of Celtic art styles in Roman Britain. His synthesis of the dragonesque brooch corpus with 270 examples includes the 73 examples recorded by the PAS. The finders were happy to loan the brooch for a surface XRF (x-ray fluorescence) analysis at the Institute of Archaeology, University College London, in order to assess the metallic composition of the artefact and to compare with other analysed brooches.

Disposition: Returned to finder.

D BOUGHTON AND S WORRELL

106. Hale, Cheshire: silver plate brooch (PAS: LVPL-035186; Treasure: 2007 T686)

Date: Roman (c. AD 50–c.300).

Discovery: Found by Thomas McCormick while metal-detecting in 2006, and reported to Frances McIntosh (North West FLO) in 2007.

Description: A silver zoomorphic plate brooch in the form of a hound catching a hare, shown in profile (Worrell 2008: 354–355, no. 4, fig. 8). The slightly stylised hound is well-observed; its long ears point upwards, the eyes are large, the body slender, the haunches prominent and its long tail curves forwards and touches the hound's back. The hound is shown biting the crouched hare's back and holds its body between its front legs, and also by its right side front and back legs. The brooch has a hinged pin secured between two lugs. Its transverse rectangular catch-plate is damaged and the pin rest is missing. The surface of the hare's body is badly corroded and that of the hound appears to have been cleaned giving an impression of two metals, copper and silver. Analysis has shown that originally the whole piece would have been silver. Dimensions: 37.9 x 24.1mm. Weight: 15g.

Discussion: Brooches depicting a hound and hare hunting scene are rare, though both animals are often depicted separately on plate brooches. A similar brooch is known from Szombathely, Hungary, also in silver and another in copper-alloy from Brigetio, Hungary (Sellye 1939: 81, nos. 6, 8, pl. 8). In Britain, a copper-alloy brooch from Piercebridge, County Durham, has a double design of a stylised hound catching a hare, but set on either side of a central bar (Butcher 2007: 11–201, no. 33, fig. D11.75). This is very closely paralleled by a further brooch from Brigetio and also an unprovenanced parallel (Murawski 2003: ref. R07-0525). Such depictions are, however, relatively common in other media, for example toilet knife handles (see 141, below).

Disposition: Acquired by the National Museums Liverpool.

R HOBBS & S WORRELL

107. Little Kimble, Buckinghamshire: copper-alloy brooch (PAS: BUC-615653)

Date: Roman (c. AD 75–c. 150).
Discovery: Found by Matthew Wildman during a metal-detecting rally in 2007, and recorded by Ros Tyrrell (Buckinghamshire FLO).
Description: A copper-alloy enamelled Headstud brooch. It has a cast-on head loop, the missing pin was hinged and its bow has a curved front surface which tapers slightly to the forward-facing, conical foot-knob. The wings are slightly D-shaped in section and concave at the back. Each wing has a longitudinal groove at its end and a circular recess perforated by an oval hole through which a setting would have been secured, which in both cases is now missing. At the top of the bow there is a prominent lozenge-shaped moulding enclosing a circular recess which would have held a setting, now missing. Below this the bow has a linear groove down each side which borders a panel of four lozenges containing traces of pale blue enamel, with infilling triangles in red enamel. At either side of the bow, beginning at the head-stud and extending down the enamelled zone, are seven square-ended projections forming a serrated edge. The foot-knob has two concentric circles of enamel, the colour of which is now unknown. Dimensions: 34.85 x 29.9 x 3.2mm.
Discussion: There is a wide variety of sub-types of Headstud brooches (Painter and Sax 1970). Most brooches of this type have a raised stud near the top of the bow, although crests, occasionally shaped like a dog, are known. Examples may be sprung or hinged, with a fixed head-loop or a loose wire loop, with studs riveted at the wings and foot, and decoration mostly in the form of a wide variety of enamel ornament. Occasionally, as in this case, the bow of a Headstud brooch has a toothed side in a similar manner to that seen on hinged T-shaped brooches, often known as the Sawfish Type, although the head-stud, head-loop and foot-knob identify the brooch from Little Kimble as a member of the diverse Headstud family. Similar brooches, but with slight variations, are known from excavations at Derby (Mackreth 1985: 287–289, no. 21, fig. 126), Dragonby (Olivier 1996: 255, no. 101, fig. 11.9) and Richborough (Bayley and Butcher 2004: 164, no. 135).
Disposition: Returned to finder.

R TYRRELL & S WORRELL

108. Seaton with Slingley, County Durham: silver trumpet brooch fragment (PAS: NCL-D28051; Treasure: 2007 T391)

Date: Roman (c. AD 75–c. 200).
Discovery: Found by Dave Scott while metal-detecting in October 2007, and reported to Rob Collins (North East FLO).
Description: Fragment of silver trumpet brooch, the head and part of the bow surviving. There are traces of copper from the spring, which is missing, alongside the lower part of the bow, foot and catch-plate. There is a series of complex mouldings on the bow, which include an acanthus moulding with five petals. There is a series of transverse grooves within circular bands on either side of the acanthus flower; the head is plain. Dimensions: 36 x 13mm. Weight: 18.3g.
Discussion: These types of brooch with acanthus flower are best known from the Backworth Treasure, and are discussed in Hattatt (1982: no. 80). Found with a silver *denarius* of Titus (minted AD 80) – see 480.
Disposition: Acquired by the British Museum.

R HOBBS

109. Inkberrow, Worcestershire: copper-alloy brooch (PAS: WAW-1DBFC0)

Date: Roman (c. AD 75–c. 200).
Discovery: Found by Phil Turner while metal-detecting in 2007, and recorded by Angie Bolton (Warwickshire & Worcestershire FLO.
Description: An unusual and almost complete zoomorphic plate brooch showing the outline of a hippocamp – a mythological creature with a horse's head and forequarters, no hind legs and the tail of a dolphin or seahorse. In the case of this brooch, a fan-shaped element instead of a tail and a moulded scroll projects and curves forwards at the junction of the body and has a cell, presumably for enamel, although no trace now survives. The creature's body has a broad diamond-shaped cell with three moulded ring-and-dot motifs in high relief which are inlaid with green enamel at the centre and surrounded by blue. A small circular cell containing traces of enamel marks the eye. Dimensions: 28.01 x 21.89 x 9.17mm. Weight: 6.3g.
Discussion: Zoomorphic plate brooches were not uncommon in Roman Britain, but examples depicting hippocamps are poorly represented. Where they are known, representations of the creature in outline form are expected, as on this example, although a brooch from Richborough, Kent (Bayley and Butcher 2004: 124, no. 354, fig. 96), has a hippocamp shown fully in the round. Four other hippocamp brooches have been recorded by the PAS from Bourne, Lincolnshire (LIN-280A34), near Steyning, West Sussex (SUSS-3F75E4), Firle, East Sussex (SUSS-962C96), and Icklingham, Suffolk (SF-12EC61).
Disposition: Returned to finder.

A BOLTON & S WORRELL

110. Highnam, Gloucestershire: copper-alloy brooch (PAS: GLO-5BBB70)

Date: Roman (c. AD 80–c. 120).
Discovery: Found by Kath Hurcombe while metal-detecting in 2007, and recorded by Kurt Adams (Gloucestershire & Avon FLO).
Description: An incomplete Polden Hill brooch with the spring and pin now missing. The wings are semicircular and the ends closed and perforated to secure the spring which was held in place by an axis bar. The external spring chord was probably held by a hook or crest on the head, much of which is truncated on this example. A recessed line runs from the top of the head down the centre of the brooch to the foot, and on either side is stepped. The catch-plate on the reverse is mostly complete with only the tip missing. Dimensions: 47 x 30 x 19mm. Weight: 14.35g.
Discussion: The Polden Hill Type of brooch, named after a particularly fine example from the Polden Hill Hoard, Somerset (Brailsford 1975: 288, fig. 6A), is a form of Colchester-derivative brooch the main development of which seems to have taken place in the West Midlands (Bayley and Butcher 2004: 160). Research by Sally Worrell (Finds Adviser) for a lecture at the Gloucestershire Roman Archaeology Day in April 2008 revealed that of the Roman brooches recorded by the PAS (up to April 2008), the Polden Hill Type was the most common brooch type found in Gloucestershire, and of the 192 brooches recorded in that county, 61 examples (37.2%) were of Polden Hill Type. This is in contrast to Somerset, where of a total of 237 Roman brooches recorded, only 6 (2.5%) are Polden Hill brooches, and Avon, where only 4 out of 54 (7.4%) examples are of Polden Hill Type.
Disposition: Returned to finder.

K ADAMS & S WORRELL

111. Sheepy, Leicestershire: gold necklace fragment (PAS: WMID-3487F6; Treasure: 2007 T41)

Date: Roman (c. AD 100–c. 200).
Discovery: Found by Wayne Burton while metal-detecting in October 2006, and reported to Caroline Johnson (Staffordshire & West-Midlands FLO) in 2007.
Description: Fragment of Roman gold necklace, consisting of three sections of loop-in-loop filigree wire. One section of wire is plain, while the central section is threaded with a blue glass polyhedral faceted bead. The final wire, probably the clasp, has an applied four-spoke wheel in plain and beaded wire, with a central bead. Length: 36.5mm. Diameter (wheel): 9.4mm. Weight: 1.5g.
Discussion: The wheel element of this fragment is closely paralleled with a wheel-clasp in the Snettisham jeweller's hoard (Johns 1997: no. 318).
Disposition: Leicestershire County Council Heritage Services hopes to acquire.

R HOBBS

112. Capel St Mary, Suffolk: copper-alloy bust (PAS: ESS-B39770)

Date: Roman (c. AD 100–c. 200).
Discovery: Found by Stuart Henderson while metal-detecting in July 2007, identified by Sally Worrell and recorded by Laura McLean (Essex FLO).
Description: A bust of a young male identified as Antinous (Worrell 2008: 363–364, no. 13, fig. 17). The face is round, the neck broad, the musculature poorly defined on the naked chest and the full hair is arranged in waves which cluster at the ears and down the back of the head. The eyes stare forward, although it is impossible to see the pupils owing to iron corrosion within their settings. The brows are finely arched, the nose straight, the lips are slightly parted and the chin prominent. Level with the centre of the shoulder blades there is a large cavity filled with corroded iron which holds the remains of a square, iron rivet that would have secured the mount to a box or piece of furniture. Dimensions: 77.2 x 50.8 x 30.39mm (across chest). Weight: 290g.
Discussion: This bust represents only the second known depiction of Antinous, Hadrian's favourite, from Britain. It is inferior in quality, but has much in common in physiognomy and detail, with the bust from Littlecote, Wiltshire (Walters and Henig 1988: 407–410), and it is particularly close in style to an unprovenanced tripod mount now in Lyons Museum (Zadoks-Josephus Jitta, Peters and van Es 1973: 24–27 nos. 1–12).
Disposition: Donated to Colchester and Ipswich Museums Service.

S WORRELL & L MCLEAN

113. Brompton, North Yorkshire: copper-alloy military diploma (PAS: YORYM-67D811)

Date: Roman (17 July AD 118).
Discovery: Found by Stuart Hodgson while metal-detecting in 2007, transcribed by Roger Tomlin (Oxford University), translated by John Pearce (King's College, London) and recorded by Liz Andrews-Wilson (North & East Yorkshire FLO).
Description: Five fragments (two joining) from the first leaf or tabella of a bronze military diploma. There is half of one binding hole in the top edge of fragment 2 (Tomlin 2008: 381–384 no. 18, figs. 17–18).
Fragment 1: Dimensions: 79.5 x 83.1 x 1.9mm. Weight: 41.3g.
Fragment 2: Dimensions: 46.6 x 48.1 x 1.7mm. Weight: 137g.
Fragment 3: Dimensions: 25.1 x 18 x 1.3mm. Weight: 22g.
Fragment 4: Dimensions: 26.4 x 15.5 x 1.7mm. Weight: 18g.
Fragment 5: Dimensions: 17.2 x 8.2 x 1.4mm. Weight: 69g.

Summary translation: 'The emperor Caesar Trajan Hadrian Augustus, son of Divine Trajan Parthicus, grandson of Nerva, Pontifex Maximus, with tribunician power for the sixth time, consul for the third time and pro-consul. For the cavalrymen and infantrymen who served in the 13 alae [cavalry units from Pannonia, Spain, Gaul and Thrace] and the 37 cohorts [from Germany, Iberia, Thrace, Africa, Gaul, Syria, Dalmatia] which are in Britain under the command of Aulus Platorius Nepos, who have spent 25 years' service are dismissed with an honourable discharge by Pompeius Falco. To those whose names are written beneath, to themselves and their children and their descendants he gave citizenship and right of legal marriage [conubium] with the wives they already had when the citizenship was given to them, or if they are unmarried he gave the right of conubium to those women married afterwards, providing it is one husband to one wife. This is done on 16th Kalends of August when Titus Julius Capito and Lucius Vitrasius Flamininus were consuls. Then [name of soldier] of 5th cohort of Raeti [Bavaria] which is commanded by Sextus Cornelius Dexter of Saldae in Mauretania ..... This document is copied and confirmed from the bronze tablet which is fixed in Rome on the wall behind the Temple of the Divine Augustus by the statue of Minerva.'

Discussion: Roman military diplomas granted Roman citizenship and the right of legal marriage to the non-citizen auxiliary soldiers upon retirement after 25 years of military service in the auxiliary forces. Enough remains of the date and the sequence of military units to show that this diploma belonged to the same issue as the Brigetio diploma now in the British Museum (JRS 1930: 20 16–22). It was therefore dated 17 July 118, and was issued to an infantry soldier of Cohors V Raetorum whose name is lost. Enough remains of the name of his commanding officer to identify him as Sextus Cornelius Dexter of Saldae in Mauretania, at the beginning of an equestrian career which culminated in the procuratorships of Asia and of Belgica and the two Germanies and who is known from other inscriptions (Tomlin 2008: 383).

Disposition: Acquired by Yorkshire Museums Trust.

R TOMLIN, J PEARCE & L ANDREWS-WILSON

---

114. Aston Clinton, Buckinghamshire: copper-alloy fastener (PAS: BUC-6D3351)

Date: Roman (c. AD 100–c. 200).
Discovery: Found by Vince Chandler while metal-detecting in 2007, and recorded by Ros Tyrrell (Buckinghamshire FLO).
Description: A copper-alloy button-and-loop fastener of Wild's (1970: 138–140) Class III. The fastener has a petal-shaped head with a domed boss at its centre and rounded moulding at the apex. The back of the head is flat and has an integral, circular-sectioned shank extending from it which is bent at 90° before forming

a triangular loop with a circular perforation at the centre. Length: 41mm. Weight: not recorded.
Discussion: Although the function of button-and-loop fasteners remains obscure, they are likely to have served as multi-purpose fasteners for clothing and harness. Fasteners of Wild's Class III are the most numerous type recorded both in Wild's study as well as by the PAS. Since 1997, the PAS has recorded 67 Class III fasteners which have a widespread distribution, but with a concentration in Yorkshire and the East Midlands. Only one other button-and-loop fastener has been reported by the PAS from Buckinghamshire – a Wild Class VIc Type from Wendover (BUC-2E01A2), which has a rectangular head decorated with a combination of two lozenges in blue enamel with six triangles in red enamel.
Disposition: Returned to finder.

R TYRRELL & S WORRELL

---

115. South Cave, East Yorkshire: copper-alloy button-and-loop fastener (PAS: YORYM-AC7061)

Date: Roman (c. AD 100–c. 200).
Discovery: Found by Roy Doughty while metal-detecting in 2007, and recorded by Liz Andrews-Wilson (North & East Yorkshire FLO).
Description: An unusually formed and highly elaborate copper-alloy double-headed button-and-loop fastener (Worrell 2008: 354, no. 3, fig. 3). There is a circular-sectioned shaft that extends from the back of the larger square head, which is bent at right angles after which it connects to the other slightly smaller square head which has a rectangular strap-bar beneath. Both heads are similarly decorated with a linear border around the edge enclosing a square with concave sides with two concentric circles within it. The central circle contains red enamel, the outer circle pale blue enamel and the enclosing field contains enamel of an unidentifiable colour. Dimensions: 46 x 17.65–18mm. Weight: 22.7g.
Discussion: This fastener is of a type not classified in Wild's (1970) corpus, although both heads resemble the button-and-loop fasteners with enamelled rectangular heads of Wild's Class VIa. Including this example, a total of five double-headed fasteners have been recorded by the PAS from Dunnington, North Yorkshire (YORYM-024128), Ravensworth, East Yorkshire (NCL-70FEC6), Piercebridge, County Durham (NCL-625592), and Waitby, Cumbria (NCL-DFC861). The published corpus is of a similar size with examples from Lowbury Hill, Berkshire, Traprain Law, East Lothian, Stanwick and Reighton, North Yorkshire, Abergavenny, Monmouthshire, and Richborough, Kent. Although an exact parallel for the South Cave fastener is not known, the double-headed fastener from Abergavenny, with each of the petal-and-boss-shaped heads decorated identically, is the closest (Savory 1993: 211–214). Liz Andrews-Wilson (North & East Yorkshire FLO) is

hoping to conduct more research on the button-and-loop fasteners that are being found in East Yorkshire as a number of those she has recorded so far are very unusual.

Disposition: Returned to finder.

L ANDREWS-WILSON & S WORRELL

---

116. Greywell, Hampshire: copper-alloy brooches and coins (PAS: SUR-DDF2B8, SUR-DF6C76, SUR-E1F317)

Date: Roman (c. AD 100–c. 200).

Discovery: Found by Chris Lacey and Mark Stonard while metal-detecting in 2007, and recorded by David Williams (Surrey FLO).

Description: 31 Late Iron Age and Roman brooches have been found at this site including three zoomorphic plate brooches representing a chicken (SUR-DF6C76), a horse (SUR-DDF2B8), a fish (SUR-36BA57), and a skeuomorphic plate brooch depicting an axe (SUR-E1F317).

Discussion: Votive gifts of jewellery and other items of personal adornment were offered at Roman temples, other less formal religious sites, household shrines and places located at natural features such as rivers, lakes and wells. The many Roman coins from Greywell are presently being sorted and studied by David Williams, Sam Moorhead (Finds Adviser) and Philippa Walton (PhD student). Taken with the brooches and other material, the group appears to represent a votive deposit centred on a valley bottom spring.

Disposition: Returned to finder.

D WILLIAMS

---

117. Gedding, Suffolk: copper-alloy zoomorphic plate brooch (PAS: SF-404EC6)

Date: Roman (c. AD 100–c. 250).

Discovery: Found by Bill Wyman while metal-detecting in 2007, and identified and recorded by Jude Plouviez (Suffolk County Council Archaeological Service).

Description: Copper-alloy flat enamelled zoomorphic brooch depicting a lion. It is missing its pin, has a damaged catch-plate and legs, and has areas of corrosion. The animal has a rounded head with an open mouth and excised areas, one of which probably leads into an eye shape. It is not clear whether there was any enamel on the head. The body is separated from the head by a straight line from which a line projects (obscured by corrosion) into the first of two enamelled cells, in which no enamel survives. The second cell contains traces of blue enamel and is partially divided by a line defining a near-circular area, perhaps representing upper limb musculature. A narrow, curving tail broadens into a tri-lobed end. Both legs are damaged, the hind one is at a definite angle, the front one is possibly also angled which might indicate a leaping pose. Dimensions: 36.5 x 17 x 1.7mm. Weight: 4.66g.

Discussion: The nearest comparable published example is by Hattatt (2000: no. 1639) which is definitely a lion with a projecting mane and the complete foreleg. However, Hattatt also refers to a brooch depicting a lion in Hull's unpublished corpus (no. 4349), as having a different head and no upstanding mane, which sounds similar to the present example. Another fragment, with a similar head (but with a closed mouth) and no mane but a different pattern of enamelled cells, is recorded from Charsfield, Suffolk (CHA 011), from a probable shrine or temple site. The British zoomorphic brooches are quite often associated with religious sites but also occur elsewhere, and can perhaps be compared to Medieval pilgrim badges.

Disposition: Returned to finder.

J PLOUVIEZ & F MINTER

---

118. Chesterton, Cambridgeshire: gold filigree necklace component (PAS: CAMHER-955025; Treasure: 2007 T411)

Date: Roman (c. AD 100–c. 300).

Discovery: Found by Andrew Mclay while metal-detecting in August 2007, and reported to Philippa Walton (Cambrigeshire FLO).

Description: Filigree necklace component. The wire has been looped to form an openwork design with a central lozenge and four corner ovals, with a loop at each end. A small fragment of the next link is preserved in one of these. The wire has been notched so as to appear beaded; much of the surface has been worn smooth. Dimensions: 24 x 8mm.

Discussion: There are exact parallels in Biroli Stefanelli (1992: nos. 240–241); no. 240 is from Syria.

Disposition: Peterborough Museum & Art Gallery hopes to acquire.

R HOBBS

---

119. Roughton, Lincolnshire: silver finger-ring fragment (PAS: NLM-A74468; Treasure: 2007 T611)

Date: Roman (c. AD 100–c. 300).

Discovery: Found by Graham Carpenter while metal-detecting in August 2006, and reported to Adam Daubney (Lincolnshire FLO) in 2007.

Description: A finger-ring fragment consisting of both shoulders and the bezel, but the whole of the bottom of the hoop is missing. The ring has an ovular swelling profile, a flattened bezel and is set with a dark stone intaglio, probably nicolo, with a very worn motif, possibly a seated figure facing left. The shoulders are decorated with lightly incised lines. Diameter (surviving): 22mm.

Disposition: Disclaimed; returned to finder.

R HOBBS

120. Hockliffe, Bedfordshire: silver 'TOT' finger-ring fragment (PAS: BH-C3A8E7; Treasure: 2007 T357)

Date: Roman (c. AD 100–c. 300).
Discovery: Found by Greg Dyer while metal-detecting in September 2007, and reported to Julian Watters (Hertfordshire & Bedfordshire FLO).
Description: A fragment of finger-ring of Keeled Type, Henig (1978) Type VIII. Only one shoulder, part of the hoop and the bezel survive. The shoulder is decorated with incised lines which run out to the edge, and the bezel consists of an octagonal moulding which is inscribed 'DEO TOTA'. The shoulder is inscribed 'FELIX'. Length: 19.5mm. Weight: 2.98g.
Discussion: The legend on the bezel refers to the Celtic deity Toutatis. The missing shoulder would have almost certainly have had the inscription 'VTERE', which, when combined with FELIX, translates as 'use (this ring) happily'. 'TOT' finger-rings are relatively common Roman finds, although the vast majority have been discovered to the east of the River Trent, in the area formerly occupied by the Iron Age Corieltauvi tribe. According to Adam Daubney (Lincolnshire FLO), this piece is significant in that it confirms that these rings, which are usually simply inscribed 'TOT', are dedicated to the warrior god Toutatis.
Disposition: Acquired by Luton Museum.

R HOBBS

121. Well, Lincolnshire: silver 'TOT' finger-ring fragment (PAS: LIN-1901F7; Treasure: 2007 T437)

Date: Roman (c. AD 100–c. 300).
Discovery: Found by Alan Eley while metal-detecting in 2007, and reported to Adam Daubney (Lincolnshire FLO).
Description: An inscribed silver finger-ring of Henig (1978) Type VIII (Tomlin 2008: 378–379 no. 14, fig. 14). Only the circular bezel and triangular shoulders remain. The shoulders are decorated with a rope-like perimeter and two triangular facets on either side. The bezel bears an inscription comprising two symbols and one letter. The symbol on the left comprises two opposing crescents set vertically; the central symbol is a '+', and the letter on the right is a capital letter 'T'. Width: 8.5mm. Weight: 2.79g.
Discussion: Finger-rings bearing the inscription 'TOT', or slight variations thereof, are well known in Lincolnshire and presumably this ring falls into this group (see discussion in 120).
Disposition: Acquired by The Collection Lincoln; finder and landowner donated their share.

A DAUBNEY

122. Gosford Farm, Nottinghamshire: silver finger-ring (PAS: LVPL-E08676; Treasure: 2007 T387)

Date: Roman (c. AD 100–c. 300).
Discovery: Found by Mike Moore while metal-detecting in August 2007, and reported to Frances McIntosh (North West FLO).
Description: Roman silver ring of Henig (1978) Type VIII; just less than half of the hoop is missing. The hoop is circular in profile and square in section and the flat, triangular shoulders are decorated with incised spirals. The circular bezel is inscribed 'TOT' inside a border of punched dots (see discussion in 120 above). Weight: 4g.
Disposition: Museum of Nottingham Life hopes to acquire.

R HOBBS

123. Wetheringsett, Suffolk: gold finger-ring (PAS: SF-F82122; Treasure: 2007 T587)

Date: Roman (c. AD 100–c. 300).
Discovery: Found by Micky Seager while metal-detecting in October 2007, and reported to Faye Minter (Suffolk FLO).
Description: A small finger-ring, the hoop is D-shaped in section and narrow at the back but flares in width into the shoulders and has a flat oval-shaped bezel. This bezel is decorated with an incised design in the form of a stylised pair of clasped hands (*dextrarum iunctio*). Dimensions (external): 14.24 x 12.51mm. Weight: 1.71g.
Discussion: The ring has parallels with a silver ring from Quenington, Gloucestershire (*TAR* 2004, no. 45), and others listed in Henig's (1978: app. 195) corpus.
Disposition: Disclaimed; returned to finder.

F MINTER

124. Irnham, Lincolnshire: copper-alloy knife handle (PAS: LIN-15BB58)

Date: Roman (c. AD 100–c. 300).
Discovery: Found by Dave Robinson while metal-detecting in 2007, and recorded with Adam Daubney (Lincolnshire FLO).
Description: A cast copper-alloy handle from a Roman folding knife which depicts a pair of naked wrestlers probably intended to represent Hercules and Antaeus (Worrell 2008: 357, no. 7, fig. 11). Hercules stands behind Antaeus with his arms wrapped around Antaeus's thighs in the process of lifting him off the ground. The right foot of the raised wrestler rests on a sub-spherical object. Down the back of the standing wrestler is a deep vertical slot into which the missing blade would have fitted when folded, and which now contains patches of iron corrosion. Dimensions: 56 x 23 x 14mm. Weight: 41.4g.

Discussion: The representation of wrestlers originates in the Hellenistic period and is a common motif in Roman times. Discussions of similar scenes identify the combatants as either generic wrestlers or as Hercules and Antaeus, as described by Apollodorus (The Library ii.5.11) and Hyginus (*Fabulae* 31).

The myth surrounding Hercules and Antaeus is not commonly represented in any media in what were the western provinces of the Roman Empire. A well-preserved knife handle from Alsenz, Rhineland-Pfalz, which depicts the struggle between Hercules and Antaeus, shows the latter with his right foot resting on a spherical object representing the earth, suggesting that the Irnham wrestlers should also be identified as the hero and the giant. The example from Irnham is the first knife handle of its type known from Britain, although the same scene is shown on a medallion from Capheaton, Northumberland (Brailsford 1964: 41, pl. x, no. 50), a Late Roman silver-gilt pepper-pot found in the Hoxne Hoard, Suffolk (Bland and Johns 1993: 25–26), and a figurine from Bavay (Boucher and Oggiano-Bitar 1993: 29, no. 5).

Disposition: Returned to finder.

A DAUBNEY & S WORRELL

---

125. Andover, Hampshire: copper-alloy figurine (PAS: HAMP-378231)

Date: Roman (c. AD 100–c. 300).

Discovery: Found by Alec Doris while metal-detecting in about 2005, and recorded with Rob Webley (Hampshire FLO) in 2007.

Description: Cast copper-alloy Roman bound captive figurine (Worrell 2008: 365, no. 15, fig. 19). The naked, crouched man's legs are drawn up and he is bound with a rope at the neck, wrists and ankles. There is a large, circular perforation piercing the abdomen transversally, which is met by a circular perforation running vertically from the captive's head to the bottom. Such perforations on figurines of this type enabled them to be secured to another object, probably using wooden pegs. The head has 'Celtic'-style features, including small, circular eyes in hollow sockets, a short nose, strong chin and curved ears. The hairstyle is also distinctively 'Celtic' with the hair brushed onto the forehead in straight lines, although it finishes just beyond the circular perforation, where the smooth surface may suggest that the back of the head was shaved. Dimensions: 34 x 21mm. Weight: 19.93g.

Discussion: A total of sixteen bound captive figurines are known with a distribution limited to the Rhine/Danube frontier and Britannia (Jackson 2005). This example is the seventh of Jackson's Type II recorded from sites in the north-west provinces of the Roman Empire. Type II bound captives are characterised by a diminutive size, the stylised facial features and hairstyle, and the position of the vertical perforation (Jackson 2005: 147, fig. 6). This find represents the most southerly example of a Type II figurine found in Britain. Two other bound captive figurines, also of Type II, have been recorded by the PAS from Thonock (NLM-2845) and Harmston (DENO-9632F6), both in Lincolnshire.

Disposition: Acquired by Hampshire Museum Service.

R WEBLEY

---

126. Stepney, London: mosaic fragments (PAS: LON-7FB541)

Date: Roman (c. 100–c. 300 AD).

Discovery: Found by Kobi Draper Romm while searching the Thames foreshore in 2007, and recorded by Kate Sumnall (London FLO).

Description: Three Roman mosaic fragments, each of which comprises either black-and-white or red-and-black tesserae set within white mortar. The mortar fabric has frequent inclusions of ground brick/tile. The tesserae are roughly square. Dimensions: ranging from 12.4 x 12.2mm to 18.6 x 17.4mm.

Discussion: Kobi Draper Romm was on a trip to the foreshore organised by the Thames Explorer Trust for local children. He discovered four fragments of mosaics, three of which turned out to be Roman, probably from a known local bath house, and one fragment was Victorian.

Disposition: Returned to finder.

K SUMNALL

---

127. Huncote and Leighfield, Leicestershire: two greyware kiln bars (PAS: LEIC-574128 & B19972)

Date: Roman (c. AD 100–c. 400).

Discovery: Found by Mick Morris (LEIC-574128) and Andy Tansley (LEIC-B19972) while metal-detecting and field-walking in 2007, and recorded by Wendy Scott (Leicestershire & Rutland FLO).

Description: Two greyware kiln bars, both of which have a rectangular section with tapering edges, giving them a 'cigar' shape and the appearance of pumice. Dimensions: Huncote (LEIC-574128): 64 x 27 x 27mm. Weight: 53g. Leighfield (LEIC-B19972): 69 x 39 x 24mm. Weight: 54.83g.

Discussion: Kiln bars are the most frequently encountered items of kiln furniture; on unexcavated sites they are often the only indication of a probable kiln site (Swan 1984: 62). This is probably the case with the two new Leicestershire kiln bars. Kiln bars were shaped by hand and their most popular arrangement within the kiln was radiating from a central pedestal. As kilns got deeper, the tapering 'cigar-shaped' bars with narrow ends were thrust into the wet clay of the kiln wall. Alternatively, bars of this type were permanently attached to the supports and kiln wall and their ends luted with clay. 'Cigar-shaped' kiln bars have a concentrated distribution pattern focusing on the middle Trent Valley and other river valleys in south

Lincolnshire, Nottinghamshire, Leicestershire, Rutland, Northamptonshire, north-west Norfolk, north-east Buckinghamshire, and Bedfordshire (Swan 1984: 63). The kiln bar from Huncote has helped to identify a new kiln site on the edge of Leicester Forest, an area that contains most of the known Roman kilns in the county.
Disposition: Returned to finders.

W SCOTT & S WORRELL

---

128. Bures area, Essex: gold finger-ring (PAS: ESS-455767; Treasure: 2007 T386)

Date: Roman (probably c. AD 150–c. 250).
Discovery: Found by Mick Mathews while metal-detecting in July 2007, and reported to Laura McLean (Essex FLO).
Description: A Roman gold finger-ring with oval hoop, slightly distorted, which expands to form rounded, keeled shoulders flanking a flat, slender, elongated ovoid bezel incised with the Greek word 'EUTYXI' (Good fortune to you [the wearer], or May you [the wearer] prosper (Tomlin 2008: 375, no. 8, fig. 8). The size and spacing of the letters is a little irregular but they are neatly cut with well-formed serifs. They retain much of their black *niello* inlay. Diameter (external): 21.7 x 15.3mm. Weight: 4.04g. Surface analysis: gold content of 94–97% and confirmed the inlay material.
Discussion: For the ring type, though with different inscription, see Marshall (1907: no. 582, fig. 92). Several gold finger-rings from Roman Britain bear Greek inscriptions, including those from Corbridge, Northumberland, Whittlesey, Cambridgeshire, and Stonham Aspal, Suffolk (Collingwood and Wright 1991: nos. 2422.1, 12, 6 & 10). The *niello* inlay in Greek lettering can be paralleled by a gold-plated silver finger-ring from Corbridge (RIB II, 3: no. 2422.43), while the EUTYXI formula is quite often found either standing alone or as part of a longer inscription on onyx and sardonyx cameos (Henig 1990: nos. 29–39). British examples include an engraved sardonyx cameo set in a gold ring found near the Roman villa at Keynsham, Avon, and a relief-carved onyx cameo found at the Roman villa at North Wraxall, Wiltshire (RIB II, 3: nos. 2423.10 & 11).
Disposition: Acquired by Braintree Museum.

R JACKSON

---

129. Yscir, Powys: copper-alloy military horse harness fitting (PAS: NMGW-8487B1)

Date: Roman (c. AD 150–c. 300).
Discovery: Found by Mr Hingley while metal-detecting in 2007, and recorded by Mark Lodwick (Finds Co-ordinator, Wales).
Description: An incomplete military fitting (*phalera*), comprising three surviving pieces that would have had two further strap loops. The central cruciform component has three loops composed of curved side arms, each terminating in a loop containing a copper-alloy pin, of uncertain function, possibly decorative. The outside edge of the loops have a rounded bar, upon which a copper-alloy strap fitting is attached. At the centre of the mount is a domed boss, which has surviving traces of silvering. The rear of the central mount has a central perforation, the function of which is uncertain. The unlooped arm of the mount has a rectangular ribbed panel before a hinge with an iron axis bar. The fitting is hinged to a broken flat plate with curved sides. The bottom of the plate has an original, unbroken edge. The plate would have been a harness pendant of crescentic form or teardrop shaped with a central opening. Both faces of the plate are plain. Looped around the opposite side of the fitting is a simple copper-alloy strip. The strip is decorated with raised concentric circles around perforations, which would have contained attachment rivets. At the base of the fragmentary strip is a surviving attachment rivet, which may be a later repair. The fitting has variable surface preservation with a dark grey to green patina. Dimensions: 40.9 x 36.6 x 5.9mm. Weight: 35.8g.
Discussion: The fitting is unusual and would have been a strap distributor with associated harness pendant, probably positioned on the breast of the horse. While numerous examples of military harness fittings are known from the 1st and early 2nd century (Bishop 1988), few later examples are recorded. During the Antonine Period (mid-2nd century) there was a change from junction loops or phalerae with concealed loops to phalerae with loops around the edge. This example is similar to examples from Newstead (Bishop and Coulston 2006: 147, fig. 90) and Seven Sisters, Glamorgan (Chapman 2005: 133, no. Tc01).
Disposition: Returned to finder.

M LODWICK

---

130. Northwich, Cheshire: copper-alloy brooch (PAS: LVPL-F52FB5)

Date: Roman (c. AD 190–c. 260).
Discovery: Found by John Watts while metal-detecting in 2005, and recorded by Frances McIntosh (Cheshire, Greater Manchester and Merseyside FLO) in 2007.
Description: A complete copper-alloy brooch in the form of a swastika with its arms turned to the right. The pin is hinged and mounted between two pierced lugs and has seized due to corrosion. The extended catch-plate is in the same plane as the bottom edge of the brooch and has a slot cut for the pin. Dimensions: 26 x 24.5 x 3mm. Weight: 12.5g.
Discussion: Swastika brooches, or Hakenkreuzfibel, are not common in Britain, but are found along the Rhine-Danube frontier. A swastika brooch, but with a sprung pin, is known from Derby (Mackreth 1985: 297, no. 39, fig. 129) and a similar example is known from Syria (Hattatt 1987: 222, no. 1145, fig. 70). The swastika, or *crux grammatica* (a cross formed from four

Greek capital gamma characters), was widely used long before the Christian period, possibly in pagan religious contexts. It did however continue in use into the early Christian period as a veiled symbol of the Cross (Hattat 1987: 222).

Deposition: Returned to finder.

F MCINTOSH

---

131. North Nibley, Gloucestershire: silver finger-ring (PAS: GLO-EF3774; Treasure: 2007 T261)

Date: Roman (c. AD 200–c. 300).

Discovery: Found by Tim Stokes while metal-detecting in January 2007, and reported to Kurt Adams (Gloucestershire FLO).

Description: Roman silver finger-ring of Henig Type (1978) VIII. An oval hoop, rectangular in section, expands via a sharp carination to triangular shoulders with shallow mouldings and feathered edges. The flat ovular bezel is plain and undecorated. Diameter (exterior): 24.9mm. Weight: 5.6g.

Disposition: Acquired by the Museum in the Park, Stroud.

R HOBBS

---

132. Maryport, Cumbria: copper-alloy mount (PAS: LANCUM-BA4D32)

Date: Roman (c. AD 200–c. 300).

Discovery: Found by Graham Ryan while metal-detecting in 2007, and recorded by Dot Boughton (Lancashire & Cumbria FLO).

Description: An incomplete cast copper-alloy circular mount of Allason-Jones (1986: 68–69) Type 1 depicting an eagle standing facing, looking to the left and with its outstretched wings held away from its body with the tips touching a thunderbolt. It is quite worn and has no grooves or mouldings to indicate features such as the eye or feathers. The outline of the eagle tapers towards a flat disc with broken-off sides, indicating a thunderbolt. When complete, the eagle would have formed the centrepiece of a circular mount and would have been framed by the letters 'OPTIME MAXIME CONSERVA', no trace of which now survives. Extending from the back is a plain, tapering spike at the centre which was probably used for attachment to a leather strap or belt. Dimensions: 30.18 x 26.44 x 9.18mm. Weight: 7.84g.

Discussion: This mount would originally have been part of a set of three openwork mounts belonging to a Roman *balteus* (military belt) which took the form of an inscription divided between three elements. The full motto was (circular): 'OPTIME MAXIME CONSERVA'; (rectangular): 'NUMERUM OMNIUM'; (triangular): 'MILITANTIUM' (Jupiter Best (and) Greatest protect (us) a troop of fighting men all). 'Best and Greatest' is an allusion to Jupiter, traditionally the god of the empire and the army. No complete set has been found in Britain, but individual Type 1 mounts are known from various sites including a complete mount found at the Swifts, Carlisle (Allason-Jones 1986); other examples are known from both military and civilian contexts from Aldborough, North Yorkshire (Bishop 1996), and Silchester, Hampshire (Boon 1974: 66f, fig. 8,3).

Disposition: On loan to Senhouse Roman Museum.

D BOUGHTON & S WORRELL

---

133. Cherington, Gloucestershire: limestone tombstone fragment (PAS: NMGW-552838)

Date: Roman (c. AD 200–c. 300).

Discovery: Found by Brian Vaughan while metal-detecting in 2007, identified by Mark Lodwick and Roger Tomlin (University of Oxford) and recorded by Mark Lodwick (Finds Co-ordinator, Wales).

Description: A fragmentary slab representing a side fragment from a Roman tombstone. The stone is a coarse Jurassic limestone and was probably quarried locally. The face of the stone has a raised vertical border with a rounded top. The remnants of three lines of inscription survive on the fragment '[...] / [...]VS / [...] N.XII / [...] V / [.] perhaps [D(is) M (anibus) / ...]us / [vix (it) a]n(nos) XII / [m(enses)...d(ies)....V [...]' (To the shades of the dead. [....]us lived 12 years, ...months, 5(or more)days ...) (Tomlin 2008: 370, no. 2, fig. 2). Dimensions: 250 x 238 x 80mm. Weight: not recorded.

Discussion: The top line of the inscription denotes the end of the name of the deceased, above [a]n(nos) XII, indicating the length of military service. The XV may indicate part of the soldier's age. The reverse of the stone has not been modified. The breaks on the stone are all of some age but there has been some recent plough damage to the surface. The tombstone is unlikely to have travelled very far.

Disposition: Returned to finder.

M LODWICK & R TOMLIN

---

134. Lacock, Wiltshire: silver finger-ring with intaglio (PAS: WILT-6DF737; Treasure: 2007 T112)

Date: Roman (c. AD 200–c. 300).

Discovery: Found by Dave Crisp while metal-detecting in February 2007, and reported to Katie Hinds (Wiltshire FLO).

Description: A silver finger-ring with an ovular hoop, a flattened bezel and smoothly swelling profile of Henig (1978) Type XI. The bezel is set with an orange carnelian intaglio, depicting a bird on a branch. The bottom of the hoop is broken with two loose fragments, although complete. Diameter: 21.4 x 15.5mm. Weight: 5.19g.

Discussion: The intaglio on this finger-ring has parallels with a series of intaglios depicting a parrot standing on a branch with two examples from Colchester and another from the Walbrook, London (Henig 1978: 268–269, nos. 685–687).

Disposition: Acquired by the British Museum.

K HINDS & R HOBBS

135. South Oxfordshire: gold foil amulet (PAS: BERK-0B6771; Treasure: 2007 T1)

Date: Roman (c. AD 200–c. 400).

Discovery: Found by David Livingstone while metal-detecting in November 2006, and reported to Fi Hitchcock (Treasure Registrar).

Description: A Roman amulet comprising a rectangular sheet (*lamella*) cut from gold foil, with 16 lines of incised text along the short axis (width). Twelve magical 'characters' on lines 1–3 are followed by the main text on lines 3–16 in Greek cursive lettering. The *lamella* is complete though with extensive rolling creasing and post-depositional crumpling. Height: 63.1mm. Width: 28.3mm. Weight: 1.41g. Surface analysis: gold and silver contents of approximately 90–93 % and 6–8% respectively.

Discussion: This is the third such amulet (not including fragmentary examples) to be found in Britain. The other examples are from Caernarvon (RIB 436) and Billingford, Norfolk (*TAR* 2003, no. 67, where references to the fragmentary examples from Britain are also given). Another fragment, barely legible, was found in the Torksey area (*TAR* 2004, no. 71). The standard corpus of precious-metal amulets of known provenance (Kotansky 1994) contains only 68 items, so they are quite rare.

The 16 lines of text have been inscribed with a fine-pointed stylus. Lines 1–3 consist of twelve magical 'characters', adapted from Greek letters or simple geometrical figures, which can be paralleled in other amulets; lines 4–5 are 'magical names' in Greek, but ultimately derived perhaps from Egyptian; lines 7–16 are a more grammatical appeal to the 'holy names' to protect a pregnant woman called Fabia, the daughter of Terentia. They are written in Greek cursive, reasonably legible but not particularly accomplished. The text is formulaic, but its formulas are difficult to parallel. There are some vulgarisms of spelling, which reflect the spoken language, and at least two errors. The amulet is apparently a charm to ensure safe childbirth. Like other examples of amulets, it was rolled up and was probably worn in a cylindrical amulet-case from the neck. Whether it was inscribed in Britain or imported by the wearer is uncertain. To judge by its handwriting the amulet probably dates as above (Roger Tomlin, University of Oxford, *personal communication*). When found, the *lamella* was tightly rolled, and later completely unrolled in the Department of Conservation, Documentation and Science at the British Museum.

Disposition: British Museum hopes to acquire.

R JACKSON & R TOMLIN

136. Godmanchester, Cambridgeshire: silver finger-ring with intaglio (PAS: CAMHER-94F877; Treasure: 2007 T131)

Date: Roman (c. AD 200–c. 400).

Discovery: Found by Simon Ashford while metal-detecting in February 2007, and reported to Philippa Walton (Cambridgeshire FLO).

Description: A finger-ring lacking most of the hoop. One shoulder survives, in the form of the stylised head and upper curved neck of a water bird, a duck or swan, with marked brow ridge and broad splayed bill which supports the bezel. The high-projecting box bezel has angled octagonal walls and a rubbed-over setting. It contains an oval *nicolo* intaglio with black substrate and light blue surface layer. The sides are bevelled and the surface is flat. Deterioration of the edges, especially in the lower arc where two red-coloured inclusions (flaws) are revealed, combined with the 'softened' nature of the impression, make it hard to identify the image, which appears to show a standing, possibly male figure, possibly with a staff. Width (original, by extension): 27mm approx. Bezel: 14.8 x 12.5mm. Weight: 6.2g.

Discussion: Zoomorphic or ornithomorphic shoulders are an occasional feature of later Roman rings, as, for example, in the Thetford Treasure, in which dolphins and woodpeckers occur on rings 5–7 (Johns and Potter 1983: 82–85).

Disposition: Acquired by the British Museum.

R JACKSON

137. Aldbrough area, North Yorkshire: gold finger-ring (PAS: YORYM-1CD342; Treasure: 2007 T335)

Date: Roman (c. AD 200–c. 400).

Discovery: Found by Jason Ashley while metal-detecting in May 2007, and reported to Beth Echtenacher (North & East Yorkshire FLA).

Description: A small, distorted finger-ring with an undecorated hoop of planoconvex cross-section, which swells towards the small flat bezel. The bezel is ornamented with a simple granulated motif – a stylised bunch of grapes in the form of a symmetrical diamond-shaped cluster of nine pellets. Width (maximum): 21.5mm. Weight: 3.1g.

Discussion: Vine motifs, such as grapes, tendrils, leaves etc., were popular in various media in the Roman period. It is likely that many were of purely decorative intent but some may have incorporated or projected a specific link to the cult of Bacchus, god of wine.

Disposition: British Museum hopes to acquire.

R JACKSON

138. Lacock, Wiltshire: silver finger-ring (PAS: WILT-6D7DE7; Treasure: 2007 T54)

Date: Roman (c. AD 200–c. 400).

Discovery: Found by Dave Crisp while metal-detecting in October or November 2006, and reported to Katie Hinds (Wiltshire FLO) in 2007.

Description: A base-silver finger-ring probably of Henig (1978) Type VIII. The hoop is slightly squashed, but is otherwise complete. The bezel is flat and circular and is supported on opposite sides by triangular shoulders which are decorated with a groove flanking each outer edge. Diameter: 21.1mm. Weight: 3.59g.

Disposition: Acquired by Wiltshire Heritage Museum.

K HINDS

139. Chettle, Dorset: iron hipposandal (PAS: DOR-002402)

Date: Roman (c. AD 200–c. 410).

Discovery: Found by Margaret Hamilton while metal-detecting in 2007, and recorded by Ciorstaidh Hayward Trevarthen (Dorset FLO).

Description: Incomplete Roman iron hipposandal (type of horseshoe) of Manning's (1985: 65, fig. 16) Type H1. The hooked heel and part of the plate remains. The plate has incurved sides with the remnants of a flared wing at one side. At the back the plate curves upwards into a flared, convex heel plate with an incomplete backward projecting hook at the mid point of the upper edge. The hook is tapering and square sectioned. Dimensions: 104.5 x 80.9 x 44.1mm. Weight: 130g.

Discussion: Examples of the same type of hipposandal (with a front hook at the top of a vertical triangular neck and with wings that are narrow at the rear of the hook) are known from London (Manning 1985: 65, fig. 16) and Colchester, Essex (Crummy 1983: 105, fig. 108). This hipposandal is one of only four recorded on the PAS database, with the other examples reported from Ilam, Staffordshire (WMID-1F5906), Takeley, Essex (ESS-8CE256), and Little Hadham, Hertfordshire (BH-4827E4).

Disposition: Returned to finder.

C HAYWARD-TREVARTHEN

140. Wickham Skeith, Suffolk: copper-alloy folding knife handle (PAS: SF-CA2A74)

Date: Roman (c. AD 250–c. 410).

Discovery: Found by Trevor Southgate while metal-detecting in 2007, and recorded by Faye Minter (Suffolk FLO).

Description: A copper-alloy folding knife handle in the form of a three-dimensional standing panther, depicted facing forward and with a deeply curved, S-shaped form. The panther has a broad head with small ears, moulded eyes, a short snout and rounded nostrils; there are three circular drilled holes along the line of the mouth, giving the impression that it is open. The function of these holes is unclear; they may have originally held decorative inset gems and are not in an obvious place to be associated with the suspension of the knife. The body of the panther is swollen and arched forwards. Moulding represents the legs, which terminate in one large foot, which has four paws and a suggestion of claws. The underside of this foot is slightly rounded. A longitudinal slot runs down the back of the handle for its entire length. The upper terminal, above the panther's head, is rectangular with a transverse moulding at its top and base; there is also a rivet hole. The iron blade was hinged and there are remains of the rectangular iron blade projecting from the upper terminal. Dimensions: 63.08 x 11.81 x 16.81mm. Weight: 29.3g.

Discussion: This folding knife is likely to have been used ritually and folding knives are often found at temple sites. This example is very similar to another from Standon, Hertfordshire (BH-EIA355), which again depicts a standing panther and has three drilled holes in the mouth area.

Disposition: Returned to finder.

F MINTER

141. Ropley, Hampshire: copper-alloy folding knife handle (PAS: SUR-E90A93)

Date: Roman (c. AD 250–c. 410).

Discovery: Found by Mr D Chapple while metal-detecting in 2007, and recorded by David Williams (Surrey FLO).

Description: A complete handle in the form of a hound chasing a hare, from a folding knife. The handle is very well preserved and remains of the iron blade survive in a slot below the figures. Both animals are schematically rendered; each has prominent ears and the hound's nose touches the hare's tail. There is a series of small notches on the lower sides adjacent to the folded blade; behind the hound is a plain rectangular extension bordered by a pair of collars and on this is the iron pin on which the blade pivots. Dimensions: 67.6 x 14.5mm. Weight: 20.86g.

Discussion: The representation of the hound and hare hunting scene was a popular theme throughout Roman material culture, particularly in the 4th century. This form of folding knife is relatively common, and over 40 such handles are recorded on the PAS database.

Disposition: Returned to finder.

D WILLIAMS

142. Bedford area, Bedfordshire: copper-alloy mount (PAS: BH-22D0A3)

Date: Roman (c. AD 250–c. 410).

Discovery: Found by Peter Salvia while metal-detecting in 2007, and recorded by Julian Watters (Hertfordshire & Bedfordshire FLO).

Description: A copper-alloy mount depicting a stylised anthropomorphic head, perhaps from either a vessel or a casket. The face is sub-oval in plan, tapering slightly towards the chin and with a semicircular, hollow cross-section. The hair is incised and depicted as short and wavy; the large, almond-shaped eyes are defined by a groove. The flat, wedge-shaped nose is wide and the mouth is represented by a short, horizontal groove. The reverse of the mount is hollow and contains a white material which is probably a corroded solder or paste for attaching the mount to a bucket. Dimensions: 33.1 x 30.4 x 11.6mm. Weight: 25.96g.

Discussion: Two almost identical examples found near Upton Snodsbury, Worcestershire, are recorded on the PAS database (WAW-2EFFB6 & 2F4145; Worrell 2006: 442–443, no. 10, fig. 11). The striking similarities between this piece and the Worcestershire examples, in terms of their form, dimensions and the manner of fixing, perhaps suggest that all three artefacts may have originated from the same workshop. The facial features and depiction of the hair of the three mounts recorded by the PAS resemble in style those of the horned head on the bucket mount from West Hill, Uley, Gloucestershire (Henig et al. 1993: 98, no. 2, figs. 83 & 85).

Disposition: Returned to finder.

J WATTERS

143. Mansfield Woodhouse area, Nottinghamshire: lead amulet (PAS: DENO-120680)

Date: Roman (c. AD 250–c. 410).

Discovery: Found by Daniel Pegg while metal-detecting in early 2007, and recorded by Anja Rohde (Derbyshire & Nottinghamshire FLO).

Description: A cast lead amulet depicting a human head. The object is pear-shaped and has a planoconvex section. It has moulded and incised facial features on the upper surface representing the stylised hair, eyes, nose, mouth, chin and cheeks. The back surface is flat and undecorated. There is no means of attachment and the object does not seem to be broken, suggesting that this is the original form of the object. Dimensions: 23 x 20.27mm. Weight: 10.62g.

Discussion: This object is very similar to another which was recorded on the PAS database in 2006 (DENO-0E4A27). Discussing the earlier find, Martin Henig (University of Oxford) suggested that these may be protective amulets intended to ward off evil.

Deposition: Returned to finder.

A ROHDE

144. Chenies area, Buckinghamshire: copper-alloy dog figurine (PAS: BUC-3ECE21)

Date: Roman (c. AD 300–c. 410).

Discovery: Found by Matthew Wildman while using a metal-detector, and recorded by Ros Tyrrell (Buckinghamshire FLO).

Description: A small copper-alloy figurine of a dog seated on its haunches and with its forelimbs raised in the air. The animal has a long snout and pointed ears, but no facial features are indicated, other than a horizontal incised line for the mouth. No attempt to represent the animal's coat is visible, but the surface is pitted by corrosion. The legs are rather roughly moulded with no joints shown. There is a scar where the tail has broken off. Dimensions: 49.58 x 42.92mm. Weight: 29.33g.

Discussion: In the Classical world the dog was the traditional animal-emblem of Aesculapius, god of medicine and healing, and of Diana the Huntress, and it also had links to the Underworld. In Britain, there are several instances of non-iconographic evidence for an Underworld dog-cult, such as the burial of eight dog skeletons, seven of them puppies, interned in urns in the Upchurch Marshes, Kent (Green 1977: 313; Hume 1956). Roman figurines of dogs are not common. A very fine figurine representing a lithe animal which is naturalistic in style with long ears, a long pointed muzzle, powerful legs and a collar around its neck is known from the temple of Nodens at Lydney, Gloucestershire (Wheeler and Wheeler 1932: 88–89, 114–120, pls. XXV–XXVI). Other dog figurines, all probably intended as votives, are recorded from Aldborough, Carrawburgh and Kirkby Thore (Toynbee 1962: 126–127). The PAS has recorded four other dog figurines, all of differing styles. The example found at Newchurch, Isle of Wight (IOW-B354E4), also depicts a seated hound, in a different pose to the Lydney dog, but equally successful in its naturalism and with similar features. The Chenies dog is a much cruder piece, but is still an interesting example of a rare type.

Disposition: Returned to finder.

R TYRRELL & S WORRELL

145. Narborough, Leicestershire: copper-alloy seal-ring (LEIC-5FC533)

Date: Roman (c. AD 300–c. 410).

Discovery: Found by Wayne Gemmell while metal-detecting in 2007, and recorded with Wendy Scott (Leicestershire FLO).

Description: A copper-alloy seal-ring with the bezel engraved with a chi-rho motif (Worrell 2008: 361, no. 10, fig. 14). The bezel has eight projecting lugs, four of which are at the shoulders creating an indented edge. The bezel rises 3.5mm above the hoop and is engraved with a chi-rho with serifs within a circular beaded border. Diameter (ring): 23mm. Diameter (bezel): 13mm. Weight: 5.56g.

Discussion: This finger-ring represents a significant addition to the corpus of early Christian symbols from Britain. In form, this ring is similar to a copper-alloy example decorated with two fish flanking an anchor which was excavated at the villa at Moor Park, Hertfordshire (Henig 1987: 184–185, pls. 1–2). Other rings engraved with a chi-rho include a gold ring from Brentwood, Essex, silver rings from Fifehead Neville, Dorset, and Thruxton, Hampshire, and a copper-alloy ring from Silchester, Hampshire (Mawer 1995: 67, 72–74, D3. Go. 3, D3. Si. 5, D3. Si. 10, D3. Br. 6).
Disposition: Returned to finder.

W SCOTT & S WORRELL

---

146. Alcester, Warwickshire: silver spoon fragment (PAS: WAW-D04DD6; Treasure: 2007 T352)

Date: Roman (c. AD 300–c. 400).
Discovery: Found by Bob Laight while metal-detecting between January and March 2007, and reported to Angie Bolton (Warwickshire & Worcestershire FLO).
Description: A spoon fragment consisting of the offset, part of the bowl and the handle. The bowl has a concave upper surface, and the underside has a moulded rectangular ridge which leads to the stem. The offset forms a curvaceous L shape in profile. The stem continues from the upper edge of the junction, and both the junction and stem are rectangular in section. The upper face of the stem is decorated with two transverse grooves and a small spur which overhangs the junction. The opposite terminal of the stem is broken, which appears to be recent damage. Length: 30.52mm. Weight: 2.4g.
Discussion: The shape of the offset and the remains of the bowl suggest that the bowl was originally oval in shape, which is a late Roman type.
Disposition: Acquired by Warwickshire Museum.

A BOLTON

---

147. Horton, south Gloucestershire: copper-alloy buckle (PAS: GLO-FA9938)

Date: Roman (c. 330–c. 400 AD).
Discovery: Reported by the landowner who was given the object by a local metal-detectorist in 2007, and subsequently recorded by Kurt Adams (Gloucestershire & Avon FLO).
Description: A copper-alloy buckle with a D-shaped frame and integral, openwork triangular plate of Hawkes and Dunning (1961) Type IIB. The buckle frame and plate have bevelled edges resulting in a trapezoidal cross-section. The bar between the frame and the plate has a construction in the centre for the pin; the construction is circular in cross-section and the pin is now missing. Flanking the plate just beyond the pin bar are two semicircular lugs, each of which have a circular rivet hole in the centre; there is a third circular lug at the apex of the plate, again with a circular rivet

hole in the centre. The reverse of the buckle is flat and undecorated. Dimensions 58 x 36mm. Weight: 15g.
Discussion: H W Böhme (1986, Liste 1, Abb. 5, Abb. 14) studied buckles of this type as part of a survey of late Roman artefacts. Although this type of buckle is found in small numbers in England and South Wales, it has a vast distribution along the European frontier of the Roman Empire, along the Rhine and Danube rivers to Pannonia. A similar buckle is known from Richborough, Kent (Lyne 1999: 108, no. 65), and an example recorded by the PAS was found at Hinton in the Hedges, Northamptonshire (NARC-C6E5B8).
Disposition: Returned to landowner.

K ADAMS

---

148. Gunthorpe, Norfolk: gold brooch (PAS: NMS-E7D687; Treasure: 2007 T236)

Date: Roman (c. AD 340–c. 380).
Discovery: Found by Paul Buckenham while metal-detecting in April 2007, and reported to Erica Darch (Norfolk FLO).
Description: An incomplete gold crossbow brooch with a sheath foot, probably of Keller (1971) Types 3–4. Its narrow upper bow is highly arched with a trapezoidal section and broadens to a bifurcation. Both bifurcated ends appear to have curved round the missing crossbar. The pin is also missing. On both sides of the bifurcation there is chip-carved decoration with three V-sectioned notches on both edges; between them is an engraved saltire and single horizontal line. The foot is simply decorated with three faintly engraved, transverse median lines and both edges are lined with short transverse and V-shaped notches. Length: 39mm. Width (foot): 7.5mm. Weight: 10.56g.
Discussion: Although incomplete, this brooch, with its highly arched bow and long, decorated foot, has several features in common with a complete developed crossbow brooch excavated at Richborough, Kent (Bayley and Butcher 2006: 118, no. 321, fig. 91). Late bow brooches classed as sheath-footed brooches of Hull's (unpublished) Group 11 include all P-profiled brooches with a sheath foot, in particular the range of P-shaped brooches with a divided bow or crossbow. The majority of the brooches that have had their composition analysed are of leaded bronze or leaded gunmetal (Bayley and Butcher 2006: 181–185, figs. 157–158). Only a very small number of high status late Roman brooches in solid gold or silver are known. The only other gold crossbow recorded in Britain is an example with acorn-shaped terminals, impressed triangles decorating the bow and foot, and circular cut-outs and scalloped edges from Odiham, Hampshire (Kent and Painter 1977: 28, no. 20).
Disposition: Norwich Castle Museum hopes to acquire.

A ROGERSON & S WORRELL

149. South Brent, Devon: copper-alloy brooch (PAS: DEV-E1A6A8)

Date: Roman (c. AD 350–c. 380).

Discovery: Found by Semaj Dance while metal-detecting in 2007, and recorded with Danielle Wootton (Devon FLO).

Description: An incomplete cast copper-alloy developed crossbow brooch of Keller (1971) Types 3–4. The highly arched upper bow is narrow and undecorated; both the bow and crossbar are of square section. An onion-shaped head-knob and a similar end-knob are intact on the upper bow. There are two holes at the centre of the crossbar positioned at either side of the head-knob. The lower bow and hinged pin are now missing; there are traces of iron corrosion on the crossbar and end knob from the iron axis bar. Dimensions: 37.5 x 29.5 x 4.5mm. Weight: 15.08g.

Discussion: Features of developed crossbow brooches of Keller's Types 3 and 4 include a highly arched upper bow, a longer lower bow, elaborate foot decoration and terminal knobs on the ends of the crossbow and at the centre of the upper bow (Swift 2000: 14–15, Table A). The two holes on the crossbar of this example are unusual features suggestive of a further decorative casting on what originally would have been an elaborate crossbar. A similar brooch found at Richborough, Kent, also has two holes in the crossbar (Bayley and Butcher 2006: 117, no. 322, fig. 91). In comparison to many other counties, there is not a large quantity of Roman objects recorded in Devon and finds such as this brooch therefore contribute to our understanding of the late Roman period in this region.

Disposition: Returned to finder.

D WOOTTON & S WORRELL

150. Warmington, Warwickshire: copper-alloy buckle plate (PAS: WAW-5AEF78)

Date: Roman (c. AD 350–c. 425).

Discovery: Found by Keith Bennett while metal-detecting in 2007, and recorded with Angie Bolton (Warwickshire & Worcestershire FLO). The object was identified by Jenny Hall (Museum of London).

Description: An openwork buckle plate which also features an integral half propeller belt stiffener with a stamped ring-and-dot at its centre, and with circular rivet hole at each corner, of Hawkes and Dunning (1961: 50–57, figs. 17–18) Type IIA. The plate is rectangular with four loops for the attachment of the missing buckle, which was held by an iron bar, traces of which survive between the loops. Each loop is decorated with fine, transverse grooves. At the opposing edge there is a pair of wide transverse ridges. The plate has a triple arcade of openwork perforations; at the centre there is a motif with a rectangular and circular terminal and a detached circular perforation close to the square end. At either side there is a motif with

rectangular and circular terminals. Pairs of ring-and-dot stamps in four rows decorate the plate between the openwork areas. The reverse of the buckle plate is undecorated. Dimensions: 30.9 x 29.42 x 4.32mm. Weight: 12.4g.

Discussion: There are many variations in the nature and combination of the decorative motifs used on buckles of Type IIA, although the rectangles and circles which often run together are common. The buckle plate discovered at the Roman villa at West Dean, Hampshire with late 4th-century coinage (Hawkes and Dunning 1961: 52, no. 8, fig. 17,h), is particular close in style to the Warmington buckle. The missing buckle is likely to have been formed by a pair of confronted dolphins with tails making involuted terminals of Type IA (Hawkes and Dunning 1961: 41–45, figs.13–14).

Disposition: Returned to finder.

A BOLTON & S WORRELL

151. Urchfont, Wiltshire: silver buckle (PAS: WILT-773952; Treasure: 2007 T590)

Date: Roman (c. AD 350–c. 450).

Discovery: Found by Keith Palmer while metal-detecting in September 2007, and reported to Katie Hinds (Wiltshire FLO).

Description: The buckle consists of a D-shaped loop with the remains of two hinge loops attached to the hinge bar. The base of the tongue has a raised square which is notched at the sides into an hourglass shape. The plate for attachment to a belt is missing. Height: 19mm. Weight: 4.1g.

Discussion: The form of the loop and the lateral notches in the base of the tongue are typical of buckles of the very end of the Roman period in Britain, though continuing later on the Continent, e.g. a buckle with a circular plate from a grave at Kingsholm, Gloucester, and another with a triangular plate, presumably also from a British findspot (Hills and Hurst 1989: fig. 1, bottom left; Appels and Laycock 2007: 226, fig. SL10.20). This type of buckle can be dated as above, and possibly reflects the presence of soldiers from eastern Europe serving in the Roman army here.

Disposition: Wiltshire Heritage Museum hopes to acquire.

B M AGER

152. Stiffkey, Norfolk: copper-alloy pendant (PAS: NMS-E0FC97)

Date: Roman (c. AD 375–c. 425).

Discovery: Found by Mr N Peel while metal-detecting before May 2007, reported to Norfolk Museums and Archaeology Service and identified by Andrew Rogerson.

Description: Cast pendant in the form of a pair of addorsed horse-heads modelled in the round, above a tapering, baluster moulded, circular-sectioned spike,

with a centrally placed suspension hole. The eyes are represented by ring-and-dot motifs and both sides of the horses' necks are decorated with three ring-and-dots and smaller annulets. The manes are indicated by engraved V-sectioned grooves. Dimensions: 39.5 x 33.5 x 7.5mm. Diameter (suspension): 3mm. Weight: 16.97g.
Discussion: The spike is paralleled by that on a bird's head pendant from Deopham (Gurney 2006: 117, fig. 3D). The horse-heads are very strikingly reminiscent of those that project from late Roman military buckle frames of Hawkes and Dunning (1961) Type 1B of the late 4th or early 5th century and considered to be an 'exclusively British innovation' (Clarke 1979: 275). Other examples recorded by the PAS include those from Broadholme, Lincolnshire (LIN-C83398), and Milton Keynes, Buckinghamshire (BH-E44A46), both of which have long spikes.
Disposition: Returned to finder.

A ROGERSON

---

153. Vindolanda, Northumberland: silver ingot (PAS: NCL-62C367; Treasure: 2007 T111)

Date: Roman/Early Medieval (c. AD 400–c. 500).
Discovery: Found by the Vindolanda Trust during controlled archaeological excavation in July 2005, and later realised through conservation work to be precious metal, and subsequently reported as Treasure.
Description: Silver ingot, complete. Length: 92mm. Weight: 60g.
Discussion: The ingot was discovered on the western rampart mound, near to a small stone-built cooking oven which may have been used to melt down defunct Roman coinage to produce the ingot. This practice was not unknown in the 5th century as Roman coins were worthless as currency apart from their silver content.
Disposition: Disclaimed, to be retained with main site archive at Vindolanda; landowner donated his share.

A BIRLEY

Section editor and further research: Sally Worrell.
Editor: Michael Lewis.

This has been an interesting year with some important discoveries alongside the steady, ongoing, increase in knowledge that has been a feature of the PAS recording of Early Medieval finds, and also those reported Treasure. The most significant discovery must be the Viking hoard from the Vale of York (217). Coins allowed this hoard to be dated to c. 928 and it was mostly found within a remarkable Carolingian silver-gilt bowl. Other finds of Carolingian metalwork like the strap-end from North East Suffolk (186) and the Frankish sword scabbard chape from Greywell, Hampshire (155), allow British finds to be seen in their European context.

While many of the finds were located by metal-detector users some important groups of material were recovered during archaeological excavations carried out prior to development. These included grave assemblages from Ely, Cambridgeshire (185) and Streethouse area, Redcar and Cleveland, grave assemblage (184). Other important cemetery finds have been recorded by detectorists as at West Wight, Isle of Wight (158), where 105 objects were recovered from dispersed Anglo-Saxon graves. In both cases the material was rescued from destruction.

A type of object that is becoming more common is copper-alloy dies for making *Pressblech* mounts represented by the example from Carisbrooke, Isle of Wight (175). These objects were previously rare but it now appears that they, and the foil mounts made off them, must have been more common than suspected. Various forms of gold pendant are being regularly reported, as are sword pyramids, all of which are filling out our knowledge of 7th-century England.

It is interesting to be seeing finds of Early Medieval Celtic material from England, such as the silver hand pin-head from Chilton Trinity, Somerset (167), and the hanging bowl mount from Binbrook, Lincolnshire (173). Not all of the Celtic metalwork is British; objects such as the enamelled hanging-bowl escutcheon from Broughton, Hampshire (182), and the copper-alloy mount from Whitchurch area, Shropshire (195), are likely to have originated in Ireland and were probably imported by the Vikings.

Viking activity is being traced by Treasure finds with hack-silver becoming increasingly informative, for instance the brooch fragment from Snape with Thorpe, North Yorkshire (208), and the silver ingot fragment from Roxby cum Risby, North Lincolnshire (206). On a larger scale the group of hack-gold, hack-silver and other finds from the North Yorkshire area (197) help fill out the record.

Not all of the interesting finds were Treasure, the lead vat from Corby area, Northamptonshire (207), is the first example of this type of object that can be

EARLY MEDIEVAL

internally dated. The lead cruciform brooch from East Yorkshire (162) represents another type of object of which the function, at present, is not understood but, as in other areas, there is a good chance that future finds will help resolve the mystery.

---

154. Newby Wiske, North Yorkshire: copper-alloy brooch (PAS: NCL-030777)

Date: Early Medieval (c. 300–c. 600).
Discovery: Found by Michael Storey while metal-detecting in May 2007, and reported to Rob Collins (North East FLO).
Description: Fowler (1960) Type G penannular brooch, with a ribbed hoop and terminals, decorated to produce a lozenge effect on each face, and a barrel pin. Diameter: 27.4mm. Weight 10.7g.
Discussion: Type G penannular brooches are uncommon finds in northern England, with the main group distributed around the River Severn. These brooches are important as they point to a British survival in Anglo-Saxon England.
Deposition: Returned to finder.

R COLLINS

---

155. Greywell, Hampshire: copper-alloy sword scabbard chape (PAS: SUR-72CF23)

Date: Early Medieval (c. 400–c. 600).
Discovery: Found by Chris Lacey while metal-detecting in 2007, and recorded with David Williams (Surrey FLO).
Description: A cast copper-alloy openwork Frankish scabbard chape of Menghin (1983) Type 3a. The chape is decorated with a stylised human head, either side of which are what look like birds' heads. Dimensions: 35.3 x 24.7 x 9.6mm. Weight: 8.88g.
Discussion: This find was imported, demonstrating links between England and Francia during the 5th or 6th century.
Deposition: Returned to finder.

D WILLIAMS

---

156. North Kesteven, Lincolnshire: copper-alloy supporting arm brooch (PAS: LIN-A5C801)

Date: Early Medieval (c. 425–c. 475).
Discovery: Found by Rob Marshall while metal-detecting in 2007, and recorded by Adam Daubney (Lincolnshire FLO).
Description: An incomplete cast copper-alloy supporting arm brooch of Mahndorf Type (Böhme 1974: 13–14). The brooch's two wings have a semicircular section and each ends in a circular plate, perforated to support the spring mechanism. The foot is slightly splayed and bears long side facets and a transverse moulding. Dimensions: 33 x 18mm. Weight: 7.82g.

Discussion: Supporting arm brooches take their name from the wide head-plate which 'supports' the axis bar and spring. These brooches date to the early to mid 5th century and were derived from Roman prototypes. They are uncommon in England, coming from northern Germany between the mouths of the Elbe and Weser rivers – the traditional homelands of the Saxons. In recent years, however, increasing numbers of these brooches have been recorded from England by the PAS.
Deposition: Returned to finder.

A DAUBNEY

---

157. Ringlemere, Kent: six grave groups (Treasure: 2005 T395; 2006 T390; 2005 T452; 2006 T30; 2006 T31; 2006 T32)

Date: Early Medieval (c. 450–c. 525).
Discovery: Found by Canterbury Archaeological Trust between October and November 2005, during the course of controlled archaeological excavations, and reported to Andrew Richardson (Kent FLO).
Description: With the kind permission of the landowners, the Smith family, the British Museum in conjunction with Canterbury Archaeological Trust carried out a research excavation at Ringlemere for several seasons. In 2004 the remains of an Anglo-Saxon cemetery were discovered, which in 2005 led to the excavation of a number of graves containing objects qualifying as Treasure. These are Graves 34, 36, 39, 40, 41 and 44.
Precious metal objects discovered included a silver-gilt belt buckle, a number of silver brooches, one silver bead, a small Roman silver plaque, several small silver (possible) dress-pins, a small number of silver studs and fittings (of as yet unknown use), and numerous silver slipknot necklace rings onto which glass or amber beads were threaded. Other grave goods found in these graves include copper-alloy dress accessories, glass vessels and large numbers of glass and amber beads.
Discussion: Post-excavation analysis, with a view to eventual publication of the site as well as conservation, is still underway at the British Museum. At present, it seems that all graves date between the second half or late 5th century and the early 6th century but not later (for more information see Corke 2004; Parfitt and Needham 2005; Marzinzik 2006; Needham *et al.* 2006; Marzinzik 2007).
Disposition: The British Museum hopes to acquire.

S MARZINZIK

---

158. West Wight, Isle of Wight (addenda): 110 gold, silver, copper-alloy and non-metal finds from a group of dispersed Anglo-Saxon grave assemblages (PAS: IOW-244C13; Treasure: 2007 T203)

Date: Early Medieval (c. 450–c. 600).
Discovery: Found by Stewart Thompson and other members of the Isle of Wight Metal Detecting Club

while metal-detecting in April 2007, and reported to Frank Basford (Isle of Wight FLO).

Description and Discussion:

1. Gold 6th-century Gallic imitative *solidus* in the name of the Roman emperor Anastasius I (r. 491–518) (but the coin might post-date his rule). Diameter: 21mm. Weight: 4.18g.

Obv: D N ANASTA-SIVS PP AVG (helmeted, diademed, and cuirassed bust, facing, holding spear and shield).

Rev: VICTORA-AAVG (GGAI) (Victory standing, left, holding long cross).

Mintmark: *//CO(MOB) (Grierson and Blackburn 1986: no. 343, pl. 17).

This coin is attributed to the Merovingians, and dates to c. 500–580, but it is possible that the series was issued by the Visigoths or the Burgundians. The coin may have come from the nearby 'warrior' Grave 69 (for the finds from the grave, see *TAR* 2004: no. 88 K & vii). This was a Continental elite burial rite which rarely occurs in England and would be in keeping with the possible Frankish origin of the occupant of the grave.

2. Silver fragment of the bow and part of the semicircular head-plate of a miniature brooch; a semicircular collet in the centre of the plate contains a tiny fragment of red glass or garnet. This type of brooch occurs with or without lobes in both Kent and France. Length: 17mm. Weight: 1.52g. Surface analysis: silver content over 95%.

3. Silver fragment of a gilt square-headed brooch consisting of the hollow-backed bow and the upper end of the foot-plate. The bow is indistinctly decorated with panels of close transverse ribbing flanking a median rib and perhaps derives from a Continental imitation of a Scandinavian type. Length: 35mm. Weight: 7.23g. Surface analysis: silver content of over 90%.

4. Fragment of a silver miniature square-headed brooch with punched decoration (this possibly joins *TAR* 2004: no. 88 D). Length: 20mm. Weight: 1.7g

5. Silver fragment from the foot-plate of a (probable) miniature square-headed brooch. Length: 17mm. Weight: 2.42g. Surface analysis: silver content of approximately 95%.

6. Silver fragment of miniature bow brooch with part of a plain, semicircular head-plate, bow with midrib, and top end of an expanding foot-plate remaining. This is probably a 5th- or 6th-century Continental import, but with the foot missing it is difficult to assign it to a particular type. Length: 25mm. Weight: 1.9g. Surface analysis: silver content of approximately 95%.

7. Silver fragment of one end of a sword pommel with traces of gilding and borders of *nielloed* interlocking triangles. There are three elongated tear-shaped slashes on the shoulder. This object is possibly associated with the sword-ring (no. 9). The pommel is an example of Menghin's (1983) Kentish Bifrons-Gilton Type. Length: 26mm. Weight: 4.2g.

8. One end of a silver sword pommel, with two lentoid slashes on the shoulder and traces of gilding. The pommel is an example of Menghin's (1983) Bifrons-Gilton Type, and the double slashes can be compared with swords from Faversham, Dover and Sarre, in Kent (Evison 1967: pl. 8a, figs. 3i, 4b & 10d). Length: 28mm. Weight: 6.2g.

9. Silver ring from the pommel of a ring-sword with gilding in grooves on either side and decorated with two rows of punched interlocking triangles round the edge, possibly associated with pommel fragment (no. 7). Diameter: 15mm. Weight: 3.9g.

10. Silver fragment of bow from a brooch, with midrib and traces of gilding. Length: 18mm. Weight: 2.7g.

11. Silver fragment of one end of the head-plate of a square-headed brooch, with an empty square collet in one corner and remains of zoomorphic decoration (this is a missing fragment of *TAR* 2004: no. 88 A). Length: 25mm. Weight: 4.1g.

12. Silver semicircular head-plate from a miniature bow brooch decorated with a zigzag ridge and a knob at the top. The geometric decoration is typical of the western variant of a southern English type and is similar to a brooch excavated at Chessell Down (Parfitt and Brugmann 1997: 39). Width: 19mm. Weight: 2.4g.

13. Silver terminal from the foot-plate of a small square-headed brooch with traces of *niello* and gilding. It is tongue-shaped with a raised circular frame decorated with punched triangles projecting along the sides. Length: 23mm. Weight: 2.7g.

14. Silver fragment of the head-plate and bow of a miniature square-headed brooch, with a raised border enclosing a quatrefoil scroll and half a circle (this joins to the other half of the head-plate in *TAR* 2004: no. 88 E). Length: 24mm. Weight: 3.1g.

15. Gilded silver bow fragment from a miniature square-headed brooch, with midrib. Length: 13mm. Weight: 1.7g.

16. Silver bow of a square-headed brooch with raised oval panel enclosing a face mask and traces of mercury gilding. Length: 25mm. Weight: 4.57g (uncleaned). Surface analysis: silver content of approximately 90%.

17. Silver fragment, roughly trapezoidal, possibly from the head-plate of a square-headed brooch, with double zigzag border along straight edge. Length: 14mm. Weight: 1.8g.

18. Silver mushroom-shaped knob with milled collar round the base. This is possibly from the head-plate of a 6th-century brooch of Lombardic Type, but there are no other fragments of such a brooch from the cemetery. Height: 14mm. Weight: 4.23g. Surface analysis: silver content of approximately 90%.

19. Silver fragment possibly from the foot-plate of a miniature square-headed brooch with a raised S-scroll to one side of a rib decorated with interlocking punched triangles. Length: 11mm. Weight: 0.8g.

20. Silver fragment from the centre of the foot-plate of a miniature square-headed brooch, with a raised cross motif. Width: 17mm. Weight: 2.1g.

21. Silver fragment of the head-plate and bow of a miniature square-headed brooch decorated with two transverse bars. Length: 14mm. Weight: 1g.

22. Copper-alloy radiate-headed brooch of 'western Hahnheim' Type with stubs of five knobs round the head-plate, a broad bow and lozenge-shaped foot-plate with traces of chip-carved decoration; the terminal and lateral lobes are missing. A 6th-century Frankish import to Anglo-Saxon England; a fragment of a similar brooch was found at the Chessell Down cemetery, Isle of Wight (Koch 1998: map 16, pls. 29.8–31.6). Length: 65mm. Weight: 18.4g.

23. Copper-alloy gilded fragment from the centre of a saucer brooch with remains of a central roundel and indistinct ornament including a barred triangular panel (part of the same brooch as *TAR* 2004: 88 i). Width: 29mm. Weight: 3.5g.

24. Copper-alloy fragment of a small circular brooch decorated with around four concentric beaded ridges; the edges damaged. This may represent a Frankish import related to a pair of brooches with concentric decoration from Rhenen, Netherlands (Böhme 1974: pl. 64, 3–4). Diameter (surviving): 14mm. Weight: 1.5g.

25. Copper-alloy fragment of a circular brooch with central boss and projection on one side; traces of gilding survive. Diameter: 9mm. Weight: 0.9g.

26. Copper-alloy head-plate of a cruciform brooch of Åberg's (1926) Group II or III, with two of three half-round knobs remaining. Width: 37mm. Weight: 17.9g.

27. Copper-alloy fragment of miniature square-headed brooch consisting of the head and the top end of the bow, with traces of gilding and decorated with four vertical bars in a central rectangle. A similar example was found at the Chessell Down cemetery (Arnold 1982: fig. 26, 17). Length: 15mm. Weight: 1.5g.

28. Copper-alloy head-plate and bow of a miniature square-headed brooch with milled frame round a central panel of vertical bars; traces of gilding survive. Length: 23mm. Weight: 5g (uncleaned).

29. Copper-alloy gilded button brooch decorated with a profile human head; its rim is missing. An example of Avent and Evison's (1982) late 5th- to early 6th-century Class L, occurring also at Chessell Down. Diameter: 14mm. Weight: 1.3g.

30. Copper-alloy gilded fragment of a button brooch decorated with a sharply featured human face. An example of Avent and Evison's (1982) Class Ai of the late 5th or early 6th century. Width: 16mm. Weight: 1.1g.

31. Copper-alloy button-type brooch with indistinct raised square possibly with projecting corners enclosing a central boss; its rim missing. Similar to a brooch from Marchélepot, France (Avent and Evison 1982: pl. 18d). Diameter: 17mm. Weight: 3.1g.

32. Copper-alloy button brooch with indistinct design; its rim is missing. Diameter: 18mm. Weight: 2.2g.

33. Copper-alloy D-shaped buckle with a tongue with a basal shield. Width: 30mm. Weight: 17.8g (uncleaned).

34. Copper-alloy buckle with D-shaped loop and club-shaped tongue; the tip is missing. Length: 38mm. Weight: 20.7g.

35. Copper-alloy buckle plate with two fragments of a stout wire loop; probably of Frankish origin. Length: 33mm. Weight: 13g.

36. Copper-alloy tinned club-shaped buckle tongue and hinge-bar. Lengths: 24 & 18mm. Weight: 6.1g. Also found was a possible brooch pin (36a), an empty collet (36b) and one unidentifiable fragment (36c).

37. Copper-alloy fragment of a buckle tongue with a basal square with a circular setting; comparable with Visigothic buckles, such as those from Majazala, Spain, and France (Zeiss 1934: pl. 9,1). Length: 23mm. Weight: 6g.

38–41. Four copper-alloy club-shaped buckle tongues; one is gilded and bears a median ridge, and one with a hooked tip. Lengths: 23–32mm. Weights: 2.6g, 3g, 3.5g & 5.5g.

42–50. Nine copper-alloy buckle tongues; eight with a basal shield, one of these with tip missing. Lengths: 24–37mm. Weights: 2g, 4g, 4.6g, 4.9g, 5.8g, 6.4g, 6.7g, 7.4g & 10.4g.

51–53. Three copper-alloy fragments of buckle tongues. Lengths: 18–22mm. Weights: 2.1g, 3.8g & 5g.

54–62. Nine copper-alloy D-shaped buckle loops. Lengths: 20–38mm. Weights: 4.3g, 5.3g, 6g, 6.5g, 6.7g, 8g, 17.4g, 34.4g & 43.7g (uncleaned).

63–69. Seven copper-alloy oval buckle loops. Lengths: 20–44mm. Weights: 4.1g, 5.3g, 6.2g, 7.3g, 10.4g, 14.2g & 15.7g.

70–77. Eight incomplete or fragments of copper-alloy buckle loops. Lengths: 19–28mm. Weights: 1.6–15.4g.

78. Fragment of a copper-alloy strap-end with incised saltire and double lines across wide end. Length: 23mm. Weight: 3.2g.

79. Fragment of a copper-alloy tongue-shaped strap-end with median ridge. Length: 34mm. Weight: 4.1g.

80. Fragment of a copper-alloy tubular strap-mount of D-shaped section, of 5th-century Quoit Brooch Style Type. Length: 33mm. Weight: 12.5g (uncleaned).

81. Copper-alloy heart-shaped belt mount with three dome-headed rivets. Length: 18mm. Weight: 3.4g (uncleaned).

82. Copper-alloy convex ovoid mount with crudely cast details of a bearded man's head. Height: 22mm. Weight: 7.7g.

83. Copper-alloy disc with damaged edges and stub of a rivet on the back; possibly from the boss or handle of a shield. Diameter: 18mm. Weight: 2.8g.

84–88. Five copper-alloy rivets; three disc-headed and two domed. Diameters: 10–26mm. Weights: 2.4g, 2.9g, 2.9g, 3g & 6.5g.

89–90. Two copper-alloy studs; one circular, one sub-triangular. Diameters: 10–22mm. Weights: 0.8g & 1.2g.

91. Copper-alloy ring with a ridge round the girth, incised with radiating grooves on one side and a criss-cross pattern on the other. Diameter: 13mm. Weight: 1.2g.

92–93. Two copper-alloy rings; one ovoid, one with remains of tinning. Diameters: 22 & 29mm. Weights: 3.5g & 9.6g.

94. Copper-alloy bracelet fragment of rod. Length: 34mm. Weight: 2.7g.

95–96. Two copper-alloy joining fragments of strip. Length: 70mm. Weights: 10g (in total).

97. Copper-alloy curved strip with median groove on one side. Length: 63mm. Weight: 6.1g.

98. Copper-alloy sub-rectangular fragment decorated with two transverse beaded lines. Length: 22mm. Weight: 3.7g.

99–100. Two copper-alloy sheet fragments of vessel, one with remains of repoussé decoration possibly representing a bust and possibly late Roman in date with later re-use. Lengths: 21 & 87mm. Weights: 0.7g & 10.2g.

101. Lentoid artefact of sheet copper-alloy with a central oblique slot; perhaps from a knife. Length: 25mm. Weight: 0.79g.

102–104. Three further copper-alloy fragments. Lengths: 15–29mm. Weights: 5g, 5.8g & 7.1g.

105–106. Two fragments of an iron buckle loop, inlaid with keystone-shaped garnets on grid-patterned foils, once possibly joining one another; one is about half the buckle and has the corroded remains of silver cloisons. This is a Frankish import dating to the early 6th century and can be compared with buckles from Caours and Barleux, Somme, France (Bayard *et al.* 1986: figs. 70 & 91). Length of each: 30mm. Weights: 7.4 & 6.8g (uncleaned).

107. Iron shank of nail or pin of uncertain date. Length: 35mm. Weight: 1.8g.

108. Domed lead stud with circular indentations. Diameter: 7mm. Weight: 1.7g.

109–110. Two annular glass beads; one is blue, the other green with white zigzag trail. Diameters: 10 & 16mm. Weights: 0.5g & 3.1g.

Discussion: The majority of the above finds are early Anglo-Saxon, with a few contemporary imports from the Continent. They predominantly date to the 6th century, though one or two objects are possibly of the 5th century (see the original find and first addenda in *TAR* 2004: no. 88; *TAR* 2005/6: no. 221).

Disposition: Acquired by the British Museum.

B M AGER & R ABDY

---

159. Wendover, Buckinghamshire: gilded copper-alloy brooch (PAS: BUC-1FB411)

Date: Early Medieval (c. 470–c. 570).

Discovery: Found by Martin Whaley while metal-detecting in 2007, and recorded by Ros Tyrrell (Buckinghamshire FLO).

Description: Gilt copper-alloy brooch of unusual form. Lozenge-shaped with circular terminal, set slightly lower at each end. The back is flat and bears an integrally cast pierced lug and catch plate. The face of

the lozenge has carved decoration in the form of two concentric lozenges around a central quatrefoil. Traces of gilding survives on the upper surface. Dimensions: 41.7 x 15mm.

Discussion: This brooch is difficult to parallel but is an unusual variant of the Early Anglo-Saxon equal armed brooch.

Disposition: Returned to finder.

R TYRRELL

---

160. Mildenhall, Wiltshire: copper-alloy bowl with an iron handle (PAS: WILT-7E5176)

Date: Early Medieval (c. 475–c. 600).

Discovery: Found by David Phillips while metal-detecting in 2007, and recorded with Katie Hinds (Wiltshire FLO).

Description: Globular sheet copper-alloy bowl with a flat-sectioned, iron handle, attached by way of two triangular lugs on the upper rim. Dimensions: 210 x 115mm, excluding the lugs. Weight: 310.31g.

Discussion: Bruce Eagles (1986: 106 & 117, no. 133) dated such bowls found in England to the late 5th or 6th century, noting 'this type of cauldron belongs to the widely distributed Vestland-Kessel Group, a form which appears to have originated in northern Gaul in the late 4th century and to have been manufactured throughout the 5th'. Examples have been recorded in later burials in Cambridgeshire, Suffolk and Warwickshire. This is probably only the third known in Wiltshire.

Disposition: Returned to landowner.

K HINDS

---

161. Haversham, Buckinghamshire: copper-alloy belt mount (PAS: BUC-215ED8)

Date: Early Medieval (c. 480–c. 570).

Discovery: Found by Ivan Clark while metal-detecting some years ago, and recorded with Ros Tyrrell (Buckinghamshire FLO) in 2007.

Description: Rectangular copper-alloy mount, with fine, chip-carved decoration. At each end is a thin tab with a rivet through it. The decorative panel contains the figure of a crouching animal in Anglo-Saxon Style I; its head is to the right and leaf-like legs or feet can be seen along the lower edge. Dimensions: 37 x 14 x 2mm.

Discussion: This is a lovely example of early Anglo-Saxon zoomorphic decoration. The animal is crisply cut and has been skilfully fitted into the rectangular panel.

Disposition: Returned to finder.

R TYRRELL

162. East Yorkshire: A lead-alloy cruciform brooch (PAS: SWYOR-B40A88)

Date: Early Medieval (c. 500–c. 570).
Discovery: Found by Mark Bell while metal-detecting in 2007, and recorded with Amy Cooper (South & West Yorkshire FLO).
Description: Fragments of a lead-alloy cruciform brooch of 'Florid Style', decorated with devolved zoomorphic motifs. On the back of the brooch are two unperforated, semicircular lugs which, on a copper-alloy brooch, would have been pierced to hold the pin mechanism (as on 165). On the lead brooch these lugs are not pierced showing that it could not have fitted with a pin or attached to clothing. Dimensions: 78.7 x 66.1 x 8.5mm.
Discussion: Lead-alloy cruciform brooches are becoming increasingly common finds and there is some debate over their function. Leahy (2005: 337) describes other discoveries of lead alloy cruciform brooches. It has been suggested that the lead-alloy examples were patterns or models used in the casting process of copper-alloy brooches. The evidence for this is the unfinished pin lugs and catch-plates which make the brooch unusable. However, some examples bear incised decoration which was usually done after casting, and imply an object beyond the stage of a rough model. Lead brooches have been found on what are likely to be cemetery sites, although one is yet to be found in a grave. It is possible that lead brooches had some sort of symbolic use.
Deposition: Returned to finder.

A COOPER

163. Marham, Norfolk: silver brooch fragment (PAS: NMS-1E5E68; Treasure: 2007 T552)

Date: Early Medieval (c. 500–c. 625).
Discovery: Found by Ian Goodger while metal-detecting between July and September 2007, and reported to Erica Darch (Norfolk FLO).
Description: A silver knob, probably from a radiate-headed brooch, its face decorated with a mask consisting of two pairs of eyes in counter relief, and with ribbed eyebrows. In the absence of a rivet hole in the flat end, it is difficult to see how the knob was attached to the head-plate, however knobs of this type are found on some Lombardic brooches, and this could be an unfinished piece. There is a protruding ledge at the back on the flat end of the object and its underside is hollow. Dimensions: 14.5 x 6mm. Weight: 1.99g.
Disposition: Acquired by Norwich Castle Museum.

A ROGERSON

164. Worth, Kent: gold coin pendant (PAS: KENT-C37138; Treasure: 2007 T673)

Date: Early Medieval (c. 500–c. 625).
Discovery: Found by Andy Sales while metal-detecting in October 2007, and reported to Andrew Richardson (Kent FLO).
Description: A gold pendant, incorporating a Visigothic gold tremissis in the name of the Roman emperor Anastasius I of Byzantium (r. 491–518). The workmanship suggests that this is a Visigothic imitation, probably minted in Toulouse or Narbonne, rather than an official Byzantine issue.
Obv: DN ___STASIUSPPAVG, diademed bust right
Rev: VICT____VGOSTORVM____, Winged Victory, facing right, holding wreath
Diameter: 14.5mm. Weight: 1.39g. Die axis 180˚.
Discussion: The coin has been made into a pendant, showing the Victory reverse, probably in England in the 6th or early 7th century, when coin-jewellery of this type was fashionable. It shows two suspension points, which may have been made at the same time. It appears to have a gold suspension loop, but only a small piece now survives; this is plainer than is usual for the period, being a simple flat bar soldered to one side of the coin only, and unattached on the other. Below this are two holes, around which are signs of wear and damage; it is not apparent whether the damage is a result of wear, or caused when the suggested rivets were removed.
Disposition: British Museum hopes to acquire.

G WILLIAMS

165. Treswell, Nottinghamshire: gilt copper-alloy cruciform brooch (PAS: DENO-4EF591)

Date: Early Medieval (c. 575–c. 600).
Discovery: Found by Daniel and Christopher Healey while metal-detecting in November 2007, and recorded with Anja Rohde (Derbyshire & Nottinghamshire FLO).
Description: Cast copper-alloy cruciform brooch in 'Florid Style'. This large brooch was cast in one piece and bears elaborate zoomorphic designs. In addition to the animal art, the face of the brooch was gilded and pieces of sheet silver attached to panels on the ends of its arms, foot-plate and the lappets on either side of the foot. On the back of the brooch are two lugs, perforated to hold the iron pin and spring and a catch-plate to secure the end of the pin. Dimensions: 155.4 x 90.1 x 13.1mm. Weight: 144.1g.
Discussion: The use of gilding and silvering gave this brooch a striking bichrome appearance. While its decoration is complex it is not unique bearing a close resemblance to the brooch from near Bingham, Nottinghamshire (DENO-2AB607).
Deposition: Returned to finder.

A ROHDE

166. North Hertfordshire: silver-gilt pyramidal mount (PAS: BH-460DE6; Treasure: 2007 T25)

Date: Early Medieval (c. 575–c. 600).
Discovery: Found by Luke Denham while metal-detecting in December 2007, and reported to Julian Watters (Hertfordshire & Bedfordshire FLO).
Description: A silver, parcel gilt Anglo-Saxon pyramidal mount, presumably from a sword scabbard. Each side of the pyramid is decorated with two chip-carved standing triangles, with a small hanging one between them. The ridges separating them are decorated with incised lines and the triangles themselves are gilt. A rectangular, deep cell in the apex of the pyramid would have contained a setting, perhaps a garnet. The pyramid is hollow and the original transverse bar for attachment has broken off, leaving only two opposing stumps behind. Dimensions: Base: 13 x 13mm; Height: 10mm. Weight: 2.3g.
Discussion: Sword pyramids are small fittings used in connection with the straps on a sword scabbard. They are now relatively common finds (some 11 having been reported Treasure between 1998 and 2004) and were apparently very prone to loss. The present piece is close in appearance to the recent find from Cambridgeshire (see 169) and to others from Flixton, North Yorkshire (*TAR* 2002: no. 67), which, however, was niello-inlaid and gilt around the lower edge; and Headbourne Worthy, Hanmpshire (*TAR* 2003: no. 116). They are widespread on the Continent, usually made from silver or copper-alloy (Menghin 1983: map 22).
Disposition: North Hertfordshire Museums Service had hoped to acquire but withdrew; returned to finder.

S MARZINZIK

167. Chilton Trinity, Somerset: silver hand pin-head (PAS: SOMDOR-D60932; Treasure: 2007 T109)

Date: Early Medieval (c. 575–c. 625).
Discovery: Found by Tim Phillips while metal-detecting in September 2006, and reported to Naomi Payne (Somerset FLO) in 2007.
Description: Cast head of a silver dress-pin of the form known as a 'hand pin' from their resemblance to a fist with the fingers sticking out horizontally. The missing pin-shaft had a circular section and was offset from the head by a short arm projecting at right angles to the plate. The lower plate has a reserved pattern with three interlocking scrolls each ending in pairs of dotted lobes. The larger motif ends in single lobed terminals in the upper corners of the plate. The dots and background originally held opaque red enamel, some of which remains. Dimensions: 17.4 x 16.1mm. Weight: 5.12g. Surface analysis: silver content of 87–91%.
Discussion: The lobes or 'dodo heads' are a motif of considerable antiquity in Celtic ornament and the use of red enamel is also in the Celtic tradition. This

fragment is an interesting addition to a small group of distinctive post-Roman native dress-pins. It may have been preserved as a decorative trinket or bead strung on a thread.
Disposition: Acquired by Somerset County Museum.

N PAYNE & S YOUNGS

168. Fransham, Norfolk: silver-gilt fragment, probably from a brooch (PAS: NMS-41D482; Treasure: 2007 T674)

Date: Early Medieval (c. 575–c. 625).
Discovery: Found by Vincent Butler while metal-detecting in October 2007, and reported to Erica Darch (Norfolk FLO).
Description: A detached knob with a simple cast animal head motif inlaid with *niello*. The object is hollow-backed and both the straight ends are pierced. Probably from an Anglo-Saxon radiate brooch of Lombardic type (see Ashley *et al.* 1990: fig. 1 no. 3; also Åberg 1923: fig. 89). Dimensions: 10 x 4.5mm. Weight: 1.64g.
Discussion: While only a fragment survives it does provide further evidence of cross-channel links during the Early Medieval period.
Disposition: Norwich Castle Museum hopes to acquire.

E B DARCH

169. Weston Colville, Cambridgeshire: silver-gilt pyramidal mount (PAS: CAMHER-9583E3; Treasure: 2007 T188)

Date: Early Medieval (c. 575–c. 700).
Discovery: Found by Len Eeles while metal-detecting in April 2007, and reported to Philippa Walton (Cambridgeshire FLO).
Description: A parcel gilt Anglo-Saxon pyramidal mount, presumably from a sword scabbard, each side decorated with two chip-carved standing triangles with a small, hanging triangle between them. The ridges separating them bear incised lines and the triangles themselves are gilt. A deep, rectangular cell in the apex of the pyramid would have contained a setting, perhaps a garnet. The pyramid is hollow and has a transverse bar for attachment across the back. Dimensions: 13 x 13 x 7mm.
Discussion: See 166, which provides further discussion and parallels.
Disposition: Ely Museum hopes to acquire.

S MARZINZIK

170. Otford, Kent: silver-gilt zoomorphic pin-head (PAS: KENT-020610; Treasure: 2007 T421)

Date: Early Medieval (c. 575–c. 700).

Discovery: Found by Lesley Burr while metal-detecting in August 2007, and reported to Andrew Richardson (Kent FLO).

Description: A flat, openwork relief-decorated head from a pin. It is parcel gilt, with *niello* inlay and two garnet roundels set back to back. It is damaged, missing about one third, but with part of the pin shaft preserved. The decoration originally consisted of two birds, one now lost, executed in *niello* inlay framed by a fine gold border. The preserved bird has an open beak and seems to hold it above a gilt motif, perhaps a small figure. Between the birds is a garnet roundel enclosed by a plain and a beaded frame. The decoration on the back of the pin is similar to the face. About 7mm of the round, grooved, *nielloed* pin shaft are preserved, which still shows traces of gilding. Length: 22.5mm. Weight: 3.9g. Surface analysis: silver content of approximately 94%, confirming mercury in the gilding, and that the stones were garnets and probably set on foils.

Discussion: The arrangement of the birds can be compared to Frankish garnet-inlaid or gilt bird and bird-headed pins with very similar shafts (for example, Menghin 2007: nos. VII.10.23 & VII.48.31). Kentish examples of bird and bird-headed pins can also be cited, such as a 7th-century example from Wingham, now in the British Museum. An example of a single, late 5th- to 6th-century, bird-headed pin terminal from Nottinghamshire was recorded in 2002 (*TAR* 2002: no. 46). The Otford pin, however, differs from many other finds in that it has decoration on both sides. Also it has two complete antithetic birds, rather than just paired bird heads.

Disposition: Acquired by Maidstone Museum; both landowner and finder donated their share.

S MARZINZIK

171. Diss area, Norfolk silver-gilt pyramidal sword mount (PAS: SF-9242E2; Treasure: 2007 T477)

Date: Early Medieval (c. 575–c. 700).

Discovery: Found while metal-detecting in August 2007, and reported to Faye Minter (Suffolk FLO).

Description: A parcel gilt Anglo-Saxon pyramidal mount, probably from a sword scabbard, each side decorated with a large garnet-inlaid field in what is likely to be a gold frame. The square cell at the apex of the pyramid is also framed by narrow gold wire. No backing foils are visible beneath the garnets. There is a transverse bar across the underside of the object which is slightly higher towards its middle, possibly as a consequence of wear. Dimensions: 13 x 10mm. Weight: 3.2g.

Discussion: See 166, which provides further discussion and parallels.

Disposition: Acquired by Colchester & Ipswich Museums Service.

S MARZINZIK

172. Ramsgate, Kent: gold annular pendant (PAS: KENT-F5A964; Treasure: 2007 T502)

Date: Early Medieval (c. 575–c. 700).

Discovery: Found by James Cooper while metal-detecting in September 2007, and reported to Andrew Richardson (Kent FLO).

Description: A round, Anglo-Saxon gold pendant with damaged attachment loop. The annular pendant is formed by three spiral turns of gold wire fused together; the wire is beaded for most of its length but with some plain sections for contrast. The attachment loop resembles the tubular fittings on bracteates, but is damaged. On one face of the attachment loop is a small, flattened, gold pellet, probably indicating the pendant's front. The loop is more abraded on the other side and there are traces of wear around the edge. Diameter: 13mm. Weight: 2.5g.

Discussion: Round pendants commonly formed part of necklaces in the Anglo-Saxon period, especially in the late 6th to 7th centuries. They were often set with gem stones, but there is no sign of the present object having had a setting and/or backing plate. Slightly larger, and more elaborate pendants, with a cross inscribed into the centre, were found in Grave 28 at Harford Farm, Norfolk (Penn 2000: fig. 93, pl. XVIII), and at several Kentish sites. Such cross-in-circle pendants are also known from Scandinavia and France, where about a dozen examples have been found (Penn 2000: 51; Menghin 2007: nos. V.3.4.3 & V.3.6.2).

Disposition: British Museum originally hoped to acquire but withdrew; returned to finder.

S MARZINZIK

173. Binbrook, Lincolnshire: copper-alloy hanging bowl mount (PAS: NLM-A6E546)

Date: Early Medieval (c. 580–c. 660).

Discovery: Found by Stanley Little while metal-detecting in 2007, and recorded by Lisa Staves (North Lincolnshire FLO).

Description: Complete cast copper-alloy mount from an Anglo-Saxon hanging bowl. The disc is slightly planoconvex, its face silvered and inlaid with champlevé enamel. On its back are traces of what appear to be solder. The decoration is divided by a three-armed, concave-sided device, in the centre of which is an annulet. Each arm has an anchor-shaped terminal made up of a pair of two strand whorls. Between each of the arms is a further whorl, in the centre of which is a claw-like terminal. It is not possible to define the original colour of the enamel but it appears that both red and green were used. Dimensions: 40.2 x 2.9mm. Weight: 27.8g.

Discussion: Three fragments of a copper-alloy sheet hanging bowl were found by the same finder in close proximity to the mount. As is typical of hanging bowl mounts the decoration is, with its spirals, late Celtic in style. Many of these bowls have been found in Lincolnshire and this find represents a useful addition to the corpus.

Disposition: Returned to finder.

L STAVES

---

174. Woodbridge area, Suffolk: silver-gilt sword pommel fragment (PAS: SF-DB2F43; Treasure: 2007 T292)

Date: Early Medieval (c. 600)

Discovery: Found by James Burvill while metal-detecting in April 2007, and reported to Faye Minter (Suffolk FLO).

Description: Part of a sword pommel, silver, parcel gilt. The pommel is decorated with three parallel, gilt ridges framing its lower edge and with two gilt slashes on its side. Remains of gilding are also visible around the two rivet sleeves in which the side of the pommel terminates. Dimensions: 46 x 15mm. Weight: 9.3g.

Discussion: This shape of 'cocked hat' pommel is a good example of Menghin's Type Beckum-Vallstenarum. Fischer (n.d.: Carte 13) categorises pommels of this form as Type Bifrons-Gilton à échancrures and has mapped examples with this typical slashed decoration on the sides. English finds are known from several sites in Kent, while there are further examples from both Germany and France.

Disposition: Acquired by Woodbridge Museum; landowner donated his share.

S MARZINZIK

---

175. Carisbrooke, Isle of Wight: copper-alloy Pressblech die (PAS: IOW-3AB946)

Date: Early Medieval (c. 600–c. 625).

Discovery: Found by Pete Sivell while metal-detecting in 2007, and recorded by Frank Basford (Isle of Wight FLO).

Description: A copper-alloy plate with damaged sides. On its face is a panel decorated in Anglo-Saxon Style II interlace executed in low relief and showing two interlaced serpents, their heads at the broader end of the plate. On each side of the plate is a small, flat roundel. Close to the edge of the wider end are three circular holes, one at the centre and one at each side. Dimensions: 33 x 24.1 x 3.4mm. Weight: 27.28g.

Discussion: The thickness of this find and its distinctly unfinished appearance, suggest that it was probably used in producing gold Pressblech foils of the sort used on the triangular buckle plate from Taplow, Essex (Speake 1980: pl. 7f) and similar objects. The foils, pressed from the die, would then have filigree soldered to the top of the ridges to complete the decoration.

If this die were complete, it would be about the right size for the foil from the Taplow buckle plate, which is about 40mm long.

Disposition: Returned to finder.

F BASFORD

---

176. Mileham, Norfolk: silver-gilt sword pommel cap (PAS: NMS-BE3EB3; Treasure: 2007 T9)

Date: Early Medieval (c. 600–c. 700).

Discovery: Found by Andrew Athow while metal-detecting in October 2006, and reported to Erica Darch (Norfolk FLO).

Description: The pommel cap is hollow with an elliptical plan, and a tapering, ogival, section. There is a perforation in the top for the tang, and a small hole on each of its two faces, one of which is filled with hard grey material. Ribbon-like zoomorphic decoration, in Anglo-Saxon Style II, has been lost through wear from the top and almost all of one face. On the better preserved face, two interlacing beasts, with a head and a tail at both ends, arch over a semicircular border, framing a space around the small hole. On the other face only one small area of decoration survives, consisting of a three-toed foot and a tail. This face bears deep scratch marks suggesting that the decoration has been obliterated. The holes in the two faces lie in roughly circular recesses which may have held decorative inlays. These holes probably contained rivets securing the cap to the organic material of the hilt. However, the cap may have been held by simply expanding the tang with the rivets being only decorative. Dimensions: 23.5 x 11.5mm. Weight: 6.54g.

Discussion: No parallel for the form has been noted, the large majority of contemporary pommel caps being of 'cocked hat' type. The style of animal ornament suggests the above date.

Disposition: Acquired by Norwich Castle Museum.

A ROGERSON

---

177. Frisby and Kirby, Leicestershire: copper-alloy mount (PAS: LEIC-40DB05)

Date: Early Medieval (c. 600–c. 700).

Discovery: Found by Chris Bursnall while metal-detecting in August 2007, and recorded by Wendy Scott (Leicestershire & Rutland FLO).

Description: A mount in the form a horned head, with a raised angular nose (or perhaps nasal guard) flanked by raised circular eyes. The face has a long moustache protruding slightly out at each side; this sits above an open lentoid mouth and a triangular bearded chin. On other mounts of this type the helmet horns terminate in Anglo-Saxon Style II birds' heads, which may have once been present on this object. Dimensions: 35 x 24 x 3mm. Weight: 5.44g.

Discussion: Warriors wearing horned helmets, like this example, are a well known motif in Early Medieval art and appear on objects such as the helmet from Sutton Hoo. However, no Anglo-Saxon or Viking Age horned helmets are known and the mount may represent a god, perhaps Woden.

Disposition: Returned to finder.

W SCOTT

---

178. Tuxford area, Nottinghamshire: silver and glass setting (PAS: DENO-633A60; Treasure: 2007 T78)

Date: Early Medieval (c. 600–c. 700).

Discovery: Found by Clifford Hancock while metal-detecting in October 2006, and reported to Anja Rohde (Derbyshire & Nottinghamshire FLO).

Description: An Anglo-Saxon glass cabochon in a silver setting. The cabochon is made from green, translucent, bubbly glass, with three twisted, opaque, blue-and-white cable trails fused into its slightly pitted surface. The oval silver setting consists of a plain upstanding frame inside of a fine twisted cable border. Approximately half of the back-plate is missing; the remainder is plain and very fragile. There is no obvious means of attachment, but the metal setting shows the remains of a possible tab on one of its rounded ends, perhaps representing an attachment hoop. Dimensions: 17 x 6mm. Weight: 1.8g.

Discussion: This setting is likely to represent an Anglo-Saxon pendant of a type popular in the 7th century. Pendants with a cabochon-cut stones occur in women's graves of the period, and, although often made of garnet with gold mounts, glass with either silver or copper-alloy mounts are also known. These pendants may represent the introduction of a Frankish custom, based on Mediterranean fashions.

Disposition: Acquired by Bassetlaw Museum, Retford.

S MARZINZIK

---

179. Chelmsford area, Essex: gold and garnet *cloisonné* setting (PAS: ESS-458378; Treasure: 2007 T149)

Date: Early Medieval (c. 600–c. 700).

Discovery: Found by Rob Abbott while metal-detecting in March 2007, and reported to Laura McLean (Essex FLO).

Description: A fragment of a *cloisonné* gold setting, still containing some of the original garnets. The setting appears to have been one end of an oval object, but is distorted with the wider end of the oval torn off, severely damaging the object and leaving a jagged edge. Set on an open, horizontal flange are a number of cells, one of them still containing a grid-patterned gold foil which lines the back and sides of the cell. The setting may have been fitted inside another, larger object, as it is not clear how inlays on the outer flange could have held fast. Inside the flange, and above it, there is what appears to be a plain rim, which is actually the back-plate of the object. Onto this back-

plate has been set an oval arrangement of *cloisonné* cells. Four of these still contain garnets and it appears that only two of them are set onto a backing foil. The back shows a raised rim, to which the horizontal flange of the object is fixed. In the middle of the back-plate is a large opening, presumably a rivet hole and a small opening, perhaps also a rivet hole, towards the edge. Dimensions: 21 x 9mm. Weight: 1.06g.

Discussion: Most gold and garnet settings are in the form of round, dome-headed studs, rather than this flat piece. The function of such settings is unknown. They may have come from disc brooches or pendants, but due to the size of the present object, that seems unlikely. The possibility that the mount belonged to a belt buckle of late 5th-century Type cannot entirely be discounted, although too little of the object is preserved to substantiate this suggestion and the potentially mushroom-shaped cell in the centre of the fitting would counter an early dating.

Disposition: Chelmsford Museum hopes to acquire.

S MARZINZIK

---

180. Hatton, Lincolnshire: gold gem-set setting (PAS: LIN-0FB775; Treasure: 2007 T505)

Date: Early Medieval (c. 600–c. 700).

Discovery: Found by Jethro Carpenter while metal-detecting in September 2007, and reported to Duncan Slarke (Staffordshire & West Midlands FLO).

Description: A square jewel, which is damaged on one corner. It is set with a square, dark-coloured cabochon glass gem set within a multiple frame made up of an upstanding plain rim edged by two rows of beaded wire. The whole is mounted on a square base-plate. Its back is plain but has an elongated metal tab running diagonally from the damaged corner to the mid point. There is also a single rivet hole through the back-plate. Dimensions: 11 x 11mm. Weight: 2.36g. Surface analysis: gold and silver content of approximately 61–66% and 30–33% respectively, and confirms the gem as glass.

Discussion: It is not clear what this object is. It may have been a pendant, with an attachment loop on the missing corner. Square Anglo-Saxon pendants with similar settings occur elsewhere, as on the Desborough, Northamptonshire, necklace (Webster and Backhouse 1991: 28). The rivet hole in the base-plate, the slight edge damage in the middle of one side and the warping of the base-plate on the opposite side may suggest that the stud was originally fixed to something and torn off.

Disposition: British Museum hoped to acquire, but withdrew; to be returned to finder/landowner.

S MARZINZIK

181. Newark area, Nottinghamshire: gold and garnet cross-pendant (PAS: DENO-89E427; Treasure: 2007 T594)

Date: Early Medieval (c. 600–c. 700).
Discovery: Found while metal-detecting in September 2007, and reported to Anja Rohde (Derbyshire & Nottinghamshire FLO).
Description: A damaged gold Anglo-Saxon cross-pendant, set with five garnets, one of which is missing. The cross's arms are of almost equal length and have concave ends. Each arm bears a round setting, two containing small cabochon garnets, a third a flat garnet. A fourth, larger stone is crudely mounted at the centre of the cross. The cross's arms are filled with filigree wire, while a grooved gold band runs around the sides of the cross. The back of the object is plain and concave, with a tear in one of the cross angles. There is some slight distortion, as the grooved gold band is torn in one of the cross angles and the attachment loop is missing. Traces of the latter can still be seen on the face and in a triangular attachment on the back of the cross. Dimensions: 28.5 x 4.9mm. Weight: 5.8g. Surface analysis: gold and silver contents of approximately 77–81% and 17–19%, and confirms the stones as garnet.
Discussion: All four garnets are poorly mounted; the settings are squeezed around stones which were too small. The empty setting has a regular, unsquashed frame. This, together with the unsuitable size of the other stones and the presence of a flat, rather than cabochon gem, suggests that the garnets may be replacements or that the goldsmith could not obtain appropriate stones. The low gold content of the object is notable and may be connected to the debasement of Merovingian gold coinage during the 7th century, these coins providing the metal for jewellery.

A number of cross-pendants are known from early Anglo-Saxon contexts and have been found on necklaces, most notably at Desborough, Northamptonshire (Webster and Backhouse 1991: 28). Other prime examples are finds from Ixworth, Suffolk, and Wilton, Norfolk (Webster and Backhouse 1991: nos. 11 & 12). The most closely related are a pendant cross with intact loop, set with filigree and one garnet from Winster Moor, Derbyshire (Campbell 1982: fig. 41), and a possible reliquary cross-pendant with a cross-shaped opening on the back from Newball, Lincolnshire (*TAR* 2005/6: no. 272).
Disposition: Newark Museum hopes to acquire.

S MARZINZIK

182. Broughton, Hampshire: copper-alloy enamelled hanging-bowl escutcheon (PAS: WMID-B145A3)

Date: Early Medieval (c. 600–c. 800).
Discovery: Found by Patrick Dunne while metal-detecting in December 2007, and recorded by Duncan Slarke (Staffordshire & West Midlands FLO).
Description: A hanging bowl escutcheon, with a flat sub-oval body, broken at the base, with an integral hook at its apex. The hook terminates in a head – possibly that of a bird – with recessed eyes and a beak or snout, which is bent downwards to rest on the rim of the bowl; a similar escutcheon was found at St Paul-in-the-Bail, Lincoln (Bruce-Mitford 2005: 191, fig. 202). The face of the escutcheon has recessed cells containing traces of *champleve* red enamel.
Dimensions: 45.1 x 25.8mm. Weight: 15.17g.
Discussion: The function of hanging bowls has been the subject of much discussion. While they often bear Celtic-style decoration, they are commonly found in Anglo-Saxon graves. Their function is also a mystery. Jane Brenan (1991: 134–135) considered that the earliest hanging bowls were made for some practical purpose (or purposes) and it was only during the 7th century that they became associated with wealth and status. Susan Youngs (formerly British Museum, personal communication) commented that while cell work similar to this escutcheon is found on British metalwork of the 7th century, it is a feature of Irish enamelling of the 8th century. Both Youngs and Kevin Leahy (National Finds Adviser) feel that the escutcheon may therefore be from the tail end of British bowl manufacture, or an import from Ireland.
Disposition: Returned to finder.

D SLARKE

183. Llanbedrgoch, Anglesey (addenda): Hack-silver and other finds (PAS: NMGW-9C0D76; Treasure: Wales 07.15)

Date: Early Medieval (c. 850–c. 1000).
Discovery: Found by Archie Gillespie in 2007 during a metal-detecting survey, as part of continuing archaeological project.
Description:
1. Drop of silver waste. Weight: 1.3g.
2. Silver casting waste. Weight: 1.8g.
3. Hack-silver ingot section, cut both ends, with one hesitant cut mark across one end. Weight: 3.3g.
4. Hack-silver ingot section, cut both ends. Weight: 3.5g.
5. Disc, cut in half with perforation; uncertain function. Weight: 1.2g.
Disposition: Acquired by the National Museum of Wales.

M REDKNAP

184. Streethouse area, Redcar and Cleveland (addenda): grave assemblage with a gold pendant (PAS: NCL-A09134; Treasure: 2007 T498)

Date: Early Medieval (c. 630–c. 650).
Discovery: Found by Stephen Sherlock Services Ltd during the archaeological excavation of a site (prior to development), with Iron Age buildings and an Anglo-Saxon cemetery, in August 2007, and reported to Fi Hitchcock (Treasure Registrar).
Description:
Grave no. 70:
1–2. Gold pendant and chain fragment. The pendant is decorated with filigree and garnet inlay. Its central setting is surrounded by a ring of garnet-filled cells from which extend four parabola-shaped settings at the end of each is a circular setting. One of these still contains a garnet, and two small fragments of others were found in the grave fill. The garnets are much smaller than the settings, leaving an empty annular zone around them. This must have contained a material that is now missing. Each of the garnets was set on a small piece of grid-marked gold foil. The area between each circular setting is decorated with two panels of Anglo-Saxon Style II filigree, made up of reeded gold wire. The pendant is divided into four fields by three radial lines of granulated pellets, either side of which is a strip of filigree. At the top of the pendant this is replaced by a narrow trapezoid panel, also filled with granulation. Above this is a sheet-gold suspension loop. The back of the pendant is plain but with a thin L-shaped strip of gold sheet in the area of the loop which probably represents a repair. Diameter: 44mm. Weight: 11g.
3. A small fragment of folded gold wire, which could be part of the chain from which the pendant was suspended or may have been part of a fastening device from a simpler fabric chain.
4. A glass bead wrapped with gold wire.
5. A long gold cylindrical tube used as a bead. Length: 11mm.
6–7. Two blue glass submelon beads; a green barrel-shaped glass bead, and a glass annular bead with a black background and a green cable pattern, broken in antiquity and perhaps worn as an amulet, possibly suspended from the waist.
8. Ironwork in very poor condition, thought to represent part of a chatelaine or ladies' key set.
9. A small sherd of coarse fired pottery.
Discussion: The dress accessories are of a type worn by a woman in the mid-7th century. As no human bones survived on the site it was not possible to verify the sex of the individual in the grave. Objects of this type are rare in north-east England but other burials in the cemetery contained high status items (see *TAR* 2005/6: no. 226 for the previous finds from the site).
Disposition: Kirkleatham Museum hopes to acquire with the main site archive.

S J SHERLOCK & K A LEAHY

185. Ely, Cambridgeshire: grave assemblage including a gold necklace, silver pin and chain and other grave goods (PAS: CAMHER-9C4BA8; Treasure: 2007 T349)

Date: Early Medieval (c. 650–c. 700).
Discovery: Found by the Cambridge Archaeological Unit during excavation (prior to development) of a small Anglo-Saxon inhumation cemetery in December 2006, and reported to Philippa Walton (Cambridgeshire FLO) in 2007.
Description: Objects found with the supine inhumation of a (presumed) female, aged 10–12 years old; the grave was aligned west to east.
1. A necklace comprising a gold pendant in the form of a cross; the original garnet settings from the arms and centre are now missing. Also a gold pendant with a D-shaped cabochon garnet setting. One gold *bulla* pendant. Six silver *bullae*.
2. A silver pin and chain (found laid across the chest).
3. Iron fittings from a wooden box; also identified by a stain in the earth.
4. Two blue-green glass palm cups; both plain and with out-folded rims (once contained in the box).
5. A bone, single-sided comb with slightly curved back, and with a small copper-alloy ring through one end, probably for suspension (once contained in the box).
6. Iron chatelaine, or keys, and knife (both probably once suspended from the belt).
7. An iron fitting with attached chains (found placed above the head).
Discussion: *Bullae* pendants are widespread across England, and usually dated to the second half of the 7th century (Geake 1997: 36). Gold and garnet pendants are also found in many other 7th-century burials. The most elaborate necklace recorded is that from Desborough (Webster and Backhouse 1991: fig. 13). The Ely pendant is odd in that it is missing the fourth arm, suggesting the shape of a 'Tau' cross, but it may have been damaged and the suspension loop a replacement. If this is the case then it takes the shape of a Celtic-style cross, like other more elaborate gold and garnet pendants, such as Ixworth (Webster and Backhouse 1991: fig. 11). An intriguing aspect of this site is the elaborate burial of a young (presumably female) member of the community, among other older female and male individuals in the cemetery which are barely furnished, or are buried unaccompanied.
Silver or copper-alloy pins linked by chains are known from 7th- and 8th-century burials and settlement contexts. At Harford Farm (Penn 2000), linked pins were found in Grave 18, together with a workbox, pendants and coins.
Disposition: To be determined.

C HILLS & S LUCY

186. North East Suffolk: silver strap-end (PAS: SF-1E8422; Treasure: 2007 T245)

Date: Early Medieval (c. 700–c. 800).
Discovery: Found while metal-detecting in April 2007, and reported to Faye Minter (Suffolk FLO).
Description: An incomplete silver strap-end, with half of the attachment end missing. It is rectangular with a raised panel bearing reserved decoration consisting of a highly devolved leaf design of Carolingian origin. The strap-end was attached to the belt by means of separate top-plate secured by four silver rivets. Dimensions: 29.5 x 18mm. Weight: 8.92g.
Discussion: This strap-end is characteristic of Carolingian work and represents a useful addition to the corpus of imported material of middle Anglo-Saxon date.
Disposition: Acquired by the British Museum.

K LEAHY

---

187. Denton with Wootton, Kent: silver hooked-tag (PAS: KENT-C30984; Treasure: 2007 T578)

Date: Early Medieval (c. 700–c. 900).
Discovery: Found by Dale Smith while metal-detecting in October 2007, and reported to Andrew Richardson (Kent FLO).
Description: A hooked-tag with a round head-plate and a rectangular extension to the head-plate, which contains one rivet hole. The front is decorated with tiny, irregular dots arranged in a circle along the edge of the head-plate. Length: 17mm. Diameter: 7.5mm. Weight: 0.44g. Surface analysis: silver content of 92–97%.
Discussion: Hooked-tags are all-purpose fasteners, used to secure small bags or purses and also clothing.
Disposition: Acquired by Canterbury Museum.

S MARZINZIK

---

188. Coberley, Gloucestershire: silver hooked-tag (PAS: BERK-BB9E23; Treasure: 2007 T500)

Date: Early Medieval (c. 700–c. 900).
Discovery: Found by Brian McIntyre while metal-detecting in September 2007, and reported to Charlotte Burril (Berkshire & Oxfordshire FLO).
Description: An Anglo-Saxon hooked-tag of sub-triangular shape, with incised interlace decoration. There is some damage at the left-hand top corner and left side. Two attachment holes are preserved; a third hole is damaged. The back is plain and the short hook preserved, although its tip is blunted. Length: 17mm. Weight: 0.6g.
Discussion: Hooked-tags are all-purpose fasteners, used to secure small bags or purses and also clothing. They occur in various forms from the 7th century onwards, but those with a triangular head-plate seem to become popular only from the 9th century.
Disposition: Corinium Museum hopes to acquire.

S MARZINZIK

---

189. North Tuddenham, Norfolk: silver brooch fragment (PAS: NMS-412F26; Treasure: 2007 T464)

Date: Early Medieval (c. 700–c. 900).
Discovery: Found by Ronald Nelson while metal-detecting in July 2007, and reported to Erica Darch (Norfolk FLO).
Description: Fragment of silver ansate brooch, with a flat terminal in the form of a rectangular panel containing a moulded twelve-petalled flower. The slightly narrowed rectangular sectioned bow is broken across the beginning of its central expansion, probably losing a central decorative rectangle, matching that on the terminal. There is an incomplete narrow catch-plate on reverse of the terminal. Length: 20mm. Weight: 4.28g.
Discussion: This piece is similar to an example in Thörle (2001: taf. 57, 4).
Disposition: Acquired by the British Museum, following withdrawal by Norwich Castle Museum.

E B DARCH

---

190. Long Sutton, Somerset: silver hooked-tag (PAS: SOM-D90C24; Treasure: 2007 T431)

Date: Early Medieval (c. 700–c. 900).
Discovery: Found by Nigel Peters while metal-detecting in May 2007, and reported to Naomi Payne (Somerset FLO).
Description: A late Anglo-Saxon hooked-tag, sub-triangular-to-round head-plate, with two lugs. The back and front are both plain, the hook intact. Length: 16mm. Weight: 0.7g.
Discussion: see 188.
Disposition: Somerset County Museum hopes to acquire.

S MARZINZIK

---

191. Woodbridge area, Suffolk: silver polyhedral pin (PAS: SF-E0A036; Treasure: 2007 T210)

Date: Early Medieval (c. 700–c. 925).
Discovery: Found while metal-detecting in April 2007, and reported to Faye Minter (Suffolk FLO).
Description: An incomplete Anglo-Saxon silver pin, its circular shaft broken in antiquity. The head is polyhedral with 13 faces, the upper face and the four main faces are lozenge-shaped with a raised border. A grid of recessed grooves divides each face into four lozenges and there are traces of *niello* within the arms of the cross. There is a collar where the head joins the shaft. Dimensions: Length: 18.9mm; Head: 7.8 x 8.2mm. Weight: 3.13g.
Discussion: Silver pins with faceted heads are believed to be later Anglo-Saxon. This example is similar to others from Suffolk and most similar to one from Bury St Edmunds area (*TAR* 2004: no. 126), which also has a geometric design in *niello* in the form of a St Andrew's-type cross within each lozenge-shaped face.

Disposition: Acquired by the British Museum.

F MINTER

---

192. Southampton area, Hampshire: silver strap-end (PAS: HAMP-ECE595; Treasure: 2007 T265)

Date: Early Medieval (c. 775–c. 900).
Discovery: Found by Mark Duell while metal-detecting the spoil heap from the construction of a patio in May 2007, and reported to Rob Webley (Hampshire FLO).
Description: A strap-end with four rivet holes; two at one end, the others along the axis of the body, but only one flat-headed silver rivet survives. The face of the strap-end bears incised geometric ornament and curvilinear scrollwork resembling floral fronds along its edges. No trace of inlay remains, but *niello* may have been used. Impressions on the back of the strap-end around the two axial rivet holes suggest that there was a large washer around each of the openings. The tip of the strap-end is worn thin and damaged, as is the top of the strap-end above the left rivet. Length: 42mm. Weight: 3.3g.
Discussion: With its split end, convex sides and geometric patterning this strap-end belongs to Thomas's (2003) Class A, Type 2. The two rivet holes on the strap-end's body are unusual, perhaps a sign that it was reused at some point or that some supplementary decoration had been applied.
Disposition: Disclaimed; returned to finder.

S MARZINZIK

---

193. Urchfont, Wiltshire: copper-alloy mount from a hanging bowl (PAS: WILT-1E76E1)

Date: Early Medieval (c. 775–c. 900).
Discovery: Found by Mike Apps while metal-detecting in 2007, and recorded with Katie Hinds (Wiltshire FLO).
Description: Copper-alloy mount from a hanging bowl in the form of two opposed bearded heads, separated by a length of plain U-shaped bar. The back of the mount is hollow and divided into three boxes by transverse plates at the bases of the heads. The two heads extend back, behind the line of the central bar, to form a gap between them and the side of the vessel. One of the heads has a flat back and would have fitted tightly against the side of the vessel. The other has a recess into which the rim of the vessel could be fitted. There are holes for three rivets. Dimensions: 41.7 x.11.7 x 11.9mm. Weight: 14.11g.
Discussion: Susan Youngs (*personal communication*, formerly British Museum) comments there is a strong similarity between this mount and those from the bowl at Myklebostad, Sogn og Fjordanen, Norway. These mounts feature a single head, but the profile for the reverse is the same. A double-headed detached mount, found near York, is a cruder version of this find. Youngs noted, 'there are two more bowl mounts from Norwegian Viking contexts which also have a head at

each end – Hommersåk, Rogaland, and Løland, Vest Agder. These date to the late 8th or 9th century on the basis of end-use, enamelling and art-historical elements, and show that late hanging-bowls from the Irish series were clearly much liked by the Norwegian Vikings'.
Disposition: Returned to finder.

K HINDS

---

194. Crawley, Hampshire: silver hooked-tag (PAS: SUSS-69F7E8; Treasure: 2007 T281)

Date: Early Medieval (c. 775–c. 1000).
Discovery: Found by Tim Chandler while metal-detecting in April 2007, and reported to Liz Andrews-Wilson (Sussex FLO).
Description: A silver hooked-tag with a circular head and two semi-circular attachment loops. The hook is intact and is linked to the head through a small rectangular plate. The head is decorated with a circle, within which there is a stylised floral motif inlaid with niello. The reverse is undecorated. Dimensions: 24.2 x 17.6mm. Weight: 2.63g.
Discussion: Hooked-tags were an all-purpose fastener used to secure clothing and purses.
Disposition: Acquired by Winchester Museums Service.

L ANDREWS-WILSON

---

195. Whitchurch area, Shropshire: copper-alloy mount (PAS: HESH-E9D295)

Date: Early Medieval (c. 780–c. 920).
Discovery: Found by Peter Williams using a metal-detector in 2007, and reported to Peter Reavill (Herefordshire & Shropshire FLO).
Description: A cast copper-alloy Irish mount with an original diameter of c. 49mm, now broken; only about quarter survives. The face of the mount had chip-carved zoomorphic decoration and glass inserts. This decoration was symmetrical, consisting of a central cross and recessed panels. The arms of the cross are decorated with incised horizontal lines creating a rope-like pattern. At its centre is a large setting forming a boss. On the face of the mount were four recessed panels set between the arms of the cross. The surviving panel has an intricate chip-carved design showing an interlaced animal with open mouth and protruding tongue. On the outer edge of the mount were originally four circular, cup-like settings, probably for glass 'jewels', two of which survive without the jewels. Traces of gilding are present over most of the reserved areas of this object. On the back of the mount is what may be the remains of a single stud. Dimensions: 45.4 x 34.9 x 4mm. Weight: 11.59g.
Discussion: Parallels for this mount have not been found, but both the form of the interlaced animal and the use of (possible) glass settings have led Kevin Leahy (Finds National Adviser) to suggest an Irish origin and a

9th-century date. The mount may have originally been part of a casket or shrine. It is likely that this object was brought from Ireland to Shropshire by the Vikings and, if this is the case, this artefact joins a small but growing collection of finds hinting at Viking activity in the county during the 9th to 10th centuries.

Disposition: Shropshire County Museum Service hopes to acquire.

P REAVILL

196. South Gloucestershire: copper-alloy strap-end (PAS: GLO-922543)

Date: Early Medieval (c. 800–c. 900).

Discovery: Found by Peter Twinn while metal-detecting in 2006, and recorded by Kurt Adams (Gloucestershire & Avon FLO) in 2007.

Description: Sub-rectangular strap-end, gently narrowing towards its forward edge. The strap-end is decorated with the face of an animal with a pointed snout and ears, represented by two crescents separated by a line, but lacking eyes and other facial features. The main decoration consists of a chip-carved knotwork motive with an incised line running down either side. Dimensions: 35 x 8 x 4mm. Weight: 2.42g.

Discussion: Prior to the inception of the PAS no strap-ends of this type had been recorded with Bristol City Museum and Art Galley or South Gloucestershire Sites and Monuments Record. Over the past four years Mr Twinn has donated six of them to the museum. His generosity with these and other finds has more than doubled the museum's collection of Late Anglo-Saxon non-ferrous metalwork, resulting in a collection that has inspired MA students at Bristol University to study this period.

Disposition: Donated to Bristol City Museum and Art Gallery.

K ADAMS

197. North Yorkshire: group of hack-gold, hack-silver and other finds (PAS: YORYM-68FFE3; Treasure: 2007 T186)

Date: Early Medieval (c. 800–c. 900).

Discovery: Found by Geoff Bambrook and partner while metal-detecting in 2007, and reported to Simon Holmes (North & East Yorkshire FLO).

Description: A series of mostly Viking Age or Late Anglo-Saxon finds from a productive site.

1–2. Two hack-gold fragments of round and square-sectioned rods. Lengths: 13mm & 7mm. Weights: 2.49g & 0.86g.

3–5. Three hack-silver fragments of rods of angular section. Lengths: 8mm, 8mm & 11mm. Weights: 0.27g, 0.7g & 1.94g.

6–28. 23 droplets and fragments of silver metalworking debris. Lengths: 4–20mm. Weights: 0.18–3.96g.

29–35. Seven hack-silver fragments, unidentifiable.

Lengths: 5–9mm. Weights: 0.27–1.6g.

36–51. Six hack-silver fragments of ingots; three of which bear testing nicks and one of which has unusually high copper content. Lengths: 5–21mm. Weights: 0.74–11.18g.

52–53. Two hack-silver sheet fragments, joining together and lightly incised with circles on the inner side. These fragments possibly derive from an ornamental disc of a type found in Viking hoards in Sweden, such as that from Assartorp and Ö. Herrestad (Hårdh 1976: pls. 33, 9 & 52: I, 8). Lengths: 14 & 13mm. Weights: 0.5g & 0.35g.

54–57. Four hack-silver fragments, cut from band-shaped arm-rings with punched decoration. Lengths: 11–12mm. Weights: 0.63–1.46g.

58. Silver tongue from a buckle or pin of a brooch. Length: 2mm. Weight: 1.2g.

59–61. Three hack-silver fragments, cut from angular-sectioned arm-rings, all with testing marks. Lengths: 22mm, 24mm & 15mm. Weights: 7.95g, 3.05g & 4.77g.

62. Silver ball-headed pin with collar and broken shaft, comparable with 9th-century bronze examples from Whitby monastery, North Yorkshire. Length: 24mm. Weight: 2.36g.

63. Silver fragment of uncertain date that is dumbbell shaped with pierced ends. Length: 12mm. Weight: 0.74g.

64. Hack-silver fragment, cut from a lozenge-sectioned ring. Width: 5mm. Weight: 0.65g.

65. Hack-silver fragment of cylindrical rod, possibly cut from the shank of a pin. Length: 13mm. Weight: 0.86g.

66. Silver fragment with incised geometric ornament, broken from a spherical object of possibly Late Anglo-Saxon date. Width: 12mm. Weight: 0.78g.

67–69. Three silver droplets, or pinheads. Although not certainly Viking Age, it is likely that they are contemporary with the above finds. Diameters: 8–9mm. Weights: 1.65–2.05g.

70. Silver pinhead, with stub of bronze shank. Diameter: 8mm. Weight: 1.32g.

71. Broken silver pinhead, with stub of iron shank. Diameter: 11mm. Weight: 2.37g.

72. Corroded fragment of a small Late Anglo-Saxon silver finger-ring, with a circular bezel engraved with a back-turned animal in 9th-century Trewhiddle Style. Length: 14mm. Weight: 0.4g.

Discussion: The find comprises 72 individual finds of precious metal from a productive site, rather than a hoard. They derive from the same 9th-century Viking Age or Late Anglo-Saxon period cultural horizon, with the exception of part of a Medieval buckle or brooch (no. 58). James Graham-Campbell has helped in identifying the finds, which, along with other objects from the site, will be published in more detail as part of a collaborative project between the British Museum and the York Archaeological Trust.

Disposition: British Museum hopes to acquire.

B M AGER & G WILLIAMS

198. Willington area, Derbyshire: two silver *nielloed* mounts (PAS: DENO-838F80; Treasure: 2007 T194)

Date: Early Medieval (c. 800–c. 900).

Discovery: Found by Keith Parker while metal-detecting around 1990, and reported to Rachel Atherton (Derbyshire & Nottinghamshire FLO) in 2007.

Description: Two engraved silver mounts with remains of *niello* inlay. One of the mounts is a flat, oval plaque, the other one consists of a silver band forming an oval and cracked at one of the narrow ends of the oval. The band is lacking a portion at this end and further, fine cracks in the metal are visible here and in other places, running perpendicular to the edge. Four rivet holes are visible close to one edge of the band. The cross-section of the band here is slightly wider than that on the other edge. This thinner edge is abraded in a number of places; due to the shiny nature of the abrasions, presumably these are recent. The inside of the band is plain, with accretions in some places near the thinner edge, perhaps traces of solder.

The oval plaque fits rather well over the opening of the band, but as the band is broken it is not now possible to say whether the plaque would have fitted better over one side of the band or the other. The back of the plaque is plain. The middle of the mount is shiny and shows blunt grooves, perhaps tool marks. Around the edge, there are accretions, including apparent traces of solder. Both mount and plaque are decorated with elaborate ornament. Roundels at the four compass points of the mount contain equal-armed crosses and are flanked by backward-looking quadrupeds and intricate knotwork. The ornament is abraded in places and some of the *niello* has fallen out, while where it is still preserved it has sometimes turned to a silvery appearance.

The plaque features an equal-armed cross inscribed into a square with concave sides, which is surrounded by geometric ornament filling a circular field. Antithetically set scrolls frame the circular field at the narrow ends of the oval plaque. Again, some of the niello is missing and the ornament is partly obscured by adhering soil and, in places, possibly by corrosion. One section of the plaque's edge appears to be freshly abraded. Dimensions: Band: 26 x 17mm. Weight: 3.38g. Plate: 22 x 17mm. Weight: 2.4g. Surface analysis: silver content (for both pieces) approximately 95%, and confirmed the identity of the inlay and solder.

Discussion: The band and plaque are likely to have formed part of one object, perhaps decorating a handle of some sort. These mounts compare closely with objects from the Trewhiddle Hoard from Cornwall, dated to c. 868. A very similar mount with a separate (possible) lid was found there and it also relates well to the Willington mounts in size (Webster and Backhouse 1991: no. 246d). The ornament on the present mounts is comparable to the animals on the arcaded mounts as well as a flat silver strip from the hoard (Wilson 1964:

no. 96). Like the latter, the Willington mounts do not feature the beaded ornament or stippled backgrounds often associated with Trewhiddle Style, as featured on other pieces from the eponymous hoard and much of the mid-Saxon metalwork recently discovered. Traditionally, a 9th-century date has been ascribed to Trewhiddle Style metalwork. Given the similarity of the present fittings to the mount from Trewhiddle, there is no reason to assume that this date would not fit for Willington, even if the date range for the Style has recently been extended (Thomas 2006: 156f).

Disposition: As this object was found prior to the Treasure Act 1996, it was considered not to be Treasure Trove and was returned to the finder.

S MARZINZIK

199. Milborne Port, Somerset: silver hooked-tag (PAS: SOM-65C991; Treasure: 2007 T528)

Date: Early Medieval (c. 800–c. 900).

Discovery: Found by Hugh Vincent while metal-detecting in August 2007, and reported to Naomi Payne (Somerset FLO).

Description: A triangular hooked-tag, with two rivet holes on its top edge and intact hook. The object's face bears two simple incised lines running along each of the long sides of the triangle. A deep notch separates the lower edge of the triangle from the hook. The back is plain. Length: 27.5mm. Weight: 2.2g.

Discussion: Hooked-tags are all-purpose fasteners, used to secure small bags or purses and also clothing. They occur in various forms from the late 8th century onwards, but those with triangular head plate seem to become popular only from the 9th century.

Disposition: Somerset County Museum hopes to acquire.

S MARZINZIK

200. Charminster, Dorset: silver hooked-tag (PAS: DOR-36DDA4; Treasure: 2007 T531)

Date: Early Medieval (c. 800–c. 900).

Discovery: Found by Martin Savage while metal-detecting in September 2007, and reported to Claire Pinder (Senior Archaeologist, Dorset County Council).

Description: A solidly made Late Anglo-Saxon double hooked-tag with trapezoid plate, scalloped upper edge, three rivet holes. The front is decorated with a vase containing a flower. Some of the curving leaves and flower stems of the plant are decorated with fine dots and incisions. A dotted and a beaded bar frame the composition on either side. Below are two stylised animal heads that extend into hooks, one of which has lost its tip. The back of the object is plain. Length: 35mm. Weight 4.81g. Surface analysis: silver content of approximately 94%, and no evidence for either gilding or inlay.

Discussion: Hooked-tags are all-purpose fasteners,

they occur in various forms from the late 8th century onwards. The animal heads forming the base of the hooks on this example can be paralleled on a hooked-tag from Hampshire, which is dated to the 10th century on the basis of its Winchester Style ornament (*TAR* 2000: no. 50). The beaded border and finely stippled ornament of the Charminster piece are characteristic of the Trewhiddle Style, which is commonly dated to the 9th century, although the date range for the style has recently been extended (Thomas 2006: 156f). Its larger size, ornament and the presence of two hooks distinguish this object from the majority of hooked-tags.
Disposition: Acquired by the British Museum.

S MARZINZIK

---

201. Weston Colville, Cambridgeshire: silver strap-end fragment (PAS: CAMHER-9B5D02; Treasure: 2007 T536)

Date: Early Medieval (c. 800–c. 900).
Discovery: Found by Len Eeles while metal-detecting in September 2007, and reported to Sarah Poppy (Senior Archaeologist, Cambridgehsire County Council.
Description: Fragment of an Anglo-Saxon strap-end, missing both its tip and the strap attachment. Its convex edges are beaded, and inside a framing line is a long-eared quadruped, apparently running. The back is slightly concave and heavily scratched. Length: 20mm. Weight: 3.01g. Surface analysis: silver content of 91–97%, with no evidence of inlay in the engraved design.
Discussion: The shape, beaded edge and depiction of the animal suggest that this object is a strap-end of Thomas's (2003) Class A, Type 1, characterised by a split end and Trewhiddle Style decoration.
Disposition: Fitzwilliam Museum, Cambridge hopes to acquire.

S MARZINZIK

---

202. West Acre, Norfolk: silver polyhedral pin (Treasure: 2007 T687)

Date: Early Medieval (c. 800–c. 900).
Discovery: Found while metal-detecting in October 2007, and reported to Erica Darch (Norfolk FLO).
Description: An Anglo-Saxon silver pin with a polyhedral head, separated from its bent round-sectioned shank by a collar. The head is inlaid with *niello*. The decorations consist of a saltire within a lozenge on the top side and on two opposing lateral sides, and with a cross within a lozenge on the other two. The smaller faces and the underside are left blank. The shank, bent just below the collar and again above the mid-length, is not hipped and tapers abruptly to a blunt point. Length: 42mm. Head width: 7–7.5mm. Weight: 4.40g.
Discussion: Such pins are common finds but most are made from copper-alloy; examples in silver are rare.

Disposition: Acquired by Norwich Castle Museum.

A ROGERSON

---

203. Brampton Abbotts, Herefordshire: silver hooked-tag (PAS: NMGW-A96F63; Treasure: 2007 T511)

Date: Early Medieval (c. 800–c. 900).
Discovery: Found by Maxine Jones while metal-detecting in June 2007, and reported to Mark Lodwick (Finds Co-ordinator for Wales FLO).
Description: Complete silver hooked-tag with a flat, circular plate and two attachment holes. The plate is decorated with an irregularly shaped blossom with eight petals of varying sizes and shapes, the reverse is plain. Length: 21.4mm. Weight: 0.9g.
Discussion: Hooked-tags are all-purpose fasteners, used to secure small bags or purses and also clothing.
Disposition: Hereford Museum and Art Gallery hopes to acquire.

S MARZINZIK

---

204. Newark area, Nottinghamshire: gold finger-ring (PAS: DENO-9A6C17; Treasure: 2007 T254)

Date: Early Medieval (c. 800–c. 1000).
Discovery: Found by Bill Severn while metal-detecting in April 2007, and reported to Rachel Atherton (Derbyshire & Staffordshire FLO).
Description: A Viking Age ring consisting of a broad, punch-decorated band, tapering sharply at each end to form wire terminals, originally twisted together. On either side of a worn beaded median rib are two rows of interlocking punched triangles with triple pellets in each. Width: 26mm. Weight: 6.1g.
Discussion: Both the form of the ring and the punched decoration are typical of Viking Age jewellery of the 9th to 10th century. Triple-pelleted triangles were used on a Viking silver ring from Moreton Bagot, Warwickshire (*TAR* 2002: no. 53).
Disposition: Newark Museum hopes to acquire.

B M AGER

---

205. North of Colchester, Essex: copper-alloy strap-end (PAS: ESS-D80727)

Date: Early Medieval (c. 800–c. 1000).
Discovery: Found by Andy Angus while metal-detecting in 2007, and reported to Laura McLean (Essex FLO).
Description: Copper-alloy strap-end, its face decorated with a raised design made up of projecting bosses linked by bars and its back covered with incised ringed-dots. The strap-end was originally attached to the belt by a strip of decorated copper-alloy secured by three rivets. Dimensions: 34.9 x 18.6 x 6.7mm. Weights: 18.28g.
Discussion: Gabor Thomas (University of Reading)

commented (*personal communication*) that the decoration on this strap-end recalls features seen on Continental examples, though normally acanthus leaf ornament is also used. This strap-end may therefore be an English copy, or perhaps a product of a workshop located on the fringes of the Carolingian Empire, perhaps somewhere like Domburg on the coast of Frisia.

Disposition: Originally the finder applied for an export licence, but donated the find to Colchester and Ipswich Museum Service after realising its archaeological value.

L MCLEAN

206. Roxby cum Risby, North Lincolnshire: silver ingot fragment (PAS: NLM:683755; Treasure: 2007 T682)

Date: Early Medieval (c. 800–c. 1000).
Discovery: Found by Stanley Little while metal-detecting in November 2007, and reported to Lisa Staves (North Lincolnshire FLO).
Description: One end, obliquely cut, from a cigar-shaped ingot with an ovoid section. Its top is smooth. Its under-surface is slightly pitted and flattened at the cut end. There are around five nicked testing marks along each side. Length: 23mm. Weight: 10.07g.
Discussion: The form is typical of Viking Age ingots found both singly and in hoards, mainly of the late 9th and 10th centuries in Scandinavia and the Netherlands, as well as in the British Isles, such as the hoard from Cuerdale, Lancashire (in the British Museum), deposited around 905. Such ingots could have been cut up for use as bullion in payments or trade transactions.
Disposition: Acquired by North Lincolnshire Museums Service; finder donated his share.

B M AGER

207. Corby area, Northamptonshire: lead vat or tank (PAS: WAW-A4D8D4)

Date: Early Medieval (c. 875–c. 925).
Discovery: Found by Brian Caddy while metal-detecting in 2007, and recorded with Angie Bolton (Warwickshire & Worcestershire FLO).
Description: The lead vessel is two-thirds complete, with the remaining portion in pieces. Its base is oval but incomplete and slightly crumpled. The wall of the vessel was made up of one large sheet of lead, rolled around to form a cylinder; the base was then joined to the sides with a separate fillet. There are locations for iron suspension rings on each side of the vessel. These were secured by sandwiching the fitting between the exterior of the vessel and a plain triangular pad. The exterior of the vat is decorated with eight triangular panels using two designs which alternate, point up and point down. One panel contains two confronted animals, looking down, their mouths open and their tongues pointed outwards. Below them is a quadruped,

perhaps wearing a bridle. A curved band of rope pattern separates this motif from a small panel of what is likely to be zoomorphic interlace depicting a double-headed serpent. At the foot of the panel is an animal's head that closely resembles the terminals seen on Trewhiddle Style strap-ends. The panel is edged with a raised, cabled, band. The second panel is edged with a band bearing opposed chevrons surrounding a standing human figure. He wears a skirted garment and no sign of any head-gear. His right hand is raised, while his left is lowered. Obliquely across his waist is a sword; this has the curved cross-guard characteristic of the later Anglo-Saxon period. Below the figure there is a quadruped (possibly a dog) with a long tail and slender snout, which may be associated with other, incomprehensible elements beneath. The tip of the panel is again decorated with a stylised head in Trewhiddle Style. Dimensions: 404 x 365 x 189mm. Weight: 15kg.
Discussion: There are a number of similar lead vats or tanks known from the Middle Anglo-Saxon period, such as Flixborough, Lincolnshire, Stidriggs, Dumfries, and Westley Waterless, Cambridgeshire. There are three examples from near Garton, Yorkshire (Leahy 2003: 165–166), and also from Riby Crossroads, Lincolnshire (Cowgill 1994: 267–271), Lewes, Sussex, and Nazeing, Essex (Leslie Wesbster, *personal communication*). There are also two from Willingham, Cambridgeshire, and one from Maidstone, Kent (Bartlett 1984).
The purpose of these vats or tanks is not known. Some have been deposited with iron tools within them, as at Flixborough, Stidriggs and Westerley Waterless (Leahy 2003). Other suggestions include holding fluids as a portable font (Bartlett 1984), but Cowgill (1994) commented that the construction of the Riby Crossroads vat was quite poor and would not have been a watertight vessel. This might also be true of the Corby example as the base did not appear to fit very well. The Corby find is the most highly decorated lead vat; on other examples the decoration is restricted to lines or, at most, incised stars. Leslie Webster (*personal communication*) compared the animals on the Corby vat with the animals seen on Mercian sculpture. She also observed that one of the quadrupeds 'has a very distinctive leaf protruding from its mouth, of a kind which appears on late 9th- or early 10th-century sculpture such as at East Stour, Dorset, and Colyton, Devon'.
Disposition: Returned to finder; subsequently sold at Bonhams (1 May 2008, Lot 280).

A BOLTON

208. Snape with Thorpe, North Yorkshire: hack-silver brooch fragment (PAS: YORYM-C89482; Treasure: 2007 T445)

Date: Early Medieval (c. 875–c. 950).
Discovery: Found by Vincent McLaughlin while metal-detecting in August 2007, and reported to Beth Echtenacher (North & East Yorkshire FLO).
Description: An irregular four-sided fragment of cast plate cut from the terminal of a Viking Age bossed penannular brooch with incised decoration, which includes zoomorphic motifs. Length: 20mm. Weight: 4.67g. Surface analysis: silver content of over 90%.
Discussion: Hack-silver is a common feature of hoards of this period and represents the Vikings' bullion economy. This brooch belongs to Johansen's (1973) subgroup A of the Type, which is of Irish origin. A complete example from Ireland is illustrated by Johansen (fig. 35). Scattered finds of these brooches from northern England are a result of Norse contacts with Ireland.
Disposition: Acquired by the British Museum.

B M AGER

209. Maunby, North Yorkshire: triple-coiled gold ring (PAS: NCL-FEC824; Treasure: 2007 T19)

Date: Early Medieval (c. 875–c. 950).
Discovery: Found by Andrew Swan while metal-detecting in January 2006, and reported to Rob Collins (North East FLO).
Description: The ring consists of a triple coil of thick lozenge-section wire, its face and edges decorated with punched back-to-back crescents and small triangles at the tapering ends of the coil. The ends are drawn into thin wires wound around the coil in eight turns at the back of the hoop. Dimensions: 22 x 8mm. Weight: 12.35g. Surface analysis: gold content of 95–98%.
Discussion: The form of the ring is closely comparable with two Viking Age examples, also of gold (in the British Museum), from Saddleworth Moor, Greater Manchester (Acc. no. PE 1915,12-6,1), and Ireland (Acc. no. PE 1849,3-1,27). The form is further paralleled by a distinctive type of coiled silver arm-ring made in Ireland in the late 9th or early 10th centuries and developed from a simpler Viking Age type (Sheehan 1991–2).
Disposition: Acquired by the British Museum following withdrawal by York Museums Trust.

B M AGER

210. Grindale, East Yorkshire: silver finger-ring (PAS: YORYM-8F9D92; Treasure: 2007 T180)

Date: Early Medieval (c. 875–c. 1000).
Discovery: Found by Robert Booth while metal-detecting in February 2007, and reported to Dave Evans (North & East Yorkshire FLA).
Description: A Viking Age ring made from a strip of silver, its outer surface bearing incised decoration consisting of a series of overlapping forked shapes lying on their sides and joined by short vertical grooves to grooved borders above and below. The ground is decorated with corresponding lines of punched dots. Dimensions: 21 x 7mm. Weight: 3.03g. Surface analysis: silver content of approximately 94%.
Discussion: The pattern represents a simple two-dimensional imitation of a pattern of deep undulating grooves that is typical of many Scandinavian Viking arm-rings of thick cast silver, and occurs occasionally on finger-rings too (Graham-Campbell 1980: nos. 227–229 & 237).
Disposition: Acquired by East Riding Museums Service.

B M AGER

211. Ringshall, Suffolk: silver ingot (PAS: SF-E8A3A6; Treasure: 2007 T714)

Date: Early Medieval (c. 875–c. 1000).
Discovery: Found by Jenny Wilding while metal-detecting in November 2007, and reported to Faye Minter (Suffolk FLO).
Description: A cast ingot of sub-rectangular form with rounded terminals. The upper face is rounded and the underside flatter and rough, probably due to casting in an open mould. The ingot appears to have been worked, with tiny hammer marks on the surfaces giving it a faceted appearance. Length: 24.7mm. Weight: 12.64g.
Discussion: Simple cast ingots can be difficult to date; although often found in Viking Age hoards they must also have been used at other times. However as its form is similar to other Viking Age examples, such as Haslingfield, Cambridgeshire, and Aston, Cheshire (*TAR* 2003: nos. 82–83), it is likely to be of Viking Age date. It has been calculated that a Viking ounce (*eyrir*) is equivalent to either around 24g or 26.6 g (opinions vary), and so the Ringshall ingot may have been made to weigh half a Viking ounce.
Disposition: Moyse's Hall Museum, Bury St Edmunds, had hoped to acquire but withdrew; returned to finder.

F MINTER

212. Kirk Deighton area, North Yorkshire: gold finger-ring (PAS: YORYM-32E6E6; Treasure: 2007 T334)

Date: Early Medieval (c. 900–c. 1000).
Discovery: Found while metal-detecting in May 2007, and reported to Beth Echtenacher (North & East Yorkshire FLA).
Description: A damaged and distorted gold finger-ring, with an oval hoop narrowing down to a parallel-sided hoop at both sides. Its bezel carries a damaged central glass cabochon (now dark brown) in a dog-tooth setting surrounded by a fine beaded wire. Around the cabochon, 14 gold pellets are placed inside beaded wire filigree. Originally there was at least one more pellet on one of the shoulders of the ring. The bezel is edged by a gold ribbon, which is now damaged. Its back is plain but scratched.
A central two-stranded braid runs around the hoop and butts onto the cabochon's setting. The braid is edged with strips of gold ribbon with a third ribbon placed on top of the braid. This arrangement is heavily damaged, abraded, and missing in places. Length: 44mm. Width (bezel): 22mm. Width (band): 8mm. Weight: 11.99g. Surface analysis: the cut end of the ring indicates gold and silver contents of approximately 65% and 33% respectively, and confirms the cabochon as glass.
Discussion: This ring belongs to a small group of probably Anglo-Saxon (culturally, not chronologically) rings characterised by the use of filigree and granulation. It resembles a silver and gold ring with lozenge-shaped bezel from Iona, which also has a central glass cabochon inside a dog-tooth setting (Graham-Campbell 1995: pl. 68b) and a considerably more elaborate gold ring from Hitchin, Hertfordshire, with an intaglio set in such a frame (Graham-Campbell 1995: fig. 27). The former has been assigned to the 10th century, while the latter dates to the 9th (Webster 1995: 50); the occurrence of dog-tooth settings on Ottonian brooches supports a 10th-century date. Closely related combinations of granulation and filigree work are also found on Viking jewellery, especially brooches.
Disposition: Acquired by the British Museum.

S MARZINZIK

213. Talgarth, Powys: silver ingot (PAS: NMGW-9C2070; Treasure: Wales 07.17)

Date: Early Medieval (perhaps c. 900–c. 1000).
Discovery: Found by Rodney Holt, while metal-detecting during June 2007 and reported to Mark Lodwick (Finds Co-ordinator, Wales).
Description: A complete finger-shaped metal ingot with rounded ends of silvery-grey appearance, with an irregularly pitted underside. The uneven state of the upper surface is consistent with the ingot having been cast in an open mould. There is no evidence for nicking,

slicing, pecking or bending - interventions sometimes undertaken in antiquity to test purity. Dimensions: 43.45 x 8.1 x 5.3mm. Weight: 10.2g. Surface analysis: approximate metal content of 97% silver and 3% copper.
Discussion: Ingots of this form can be difficult to date with precision. It is likely however, that this ingot is at least 500 years old, and probably older in date. In form the ingot displays features (size, shape, and casting technique) that are consistent with a Viking Age date, as seen in examples from the Viking hoards from Cuerdale, Lancashire (c. 905) and Chester (buried c. 970; Webster 1953). Parallels from Wales include Early Medieval ingots and fragments thereof found during excavations at Llanbedrgoch, Anglesey (dated to the 9th or 10th century), and a silver ingot of similar size found during the 1976 excavations at Dinorben (NMW Acc. No. 93.84H).
The silver content compares to surface analysis of silver rods from the Skaill hoard, Orkney (94.4–98.3%; Graham-Campbell 1995: 78–9). Its weight (10.2g) falls within the lower end of the range for the type, and comparable to that of complete ingots found at Haslingfield, Cambridgeshire (10.62g; *TAR* 2003, no. 82), Eccleston, Cheshire (10.5g; *TAR* 2001, no. 66), Wickham Skeith, Suffolk (10.35g; *TAR* 2001, no. 67) and Over Compton, Dorset (10g; *TAR* 2000, no. 68).
Disposition: Brecknock Museum hopes to acquire.

M REDKNAP

214. Plumpton, East Sussex: copper-alloy *cloisonné* enamelled brooch (PAS: SUSS-577951)

Date: Early Medieval (c. 900–c. 1050).
Discovery: Found by Steve Cole while metal-detecting in 2007, and recorded by Liz Andrews-Wilson (Sussex FLO).
Description: The face is decorated with a floral geometric motif executed in *cloisonné* enamelling, with the inlay applied into interlocking cells formed from metal strips. The enamelling is held in place by a folded-over strip of copper-alloy. Each of the circular projecting lobes would have held a glass setting, none of which survive. Traces of gilding can be seen on the collar around the enamelled face and on the reverse. The reverse is plain but retains the remains of the lug attachment and the catch-plate. Dimensions: 25.1 x 23.5 x 5.3mm. Weight: 4.5g.
Discussion: A number of brooches of this type have been recorded by the PAS. Attractive and skilfully made, they appear to have been produced in England.
Disposition: Returned to finder.

L ANDREWS-WILSON

215. Fylde, Lancashire: copper-alloy sword pommel cap (PAS: LANCUM-FF48A2)

Date: Early Medieval (c. 900–c. 1100).
Discovery: Found by David Hall while metal-detecting in 2007, and recorded by Dot Boughton (Lancashire & Cumbria FLO).
Description: Cast copper-alloy sword pommel cap of a hollow cast lobed type. There are no rivets and the cap was presumably held in place by hammering to expand the tang. However, flat crescent-shaped recesses at the base of each end may have also played a part in securing the cap. Dimensions: 57 x 22.5 x 22.1mm. Weight: 101.81g.
Discussion: Late Anglo-Saxon and Anglo-Scandinavian swords were studied by Petersen (1919). This one is a Petersen L Type VI pommel, a fusion of Anglo-Scandinavian and Anglo-Saxon fashions.
Disposition: Returned to finder.

D BOUGHTON

216. Bridlington area, East Yorkshire: silver finger-ring (PAS: NCL-40E866; Treasure: 2007 T599)

Date: Early Medieval (c. 900–c. 1100).
Discovery: Found by Paul Rennoldson while metal-detecting in October 2007, and reported to Rob Collins (North East FLO).
Description: A silver ring made of two plain rods and two finely twisted wires twisted together, and tapering at the back where they are hammered together. Diameter: 25mm. Weight: 5.87g. Surface analysis: silver content of approximately 98%.
Discussion: The ring is a miniature version of Viking Age gold and silver neck and arm-rings of the 10th to 11th centuries, like those from Skaill, Orkney, and Wipholm, Germany. This type of ring appears to have continued in use somewhat later in Denmark at least (Graham-Campbell 1980: nos. 217 & 221).
Disposition: Acquired by East Riding Museum Service; landowners donated their share.

B M AGER

217. Vale of York, North Yorkshire: silver-gilt cup with a gold arm-ring, five silver arm-rings, 62 further pieces of hack-silver, 617 silver coins and a fragmented lead sheet cover or container (PAS: SWYOR-AECB53; Treasure: 2007 T2)

Date: Early Medieval (deposited in c. 928).
Discovery: Found by Andrew and Dave Whelan while metal-detecting in January 2007, and reported to Amy Cooper (South & West Yorkshire FLO). James Graham-Campbell helped identify the jewellery, and St. John Simpson assisted with the discussion of Sasanian silver vessel forms and decoration.
Description and Discussion (objects found outside the cup are asterisked):

1. Silver-gilt cup of globular form with plain flat base, short, slightly convex neck, and thickened flat rim. The sides are decorated with six roundels enclosing running animals in front of a bush or tree: apparently a stag, a large feline, a doe and a deer, a lion, and a horse. There are collared, foliate sprays in the fields between the roundels and collared vine scrolls run in bands round the neck and base. There are remains of gilding both inside and out, although the extent is obscured by soil. Dimensions: 120 x 92mm. Weight: 380.2g. Surface analysis: silver content of approximately 75–78% and traces of mercury gilding on the outside of the vessel. The cup's closest parallel in both form and design is with the cup from the Halton Moor hoard, Lancashire (in the British Museum). It is certainly from the same workshop, if not made by the same hand, so the two vessels may have formed a pair, or part of a larger set. Although the Halton Moor hoard was deposited c. 1025, the cup from it was produced earlier in a Carolingian workshop in the mid 9th century (Lennartsson 1999: 54–55, 431–619, at 565, n. 54). Both cups are related to a group of six late 8th- to mid 9th-century vessels from the Continent and southern Scandinavia by their form and size, and especially by their design, to the example from Włocławek, Poland. Internal gilding and lids in some cases suggest they were made for liturgical use (Wilson 1960: 147–173, fig. 15a–b; Wamers 1991: 97–152).
The vine motif of the Vale of York cup was most likely intended as the emblem of Christ the True Vine, and the six roundels possibly represent the number of days of the Creation, but the symbolism of the animal motifs is uncertain. It has long been suggested that the Halton Moor designs reflect Oriental influence, possibly through the medium of Byzantine textiles, and there is certainly a striking similarity between the lion and 'tree' roundel and the design of a Sasanian silver dish in the Hermitage Museum (Battiscombe 1956: 419–421, pl. 37, fig. 16). Also, a degree of similarity of form may be observed with broad-bellied Sasanian silver vessels with raised necks (Marschak 1986: figs. 20–21, 57, 59 & 81). The cup from the Vale of York Hoard possibly represents loot from a church or monastery in the northern Frankish Empire, which was often raided by the Vikings during the 9th century, or may have been given as tribute.
2. Gold arm-ring consisting of a narrow strip with tapering ends which have been drawn into wires and twisted round each other. It is decorated with punched V-shapes, each enclosing a small triangle. Diameter (max): 75mm. Weight: 46.7g. Surface analysis: gold content of approximately 94–97%. The form is comparable with certain Insular and Scandinavian Viking arm-rings of the 10th to 11th centuries, such as that from the Cuerdale Hoard, Lancashire, deposited c. 905–910, and Tolstrup, Denmark (Hawkins 1847: 110–130, fig. 22; Skovmand 1942: 49–54, fig. 9). Examples of gold arm-rings found in hoards are rare.

The hoard also contained the following silver objects which include hack-silver, cut-up pieces of jewellery and ingots used as bullion in payments or trade transactions:

3. Penannular arm-ring of thick, circular-section rod. Diameter (max): 74mm. Weight: 98.3g. Surface analysis: silver content of approximately 90%. Similar examples, some with tapering ends, occur in 10th-century Insular and Scandinavian hoards, such as from Ballaquayle, Isle of Man, Skaill, Orkney, and Slemmedal, Norway (Graham-Campbell 1980: cat. 235; Roesdahl and Wilson 1992: cat. 141).

4. Plate fragment cut from the triangular terminal of a bossed penannular brooch, with three bosses surviving and decorated with an interlaced animal motif. Width: 52mm. Weight: 39.4g. The floruit of this mainly Irish type of brooch was the later 9th century, although production continued into the 10th; a similar brooch from Ireland is illustrated by Johansen (1973: 63–124, fig. 35; for production and dating see Graham-Campbell 1975: 33–47).

5. Plate fragment cut from the triangular terminal of a bossed penannular brooch, with one boss surviving enclosed by a ring knot; the back is decorated with part of a double ring and a dotted ribbon. Length: 25mm. Weight: 9g (for the type, see no. 4 above). Surface analysis: silver content of approximately 90%, with no traces of gilding.

6. Half of a plain, hollow, spherical terminal for a ball-type penannular brooch with a knobbed collar. Diameter: 24mm. Weight: 16.5g. Surface analysis: silver content of approximately 90–95%. A brooch with similar terminals comes from a hoard from Skaill, Orkney, which was deposited c. 950; hollow terminals replaced smaller solid forms in the early to mid 10th century (Graham-Campbell 1980: cat. 197; 1987: 231–246).

7. Arm-ring* consisting of a broad penannular band, with square terminals and punched decoration of rows of triple-pelleted rounded triangles and a median double row of square/triangular dots. Dimensions: 113 x 22mm. Weight: 131g. Surface analysis: silver content of approximately 90%. A plain example of the type was found in the Cuerdale Hoard, deposited c. 905–910 (see no. 2).

8. Doubled-back length cut from an arm-ring* of lozenge-sectioned rod with a scrolled, tapered terminal; several testing nicks on the edges (might join no. 21). Length: 144mm. Weight: 11.1g. Scroll-ended arm-rings are common in Scandinavian Viking contexts, such as from Gotland, Sweden (Stenberger 1947: figs. 35, 2–4; 39, 9; and 173, 14–15).

9. Barrel-shaped pendant bead* with filigree wire decoration, linked by a loop-in-loop chain to the pin from a brooch, of which only the hinge attachments for the pin survive. Length: 215mm. Weight: 16.4g.

10. Sheet fragment possibly from a disc brooch, with curved outer edge, punched decoration of triple-pelleted triangles and two hollow bosses. Length: 33mm. Weight: 3g.

11. Upper end of pin from a penannular brooch with broad, plain, looped head. Length: 67mm. Weight: 26.3g.

12. Lower end of brooch pin with long, flattened end bent back on itself and incised with a zigzag pattern; probably from no. 11 above. Length: 72mm. Weight: 15.1g.

13. Coiled-up length of neck-ring* of (possibly) six plaited wires with one long, plain, hook-ended terminal surviving. Length: 103mm. Weight: 113.3g. This was a long-lived Viking Age form, occurring in both Scandinavia and the British Isles; see examples from Ballacamaish, Isle of Man, and the Cuerdale Hoard (Roesdahl and Wilson 1992: cat. 141 & 361; Bjørn 1940, fig. 22; Hawkins 1847: figs. 58–59).

14. Hook-ended terminal of a neck-ring of flattened rectangular section; plain, with testing nicks on edges. Length: 43mm. Weight: 8g.

15–16. Two folded-up lengths of two wires twisted together; from neck- or arm-rings. Length: 92mm and 68mm; Weight: 25g and 28.1g.

17. Curved, L-shaped length of rod with finely twisted appearance, except where plain at one end; from an arm-ring of twisted rod of Permian type of the 9th or early 10th century, found both in the British Isles and Scandinavia, although probably of Russian origin, such as fragments from the Cuerdale Hoard (Graham-Campbell 2006: 73–81). Length: 101mm. Weight: 26.1g.

18. Arm-ring of two wires twisted together and tapering at back. Diameter: 71mm. Weight: 29g. The form is typically Viking, originating in the 9th century, such as from Fyrkat, Denmark (Graham-Campbell 1980: no. 218).

19–20. Two arm-rings of rod, with long tapering ends, probably originally knotted. Widths: 97 & 80mm. Weight: 24.1g & 21g. Complete examples occur in the Cuerdale Hoard (Hawkins 1847: figs. 53–54).

21. Narrow, U-shaped length of lozenge-sectioned rod, probably from an arm-ring, or perhaps from a brooch pin (possibly joins no. 8). Length: 43mm. Weight: 11.9g. Examples of simple knotted arm-rings of lozenge-sectioned rod occur in the Cuerdale Hoard (Hawkins 1847: figs. 48–50).

22–24. Three lengths of wire from neck-rings and arm-rings. Lengths: 30–47mm. Weights: 2.6–3.8g.

25–57. 32 ingots and ingot fragments, mainly of typical cigar shape. Lengths: 9–133mm. Weights: 2.6–233.5g. Silver ingots and ingot fragments often occur in Viking Age hoards in Scandinavia, Ireland and the Netherlands, as well as in Britain, such as in the Cuerdale Hoard.

58–66. Eight lengths of rod of circular and lozenge-shaped sections. Lengths: 9–32mm. Weights: 1.6–11.8g.

67. Length of bar of low triangular section with testing nicks. Length: 34mm. Weight: 6g.

68. Lead fragments of sheet covering or container*. Total weight: 2.15 kg (approx).

69–76. Possible lead scraps from all nine levels in the cup. Total weight: 27g (approx).

The hoard also contains a total of silver 617 coins, dating from the late 9th and early 10th centuries, terminating in the reign of Æthelstan (r. 924/5–939). Summary totals are as follows:

Anglo-Saxon
Alfred the Great (r. 871–899)

London monogram (c. 880)	3
Two-line (c. 880–899)	47
Rex Doro (c. 880–899)	1

Edward the Elder (r. 899–924/5)

Two-line	340
Bust	48
Floral varieties	3
Burh	2
'Rose'	9

Æthelstan (r. 924/5–939)

Two-line	67
Bust	1
'Church', with York signature	22
'Church', moneyer only	14
Rex Totius Britanniae	1
Archbishop Plegmund (890–923)	8

Anglo-Viking

Sihtric I (921–926/7)	2
Sword St Peter (Cross reverse) (c. 921–927)	22
St Martin (c. 925–930)	1
Other Sword (c. 921–927)	1
Danelaw imitation, Edward Two-line	4
Danelaw imitation, Athelstan Church	1
Carolingian	4

Islamic

Nasr b. Ahmad I (r. 864–892)	1
Ismail b. Ahmad I (r. 892–907)	3
Ahmad II b. Ismail (r. 907–914)	4
Nasr II b. Ahamad II (r. 914–943)	2
Nasr b. Ahmad (I or II) (r. 864–892 or r. 914–943)	1
Caliph Al Mu'tamid (r. 870–892)	1
Uncertain Samanid (c. 819–999)	3

Total	617

Typical of Viking mixed hoards of the early 10th century, the Vale of York Hoard contains a mixture of Anglo-Saxon, Anglo-Viking, Islamic and Carolingian coins, together with a range of silver objects from around the Viking world (Graham-Campbell 2001: 212–229). However, the mixture of coins in the hoard permits an unusually close dating for the deposit. The Anglo-Saxon types in the hoard begin with Alfred's London monogram type of c. 880, but ends strongly (17% of the coins) early in the reign of Æthelstan

(r. 924/5–939). This agrees with the fact that all of the dateable Anglo-Viking issues are of types which can be dated to the 920s (Blackburn 2006: 204–226), the majority of which appear to be comparatively freshly struck. The latest coin which is assumed to be of Danelaw type is an imitation of the so-called 'Church' type of Æthelstan, with a blundered inscription, which appears to very freshly struck. The prototype for this is regarded as one of the earliest issues of Æthelstan after his capture of York in 927 (Blunt 1974: 89–92). Together with the Danelaw issues, the different types of Æthelstan provide an approximate terminus ante quem for the deposition of the hoard. The 'Church' type is extremely well represented in the hoard, and the majority of the coins of this type carry a York mint signature, and appear freshly struck. As mentioned above, this type was probably introduced fairly quickly following Æthelstan's capture of Viking Northumbria in 927. This type was apparently followed fairly closely (probably c. 927–928) by the introduction of a type giving Æthelstan the title (in various abbreviated forms) Rex Totius Britanniae, which is normally considerably more common than the 'Church' type (Blunt 1974: 55–57); however, the Rex Totius Britanniae type is represented here by only a single coin. This combination very clearly suggests that the hoard was deposited very shortly after the introduction of the Rex Totius Britanniae type (therefore in c. 928), and this corresponds very closely with the dating suggested by the Danelaw coinage. The Carolingian and Islamic coins are also consistent with this dating.

The Vale of York hoard is the latest in a growing group of Viking hoards dating from the mid to late 920s, including Warton (Carnforth), Lancashire (c. 925), Thurcaston, Leicestershire (c. 925), Goldsborough, North Yorkshire (c. 925), Flusco Pike 2, Cumbria (c. 925), and Bossall/Flaxton, North Yorkshire (c. 927). It is also the largest of these hoards by a distinct margin, although it is considerably smaller than the better-known hoard from Cuerdale, Lancashire (c. 905–910); see Williams (forthcoming) for a fuller discussion of the coins, Ager (forthcoming 2009) for the other objects, and Williams (forthcoming 2009) on the wider significance of the hoard.

Disposition: Acquired jointly by the British Museum and Yorkshire Museums Trust.

G WILLIAMS & B M AGER

---

218. North Hertfordshire: copper-alloy openwork knife chape (PAS: BH-96B701)

Date: Early Medieval or Medieval (c. 950–c. 1100).
Discovery: Found by Dave Mance while metal-detecting in 2007, and recorded by Julian Watters (Hertfordshire & Bedfordshire FLO).
Description: A cast copper-alloy openwork object, probably part of a chape from a dagger sheath. Less than a half of the chape survives; the other part would

probably have been identical and set parallel to it, with a gap separating them. The decoration depicts a quadruped standing left; its facial features are clearly shown, and it appears to wear a pointed hat. A decorative openwork pattern surrounds the central design and there are cross-hatched mouldings and ridges on the vertical outer edge. Dimensions: 31 x 29.1 x 3.2mm. Weight: 7.96g.

Discussion: This chape would appear to be an early example from this distinctive series of artefacts. Later examples (BH-C0EBC5 & -06B7C1) are probably heavily devolved versions of the original design.

Disposition: Returned to finder.

J WATTERS

---

219. Little Laver, Essex: copper-alloy strap-end (PAS: ESS-8CA327)

Date: Early Medieval (c. 1000).

Discovery: Found by John Covill while metal-detecting in October 2005, and recorded by Laura McLean in 2007.

Description: Cast copper-alloy doubled-faced strap-end of Thomas (2004) Class E Type 2, the end of the belt being secured by a small top plate, now missing. The strap-end is decorated with a highly stylised human figure, with its arms outstretched, and flanked by two interlaced beasts. Both faces are worn. Dimensions: 55.4 x 27.1 x 5.9mm. Weight: 24.82g.

Discussion: While based on an earlier central motif, this strap-end appears to combine feature of both Anglo-Saxon and Viking Age art.

Disposition: Returned to finder.

L MCLEAN

---

220. Risby, Suffolk: copper-alloy (possible) upper sword-guard (PAS: SF-1AA037)

Date: Early Medieval (c. 1000–c. 1050).

Discovery: Found by Gary Phillips while metal-detecting in 2007, and recorded by Faye Minter (Suffolk FLO).

Description: Cast copper-alloy object, possibly an upper sword-guard, incomplete with fragments missing from its upper edges. The object is hollow with an open top. There are three rectangular holes through the lower face; these are crude, irregular and appear unfinished. Casting seams also survive on this face, all implying that it was not meant to be seen when the object was in use.

Both sides of the object bear incised decoration showing two beasts' heads in profile. Both face outwards, their snouts being in the narrower terminal ends. Each beast has open jaws and oval-shaped eyes. Behind their heads are curvilinear spiral-like grooves, which could represent ears or bodies; these flank a central vertical motif with a triangular point at its

top. This decoration is in the late Viking Age Ringerike Style, which was current during the time of Cnut (r. 1016–1035) and perhaps continued later in England. Dimensions: 86.9 x 24.5 x 24.1mm. Weight: 63.68g.

Discussion: Helen Geake (National Finds Adviser) suggests that this object is possibly the upper guard of a sword, which fitted beneath the pommel cap. Petersen (1919) sword Types L and Z and their variants offer the best parallels for this example as they appear to have an upper-guard which is curved upwards and is riveted to the pommel (Pierce 2002: 74–83 & 127). However, there is no evidence that these upper-guards were made separately, as this example was, and there is no parallel for the decoration or the form of the holes through its base. This difference perhaps indicates that this object is not a sword fitting at all, but instead some other kind of decorative mount.

Disposition: Returned to finder.

F MINTER

---

221. Ringland, Norfolk: copper-alloy staff terminal (PAS: NMS-F28FF6)

Date: Early Medieval or Medieval (c. 1000–c. 1100).

Discovery: Found by Alex Banrock while metal-detecting, and recorded with Norfolk Museums & Archaeology Service in July 2007, where it was identified by Steven Ashley.

Description: Cast copper-alloy staff or sceptre terminal with a hollow openwork body set on a rectangular socket. One face is decorated with the figure of a lion, its head arched over above his back to grip its tail, which is curled up from between its legs. Cast and engraved decoration picks out the mouth, eye, limbs and paws, emphasising the three prominent curls representing the mane. The other openwork face shows an eagle, with its neck arched up and over, with its open-beaked head resting against the back of its neck. Cast and engraved detail represents the beak, eyes and feathers on the wings and tail. The openwork sides have two S-shaped wyverns with foliate tails. Dimensions: 50 x 66 x 23mm. Weight: 118.59g.

Discussion: A similar openwork terminal decorated with birds flanking a central tree or scrolling foliage and containing lead, described as a sword pommel, is discussed by Thomas Kendrick (1938: 377–381, pl. 74, no. 5) and is dated to the 12th century. Two further examples in the British Museum were also identified as sword pommels (Ward-Perkins 1940: 25, fig. 2, nos. 1–2) but these, and two more recently discovered finds, are now thought to be terminals from cross-staffs or sceptres (Bailey 1994: 171–173). The late 'Winchester Style' or early Romanesque decoration employed on the Ringland terminal has been provisionally ascribed to c. 1050–c. 1060 (Sandy Heslop, *personal communication*).

Disposition: Returned to finder.

S ASHLEY

222. East Kirkby, Lincolnshire: copper-alloy strap-end (PAS: NCL-C53CC3)

Date: Early Medieval (c. 1000–c. 1200).
Discovery: Found by Paul Gibson while metal-detecting in September 2007, and recorded by Rob Collins (North East FLO).
Description: A copper-alloy strap accessory. It has a flat attachment plate with two rivet holes, which is defined from the decorative part by a transverse ridge. This has eight perforations encircling a rough lozenge, and central cross in relief, which avoids a central, sub-square perforation. This motif and the corners of the main plate have punched ring-and-dot decoration. The pointed terminal and its flanking outside corners have raised knops. The reverse is covered with punched ring-and-dot motifs. The object is slightly convex in section lengthways. Dimensions: 49.29 x 23.56 x 5.16. Weight: 15.6g.
Discussion: No parallel has been traced.
Disposition: Returned to finder.

R COLLINS

223. Worfield area, Shropshire: copper-alloy single looped buckle and plate (PAS: HESH-35BB80)

Date: Early Medieval or Medieval (c. 1000–c. 1250).
Discovery: Found by Frank Taylor while metal-detecting in 2007, and recorded by Peter Reavill (FLO Herefordshire & Shropshire).
Description: The buckle frame is roughly D-shaped and decorated with stylised animals' heads. It was perhaps originally tinned. Riveted to it is a folded cast metal buckle-plate decorated with a pattern of interlocking T-shapes, inlayed with niello. Traces of leather survive between its two leaves. The animal heads were cast and each shows two oval ears, and eyes and pellets representing the nostrils. Dimensions: 56.1 x 16.4 x 5mm. Weight: 7.66g.
Discussion: The stylised dog-like terminals are often associated with the Romanesque period; however, the motif is likely to have lasted much longer. David Williams (Surrey FLO) has suggested that the use of niello is common in the 11th century but the repeating interlocked design on the plate is most unusual. In view of the length of its plate, it perhaps functioned as a horse harness link.
Disposition: Returned to finder.

P REAVILL

224. Ware area, Hertfordshire: gilded silver Anglo-Saxon or Scandinavian coin-pendant (PAS: BH-E11856; Treasure: 2007 T287)

Date: Early Medieval or Medieval (c. 1040–c. 1100).
Discovery: Found by Kevin Easton while metal-detecting in May 2007, and reported to Julian Watters (Bedfordshire & Hertfordshire FLO).
Description: The coin used to make this brooch is a silver *miliaresion* of the Byzantine emperor Romanus III (r. 1028–1034), which has been gilded and mounted as a pendant by the addition of a ring, attached via a ribbed suspension loop riveted to the coin. Both the ring and the loop have been gilded. The coin had previously been pierced for suspension leaving a small hole immediately adjacent to the suspension loop. This was drilled prior to the gilding of the coin, as the gilding seals the pierced hole. The coin has been mounted so that the reverse design, showing a standing figure of the Virgin and Child, is vertical. This parallels Anglo-Saxon and Anglo-Norman coin jewellery of the 11th century, which generally show the reverse side with a cross, rather than the royal bust on the obverse.
Discussion: Although Byzantine coins of this period are rare as British finds (and this is, in any case, a comparatively rare coin), coins of this type made their way to Scandinavia in the 1040s, where they influenced the design of coins of the Danish king Sven Estridsen (r. 1047–1074). Given the contacts between England and Scandinavia during this period, the coin (if not the whole pendant) may well have come to England via Scandinavia. The coin itself is cracked and broken, with somewhere between a third and a half of the coin surviving.
Disposition: Acquired by Hertford Museum; the finder donated his share.

G WILLIAMS

225. Tarrant Rushton, Dorset: copper-alloy stirrup terminal (PAS: DOR-665D58)

Date: Early Medieval or Medieval (c. 1050–c. 1100).
Discovery: Found by David Cobb while metal-detecting in 2007, and recorded with Ciorstaidh Hayward-Trevarthen (Dorset FLO).
Description: A cast copper-alloy stirrup terminal with zoomorphic decoration. The terminal would have formed the junction between one side of the stirrup and the tread. It is in the form of a crested animal, with its head on the side of the stirrup and is curled around to look up. The crest at the base is decorated with stylised tendrils and lobes. Within the terminal is corrosion product from the missing iron stirrup. Dimensions: 43.7 x 26.4 x 13.4mm. Weight: 32.45g.
Discussion: This is an unusual find for Dorset but represents the increasing number of late Anglo-Saxon and Anglo-Scandinavian stirrup fragments recorded by the PAS. A similar more decorative example can be seen in Williams (1997: 2, fig. 3).
Disposition: Returned to finder.

C HAYWARD-TREVARTHEN

226. Eye, Suffolk: silver probable pendant
(PAS: SF-3465C7; Treasure: 2007 T653)

Date: Early Medieval (uncertain date).
Discovery: Found by Suffolk County Council
Archaeological Service while conducting systematic
metal-detecting as part of the excavation of an early
Anglo-Saxon site, in advance of development, in
September 2007. Reported to Faye Minter
(Suffolk FLO).
Description: A pendant in the form of an open stylised
hand; incomplete with the suspension loop broken
and the thumb detached. A roughly circular flat sheet
represents the palm from which project four fingers,
cut into a rectangular plate; the detached fragment
represented the thumb. The back of the pendant is flat
and undecorated. Length: 21.6mm. Weight: 0.47g.
Discussion: Other Anglo-Saxon hand-shaped pendants
are known, for example a smaller and less crude
example from Faversham, Kent (MacGregor and Bolick
1993: 164, 25.11).
Disposition: Disclaimed; to remain with the site
archive at Suffolk County Archaeological Store.

F MINTER

Section editor and further research: Kevin Leahy.
Editor: Michael Lewis.

Dress accessories are well represented amongst the objects found in 2008, including ornate buckles from South Gloucestershire (227), Betchworth, Surrey (231), and Ilam, Staffordshire (260), mounts – though possibly not for straps – from Hound, Hampshire (299), and Cerne Abbas, Dorset (311), as well as strap-ends, such as that from Maiden Newton area, Dorset (287). The precise function of a copper-alloy item, probably for dress, from Ogbourne St Andrew, Wiltshire (228), is unknown. Similarly complex to understand is an ornate high-quality buckle frame from Bradfield, Essex (288), which has parts of two common religious mottoes – 'Jesus Nazarenus' and 'Ave Maria...' –erroneously combined. The very small number of silver mounts definitely for straps (which have two 'bars') include two from near Winchester, Hampshire (259 & 273), and strap-ends from Charminster, Dorset (291), and Tower Hamlets, London (315); these objects emphasise the disproportionate rarity of such items in the later Medieval period when it was sought to restrict precious-metal versions of dress accessories to great landowners and the aristocracy, which abroad resulted in more frequent sumptuary laws than the few enacted in England.

Brooches recorded, almost all circular, have a greater spread of copper alloys, silver and gold, and include examples from Wherwell, Hampshire (245) (which has a zoomorphic frame of distinctive type), Crimplesham, Norfolk (258), and Lladdewi, Gower, Swansea (249). Notable this year is one from North Somerset (272) of copper alloy with the added feature of a pendent bird. A silver find from Binbrook, Lincolnshire (279), has an amatory legend, and another (that is gilt) from Dunstable, Bedfordshire (268), is in the uncommon form of a finger-ring, appropriate for a betrothal or wedding gift. Another from Old Kirk Field area, County Durham (278), has the common 'Ave Maria...' together with 'Jesus Nazarenus...' legends. Silver-gilt brooches from Kelvedon, Essex (274), and South Gloucestershire (276) have legends which defy interpretation, presumably magic formulae (see 'fede' rings, below). An elaborate, enamelled copper-alloy brooch from Worksop, Nottinghamshire (305), with the striking motif of a 'family' of genitalia, is a notable new addition to the repertoire – a fertility charm.

A number of finger rings, both in base and precious metals (the majority being of one metal only), but with *niello* or enamel have been recorded from Rampisham, Dorset (240), Long Whatton, Leicestershire (233), Diss area, Suffolk (236), Beverley area, East Yorkshire (237), Port Eynon, Gower, Swansea (232), and Rhoose and Llanfair, both in the Vale of Glamorgan (234 & 238). There are also gem-set versions of the common 'stirrup' form, such as those from Diss area, Suffolk (248), as well as other designs, including that from Beverley area, East Yorkshire (237). A silver one from

MEDIEVAL

Lower Dean, Bedfordshire (250), is inscribed with the name of Christ and one from Finchingfield, Essex (275), has the common alternatives 'IHC' and 'Jesus Nazarenus…' Another, just with relief decoration and apparently unfinished, from Wingfield, Wiltshire (283), is an unusual find. Signets include an example from Langley with Hardley, Norfolk (252), which has a Roman intaglio and a legend identifying it as a secret seal. Another, from Stoughton area, West Sussex (307), has a probable heraldic motif. Mainly from the top end of the market (and comparatively late in date) is a range of relatively heavy, gem-set, iconographic examples, in gold or silver gilt, with ornate designs emphasised by *niello* or enamel. Examples include those from Winwick, Cheshire (290), South Wingfield, Derbyshire (292), Bonby, North Lincolnshire (295), and Diss area, Suffolk (298); one from Lydd, Kent (308) has a legend suggesting it was a new-year gift. There are also some 'fede' rings with the motif of clasped hands, presumably amatory, from Coberley, Gloucestershire (300), Vernhams Dean, Hampshire (322) (with the hands crowned), and two from Brookland, Kent (255 & 280). Similarly ornamented brooches from Kelvedon, Essex (274), and Boxley, Kent (246), have uninterpretable legends (again, presumably magical) – the hands in several cases holding, or originally holding, gems. Inscribed rings include a few with amatory legends, from Thurlaston, Leicestershire (301), Harlaston, Staffordshire (286), and Naburn, Yorkshire (304); the example from Naburn has the back of the bezel open to the skin, allowing the gem it once held to transfer directly the virtue with which it was believed to be endowed. Another, from Dinas Powys, the Vale of Glamorgan (302), has English wording apparently influenced by Welsh pronunciation.

A silver pendant with a green intaglio from Osmington, Dorset (251), like the Naburn ring, has the back of the stone exposed for direct contact with the wearer. This, as well as a finger-ring from Theydon Garnon, Essex (254), has the magical formula against fever, AGLA. Another silver pendant from Great Smeaton, Yorkshire (293), has 'IHC' together with the Marian monogram, and one from Urchfont, Wiltshire (294), is in the form of an ivy leaf. Also mentioned in this report are four silver pendent crucifixes (some abraded from years of wear) from south-east Norfolk (247), Lancaster area, Lancashire (317), Long Marston, North Yorkshire (281), and Pontefract, West Yorkshire (296).
Other finds of interest include a copper-alloy purse bar from Telford area, Shropshire (320), which has the *niello*-inlaid, conventional inscription 'Ave Maria …', and a complete copper-alloy mirror case from Wressle, East Yorkshire (257), which is an unusual find in this state. A lead/tin pilgrim's souvenir badge from Wragby area, Lincolnshire (265), featuring Becket's head in an incomplete frame, is a reminder of the widespread popularity of this Canterbury-based cult. In contrast,

a lead *ampulla* found at Gatcombe area, Isle of Wight (256), is one of several similar pilgrim souvenirs originally from the Holy Land. Further religious brooches include a copper-alloy octagon engraved with the crucifixion from Elmstead, Essex (314), and a roundel for the Montpellier-based cult of St Roche, France, found in Lund, East Yorkshire (313). A remarkable group of at least 30 crude, anonymous *ampullae*, probably from the very end of the Middle Ages, some possibly unfinished, comes from Penllyn, the Vale of Glamorgan (312). In the ecclesiastical realm are enamelled panels from a processional cross from Kingston St Michael, Wiltshire (241), a figure of Christ crucified from Portskewett, Monmouthshire (243), a 14th-century enamelled pyx lid from Arncliffe, North Yorkshire (270), a gold mount engraved with the Trinity from Great Gaddesen, Hertfordshire (316), and another of silver with the Annunciation scene from Barham, Kent (318). Also an elaborate silver-gilt pendant with the scene of Christ's Passion, opening to reveal the figures of John the Baptist, St Catherine and Mary Magdalene, found in Kilgetty, Pembrokeshire (321), is an impressive three-dimensional devotional aid.

An ornate copper-alloy tap housing featuring a man's head from Callow, Derbyshire (253), must have been from an affluent milieu. More humble is a late Medieval rectangular lead container, perhaps for holding ink, from Brill, Buckinghamshire (306). A possible tool handle of copper alloy from Bedford area, Bedfordshire (230), has the attractive form of a stylised animal head. Likewise, an antler gaming piece from the City of London (229) has the enigmatic carved motif of an exotic, bearded head, while a bone chess piece from Beckingham, Lincolnshire (235), is either a king or a queen.

Among the seals found are lead Papal *bullae* of Celestine III (r. 1191–1198) from Rock, Worcestershire (242), and Clement VI (r. 1342–1352) from Tywardreath, Cornwall (284). Matrices of lead/tin, copper alloy and silver feature personal names (one from Leatherhead, Surrey (244), has that of a family recorded at Leatherhead), heraldry (see Nether Wallop, Hampshire (271)) and amatory mottoes (see Leziate, Norfolk (261)), while one found in Sealfield, North Yorkshire (267), depicts the martyrdom of Becket with a prayer for his intercession, complementing the pilgrim souvenir from Wragby area, Lincolnshire (265), also associated with this very popular saint.

Copper-alloy sword pommels from Blore with Swinscoe, Staffordshire (262), and Wetheringsett cum Brockford, Suffolk (269), have (respectively) engraved heraldic devices and fine, grotesque monsters. Silver scabbard chapes are unusual finds, and include examples from Wonston, Hampshire (277), and Walgrove, Northamptonshire (282). Heraldic horse pendants include one apparently with the arms of the earls of Gloucester and Hereford, found in Middleton on Sea area, West Sussex (239), and another from Churton by Aldford, Cheshire (289), which has the unusual heraldic motif of a moth. A copper-alloy harness boss from Bletchingley, Surrey (319), is engraved with initials that are probably those of Henry Stafford, second duke of Buckingham in the late 15th century.

A stylised horse-form copper-alloy object from Ludgvan, Cornwall (266), is the first recognised example in Britain of a distinctive series of what are thought to be weights, perhaps of 14th-century date, which were previously known only in Scandinavia. Also of interest is a sheet-silver representation of an armour-covered arm from Coberley, Gloucestershire (309), presumably from some kind of figurine, though its specific context is enigmatic.

---

227. South Gloucestershire: copper-alloy buckle with integral plate (PAS: GLO-927993)

Date: Medieval (c. 1050–c. 1125).
Discovery: Found by Peter Twinn while metal-detecting in 2007, and recorded by Kurt Adams (Gloucestershire & Avon FLO).
Description: A copper-alloy openwork buckle. One end of this looped object is shaped like a dragon, with its head, which has a narrow snout, arched eyebrow ridge and a small ear, on the outside. The body runs at an angle to the waist and then recurves, forming a loop. There is a row of dots along the neck and body. A wing protrudes on one side and on the other are two legs, between which is a vestigial tail. One leg is gripped in the beast's mouth to form a smaller loop. A central hole at the junction of the two loops is where a pin would have been attached if this were a buckle. On the back is an integral, square-section rivet. Dimensions: 35 x 18mm. Weight: 5.5g.
Discussion: Similar items have been found in excavations from Gotland, Sweden, in the Ringerike and Urnes Styles, which dates them to c. 1050–c. 1125, although none of these has an integral rivet. It is likely that this object represents trade with Scandinavia.
Disposition: Donated to Bristol City Museum and Art Gallery.

K ADAMS

---

228. Ogbourne St Andrew, Wiltshire: copper-alloy probable strap union or junction (PAS: WILT-266B84)

Date: Medieval (c. 1100–c. 1200).
Discovery: Found by Mark Gillett while metal-detecting in 2007, and recorded with Katie Hinds (Wiltshire FLO).
Description: A copper-alloy accessory in the form of two roughly triangular loops, with each end being

recessed to form a narrow strap bar, and linked by a central area with an animal head standing proud. To either side are what could be stylised rectilinear limbs. The lower loop is formed from two animals' bodies, each with one or two longitudinal grooves, turning to end in a pair of opposed heads which hold the narrow bar between their open jaws. The other loop comprises two tendrils curling outwards, then inwards at the top, each ending in a circular knop; between the knops is the second bar. An outer tendril emerges from each side of the central animal head and runs alongside the first before curling outwards to end in a circular knop. On the flat reverse is a central blind hole. Weight: 8.26g.
Discussion: Kevin Leahy (Finds Adviser) comments that the object looks Romanesque, although some of its features are reminiscent of late Viking Age art. The eyes look like those on Urnes Style animals and the tendrils look like Ringerike Style. A similar item, also with a central animal head, has been found in Lincolnshire (LIN-DD4333). The style of the head appears to be related to those on Williams' (1997) Class-B stirrup-strap mounts, which probably date to the 11th century.
Disposition: Returned to finder.

K HINDS

---

229. City of London: bone counter (PAS: LON-02C8B8)

Date: Medieval (c. 1100–c. 1200).
Discovery: Found by Sybil Hunot while searching the Thames foreshore in 2007, and recorded by Kate Sumnall (London FLO).
Description: A Medieval antler gaming piece with a human bust. The antler has been carved to form an irregular disc; the reverse is flat, the front is convex. The front is carved with the linear bust of a bearded figure facing left and wearing a domed headpiece. There are three curving lines radiating from the back of the headgear, presumably ribbons or ties, and a carved line forms a border around the edge of the counter. Diameter: 36.94mm. Thickness: 7.48mm. Weight: 10.99g.
Discussion: A similar gaming piece found in Southwark is illustrated in MacGregor (1985: 130, fig. 71). The Southwark example is carved on both sides with a pattern. Geoff Egan (Finds Adviser) suggests a 12th-century date; the figure is difficult to interpret though. With broad dating to the period of the Crusades, it looks more like some kind of Eastern official or military personage than a mitred, high-ranking member of the English Church.
Disposition: Returned to finder.

K SUMNALL

230. Bedford area, Bedfordshire: copper-alloy possible tool handle (PAS: BH-5DDC06)

Date: Medieval (c. 1100–c. 1200).
Discovery: Found by Peter Salvia while metal-detecting in 2007, and reported to Julian Watters (Hertfordshire & Bedfordshire FLO).
Description: A copper-alloy object, probably a tool handle. The terminal takes the form of the head of a sea monster, with large ears and an open mouth in which is held a small fish. A moulded collar separates the terminal from a curved handle of circular section. Dimensions: 80.4 x 9.5 x 11.45mm. Weight: 21.43g.
Discussion: The suggested dating of this piece is based on the Romanesque style of the animal. Although no exact parallel could be found, similar pieces, often depicting wolves holding human heads, are known.
Disposition: Returned to finder.

J WATTERS

231. Betchworth, Surrey: gilded copper-alloy buckle plate (PAS: SUR-C27225)

Date: Medieval (c. 1100–c. 1200).
Discovery: Found by Nick Green while metal-detecting in 2007, and recorded with David Williams (Surrey FLO).
Description: A high quality gilded buckle-plate, depicting a finely modelled dragon with additional punched decoration on the body. Dimensions: 32.16 x 21.46mm. Weight: 8.78g.
Discussion: The dragon is reminiscent of similar creatures found on Romanesque sculpture, for example those on the lintel at St Bees Priory church, Cumbria, and the tympanum at Southwold Minster, Nottinghamshire. Both have a scaled body and a scrolling tail, although neither tail bifurcates; these both date to c. 1120.
Disposition: Donated to Guildford Museum.

D WILLIAMS

232. Port Eynon, Swansea: silver finger-ring (PAS: NMGW-9D92B2; Treasure: Wales 07.02)

Date: Medieval (c. 1100–c. 1200).
Discovery: Found by Ronald Sanders while metal-detecting in December 2006, and reported to Mark Lodwick (Finds Co-ordinator, Wales) in 2007.
Description: Decorative silver finger-ring with six fields of crudely engraved ornament. A possible interlace motif, radiating lines and four fields with saltire and cross patterns. Now broken and flattened. Width (hoop): tapers at the shoulder from 5.4–4mm. Weight: 2.42g. Surface analysis: approximately 97% silver and 3% copper.
Discussion: Parallels include a ring from the Lark Hill Hoard, Worcester, buried in c. 1173–1174.
Disposition: Acquired by Swansea Museum.

M REDKNAP

233. Long Whatton, Leicestershire: silver finger-ring (PAS: DENO-2C0235; Treasure: 2007 T294)

Date: Medieval (c. 1100–c. 1200).
Discovery: Found by John Wardle while metal-detecting in February 2007, and reported to Anja Rohde (Derbyshire & Nottinghamshire FLO).
Description: A silver finger-ring, now slightly distorted. The ring has three oval bezels, each bearing a cross against a *niello* background. The *niello* is now worn and, in some areas, does not survive. Two of the bezels are cracked on the inside surface. Diameter: 27mm.
Disposition: Leicestershire County Council Heritage Services hopes to acquire.

B NENK

234. Rhoose, Vale of Glamorgan: gold finger-ring (PAS: NMGW-9D9A68; Treasure: Wales 07.19)

Date: Medieval (c. 1100–c.1200).
Discovery: Found by John Pugh while metal-detecting in September 2007, and reported to Mark Lodwick (Finds Co-ordinator, Wales).
Description: Decorative gold ring with a projecting facetted rectangular bezel, set with a small cabochon purple stone, probably rose quartz. Dimensions: (bezel) 10 x 8.7mm; (hoop, now distorted) 13.2 x 20.7mm. Weight: 3.6g. Surface analysis: approximately 92% gold, 7% silver and 1% copper.
Discussion: Similar in form and size to a ring from a grave (perhaps that of Bishop Ranulf Flambard, r. 1099–1128) Chapter House site, Durham Cathedral; also paralleled by three rings from the Lark Hill Hoard, Worcester (c. 1173–1174).
Disposition: Acquired by the National Museum of Wales.

M REDKNAP

235. Beckingham, Lincolnshire: bone chess piece (PAS: LIN-BC6858)

Date: Medieval (c. 1100–c. 1300).
Discovery: Found by Brian Hillier while metal-detecting in 2007, and recorded with Adam Daubney (Lincolnshire FLO).
Description: A gaming piece, which appears to be an early form of king or queen, made from a hollowed out tibia or metapodial. In section it is nearly square with rounded edges. At the (probable) lower end, in the front, are two deeply cut diagonal facets, presumably to represent a throne canopy. At the (probable) top, the natural central cavity is plugged with a flush-fitting, tapering cylindrical bone insert with a globular knop to represent the head. This fits in the other end too, but does not sit flush there.
Discussion: This piece can be compared to a number of published examples like one from Old Sarum, Wiltshire (MacGregor 2001: 15 & 17, fig. 1, no. 1). Others come from South Witham, Lincolnshire and Coventry,

associated with 14th-century pottery; other examples have been dated earlier, to the 12th century.
Disposition: Returned to finder.

A DAUBNEY

---

236. Diss area, Suffolk: gold finger-ring (PAS: SF-89F2D6; Treasure: 2007 T234)

Date: Medieval (c. 1100–c. 1300).
Discovery: Found while metal-detecting in April 2007, and reported to Faye Minter (Suffolk FLO).
Description: The hoop is narrow and D-shaped in section and has an oval bezel with an oval-shaped setting of a dark blue stone, which is perhaps most likely to be a sapphire. The bezel stands proud of the hoop and has moulded shoulders either side of it.
Dimensions: 21.1 x 20.2mm. Weight: 1.80g.
Discussion: A very similar gold finger-ring was found at Kington St Michael, Wiltshire (*TAR* 2003: no. 169).
Disposition: Acquired by Colchester and Ipswich Museum Service.

F MINTER

---

237. Beverley area, East Yorkshire: gold finger-ring (PAS: YORYM-59F421; Treasure: 2007 T561)

Date: Medieval (c. 1100–c. 1300).
Discovery: Found by Keith Scott while metal-detecting in September 2007, and reported to Beth Echtenacher (North & East Yorkshire FLA).
Description: A gold finger-ring with a small green setting, of very delicate design. Either side of the bezel there is a rectangular shoulder collar, both of which are undecorated. At the apex of the pyramidal bezel there is a small oval setting, which holds a small, crudely cut gem stone. The reverse of the bezel is flat but the edges are chamfered. The rectangular-sectioned hoop is bent slightly out of shape, and the bezel has also distorted out of its position. Dimensions: 21.3 x 19.4mm. Weight: 1.25g.
Disposition: Acquired by East Riding Museums Service: landowner donated his share.

L ANDREWS-WILSON

---

238. Llanfair, Vale of Glamorgan: gold finger-ring (PAS: NMGW-9DC905; Treasure: Wales 07.18)

Date: Medieval (c. 1100–c. 1300).
Discovery: Found by Albert Whyman while metal-detecting in July 2007, and reported to Mark Lodwick (Finds Co-ordinator, Wales).
Description: Decorative ring with a projecting oval bezel of floriate form with eleven 'petals', each engraved with a central dot, set with a small cabochon almandine garnet. Small transverse ridges either side of the bezel are engraved with transverse lines. The shoulders are engraved with short lines in a diaper pattern creating lozenges with central dots.

Dimensions: (bezel) 7 x 5.6mm; (hoop, now distorted) 14.6 x 23.7mm. Weight: 2.5g. Surface analysis: approximately 96% gold, 2% silver and 2% copper.
Discussion: The engraved steps either side of the bezel are a feature found on rings dated to the 12th and 13th centuries. One with engraved decoration on the bezel and hoop shoulders from Houghton, West Sussex (*TAR* 2004: no. 169) is attributed to the 12th century.
Disposition: Acquired by the National Museum of Wales.

M REDKNAP

---

239. Middleton on Sea area, West Sussex: copper-alloy heraldic horse harness pendant (PAS: SUSS-78B4F0)

Date: Medieval (c. 1125–c. 1350).
Discovery: Found by Seamus Lavery while metal-detecting in 2007, and recorded with Laura Burnett (Sussex FLO).
Description: A copper-alloy shield-shaped pendant with a suspension loop at the top and enamelled coats of arms on both sides, with tinctures in red enamel and the gold colour of the metal. One face has *or three chevrons gûles* (three red chevrons on a gold background) – the arms of the Earls of Gloucester and Hereford (Ashley 2002: 11, no. 59). The other face has *gûles ten bezants or* (ten gold balls on a red background, arranged four, three, two, one) – the arms of Lord de la Zouch. Dimensions: 42.35 x 26.68 x 28mm. Weight: 10.78g.
Discussion: While many enamelled horse harness pendants have been recorded by the PAS, some double sided, this one is unusual in have different coats of arms on each side. It may relate to Eleanor de Clare, co-heiress to Gilbert de Clare, Earl of Gloucester and Hereford, who married William de la Zouch in 1329.
Disposition: Returned to finder.

L BURNETT

---

240. Rampisham, Dorset: gold finger-ring (PAS: DOR-B88E77; Treasure: 2007 T296)

Date: Medieval (c. 1150–c. 1300).
Discovery: A chance find, reported to Claire Pinder (Senior Archaeologist, Dorset County Council).
Description: A finger-ring consisting of a thin wire band widening at the bezel to accommodate a deep red oval stone, probably a garnet. The shape approximates to that of the stirrup ring, which was widespread in the 13th century. Diameter: 19mm.
Disposition: Disclaimed; returned to finder.

J P ROBINSON

241. Kington St Michael, Wiltshire: gilded copper-alloy enamel panel from a processional cross (PAS: WILT-45FC93)

Date: Medieval (c. 1175–c. 1300).
Discovery: Found by Tim Storer while metal-detecting in 2007, and recorded by Katie Hinds (Wiltshire FLO).
Description: The right-hand arm panel from a cross made in Limoges, France. One corner is bent and a little torn. It depicts a winged bull, facing left, on a dark blue enamel background within a border of gilding; this is flanked by a band of green enamel and a gilded zigzag border along the edge. The bull has reddish body and wings (probably cuprous oxide caused by the gilding process) and has a halo with traces of red and blue enamel. Gilding covers much of the wings and face, as well as the outline of the body. One corner has a lozenge outline, missing its enamel and surrounded by the dark-blue enamel field. The features of the bull and the wings are picked out with light grooves. An area of enamel between the two wings is missing and was presumably a dark blue. There are four rivet holes in line with the central stem of the T. On the reverse between two of the rivet holes is a scratched, downwards-pointing arrow, presumably to align the panel on the crucifix from behind. Dimensions: 53.2 x 36.6 x 1.6mm. Weight: 16.77g.
Discussion: The winged bull represents St Luke, one of the four set on the points of the cross; the lowermost one being placed somewhat up the stem. A similar panel (DOR-C06CB4) was found in 2007 at Frampton, Dorset.
Disposition: Returned to finder.

K HINDS

242. Rock, Worcestershire: lead papal *bulla* of Celestine III (PAS: WAW-29A963)

Date: Medieval (c. 1191–1198).
Discovery: Found by Ivor Wills while metal-detecting in 2007, and recorded by Angie Bolton (Warwickshire & Worcestershire FLO).
Description: The designs of the stamps are the conventional ones for papal *bullae* of the later Medieval period. The obverse depicts the faces of Saints Peter and Paul with a patriarchal cross between them and the legend SPASPE above (an abbreviation for St Paul and St Peter); the reverse has the name of the Pope (Celestine III, r. 1191–1198) with his abbreviated title (Pastor Pastorum) – CELE/STINVS/PP• III – within a beaded border. Dimensions: 39.59 x 36.95 x 6.33mm. Weight: 48.7g
Discussion: Papal *bullae* were originally attached to documents issued by the papacy. This is the first papal *bulla* of Celestine III to be recorded by the PAS, though two others, from Norfolk and Suffolk, are known in England (Tim Pestell, Norfolk Museums Service, *personal communication*).
Disposition: Returned to finder.

A BOLTON

243. Portskewett, Monmouthshire: copper-alloy figurine of Christ (PAS: NMGW-2DDF30)

Date: Medieval (c. 1200–c. 1300).
Discovery: Found by Steven King while metal-detecting in 2007, and recorded by Mark Lodwick (Finds Co-ordinator, Wales).
Description: The figure is almost complete, but lacks both lower arms. The crucified Christ has the head angled to the right. The facial features are eroded but the eyes appear to be closed. The hair is swept back and falls onto the shoulders. The arms are perpendicular to the body, and the shoulders, chest, ribs and abdomen are detailed using incised marks. The loincloth has deep folds at the front and back (moulded by V-shaped grooves) and is secured with a knot, tied on the left hip. It extends below the slightly bent knees. The right foot is on top of the left one, with a perforation positioned above the incised toes. Dimensions: 43.2mm. Weight: 44.7g.
Discussion: The figure can be very closely paralleled with an example excavated over 100km to the west at Carmarthen Greyfriars, Carmarthenshire. That example was found below an early 14th-century floor and has a suggested mid 13th-century date. The figures appear similar enough to be considered as originating from the same workshop, if not the same mould.
Disposition: Returned to finder.

M LODWICK

244. Leatherhead, Surrey: lead seal matrix (PAS: SUR-419757)

Date: Medieval (c. 1200–c. 1300).
Discovery: Found by Kevin Grainger while metal-detecting in 2007, and recorded by David Williams (Surrey FLO).
Description: A circular lead seal, displaying a central octofoil surrounded by the legend 'S'IOHANNPINCHVN' (the seal of John Pinchun). Diameter: 31.55mm. Weight: 18.94g.
Discussion: Medieval lead seals are fairly frequently found but can rarely be related to a historical family. In the case of the surname Pinchun (from which the modern surname Pinsent derives), the Medieval document known as the 1235 Surrey Eyre indicates that a William and a Thomas Pinchun were living in Leatherhead in that year. John is likely to have been from the same family and it is interesting to see that the seal has not travelled far from where the Pinchun family lived.
Disposition: Donated to Guildford Museum.

D WILLIAMS

245. Wherwell, Hampshire: copper-alloy zoomorphic annular brooch (PAS: HAMP-384B46)

Date: Medieval (c. 1200–c. 1300).
Discovery: Found by Martin Hams while metal-detecting before 2007, and recorded with Rob Webley (Hampshire FLO) in 2007.
Description: Part of the frame of a cast copper-alloy annular brooch, originally formed of two dragons or wyverns, survives. The upper surface is finely decorated through punching and engraving. Dimensions: 37.95 x 32.6 x 9mm. Weight: 9.93g.
Discussion: Zoomorphic annular brooches are not common. An example in gold of a similar design, including the openwork quatrefoil, and said to be from Hertfordshire, gives some idea of its original appearance (Alexander and Binski 1987: 483, no. 641). The upper surface of this brooch is finely decorated through punching and engraving.
Disposition: Returned to finder.

R WEBLEY

246. Boxley, Kent: gold oval brooch (PAS: KENT-984E65; Treasure: 2007 T389)

Date: Medieval (c. 1200–c. 1300).
Discovery: Found by John Millin while metal-detecting in August 2007, and reported to Andrew Richardson (Kent FLO).
Description: A miniature brooch, roughly oval in shape, and terminating in two joined hands. It has two facets which carry an enigmatic inscription, punctuated by flowers and colons. Reading clockwise from the pin, the letters are: (on the inner band) 'N V I   V N: I I   M   I N I' and (on the outer band) 'V I I I T   I: I: I - I I   V   L V I (?)I'. The meaning of this is unclear, but may have magical or amuletic significance. The two hands may once have held a pearl, which is customary for brooches of this type (the equivalent of 'fede' rings). Dimensions: 19.97 x 13.1 x 3.99mm. Weight: 0.9g.
Disposition: Disclaimed; returned to finder.

J P ROBINSON

247. South-east Norfolk: silver-gilt pendant cross (PAS: NMS-4180B3; Treasure: 2007 T520)

Date: Medieval (c. 1200–c. 1300).
Discovery: Found by Gerry Casey while metal-detecting in September 2007, and reported to Laura McLean (Essex FLO).
Description: Medieval pendant cross, with a central roundel which is inscribed on the front with the letters 'A G' and on the back 'L A'. Each arm of the cross has a bulbous terminal. 'AGLA' was a popular amuletic charm in the Middle Ages. These letters are derived from the Latin version of the initial letters of the Hebrew words 'Ata gibor le'olam Adonai' (You are mighty forever O Lord), and were believed to be a powerful charm

against fever in the Medieval period. A large suspension loop is soldered to the top terminal. Height: 35mm. Width: 26mm.
Disposition: Acquired by Norwich Castle Museum.

J P ROBINSON

248. Diss area, Suffolk: gold finger-ring (PAS: SF-89B470; Treasure: 2007 T233)

Date: Medieval (c. 1200–c. 1300).
Discovery: Found while metal-detecting in April 2007, and reported to Faye Minter (Suffolk FLO).
Description: A gold finger-ring of stirrup shape. The hoop is D-shaped in section and expands into a bezel with an oval shaped setting of a dark blue stone, which is perhaps most likely to be a sapphire. Dimensions: 24.4 x 21.1mm. Weight: 4.18g.
Discussion: Very similar gold stirrup-shaped finger-rings have been found in Norfolk, from Norwich and Thornham (*TAR* 2004: nos. 180–181). Another from the Littleton area, Hampshire (HAMP-6EC8B4), has a semi-precious stone of irregular shape (Egan and Pritchard 1991: nos. 1608–1609).
Disposition: Acquired by Colchester and Ipswich Museum Service.

F MINTER

249. Llanddewi, Gower, Swansea: silver brooch (PAS: NMGW-9C2734; Treasure: Wales 07.09)

Date: Medieval (c. 1200–c. 1325).
Discovery: Found while metal-detecting in 2006, and reported to Mark Lodwick (Finds Co-ordinator, Wales) in 2007.
Description: Annular brooch, plain and of circular cross-section; the pin has a D-shaped cross-section, with a ridge next to the loop. Diameter: 12.2mm. Weight: 0.9g.
Disposition: Swansea Museum hopes to acquire.

M REDKNAP

250. Lower Dean, Bedfordshire: inscribed silver-gilt finger-ring (PAS: NARC-7742D7; Treasure: 2007 T62)

Date: Medieval (c. 1200–c. 1350).
Discovery: Found by William Huckle while metal-detecting in January 2007, and reported to Steven Ashby (Northamptonshire FLO).
Description: A silver-gilt finger-ring tapering into a pointed bezel, which has been sheared off. The shoulders are decorated with what appear to be two animal heads conjoined at the snout. The back of the ring carries an inscription which reads 'I E S V S C R I S T' (Jesus Christ). Diameter: 19mm.
Disposition: Acquired by Bedford Museum.

J P ROBINSON

251. Osmington, Dorset: silver-gilt pendant with intaglio (PAS: DOR-B80705; Treasure: 2007 T126)

Date: Medieval (c. 1200–c. 1350).

Discovery: Found while metal-detecting in March 2007, and reported to Claire Pinder (Senior Archaeologist, Dorset County Council).

Description: A silver-gilt pendant set with an intaglio of green stone. The mount frames the stone leaving the reverse exposed. The front is inscribed '+: A: +: G: +: L: +: A:'. The reverse of the mount has scalloped edging. Length: 35mm. Width: 17mm.

Discussion: The stone is exposed deliberately to provide contact between it and the skin of the wearer. The stone, along with the inscription (see 247), is likely to have had magical significance.

Disposition: Acquired by the British Museum (Reg. No. 2009, 8002.1).

J P ROBINSON & B NENK

252. Langley with Hardley, Norfolk: silver signet ring (PAS: NMS-1E07E1; Treasure: 2007 T483)

Date: Medieval (c. 1200–c. 1350).

Discovery: Found while metal-detecting in August 2007, and reported to Erica Darch (Norfolk FLO).

Description: An incomplete signet ring, incorporating a late Roman intaglio engraved with the figure of Fides, standing and holding corn ears and a basket of fruit. The bezel is oval in shape and has the following legend around the stone '+ SIGNV- SECRETIC ELA' (The secret sign of Ela). The hoop of the ring is broken, but a fragment remains on the right side, which shows an area of punched decoration within four half-lozenges, creating a criss-cross effect. Dimensions (bezel): 19.5 x 15.5mm. Weight: 4.12g.

Discussion: The ring was used as a counter-seal, probably in financial transactions or to seal closed correspondence. The intaglio is probably from the 2nd century AD.

Disposition: Norwich Castle Museum hopes to acquire.

J P ROBINSON, A ROGERSON & A B MARSDEN

253. Callow, Derbyshire: copper-alloy tap-housing with spout (PAS: DENO-E09322)

Date: Medieval (c. 1200–c. 1400).

Discovery: Found by Peter Needham while metal-detecting in early 2007, and recorded by Anja Rohde (Derbyshire & Nottinghamshire FLO).

Description: The tap spout is fitted into an elaborate housing – a large block cast in the form of a male human head. The spout passes through this housing and emerges from the crown of the head. It curves over and its terminal is moulded to represent the head of a beast, possibly a dog. The curve of the spout is asymmetrically placed in the human-head housing, suggesting that it originally swivelled. This may have

been the means of opening and closing the channel by releasing or blocking the flow of the water. The unit is broken off at the back of the neck of the housing. Dimensions: 87.7 x 33.5 x 34.7mm. Weight: 253.1g.

Discussion: This is a high quality item, probably imported from the Low Countries. It would most likely have come from a high status or religious site, such as the lavatorium of a monastery. A wide range of decorated taps and spouts are known from the High Medieval period, a comparable example being a female-headed 'tap handle' part from Lewes Priory (Dunning 1968).

Deposition: Returned to finder.

A ROHDE & G EGAN

254. Theydon Garnon, Essex: silver finger-ring (PAS: BH-C5AF24; Treasure: 2007 T175)

Date: Medieval (c. 1200–c. 1350).

Discovery: Found by Ruth Cattermole while metal-detecting during 2007, and reported to Julian Watters (Bedfordshire & Hertfordshire FLO).

Description: A Medieval silver finger-ring with a plain hoop of rectangular section. The ring is engraved with the inscription, now worn and difficult to read: '+:A:+:G:L:+:A:'. Diameter: 24mm. Weight: 2.87g.

Discussion: See 247 for the significance of the letters, and *TAR*: 1998–1999, no. 118 for a similar ring with the same inscription.

Disposition: Acquired by Epping Forest District Museum.

B NENK

255. Brookland, Kent: silver-gilt finger-ring (PAS: KENT-299A33; Treasure: 2007 T493)

Date: Medieval (c. 1200–c. 1400).

Discovery: Found by Mick Allen while metal-detecting in August 2007, and reported to Andrew Richardson (Kent FLO).

Description: A silver-gilt finger-ring, the bezel being a quatrilobe engraved with a cross against a hatched ground. The centre of the cross may bear an inscribed letter, but this is unclear. The hoop of the ring is engraved with a series of vertical lines separated by areas of cross-hatching; the back of the hoop bears a crude representation of clasped hands (a 'fede' ring). Diameter: 25mm. Bezel (diameter): 11mm.

Discussion: Fede (Italian, meaning 'faith') rings were a popular love token from the 12th century and the design remains popular today. The joined hands symbolise the faithful love.

Disposition: Canterbury Museum hopes to acquire.

B NENK

256. Gatcombe area, Isle of Wight: pilgrim's lead *ampulla* (PAS: IOW-083774)

Date: Medieval (c. 1200–c. 1500).
Discovery: Found by Jeremy Wilber-Smith while metal-detecting in 2007, and recorded by Frank Basford (Isle of Wight FLO).
Description: A damaged lead *ampulla*, with a distorted, circular body; the neck is incomplete and the mouth is missing. Two suspension lugs, one at either side of the neck, are also missing apart from stubs. The body has particularly thick walls. The edges are bevelled and decorated with raised diagonal hatching. One side has a 'compass-drawn' sexfoil, with the outer points of the petals joined by an arc line in a plain circle. The other side has a fleur-de-lis with the petals and stalk emanating from a central pellet and the stem flares outwards at the base. The area between each side petal and the stem is filled with cross-hatching (less conspicuous on the left side). Dimensions: 54 x 39 x 9.6mm. Weight: 60.92g.
Discussion: This is one of very few pilgrim souvenirs that can be assigned an origin in the Holy Land itself from the discovery of an *ampulla* mould with a similar sexfoil motif at a workshop excavated in Akko (Acre), Israel (Danny Syon, Israeli Archaeology Service, *personal communication*). Similar examples have been recorded from London (Spencer 1998: 205–206, fig. 214b) and Binsted, Hampshire (BERK-E3B315).
Disposition: Returned to finder.

F BASFORD & G EGAN

257. Wressle, East Yorkshire: mirror case (PAS: NLM-E452C5)

Date: Medieval (c. 1250–c. 1300).
Discovery: Found by Robert Franey while metal-detecting in 2007, and recorded by Lisa Staves (North Lincolnshire FLO).
Description: A cast copper-alloy mirror case comprising a pair of identical, shallow circular sides, both with a pair of integral lugs at one end and a single lug at the other. They are joined by a hinge in the form of a copper-alloy rivet which passes though the two lugs of one case and the single lug on the other (the opening side has the same arrangement, but with no means of securing the two parts together, as the lugs here are not pierced). The outside of both cases is decorated with the standard design of an open cross of punched triangles in four arched lines. In one side a fragment remains of a corroded, convex glass, backed with a thin foil of lead (now a deep red colour). The glass was held in place by a ring of white material, probably a calcium carbonate putty, which can be seen inside both parts; the case, lacking glass, also has traces of an orange-red material that may be lead oxide. Dimensions: 43.7 x 31.2 x 6.9mm. Weight: 18.13g.
Discussion: Several Medieval mirror cases have been recorded by the PAS (Bayley *et al.* 1984), but to find one complete with parts of the mirror still attached is unusual.
Disposition: Returned to finder.

L STAVES

258. Crimplesham, Norfolk: silver-gilt brooch (PAS: NMS-026E35; Treasure: 2007 T72)

Date: Medieval (c. 1250–c. 1300).
Discovery: Found by Keith Underdown while metal-detecting in January or February 2006, and reported to Erica Darch (Norfolk FLO) in 2007.
Description: A silver brooch. Two ends of the loop, one of which is in the form of a very simple snake head with two pellets for eyes, are joined by being twisted around each other so that the snake's own tail is wrapped around its neck. A separate piece of silver wrapped around the frame forms a second, smaller, snake, twisted around the first on one half of the frame only. The outside edge is decorated with very worn stamped dots, and there are traces of gilding. The pin is intact and has a transverse ridge. Diameter: 17–19mm. Weight: 2.14g.
Disposition: Acquired by Lynn Museum; the finder and landowner donated their share.

E DARCH

259. Winchester area, Hampshire: silver bar-mount (PAS: HAMP-4D35C0; Treasure: 2007 T264)

Date: Medieval (c. 1250–c. 1350).
Discovery: Found by Terry Hinde while metal-detecting in October 2006, and reported to Rob Webley (Hampshire FLO).
Description: A bar-mount, with a central aperture. The bar is chamfered and has two studs on the reverse. Length: 9mm. Width: 5mm. Weight: 0.38g.
Discussion: For similar examples in copper alloy, see Egan and Pritchard (1991: no. 1157).
Disposition: Acquired by Winchester Museums Service; both finder and landowner donated their share.

J P ROBINSON

260. Ilam, Staffordshire: copper-alloy oval buckle (PAS: WMID-4E9183)

Date: Medieval (c. 1250–c. 1400).
Discovery: Found by Kevin Blackburn while metal-detecting in 2006, and recorded with Caroline Johnson (Staffordshire & West Midlands FLO) in 2007.
Description: An incomplete cast copper-alloy oval buckle with ornate outside edge and attached sheet copper-alloy buckle plate. On the back of the buckle frame, the moulded decoration along the outside edge is also illustrated, although this is in a cruder style. The sheet plate is decorated with what appears to be a dragon or griffin, which appears to be lying on its

front with its legs and probably its tail stretched out behind. The beast is encompassed within a border of single incised parallel lines. The back of the plate, which has a dark green patina, is also flat and undecorated. Dimensions: 59 x 18.5 x 3.5mm. Weight: 5.3g.

Discussion: A similar buckle frame of this common form is illustrated by Egan and Pritchard (1991: 73, no. 297).

Disposition: Returned to finder.

D SLARKE

261. Leziate, Norfolk: silver seal matrix (PAS: NMS-BFE0C6; Treasure: 2007 T34)

Date: Medieval (c. 1250–c. 1400).

Discovery: Found by Albert Burkinshaw while metal-detecting in October 2006, and reported to Erica Darch (Norfolk FLO) in 2007.

Description: A concave-sided, hollow composite seal matrix, set with a classical intaglio of carnelian (broken obliquely) and with a separate, D-section loop and sexfoil on the narrowed reverse. The intaglio is oval, with a standing Mercury carrying a caduceus and holding a moneybag. The inscription reads: '* I · A · ODOR · DVLCIS · AMOR' (I am the perfume of sweet love). Dimensions: 21 x 19mm.

Disposition: Acquired by Norwich Castle Museum.

S J ASHLEY

262. Blore with Swinscoe, Staffordshire: copper/lead-alloy sword pommel (PAS: WMID-426D04)

Date: Medieval (c. 1250–c. 1500).

Discovery: Found by Paul Flowers while metal-detecting in 2007, and recorded by Duncan Slarke (Staffordshire & West Midlands FLO).

Description: A cast hollow pommel which is sub-circular, with two flat faces, and a chamfered, flat perimeter. Rectangular perforations in the base and top would have held the end of the iron tang of the sword. The two faces are decorated with copper-alloy shield-shaped panels. The more complete one is engraved with a rough chequer design (the surface of the second is not visible). The area around both panels is also decorated with linear tooling. Dimensions: 43.4 x 47.1 x 29.4mm. Weight: 83.22g.

Discussion: This is a 'wheel' pommel (Ward Perkins 1940: 22, fig. 1, Type VIII, & 28). This form appears to have evolved during the later 13th century from the simple disc pommel. Throughout the 14th and 15th centuries the cruciform sword with a wheel pommel and a straight double-edged blade was the basic type in common use.

Disposition: Returned to finder.

D SLARKE

263. Old Buckenham, Norfolk: silver coin-brooch or mount (PAS: NMS-BEA416; Treasure: 2007 T12)

Date: Medieval (c. 1275–c. 1280).

Discovery: Found by David Bailey while metal-detecting in December 2006, and reported to Erica Darch (Norfolk FLO).

Description: A demi-gros struck at Valenciennes for Margaret of Constantinople, countess of Hainaut, between 1275 and 1280. The reverse has been fitted with a silver attachment; this is most likely to be a catch-plate for a brooch but the angle at which it is affixed to the coin makes it possible that it represents one of a paid of grips by which the coin was fastened to a leather strap as a mount. Diameter: 22.5mm. Weight: 2.93g.

Discussion: This work would have been carried out soon after striking, at a period when, owing to the lack of large English silver coins. Continental coins of suitable size were being adapted into coin-brooches.

Disposition: Donated by the finder and landowner to Norwich Castle Museum.

A MARSDEN

264. Paull, East Yorkshire: gilded coin brooch (PAS: YORYM-60FCA5; Treasure: 2007 T626)

Date: Medieval (c. 1292–c. 1317).

Discovery: Found by Dave Everingham while metal-detecting in September 2007, and reported to Liz Andrews-Wilson (North & East Yorkshire FLO).

Description: A silver coin converted into a brooch by having a pin attached to one side (the pin has not survived, but the attachment is partially present) and with one side gilded. The gilded side is, as usual, the side showing the cross.

Discussion: The coin is a silver *gros tournois* type, a relatively large silver coin of the late 13th and early 14th century. Many of these coins have been found in England converted into brooches in this way, alongside similarly treated groats of Edward I (r. 1272–1307), England's own first large silver coin, introduced in 1280. Most examples of such coin-brooches are of *gros tournois* of the French kings of the period, particularly Philip III (1270–1285) and Philip IV (1285–1314), but a number are of the lesser rulers of the Low Countries region who also used the *tournois* design for their own early issues of large silver coins.

This specimen is one such piece, a *gros au portail* of Gui IV, Count of Saint-Pol (r, 1292–1317), issuing coins at his lordship of Élincourt in the Cambrésis, a region belonging to the Holy Roman Empire and technically under the suzerainty of the bishops of Cambrai. Gui IV inherited Élincourt in 1300 and opened a mint, despite the protests of the bishops.

The details of the coin are as follows: Obv: cross in centre, with the inner legend '+G COMES SPAVLI', and outer legend '+GRACIA DOmIHI DEI NPI FACTV

SS II' (no punctuation). Rev: border of five-petalled roses in circles; stylised castle in centre, with the legend '+MONE[ ]LInET (partially hidden by remains of attachment). Weight: 3.95g. Die axis: 70° (de May 1987: 89, H2, though different in details of punctuation and lettering).
Disposition: Acquired by East Riding Museums Service.

B J COOK

---

265. Wragby area, Lincolnshire: lead/tin pilgrim badge (PAS-LIN-D80A35)

Date: Medieval (c. 1300–c. 1350).
Discovery: Found by Paul Vir while metal-detecting in 2007, and recorded by Adam Daubney (Lincolnshire FLO).
Description: The badge is in the form of the bust of St Thomas Becket, who wears a mitre and drapery, and has a stern expression. The collar of the amice is decorated with a perimeter of pellets and a series of pellet-in-ring motifs, representing embroidery and gems. This feature can be dated to the first half of the 14th century. To the left of the face is a censing angel (there would originally have been another on the right). Part of the beaded frame survives.
Dimensions: 68 x 33 x 7mm.
Discussion: This is one of a well-known series of badges, which depict the life-sized, mitred bust reliquary of Thomas, kept in Canterbury Cathedral from the early 14th century to the Reformation. Offerings made at the cathedral show that the popularity of this head reliquary peaked in 1420. Hundreds of badges of this form, or less elaborate examples, have been found in London and Canterbury (Spencer 1998, 102–107, figs. 76–77; several of these retain the original, ornate frame which went with badges of this sort). The presence in Lincolnshire of the present one is not surprising given Becket's widespread popularity.
Disposition: Returned to finder.

A DAUBNEY

---

266. Ludgvan, Cornwall: copper-alloy (possible) weight (PAS: CORN-A6D554)

Date: Medieval (c. 1300–c. 1350).
Discovery: Found by Roy Powell while metal-detecting in June 2007, and recorded by Anna Tyacke (Cornwall FLO).
Description: A copper-alloy figurine of a horse, cast in the round, with moulded ears and nose, incised lines for hair of the mane on one side only, and wedge-shaped tail which appears docked. It is a heavy casting for its size. Dimensions: 53 x 20 x 40mm. Weight: 97.1g.
Discussion: This is most likely to have been a weight, as it resembles Medieval equine figures interpreted as weights, found mainly in Norway but also elsewhere in Scandinavia, where they are dated to the early 14th century (Kisch 1965: 121 & 123–124, figs. 81–82).

However, the standard represented is not clear (Petter Molaug, Norwegian Institute for Cultural Heritage Research, *personal communication*). The present find seems to be the first discovered outside Scandinavia.
Disposition: The Royal Cornwall Museum has acquired.

A TYACKE & G EGAN

---

267. Sealfield, North Yorkshire: silver seal matrix (PAS: NCL-FFF137; Treasure: 2007 T39)

Date: Medieval (c. 1300–c. 1350).
Discovery: Found by Carl Richardson and Richard Hunter while metal-detecting in November 2006, and reported to Rob Collins (North East FLO) in 2007.
Description: An oval seal matrix engraved with the scene of Thomas Becket's martyrdom. Three of the four knights responsible for the attack approach Thomas as he kneels before an altar. Edward Grimm, the cleric who witnessed the attack, stands behind the altar and holds a cross-staff. Beneath the scene, in an architectural canopy, is the half figure of a suppliant. The legend reads 'OPEM NOBIS O TOMA PORIGE' (Extend your help to us, O Thomas). On the reverse is a suspension loop. Length: 24mm. Width: 18mm.
Disposition: Acquired by Richmondshire Museum. One of the rewards was abated by 10% for a delay in reporting.

J P ROBINSON

---

268. Dunstable, Bedfordshire: silver-gilt brooch in the form of a finger-ring (PAS: BH-DE4686; Treasure: 2007 T465)

Date: Medieval (c. 1300–c. 1350).
Discovery: Found during construction work between 1970 and 1990, and reported to Julian Watters (Bedfordshire & Hertfordshire FLO).
Description: A silver-gilt brooch, which appears to have been converted from a finger-ring. The ring is slender and forms the frame of the brooch, to which a sword-shaped pin with a collar with decorative circular punch marks has been attached. The frame is narrowed for the attachment of the pin. Similar finds are known from London (that these are not adaptations of finger-rings is shown by a ceramic mould including the frame constriction for producing this distinctive form of brooch; Egan 1996: 87–88, fig. 3C). The hoop terminates in two clasped hands and has a bezel, which protrudes very much in the manner of stirrup-shaped rings. The stone that once furnished the bezel is now lost. The inscription '+ I O S _ A _ + S I N E D. A M V R' (probably intended to mean, I am a sign of love) covers the external surface of the hoop. The meaning of the inscription makes it clear that the brooch was intended as a love token, possibly a betrothal or marriage gift, for which a finger-ring would be an appropriate motif. Dimensions: 21 x 25mm. Weight: 2.3g.

Disposition: Declared not Treasure Trove; returned to finder.

J P ROBINSON & G EGAN

269. Wetheringsett cum Brockford, Suffolk: copper-alloy sword pommel (PAS: SF-15A447)

Date: Medieval (c. 1300–c. 1400).
Discovery: Found by Keith Lewis while metal-detecting in 2007, and recorded by Faye Minter (Suffolk FLO).
Description: A copper-alloy cast pommel. It is square in section with four roughly oval shaped faces and a hole through the centre for the blade tang. Each face of the pommel has an engraved grotesque, hybrid human and animal-like figure. Each of these is different but they are all in side profile, have wings and are advancing on their hind legs. They also all have second human faces in their hindquarters, some with tails projecting from the mouths. Two of the grotesques have human heads and the other two have bird- and animal-like heads.
Discussion: Parallels for the grotesques appear as marginalia of manuscripts such as the Luttrell Psalter of c. 1330 (Brown 2007).
Disposition: Returned to finder.

F MINTER, J P ROBINSON & G EGAN

270. Arncliffe, North Yorkshire: copper-alloy pyx lid (PAS: YORYM-58EB27)

Date: Medieval (c. 1300–c. 1400).
Discovery: Found by Paul Myers while metal-detecting in 2007, and recorded with Liz Andrews-Wilson (North & East Yorkshire FLO).
Description: A copper-alloy pyx lid with Limoges-style decoration, gilded inside and out. At the apex is a plain cross set on a knop. On the cone are four circles, each around an octafoil. The circles are a greyish-blue enamel, which has a gilded border, and the octafoils are slightly greener, with gilded outlines. The field between the petals is gilded, with rows of punched dots. The main circles are also surrounded by a gilded circle. Between the circles are foliate motifs, also gilded. The background enamel colour, possibly a darker blue, has mainly been lost. Around the edge of the base of the lid is a band of gilding with a pair of lines of incised dots along the middle. There are two loops on opposite sides of the base of the cone. One expands into a flat plate and further broadens into a triangle, which is riveted onto the inside of the lid. Wear is evident on the loop, indicating that the pyx was in use for some time before disuse. This loop would have formed part of a hinge mechanism, which would have fixed to the base. The second loop, of similar design, extends with a projection which would have held the lid shut. A string or pin would have been slotted through its hole to secure it.

Discussion: This object is of higher quality than might be expected in a normal parish church. The enamelling is of Limoges style (though English manufacturers were developing the technique from the late 13th century). It may have been kept in the local church for some time before it was taken away, perhaps along with a copper-alloy crown, which probably came from a wooden statue (see YORYM-5936A7). These three objects were found together, perhaps suggesting that they were either stolen from the church and discarded along the way, or removed during the Reformation. There is a parallel for the lid on the complete pyx from Godsfield (Hampshire), dated to c. 1350–c. 1400, which has a similar form and proportions, although the decoration differs (Alexander and Binski 1987: 240, no. 119).
Disposition: Returned to finder.

L ANDREWS-WILSON, J CHERRY & K LEAHY

271. Nether Wallop, Hampshire: copper-alloy seal matrix (PAS: HAMP-E43D58)

Date: Medieval (c. 1300–c. 1400).
Discovery: Found by Peter Barker while metal-detecting in 2006, and recorded with Rob Webley (Hampshire FLO) in 2007.
Description: Cast copper-alloy seal matrix engraved with a shield: (possibly) *per fess, two saltires over* (possible) *an animal's head* – the arms are unidentified – with a stylised banner finial above. The inscription reads: 'S' TOM(?)AS WELLOP' (seal of Thomas Wellop). Dimensions: 20.1 x 20.8mm. Weight: 11.35g.
Discussion: The matrix was not lost far from its presumed place of use. 'Wellop' was a common rendering of 'Wallop' in the 13th and 14th centuries. Further, a Thomas Wallop (c. 1325–1361) is documented as being from the area. His son, John, was born in Nether Wallop in 1351. This date is consistent with the object's form.
Disposition: Returned to finder.

R WEBLEY

272. North Somerset: copper-alloy annular brooch (PAS: GLO-C03D14)

Date: Medieval (c. 1300–c. 1400).
Discovery: Found by David Gad while metal-detecting in 2006, and reported to Kurt Adams (Gloucestershire & Avon FLO) in 2007.
Description: A copper-alloy brooch with four outward-tapering collets spaced evenly around the frame, which has a sub-triangular cross-section. Each collet is filled with a white paste that would have held a gem. A little distant from the constriction for the pin is a second constriction, from which a pendant, in the form of a bird displayed, is suspended. The crescentic wings are attached to the centre of the main body via small projections and the expanded body narrows towards

the tail, which is represented by a quadrangle. The head and neck are depicted by a plain rectangle. Double lines of dots down the centre of the tail, body and wings represent feathers. On the underside of the head a loop (possibly intended to be a beak) attaches the pendant to the frame. On the underside of the pendant and frame are a series of striations that are original file-finishing. Dimensions: 22 x 18 x 4mm. Weight: 2.6g.

Discussion: The basic brooch is unremarkable; similar examples of the frame are found over much of the country, furthermore the quality of the craftsmanship is rather low when compared to other brooches of the period. No parallel for the attachment of a pendant to an annular brooch of comparable date has been traced. If found separately the pendant would probably have been thought to be from an accessory for horse-harness rather than a brooch. This find of a previously unknown elaboration in an otherwise simple brooch could perhaps be a local product.

Disposition: Returned to finder.

K ADAMS

---

273. Winchester area, Hampshire: silver-gilt bar-mount (PAS: HAMP-C28BE4; Treasure: 2007 T262)

Date: Medieval (c. 1300–c. 1400).

Discovery: Found by Terry Hinde while metal-detecting in March 2007, and reported to Rob Webley (Hampshire FLO).

Description: A cast bar-mount for a strap; convex with plain arms, and end lobes perforated for rivets, one of which survives. The larger central lobe is decorated with cross-hatched diagonal lines. Length: 18.35mm. Weight: 1.3g.

Discussion: The mount can be paralleled with a number of excavated examples in copper alloy from London (Egan and Pritchard 1991: 213–214, nos. 1160–1161) and elsewhere. There is also a silver-gilt bar-mount from Churcham, Gloucestershire (*TAR* 2004: no. 216), though this example has a large perforation through the central lobe.

Disposition: Acquired by Winchester Museums Service; both landowner and finder donated their share.

R WEBLEY

---

274. Kelvedon, Essex: silver-gilt oval brooch (PAS: ESS-6EC685; Treasure: 2007 T71)

Date: Medieval (c. 1300–c. 1400).

Discovery: Found by Richard Moss while metal-detecting in February 2007, and reported to Caroline McDonald (Essex FLO).

Description: A silver-gilt brooch, roughly oval in shape and tapering to a point, which terminates in two joined hands (a 'fede' ring). The pin is missing. The back of the frame is inscribed with a repeated sequence of letters, reading clockwise from where the pin would have been attached 'IOV – VIOVIOVIO' (significance unclear). Length: 22mm. Width: 12mm.

Discussion: Similar to a brooch from mid-Norfolk (*TAR* 1998–1999: no. 155).

Disposition: Acquired by Braintree Museum.

J P ROBINSON

---

275. Finchingfield, Essex: inscribed silver finger-ring (PAS: ESS-288395; Treasure: 2007 T137)

Date: Medieval (c. 1300–c. 1400).

Discovery: Found by Michael Jones while metal-detecting in February 2007, and reported to Philip Wise (Heritage Manager, Colchester and Ipswich Museum Service).

Description: A finger-ring consisting of a simple flat band inscribed with the letters: '* I H C : N A Z A R E N U S: REX I' (to signify, Jesus of Nazareth King of the Jews). Length: 23mm.

Discussion: This inscription (though abbreviated) was placed above the head of Christ on the Cross. In the Middle Ages the phrase was used to cure or avert sickness.

Disposition: Acquired by Braintree Museum.

J P ROBINSON

---

276. South Gloucestershire: silver-gilt brooch (PAS: GLO-EF2CE8; Treasure: 2007 T208)

Date: Medieval (c. 1300–c. 1400).

Discovery: Found by Nick Keeler while metal-detecting in March 2007, and reported to Kurt Adams (Gloucestershire FLO).

Description: A circular brooch with a flat frame; the back is slightly rounded. There is a break where the missing pin would have been attached. The front carries an inscription (the letters alternating with ring-and-dot motifs) 'O . V . N . O . V . E . R . A . V . E . (meaning uncertain). Diameter: 23mm.

Disposition: Acquired by Museum in the Park, Stroud.

J P ROBINSON

---

277. Wonston, Hampshire: silver scabbard chape (PAS: HAMP-8C1E11; Treasure: 2007 T341)

Date: Medieval (c. 1300–c. 1400).

Discovery: Found by Mark Duell while metal-detecting in March 2007, and reported to Rob Webley (Hampshire FLO).

Description: A silver sheet chape, which has a cusped edge and engraved decoration on the front. Dimensions: 21.05 x 20.15 x 4.35. Weight: 3.6g.

Disposition: Winchester Museums Service hopes to acquire.

B NENK

278. Old Kirk Field area, Hartlepool, County Durham: inscribed silver brooch (PAS: NCL-D1AF46; Treasure: 2007 T361)

Date: Medieval (c. 1300–c. 1400).
Discovery: Found by Brian Leslie while metal-detecting in May 2007, and reported to Rob Collins (North East FLO).
Description: A silver brooch, circular in shape, with an open centre. The flattened frame of the brooch is inscribed on one side 'AVE MARIA GRA...' (Hail, Mary, [full of] grace), and on the other is '+IHESVS: NA: RE' (Jesus of Nazareth, King [of the Jews]).
Diameter: 21mm.
Disposition: Acquired by Hartlepool Museum and Heritage Service.

J P ROBINSON

279. Binbrook, Lincolnshire: inscribed silver brooch (PAS: NLM-FDB8B5; Treasure: 2007 T684)

Date: Medieval (c. 1300–c. 1400).
Discovery: Found by Stephen Wilkinson while metal-detecting in November 2007, and reported to Lisa Staves (North Lincolnshire FLO).
Description: Circular silver brooch that is flat, with raised edges forming a border. On the front is an inscription which reads 'AMOR VNICIT OMNA', a misspelling of the Latin Amor vincit omnia (Love conquers all). The beginning of the inscription is indicated by the positioning of the pin, which is attached to a recess in the frame by a loop. Diameter (of frame): 12mm.
Disposition: Disclaimed; returned to finder.

J P ROBINSON

280. Brookland, Kent: silver-gilt finger-ring (PAS: KENT-2963F0; Treasure: 2007 T501)

Date: Medieval (c. 1300–c. 1400).
Discovery: Found by Phil Castle while metal-detecting in September 2007, and reported to Andrew Richardson (Kent FLO).
Description: Silver-gilt finger-ring, with a bezel formed of clasped hands. The shoulders probably represent cuffs. Opposite the bezel an engraved rectangular panel covers the point at which the ends of the hoop are soldered together. The ring is slightly distorted and the gilding is very worn. Diameter: 22.19 x 21.3 x 5.96mm. Width: 6mm. Weight: 3.5g.
Disposition: Canterbury Museum had hoped to acquire, but withdrew; returned to finder.

B NENK

281. Long Marston, North Yorkshire: silver pendant-cross (PAS: YORYM-763D18; Treasure: 2007 T515)

Date: Medieval (c. 1300–c. 1400).
Discovery: Found by Frank Andrusyk while metal-detecting in September 2007, and reported to Amy Cooper (South & West Yorkshire FLO).
Description: A silver pendant-cross, with a central sexfoil collet, now missing its stone. The arms of the cross carry an inscription. Along the vertical arms is '+IESVSN' and along the horizontal arms is 'AZAREN' (Jesus of Nazareth). Dimensions: 40.1 x 33.4 x 3.6mm. Weight: 4.9g.
Disposition: Aquired by Harrogate Museum.

J P ROBINSON

282. Walgrave, Northamptonshire: silver scabbard chape (PAS: NARC-774CD2; Treasure: 2007 T212)

Date: Medieval (c. 1300–c. 1400).
Discovery: Found by Franco Ladu while metal-detecting in April 2007, and reported to Steven Ashby (Northamptonshire FLO).
Description: The chape has small rivet holes near the wider end for attachment to the scabbard. This end is engraved with two pairs of double lines and the narrow end terminates in a knop. Length: 63mm. Diameter: 10mm.
Discussion: Another incomplete silver chape, with engraved curvilinear decoration; Treasure: 2007 T440) from St Michael, Hertfordshire, and found by Mr G Jones, is assigned to the 15th century.
Disposition: Northampton Museum hopes to acquire.

M MELLOR

283. Wingfield, Wiltshire: unfinished silver finger-ring (PAS: WILT-6F3276; Treasure: 2007 T110)

Date: Medieval (c. 1300–c.1500).
Discovery: Found by Judith Jonik while metal-detecting in February 2007, and reported to Katie Hinds (Wiltshire FLO).
Description: A silver finger-ring, presumably unfinished as the decoration is asymmetrical around the hoop. The bezel comprises a point, with two flanking indentations on one side. Around the hoop are a central rib with five to six distinct areas to each side decorated with diagonal grooves and horizontal incised lines, overall giving a triangular section. One edge has a slight rebate but on the less well-executed side there is no decoration at this point, and (while also triangular in section) it is rather rounder than in the other quarters, with a slight midrib, as though it may not yet have been finished from the casting. Diameter: 25.2mm. Weight: 7.52g.
Disposition: Acquired by Wiltshire Heritage Museum.

K HINDS

284. Tywardreath, Cornwall: lead papal *bulla* (PAS: CORN-B357D6)

Date: Medieval (c. 1342–1352).
Discovery: Found by Jamie Holland while metal-detecting in February, 2007, and recorded with Anna Tyacke (Cornwall FLO).
Description: The *bulla* is from the period of Pope Clement VI (r. 1342–1352) and has 'CLE/MENS/PP VI' with a floret above and below on one side. The small floret at the start of the text and the reversed bar to the 'N' are characteristic of the *bullae* of this pope. The obverse is very worn, with only a few pellets remaining from the border around the conventionalised heads of St Peter and St Paul, which were respectively to the left and right of a central patriarchal cross.
Discussion: Despite his short period in office, *bullae* of Clement VI are relatively frequent finds and mark an upsurge in the use of papal documents around the time of the Black Death.
Disposition: Returned to finder.

A TYACKE

285. West Clandon, Surrey: silver *piedfort* (PAS: SUR-D6C932; Treasure: 2007 T339)

Date: Medieval (mid 1350s).
Discovery: Found by Mark Stonard while metal-detecting in 2006 or before, and reported to David Williams (Surrey FLO) in 2007.
Description: A piedfort striking of the coin known as a *blanc au léopard sous couronne*, Second Type, struck by King Edward III as Duke of Aquitaine (1325–1362), probably in the mid 1350s.
Discussion: This is the first find of a *piedfort* in England since the Treasure Act 1996. *Piedforts* are unusual objects and their actual purpose has never been clearly established. In most cases, they are objects struck from the dies of a currency coin, but using a blank of unusual thickness and weight. However, the weights of surviving piedforts do not seem to relate to the weights of the currency coins – they are never multiples of these. In this case, the weight of the currency coin was something around 1.7g, and the *piedfort* weighs 6.67g. The first *piedforts* are known from the later 13th century from England, France and other principalities in the region. They continued to be produced in England into the 16th century, later in France. Although all individual piedforts are rare, they are relatively common as a phenomenon in the coinage of Aquitaine in the 14th century. The specific coin involved here exists in at least 23 versions, and *piedfort* strikings of two of these are known. This example provides a third. These other *piedforts* weigh 7.85g and 6.12g. Several ideas have been put forward to explain piedforts. It is very unlikely that they are pattern coins, since they are made with currency dies, and in some cases the same die has been identified used both on normal coins and a *piedfort*. Nor is it likely that they were created as guides for mint workers. Perhaps the likeliest explanation is that they were made for the use of important officials, who might have used them as reckoning counters. This would certainly account for them turning up far from home and away from any context of currency. In the case of Aquitaine, it was normal in the 14th century for Englishmen to serve as officials there, as they were more loyal to the king and less affected by the complicated local rivalries of the duchy.
Disposition: Acquired by the British Museum.

B J COOK

286. Harlaston, Staffordshire: inscribed gold finger-ring (PAS: WMID-F4CF43; Treasure: 2007 T628)

Date: Medieval (c. 1350–c. 1400).
Discovery: Found by Jeremy Rudge while metal-detecting in November 2007, and reported to Duncan Slarke (Staffordshire & West Midlands FLO).
Description: A gold finger-ring, with a D-sectioned hoop. It is decorated on the internal and external surfaces with engraved flowers and leaves, interspersed with the words of an inscription in French. On the outside this reads '+ TANT QUE MURAI' and on the inside '+VOUZ CEROIRE', which probably means 'Until I die I will be yours'. This sentiment suggests that the find may originally have been a marriage ring. Diameter: 19mm. Weight: 2.32g.
Disposition: Potteries Museum & Art Gallery, Stoke, hopes to acquire.

J P ROBINSON

287. Maiden Newton area, Dorset: copper-alloy strap-end (PAS: DOR-B703F7)

Date: Medieval (c. 1350–c. 1450).
Discovery: Found by Simon Gover while metal-detecting in 2007, and recorded by Ciorstaidh Hayward Trevarthen (Dorset FLO).
Description: A composite strap-end with a plain front plate (recessed at the back for the strap) that terminates in a stylised, crowned human head, which is cast in the round. Details of the hair (back and front), facial features and crown have been added or emphasised by tooling. Dimensions: 45.51 x 11.89 x 5.42mm.
Discussion: For parallels see Egan and Pritchard 1991: 132–133, no. 614, which are similar but have less detailing on the heads.
Disposition: Returned to finder.

C HAYWARD TREVARTHEN

**288. Bradfield, Essex: copper-alloy buckle frame
(PAS: ESS-E89DE3)**

Date: Medieval (c. 1350–c. 1450).

Discovery: Found by David Haffenden while metal-detecting in June 2007, and recorded by Laura McLean (Essex FLO).

Description: An incomplete, cast, ring-shaped buckle frame which has a bevelled edge, an incomplete forked spacer, and an offset, constricted bar for the now missing pin. The sheet plates are missing. The frame is engraved with an inscription within a linear border (each letter is separated by three vertical lines) 'x IESVS x NAZA x IA x G' (the 'N' and 'A' of NAZA are located to either side of a pin rest in the form of an integral animal head. The reverse of the buckle is plain and undecorated. The surface is worn. Length: 58.52mm. Diameter: 37.22mm. Weight: 16.81 g.

Discussion: The inscription is a combination of two legends often found independent of each other on brooches of the same date: 'IESVS NAZARENVS' (Jesus of Narareth) with the usual ending being replaced by 'IA G', which is the end of 'AVE MARIA GRATIA PLENA' (Hail Mary, full of grace). Parts of the two distinct legends have become combined possibly by an illiterate maker who has focused on the common Rs. This may well not have mattered greatly, as most people were illiterate or sub-literate (concentrating on initial letters or patterns of letters rather than whole words for recognition of common tags).

Disposition: Returned to finder.

L MCLEAN & G EGAN

**289. Churton by Aldford, Cheshire: copper-alloy
harness pendant (PAS: LVPL-375DD7)**

Date: Medieval (c. 1350–c. 1450).

Discovery: Found by George McKean while metal-detecting in 2007, and reported to Frances McIntosh (Cheshire, Greater Manchester & Merseyside FLO).

Description: A copper-alloy shield-shaped harness pendant. The coat of arms consists of a moth or butterfly (now white) with two wings on each side, zigzag lines of red enamel for the legs and others for the antennae. Dimensions: 43 x 24 x 2mm. Weight: 10.6g.

Discussion: Insects are unusual in heraldry, which makes this pendant an unusual find. Papworth (1961: 956–957) lists only the family of Bolowre as having a single butterfly on its arms and three – Bolour, Berston and Muschamp – with three; Fox Davies (1954: 261) adds Papillon and Penhellicke to those with three.

Disposition: Returned to finder.

F MCINTOSH & G EGAN

**290. Winwick, Cheshire: gold finger-ring
(PAS: LVPL-0330D6; Treasure: 2007 T606)**

Date: Medieval (c. 1350–c. 1450).

Discovery: Found while metal-detecting in September 2007, and reported to Frances McIntosh (Cheshire, Greater Manchester & Merseyside FLO).

Description: A gold finger-ring set with a hexagonal sapphire in a bezel with a pinched border. The shoulders of the ring are divided into three bands. The raised, central band is plain, with a rouletted border, which has worn smooth in places. The two side bands are engraved with flowers and leaves, and would originally have been enamelled. The back of the hoop is decorated with diagonal bands of alternate plain and punched decoration to give the effect of cabling. Inside the hoop is the French inscription 'JOYE SANZ FYN' (joy without end). The hoop resembles a distended stirrup shape. Dimensions: 20 x 23mm.

Discussion: A closely comparable ring in the Victoria and Albert Museum (V&A M.191–1975) was owned by William Wytlesey, Archbishop of Canterbury, who died in 1374.

Disposition: Cheshire Museums Service had hoped to acquire, but withdrew; returned to finder.

J P ROBINSON

**291. Charminster, Dorset: engraved silver strap-end
(PAS: SOMDOR-D92905; Treasure: 2007 T98)**

Date: Medieval (c. 1350–c. 1500).

Discovery: Found by Robert Dixon while metal-detecting in 2006, and reported to Claire Pinder (Senior Archaeologist, Dorset County Council) in 2007.

Description: A beautifully executed strap-end. It is split for attachment to a small strap, and would have been held in place by two surviving rivets and terminate in a trefoil-shaped knop. The top plate is engraved with a shield with three stars along the upper edge and a horizontal line below, which may be a heraldic device. Dimensions: 23.4 x 12.7 x 2.4mm. Weight: 1.7g.

Disposition: Disclaimed; returned to finder.

M MELLOR

**292. South Wingfield, Derbyshire: gold finger-ring
(PAS: DENO-D1A913; Treasure: 2007 T300)**

Date: Medieval (c. 1350–c. 1500).

Discovery: Found as the result of an amateur archaeological investigation by John Hardwick in May 2007, and reported to Rachel Atherton (Derbyshire & Nottinghamshire FLO).

Description: A finger-ring fashioned into the shape of a garter. The external surface is inscribed in French '+ tout + pur + le + meus +' (probably meaning 'all for the better'). White enamel survives in the recesses of some letters. The buckle of the garter has been sheared off, but the fictive pin survives. The pendant strap of

the garter is decorated with a panel of cross-hatching. Dimensions: 19.5 x 8.1 x 2.1mm. Weight: 1.6g.
Discussion: A gold ring already in the British Museum (Dalton 1912: no. 977) carries a similar inscription (pur le meux).
Disposition: Derby Museum and Art Gallery hope to acquire.

J P ROBINSON

293. Great Smeaton, North Yorkshire: silver-gilt pendant reliquary (PAS: YORYM-6CE0B1; Treasure: 2007 T598)

Date: Medieval (c. 1350–c. 1500).
Discovery: Found by Thomas Bolam while metal-detecting in November 2007, and reported to Rob Collins (North East FLO).
Description: A circular silver-gilt pendant. The central roundel is engraved on one side 'IHC', and the other is engraved with the Marian monogram; in each case against a cross-hatched ground. Originally there would have been three loops for suspension, but only the central one survives. Dimensions: 19 x 23mm.
Disposition: Acquired by York Museums Trust.

B NENK

294. Urchfont, Wiltshire: silver ivy-leaf pendant (PAS: SOM-F52064; Treasure: 2007 T529)

Date: Medieval (c. 1400–c. 1450).
Discovery: Found by Hugh Vincent while metal-detecting in September 2007, and reported to Naomi Payne (Somerset FLO).
Description: A pendant in the form of a stylised ivy leaf. Two of the points of the leaf are slightly distorted. The pendant is likely to have decorated costume as one of a series (see Egan and Pritchard 1991: 217–218, no. 1188). The ivy leaf was often taken to signify constancy in the Middle Ages. Dimensions: 15 x 15mm.
Disposition: Acquired by Wiltshire Heritage Museum; the finder and landowner donated their share.

J P ROBINSON

295. Bonby, North Lincolnshire: silver-gilt finger-ring (PAS: NLM-688C74; Treasure: 2007 T174)

Date: Medieval (c. 1400–c. 1500).
Discovery: Found by Ken Ellis while metal-detecting in March 2007, and reported to Lisa Staves (North Lincolnshire FLO).
Description: An iconographic finger-ring. The bezel consists of two panels, the one on the left engraved with the figure of a kneeling angel, and the one on the right with two standing figures. This is likely to represent the Annunciation, the second bearded figure on the right panel possibly intended as God the Father. The hoop of the ring is made up of a series of lozenges, the shoulder lozenges decorated with three engraved

flowers on each side. This faceting of the hoop is an unusual feature and creates a very decorative effect. The ring would originally have been enamelled. Diameter: 22mm. Weight: 4.25g.
Disposition: North Lincolnshire Museum hopes to acquire.

J P ROBINSON

296. Pontefract, West Yorkshire: silver cross-pendant (PAS: SWYOR-C4E534; Treasure: 2007 T81)

Date: Medieval (c. 1400–c. 1500).
Discovery: Found by Phillip Fletcher while metal-detecting in February 2007, and reported to Amy Cooper (South & West Yorkshire FLO).
Description: A small silver cross; the suspension loop is broken. The figure of Christ on the front of the cross is intact, though much abraded. A second figure on the back is equally worn and is likely to represent the Virgin Mary. The cross itself is more elaborate on the front, with three arms terminating in a stylised trefoil. At the top is an inscription 'R I' to signify 'Rex Judeorum' (king of the Jews). Length: 25mm. Width: 18mm.
Discussion: The cross dates to a time when small, personal items of devotional art were popular.
Disposition: Acquired by Wakefield Museum.

M MELLOR

297. Aldbrough, North Yorkshire: gold finger-ring (PAS: NCL-FF8757; Treasure: 2007 T37)

Date: Medieval (c. 1400–c. 1500).
Discovery: Found by Colin Henderson while metal-detecting in November 2006, and reported to Rob Collins (North East FLO).
Description: A hollow-cast finger-ring, set with a roughly oval, pale blue stone. The shoulders are engraved with a floral motif, probably a lily. Diameter: 21mm.
Disposition: Acquired by Harrogate Museum.

J P ROBINSON

298. Diss area, Suffolk: gold finger-ring (PAS: SF-8A76E4; Treasure: 2007 T232)

Date: Medieval (c. 1400–c. 1500).
Discovery: Found while metal-detecting in April 2007, and reported to Faye Minter (Suffolk FLO).
Description: A complete gold iconographic finger-ring. The bezel is flat and rectangular and engraved with a representation of the Trinity: the haloed, seated figure of God the Father, supporting Christ on the cross, and with a dove in the top left corner, representing the Holy Ghost. The shoulders of the ring are also engraved. The inside of the hoop has an inscription, with traces of black *niello*. The black letter legend reads 'EN BON ESPOER' (in good hope). Dimensions: 21.8 x 20.7mm. Weight: 4.38g.

Discussion: Iconographic finger-rings are so called as they depict devotional images and saints. They were used at weddings and given as New Year presents in England and Scotland from the late 14th century; this type of ring did not survive the Reformation (Scarisbrick, Henig and Fenton 2003: 42–43, pl. 12, 1–4). A very similar iconographic gold finger-ring has been found at Wall, Staffordshire (*TAR* 2003: no. 187).
Disposition: Acquired by Colchester and Ipswich Museum Service.

F MINTER

---

299. Hound, Hampshire: silver mount (PAS: HAMP-E271F0; Treasure: 2007 T455)

Date: Medieval (c. 1400–c. 1500).
Discovery: Found by Mark Duell while metal-detecting before August 2007, and reported to Rob Webley (Hampshire FLO).
Description: A mount of roughly semicircular section, in the shape of an acorn, with a leaf on each side. Below, within a serrated semicircle, is a large, central aperture. This aperture may have formed one of the means of attaching the mount to whichever object it decorated. On the back are two studs. Dimensions: 16.15 x 13.85 x 5mm. Weight: 1.95g.
Disposition: Hampshire Museums Service hopes to acquire.

J P ROBINSON

---

300. Coberley, Gloucestershire: silver-gilt finger-ring (PAS: NMGW-A8C737; Treasure: 2007 T512)

Date: Medieval (c. 1400–c. 1500).
Discovery: Found by Dennis Pople while metal-detecting in September 2007, and reported to Mark Lodwick (Finds Co-ordinator for Wales).
Description: The finger-ring is intact and of the 'fede' type. The bezel comprises a crowned heart, flanked on each side by a four-petalled flower – a heart sprouting flowers. Above the heart is a three-pronged crown containing four circular perforations. These details have been enhanced with short, engraved lines. The hoop comprises two interlace strands, which join at the back with clasped hands, symbolising faith or trust. The clasped hands have cuffs, embellished with circular punched marks. Traces of gilding survive over much of the surface of the ring. Diameter: 23mm. Height (bezel): 14.3mm. Weight: 8.6g.
Disposition: Acquired by Corinium Museum, Cirencester.

M LODWICK

---

301. Thurlaston, Leicestershire: gold finger-ring (PAS: LEIC-815FF6; Treasure: 2007 T671)

Date: Medieval (c. 1400–c. 1500).
Discovery: Found by Wayne Burton while metal-detecting in November 2007, and reported to Wendy Scott (Leicestershire FLO).
Description: The finger-ring is in the form of a flattened band, which is engraved with leaves and flowers, and a French inscription, which reads '+ MON CUER AUEZ' (have my heart). It is slightly distorted. Dimensions: 19 x 14mm.
Disposition: Acquired by Leicestershire County Council Heritage Services.

J P ROBINSON

---

302. Dinas Powys, Vale of Glamorgan: gold finger-ring (PAS: NMGW-9DEB70; Treasure: Wales 07.08)

Date: Medieval (c. 1400–c. 1500).
Discovery: Found by Gwyn Rees while metal-detecting in January 2007, and reported to Mark Lodwick (Finds Co-ordinator, Wales).
Description: Gold ring with a D-shaped cross-section. Externally plain, the inner face is engraved in black letter script, though the reading is not clear. One possibility is a garbled version of 'I VOELT' (I wish it), where the 'V' has been written as an 'F' (common in Welsh) and the 'O' and 'E' are ligatured. Diameter (internal): 17mm. Weight: 2.4g. Surface analysis approximately 76% gold, 14% silver and 10% copper.
Discussion: This ring is of a long-lasting form (without an inscription. It might be ascribed to the 18th or 19th century); however, the letter forms are from the later 14th or 15th centuries.
Disposition: Acquired by the National Museum of Wales.

M REDKNAP

---

303. Swallowfield, West Berkshire: gold brooch (PAS: BERK-BB15D7; Treasure: 2007 T486)

Date: Medieval (c. 1400–c. 1500).
Discovery: A chance find in the early 1970s, and reported to Charlotte Burrill (Berkshire & Oxfordshire FLO).
Description: A circular brooch, decorated on the front with grooves alternately occupied by pellets and words from a French inscription: '+ avez tout mon coer a vre plaisir' (have all my heart at your pleasure). The back is decorated with four-petalled flowers and sprigs of foliage. It would originally have been enamelled. Diameter: 32mm.
Disposition: Declared not Treasure Trove; returned to finder.

J P ROBINSON

**304. Naburn, City of York: gold finger-ring
(PAS: YORM-74B6A8; Treasure: 2007 T179)**

Date: Medieval (c. 1400–c. 1500).
Discovery: Found by Keith Manners while metal-detecting in March 2007, and reported to Dave Evans (North & East Yorkshire FLO).
Description: A gold finger-ring, which is hollow cast, with a roughly oval aperture in the bezel, the back of which is open so that the stone it once held would have been in contact with the wearer's skin. This may indicate that the stone was thought to have magical properties. It would have been secured in place by two pins inserted through two small apertures, one at the top and one at the bottom. The external face of the hoop is decorated on the left with a double row of zigzags, which run into an inscription 'IC HOPE' (I hope). In the field after the inscription the zigzags are replaced by what appears to be a series of stylised fleurs-de-lis, the first two of which are combined, one inverted against the side of the other. This is repeated with the third and fourth fleurs-de-lis. The ring was probably originally enamelled. Dimensions: 21.9 x 4.1mm. Weight: 2.27g.
Disposition: Disclaimed; returned to finder.

J P ROBINSON

305. Worksop, Nottinghamshire: copper-alloy fertility badge (PAS: DENO-FEAA62)

Date: Medieval (c. 1400–c. 1520).
Discovery: Found by Craig Betts while metal-detecting, and recorded with Rachel Atherton (Nottinghamshire & Derbyshire FLO).
Description: A cast and enamelled roundel, which has the stub of an integral central loop that has broken off the back. The front has a large phallus centrally, pointing left into a vulva and there is a smaller phallus pointing downwards below. Above is the Lombardic-letter legend '+HAVE / PIS(?R)EO'. The surviving enamel is red. Diameter: 51.2mm. Weight 39.3g.
Discussion: This unparalleled, highly explicit badge with a family of genitalia is a most unusual find in England, where accessories featuring material that could be deemed pornographic were markedly far less common than they seem to have been in several towns across the North Sea and the English Channel. Malcolm Jones (Sheffield University) provisionally suggests that this elaborate, well-made and presumably relatively expensive badge was a fertility charm, the legend meaning something like 'May you have issue'.
Disposition: Returned to finder.

R ATHERTON, G EGAN & M JONES

306. Brill, Buckinghamshire: lead-alloy (possible) ink holder (PAS: BUC-3803B7)

Date: Medieval (c. 1400–c. 1550).
Discovery: Found by Clifford Emmett while metal-detecting in 2007, and recorded by Ros Tyrrell (Buckinghamshire FLO).
Description: A hollow-cast rectangular container, broadening at the base and open at the top, below which are two lug handles. These appear to have been intended as loops, but they are solid (possibly intended to be perforated by the owner, who did not do this). Two of the faces have an uneven zigzag, bordered by two lines, between the lugs. Below, on one side is a privy mark consisting of cross above a circle and on the other is a cross ending in an inverted V-shape and with a line across the vertical bar. There is damage to the rim and the base of the object.
Dimensions: 81 x 25 x 1.5mm.
Discussion: A similar container with different privy marks was found in Salisbury (Egan 2001: 99, fig. 34, no. 83). These objects have been dated variously from the late 14th to the late 16th century.
Disposition: Returned to finder.

R TYRRELL & G EGAN

307. Stoughton area, West Sussex: silver-gilt signet ring (PAS: SUSS-BA4106; Treasure: 2007 T239)

Date: Medieval (c. 1400–c. 1550).
Discovery: Found by Chichester District Council in April 2007, and reported to Liz Andrews-Wilson (Sussex FLO).
Description: A silver-gilt ring which has a circular bezel with the image of a bird plucking a flower. Above the head of the bird is the inscription 'I FFYNCHR', which is likely to denote a personal name: J Fincher – the bird, or finch, acting as a rebus. The shoulders have three grooves, which turn into fictive cable-work, the grooves being decorated with small punches. The back of the ring has seen a lot of wear, and the punches have, for the most part, been abraded. Dimensions: 26.2 x 25.7 x 13.6mm. Weight: 12.44g.
Disposition: Chichester District Museum hopes to acquire as part of the main site archive.

J P ROBINSON

**308. Lydd, Kent: gold finger-ring
(PAS: KENT-C343E3; Treasure: 2007 T632)**

Date: Medieval (c. 1400–c. 1550).
Discovery: Found by Chris Beever while metal-detecting in November 2007, and reported to Andrew Richardson (Kent FLO).
Description: An iconographic finger-ring with a central, engraved image of a standing saint, possibly St John the Evangelist, holding a chalice in his left hand and blessing it with his right. The ring is a highly original construction of geometric planes, creating an exaggerated point at the shoulder. Each plane is engraved with a sunburst and sprigs of foliage. The hoop is cabled and carries an inscription punctuated by engraved flowers (differently orientated from the image), reading 'EN BON AN'. Dimensions: 20.22 x 21.32 x 7.96mm. Weight: 4.8g.
Discussion: This French inscription, wishing a good year, appears on a large number of Medieval rings which are considered to have been New Year's gifts.
Disposition: Canterbury Museum hoped to acquire, but withdrew, to be returned.

J P ROBINSON

**309. Coberley, Gloucestershire: silver-gilt fragment in the form of a human arm
(PAS: WILT-116095; Treasure: 2007 T696)**

Date: Medieval or Post-Medieval (c. 1400–c. 1600).
Discovery: Found by Paul Fern while metal-detecting in September 2007, and reported to Katie Hinds (Wiltshire FLO).
Description: A hollow object in the form of a human arm, bent at the elbow and wearing armour. Two small holes near the top were presumably for attachment to the missing remainder of the figure. The armour on the upper arm is engraved and punched, representing a combination of mail and plate. The sleeve covering the lower arm is probably intended to be fabric. The edge at the top of the arm is serrated and damaged. Dimensions: 39.9 x 10mm. Weight: 5.3g.
Discussion: The original function of the object is unknown. It may have been part of a devotional figure for private worship, perhaps representing a warrior saint, or possibly a toy or table ornament.
Disposition: Acquired by Corinium Museum.

B NENK

**310. Penllyn, Vale of Glamorgan: silver brooch
(PAS: NMGW-9C3A27; Treasure: Wales 07.14)**

Date: Medieval (c. 1427–c. 1500).
Discovery: Found by Phil Smith while metal-detecting in May 2007, and reported to Mark Lodwick (Finds Co-ordinator, Wales).
Description: The frame of an annular brooch; the pin is missing. It has been made by filing down the rim of, and removing the centre from, a silver groat of Henry VI (r. 1422–1461) struck at Calais between 1427 and 1434. Diameter: 22mm. Diameter (hole): 9mm. Weight: 2.27g.
Discussion: The use of Medieval coins to form brooches is paralleled by a recent find from Covenham, Lincolnshire (2007 T434), created from a Short Cross penny of 1205–1209 and by two converted coins of the Teutonic Orders from the late 14th and early 15th centuries in the Ducker Hoard (Bunge, Gotland), deposited in the early 16th century. These feature constrictions or piercing to accommodate a pin, lacking on the Cowbridge example. While this feature is not essential, its absence here raises the possibility that the conversion was not completed.
Disposition: Acquired by the National Museum of Wales.

E M BESLY & M REDKNAP

**311. Cerne Abbas, Dorset: silver-gilt dress fitting
(PAS: DOR-B85D80; Treasure: 2007 T196)**

Date: Medieval (c. 1450–c. 1500).
Discovery: Found by Mr A Davis while metal-detecting in April 2007, and reported to Claire Pinder (Senior Archaeologist, Dorset County Council).
Description: A lozenge-shaped dress fitting with a knop at each corner and a central collet set with a pale pink stone (two of the corners have been bent). The front is decorated with roughly incised lines and the edges are serrated. On the back are the remains of two attachment bars. The dress fitting is silver gilt apart from the knops, which are plain silver and possibly intended to simulate pearls. Length: 13mm. Width: 14mm.
Disposition: Acquired by the British Museum.

D THORNTON

312. Penllyn, Vale of Glamorgan: hoard of over 30 lead *ampullae* (PAS: NMGW-504A65, 505AC2, 501A31, EBBC07 etc)

Date: Medieval (c. 1450–c. 1525).
Discovery: Found by Norman and Ann Oxley, Denis and Tina Pople and Tony Jones while metal-detecting in 2007, and recorded by Mark Lodwick (Finds Co-ordinator, Wales). In a combined effort by the primary finders and members of Rhondda Artefacts and Research Enthusiasts, and attended by Mark Lodwick, the findspots of 13 of the *ampullae* were recorded.

Description: Crude *ampullae*, blank on one side. On the other sides, the scallop-shell emblem of St James, which had come to represent pilgrimage.

Discussion: All 35 complete or fragmentary *ampullae* (representing at least 31 original containers) were recovered from ploughsoil from within a 50m² area, with most concentrated in a 15m² area. They are all of the same form and basic dimensions, sharing many features – including the loss or miscasting of the side loops – suggesting they were unfinished. They presumably came from one workshop or casting site. The discovery of more than a single *ampulla* in one place is very unusual, and this sizeable multiple find (away from any known shrine) is unparalleled.

Disposition: The finds have been donated to the National Museum of Wales.

M REDKNAP

---

313. Lund, East Yorkshire: copper-alloy pilgrim badge (PAS: YORYM-CEA5E7)

Date: Medieval (c. 1475–c. 1525).

Discovery: Found by Gary Crowther while metal-detecting in 2007, and recorded with Liz Andrews-Wilson (North & East Yorkshire FLO).

Description: A cast badge, in the form of a button, formed from a flat, circular plate of copper alloy, with an iron attachment loop cast into the centre of the reverse. The front of the badge has an engraved image of St Roche in a circular border. The saint, whose cult was based at Montpelier in France, was himself a pilgrim, as is shown by his clothing. He wears a long, flowing tunic and a large rounded headdress, and carries a round-topped staff in his left hand, which has a string of rosary beads daggling from it. Roche suffered from a sore on the upper leg, which he is exposing, and he had a companion dog, which was apt to lick the wound (a comfort of a kind). He is a patron of those with stubborn, non-healing wounds and apparently untreatable sores. There is an attendant angel kneeling on his right side and a scroll above the angel, which reads 'SROC', indicating the saint's name. Dimensions: 32.2 x 30.9 x 1.3mm. Weight: 6.7g.

Discussion: This is only the second St Roche souvenir recorded from England. The other was found in South Petherton, Somerset (SOMDOR905).

Disposition: Returned to finder.

L ANDREWS-WILSON & G EGAN

---

314. Elmstead, Essex: copper-alloy devotional badge depicting the Crucifixion (PAS: ESS-302D31)

Date: Medieval (c. 1450–c. 1530).

Discovery: Found by Stuart Elton while searching with a metal-detector in 2007, and recorded by Laura McLean (Essex FLO).

Description: Octagonal devotional badge of button form. It is engraved with the Crucifixion: the central figure is of Christ on the cross, with robed figures standing to the sides, St John to the right, holding his gospel book, while to the left the Virgin has her hands clasped in prayer. The figure of Jesus has his right leg crossing over the left one, with the nail showing. The nails are also clear on the palm of each hand, with the fingers closing around them. A small panel at the top of the cross reads 'INRI' – reversed 'N' – (Jesus of Nazareth, King of the Jews). The entire design is bordered by an engraved double line, with cording along the edge. There is some damage at the base and the surface is slightly worn. The central stem/attachment loop has been broken off. Diameter: 31.43mm. Thickness (including broken shank): 3.96mm. Weight: 6.91g.

Discussion: This is one of many copper-alloy religious badges dating from the last generation before the Reformation.

Disposition: Donated to Colchester & Ipswich Museum Service.

L MCLEAN

---

315. Tower Hamlets, London: silver girdle terminal (PAS: LON-8809F7; Treasure: 2007 T204)

Date: Medieval (c. 1450–c. 1550).

Discovery: Found by Alan Place while metal-detecting in January 2007, and reported to Kate Sumnall (London FLO).

Description: A silver girdle terminal, which consists of a tapering rectangular shaft terminating in a hexagonal knop. Each edge is decorated with two semicircular protuberances positioned close to the knop. On each face there is a central band of decoration, with an engraved design resembling tears, between two narrow bands of engraved decoration resembling rope work. On one side there is a large hole (diameter: 5mm) presumably for the attachment of fabric. Dimensions: 39.55 x 15.93 x 10.43mm. Weight: 14.54g.

Discussion: For a comparable example, with tear decoration in relief, see *TAR* 2004: no. 223.

Disposition: Disclaimed, returned to finder.

J P ROBINSON

316. Great Gaddesen, Hertfordshire: gold rectangular mount (PAS: BH-DE1292; Treasure: 2007 T224)

Date: Medieval (c. 1450–c. 1550)
Discovery: Found by Mary Hannaby while metal-detecting in April 2007, and reported to Julian Watters (Bedfordshire & Hertfordshire FLO).
Description: The mount is rectangular in shape and slightly distorted. The front surface is engraved with a depiction of the Holy Trinity, showing the seated figure of God the Father, holding aloft the crucified Christ. The engraving was originally enamelled, and significant traces of black enamel remain in the recesses of the design. The mount is likely to have decorated a reliquary or a book cover. Height: 29mm. Width: 23mm. Weight: 9g.
Disposition: Dacorum Heritage Trust, Berkhamsted, had hoped to acquire but withdrew; returned to finder.

J P ROBINSON

317. Lancaster area, Lancashire: silver crucifix pendant (PAS: LANCUM-354065; Treasure: 2007 T657)

Date: Medieval (c. 1450–c. 1550).
Discovery: Found by Martin Rowson while metal-detecting in November 2007, and reported to Dot Boughton (Cumbria & Lancashire FLO).
Description: The pendant has trefoil terminals and a suspension loop. The figure of Christ has its right arm broken at the shoulder. On the back is a figure of the Virgin and Child. Dimensions: 40 x 23mm.
Disposition: Lancaster City Museum hoped to acquire, but withdrew; returned to finder.

J P ROBINSON

318. Barham, Kent: engraved silver mount (PAS: KENT-6D9885; Treasure: 2007 T699)

Date: Medieval (c. 1450–c. 1550).
Discovery: Found by Steven Long while metal-detecting in November 2007, and reported to Andrew Richardson (Kent FLO).
Description: A lozenge-shaped mount, slightly distorted in the centre. It is engraved with the scene of the Annunciation: the Archangel Gabriel kneels on the left, greeting the Virgin Mary, who is at a lectern on the right. They are separated by a vase containing a lily, the symbol of the Virgin. Above the pair is the Holy Spirit in the form of a dove. Each corner of the mount is perforated by a small hole, which was the means of attachment. This may have been, for example, an item of dress, a book cover or a casket. It would originally have been enamelled. Dimensions: 20.78 x 19.12 x 0.8mm. Weight: 1.6g.
Disposition: Acquired by Canterbury Museum.

J P ROBINSON

319. Bletchingley, Surrey: copper-alloy harness boss (PAS: SUR-A033A8)

Date: Medieval (c. 1475–c. 1525).
Discovery: Found by Chris Andre while metal-detecting in 2007, and recorded by David Williams (Surrey FLO).
Description: A copper-alloy roundel from a horse harness, probably from the bridle set. The boss is circular with a wide brim and a hemispherical central dome. There are no signs of the method of attachment. The boss has been extensively engraved. On the rim is a sequence of four lions passant guardant, which alternate with the letters 'H' and 'B'. On the dome are two more lions and the letters 'HB' occur again. On the rim the field has been filled with closely spaced zigzag (or rocked tracer) work. Diameter: 79.33mm. Weight: 46.83g.
Discussion: The letter forms, with their distinctive lobed extensions, can be dated to c. 1470–c. 1510 (John Cherry, *personal communication*). With its extensive decoration the boss is likely to have been owned by a member of the nobility. In view of the location of the findspot, near Bletchingley, the initials 'HB' are probably those of Henry Stafford, second Duke of Buckingham; Edward, third Duke of Buckingham, always signed each page of his accounts with the initials 'EB' (Mary Saaler, *personal communication*). Henry was the Lord of the Manor of Bletchingley from 1460, when he succeeded his grandfather Humphrey, until his execution in 1483. Henry, however, is not known to have visited Bletchingley and the boss was probably lost by a member of his retinue who would have worn their lord's livery (information on the Bletchingley Manor was provided by Mary Saaler). Henry Duke of Buckingham was heavily involved in the Wars of the Roses and was a key supporter of Richard III who came to the throne in June 1483. Buckingham soon attempted a rebellion in the Midlands and Wales. Richard moved against him in October and Buckingham's support deserted him. He was executed in Salisbury in November of the same year. Henry is also one of the prime suspects in the murder of the two princes in the Tower of London and he appears prominently in Shakespeare's Richard III.
Disposition: Returned to finder.

D WILLIAMS

320. Telford area, Shropshire: copper-alloy purse bar (PAS: HESH-C72F24)

Date: Medieval (c. 1475–c. 1550).
Discovery: Found by Paul Mower while metal-detecting in 2007, and recorded with Peter Reavill (Herefordshire & Shropshire FLO).
Description: A copper-alloy purse bar, almost complete, with parts of both ends missing. It has an expanded, sub-rectangular terminal at either end. On the lower edge of each arm are two small, sub-rectangular, integrally cast loops, from which leather or cloth pouch would have been suspended. At the centre of the bar is a shield-shaped element with a hole for

the rotating suspension loop. Both sides of the bars arms have an inscription inlaid with *niello*: on one side '[A]VE MARIA / GATIA PLE..' (underlined letters are ligatured) and on the other 'DOMINV / S / TECVM' (Hail Mary Full of Grace, the Lord is with you). The central element has a *niello* fleur-de-lis.

Dimensions: 137.5 x 57.8 x 9.4mm. Weight: 62.9g.

Discussion: Similar purse bars have been discussed by Ward Perkins (1940, 163–165), who classifies this form as Type A2 – distinguished by the presence of an inlaid religious or talismanic inscription and a lack of ornament – and dates it to *c.* 1490.

Disposition: Returned to finder.

P REAVILL

---

321. Kilgetty, Pembrokeshire: silver-gilt pendant (PAS NMGW-9E8024; Treasure: Wales 07.7)

Date: Medieval (c. 1500–c. 1550).

Discovery: Found while metal-detecting in January 2007, and reported to Mark Lodwick (Finds Co-ordinator, Wales).

Description: A silver-gilt devotional pendant, of rounded arch niche form, with one hinged door. The door is opened by removing a pin which slides through retaining tubes on the left of the pendant, which mirror the appearance of the hinge on the right. The door has a damaged openwork panel in its centre. Two cast, haloed figures kneel within a beaded circular frame. The figure on the left appears to be praying; the one on the right appears to have arms crossed on the chest. When the pendant is closed, these small figures appear to flank a central figure visible inside.

The main external faces, front and back, are engraved with flower motifs in the lower corners. On the front, a bird with nimbus, wings outspread sits slightly off-centre above the circular frame, in the top panel. The back is engraved with a scene from the Passion of Christ, again within a plain circular frame. The knotted rope binding Christ is depicted wrapped around the lower shaft of the cross, which has a stylised rendering of wood grain and knots. The head of Christ in Majesty, flanked by John (left) and (possibly) Mary or angels (right), fills the upper panel. This is probably a dove, representing the Holy Spirit.

When the pendant is opened, a Trinity of haloed saints, each standing on a small pedestal, is revealed. The central figure is John the Baptist. His long hair extends below the shoulders, and he appears to wear a long cloak. Some of the moulding suggests a camel-hair robe below his knee. John holds his emblem, an *Agnus Dei* on a book, to which his right hand appears to be pointing. To his left stands St Catherine, supporting her symbols – a broken wheel in her right hand, and her martyr's palm leaf in her left hand. To John's right stands Mary Magdalene. Tresses of her long hair are suggested between the fingers of her right hand, and she holds a cylindrical jar in her left hand. This recalls her anointing the feet of Christ with ointment and wiping them with her long hair. Transverse moulding

on the jar resembles the turned decoration found on other representations of ointment jars (e.g. St Mary Magdalene, c. 1450, on London, British Museum, Harley 2915, fol. 152r).

The missing suspension loop was probably lost in antiquity from the attachment lug, and may have been the reason for the loss of the reliquary itself.

Height: 38mm. Width: 30mm. Thickness: 0.5mm. Weight: 17.61g.

Discussion: The design and style of the iconography of the pendant suggest it was probably made during the first half of the 16th century. Similar representations from the Passion cycle appear in printed sources such as *The Passyon of Christ* (published by Wynkyn de Worde in 1532) and *Meditationes Jordani de vita et passione Iesu Christi* (published by Richard Pynson in 1513). The style of the flower designs is reminiscent of those in early 16th-century painted border patterns from Llandeilo Tal-y-bont church, Pontarddulais. For an engraved scene on a silver-gilt pendant within a plain circular border, dated to c. 1520, see Lightbown (1992: cat. no. 68). Circular frames also occur on late 15th-century reliquary pendant capsules.

During the early 16th century, reliquary pendants with miniature cameo scenes, sometimes in enamelled gold, were particularly popular. Many post-date a change in liturgy that rendered osculatories obsolete, though the form of the Pembrokeshire pendant copies those of larger paxes (which were also kissed to celebrate the unity of the church through the bond of charity) – for example, the retable for private devotion set as a pax from the mid-15th century from the Ernest Brummer Collection (Spink and Son 1979: no. 252). Many such objects were converted into reliquary pendants, intended to be worn as items of personal adornment and for devotional purposes such as meditation.

Disposition: Acquired by the National Museum of Wales.

M REDKNAP

---

322. Vernhams Dean, Hampshire: silver-gilt finger-ring (PAS: WILT-BAB214; Treasure: 2007 T533)

Date: Medieval/Post-Medieval (c.1500–c.1600).

Discovery: Found by Michael Ashton while metal-detecting in September 2007, and reported to Katie Hinds (Wiltshire FLO).

Description: The 'fede' finger-ring's bezel is formed of clasped hands surmounted by a crown, and the hoop is decorated with alternating floral and foliate motifs. Much of the gilding remains on both the inner and outer surfaces. Diameter: 22mm. Weight: 4g.

Discussion: The love symbolised by the joined hands is here emphasised by a crowned heart between the hands.

Disposition: Hampshire Museums Service hopes to acquire.

N AWAIS-DEAN

Section editor and further research: Geoff Egan
Editor: Michael Lewis

Dress accessories again comprise the largest single category of finds recorded with the PAS and reported Treasure in 2007. A buckle frame enamelled in black and white from Mildenhall, Wiltshire (381), almost certainly made in London by makers recently identified from documentary sources, seems appropriate for the puritan taste of the mid 17th century. Despite the clear hallmarks on a late 17th-century silver shoe buckle from Newport area, Isle of Wight (399), its maker has not been traced. From the Medieval/post-Medieval transitional period is a signet finger-ring with a crowned initial from Paul, Cornwall (323), from a well known series. Later signet rings of gold are armorial, such as that from Oulton, Staffordshire (343), while another gold ring from Winterbourne, Wiltshire (345), has 19 non-matching diamonds, which may have been acquired over a period of time. The finger-rings of precious metals include several with amatory legends and, from the late 17th and 18th centuries, mourning rings named the deceased they commemorate: from Kensworth, Bedfordshire (402), Hawton, Nottinghamshire (403), Milbourne Port, Somerset (410), Boxgrove, West Sussex (395), and Buttercrambe with Bossal, North Yorkshire (408). A silver decade ring from Wootton Wawen, Warwickshire (351) is an unusual accessory from the late 16th- or 17th-century Catholic community, and from the mid 17th century is another silver ring from Penllyn, Vale of Glamorgan (366), with a pious motto on the inside. Also from the 17th century are a multiple-signet ring (awkward to wear) and a similar item with a much smaller central hole, respectively from Brearton, North Yorkshire (372), and Stanton Drew, Gloucestershire (373), both of copper alloy and both with four different die motifs.

From the early part of the period are further hooked clasps, including ones of silver from east Hertfordshire (330), Carnforth, Lancashire (331), Kelsale, Suffolk (329), and, with an early non-letter mark, from Wentlooge, Monmouthshire (332), and a contemporary cap hook, again of silver, from North Yorkshire area (333), which have been the subject of a major synthesis (Read 2008). Also among Treasure items are two silver filigree pins of similar date from Mercaston, Derbyshire (335), and Durnford, Wiltshire (334), and a silver whistle of so-called 'bosun's' type, though this one was found, land-locked, at Garthorpe, Leicestershire (337). More familiar are a pair of silver cufflinks from the late 17th century from south-east Lancashire (396). A copper-alloy clog clasp from Guildford, Surrey (411), stamped 'Liberty to America', is a rare instance in this country of an everyday, lower-class dress item with a slogan advocating American independence in the late 18th century. A large, silver-gilt and enamelled, jewelled pendant from Padstow, Cornwall (417), submitted as possible Treasure, is a 19th-century baroque-revival piece, as produced in several European centres at that time.

A large, Midlands-purple, ceramic domestic storage vessel from Atcham, Shropshire (377) is of a form apparently previously unknown, while a small, decorative glass bottle from Wimborne Minster, Dorset (400), probably from the late 17th or 18th century, is probably of Iberian origin. The range of decorative knife handles continues to expand, this year with one bearing the date 1526 from Gussage All Saints, Dorset (346), and a 17th-century find from London (371) has re-used a thimble to strengthen the shoulder. A silver-gilt seal-top spoon from Oving, West Sussex (378), was, from the marks stamped on it, probably made by Robert Cotton in London in 1615–1616. A silver thimble from Kelvedon, Essex (369), also from the 17th century, provides a further pious motto – 'fear God only'. A possible 16th-century lead bird-feeder or water trough from Alberbury with Cardeston area, Shropshire (338), probably for a caged pet, is decorated with unidentified arms. More upmarket are two silver shield-shaped vervel (hunting bird's identification tag) pendants, from south Herefordshire (339) and Foulsham, Norfolk (347), which probably respectively refer to Thomas, 4th duke of Norfolk (1536–1576), and to Francis Mannock of Gifford's Hall, Suffolk, also in the late 16th century, and there is an inscribed silver vervel ring inscribed to show it was from Chicheley, Berkshire, found in Emneth, Norfolk (352). Of related interest is a silver hawking whistle from Old Radnor, Powys (386). Silver seal matrices with unidentified arms come from Ropley, Hampshire (397), Shenley, Hertfordshire (374), Thurlaston, Leicestershire (393), and Udimore, East Sussex (342), and another, from Coxhoe, County Durham (376), has the motif of a skeleton holding an hourglass. A base-metal fob seal from Broughton-in-Furness, Cumbria (406), with a stone, probably of glass, reading 'If I dare', is likely to be a mass-produced item, and another of gold from Landford, Wiltshire (418), reading 'Remember me' on a possible amethyst, was a more expensive version; one of silver from Wantage Down area, Oxfordshire (370), has an exotic script which has not yet been identified.

A lead/tin 'pilgrim' badge from Barrow, Suffolk (327), from the politically inspired cult for Henry VI based at Windsor under the early Tudors, is a reminder of its brief but wide popularity. From the middle of the next century, from Tendring area, Essex (379), and Drayton Bassett, Staffordshire (380), are a couple of silver pendants with the head of Charles I. Also, from east of Colchester, Essex (382), is a heart-shaped pendant with an inscription to the same monarch, and from the Itchen Valley, Hampshire (384), comes a slightly later silver medal of Charles II. Another silver medal, from Runhall, Norfolk (383), is dated 1650, but this time with a pious inscription in German.

Lead cloth seals, which provide detailed evidence for traded textiles, include the first known for a textile woven in Courtenay in France, found in Nash Mills, Hertfordshire (387). A copper-alloy crotal bell from Great Barton, Suffolk (325), perhaps for a horse harness, has the arms of Nuremburg, and is a newly identified category of import from this important manufacturing centre in south Germany.

Toys include two fragments of possibly late 16th- to early 17th-century lead 'flat' women figures from Chiseldon, Wiltshire (355), and Pocklington area, East Yorkshire (356), while from Higher Kinnerton, Flintshire (354), is a solid lead three-dimensional figurine, also of a woman, but apparently imitating the form of finely detailed, hollow-cast late 16th-century versions (so far only found in London). A miniature, multiple copper-alloy cauldron from Crowle, North Lincolnshire (357), and of late 16th- or 17th-century date, combining four vessels, may have been an unusual toy for a child or a novelty for adults. A lead 'hornbook' from Belton and Manthorpe, Lincolnshire (389), from the reign of Charles II, adds to the rural focus of previous finds of these educational toys, and there is a probable handle from another from Penkridge, Staffordshire (394). An incomplete lead-alloy figurine of the noted early 19th-century Afro-Caribbean pugilist and former slave, Tom Molineaux, from Ryde, the Isle of Wight (414), is a rare survival of the sort of souvenir figure more familiar in ceramic form. A silver spur for cock-fighting from Snape, North Yorkshire (388), is difficult to date accurately, but probably earlier than the ban which went onto the Statute Book in 1835. A copper-alloy pipe tamper in the form of an embracing couple, from about the turn of the 19th century, from Bures area, Essex (405), parallels a previous find and adds to the erotica of this date. A small copper-alloy coffin from Kirkham, Lancashire (420), was probably used for a pet in the 19th century.

A stone mould for casting single shot balls from London (375) is an unusual item. A decorative sword found in Woolley, West Yorkshire (415), is of Indian origin and probably dates to the 19th century. A copper-alloy manilla (currency arm-band from West Africa) found in Ilam, Staffordshire (353), follows others reported in previous years. A lead gaming piece for spinning, with Hebrew letters to determine particular outcomes, from Shalfleet, Isle of Wight (423), is probably of 19th-century date and would have been used within the Jewish community, sanctioned for gambling on a modest scale by the religious authorities.

323. Paul, Cornwall: copper-alloy signet finger-ring (PAS: CORN-67B346)

Date: Medieval/post-Medieval (c. 1450–c. 1550).

Discovery: Found by Harry Manson while metal-detecting in August 2007, and recorded by Anna Tyacke (Cornwall FLO).

Description: Cast copper-alloy signet finger-ring, with an oval bezel with an incuse lombardic letter 'R' and crown above. The hoop is semicircular in section, but is mainly missing. Diameter: 25mm. Dimensions (bezel): 17 x 11.7 x 9mm. Weight: 5.97g.

Discussion: This type of signet ring was popular in the late Medieval period (e.g. Saunders 1991: 46, fig. 12, no. 19, from Wilton, Wiltshire, and another in the Salisbury Museum collections is dated to the 15th century; Egan 2005: 53, fig. 39, no. 236 from London, residual in a later context, is similar but without a crown).

Disposition: Returned to finder.

A TYACKE

324. Chettle, Dorset: copper-alloy pen (PAS: DOR-173638)

Date: Medieval/post-Medieval (c. 1450–c. 1550).

Discovery: Found by David Cobb while metal-detecting in 2007, and recorded by Ciorstaidh Hayward Trevarthen (Dorset FLO).

Description: A cast copper-alloy pen with a lozenge faceted shaft, now distorted. The shaft narrows into a plain rod at the distal end and terminates in a rounded knop. There is a similar plain section between the faceting and the lanceolate end. The latter has four curving, flat foils to hold the ink and tapers to a point. Dimensions: 84.66 x 6.3 x 6.27mm. Weight: 5.96g.

Discussion: A relatively unusual find in good condition. There is a monastic site in the vicinity, from which this clerkly tool may have come (Egan 1998: no. 898 from London; see also NARC-7DB472).

Disposition: Returned to finder.

C HAYWARD TREVARTHEN

325. Great Barton, Suffolk: copper-alloy bell with heraldic arms (PAS: SF-A43191)

Date: Medieval/post-Medieval (c. 1450–c. 1650).

Discovery: Found by Hugh Howcutt while metal-detecting in 2007, recorded by Faye Minter (Suffolk FLO) and identified by Edward Martin (Suffolk County Council Archaeological Service).

Description: Cast copper-alloy clapper bell. It has a silvery colour, perhaps due to a high lead/tin content. It has an integral suspension loop and is semicircular in shape, with the lower edge having eight stepped, almost semicircular arches. The hollow inside of the bell has a copper-alloy wire loop attached to the apex and hanging from this is a solid copper-alloy pea. The outer face of the bell is decorated with four integrally moulded roundels, each with the same heraldic arms – per pale, a demi eagle displayed, and three bends – the arms of Nuremberg, Germany, where this object was presumably made. Dimensions: 29.04 x 28.26mm. Weight: 27.98g.

Discussion: Similar bells from Ickingham, Suffolk (SF-BC7AB1), Gatcombe, Isle of Wight (IOW-D712F1), and Compton Abbas, Dorset (SOMDOR-0B1D95), have been recorded. They may have been for horse harnesses and may well date from the 15th to early 17th century, when jettons, thimbles and fustian textiles were being traded to England from southern Germany.

Disposition: Returned to finder.

F MINTER

326. Harlaston, Staffordshire: silver coin brooch (PAS: WMID-F4E937; Treasure: 2007 T627)

Date: Post-Medieval (c. 1501–c. 1521).

Discovery: Found by Jeremy Rudge while metal-detecting in June 2007, and reported to Duncan Slarke (Staffordshire & West Midlands FLO).

Description: A silver *soldino* of Doge Leonardo Loredano of Venice (r. 1501–1521), which has been converted into an item of jewellery by the addition of a decorative and shaped face covering one side which, presumably, was intended to be on view, whilst the actual coin face was not. The most likely interpretation is that it has been made into a button, or maybe some other type of dress fastening. Dimensions: 12.8 x 3.97mm. Weight: 0.77g.

Discussion: The *soldini* of early 16th century Venice, especially those of Leonardo Loredano, were present in English currency in very large numbers. Known as 'galley-halfpence', they functioned as unofficial halfpenny substitutes, since official small change was in short supply. As English coin finds, such *soldini* are probably more common than the contemporary English halfpennies. Despite their ubiquity, the English government opposed the use of *soldini* and launched a campaign in the 1520s to prohibit their import and chase them out of currency, with apparent success. The main question for this object would be when the coin was converted into an item of jewellery. In principle, this could have happened at any time between the 16th and 18th centuries, since there seem to be no parallels that permit a more precise dating of the ornamental addition. However, cautiously, it may seem likely that the conversion would have occurred reasonably close to the coin's period of English currency and could even have come about as a consequence of the official campaign against its use. Thus a date in the early decades of the 16th century would seem probable.

Disposition: Disclaimed; returned to finder.

B COOK

327. Barrow, Suffolk: lead pilgrim badge (PAS: SF-461CD7)

Date: Post-Medieval (c. 1500–c. 1530).

Discovery: Found by Mr Frankham while metal-detecting in 2007, and recorded by Faye Minter (Suffolk FLO).

Description: A cast lead pilgrim badge, now worn. It is circular with a border of three concentric circles, each of small pellets around a (possible) standing facing figure. On the back are an integrally cast pin and clasp. Diameter: 17mm. Weight: 1.78g.

Discussion: This badge is similar to a slightly larger one from London, which depicts Henry VI (r. 1422–1461 & 1470–1471) holding an orb, which was excavated from an early 16th-century context (Spencer 1998: 189–190 & 208). A politically inspired cult celebrating Henry VI was developed under the early Tudors.

Disposition: Returned to finder.

F MINTER

328. Bluntisham, Cambridgeshire: silver trefoil hooked clasp (PAS: BH-01C693; Treasure: 2007 T26)

Date: Post-Medieval (c. 1500–c. 1600).

Discovery: Found by Luke Denham while metal-detecting in 2006, and reported to Julian Watters (Bedfordshire & Hertfordshire FLO) in 2007.

Description: A silver dress-hook with a triangular, nicked back-plate. The trefoil ornament comprises three lobes with applied filigree knops and spiral decoration. At the centre a dome-headed pin is attached with a butterfly clip to the back-plate, holding a small silver petal-shaped element at the centre front. On the back, a recurving hook and a rectangular bar for attachment are soldered on. Dimensions: 22.2 x 16.8 x 8.6mm. Weight: 3.76g.

Discussion: This is a classic 16th-century type often reported as Treasure.

Disposition: Disclaimed; returned to finder.

D THORNTON

329. Kelsale cum Carlton, Suffolk: silver-gilt circular hooked clasp (PAS: SF-E85546; Treasure: 2007 T713)

Date: Post-Medieval (c. 1500–c. 1600).

Discovery: Found by Richard Calver while metal-detecting in October 2007, and reported to Faye Minter (Suffolk FLO).

Description: An incomplete, composite silver-gilt dress-hook, comprising a circular front-plate with seven evenly spaced knops and a central floral motif with eleven oval petals, and a separate domed rivet which holds the front-plate to a flat back-plate. Projecting from the upper edge of the former are the remains of an integral, transverse rectangular loop. The recurving hook is soldered to the back plate opposite the incomplete loop. Length: 21.4mm. Weight: 2.16g.

Discussion: This hooked tag appears to be a variation on the typology proposed by Gaimster *et al.* (2002). As it is composite it would belong to Group I, but it differs in that its transverse loop is integral to the front-plate rather than soldered onto the back-plate. This position, and its being in one with the front-plate, is more typical of accessories of Group II versions, which are normally cast in one.

Disposition: Acquired by Colchester & Ipswich Museum Service.

F MINTER

330. East Hertfordshire: silver-gilt hooked clasp (PAS: BH-E15835; Treasure: 2007 T211)

Date: Post-Medieval (c. 1500–c. 1600).

Discovery: Found while metal-detecting in April 2007, and reported to Julian Watters (Bedfordshire & Hertfordshire FLO).

Description: A silver dress-hook, book-shaped with projecting knops and foliate elements supporting a hook at the top. The front is gilt, with a heart and three lobes in filigree. On the back is a rectangular bar attachment. For a more complex example of this form see *TAR* 2003: no. 239 (also two in the British Museum: 2003, 3–1,1 & 2003, 3–1,2).

Disposition: Acquired by Ware Museum; both finder and landowner donated their share.

D THORNTON

331. Carnforth area, Lancashire: silver hooked clasp (PAS: LANCUM-6E9692; Treasure: 2007 T319)

Date: Post-Medieval (c. 1500–c. 1600).

Discovery: Found by Martin Head while metal-detecting in March 2007, and reported to Dot Boughton (Cumbria & Lancashire FLO).

Description: A cast silver dress-hook composed of a lozenge-shaped plate, with circlets and knops on the outer edge. It is likely the object would originally have had a central quatrefoil flower (this would have been attached by the rivet, which survives, through the perforation in the centre). On the back is a simple knop. Its transverse bar and hook are intact. Dimensions: 30.93 x 23.4mm. Weight: 6.31g.

Discussion: Similar are examples from Chelsham Court Farm, Surrey (Gaimster *et al.* 2002), which retains the central quatrefoil flower, and a dress-hook from East Keal, Lincolnshire (*TAR* 2004: no. 270).

Disposition: Acquired by Lancashire County Museums Service.

D BOUGHTON

332. Wentlooge, Monmouthshire: silver-gilt hooked-clasp (PAS: NMGW-9F0C64; Treasure: Wales 07.22)

Date: Post-Medieval (c. 1500–c. 1600).

Discovery: Found by James Manley while metal-detecting during October 2007, and reported to Mark Lodwick (Finds Co-ordinator, Wales).

Description: Silver-gilt dress-hook with a trefoil back-plate cut from a sheet and indented by filing, to which a separate hook and bar loop have been soldered on the reverse. Soldered to the front are three hollow, hemispherical bosses, each decorated with three single-strand 'rope-twist' filigree wire circlets, arranged around a small granulated pellet at the mid-point of each dome. Holding a flat, central disc is a dome-headed split pin, which passes through the centre of the back-plate, between the three bosses. The gilding does not appear to extend to the hook.

A maker's mark has been punched onto the hook's shaft, at the point where it has been attached to the back-plate. This is in the unusual, presumably early, form of four triangular indents, making a cruciform stamp. Length (including hook): 19.5mm. Width (back-plate): 14.4mm. Weight: 3g. Surface analysis: approximately 97% silver and 3% copper.

Disposition: Newport Art Gallery & Museum hopes to acquire.

M REDKNAP

333. North Yorkshire: silver-gilt cap hook (PAS: YORYM-68E976; Treasure: 2007 T182)

Date: Post-Medieval (c. 1500–c. 1600).

Discovery: Found by Geoff Bambrook while metal-detecting in November 2004, and reported to Dave Evans (North & East Yorkshire FLA) in 2007.

Description: A silver accessory, cast in one in the form of a rose with radiating petals and projecting knops. There are traces of gilding on the front. On the back are the remains of a single hook, suggesting that this may have been a cap accessory in which the hook doubled back on itself.

Discussion: For a comparable item, with the hook still in situ, but with a scene of the Crucifixion, see *TAR* 2003: no. 240, from Raydon, Suffolk.

Disposition: British Museum hopes to acquire.

D THORNTON

334. Durnford, Wiltshire: silver-gilt dress-pin (PAS: WILT-6E7454; Treasure: 2007 T89)

Date: Post-Medieval (c. 1500–c. 1600).

Discovery: Found by David Martin while metal-detecting in January 2007, and reported to Katie Hinds (Wiltshire FLO).

Description: A silver-gilt dress-pin with a heavy spherical head, decorated with applied filigree ornament on two hemispheres. Each hemisphere

has five circles surrounding a central cinquefoil, each containing a quatrefoil. At the centre of each foil and above and below each foil is a knop (though some are missing through wear). The pin-head is still gilded but this has worn off the knops. The shank of the pin, which narrows towards the point, is slightly damaged and a little bent. Diameter (head): c. 15mm. Length (shank): c. 52mm. Weight: 6.53g.

Disposition: Salisbury & South Wiltshire Museum hopes to acquire.

K HINDS

335. Mercaston, Derbyshire: silver-gilt dress-pin (PAS: DENO-D3CCD3; Treasure: 2007 T192)

Date: Post-Medieval (c. 1500–c. 1600).

Discovery: Found by Harry Taylor while metal-detecting in March 2007, and reported to Rachel Atherton (Derbyshire & Nottinghamshire FLO).

Description: A silver pin with a spherical head divided into two halves, each decorated with applied filigree and spiral ornament, and a knop at the top. The tip of the shaft has been bent back on itself. Diameter (head): 7mm.

Discussion: A relatively small example of a type frequently reported as Treasure.

Disposition: Acquired by Derby Museum and Art Gallery.

D THORNTON

336. Emneth, Norfolk: silver rumbler bell (PAS: NMS-2C2226; Treasure: 2007 T306)

Date: Post-Medieval (c. 1500–c. 1600).

Discovery: Found while metal-detecting in May 2007, and reported to Erica Darch (Norfolk FLO). Found with 352.

Description: A spherical silver rumbler bell, cast in two halves and soldered together, now in two pieces. There is a slot with rounded ends cut into the base, and a circular suspension loop is integrally cast with the upper half. The bell has a cylindrical copper-alloy pea, and a separate applied corded rib on the upper half at the seam, part of the way around the girth. Dimensions: 15 x 12mm. Weight: 1.54g.

Discussion: Copper-alloy bells of similar construction but with separately made suspension loops and iron pea (normally rather larger than this one) were in use as dress accessories in the 16th century (Egan and Pritchard 1991: 337–339; Egan 2005: 57).

Disposition: Acquired by Norwich Castle Museum.

S J ASHLEY

337. Garthorpe, Leicestershire: silver 'bosun's' whistle (PAS: LEIC-757733; Treasure: 2007 T707)

Date: Post-Medieval (c. 1500–c. 1600).
Discovery: Found by Ray Howitt while metal-detecting in September 2007, and reported to Wendy Scott (Leicestershire FLO).
Description: A complete silver whistle of tapering form, cut from sheet, with two collars, opening out into a hollow-cast sphere with an opening on the upper surface. There is an S-shaped grip soldered at two points on the lower side.
Discussion: This is, in form at least, a bosun's whistle, as used for giving orders and other signalling on board ship and as a badge of status in the navy, though this one was found in a land-locked county. They are generally dated to the 16th century, but the form continues today. Similar whistles are in the collections of the National Maritime Museum (PT 0457) and Museum of London – six have been found on the Thames foreshore and during archaeological excavation (Egan 2005: 124, fig. 118, nos. 594 & 596–597), a couple being from late 16th- to early 17th-century contexts. All of these are of lead/tin (see also *TAR* 2002: no. 125, which may be of similar date).
Disposition: Disclaimed; returned to finder.

D THORNTON

338. Alberbury with Cardeston area, Shropshire: lead-alloy bird-feed or water container (PAS: HESH-005348)

Date: Post-Medieval (c. 1500–c. 1600).
Discovery: Found by Ian Collins while metal-detecting in 2007, and recorded by Peter Reavill (Herefordshire & Shropshire FLO).
Description: A slightly distorted container, originally D-shaped in plan. The right-angled rim is slightly bent over. There is a casting seam on the two long sides and the base. The container is still about half-filled with soil, the upper part of which was subject to flotation, but no organic material was present. The back, sides and base are flat and undecorated, while the front, originally curved, has a chevron, with two crosses and an indistinct motif above and five pellets below, perhaps as a foliate design. Dimensions: 42.7 x 36.5 x 21.4mm. Weight: 94.47g.
Discussion: Similar containers have been found in London and Devon; (Read 1995: 127–128, fig. 811).
Disposition: Returned to finder.

P REAVILL

339. South Herefordshire: enamelled silver armorial (possible) vervel pendant (PAS: HESH-A49557; Treasure: 2007 T544)

Date: Post-Medieval (c. 1500–c. 1600).
Discovery: Found by Chris Chandler while metal-detecting in 2007, and reported to Peter Reavill (Shropshire & Herefordshire FLO).
Description: Cast and enamelled silver shield-shaped pendant with attachment ring. The front is engraved with a lion rampant on a field of red enamel. Areas of the enamel have been lost from the upper parts of the shield, showing that the surface beneath was roughened as keying. The back is inscribed on four lines: T / NOR/FOC/K. The workmanship is of a high quality. Dimensions: 19.6 x 1.3mm. Weight 1.31g.
Discussion: Vervels, most commonly in the form of rings, would have been attached to the legs of hunting birds to identify the owner. They are often inscribed with the owner's name, residence or coat of arms. They fulfil the same function as modern racing pigeon rings. The arms *gules a lion rampant argent* are those of the FitzAlan earls of Arundel, a title inherited by the Howard dukes of Norfolk with the marriage of Thomas, the 4th duke (1536–1576), to Mary FitzAlan.
Disposition: Hereford Museum & Art Gallery hopes to aquire.

P REAVILL

340. Llancarfan, Vale of Glamorgan: silver-gilt dress-hook loop (PAS: NMGW-B0C420; Treasure: Wales 07.01)

Date: Post-Medieval (c. 1500–c. 1600).
Discovery: Found by Mr P D Halford while metal-detecting in November 2006, and reported to Mark Lodwick (Finds Co-ordinator, Wales).
Description: Silver-gilt decorative roundel which once adorned the front of a dress-hook loop, to the back of which are soldered three sections of wire (which when complete formed the trefoil loop for the hook). The slightly domed silver-gilt boss has a border of 'cable-twist' filigree wire, wound in a spiral to create two strands. Within this, there are five cable-twist 'filigree' wire circlets, and a small granulated pellet in the interspace. Diameter: 9.4mm. Weight: 0.49g. Surface analysis: approximate metal content of 96% silver and 4% copper.
Disposition: National Museum of Wales hopes to acquire.

M REDKNAP

**341. Whitchurch area, Cheshire: gold finger-ring
(PAS: LVPL-00A457; Treasure: 2007 T156)**

Date: Post-Medieval (c. 1500–c. 1650).
Discovery: Found by Barry Lambert while metal-detecting in March 2007, and reported to Frances McIntosh (North West FLO).
Description: A small gold finger-ring, now slightly distorted, with a foliate design on the external surface and inscribed inside '+ DON + DAMI' (gift of a friend) followed by a sprig. Very slight traces of black enamel are visible on both the inner and outer faces.
Discussion: The style of the capital letter inscription is comparable with those on several rings of similar date.
Disposition: Nantwich Museum hoped to acquire, but withdrew; returned to finder.

N AWAIS-DEAN

**342. Udimore, East Sussex: silver seal matrix
(PAS: SUSS-70D736; Treasure: 2007 T95)**

Date: Post-Medieval (c. 1500–c. 1700).
Discovery: Found by Alan Charman while metal-detecting in December 2006, and reported to Liz Andrews-Wilson (Sussex FLO) in 2007.
Description: A silver seal matrix with an incomplete, decorative handle and oval face, which has the crude image of a bee keeper, standing on an exergue line. In front of him is a bell-shaped beehive, mounted on four thin legs, formed from two A-frames. There are seven stylised bees flying above, and the whole design is enclosed within a plain border. Dimensions: 16.5 x 15.4 x 11.8mm. Weight: 5.5g.
Disposition: Disclaimed; returned to finder.

L ANDREWS-WILSON

**343. Oulton, Staffordshire: gold finger-ring
(PAS: WMID-3DDE65; Treasure: 2007 T385)**

Date: Post-Medieval (c. 1500–c. 1700).
Discovery: Found by Sylvia Harris while gardening in October 2005, and reported to Angie Bolton (Warwickshire & Worcestershire FLO) in 2007.
Description: A gold signet ring, the hoop expanding at the shoulders to the oval bezel, which is set vertically. The bezel is engraved as a shield with a coat of arms: per pale, a tower of three turrets set on rocks, with a lozenge to either side of the tower; a lion rampant. The bezel is edged by a beaded border.
Disposition: Disclaimed; returned to finder.

N AWAIS-DEAN

**344. Holme, North Lincolnshire: gold finger-ring
(PAS: NLM-BE8630; Treasure: 2007 T120)**

Date: Post-Medieval (c. 1500–c. 1700).
Discovery: Found by Reg Robinson while metal-detecting in February 2007, and reported to Lisa Staves (North Lincolnshire FLO).
Description: A finger-ring with a D-shaped band, now squashed slightly out of shape, the exterior chased with scrolls. An inscription engraved on the inside of the hoop reads
'IN+TEMPORE+CAVE' (beware in time) and is framed by stars. The words are followed by a scroll. Diameter (external): 19.8mm. Weight: 1.83g.
Discussion: The scrollwork is similar to that on a couple of rings published by Dalton (1912: nos. 1902 & 2025).
Disposition: Acquired by North Lincolnshire Museums Service.

N AWAIS-DEAN

**345. Winterbourne, Wiltshire: gold finger-ring
(PAS: WILT-637426; Treasure: 2007 T317)**

Date: Post-Medieval (c. 1525–1575).
Discovery: Found by Simon Law while metal-detecting in 2007, and reported to Katie Hinds (Wiltshire FLO).
Description: Gold finger-ring with 19 diamonds of various cuts set around the hoop. One stone is missing from the back of the hoop. The style of the ring is reminiscent of a belt and the bezel is in the form of a buckle. The inside, as well as the top and bottom of the hoop, have also been enamelled in black to continue this effect of a belt and buckle. Dimensions: 26 x 18mm. Weight: 3.5g.
Discussion: A ring with stones set around the hoop is a rare survival. Regular wear could explain the missing stone. The belt-and-buckle motif was fairly common, used in the Middle Ages and continuing today. The stones have been set deeply and it appears as if they have been pushed into pitch. The variation in the cuts of the stones points to the mid 16th century (by the early part of the next century cutting had become more regularised). Given the crudeness of the goldwork and the poor quality of the enamel used, it is possible that the diamonds were bought loose, perhaps over a period of time, to be set into the ring as a display of the owner's wealth.
Disposition: Salisbury & South Wiltshire Museum hopes to acquire.

N AWAIS-DEAN

346. Gussage All Saints, Dorset: copper-alloy knife-handle terminal (PAS: DOR-55A6C1)

Date: Post-Medieval (c. 1526).
Discovery: Found by Martin Green while metal-detecting in 2007, and recorded by Ciorstaidh Hayward Trevarthen (Dorset FLO).
Description: Copper-alloy knife-handle terminal, with the stub of the iron tang. The object is sub-oval and is open at one end for attachment of the tang. Both faces have the date 1526 recessed, with a white inlay. Above and below the date, on both sides, is a linear groove and the flat top edge also has three oblique grooves. Dimensions: 14.83 x 14.01 x 6.9mm. Weight: 6.37g.
Discussion: While knife-handle terminals are found in great variety, it is unusual to find such an early dated example. It is possible that this was from one of a pair for a wedding or other commemorative gift.
Disposition: Returned to finder.

C HAYWARD TREVARTHEN

347. Foulsham, Norfolk: silver shield-shaped vervel (PAS: NMS-1EB356; Treasure: 2007 T679)

Date: Post-Medieval (c. 1550–c. 1625).
Discovery: Found by Andrew Carter while metal-detecting in October 2007, and reported to Erica Darch (Norfolk FLO).
Description: A silver pendant shield, probably from a vervel, with an integral loop at the top. The shield is engraved on both faces: 'Fr Man / nock of / giffardes / hall // in Stoke / in Suf. / esquire'. Dimensions: 10 x 17mm. Weight: 0.46g.
Discussion: Two similar objects are illustrated in *TAR* 2004, nos. 319 & 320; see also 339 in this report. The owner was either Francis Mannock of Gifford's Hall, Stoke by Nayland, Suffolk, who inherited the property in 1558, or his grandson, Sir Francis Mannock, who inherited in 1616, referring to a time before he was created a baronet in 1627. Of the two, the first seems the more likely.
Disposition: Acquired by Norwich Castle Museum.

S J ASHLEY

348. Newent, Gloucestershire: silver-gilt finger-ring (PAS: GLO-19A336; Treasure: 2007 T383)

Date: Post-Medieval (c. 1550–c. 1660).
Discovery: Found by Mark Powles while metal-detecting in June 2007, and reported to Kurt Adams (Gloucestershire FLO).
Description: The ring is formed of a broad flat band with exterior ridges in relief at the top and bottom. In between is the inscription: '+ HART x...x TRV'. The inscription is set between two bands of raised circular bosses, and here and along the edges the gilding is worn. The hoop has been neatly cut through

transversely between the surviving words. Dimensions: 23 x 9 x 1mm.
Discussion: For a similar example see *TAR* 2004: no. 300. Evans (1931) records a number of spelling variations of the inscription 'Be True in Heart' but none matches this one exactly. It is possible, but purely speculative, that 'be' has been removed by the cutting of the ring (Spencer 1998: 322–323, fig. 321d).
Disposition: Acquired by Gloucester City Museum; the landowner donated their share.

N AWAIS-DEAN

349. Swallowfield area, Oxfordshire: gold finger-ring (PAS: BERK-BAB9D4; Treasure: 2007 T489)

Date: Post-Medieval (c. 1550– c. 1700).
Discovery: Found while gardening in 2007, and reported to Charlotte Burrill (Berkshire & Oxfordshire FLO).
Description: A gold posy ring, slightly distorted. The hoop is decorated with flower designs, hearts and other decorative motifs. Some enamel has survived on the outside – colours that remain are white, green, blue and black. The inside is inscribed 'Kindly take this for my sake'. Traces of black enamel remain in the lettering. Dimensions: 20 x 3.7 x 1.15mm. Weight: 2.3g.
Discussion: The internal inscription, as on many lovers' rings and some others, remained secret to all but the wearer and donor.
Disposition: Oxfordshire Museums Service hopes to acquire.

N AWAIS-DEAN

350. Edgefield, Norfolk: gold finger-ring (PAS: NMS-411415; Treasure: 2007 T359)

Date: Post-Medieval (c. 1550– c. 1700).
Discovery: Found while metal-detecting in June/July 2007, and reported to Erica Darch (Norfolk FLO).
Description: An enamelled gold finger-ring in the form of a belt and buckle, inscribed on the inside 'TOVT + PAR + AMOVR +' (all through/for love). The slightly distorted hoop (the belt) is formed from two strips and is decorated with a running vine scroll, except beyond the buckle, where four pin holes are represented by double concentric rings (separated by transverse lines). The buckle is shown as double-looped with pointed ends, and large lobes at both ends of the bar. The belt passes through the buckle to be folded over and tucked back under itself. The rounded end is decorated with a motif that perhaps represents a strap-end. A small patch of white enamel survives within the buckle, and part of a ring of blue around one pin hole. A thick line of blue enamel is visible along the edges of the gap between two lengths of belt, while a minute speck of green enamel on the inner face is perhaps accidental. Diameter (internal): 15.5–17.5mm. Weight: 4.3g.

Discussion: Rings in the form of a belt and buckle, often for lovers, were popular in Europe from around the 14th century onwards.

Disposition: Acquired by Norwich Castle Museum; landowner donated his share.

A ROGERSON & N AWAIS-DEAN

351. Wootton Wawen, Warwickshire: silver decade finger-ring
(PAS: WAW-CB51A1; Treasure: 2007 T207)

Date: Post-Medieval (c. 1550–c. 1700).

Discovery: Found by Don Fowkes while metal-detecting in March 2007, and reported to Angie Bolton (Warwickshire & Worcestershire FLO).

Description: A silver decade ring, comprising a large D-section hoop with ten knops riveted to the exterior at regular intervals. The bezel is a larger flattened knop engraved with the sacred monogram 'I-H-S', above which is a cross; to the base of the monogram are three nails. On the internal face are slight indications of the rivets at the points corresponding to the knops on the exterior.

Discussion: Decade rings were a form of rosary used for repeating Ave and Paternoster prayers. The smaller knops were to count the Aves and the larger bezel represents the Paternoster. They were introduced around the 10th century. Since they were more discreet than rosary beads they became popular during times of religious persecution, particularly in the 16th century. There is one comparable example in British Museum (Dalton 1912: no. 800), but this has a cruder inscription on the bezel and was cast in one piece (see also SOMDOR-7E6495).

Disposition: Warwickshire Museum hopes to acquire.

N AWAIS-DEAN

352. Emneth, Norfolk: silver hawking vervel
(PAS: NMS-2C1204; Treasure: 2007 T305)

Date: Post-Medieval (c. 1550–c. 1700).

Discovery: Found while metal-detecting in May 2007, and reported to Erica Darch (Norfolk FLO). Found with 336.

Description: Silver hawk-ring or vervel, flat-sectioned with an engraved inscription around one face that reads '·m' Come·buck of Chichly' (Chicheley, Berkshire); there is a small nick above the initial m. Diameter: 11mm. Weight: 0.57g.

Disposition: Acquired by Norwich Castle Museum.

S J ASHLEY

353. Ilam, Staffordshire: copper-alloy manilla
(PAS: WMID-22DE66)

Date: Post-Medieval (c. 1550–c. 1945).

Discovery: Found by Julian Lee while metal-detecting in 2007, and recorded by Caroline Johnson (Staffordshire & West Midlands FLO).

Description: A complete cast copper-alloy manilla with probable silver coating. This is a small penannular arm bangle/bracelet comprising a circular-sectioned curved rod of a standard thickness, with expanded and flattened sub-oval terminals. There is a slight ridge from the casting seam running the length of each terminal base, which has been filed down leaving numerous marks. The object is overall slightly worn but in good condition with a smooth light grey/green patina. Dimensions: 57.5 x 59.5 x 8.5mm. Weight: 73.7g.

Discussion: Manillas were used as a form of money on the West African coast from the 16th century to the mid 20th century. They are hard to date as they were made in the same way, using the same metals with the same decoration over a long period (Anna Tyacke, Cornwall FLO, *personal communication*). This present find is similar to an example in the Royal Institution of Cornwall's collections that was recorded with the PAS (CORN-31B3A7) which came from the shipwreck of the Duoro, which was lost off the Isles of Scilly on 27 January 1843 en route to Africa.

Disposition: Returned to finder.

C JOHNSON

354. Higher Kinnerton, Flintshire: lead toy figurine
(PAS: LVPL-834150)

Date: Post-Medieval (c. 1575–c. 1600).

Discovery: Found by Lawrence Moulsdale while metal-detecting in 2007, and recorded by Frances McIntosh (Cheshire, Greater Manchester & Merseyside FLO).

Description: Solid lead figurine of a lady wearing a full-length, pleated dress. The head is slightly damaged. It is similar to, but cruder than, several highly detailed hollow versions from London, which are assigned to the late Elizabethan period. Dimensions: 62 x 21mm. Weight: 86.4g.

Discussion: It is significant as it is the first solid example of the series recorded, and also the first outside London. This is presumably a cheaper version than the London finds, but more sophisticated than the 'flats', like 355–356 (see Forsyth and Egan 2005: nos. 4.13–16 & 4.19 for examples of the finer ones found in London).

Disposition: Returned to finder.

F MCINTOSH

355. Chiseldon, Wiltshire: lead toy figurine (PAS: WILT-1C62D7)

Date: Post-Medieval (c. 1575–c. 1700).
Discovery: Found by Mark Gillett while metal-detecting in 2007, and recorded by Katie Hinds (Wiltshire FLO).
Description: Fragment of a flattish lead female figurine comprising torso and arms. Inverted Vs fill the V-shaped body on the front and back. The body has a slightly trapezoidal section and the triangular-section arms are flat at the back and angled at the front. The back has a central vertical rib, which on the front is wider and less pronounced. The arms are angled outwards then inwards to rest on the narrow waist; they have transverse hatching on the back. The breaks at top and bottom of the body at the neck and waist are old. Dimensions: 18 x 26mm. Weight: 3.5g.
Discussion: This is similar to hollow examples from London published by Forsyth and Egan (2005: 155, fig. 4.19), who suggest these are cheaper versions of hollow three-dimensional figurines from the late 16th to late 17th centuries.
Disposition: Returned to finder.

K HINDS

356. Pocklington area, East Yorkshire: lead toy figurine (PAS: YORYM-5C25C7)

Date: Post-Medieval (c. 1575–c. 1700).
Discovery: Found by Bernard Ross while metal-detecting in 2007, and recorded by Liz Andrews-Wilson (North & East Yorkshire FLO) and Jim Halliday (finds expert).
Description: A cast lead toy fragment. This is part of the skirt from a flat female figurine, decorated on both sides. One face has a grid pattern and the other has four parallel lines, two on either side, flanking a zigzag design. The remains of four copper-alloy rivets with lead caps suggest that this example had been attached to a base enabling it to stand up. Dimensions: 39 x 22 x 2.6mm. Weight: 11.64g.
Discussion: Similar toys can be seen in Forsyth and Egan (2005: 155, fig. 4.19). Although few lead toys of this period are found outside London in rural locations, there is a concentration in Yorkshire. No parallel is known for the riveting.
Disposition: Returned to finder.

L ANDREWS-WILSON

357. Crowle, North Lincolnshire: copper-alloy toy multiple cauldron (PAS: NLM-5A2185)

Date: Post-Medieval (c. 1575–c. 1700).
Discovery: Found by David Seddon while metal-detecting in 2007, and recorded by Lisa Staves (North Lincolnshire FLO).
Description: Incomplete cast copper-alloy miniature cauldron, cast in a quadruple form. Each of the four cauldrons has a rectangular foot decorated with three incised lines and a handle on the side, though two handles are missing. Dimensions: 38.7 x 29.7mm. Weight: 56.86g.
Discussion: The purpose of creating a quadruple form of the cauldron toy is still unclear. However, vessels known as 'fuddling' vessels have been recorded as full size ceramics and were produced from the 17th century as novelty pieces. These 'fuddling cups' were vessels with three or more small cups with interlinked handles and joined together through small holes in the walls (see SWYOR-6C64B4 for a three-cup miniature). The idea was to drink from one without spilling the contents of the others. Although cooking vessels have no 'fuddling cup' parallel, it seems that this miniature is some sort of novelty piece.
Disposition: Returned to finder.

L STAVES

358. Beaumont area, Essex: copper-alloy socketed candlestick (PAS: ESS-C40E64)

Date: Post-Medieval (c. 1575–c. 1700).
Discovery: Found by Peter Bohannon while metal-detecting in Autumn 2007, and recorded by Laura McLean (Essex FLO).
Description: Cast copper-alloy candlestick. The incomplete socket has an everted rim and an expanded moulding at the bottom. The stem has a bladed knop and a lower, bulbous moulding, from which the rebated attachment rivet protrudes; the basal dish is missing. It has a dull grey patina with small flecks of green copper corrosion. A break at the base of the stem is old but those in the socket appear more recent, though there is some wear. Length: 96.33mm. Weight: 122.61g.
Disposition: Donated to Colchester and Ipswich Museums Service.

L MCLEAN

359. Stoulton, Worcestershire: lead cloth seal (PAS: WAW-79D3C6)

Date: Post-Medieval (c. 1590–c. 1620).
Discovery: Found by John Bridgewater while metal-detecting in 2007, and recorded by Angie Bolton (Warwickshire and Worcestershire FLO).
Description: A fragment of a proforma cast lead cloth seal. The seal is a sub-rectangular spade shape. The integrally cast legend reads '[...] / XXII / XVIII / ?E'. The second disc is missing but the flattened rivet shows the seal had been attached to a cloth. Dimensions: 23.14 x 18.42mm. Weight: 4.4g.
Discussion: The numerals on this cloth seal are the dimensions, as required by law, of a particular variety of cloth; 22 is probably the length in yards while 18 is probably its weight in pounds. The 'E' could well be from 'searched', meaning the cloth had been examined by the government's textile officials, who measured and weighed each cloth to check it conformed to the specifications. 'Searched' was then stamped in the blank area below the figures when the seal was fixed to the textile, so it could be seen on the market stall. This seal dates from the late 16th century to about 1620, and is probably the first of this type discovered in Worcestershire. The PAS has recorded four other similar proforma cloth seals: LIN-57C813 from Lenton Keisby and Osgodby, Lincolnshire; WAW-F76B32 from Evesham, Worcestershire; NMS-C9B764 from Quidenham, Norfolk; and SWYOR-DAB180 from Clifton, South Yorkshire (Egan 1996: 58–59, fig. 26, nos. 117–119).
Disposition: Returned to finder.

A BOLTON

360. Market Rasen, Lincolnshire: gold finger-ring (PAS: 1917F7; Treasure: 2007 T143)

Date: Post-Medieval (c. 1600–c. 1700).
Discovery: Found by Dean Wilson while metal-detecting in March 2007, and reported to Lisa Staves (North Lincolnshire FLO).
Description: A gold finger-ring with a D-shaped band. The complex bezel holds out a colourless cut stone and it is backed by a heart with pale blue enamel covering most of it, although much is chipped. Two tapered grooves run along the top and bottom of each shoulder, and within these, further pale blue enamel is evident; there are also very slight traces of black enamel. Diameter: 18.2mm. Weight: 2g. Analysis revealed the transparent stone to be rock crystal.
Discussion: This finger-ring is very similar to an example found in Hawkhurst, Kent (*TAR* 2004: no. 313), and there are many comparable examples in the British Museum dated to the 1600s (Dalton 1912).
Disposition: Disclaimed; returned to finder.

N AWAIS-DEAN

361. Everleigh, Wiltshire: gold finger-ring (PAS: WILT-BA3553; Treasure: 2007 T516)

Date: Post-Medieval (c. 1600–c. 1700).
Discovery: Found while metal-detecting in September 2007, and reported to Katie Hinds (Wiltshire FLO).
Description: A gold posy ring with a D-section hoop, slightly distorted, engraved on the inside 'the love Is true that I ☉ U x'. Preceding the inscription is a damaged word; all that can be discerned are flourishes of the initial capital, possible 'T', and an end letter, possibly 'e', perhaps for 'Trust'. Following this is an illegible stamp, probably a maker's mark. Diameter: 22mm. Weight: 2.6g.
Discussion: This particular inscription is recorded by Evans (1931: 95), and a ring in the British Museum has the same inscription, although the final three letters are in lower case.
Disposition: Wiltshire Heritage Museum hoped to acquire, but withdrew; returned to finder.

N AWAIS-DEAN

362. Kenn, North Somerset: gold finger-ring (PAS: GLO-EF2971; Treasure: 2007 T5)

Date: Post-Medieval (c. 1600–c. 1700).
Discovery: Found by Jon Hill while metal-detecting in October 2006, and reported to Kurt Adams (Gloucestershire FLO).
Description: A gold finger-ring, with a plain band with a D-shaped cross-section, and an inscription in the inside face which reads 'A frindes gifte' (a friend's gift). Diameter: 15mm. Weight: 1.5g.
Disposition: Acquired by North Somerset Museum.

K ADAMS

363. Westbury-on-Severn, Gloucestershire: gold finger-ring (PAS: GLO-195C52; Treasure: 2007 T333)

Date: Post-Medieval (c. 1600–c. 1700).
Discovery: Found by Timothy Denning while metal-detecting in May 2007, and reported to Kurt Adams (Gloucestershire FLO).
Description: A small gold ring with a D-shaped hoop. Inscribed on the inside is 'Thy light is my delight'. There are traces of black enamel within the lettering. Dimensions: 18 x 2.5mm.
Disposition: Dean Heritage Centre hoped to acquire, but withdrew; returned to finder.

N AWAIS-DEAN

364. Soham area, Cambridgeshire: gold finger-ring (PAS: SF-3A8B11; Treasure: 2007 T163)

Date: Post-Medieval (c. 1600–c. 1700).
Discovery: Found by Jeffery Banks while metal-detecting in March 2007, and reported to Faye Minter (Suffolk FLO).
Description: A gold finger-ring, now distorted. The outer face of the band has eight evenly spaced circular bosses with a twisted rope-like motif around each one. The edges of the band are moulded, and there are opposing pairs of small rectangular knops between each circular boss. The inner face of the ring is inscribed 'No fancy Strang Shall make me chang' (I will love no other). Some of the letters contain traces of the original black enamel. Dimensions: 23.6 x 18.3mm. Weight: 8.88g.
Discussion: The style of the lettering is similar to examples from Pinhoe, Devon, and Bungay, Suffolk (*TAR* 2003: nos. 271 & 272), although these have less elaborate D-shaped sectioned hoops. No parallel for the inscription has been traced.
Disposition: Acquired by Ely Museum.

F MINTER & N AWAIS-DEAN

365. Buckingham, Buckinghamshire: gold finger-ring (PAS: BUC-068008; Treasure: 2007 T436)

Date: Post-Medieval (c. 1600–c. 1700).
Discovery: Found by Gareth Jarvis while metal-detecting in March 2007, and reported to Ros Tyrrell (Buckinghamshire FLO).
Description: A small gold ring with a D-section hoop, now slightly distorted. An inscription on the inside reads 'x BE x FAITHFULL'. There are tiny traces of black enamel in the lettering. Dimensions: 15 x 2mm.
Discussion: The style of the lettering is consistent with that on other rings of this date. The motto is recorded in Evans (1931: 25), although in that case the inscription is in lower case italic and there is only a single 'l' in 'faithful'. Another ring in the British Museum reads 'Be.faithfull.and.louing'.
Disposition: Acquired by Buckinghamshire County Museum.

N AWAIS-DEAN

366. Penllyn, Vale of Glamorgan: silver-gilt finger ring (PAS: NMGW-9F38B2; Treasure: Wales 07.16)

Date: Post-Medieval (c. 1600–c. 1700).
Discovery: Found by Tony Jones while metal-detecting in May 2007, and reported to Mark Lodwick (Finds Co-ordinator, Wales).
Description: A silver-gilt ring in the form of a broad band with beaded edges. The inner face is engraved 'LEVE +TO +DYE' with crosslets between words and a trefoil at the end. The hoop is fractured. Diameter (internal): 18.6mm. Weight 5.1g. Surface analysis: approximately 98% silver and 2% copper.

Discussion: The ring has a form and style of lettering typical for the 17th century. The style of lettering may be compared with that on a 17th-century posy ring inscribed 'PITYE THE POOWR', with similar crosslets and floral stop, from London (Murdoch 1991: no. 124).
Disposition: Acquired by the National Museum of Wales.

M REDKNAP

367. Emneth, Norfolk: silver-gilt finger-ring (PAS: NMS-2C5DA4; Treasure: 2007 T307)

Date: Post-Medieval (c. 1600–c. 1700).
Discovery: Found while metal-detecting in May/June 2007, and reported to Erica Darch (Norfolk FLO).
Description: A silver finger-ring with a circular-section hoop (now slightly distorted) and a separate soldered, gilded openwork bezel in the form of a knot decorated with filigree. Dimensions: 25 x 20mm. Weight: 1.77g.
Discussion: The ring is similar to a larger and more elaborate mid 17th-century example with an internal inscription (Oman 1974: pl. 59f).
Disposition: Acquired by Norwich Castle Museum.

E B DARCH

368. Lapley, Stretton and Wheaton Aston, Staffordshire: silver bell (PAS: WMID-345AB7; Treasure: 2007 T42)

Date: Post-Medieval (c. 1600–c. 1700).
Discovery: Found while metal-detecting in October 2006, and reported to Caroline Johnson (Staffordshire & West Midlands FLO) in 2007.
Description: A small bell in the form of a thistle head, made from engraved silver sheet; the clapper survives inside, as does a small loop for suspension. There are two small holes in vertical alignment on the body.
Discussion: This bell does not correspond with recorded hawking types, which are simple round bells in copper-alloy, or with ones worn as fashionable accessories in late Medieval dress.
Disposition: Disclaimed; returned to finder.

D THORNTON

369. Kelvedon, Essex: inscribed silver thimble (PAS: ESS-6EC030; Treasure: 2007 T80)

Date: Post-Medieval (c. 1600–c. 1700).
Discovery: Found by Tony Gilson while metal-detecting in February 2007, and reported to Caroline McDonald (Essex FLO).
Description: A complete open-ended silver thimble. It is now slightly flattened and split along the original join. It is decorated with four running crosses which divide the design into ten square fields which are filled with raised, sub-square dots. A double border runs around the lower edge. The upper border contains the inscription '+ FARE GOD ONLY' (fear God only). Height: 20mm. Weight: 4.99g.

Disposition: Acquired by Braintree Museum; landowner donated their share.

C MCDONALD

---

370. Wantage Down area, Oxfordshire: inscribed silver seal matrix (PAS: BERK-B9F5A5; Treasure: 2007 T487)

Date: Post-Medieval (c. 1600–c. 1700).
Discovery: Found while metal-detecting in September 2007, and reported to Charlotte Burrill (Berkshire & Oxfordshire FLO).
Description: A fob seal, perhaps of base silver. The fluted handle has an integral suspension loop. The face is roughly engraved with three letters and four stars within pearled border. The non-European script, possibly Armenian, has so far not been identified definitively, but the shape of the seal suggests roughly the date above. Dimensions: 21.4 x 18.8mm. Weight: 8.5g.
Disposition: Oxfordshire Museums Service hopes to acquire.

D THORNTON

---

371. City of London, London: iron knife (PAS: LON-AEEE42)

Date: Post-Medieval (c. 1600–c. 1700).
Discovery: Found by Tony Pilson and Ian Smith while searching the Thames foreshore in 2007, and recorded by Kate Sumnall (London FLO).
Description: Fragment of an iron knife with remains of a wooden handle and a copper-alloy shoulder/hilt band. This hilt band is a re-used thimble. It has a triple line border below the fine, regular circular pits; the top has been irregularly trimmed off. When the object was found all the elements were tightly fitted together; now they are loose. Since the blade is very thin its function may have been for precision work. Diameter: 12.41mm. Length: 51.94mm. Weight: 4.05g.
Discussion: Recycling is nothing new, as is shown by this thimble that has been pressed into service as a hilt band on this knife. If this had been found on agricultural land it is doubtful it would have be so readily recognisable; the iron probably at best being a corroded lump adhering to the thimble, or else only a very worn and damaged thimble would have survived.
Disposition: Returned to finders.

K SUMNALL

---

372. Brearton, North Yorkshire: copper-alloy ring with four seal matrices (PAS: SWYOR-6C2985)

Date: Post-Medieval (c. 1600–c. 1700).
Discovery: Found by Jeff Warden while metal-detecting in 2007, and reported to Amy Cooper (South & West Yorkshire FLO).
Description: A copper-alloy (possible) finger-ring, with four bezels, each a seal matrix. The ring is a plain band, slightly oval in section. Each bezel is oval and each has a different design cut into it. They are all arranged with the long axis along the band of the ring, but the designs have different orientations. The first is orientated with the narrow ends forming the top and bottom – the design is a shield with: a bird (probably a hunting bird) facing left (described from the matrix) with the letters 'IW' above (on the impression); the next bezel is horizontally aligned, with a cockerel facing left (described from the matrix); the next, also horizontal, shows a bird of prey advancing to the left (from the matrix) holding a small animal in its beak; the final matrix is horizontal but the opposite way up to the others, and it shows a quadruped with a long tail, passant left (from the matrix) – it looks like a dog but may be intended to be a lion. Dimensions: 34.1 x 33.5 x 13.4mm. Weight: 24.8g.
Discussion: Several seal matrices with multiple designs are known, such as 373, but no parallel for a multiple-device finger-ring has been traced.
Deposition: Returned to finder.

A COOPER

---

373. Stanton Drew, Gloucestershire: copper-alloy quadruple seal matrix (PAS: GLO-F89AF1)

Date: Post-Medieval (c. 1600–c. 1700).
Discovery: Found by Martin Elsbury while metal-detecting in September 2007, and recorded by Kurt Adams (Gloucestershire & Avon FLO).
Description: Four conjoined dies emanating from a central perforated hub. The arms are oval in cross-section and expand to a flattened-oval terminal, the face of each containing a low-relief device in a border, as follows: a three-masted ship in sail; a crown; a bird (possibly a dove) standing, facing left with a palm branch before and above; a heart flanked by two chevrons and pierced by two saltire arrows, the fletching uppermost, and a cross in a square (possibly a flag) above. Dimensions: 31 x 31 x 13mm. Weight: 14.65g.
Discussion: Similar dies have been recorded by the PAS (see ESS-393EF8, WILT-D1D4D6 & WAW-BC0821); see also 372.
Disposition: Returned to finder.

K ADAMS

---

374. Shenley, Hertfordshire: silver seal matrix (PAS: BH-C54352; Treasure 2007 T404)

Date: Post-Medieval (c. 1600–c. 1700).
Discovery: Found by Graham Batt while metal-detecting in 2007, and reported to Julian Watters (Hertfordshire & Bedfordshire FLO).
Description: A silver seal matrix depicting a shield bearing the arms: a chevron with a star at the angle, three scorpions two and one. The tapering handle is of hexagonal section, the upper part being swollen and

with a double horizontal groove. The openwork lug is incomplete. Dimensions: 16.4 x 14mm. Weight: 6.26g.
Discussion: Attempts to identify the family to whom this distinctive crest belonged have not been successful.
Disposition: Acquired by Bushey Museum.

D THORNTON

375. City of London: stone musket ball mould (PAS: LON-763F17)

Date: Post-Medieval (c. 1600–c. 1700).
Discovery: Found by Tony Pilson and Ian Smith while searching the Thames foreshore in 2007, and recorded by Kate Sumnall (London FLO).
Description: Half a stone mould for a single musket ball. The mould is an irregular cuboid with a carved hemispherical recess and a wedge-shape funnel to pour the liquid lead in to form the ball. In addition there are two recesses for pins to hold the two parts comprising the complete mould together, and two notches on the outside surface for a wire binding, again to secure the two mould halves firmly together. Dimensions: 35.73 x 27.84 x 21.42mm. Weight: 47.02g.
Discussion: This well-made mould is unusual in being of stone for a single ball; the finders had previously discovered a musket-ball mould made of iron of a form similar to a pair of pliers.
Disposition: Museum of London hopes to acquire.

K SUMNALL

376. Coxhoe, County Durham: silver seal matrix (PAS: NCL-C27BA0; Treasure: 2007 T86)

Date: Post-Medieval (c. 1600–c. 1750).
Discovery: Found by Carl Richardson while metal-detecting in December 2006, and reported to Rob Collins (North East FLO) in 2007.
Description: A fragmentary oval seal-die engraved on the face with a skeleton holding an hourglass in one hand, and flanked by flower sprays. The remains of the handle on the back are from a fluted shank and what would have originally been a loop terminal.
Discussion: A silver seal with a similar motif has been excavated at the colonial site of Jamestown, Virginia, USA (Beverley Straube, *personal communication*).
Disposition: Acquired by Bowes Museum, Barnard Castle; landowner donated his share.

D THORNTON

377. Atcham, Shropshire: ceramic vessel (PAS: HESH-8B2EA1)

Date: Post-Medieval (c. 1600–c. 1800).
Discovery: Found by Jo Marvel while gardening in 2007, and recorded by Peter Reavill (Shropshire & Herefordshire FLO).
Description: A large pottery vessel or jar, probably for storage, transportation, and dispensing of liquids (possibly milk or cider). The vessel is of Midlands-purple fabric. The precise dating is difficult with functional wares. It is globular, with a relatively wide base with evenly expanded walls, which taper to a mouth with an inverted rim. On the front is a raised, U-shaped applied 'pie crust' ridge, to the upper left of which is a small, tapered hole (presumably to stop a vacuum being formed within the vessel). Below the pie-crust decoration is a small spigot hole, presumably to take a tapered tap. The rim of the aperture has been reinforced with additional clay to strengthen its outer edge. To either side of the pie-crust decoration are two applied strap handles with thumb impressions along the edges. The outer surface has been burnished and the upper part has splashed decoration. The inner surface is glazed in a thick, dark brown/purple glaze evenly applied and creates an even coat. The rim is recessed to take a small lid, now lost (of pottery or wood). The fabric is a relatively hard earthenware with a number of small angular and sub-angular grit and quartz inclusions, and there is also a large amount of mica in the fabric. Dimensions: Diameter: 295mm. Height: 400mm. Thickness: 13.4mm. Weight: 9.4kg
Discussion: No direct parallel has been found and this functional vessel form would have remained current for a long time. Midlands-purple ware is usually dated to c. 1500–c. 1800, and it is most likely that this example dates to the later part of the period, probably post-1650. It is a relatively unusual survival of functional rural pottery.
Disposition: Returned to finder.

P REAVILL

378. Oving, West Sussex: silver seal-top spoon (PAS: SUSS-BC6F54; Treasure: 2007 T345)

Date: Post-Medieval (1615–1616).
Discovery: Found by Marcus Kelland while metal-detecting in June 2007, and reported to Liz Andrews-Wilson (Sussex FLO).
Description: A silver seal-top spoon with a gilt finial and a stem of hexagonal section; the stem is bent over and the bowl torn and crushed. In the bowl on the front can be seen the mark of the leopard's head crowned; on the back of the stem the London date letter 'S' in a shield (for 1615–1616) and the maker's mark 'RC'. Dimensions: 82.8 x 50.4mm. Weight: 37.3g.

Discussion: The maker was probably Robert Cotton, who is known on other seal-top London spoons hallmarked for 1618–1619 and 1632–1633.
Disposition: Disclaimed; returned to finder.

D THORNTON

379. Tendring area, Essex: silver pendant of Charles I (PAS: ESS-6ECE34; Treasure: 2007 T15)

Date: Post-Medieval (c. 1640–c. 1660).
Discovery: Found by Keith Leeders while metal-detecting in September 2006, and reported to Caroline McDonald (Essex FLO) in 2007.
Description: A silver pendant, oval with small projections at the side, now damaged. The pendant is cast with a bust of Charles I (r. 1625–1649) on one side and engraved on the other with initials 'CR' conjoined for Carolus Rex (King Charles). Length: 13.54mm. Weight: 0.58g.
Discussion: Though lacking a suspension loop, comparison with heavier, more sculptural versions with a similar bust and the royal arms as used in the reign of Charles I would lead one to think that this was originally a pendant. The bust is similar to ones on Civil War medal designs (Hawkins 1885: 348, no. 203). Heavier versions sometimes combine personal arms on one side with owner's initials indicating royalist allegiance (*TAR* 2003: no. 274). The pendant therefore dates as above, when badges, buttons and other objects record allegiance to the monarchy and to the future King Charles II.
Disposition: Acquired by Colchester & Ipswich Museum Service.

D THORNTON

380. Drayton Bassett, Staffordshire: silver pendant of Charles I (PAS: WMID-338537; Treasure: 2007 T324)

Date: Post-Medieval (c. 1640–c. 1660).
Discovery: Found while metal-detecting in February 2007, and reported to Caroline Johnson (Staffordshire & West Midlands FLO).
Description: A damaged, double-sided silver pendant with a bust of Charles I (r. 1625–1649) in profile on one side, and on the other side, a three-quarter face of his consort Henrietta Maria. The decorative border is damaged at the top and bottom, but would probably have included mounts for attachment.
Dimensions: 18.9 x 19.2 x 3.2mm. Weight: 2.57g.
Discussion: This is a common form dating to the Civil War period. Some examples (e.g. *TAR* 2003: no. 274) have ownership initials or arms, suggesting that they were worn to show Royalist allegiance. Similar portraits have been published by Hawkins (1885: 357, nos. 203, 223 & 348).
Disposition: Acquired by Potteries Museum & Art Gallery, Stoke.

D THORNTON

381. Mildenhall, Wiltshire: copper-alloy enamelled buckle (PAS: SOM-BB0BB4)

Date: Post-Medieval (c. 1640–c. 1700).
Discovery: Found by Anne Morgan while metal-detecting in 2007, and recorded by Naomi Payne (Somerset FLO).
Description: An enamelled cast copper-alloy rectangular double loop buckle. The outside edges are trefoil shaped and there are external knops at each end of the narrowed strap bar. The pin is missing. The front of the buckle is decorated with moulded scrollwork and in between the raised scrolls the recesses are filled alternately with black and white enamel. Dimensions: 39.6 x 26.4 x 3.3mm. Weight: 9.8g.
Discussion: The London manufacturers of these buckles are known to have also produced enamelled buttons, stirrups and ornate candlesticks. This material was being made at the time of the Commonwealth (1649–1660) and later (if not slightly earlier as well). The range was formerly known as 'Surrey enamels' from a mistaken attribution to a foundry there, but it has recently come to light that known makers in the capital were responsible (Blair 2005: 2–9; Blair 2006: 10–21). A similar (although incomplete) buckle was found at Horsham St Faith and Newton St Faith, Norfolk (NMS-CDABE7).
Disposition: Returned to finder.

N PAYNE

382. East of Colchester, Essex: silver locket fragment (PAS: ESS-259730; Treasure: 2007 T496)

Date: Post-Medieval (c. 1649–c. 1675).
Discovery: Found while metal-detecting in September 2007, and reported to Laura McLean (Essex FLO).
Description: A thin, silver, heart-shaped plaque, engraved 'prepared be to follow me', and below, the initials 'CR'. Dimensions: 19.5 x 18.96 x 2.83mm. Weight: 0.85g.
Discussion: A common type of memorial for Charles I (r. 1625–1649), made either during the Commonwealth (1649–1660) or after the Restoration in 1660. The plaque is probably part of a locket. The same inscription occurs on memorial rings for Charles I.
Disposition: Acquired by Colchester and Ipswich Museum Service.

J A RUDOE

383. Runhall, Norfolk: silver pendant medallion (PAS: NMS-BFBA71; Treasure: 2007 T33)

Date: Post-Medieval (1650).
Discovery: Found by Kelvin Boldero while metal-detecting in September 2006, and reported to Erica Darch (Norfolk FLO) in 2007.
Description: A silver pendant medallion in the form of a disc, with a separate flat-sectioned loop soldered to the apex, now broken in two pieces. The pendant is inscribed on both sides. The obverse reads '1650 (with

orb between) / FORDERT SE/INE FURCHT UND / EHR SONST BE/STEHT ER NIM/MER MEHR' (Promote/ Demand Fear/Respect and Honour for Him or He will cease to be). The reverse has a shield between two fronds which bears the arms of Saxony, and reads 'GOTT DEN / HERRN LOBT UND / EHRT DER DEN / FRIEDEN UNS / BESCHERT. / (possible small B in base)' (Praise and honour God the Lord who brings/gives us Peace). Each is a rhyme of two lines in old-fashioned German – a prayer/motto or commandment for devout living. Diameter: 22mm. Weight: 1.98g.
Disposition: Acquired by Norwich Castle Museum; the landowner donated their share.

S J ASHLEY & K FELDER

---

384. Itchen Valley, Hampshire: silver medal of Charles II (PAS: HAMP-604ED1; Treasure: 2007 T522)

Date: Post-Medieval (c. 1650–c. 1660).
Discovery: Found by Terry Stone while metal-detecting in September 2007, and reported to Rob Webley (Hampshire FLO).
Description: A cast, oval silver medal, tarnished and with its upper part and suspension loop broken off. The obverse bears an uncrowned bust of Charles II (r. 1660–1685) facing right, with a raised border, and the reverse has a phoenix rising from the flames with rays of light above and an oval border around, all incised. Height: 18.8mm. Thickness: 1.35mm. Weight: 1.55g.
Discussion: This royalist medal would have been made after the execution of Charles I (1649) and before the Restoration of the monarchy (1660). The reverse expresses the hope that the monarchy will rise again, like the phoenix. A similar example is published by Hawkins (1885: 443, no. 15).
Disposition: Acquired by Winchester Museums Service.

P ATTWOOD

---

385. South Creake, Norfolk: gold finger-ring (PAS: NMS-2AD401; Treasure: 2007 T217)

Date: Post-Medieval (c. 1650–c. 1700).
Discovery: Found by Robert Green while metal-detecting in March 2007, and reported to Erica Darch (Norfolk FLO).
Description: A gold ring with a D-shaped band, inscribed on the inside 'A vertuous wife preserveth life'. There is a possible maker's mark in the form of a very worn stamped 'H' between the beginning and end of the inscription (see Oman 1974: pl. 58, H for a similar example). Diameter: 21mm. Weight: 3.8g.
Discussion: Inscriptions declaring that a virtuous wife preserved or comforted life, or banished strife are frequently found on marriage rings (Evans 1931), and there are several such examples in the British Museum.
Disposition: Acquired by Lynn Museum.

E B DARCH

---

386. Old Radnor, Powys: silver hawking whistle (PAS: NMGW-9F1A17; Treasure: Wales 07.21)

Date: Post-Medieval (c. 1650–c. 1700).
Discovery: Found by Ian Cole while metal-detecting during September 2006, and reported to Peter Reavill (Herefordshire & Shropshire FLO) and to the National Museum Wales, where it was identified by Mark Redknap.
Description: Complete small whistle made of silver sheeting, retaining a small suspension ring on its underside. It is plain, with a domed end that has been soldered to the pipe. Length: 30.02mm. Width: tapers 7.5–5.7mm. Weight 3.1g. Surface analysis: approximately 97% silver and 3% copper.
Disposition: Acquired by Radnorshire Museum, Llandrindod Wells.

M REDKNAP

---

387. Nash Mills, Hertfordshire: lead cloth seal (PAS: BH-0A8713)

Date: Post-Medieval (c. 1650–c. 1750).
Discovery: Found by Richard Shelton while metal-detecting in 2007, and recorded by Julian Watters (Hertfordshire & Bedfordshire FLO).
Description: A lead two-disc cloth seal from Courtenay, near Paris. One disc bears the legend 'BU[R..]/DE COU[R]/TNAY/TRANSI...', which indicates that it was issued, perhaps for customs in transit, by the bureau at Courtenay. The other disc bears a crowned saltire cross, with the letters 'C' in the left-hand angle, 'D' underneath and 'C/G' in the right-hand angle. Rope-work borders enclose the designs on both sides. Dimensions: 35.4 x 29.4 x 7.1mm. Weight: 24.24g.
Discussion: This is the first Courtenay seal to have been found in Britain. It is uncertain what sort of textile it would have been attached to as no reference has been traced to the import of cloths from this French town.
Disposition: Returned to finder.

J WATTERS & G EGAN

---

388. Snape, North Yorkshire: silver (possible) cockspur (PAS: SWYOR-B06054; Treasure: 2007 T451)

Date: Post-Medieval (c. 1650–c. 1835).
Discovery: Found by Kevern George while metal-detecting in August 2007, and reported to Amy Cooper (South & West Yorkshire FLO).
Description: A silver object with a slightly curved shaft tapering to a point, with a ridge pierced for attachment at the other end.
Discussion: This may be a spur for use in cockfighting that would have been attached by the hole at the back onto a leather strap around the cock's leg, to lengthen the natural spur. The only one in the British Museum is made of steel, which might seem a more

suitable material; however, silver ones were thought suitable for gentlemen's specially bred game-cocks. By the late 17th century, cockfighting was considered a gentlemanly pastime, with opportunities for gambling. A reference appears in George Powell's play, A Cornish Comedy, performed in 1696, in which one of the characters states 'Hawks, hounds, setting dogs and cocks, with their appurtenances are the true marks of a country gentleman' (Strutt 1801: xxviii). Cockfighting was popular in England from Roman times until it was banned by Act of Parliament in 1835. References to cockfighting appear in Shakespeare (Hamlet V, 2 and Anthony and Cleopatra 11, 3.36) and it is frequently mentioned as a popular rural and city pastime of the common people into the 19th century. Given the unchanging design of the spurs it is difficult to date this one precisely.
Disposition: Disclaimed; returned to finder.

D THORNTON

389. Belton and Manthorpe, Lincolnshire: lead hornbook (PAS: LIN-16BF84)

Date: Post-Medieval (c. 1660–c. 1685).
Discovery: Found by David Baker while metal-detecting in 2007, and recorded by Adam Daubney (Lincolnshire FLO).
Description: Complete cast lead 'hornbook', which is flat, rectangular and decorated on both sides. One side has a crude depiction of Charles II (r. 1660–1685) shown in profile, facing left, in an ornate border, wearing a large double-arched crown with two crosses. His face is cartoon-like and is shown smiling. The other side is taken up with the alphabet on five lines, each separated by a horizontal line; the letters J and V are missing, and so reads as follows 'ABCDEF/GHIKL/MN(reversed)OPQ/RSTVW/XYZ'. Next to the letter 'Z' are four vertical lines with a diagonal. Dimensions: 37 x 16 x 3mm.
Discussion: Hornbooks were children's teaching tablets that usually contained the alphabet and the Lord's prayer. They became available during the 16th century. Although the term hornbook is commonly used for lead tablets, it is a slightly misleading name. True hornbooks were made out of wood onto which the printed paper would have been mounted, and then covered with a thin sheet of transparent horn for protection. The lead tablets are presumably cheaper versions of these books; see 394.
Disposition: Returned to finder.

A DAUBNEY

390. Holmer area, Herefordshire: silver seal matrix (PAS: HESH-1D4423; Treasure: 2007 T403)

Date: Post-Medieval (c. 1660–c. 1685).
Discovery: Found by Simon Sloan while metal-detecting in June 2007, and reported to Peter Reavill (Herefordshire & Shropshire FLO).
Description: A silver pedestal, or pendant, seal matrix. The die face is oval and the handle rises to a double-moulded band which terminates in a suspension loop. The die is well cut and displays two hearts with a crown above (with a central fleur-de-lis and a series of wedges in the arches). Dimensions: 11.9 x 11.4 x 19.6mm. Weight: 3.94g.
Discussion: This motif is often associated with the marriage between Charles II and Catherine of Braganza (1662). For a comparable example see *TAR* 2003: no. 282, from Metfield, Suffolk. The device is stylistically similar to those on a number of silver buttons/cufflinks reported as Treasure; see 393.
Disposition: Hereford Museum and Art Gallery hopes to acquire.

P REAVILL

391. Droxford, Hampshire: silver shoe buckle (PAS: HAMP-E23148; Treasure: 2007 T453)

Date: Post-Medieval (c. 1660–c. 1700).
Discovery: Found by Mark Duell while metal-detecting in August 2007, and reported to Rob Webley (Hampshire FLO).
Description: An incomplete, silver double-looped buckle with a sub-triangular chape which has a large stud stamped with the maker's mark 'WW' conjoined. The pin and outer edge of the buckle are missing. Length: 27.9mm. Weight: 4.35g.
Discussion: Murawski (2003: 579) published a complete oval buckle with an iron rivet, apparently having the same maker's mark.
Disposition: Winchester Museums Service hopes to acquire.

D THORNTON

392. Binton, Warwickshire: copper-alloy spoon (PAS: WAW-06E0C0)

Date: Post-Medieval (c. 1660–c. 1700).
Discovery: Found by Mark Pugh while metal-detecting in 2007, and recorded by Angie Bolton (Warwickshire & Worcestershire FLO).
Description: A cast copper-alloy spoon, with a sub-oval shape bowl. The end is asymmetrically worn (suggesting the user was right-handed). A maker's mark on the bowl is not clear, but may read 'FT'. The stem is sub-oval in section, tapering slightly in the middle, with a slip-top terminal. The surface has a green patina. Dimensions: 164 x 47.96mm. Weight: 42.6g.

Discussion: Egan (2005: 117) notes that, since the 1560s, the Pewterers' Guild had tried to prevent copper-alloy spoons being made and was effective in this until the late 17th century.
Disposition: Returned to finder.

A BOLTON

---

393. Thurlaston, Leicestershire: silver double-sided seal matrix (PAS: LEIC-964413; Treasure: 2007 T525)

Date: Post-Medieval (c. 1664–c. 1685).
Discovery: Found by Bill H Riley while metal-detecting in June 2007, and reported to Wendy Scott (Leicestershire FLO).
Description: A silver double-sided seal die made of two parts: a disc and a curved frame with foliate scrolls framing a pierced loop for suspension. The die is engraved on one side with two hearts conjoined, pierced by an arrow and bleeding, surmounted by a crown; on the other side is an animal head, possibly that of a griffin. Dimensions: 22 x 13mm.
Discussion: The 'crowned hearts' motif is often associated with Charles II and his consort, Catherine of Braganza (1662); see 390 and 397.
Disposition: Leicestershire County Council Heritage Services had hoped to acquire but withdrew; returned to finder.

D THORNTON

---

394. Penkridge, Staffordshire: lead, possible hornbook handle (PAS: DENO-EB9B13)

Date: Post-Medieval (1669).
Discovery: Found by Eric Pursglove while metal-detecting in early 2007, and recorded by Anja Rohde (Derbyshire & Nottinghamshire FLO).
Description: This fragment is a flat, sub-rectangular, cast lead plate with a short, narrow projection from the centre of one edge. The opposite edge has a rough, unformed area in the centre, which may indicate where it has broken away from the rest of the object. The plate has a large, heart-shaped hole and is decorated around this with cast roundels, lines and pellets on both faces. One face has the date '1669' and the other has the letters 'R + I', presumably the initials of the maker. Dimensions: 30.2 x 22.3 x 2.8mm. Weight: 9.25g.
Discussion: This may be part of a hornbook; see 389. The presence of a date and maker's initials is paralleled on other finds.
Deposition: Returned to finder.

A ROHDE

---

395. Boxgrove, West Sussex: gold mourning ring (PAS: SUSS-356DB0; Treasure: 2007 T29)

Date: Post-Medieval (1670).
Discovery: Found by Stephen Underwood during construction work in March 2006, and reported to Liz Andrews-Wilson (Sussex FLO) in 2007.
Description: A gold finger-ring, inscription on the inside of the hoop with the legend 'JOHN KING ESQ obijt 10 March 1670'. There is a marker's mark after the legend, the unidentified initials 'CE' conjoined within an oval. The hoop is bent at several points (giving a hexagonal appearance), D-shaped in section and has an engraved skull on the exterior.
Disposition: Acquired by Chichester District Museum.

L ANDREWS-WILSON

---

396. South-east Lancashire: silver cufflinks (PAS: LANCUM-362FE5; Treasure: 2007 T77)

Date: Post-Medieval (c. 1670–c. 1700).
Discovery: Found by Steven Moody while metal-detecting in April 2007, and reported to Dot Boughton (Cumbria & Lancashire FLO).
Description: A complete cast silver cufflink composed of two small decorated button-like discs, each with a loop on the reverse. They are linked by an oval silver-wire chain link. The discs have down-turned edges and are both decorated with two hearts (not conjoined), with a single crown which has two arches bridging two small fleurs-de-lis. Dimensions: Length: 36mm. Diameter 18mm. Weight 2.2g.
Discussion: For several cufflink components of a very similar type see *TAR* 2004: nos. 235–243 & *TAR* 2005/6: nos. 612–641 (of these only *TAR* 2005/6: no. 615 is complete).
Disposition: Disclaimed; returned to finder.

D BOUGHTON

---

397. Ropley, Hampshire: silver double-sided seal matrix (PAS: SUR-7D6293; Treasure: 2007 T406)

Date: Post-Medieval (c. 1670–c. 1720).
Discovery: Found by Christopher Kislingbury while metal-detecting in August 2007, and reported to David Williams (Surrey FLO).
Description: A flat, double-sided fob seal, cut from sheet silver, with a suspension loop at the top. The swivelling seal is engraved on both sides with scrolling ornament at the outer edge, and on one side with a cupid with bow and arrow, and on the other with two hearts pierced by a single arrow, bleeding, surmounted by a crown. The scrolling ornament on the handle and the style and subject of the engraved seal suggest the above date. Dimensions: 23.47 x 13.39mm. Weight: 2.61g.
Discussion: See 393.
Disposition: Acquired by Hampshire Museums Service.

D THORNTON

398. Phillack, Cornwall: silver bodkin
(PAS: CORN-943711; Treasure: 2007 T222)

Date: Post-Medieval (1672).
Discovery: Found by Graham Dyer while metal-detecting in April 2007, and reported to Anna Tyacke (Cornwall FLO).
Description: A silver bodkin with a round knop, a semicircular terminal, a round hole and a longitudinal slot. Initials on one side are dot-punched 'A' and 'H' with a cross and the date '1672'. On the other side of the shaft is a maker's mark, possibly a pomegranate or a thistle with a crescent. Dimensions: 118 x 4 x 2.4mm. Weight: 7.34g.
Discussion: This is a rare dated example of a fairly common object, usually found in East Anglia or the South East, rather than Cornwall.
Disposition: Acquired by Royal Cornwall Museum.

D THORNTON

399. Newport area, Isle of Wight: silver shoe buckle
(PAS: IOW-4074C3; Treasure: 2007 T607)

Date: Post-Medieval (c. 1675–c. 1700).
Discovery: Found while metal-detecting in 2007, and reported to Frank Basford (Isle of Wight FLO).
Description: Incomplete silver shoe buckle of baroque form. The buckle is decorated with scrolls and shells on the frame; the chape has a stud with radiating lines and is stamped twice on the back with lion passant mark and the maker's initials 'RM' above a star in a shield. Dimensions: 44.8 x 21.8 x 9.9mm. Weight: 13.16g.
Discussion: The maker's mark does not appear to have been recorded previously. This would seem to be a man's shoe buckle. From the late 17th century men wore shoe buckles, which are characterised by their small size and delicacy. This buckle is similar to slightly later example from Greinton, Somerset (SOMDOR-DA1AE6).
Disposition: Disclaimed; returned to finder.

F BASFORD

400. Wimborne Minster, Dorset: glass bottle
(PAS: DOR-23C926)

Date: Post-Medieval (c. 1675–c. 1800).
Discovery: Found by Sharon Rowland, by chance, before 2007, and recorded by Ciorstaidh Hayward Trevarthen (Dorset FLO).
Description: A small colourless and blue glass drop-shaped, blown bottle. The body flares out at the sides into a rounded drop shape, which is flattened at the front and back. At the base is an applied flat foot which is uneven so that the vessel will not stand on it. It is crudely decorated with two applied blue-glass sub-circular prunts, one each face, each with an impressed linear grid. There are applied trails of colourless glass along each side, forming double loops at the neck and attached along the sides on the bottle's main body (one loop is broken off at the base the neck). The trails along the body have been tooled to produce a series of ridges. Dimensions: 58.63 x 36.73 x 21.4mm. Weight: 26.75g.
Discussion: The bottle is made in lead glass and is therefore late 17th century or later. The looped trails along the side are common features on Spanish glass (Hugh Wilmot, *personal communication*). It may possibly be post-1700, as the tooled trailing and blue prunts were popular then, although this is quite a crude example (Rachel Tyson, *personal communication*). The bottle was possibly used for scent.
Disposition: Returned to finder.

C HAYWARD TREVARTHEN

401. Overton, Flintshire: gold touch-piece of James II (PAS: NMGW-DDBBF5; Treasure: Wales 07.11)

Date: Post-Medieval (c. 1685–8).
Discovery: Found whilst metal-detecting in July 2007, and reported to Mark Lodwick (Finds Co-ordinator, Wales)
Description: A gold touch-piece of James II (r. 1685–8).
Discussion: Such pieces formed part of the ceremony of 'touching for the King's Evil' (scrofula, believed to be cured by the monarch's touch); patients received a memento in the form of a 'touch-piece', suspended on a white ribbon. The early Stuart monarchs (James I, Charles I) used gold coins (angels), pierced to take a ribbon. After the Restoration of Charles II (1660) special non-monetary gold pieces were made for the ceremony.
Disposition: Acquired by the National Museum of Wales.

E M BESLY

402. Kensworth, Bedfordshire: gold mourning ring
(PAS: BH-4B0E12; Treasure: 2007 T16)

Date: Post-Medieval (1700).
Discovery: Found while metal-detecting in June 2005, and reported to Mark Lodwick (Finds Co-ordinator for Wales) in 2007.
Description: A gold mourning ring formed of a thin, flat band engraved with a skull on the exterior, now squashed out of shape. The interior is inscribed 'Prepare to follow M.B. obt 28 Augt 700. aet IX' (MB died on 28 August 1700 aged 9).
Disposition: Acquired by Luton Museum.

J A RUDOE

403. Hawton, Nottinghamshire: gold mourning ring (PAS: SWYOR-C542C8; Treasure: 2007 T375)

Date: Post-Medieval (1700).
Discovery: Found by Andrew Diamond while metal-detecting in March 2007, and reported to Amy Cooper (South & West Yorkshire FLO).
Description: A gold mourning ring with a D-section hoop that is inscribed to the inside 'S P obijt 20 June j700 aeta 28' (SP died on 20 June 1700 aged 28), followed by a maker's mark 'M' in a rectangle. There are traces of black enamel within the lettering and the rectangle.
Discussion: The maker is unidentifiable from those listed by Grimwade 1990 and Jackson 1964.
Disposition: Acquired by Newark Museum.

N AWAIS-DEAN

404. West Crewkerne, Somerset: silver thimble (PAS: SOM-574036; Treasure: 2007 T678)

Date: Post-Medieval (c. 1700–c. 1725).
Discovery: Found by Michael Charles while metal-detecting in November 2007, and reported to Naomi Payne (Somerset FLO).
Description: A silver thimble formed from thin sheeting soldered together, the dome missing. There are regular indentations on the body except for area near the border on one side with two birds flanking a cartouche left blank for owner's initials; above this there is a maker's stamp 'DS'. Dimensions: 14.2 x 17.4 x 0.6mm. Weight: 3g.
Discussion: For a similar thimble, see an example formerly in the Holmes collection (sold at Christies's on 31 May 1995, lot 62).
Disposition: Acquired by Somerset County Museum.

D THORNTON

405. Bures area, Essex: copper-alloy pipe tamper (PAS: ESS-FE21B0)

Date: Post-Medieval (c. 1700–c. 1800).
Discovery: Found by Mick Mathews while metal-detecting in October 2007, and recorded by Laura McLean (Essex FLO).
Description: Cast copper-alloy pipe tamper. The handle is formed of the figure of St George standing upon a dragon, which he is slaying with a spear. The triangular, round-section shaft of the tamper extends below the dragon's body. It has a collar at the base before a flattened circular terminal. The surface is worn. Dimensions: 60.03 x 24.37 x 4.85mm. Weight: 13.91g.
Discussion: The patriotic figure of St George seems to have been particularly popular for tampers.
Disposition: Returned to finder.

L MCLEAN

406. Broughton-in-Furness, Cumbria: gilt copper-alloy seal matrix (PAS: LANCUM-94C1F7)

Date: Post-Medieval (c. 1700–c. 1800).
Discovery: Found by Vera and Brian Rendall while metal-detecting in 2007, and recorded by Dot Boughton (Lancashire & Cumbria FLO).
Description: Gilt cast copper-alloy seal matrix inscribed 'If I Dare', above a lion couchant facing right (left on the seal). It is undamaged and much of the gilding remains in the grooves and cavities of the base-metal casting. The seal matrix itself is probably made from white cloudy glass or (less likely) a semi-precious gemstone. Dimensions: 27.71 x 17.78mm. Weight: 10.28g.
Discussion: This is a further find of a probably mass-produced matrix from a period when these were in widespread use.
Disposition: Returned to finder.

D BOUGHTON

407. Plumley, Cheshire: lead owl figurine (PAS: LVPL-555B72)

Date: Post-Medieval (c. 1700–c. 1900).
Discovery: Found by Aleks Wijs while metal-detecting in 2007, and recorded by Frances McIntosh (Cheshire, Greater Manchester & Merseyside FLO).
Description: Cast lead owl. It is solid and has detailing on both faces, which allow it to be identified as a long-eared owl (Asio otus). The bird is depicted standing, with the tail in side view. Dimensions: 40 x 16 x 12mm. Weight: 40g.
Discussion: It seems likely that it is a toy, similar to a shy cock.
Disposition: Returned to finder.

F MCINTOSH

408. Buttercrambe with Bossall, North Yorkshire: gold mourning ring (PAS: LVPL-E05136; Treasure: 2007 T116)

Date: Post-Medieval (c. 1705–c. 1750).
Discovery: Found by Hal Roach while metal-detecting in January 2007, and reported to Frances McIntosh (North West FLO).
Description: A D-section hoop with a skull on the bezel, showing traces of white enamel. There are also traces of black enamelling within cross-hatching on the outside of the band. On the inside is the inscription 'sic omnibus' (so it is for everyone), with the maker's mark 'DA'. There are slight traces of black enamel within the lettering.
Discussion: The maker's mark is likely to be that of Isaac Davenport, who registered his mark as a 'smallworker' in 1705 (Grimwade 1990: no. 434).
Disposition: British Museum had hoped to aquire, but withdrew; returned to finder.

N AWAIS-DEAN

409. Bridestowe, Devon: ceramic jug (PAS: DEV-E10118)

Date: Post-Medieval (c. 1720–c. 1800).
Discovery: Found by Mr de Courcey whilst carrying out farm work with a tractor in the 1970s, which was subsequently recorded by Mr Harrison with Danielle Wootton (Devon FLO).
Description: A South Somerset ware jug; typical of these wares, particularly those from Donyatt. White slip bands under an amber glaze survive on the neck and shoulder of the jug. There is one turned line around the body. Diameter: 220mm. Length: 200mm.
Discussion: Although sherd fragments of this type of pottery are found in Devon relatively frequently, it is unusual for a complete vessel to be recovered from the ground. It is remarkable that this one survived in this state. The jug can be closely paralleled with one published by Coleman-Smith and Pearson (1988: 152–153, no. 4/266).
Disposition: Returned to finder.

D WOOTTON

410. Milborne Port, Somerset: gold and *niello* mourning ring (PAS: SOM-FA3D08)

Date: Post-Medieval (1753).
Discovery: Found by Hugh Vincent while metal-detecting in 2007, and recorded by Naomi Payne (Somerset FLO).
Description: A gold and *niello* mourning ring. The band is divided into five curvilinear scrolls, which contain a legend in gold, highlighted by *niello* which reads 'WM BYSHOP OB:24 JULY.1753 AE:40' (William Byshop who died on 24 July 1753 aged 40). On the inside of the band there is a maker's mark 'IW' within a simple rectangle. Diameter (external): 21.6mm. Width (band): 3.3mm. Thickness (band): 2.1mm. Weight: 4.2g.
Discussion: The finder checked the parish registers for Milborne Port and discovered that a William Byshop married a Sara Hallet on 23 October 1739. This ring presumably belonged to Sara, who had it made after the death of her husband. The maker's initials are not uncommon, but perhaps refer to John Webber of Plymouth, who entered his name and mark at the assay office in 1724. A number of London goldsmiths who were operating at this date had the same initials.
Disposition: Returned to finder.

N PAYNE

411. Guildford, Surrey: copper-alloy clog clasp (PAS: SUR-A665E0)

Date: Post-Medieval (c. 1770–c. 1800).
Discovery: Found by Mark Stonard while metal-detecting in 2007, and recorded by David Williams (Surrey FLO).
Description: One of an original pair of clog fasteners. This clasp bears the punched legend 'LIBERTY TO AMERICA' within a wreath. Dimensions: 26.19 x 15.48mm. Weight: 2.56g.
Discussion: This is an unusual instance of an everyday object with a motto favouring American independence found in Britain. It suggests radical, non-patriotic political sentiment among the lower classes.
Disposition: Returned to finder.

D WILLIAMS

412. Brecon, Powys: silver finger-ring bezel with intaglio (PAS: NMGW-9A96E6; Treasure: Wales 07.10)

Date: Post-Medieval (c. 1775–c. 1800).
Discovery: Found by Steven Williams and John Thomas while metal-detecting in August 2007 and reported to Mark Lodwick (Finds Co-ordinator, Wales).
Description: Silver bezel of a finger-ring containing an orangey-red cornelian intaglio. The edge of the bezel is decorated by a line of triangles running round its bottom edge and the back by an engraved floral pattern. The intaglio depicts a winged male figure, probably Cupid, a large bunch of grapes and an animal, probably a hare. Dimensions: 14 x 11 x 5mm. Weight: 1.4g.
Discussion: The intaglio would appear to be Roman; the same design elements can be seen on an intaglio from Bath (Henig 1978: 200, no. 113) where Cupid is holding a bunch of grapes and a hare is jumping up to reach it. On the present intaglio the hare is more fortunate and has got the bunch of grapes. The size, shape and decoration of the bezel do not appear to be Roman and would fit better with an 18th- or 19th-century date.
Disposition: Not Treasure; returned to finders.

E M CHAPMAN

413. Ambleside, Cumbria: copper-alloy pipe tamper (PAS: LANCUM-F58134)

Date: Post-Medieval (c. 1775–c. 1820).
Discovery: Found by Peter Adams while metal-detecting in 2007, and recorded by Dot Boughton (Lancashire & Cumbria FLO).
Description: A copper-alloy pipe tamper with its handle cast into the form of two lovers kissing. The male figure stands upright while the female's legs are bent giving her the look of being seated, suggesting a more erotic interpretation. The figures stand at a height of 40mm. The shaft is smooth and expands to a

flattened circular terminal. The shaft measures 31mm forming an overall length/height for the tamper of 71mm. Weight: 16.73g.

Discussion: A precise parallel comes from the wreck of the Colossus, which sank in 1798. This find adds to the growing, often tavern-related pornographic items of similar date.

Disposition: Returned to finder.

D BOUGHTON

414. Ryde, Isle of Wight: lead pugilist figurine (PAS: IOW-40D6F1)

Date: Post-Medieval (c. 1800–c. 1825).

Discovery: Found by Dorothy Hewison while gardening in 2007, and recorded by Frank Basford (Isle of Wight FLO).

Description: Incomplete lead male figure, with a robust body and head facing forwards. The hair is tightly curled and the facial features appear to be Afro-Caribbean. The right arm is broken just below the elbow and the left arm just above the elbow, and both legs are broken off close to the knee. The figure is attired in tightly clad boxing shorts with a high waistline and a prize-fighter's belt. When complete, the figure would have had a boxing stance with the left leg placed slightly forward and right arm raised at the elbow. Although incomplete and with old breaks, this figurine is in fair condition. Originally it was coated in a black substance; however, much of this has worn off. Dimensions: 91 x 44 x 23mm. Weight: 185.86g.

Discussion: The figurine is probably a representation of the celebrated American pugilist, Tom Molineaux. Born a slave on a Virginia plantation, Molineaux (1784–1818) fought fellow slaves while plantation owners wagered on the contests. After winning one of these matches against a rival, he was granted his freedom and the sum of $500 by his owner, Algernon Molineaux. By 1809, he had travelled to New York and subsequently to England where he became a notable prize fighter. Two notorious fights with English champion Tom Cribb in 1810 and 1811 won Molineaux a place in boxing history and he became a celebrity in England. He fought only sporadically, opting to engage in numerous sparring exhibitions. He died in Dublin, Ireland, and his death was reported in the 13 October 1818 edition of the New York Spectator. A hand-coloured etching showing Tom Molineaux in a similar stance to that of the figurine is in the Collections of Virginia Historical Society, Richmond, USA. Porcelain figures of Molineaux are also known (Halfpenny and Beddoe 1990: pl. S12; Miranda Goodby, *personal communication*).

Disposition: Returned to finder.

F BASFORD

415. Woolley, West Yorkshire: iron sword (PAS: SWYOR-398C11)

Date: Post-Medieval (probably c. 1800–c. 1900, but possibly as early as c. 1600).

Discovery: Found at the bottom of a pond by workers clearing it out, and reported by the landowner, Phillip Rowbottom, to Amy Cooper (South & West Yorkshire FLO) at Wakefield Museum.

Description: An iron sword which is full length with all the iron parts surviving. It has a straight blade, which tapers to a point. The metal is extremely fragile at the join between the blade and the hilt. The pommel and guard are discoid and are joined by a curving hand guard on one side. Beyond the pommel is a long, tapering projection which is circular in section and terminates in a pointed knop. The iron is generally in very good condition and there is a layer of concretion round the guard with roots trapped in it. Length: 980mm.

Discussion: This sword from India known as a *firangi* or *farang* (the term supposedly means 'foreigner'). The distinctive disc pommel and guards are indicators of types of swords from the Hindu areas of India. The indigenous broad, straight-bladed version is known as a *khanda* (as depicted in the centre of the common Hindu religious symbol). This, though, is a variant with a European-style straight-edged blade. The pommel extension is to enable both hands to guide the sword. They date from the 17th century to the present day, and most in this country are 19th-century souvenirs of empire. Most of these swords were decorated in some way, many with inlay or gilding, especially at the hilt or on the blade immediately below the guard. No decoration is visible on this example, though rust and concretion may obscure details.

Deposition: Returned to landowner.

A COOPER & K MATTHEWS

416. Twickenham, London: leather shoe (PAS: SUR-FFE5A2)

Date: Post-Medieval (c. 1800–c. 1900).

Discovery: Found by Jacqui Hill while digging in their former garden in waterlogged soil adjacent to the River Thames, and recorded by David Williams (Surrey FLO) in 2007.

Description: Child's leather shoe, originating in eastern Europe, and made in the late 19th century. It has stamped decoration, and a copper-alloy buckle and rivets. The number 2 is stamped on the sole.

Discussion: Being of unusual construction, the shoe was sent for comment to June Swann (formerly Northampton Museum) who identified its origin and date.

Disposition: Returned to finder.

D WILLIAMS

417. Padstow, Cornwall: silver-gilt jewelled pendant (PAS: CORN-FA0676; Treasure: 2007 T643)

Date: Post-Medieval (c. 1800–c. 1900).

Discovery: Found by Jonathan Clemes while metal-detecting in October 2007, reported to Anna Tyacke (Cornwall FLO), and identified by Dora Thornton (British Museum).

Description: Silver-gilt pendant with ornate cherub and foliage openwork detail, and *niello* inlay, surrounding settings of crude rectangular collets with five emeralds, one ruby, two garnets, and two citrine quartz around a central amethyst in a ropework setting, with two settings missing their stones. The gems all look re-used and have been replaced into these settings as they are scratched and worn (Sara Chambers, gemmologist, *personal communication*). The attachment loop at the top of the pendant has been damaged and is missing, and there are two small suspension loops at the bottom of the pendant, below each emerald, which would have had drop pendants attached, perhaps pearls. The frame appears to be made up of a cast element, roughly the bottom half of the piece, along with the cast settings, that have then been mounted and soldered onto an earlier handmade element, roughly the top half of the pendant, which was probably weakened by the process.
Dimensions: 48 x 40mm.

Discussion: Although the pendant is made in a baroque style appropriate for the 17th century, several features suggest that it is not what it claims to be. The whole object is crudely made and the back has a look suggesting it may have been moulded .The cherub head is not winged in the way one would expect of jewellery of this type and the fact that the jewel is silver, not gold, all argue for its being a 19th-century copy. Similar neo-baroque jewels were made all over Europe in the mid 1900s, in cities such as London, Vienna, Rome, Venice, Aachen, Munich and Paris.

Disposition: Returned to landowner.

D THORNTON

418. Landford, Wiltshire: gold fob-seal matrix (PAS: HAMP-609305)

Date: Post-Medieval (c. 1800–c. 1900).

Discovery: Found by Mark Duell while metal-detecting in 2006, and recorded by Rob Webley (Hampshire FLO) in 2007.

Description: Ornate cast gold fob-seal matrix with inset gem die. Its lower element features the plea 'Remember me' engraved in Gothic script on a (possible) amethyst. Uppermost within this element is a small plait of hair under glass. It is revealed by opening the moulded foliate upper element around its hinge. Dimensions: 28.82 x 18.85mm. Weight: 11.7g.

Discussion: This object unusually combines a practical seal with a container for a sentimental keepsake of the hair of a beloved relative or close acquaintance.

Disposition: Returned to finder.

R WEBLEY

419. Hurst Green, East Sussex: lead/tin toy milk churn (PAS: SUSS-753154)

Date: Post-Medieval (c. 1800–c. 1900).

Discovery: Found by Trish McLaughlin while metal-detecting in 2007, and recorded by Laura Burnett (Sussex FLO).

Description: Cast lead-tin alloy model milk churn, probably Georgian or Victorian. The item is conical with a flared rim. At each side are delicately moulded handles cast integrally with the body, the base has been broken and there is some damage at the rim. Dimensions: 35.2 x 22.7 x 0.8mm. Weight: 17.1g.

Discussion: Lead-tin toys are occasional detector finds and often echo contemporary household items as in this example. An almost identical churn is recorded from East Sussex (SUSS-949A95).

Disposition: Returned to finder.

L BURNETT

420. Kirkham, Lancashire: copper-alloy pet coffin (PAS: LANCUM-1A3576)

Date: Post-Medieval (c. 1800–c. 1900).

Discovery: Found by Roy Lewis while metal-detecting in 2007, and recorded by Dot Boughton (Lancashire & Cumbria FLO).

Description: Small cast copper-alloy coffin which comprises three different parts: the casket, a lid and a (possible) head-plate. All three parts are held together by a small, cast copper-alloy rivet at the head end of the coffin and all can swivel independently. The 'head-plate' is thinner than the body and lid, and may have protected a message wedged between it and the lid (any such a message probably rotted away). Dimensions: 82.3 x 3.85 x 3.55mm.

Discussion: The shape of the coffin is recent and from the size it is likely that it was meant for a small pet or possibly the ashes of a bigger one. Pet burials and coffins for pets are not unusual, but do not have a long tradition. It is unlikely that this object dates from before 1800.

Disposition: Returned to finder.

D BOUGHTON

421. Duffryn Ardudwy, Gwynedd: silver finger-ring (PAS: NMGW-9ABD00; Treasure Wales 07.20)

Date: Post-Medieval (c. 1800–c. 1900).
Discovery: Found by Andrew Bentley while metal-detecting during May 2007, and reported to David Williams (Surrey FLO) and then Mark Lodwick (Finds Co-ordinator, Wales).
Description: Decorative silver ring with an oval bezel, set with a garnet.
Discussion: The construction of the ring and regular oval stone with flat underside suggest a 19th-century date.
Disposition: Not Treasure; returned to finder.

M REDKNAP

422. City of London: stone scarab (PAS: LON-AF19A7)

Date: Post-Medieval (c. 1800–c. 1925).
Discovery: Found by Terry Greenwood while searching the Thames foreshore in 2007, and recorded by Kate Sumnall (London FLO).
Description: An Egyptian stone scarab with cartouche on the base. Dimensions: 66.48 x 54.85 x 36.62mm. Weight: 147.09g.
Discussion: Stephen Quirke (Petrie Museum) identified the object as 'an interesting example usually discarded from collections as not ancient. The cartouche (name-ring) containing the hieroglyphs is an often-copied motif – the signs themselves are accurate enough and read Menmaatra, which is the throne-name of King Sety I, c. 1290 BC, father of King Ramses II; the hieroglyph under the name-ring is the sign for 'gold' (Egyptian *nbw*). The criteria for considering it not ancient are the criss-cross interior of the gold hieroglyph and lower sign in the cartouche; the material, which looks like limestone, not usually used for Sety I-Ramses II ancient scarabs; the rough cutting, partly caused by the material; the feather on the head of the goddess-hieroglyph (*Maat*) is a simple triangle which is unknown on an ancient scarab (it should have the rounded tip of a plum). There are also many 'rustic' ancient scarabs, and many ancient copies made outside Egypt'.
Disposition: Returned to finder.

K SUMNALL & S QUIRKE

423. Shalfleet, Isle of Wight: lead gaming piece (PAS: IOW-918A57)

Date: Post-Medieval (c. 1800–c. 1925).
Discovery: Found by Cass Davis while metal-detecting in 2007, and recorded by Frank Basford, (Isle of Wight FLO).
Description: Roughly cube-shaped with a pointed base and a small handle at the top. The upper part of the cube is hollow and the central handle, now incomplete, is sub-circular in cross-section. The base is formed by a rib at each corner. Each rib extends downwards and meet at the centre to form a point that enabled the piece to spin in a similar way to that of a spinning top. Each face has a Hebrew letter in raised relief that represents the initials of the phrase 'Nes Gadol Haya Sham' (a great miracle happened there) indicating the following values: nicht = nothing, gimmel = double, halb = half, stell ein = put back in (throw again). Dimensions: 23.2 x 13.9 x 12.2mm. Weight: 13.56g.
Discussion: The use of the Dreidel, an elaborate form of dice with different letters on the four sides, began in Germany centuries ago. Rabbis there allowed their community to gamble only during Hanukkah. The Jewish people transliterated the initials into their Hebrew equivalents as preceding, using them as a reminder of the miracle of Hanukkah, the Festival of Lights. This is an eight-day holiday celebrating the re-kindling of the Temple menorah at the time of the Maccabee rebellion in the 1st century AD. The festival is observed in Jewish homes by the kindling of one more light on each night of the holiday.
Disposition: Returned to finder.

F BASFORD

424. Penrith, Cumbria: ceramic gaming piece (PAS: LANCUM-A84751)

Date: Post-Medieval (c. 1850–c. 1900).
Discovery: Found by Sue Convey while gardening in the 1980s or 1990s, recorded by Dot Boughton (Lancashire & Cumbria FLO), and identified by Jo Dawson (Greenlane Archaeology Ltd).
Description: Cuboid gaming piece made from glazed white ceramic and with four parallel-grooved faces. Dimensions: 15 x 15 x 19.1mm. Weight: 15g.
Discussion: Such objects were used to play 'dibs', a game similar to jacks or fivestones. The player throws a bunch of five pieces in the air, and sees how many they can catch on the back of the hand. There are many variations and refinements to this simplest version.
Disposition: Returned to finder.

D BOUGHTON & J DAWSON

425. Exeter, Devon: tin ration container (PAS: DEV-0B0D26)

Date: Post-Medieval (c. 1899–c. 1902).

Discovery: Found by Peter Edwards while gardening several years ago, and recorded by Danielle Wootton (Devon FLO) in 2007.

Description: This ration tin most probably dates to the Boer War period (1899–1902), and is sometimes referred to as an 'iron' ration. At one end of the tin is the word 'COCOA' in relief, while the other end has the word 'DINNER'. Internally, the tin is divided into two sections, the 'dinner' containing a beef extract and the 'cocoa' compartment having compressed cocoa powder. There is a soldered tin strip at each end of the tin, which would have been opened with a small key, similar to the way some modern cans are opened today. Dimensions: 120 x 70 x 40mm.

Discussion: Because the tin is still sealed, the food ration is probably still inside. The tin would originally have had a paper label with the instructions 'EMERGENCY RATION. Field Service. This ration is not to be opened except by order of an officer or in an extremity. It is to be carried in the haversack and produced at inspections etc. The ration is calculated to maintain strength for 36 hours if eaten in small quantities at a time.'

Discussion: Similar examples, which are held at the National Army Museum, London, were made by the Bovril Company of London.

Disposition: Returned to finder.

D WOOTTON

426. Wellingore, Lincolnshire: white-metal German military tag (PAS: LIN-75CDB6)

Date: Post-Medieval (c. 1939–1945).

Discovery: Found by Ron Teather while metal-detecting in 2007, and recorded by Adam Daubney (Lincolnshire FLO).

Description: Upper half of a Second World War German military tag. The tag is flat, crescentic and has two holes at the curved edge. There are two tabs of metal protruding from the straight edge, which originally would have attached to the opposing crescentic side. One face is stamped with the owner's details. The top line reads '..6664', which is the soldier's personal number. The bottom line reads '...p Ld Schutz Ers Batl 13(?4)'. The letter 'p' at the far right next to the break would have been the last letter of the abbreviated word Komp[anie], and so in full the inscription would reads *Kompanie Landeschutz Ersatz Bataillon* (Company Land Defence Drafting Battalion). Dimensions: 46.4 x 25.84 x 1.29.

Discussion: Another German identity tag and an infantry badge were also found in the same field (LIN-CE1D45 & CE8D25). An image of the former tag was sent to the Deutsche Dienststelle, who wrote back to say that the wearer of that *Erkennunsmarke* reappeared in Germany in 1956, proving that despite being the upper portion, the tag was not part of a burial.

Disposition: Returned to finder.

A DAUBNEY

Section editor and further research: Geoff Egan.
Editor: Michael Lewis.

Key to abbreviations:

General:
m. = mint
im. = initial mark
mn. = moneyer
Obv: = obverse
Rev: = reverse
* (asterisk) = fragmentary coins
† (cross) = clipped (Medieval only)

Roman denominations:
as = *as*
aur = *aureus*
den = *denarius*
dup = *dupondius*
num = *nummus*
sest = *sestertius*
sil = *siliquae*

IRON AGE
(AND OTHER PRE-ROMAN) COINS

In 2007, nine Treasure cases involving Iron Age coins were reported, covering a total of 36 coins. Among these cases are six addenda, which underline the importance of recording all Iron Age coins, as many come from dispersed hoards or votive deposits which have often been ploughed out. In the cases of Beverley, East Yorkshire (431), and Driffield, East Yorkshire (434 & 435), coins have been recorded for almost a decade from these findspots.

In addition 443 single finds of Iron Age coins have been recorded on the PAS database in 2007. This report also includes a Carthaginian coin found at Nettleton, Lincolnshire (436), which probably arrived in Britain during the Iron Age. A number of other Greek and Carthaginian coins have been recorded over the years from Britain but this piece has one of the most northerly findspots. An example of Britain's earliest coin issue, the so-called 'Thurrock' type *potin* cast in Kent, has also travelled a considerable distance to its resting point in Osbournby, Lincolnshire (440). The PAS continues to record a significant number of Continental Iron Age coins. This report contains Gallo-Belgic gold *staters* found in Sissinghurst, Kent (437), and the Calbourne area, Isle of Wight (438); Continental silver coins from West Sussex (441), the Isle of Wight (454) and Gwithian, Cornwall (446); and Continental base-metal issues found in Longwick cum Ilmer, Buckinghamshire (439), and Micheldever, Hampshire (443). These records continue to enhance research into the circulation of Gaulish coins in Britain.

Treasure and PAS finds continue to include unpublished and rare coins. The Saxilby Hoard, Lincolnshire (428), contains two previously unrecorded north-eastern gold *staters* that the British Museum hopes to acquire. A rare Gallo-Belgic D gold quarter *stater* has been found at Willingdon and Jevington, Sussex (444), while near Eastbourne was found another Atrebatic silver unit (449) which is known from only a handful of examples. The British Museum has also acquired a gold 'scyphate' quarter *stater* from Welbourn, Lincolnshire (447), which is only normally found in that county. A find from Shoreham by Sea, West Sussex (455) has the clearest reading of the inscription for the British king Tincomarus on a silver issue, while possibly the best example of a Tincomarus gold *stater* has been recorded from the Newchurch area, Isle of Wight (456).

Research by many scholars, for example Ian Leins (British Museum & Newcastle University), is reliant on the accurate recording of findspots, and it is welcome that increasing numbers of detectorists are now providing very precise National Grid References

COINS

by plotting finds using a map or (better still) using handheld Global Positioning Systems (GPS) devices. In years to come, this recording will become increasingly important. The Iron Age coins recorded with the PAS and Celtic Coin Index (CCI) are now better integrated as the CCI is now hosted by the PAS (www.finds.org.uk/cci) and currently catalogues over 37,925 pieces. This represents the most comprehensive archaeological database of its kind in the world. Iron Age numismatics is growing from strength to strength with PAS records playing a central role.

A number of the single finds have been included in the 'Coin Register' in the *British Numismatic Journal* 78 (2008).

HOARDS

427. Little Horwood (addenda), Buckinghamshire: two gold *staters* (PAS: BUC-6CFB85; Treasure: 2007 T608)

Date: Iron Age (c. 60–c. 20 BC).
Discovery: Found by Andrew Clarkson, Edward Clarkson and Gordon Heritage while metal-detecting in October 2007, and reported to Ros Tyrrell (Buckinghamshire FLO).
Description: Both coins are British gold *staters* of a type known as 'British LA' or 'Whaddon Chase' (BM 295; VA 1476). Similar coins accounted for 60 of the 73 coins reported in the original find.
Discussion: The coins' type and the circumstances of their discovery suggest that they are related to both the earlier discovery and the original Whaddon Chase Hoard, discovered in 1849 (for the original find and further discussion, see *TAR* 2005/6, no. 1042).
Disposition: Acquired by Buckinghamshire County Museum.

I LEINS

428. Saxilby, Lincolnshire: four gold *staters* (PAS: LIN-3400F2; Treasure: 2007 T602; CCI: 08 6258-62)

Date: Iron Age (c. 60–c. 50 BC).
Discovery: Found by Geoffry Rippon and Paul Virr while metal-detecting in October 2007, and reported to Adam Daubney (Lincolnshire FLO).
Description: Four gold *staters* and one gold pellet or droplet. The *staters* are early uninscribed North-East coast types. Two are of the recorded type 'British H' and two are of an unrecorded type, differing from the published type 'British I' in the choice of an entirely new obverse design.
1. Early uninscribed 'British H' gold, 'North-East coast Type' (VA 800.03; BMC 182). Diameter: 20.59mm. Weight: 6.15g. Registered as CCI 08.6258.
2. Early uninscribed 'British H' gold, 'North-East coast Type' (VA 800.11; BMC 190). Diameter: 20.04mm. Weight: 5.87g. Registered as CCI 08.6259.

3. Early uninscribed North-East coast gold (new type; not catalogued in VA/BMC). Diameter: 20.22mm. Weight: 6.24g. Registered as CCI 08.6260.
4. Early uninscribed North-East coast gold (new type; not catalogued in VA/BMC). Diameter: 18.45mm. Weight: 6.21g. Registered as CCI 08.6261.
5. Gold pellet. Dimensions: 10.91 x 13.64 x 6.71mm. Weight: 5.33g. Registered as CCI 08.6262.
Discussion: The presence of the gold pellet in the hoard may suggest an industrial process, such as the melting down of gold coins into pellets ready for the striking of new issues, or even making jewellery. Pellets of this kind have been found with other coin deposits, including the well-known East Leicestershire Hoard (Leins 2007a; 22–48).
Disposition: British Museum acquired coin no. 4.

A DAUBNEY & I LEINS

429. Urchfont, Wiltshire: two silver units (PAS: WILT-CDD3C6; Treasure: 2007 T55)

Date: Iron Age (c. 50–c. 20 BC).
Discovery: Found by Keith Palmer while metal-detecting in December 2006, and reported to Katie Hinds (Wiltshire FLO) in 2007.
Description: Two silver coins of the uninscribed 'Irregular Western series'. Both coins are of the same type and would have been produced around 50–20 BC. Diameters: 12mm & 11mm. Weights: 0.93g & 0.71g.
Discussion: This type of coin is not published in the main catalogues of Iron Age coinage, but examples have been recorded on the CCI (e.g. CCI 99.1932).
Disposition: Wiltshire Heritage Museum hopes to acquire.

D ALGAR & I LEINS

430. Westerham (3rd addenda), Kent: fourteen gold quarter *staters* (PAS: KENT-049BF3; Treasure: 2007 T624)

Date: Iron Age (c. 20 BC–c. AD 10).
Discovery: Found by Nick Moon while metal-detecting between April and September 2007, and reported to Andrew Richardson (Kent FLO).
Description: The composition of the present group is similar to the earlier finds (see *TAR* 2003, no. 351; *TAR* 2005/6, nos. 1047 & 1048) and can be summarised as follows:
1. Gold quarter *stater*, 'British LY3' (VA 158; BMC 371).
2.–14. Gold quarter *staters*, 'British LZ2' (VA 151; BMC 2469).
Discussion: All of the coins are early uninscribed gold quarter *staters* of types associated with the Cantii (peoples from modern Kent). All were produced towards the end of the first century BC, but as none have inscriptions they cannot be directly associated with a historically attested ruler.
Disposition: Acquired by Maidstone Museum.

I LEINS

431. Beverley (addenda), East Yorkshire: three North-Eastern (Corieltavian) gold *staters* (PAS: YORYM-1EC684; Treasure: 2007 T660)

Date: Iron Age (c. 50 BC–c. AD 10).
Discovery: Found by Jack Cooper and Alec Thompson while metal-detecting in October 2007, and reported to Liz Andrews-Wilson (North & East Yorkshire FLO).
Description: Three North-Eastern (Corieltauvi) gold *staters*, one of the 'South Ferriby' type (VA 811) and two of the 'Domino' type (VA 829-1).
Discussion: This is a further addenda to coins found on the site since 2001 (for summaries of earlier finds, see *TAR* 2005/6, no. 1049; Leins 2007b, 244–245, nos. 8–9). The coins are similar to pieces already recorded and do not change the dating of the hoard.
Disposition: Disclaimed; returned to finder.

I LEINS

---

432. East Leicestershire (1st addenda): two silver units (PAS: WAW-A89225 & A87636; Treasure: 2007 T274)

Date: Iron Age (c. AD 30–c. 60).
Discovery: Found in November 2006, and reported to Angie Bolton (Warwickshire & Worcestershire FLO). The coins were about 500m apart from each other on opposite sides of the same field, on an adjacent field to the findspot of an earlier hoard recovered from 2001 onwards and declared Treasure in 2003 (Leins: 2007a).
Description: Two silver units of North-Eastern type; they originated in the East Midlands and are generally attributed to a tribe known as the Corieltauvi.
1. uninscribed silver unit (Leicestershire hoard type uninscribed 3a) (VA 877; BMC 3218). Weight: 1.04g.
2. silver unit inscribed 'AVN COST' (VA 914; BMC 3261). Weight: 0.96g.
Discussion: The site of the earlier find declared Treasure (Leins 2007a: 22–48) was the subject of archaeological investigation, which suggested that the majority of the coins were deposited in a series of discrete groups as part of a ritual act or religious observance in the middle decades of the 1st century AD. The geographical extent of this activity has not been determined and may have been spread over a wide area. The fact that these two coins are of types contained in the earlier hoard, suggests that they are likely to have been part of this ritual activity.
Disposition: Leicestershire County Council Heritage Service hopes to acquire.

E GHEY & I LEINS

---

433. North Dalton, East Yorkshire (1st addenda): four North-Eastern (Corieltavian) coins (PAS: NCL-63DA22; Treasure: 2007 T600; CCI: 08 6254-7)

Date: Iron Age (c. AD 30–c. 60).
Discovery: Found by Paul Rennoldson and Thomas Bolam while metal-detecting in 2007, and reported to Rob Collins (North East FLO).
Description: Four of the five coins declared are Iron Age (the Roman coin is covered in 2008 T153).
1. Gold-plated copper-alloy 'South Ferriby' type *stater* (VA 811.23; BMC 3149; CCI 08.6254). Diameter: 21mm. Weight: 5.23g.
2. Gold 'Kite' type *stater* (VA 825.09; BMC 3184; CCI 08.6255). Diameter: 19mm. Weight: 5.33g.
3. Gold-plated copper-alloy VOLISIOS DVMNOCOVEROS *stater* (VA 978.02; BMC 3337; CCI 08.6257). Diameter: 19.2mm. Weight: 5.27g.
4. Silver AVN COST unit (VA 914.03; BMC 3261; CCI 08.6256). Diameter: 14.7mm. Weight: 0.74g.
Discussion: These coins represent addenda to 2006 T494 (*TAR* 2005/6, no. 1050).
Disposition: Disclaimed; returned to finder.

I LEINS

---

434. Driffield area (addenda), East Yorkshire: three North-Eastern (Corieltavian) gold *staters* (PAS: NCL-001A42; Treasure: 2007 T48)

Date: Iron Age (c. AD 30–c. 60).
Discovery: Found by David Scott while metal-detecting in October 2006, and reported to Rob Collins (North East FLO).
Description: Three North-Eastern (Corieltavian) gold *staters*, two 'Kite' types (VA 825) and one VOLISIOS DVMNOVELLAVNOS type (VA 988).
Discussion: These coins clearly represent further addenda to a hoard which has been found in batches since 2002 (for latest addenda see *TAR* 2005/6, no. 1053. For a further addendum see 435).
Disposition: Disclaimed; returned to finder.

I LEINS

---

435. Driffield area (addenda), East Yorkshire: two North-Eastern (Corieltavian) gold *staters* (PAS: YORYM-1C8AA2; Treasure: 2007 T597)

Date: Iron Age (c. AD 30–c. 60).
Discovery: Found by David Scott while metal-detecting in August 2007, and reported to Rob Collins (North East FLO).
Description: Two uninscribed North-Eastern (Corieltavian) gold *staters*, one of the 'Kite' type (VA 825) and one of the 'Domino' type (VA 829).
Discussion: These coins represent further addenda to a hoard which has been found in batches since 2002 (for latest addenda see *TAR* 2005/6, no. 1053. For a further addendum see 434).
Disposition: Disclaimed; returned to finder.

I LEINS

SINGLE FINDS

436. Nettleton, Lincolnshire: Carthaginian copper-alloy unit (PAS: LIN-C0E9D7)

Date: Iron Age (c. 300–c. 264 BC).
Discovery: Found by Michael O'Bee while metal-detecting, and recorded by Adam Daubney (Lincolnshire FLO).
Description: Copper-alloy unit of the Carthaginian Empire, struck in Sardinia. Diameter: 18mm.
Discussion: Carthaginian and Numidian coins are occasionally found in Britain, dating from the 3rd and 2nd centuries BC. A Numidian piece was found in excavations at Carn Brea, Cornwall, and two smaller Carthaginian coins were found many years ago in the temple assemblage from Castle Combe, North Wraxall, Wiltshire (Moorhead 2001: 112, no. 8). Most recently, several similar coins have been recorded in Kent (Holman 2005: 5, fig. 2, no. 14; 40–41). Traditionally, it has been assumed that these coins reflect the tin trade between south-west Britain and the Mediterranean.
Disposition: Returned to finder.

A DAUBNEY & S MOORHEAD

437. Sissinghurst, Kent: Gallo-Belgic gold *stater* (PAS: KENT-3F6108)

Date: Iron Age (c. 175–c. 100 BC).
Discovery: Found by Bob Sharp while metal-detecting in August 2007, and recorded by Andrew Richardson (Kent FLO).
Description: Gold Gallo-Belgic AB 'Broad Flan' *stater* (Sills Ab1, class 5). Diameter: 21.69mm. Weight: 7.1g.
Discussion: The findspot of this coin is entirely consistent with the known distribution of Gallo-Belgic AB *staters*, which is centred on Kent, London and Essex.
Disposition: Returned to finder.

A RICHARDSON & I LEINS

438. Calbourne area, Isle of Wight: Gallo-Belgic gold *stater* (PAS: IOW-D35422)

Date: Iron Age (c. 200–c. 125 BC).
Discovery: Found by Kevin Tigwell while metal-detecting in 2007, and recorded by Frank Basford (Isle of Wight FLO).
Description: A Continental Gallo-Belgic XB1 gold *stater* of Scheers 15 type. Diameter: 12mm. Weight: 7.48g.
Discussion: This type has been traditionally associated with the Suessiones, Senones and other tribes of the southern part of Gallia Belgica. It is in good condition but is slightly worn overall.
Disposition: Returned to finder.

I LEINS & F BASFORD

439. Longwick cum Ilmer, Buckinghamshire: Gaulish copper-alloy *potin* (PAS: BERK-9FD3C7)

Date: Iron Age (c. 175–c. 125 BC).
Discovery: Found by Stephen Palmer while metal-detecting before March 2007, and reported to Charlotte Burrill (Oxfordshire & Berkshire FLO).
Description: *Potin*, attributed to the Remi tribe (Gaul). Obv: figure running right, holding torc and spear. Rev: animal right (Delestrée and Tache: no. 154).
Discussion: A number of other British provenances have been recorded for this type, for example at Offley, Hertfordshire (CCI 69.0640).
Disposition: Returned to finder.

I LEINS & S MOORHEAD

440. Osbournby, Lincolnshire: copper-alloy *potin*, (PAS: LIN-73E287)

Date: Iron Age (c. 100 BC)
Discovery: Found by Tim Camm while metal-detecting, and reported to Adam Daubney (Lincolnshire FLO).
Description: British 'Thurrock type' *potin*. Obv: head left, obscured by casting sprue. Rev: bull, obscured by casting sprue (closest parallel for the coin is CCI 00.0452). Diameter: 17mm.
Discussion: This example, like others recently recorded with the PAS, demonstrates the penetration of these types well beyond their south-eastern origins.
Disposition: Returned to finder.

I LEINS & A DAUBNEY

441. West Sussex: silver unit of Eastern Gaul (PAS: SUSS-65D368)

Date: Iron Age (c. 100–c. 50 BC).
Discovery: Found by Garry Crace while metal-detecting in July 2007, and reported to Liz Andrews-Wilson (Sussex FLO)
Description: Obv: head left. Rev: horse left with ?KA above and blundered Greek letters below (c.f. Delestrée and Tache: no. 3196ff). Diameter: 12.5mm. Weight: 1.87g.
Discussion: This type belongs with the coinage of eastern Gaul, usually associated with the Lingones or Aedui. The reverse includes a corruption of the Greek 'Kaletedou'. Around 10 examples of this type are known from Britain.
Disposition: Returned to finder.

I LEINS & L ANDREWS-WILSON

442. North Hertfordshire area: contemporary copy (gold plated *stater*) of Addedomaros (PAS: BH-318E56)

Date: Iron Age (c. 30–c. 10 BC).
Discovery: Found by Harvey Cross while metal-detecting in 2006 and recorded by Julian Watters (Hertfordshire & Bedfordshire FLO) in 2007.
Description: A contemporary copy of a gold *stater* of the Eastern coin region (the tradition centred on Essex, Hertfordshire and surrounding counties). Although the coin is in very poor condition, it almost certainly copies a gold *stater* of the ruler Addedomaros (cf. VA 160; BMC 2390). Diameter: 18.5mm. Weight 2.89g.
Discussion: None of the gold plating or the design survives on the obverse of the coin, but enough of the design is visible on the plated areas of the reverse to identify it. Addedomaros was the first ruler and issuer of coins to the north of the River Thames to place his name on his coins.
Deposition: Returned to finder.

I LEINS & J WATTERS

443. Micheldever, Hampshire: copper-alloy *potin* (PAS: HAMP-6152A2)

Date: Iron Age (c. 70–c. 50 BC).
Discovery: Found by Mark Duell while metal-detecting in 2007, and recorded with Rob Webley (Hampshire FLO).
Description: Cast copper-alloy *potin*. Obv: a stylised head. Rev: wild boar above pellets and torc. Diameter: 18.25mm. Weight: 3.66g.
Discussion: It is currently thought that this coin was minted in Belgium (Delestrée and Tache: no. 531A). At least ten other examples have been recorded from Britain, including one now in the collections of Winchester Museums Service and another from Hampshire recorded with the PAS (HAMP432).
Disposition: Returned to finder.

I LEINS & R WEBLEY

444. Willingdon and Jevington, East Sussex: Gallo-Belgic gold quarter *stater* (PAS: SUSS-23B126; CCI: 00.0490)

Date: Iron Age (c. 60–c. 50 BC).
Discovery: Found by Roy Lock (deceased) while metal-detecting in 2000, and recorded with Liz Andrews-Wilson (Sussex FLO).
Description: Gallo-Belgic D variant gold quarter *stater*. Obv: three dot-in-ring motifs (VA 67–3). Rev: complex pattern derived from Roman trophy. Diameter: 9.48mm. Weight: 1.2g.
Discussion: This is a rare variety with three dot-in-ring motifs on the obverse. The weight of this coin is closer to the British uninscribed P 'Trophy type'.
Disposition: It is hoped this coin will be donated to the British Museum.

L BURNETT & L ANDREWS-WILSON

445. Chichester area, West Sussex: Gallo-Belgic gold *stater* (PAS: SUSS-4E9F15; CCI: 06.0587)

Date: Iron Age (c. 60–c. 50 BC).
Discovery: Found by Peter Sheffield while metal-detecting before January 2001, and reported to Liz Andrews-Wilson (Sussex FLO).
Description: Gallo-Belgic E 'Gallic War' gold *stater*. Obv: blank. Rev: abstract horse with stylised charioteer right (VA 54–1). Diameter: 17.1mm. Weight: 5.80g.
Discussion: Coins of this type continue to be recorded in significant numbers, enabling the creation of fuller distribution maps.
Disposition: Returned to finder.

L ANDREWS-WILSON & I LEINS

446. Gwithian, Cornwall: Armorican base-silver *stater* (PAS: CORN-0FCF32)

Date: Iron Age (c. 60–c. 50 BC).
Discovery: Found by Graham Dyer while metal-detecting in April 2007, and recorded by Anna Tyacke (Cornwall FLO).
Description: Armorican base-silver *stater*. Obv: abstract head right, boar above. Reverse: human-headed horse with rider right, lyre symbol below. Diameter: 20mm. Weight: 7.38g.
Discussion: The coin is a variant of published types (the nearest parallels are Delestrée and Tache: nos. 2284–2285). The type originated from the Channel Islands or Cotentin region.
Disposition: Acquired by Royal Institution of Cornwall.

A TYACKE & I LEINS

447. Welbourn, Lincolnshire: North-Eastern (Corieltavian) gold quarter *stater* (PAS: LIN-AC3623)

Date: Iron Age (c. 60–c. 50 BC).
Discovery: Found by Ron Teather while metal-detecting in 2007, and recorded by Adam Daubney (Lincolnshire FLO).
Description: North-Eastern (Corieltavian) gold 'scyphate' quarter *stater*. Obv: abstract pattern based on a boar. Rev: pattern with prominent retrograde S-shape (cf. CCI 94.0765). Diameter: 16.18mm. Weight: 1.35g.
Discussion: Around 35 examples of this coin have been recorded, mostly from Lincolnshire.
Disposition: Acquired by the British Museum.

A DAUBNEY & I LEINS

448. Chichester area, West Sussex: copper-alloy unit (PAS: SUSS-4ECF02; CCI: 06.0588)

Date: Iron Age (c. 50–30 BC).
Discovery: Found by Peter Sheffield while metal-detecting before January 2007, and recorded by Liz Andrews-Wilson (Sussex FLO).
Description: Early uninscribed British copper-alloy unit. Obv: abstract head right. Rev: cock left.
Diameter: 15.8mm. Weight: 2.3g.
Discussion: This type appears to be known from Belgic Gaul, and was published as a coin of the Ambiani in the British Museum catalogue (Allen and Mays: 1995, 64 no. 31). The six other examples recorded by the CCI are all British finds, from Wiltshire, Sussex and possibly Hampshire. These coins almost certainly fit alongside more common issues such as the so-called 'Chichester cock' bronzes. They were based on Belgic prototypes, but produced in southern Britain, somewhere in the Solent hinterland.
Disposition: Returned to finder.

L ANDREWS-WILSON & P DE JERSEY

449. Eastbourne area, East Sussex: Southern (Atrebatic) silver unit (PAS: SUSS-92DEC6)

Date: Iron Age (c. 50–c. 20 BC).
Discovery: Found by David Wootten while metal-detecting in 2007, and recorded with Liz Andrews-Wilson (Sussex FLO).
Description: Southern (Atrebatic) uninscribed silver unit. Obv: two opposed animals, possibly ducks. Rev: horse advancing left. Diameter: 10.9mm. Weight: 1.3 g.
Discussion: This type has not been published in any catalogues. The first one was found in 2000 and several have been found since. A partial search of the CCI has revealed seven other examples (CCI 000941; 920063; 930682; 930995; 950257; 970995 & 980346). This coin is also identical to a find from East Dean and Friston, Sussex (SUSS-186B34).
Disposition: Returned to finder.

L ANDREWS-WILSON & I LEINS

450. Cliffe, Kent: Kentish (Cantii) silver unit (PAS: KENT-1B82D0)

Date: Iron Age (c. 50–c. 20 BC).
Discovery: Found by Cliff Turner while metal-detecting before April 2007, and recorded by Andrew Richardson (Kent FLO).
Description: Kentish (Cantii) silver unit. Obv: head, with torc around neck, right. Rev: winged horse right.
Diameter: 11.68mm. Weight: 1g.
Discussion: A number of examples of this uncatalogued type are now known from archaeological sites in Kent.
Disposition: Returned to finder.

A RICHARDSON & I LEINS

451. Wickham Skeith, Suffolk: Kentish (Cantii) copper-alloy unit (PAS: SF-DABE83)

Date: Iron Age (c. 50–c. 20 BC).
Discovery: Found by Trevor Southgate while metal-detecting in April 2007, and recorded by Faye Minter (Suffolk FLO).
Description: Kentish (Cantii) copper-alloy unit. Obv: wolf right. Rev: bull right (VA 154–3; BMC 2484).
Diameter: 16mm. Weight: 1.77 g.
Discussion: Around 35 coins of this type are listed on the CCI, the majority of which are located in Kent and two from Essex. This is the most northerly find to date.
Disposition: Returned to finder.

F MINTER & I LEINS

452. Findon area, West Sussex: South Western (Durotrigan) silver half unit (PAS: SUSS-301B12)

Date: Iron Age (c. 50–c. 20 BC).
Discovery: Found by Richard Lyon, while metal-detecting in 2007, and recorded with Laura Burnett (Sussex FLO).
Description: South Western (Durotrigan) 'Hampshire Thin' silver half unit. Obv: complex pattern of pellets. Rev: horse left (BMC 2782; VA 1280). Diameter: 16.44mm. Weight 0.7g.
Discussion: A relatively rare type of Iron Age coin, most previous examples for which findspots are known come from Hampshire or the Isle of Wight (as the name suggests) or bordering districts. This is markedly further east; a coin of this type from Lewes, East Sussex (SUSS-A82BC4) helps establish the wider circulation area of these coins. These coins have recently been reattributed from the Durotriges to the Belgae by Chris Rudd (coin-dealer).
Disposition: Returned to finder.

L BURNETT & I LEINS

453. Tarrant Monkton, Dorset: South Western uninscribed silver *stater* (PAS: DOR-2AF3C2)

Date: Iron Age (c. 50 BC–c. AD 10).
Discovery: Found by Robert Tydeman while metal-detecting in 2006, and recorded with Ciorstaidh Hayward Trevarthen (Dorset FLO).
Description: South Western uninscribed type silver *stater* with stylised head and horse (BMC 2711).
Diameter: 20.21mm. Weight: 4.98g.
Discussion: This is a good, clear, example of this uninscribed type and is one of ten Iron Age coins recorded in Dorset in 2007.
Disposition: Returned to finder.

C HAYWARD TREVARTHEN

454. Isle of Wight: Armorican silver fractional unit (PAS: IOW-31E7D6; CCI: 07 0062)

Date: Iron Age (c. 40–c. 20 BC).
Discovery: Found by Tom Winch while metal-detecting around May 2007, and recorded by Frank Basford (Isle of Wight FLO).
Description: Armorican silver fractional unit. Obv: abstract head derived from head of Athena left. Rev: horse galloping left. Diameter: 10.5mm. Weight: 0.94g.
Discussion: This coin is of the type Delestrée and Tache: 2369 (see also De Jersey: 1994, 114 for illustration, and a discussion in Gruel and Taccoen: 1992).
Disposition: Returned to finder.

F BASFORD & P DE JERSEY

455. Shoreham by Sea, West Sussex: silver unit of Tincomarus (PAS: SUSS-2BF306)

Date: Iron Age (c. 20 BC–c. AD 10).
Discovery: Found by John Kempshall while metal-detecting in 2007, and recorded with Liz Andrews Wilson (Sussex FLO).
Description: British Iron Age silver unit of Tincomarus, associated with the Southern (Atrebatic) regional series. The inscription TINCOMAR[VS] can be seen around the head. Diameter: 12.2mm. Weight: 1.3g.
Discussion: These silver units were published by Van Arsdell (1989) as coins of Verica (VA473–1) but later reinterpreted as issues of Tincomarus. It is probably one of the earliest Iron Age coins to include a labelled portrait of a British ruler. 28 are now known, of which 16 have provenances, mainly in the South Downs and West Sussex area. The present coin is the clearest representation of Tincomarus's name on a silver coin.
Disposition: Acquired by the British Museum.

L ANDREWS-WILSON & I LEINS

456. Newchurch area, Isle of Wight: Southern (Atrebatic) gold *stater* of Tincomarus (PAS: IOW-D8AA20)

Date: Late Iron Age (c. 20 BC–c. AD 10).
Discovery: Found by Alan Rowe while using a metal-detector in 2007, and recorded by Frank Basford (Isle of Wight FLO).
Description: Southern (Atrebatic) gold *stater* of Tincomarus. Obv: wreath pattern. Rev: horse right and inscription TINC-O-MARVS around (BMC 765). Diameter: 20mm. Weight: 5.42g.
Discussion: The coin is similar to an example that was acquired by the British Museum, part of the Alton hoard (1996). The Alton find was the first coin to reveal the correct form of the name TINCOMARVS, which had previously been read as Tincommius by 19th- and 20th-century historians. However, this Isle of Wight find is probably the finest example of a Tincomarus coin with the full legend yet found.

Disposition: Returned to finder.

F BASFORD & I LEINS

457. Newton Blossomville, Buckinghamshire: Eastern (Trinovantian) gold *stater* of Andoco (PAS: BUC-FDAF75)

Date: Iron Age (c. 10 BC–c. AD 10).
Discovery: Found by Barrie Plasom while metal-detecting in August 2007, and recorded by Ros Tyrrell (Buckinghamshire FLO).
Description: Eastern (Trinovantian) gold *stater* of Andoco. Obv: wreath pattern. Rev: horse right, ANDO below and in front (VA 1860–1; BMC 2011). Diameter: 17.77mm. Weight: 5.46g.
Disposition: Returned to finder, and subsequently sold.

R TYRRELL & I LEINS

458. Isle of Wight: Southern (inscribed) silver unit (PAS: IOW-DA10F4)

Date: Iron Age (c. AD 30–c. 45).
Discovery: Found by Alan Rowe while metal-detecting in April 2007, and recorded by Frank Basford (Isle of Wight FLO).
Description: Southern silver unit. Obv: cross of pellets, C R A B in angles. Rev: eagle (VA 1285; BMC 2788). Diameter: 13mm. Weight 0.89g.
Disposition: Returned to finder.

F BASFORD & I LEINS

Section editor and further research: Sam Moorhead.
Editor: Michael Lewis.

ROMAN COINS

Listed below are 41 hoards, or other groups of coins, containing 6,417 coins. Seven are addenda to earlier finds, one is an earlier find from Sible Hedingham, Essex which has not been published (524), one, from Whittington, Northumberland (527) contains only eight base-metal coins so is not Treasure, and one from Hawkesbury, South Gloucestershire (520) is probably not a hoard. The groups of coins can be broken down as follows:

Century AD	No. of hoards /groups	Total number of coins
1st	3	49
2nd	11	254
3rd	9	c. 2,608
4th	10	3,313
5th	8	193
Totals	41	c. 6,417

In 2007, 20,675 Roman coins were recorded on the PAS database (including around 11,000 coins from Norfolk found in previous years), bringing the total to about 55,000 coins. This dataset is now by far the largest for coins found on rural sites in Britain and is the focus for a PhD thesis being written by Philippa Walton (University College London & Department of Portable Antiquities and Treasure, British Museum). A number of the coins listed below as single finds have been included in the 'Coin Register' in the British Numismatic Journal 78 (2008).

Republican and 1st century AD

Roman Republican coins continue to be found in considerable numbers with well over 400 recorded on the PAS database. Coins of Mark Antony, such as that from Lanivet, Cornwall (463), struck in 32–31 BC, are the most commonly recorded from this period; because they were struck in debased silver they continued to circulate until the 3rd century AD. However, the coin of the little-known *triumvir* (one of the three leaders of Rome) Lepidus (the other *triumvirs* were Octavian and Mark Antony) from Cotton, Suffolk (462) is much rarer. A hoard from the Mansfield Woodhouse area, Nottinghamshire (459) contains mainly Republican issues, but also has three pieces of Tiberius (r. AD 14–37). It is most likely that this hoard was buried after the Roman invasion of AD 43, *denarii* of Caligula and Claudius being incredibly rare in Britain. The Annesley Hoard, Nottinghamshire (460) shows how Republican coins were still in circulation in the Flavian period (AD 69–96). There is one notable coin of Augustus (r. 27 BC–AD 14), a silver *denarius* from near Calbourne, Isle of Wight (464) which was previously only known from one specimen in Paris and was found in a detectorist's collection of lesser-regarded finds. There is also an as of either Augustus or Tiberius from Niton and Whitwell,

Isle of Wight (465) which had been countermarked by the Roman army on the Rhine; such coins are unusual in Britain. Another very rare silver *denarius*, found at Great Hale, Lincolnshire (467) was minted for Galba during the Civil War of AD 69, which is struck from dies which are not recorded in the British Museum or Paris. The smallest denomination of the Augustan monetary system was the *quadrans*, 64 making up a *denarius*. These coins were mainly struck for use in Italy and are very rarely found in Britain. However, this report includes two such coins, one of Claudius from Dorchester, Oxfordshire (466) and the other from an anonymous issue found at Goosetry, Cheshire (468); there are five in total now recorded on the PAS database.

HOARDS

---

459. Mansfield Woodhouse area, Nottinghamshire: 22 silver *denarii* (PAS: DENO-73ECB4; Treasure: 2007 T260)

Date: Roman (deposited in c. AD 37).
Discovery: Found by Daniel and Stephen Pegg while metal-detecting in April 2007, and reported to Anja Rohde (Derbyshire & Nottinghamshire FLO).
Description: A small hoard of 19 Republican and three Imperial *denarii*. This hoard was originally reported as a hoard only of Republican *denarii* but the presence of three pieces of Tiberius means that the date of disposition now stands at around AD 37.
1–19. Republic (before 44 BC) 19
20–3. Tiberius (r. AD 14–37) 3
Disposition: Acquired by Mansfield Museum and Art Gallery.

R ABDY & N BAUER

---

460. Annesley, Nottinghamshire: four silver *denarii* (Treasure: 2005 T194)

Date: Roman (deposited in c. AD 75).
Discovery: Found by Mr R Scothern while metal-detecting in May 2003. This find was not included in the *TAR* 2003, and hence is published here.
Description: 4 silver *denarii*:
Republic:
1. L. RVTILI FLAC (77 BC) (RRC 387)
2. *L. PLAVTIVS PLANCVS (47 BC) (RRC 453)
Imperial:
3. Nero (r. AD 54–68)
4. Vespasian (r. AD 69–79)
Disposition: Disclaimed; returned to finder.

R ABDY

461. Shorwell, Isle of Wight (addenda): One copper-alloy sestertius and 22 silver *dupondii/asses* (PAS IOW-2CE096; Treasure: 2007 T197)

Date: Roman (deposited in c. AD 98).

Discovery: Found by Brian Hawkes and fifteen other members of the Isle of Wight Metal Detecting Club while metal-detecting in April 2007, and reported to Frank Basford (Isle of Wight FLO). The coins were found in a 20m radius in ploughsoil. The original hoard was found in 2006 (*TAR* 2005/6, no. 1065) in the same area.

Description: Summary of the entire hoard, addenda numbered and marked as †:

	Sest	Dup/As	Total
1. Caligula (r. AD 37–41)		1†	1
2. Claudian copies (c. AD 41–64)	1†	2	3
Nero (r. AD 54–68)	1	6	7
3–8. Vespasian (r. AD 69–79)		4, 6†	10
9. Domitian Caesar (r. AD 73–81)		1, 1†	1
10–16. Uncertain Flavian (AD 69–81)		15, 7†	22
17. Domitian (r. AD 81–96)		12, 1†	13
18. Nerva (r. AD 96–98)		1†	1
19–23. Uncertain emperor		10, 5†	15
Total	2	72	74
Non-hoard coins			7 (inc. 2†)

Discussion: The date the hoard was deposited can be moved to AD 98 by the presence of the coin of Nerva, and it is extended at the beginning by one of Caligula, a fairly rare coin for Britain.

Disposition: Disclaimed; returned to finders.

R ABDY

SINGLE FINDS

462. Cotton, Suffolk: Republican silver *denarius* of Lepidus (PAS: SF-7DD9F2)

Date: Roman (42 BC).

Discovery: Found by Chris J Bayliss while metal-detecting in May 2007, and recorded by Faye Minter (Suffolk FLO).

Description: This coin, which is struck in Italy, shows the heads of two *triumvirs*, Lepidus and Octavian (later Augustus) (r. 43–36 BC) (RRC 495/2d). Diameter: 17.28mm. Weight: 3.35g.

Discussion: This piece is from a small issue, there being only about 30 obverse and reverse dies issued.

Disposition: Returned to finder

F MINTER & S MOORHEAD

463. Lanivet, Cornwall: Republican silver *denarius* of Mark Antony (PAS: CORN-744206)

Date: Roman (c. 32–31 BC).

Discovery: Found by Philip Steele while metal-detecting in March 2007, and recorded by Anna Tyacke (Cornwall FLO).

Description: Silver Republican legionary *denarius* of Mark Antony, struck at a travelling mint, and honouring Legio XII. Stamped with an 'N' on the obverse which is a banker's, or private control, mark (RRC 544/26). Diameter: 18.4mm. Weight: 3.06 g.

Discussion: This coin is likely to have come to Britain with the Roman army during the 1st century AD, but Mark Antony *denarii* are known to have circulated until the 3rd century AD.

Disposition: Acquired by Royal Institution of Cornwall.

A TYACKE & S MOORHEAD

464. Calbourne, Isle of Wight: silver *denarius* of Augustus (PAS: IOW-0D5931)

Date: Roman (c. 27 BC–c. AD 14).

Discovery: Found by Rob Gates while metal-detecting in 2007, and recorded by Frank Basford (Isle of Wight FLO).

Description: An incomplete silver *denarius* of the emperor Augustus (r. 27 BC–AD 14). Obv: Laureate head of Augustus, right. Rev: Capricorn right; above, a star (RIC I: 542). Diameter: 17mm. Weight: 2.79g.

Discussion: This coin is very rare, the only other known example being in the Bibliotheque Nationale in Paris. Its mint is unknown, but it is probably from the western half of the Roman Empire. Given that the other example is in a French museum, the most likely mint might be Lyon (Lugdunum).

Disposition: Donated to the British Museum.

F BASFORD & S MOORHEAD

465. Niton and Whitwell, Isle of Wight: copper *as* of Augustus or Tiberius (PAS: IOW-F52A23)

Date: Roman (c. 15 BC–AD 15); countermarked either AD 41–54 or 79–81.

Discovery: Found by Keith Stuart while metal-detecting in November 2007, and recorded by Frank Basford (Isle of Wight FLO).

Description: A copper *as*; the bust and altar are just visible. The countermark TI.C.A probably stands for Tiberius Claudius Augustus (i.e. Claudius, r. AD 41–54) or Titus Caesar Augustus (r. AD 79–81) (RIC I: Augustus 230ff & Tiberius 95; BMC: Roman I, xxxv; *Pangerl*: 266–268, nos. 58a–f). Diameter: 22mm. Weight: 4.05 g.

Discussion: *Asses* were commonly countermarked by the Roman army on the Rhine frontier, in this case probably to signify that the coin was still good for circulation.

Disposition: Returned to finder.

F BASFORD & S MOORHEAD

466. Dorchester, Oxfordshire:
copper *quadrans* of Claudius (PAS: LON-EDEF06)

Date: Roman (AD 41–54).
Discovery: Found by Roger Smith and Sue Anderson while metal-detecting, and recorded by Kate Sumnall (London FLO).
Description: Copper *quandrans* of Claudius (r. AD 41–54). Obv: TI CLAVDIVS CAESAR AVG; three-legged *modius* (corn measure). Rev: PON M TR P IMP COS DES IT around S C (RIC I: 184). Diameter: 19.64mm. Weight: 2.88g.
Discussion: This is one of only five *quadrantes* recorded with the PAS. These small coins were most commonly used in Italy and are rarely found in Britain. There were four *quadrantes* to the *as*, and 64 to the *denarius*.
Disposition: Returned to finder.

K SUMNALL & S MOORHEAD

467. Great Hale, Lincolnshire:
silver *denarius* of Galba (AD 68) (PAS: LIN-898441)

Date: Roman (c. AD 68).
Discovery: Found by Dave Panton while metal-detecting in 2007, and recorded by Adam Daubney (Lincolnshire FLO).
Description: A silver *denarius* of Galba (r. AD 68). Obv: female bust of Bonus Eventus right, diademed and draped, with hair in plait above neck. Rev: a pair of clasped right hands holding a *caduceus* (RIC I: c.f. 6). Diameter: 18.53mm.
Discussion: This rare piece was struck between April and June AD 68 in the name of Galba in Spain. Galba had agreed to join the revolt against Nero so started to strike coins. Some of the early coins did bear his name and portrait, but others looked back to the past. This particular coin is copied from a Republican coin of L. Scribonius Libo (moneyer in 62 BC) which also depicts Bonus Eventus (RRC: 416/1). There is no coin in the British Museum or the Bibliotheque Nationale, Paris, that is struck from the same dies.
Disposition: Returned to finder.

A DAUBNEY & S MOORHEAD

468. Goostrey, Cheshire: copper-alloy *quadrans*
(LVPL-05B7D1)

Date: Roman (c. AD 81–161).
Discovery: Found by John Grassby while metal-detecting in 2007, and recorded by Frances McIntosh (Cheshire, Greater Manchester & Merseyside FLO).
Description: This anonymous coin shows the winged hat and *caduceus* of Mercury, but does not name an emperor, hence its general date as above (RIC II: 32). Diameter: 15mm. Weight: 2.3 g.
Discussion: See 466.
Disposition: Returned to finder.

F MCINTOSH & S MOORHEAD

469. Clipstone, Nottinghamshire: silver *drachm* of
King Nahapana (PAS: DENO-1080E2)

Date: c. AD 40–78.
Discovery: Found by Pete Reid while metal-detecting in 1998, and recorded by Anja Rohde (Derbyshire & Nottinghamshire FLO).
Description: A struck silver *drachm* of the Western Ksatraps of Gujurat in western India in the name of King Nahapana (r. c. AD 40–78). Obv: diademed bust facing right with a Greek inscription. Rev: arrow and a thunderbolt with inscriptions in Kharoshthi and Brahmi script. Diameter: 15.9mm. Weight: 2.3g.
Discussion: Many publications date this coin to the 2nd century AD. It is a very unusual coin to turn up as a British find. It seems unlikely that it came to Britain during the Roman period, although that idea cannot be entirely discounted. However, it is more likely that this represents a coin acquired at a later date, possibly as a souvenir or part of a collection, brought to England and subsequently lost.
Deposition: Returned to finder.

A ROHDE & S MOORHEAD

2nd century AD

As is normally the case, the majority of the 2nd-century AD hoards contain silver *denarii*, one from Westgate area, County Durham (474) having a new variety for Hadrian. However, two hoards terminating in the reign of Commodus (r. AD 180–192) do contain copper-alloy *sestertii*, one from Ellesmere, Shropshire (475) and the other from Kingskerswell, Devon (477). A third *sestertius* hoard from Newchurch, Isle of Wight (479) terminates in the early years of the reign of Septimius Severus (r. AD 193–211), a time when the supply of *sestertii* to Britain began to dry up. The single finds in this report have an eastern flavour, including a *dupondius* of Trajan, found in Wigginton, Hertfordshire (481), which has a countermark apparently applied at Antioch (south-eastern Turkey) in Hadrian's reign during the second Jewish Revolt (AD 132–135).

HOARDS

470. Whitchurch area, Cheshire: three silver *denarii*
(PAS: LVPL-B8BD62, 8B6538 & EB9A86;
Treasure: 2007 T315)

Date: Roman (deposited in c. AD 111).
Discovery: The coins were found at different times during a metal-detecting rally on 25 March 2007. Another four or five were briefly shown to Frances McIntosh (Cheshire, Greater Manchester & Merseyside FLO) at the end of the day; however, subsequent attempts to recover these coins have failed.

Description:
1. Galba (r. AD 68–69) (RIC I: 143)
2. Domitian (r. AD 81–96) (RIC II: 691)
3. Trajan (r. AD 103–111) (RIC II: 115var; RIC: 115 has a draped bust, this coin only has a draped left shoulder)
Disposition: Returned to finders.

F MCINTOSH, D SHOTTER & S MOORHEAD

---

471. Selsey area, West Sussex: three silver *denarii* (PAS: SUSS-B27B77; Treasure: 2007 T377)

Date: Roman (deposited in c. AD 117).
Discovery: Found by Martin Homer while metal-detecting in July 2007, and reported to Liz Andrews-Wilson (Sussex FLO).
Description: Trajan (RIC: 13, 118 & uncertain).
Disposition: Acquired by Chichester District Museum.

L ANDREWS-WILSON & I LEINS

---

472. Petworth area, West Sussex: 103 silver *denarii* and associated pottery (PAS: SUSS-C3BB17; Treasure: 2007 T106)

Date: Roman (deposited in c. AD 134).
Discovery: Found by Malcolm Douglas while metal-detecting in November 2006, and reported to Liz Andrews-Wilson (Sussex FLO).
Description: The coins range from the Roman Republic to the 2nd century AD. The latest coin is of Hadrian (r. AD 117–138), and is the sole example in the hoard of the late obverse group of AD 132/4–138 with a type of 'Fortune the homebringer' that was probably made before the emperor's final return to Italy. Seven very abraded pieces of coarseware pottery were found with the hoard. One piece is diagnostic, forming part of the base of a jar or bowl. It is not certain that the fragments come from the original hoard container, but this seems possible as the dating is consistent with the coins.

1–10. Republic	10
11–15. Mark Antony (minted 32–31 BC)	5
16–18. Augustus (r. 31 BC–AD 14)	3
19. Nero (r. AD 45–68)	1
20–46. Vespasian (r. AD 69–79)	27
47. Titus Caesar (r. AD 71–79)	1
48–51. Domitian Caesar (r. AD 73–79)	4
52–53. Titus (r. AD 79–81)	2
54–60. Domitian (r. AD 81–96)	7
61–63. Nerva (r. AD 96–98)	3
64–91. Trajan (r. AD 98–117)	28
92–103. Hadrian (r. AD 117–138)	12

Disposition: Chichester District Museum hopes to acquire.

R ABDY & R HOBBS

---

473. North Dalton area (1st addenda), East Yorkshire: three silver *denarii* (PAS: YORYM-109BE5; Treasure: 2007 T185)

Date: Roman (deposited in c. AD 161).
Discovery: Found by Daniel Crowe while metal-detecting in March 2007, and reported to Dave Evans (North & East Yorkshire FLO).
Description: The coins probably represent addenda to the Pocklington area Hoard (*TAR* 2005/6: no.1073), being Roman silver *denarii* of similar date to those in the earlier find, which comprised coins issued between the reigns of Galba (r. AD 68–69) and Marcus Aurelius (r. AD 161–180).
1. Vespasian (AD 74) (RIC 2.i: 702)
2. Vespasian (AD 75) (RIC 2.i: 777)
3. Hadrian (AD 119–122) (RIC 2: 98(b))
Discussion: A silver *siliqua* of the House of Constantine I, produced c. AD 340s/350s at Arles (mintmark: SAR[L]) was also found. Weight 0.17g. A coin of this type would not have circulated or been hoarded with earlier *denarii* (coins 1–3) and is a later casual loss rather than as part of the hoard. The site has also produced several further groups of Iron Age and Roman coins (see *TAR*: 2005/6, no. 1050).
Disposition: Acquired by East Riding Museum Service.

I LEINS

---

474. Westgate area, County Durham: eleven silver *denarii* (PAS: NCL-62EF85; Treasure: 2007 T198)

Date: Roman (deposited in c. AD 176).
Discovery: Found by Dave Scott while metal-detecting in March 2007, and reported to Rob Collins (North East FLO).
Description: All the coins are from the 2nd century AD; the latest an issue of Marcus Aurelius (r. AD 161–180) for his wife Faustina II, issued before her death in AD 176. In terms of composition this group of coins is consistent with other hoards of this period.

1–2. Trajan (r. AD 98–117)	2
3–5. Hadrian (r. AD 117–138)	3
6. Sabina	1
7–10. Antoninus Pius (r. AD 138–161)	4
– Marcus Aurelius (r. AD 161–180)	
11. Faustina II	1

Discussion: No. 5 – Hadrian, IVSTITIA AVG COS III P P (with COS III in the legend rather than the exergue) is a new variety (RIC: 214var).
Disposition: British Museum acquired no. 5.

R ABDY

475. Ellesmere, Shropshire: 13 copper-alloy *sestertii* (PAS: HESH-887B04; Treasure: 2007 T667)

Date: Roman (deposited in c. AD 180).

Discovery: Found by George Bennett, Gordon Griffiths, Roy Griffiths, Martin Punnett and Terry Ransome while metal-detecting in August 2007, and reported to Peter Reavill (Herefordshire & Shropshire FLO).

Description: This small group of 2nd-century AD brass *sestertii* spans the reigns of Hadrian, Antoninus Pius, Marcus Aurelius and Commodus, and includes coins of other members of their families. A high degree of corrosion prevents close catalogue identification in many cases. The latest identifiable coin is for the deified Marcus Aurelius, probably produced very soon after his death in AD 180.

1. Hadrian (r. AD 117–138)	1
2. Antoninus Pius (r. AD 138–161)	1
3. Faustina I	1
4. Marcus Aurelius (r. AD 161–180)	1
5. Faustina II	1
6. Lucilla	1
– Commodus (r. AD 180–192)	
7. Divus Marcus	1
8–13. Uncertain emperor	6

Disposition: Shropshire County Museums Service hopes to acquire.

R ABDY

476. Ugthorpe, North Yorkshire (addenda): 47 silver *denarii*, two silver fragments and a copper-alloy brooch fragment (PAS: YORYM-743FA7; Treasure: 2007 T416)

Date: Roman (deposited in c. AD 192).

Discovery: Found by Russell Willis and Trevor Pye while metal-detecting in July 2007, 30m from the original hoard findspot, and reported to Philippa Walton (Cambridgeshire FLO).

Description and discussion: The earliest coin is of the emperor Nero (r. AD 54–68), and the latest is a COS VII issue of Commodus (r. AD 180–192), dateable to AD 192. In terms of composition this group of coins is consistent with other hoards of this period and with the 1998 Ugthorpe hoard in which the last coin dated to AD 185 (Barclay: 121–124).

	1998	2007 addenda
1. Nero (r. AD 54–68)	-	1
2–3. Vespasian (r. AD 69–79)	2	2
4. Titus Caesar	-	1
- Domitian Caesar	3	-
5. Domitian (r. AD 81–96)	1	1
- Nerva (r. AD 96–98)	1	-
6–14. Trajan (r. AD 98–117)	3	9
15–16. Hadrian (r. AD 117–138)	3	2
17–23. Antoninus Pius (r. AD 138–161)	3	7
24–28. Diva Faustina I	-	5
29–31. Aurelius Caesar	-	3
32–34. Marcus Aurelius (r. AD 161–180)	1	3
35. Lucius Verus	-	1
36. Divus Pius	-	1
37–40. Faustina II	-	4
41–42. Lucilla	1	2
43–45. Commodus (r. AD 180–192)	2	3
46. Divus Aurelius	-	1
47. Uncertain emperor	1	1
- Imitation	1	-
48–49. Uncertain fragments	-	2

50. Fragment of a copper-alloy trumpet brooch, with only the head and part of the bow remaining; the head has traces of an iron spring attachment. Weight: 11.3g.

Discussion: The date the hoard was deposited now stands at AD 192, as opposed to AD 185 for the original hoard. Many of the coins are fairly corroded (as was the case with the original find).

Disposition: Whitby Museum hopes to acquire.

R ABDY & R HOBBS

477. Kingskerswell, Devon: one silver *denarius* and 12 bronze *sestertii*, and copper-alloy fragments (Treasure: 2007 T134)

Date: Roman (deposited in c. AD 192).

Discovery: Found with a metal-detector in about 1988, and reported to the Royal Albert Memorial Museum in March 2007.

Description:

1. Antoninus Pius (r. AD 138–161)	1 *sest*
2. Commodus (r. AD 180–192)	1 *sest*
3. Crispina (c. AD 180–183)	1 *sest*
4–5. Uncertain Antonine	1 *den*, 2 *sest*
6–12. Uncertain emperor	7 *sest*

Discussion: A copper-alloy brooch and loop declared with the hoard are probably random losses not associated with the find. The hoard was found prior to the Treasure Act of 1996 (therefore Treasure under Treasure Trove), and was conserved by Pippa Pearce (British Museum).

Disposition: Not Treasure Trove; returned to finder.

R ABDY & R HOBBS

478. Postwick, Norfolk (addenda): four silver *denarii* (PAS NMS-D537C1; Treasure: 2007 T220)

Date: Roman (the latest coin in the addenda is AD 156/7; the latest coin in the original hoard is AD 192).

Discovery: Found by Roy Crawford while metal-detecting on the site of an earlier hoard discovered in 1986 (Burnett and Gregory 1988: 33–36), and reported to Erica Darch (Norfolk FLO). Subsequent groups from the hoard have been found (*TAR* 2005/6, no. 1079; 2004, no. 436), but none of them affect a date of disposition of AD 192.

Description:
4 silver *denarii* of:
1. Mark Antony (31 BC) (RRC 544/22)
2. Vespasian (AD 75) (RIC: 161)
3. Diva Faustina (c. AD 141–150) (RIC: 362)
4. Antoninus Pius (AD 156/7) (RIC: 261)
Disposition: Disclaimed; returned to finder.

A MARSDEN & R ABDY

---

479. Newchurch, Isle of Wight: 57 copper-alloy *sestertii* and *sestertius* fractions (PAS: IOW-841278; Treasure: 2006 T29 & 2007 T289)

Date: Roman (deposited in c. AD 197).
Discovery: Found by Terry Barrett, Harry Bragg, Derek Johnson, Tony Perez and David Walker while metal-detecting on 13 December 2005 (38 coins) and 26 April 2007 (19 coins), and reported to Frank Basford (Isle of Wight FLO).
Description: The coins cover the period from Trajan (r. AD 98–117) to Septimius Severus (r. AD 193–211), the latest coin dating to AD 197.

	Sest	Dup/As	Uncertain
1. Trajan (r. AD 98–117)	1	-	-
2–7. Hadrian (r. AD 117–138)	3	2	1
8–12. Antoninus Pius (r. AD 138–161)	4	1	
13. Faustina I	1	-	-
14. Marcus Caesar	-	1	-
15–9. Marcus Aurelius (r. AD 161–180)	4	1	-
20–1. Commodus Caesar	2	-	-
22–3. Faustina II	1	1	-
24–5. Lucilla	2	-	-
-. Commodus (r. AD 180–192)	-	-	-
26. Divus Marcus	1	-	-
27–9. Uncertain Antonine	3	-	-
30. ?Clodius Albinus (r. AD 195–197)	1	-	-
31. Septimius Severus (r. AD 193–211)	1	-	-
32–57. Uncertain emperor	15	10	1
Total	39	16	2

Disposition: Disclaimed; returned to finders.

M LYNE & R ABDY

---

480. Seaton with Slingley, County Durham: a silver *denarius* and silver trumpet brooch (PAS: NCL-D488D8; Treasure: 2007 T391)

Date: Roman (AD 80 (coin) and AD 100–200 (brooch)).
Discovery: Found by Dave Scott while metal-detecting in October 2000, and reported to Rob Collins (North East FLO) in 2007.
Description: A silver *denarius* of Titus (minted AD 80).
Discussion: Found with 108.
Disposition: British Museum hopes to acquire.

R ABDY

SINGLE FINDS

---

481. Wiggington, Hertfordshire: copper-alloy *dupondius* of Trajan (PAS CORN-5E39D1)

Date: Roman (AD 98–117); countermarked AD 117–138.
Discovery: Found by Steve Collins while metal-detecting in November 2007, and recorded by Anna Tyacke (Cornwall FLO).
Description: Copper-alloy *dupondius* of Trajan (r. AD 98–117). Obv: either side of Trajan's worn head are two countermarks, one a laurel branch, the other possibly similar or even a small head. Rev: worn out. Diameter: 25mm. Weight: 10.2g.
Discussion: The laureate countermark is associated with Antioch and was apparently applied in Hadrian's reign prior to the Jewish Revolt of AD 132–135 (Howgego 1985: no. 378). This coin obviously travelled a long way after being countermarked.
Disposition: Returned to finder.

A TYACKE & S MOORHEAD

3rd century AD

The largest hoards from this period comprise 3rd-century radiate coins from Bath, Bath and North East Somerset (483). Cotswold Archaeology Ltd have excavated around 30,000 coins in a block of soil which awaits conservation and analysis at the British Museum. A further 1,030 coins were found in East Sussex (485) giving the entire hoard 2,893 pieces, and thus making it the largest base-silver radiate hoard of its kind since the famous Dorchester Hoard found in 1936. One of the most exciting hoards includes two gold *aurei* of Carausius (r. AD 286–93) from Ashbourne area, Derbyshire (490), bringing the total known gold pieces of Carausius to 25. One coin is from the mint of Rouen, struck from dies already recorded; the other is a new type from the mint of London. There are also five *radiates* of Carausius, from Chichester area, West Sussex (494), Shalfleet, Isle of Wight (495), Chedzoy, Somerset (496), Greywell, Hampshire (497) and Hinton on the Green, Worcestershire (498) which are new varieties, highlighting how detector finds are increasing the knowledge of his coinage. There is another gold *aureus* for Gordian III (r. AD 238–244) from Lutterworth, Leicestershire (491) and a new type for an as of Philip I (r. AD 244–249) from Pavenham, Bedfordshire (492). Possibly the most interesting contemporary copy found in 2007 is a 'Limesfalschungen' copper-alloy cast as found at Crondall, Hampshire (493) which was probably made on the Rhine or Danube frontier. Bizarrely, it shows the bust of Nero (r. AD 54–68) on one side and the bust of Otacilia Severa (r. AD 244–249) on the other. It might be the latest example of these casts to be found in Britain.

HOARDS

---

482. Twycross, Leicestershire: 29 base-silver *denarii* and *radiates* (PAS: NMGW-29BDC6; LEIC-215B27, 206F66, 213D57, 21A411 & 2228A4; WMID-909D93, D22C67 & D212F4; Treasure: 2007 T312)

Date: Roman (deposited in c. AD 253).

Discovery: Found by Fred Cooper, Chris Hemus, Enid Homer, Darren Hoyle, David Onens, Gary Thompson, Hugh Vincent, and others while metal-detecting at a rally in June 2007, and reported to multiple FLOs, local to each finder.

Description: This hoard contains 23 *denarii* from the period between Hadrian (r. AD 117–138) and Gordian III (r. AD 238–244) and 6 *radiates* from the period between Gordian III and Trebonianus Gallus (r. AD 251–253).

Denarii:

1. Hadrian (r. AD 117–138)	1
2. Sabina	1
- Commodus (r. AD 180–192)	
3. Divus Marcus Aurelius	1
4–8. Septimius Severus (r. AD 193–211)	5
9–10. Julia Domna	2
11. Caracalla (r. AD 195–217)	1
12–13. Elagabalus (r. AD 218–222)	2
14. Julia Maesa	1
15. Julia Soemias	1
16–17. Severus Alexander (r. AD 222–235)	2
18–19. Julia Mamaea	2
20. Maximinus I (r. AD 235–238)	1
21. Gordian III (r. AD 238–244)	1
22–23. Uncertain	2

Radiates:

24–25. Gordian III (r. AD 238–244)	2
-. Philip I (r. AD 244–249)	
26. Otacilla Severa	1
27. Philip II Caesar	1
28. Decius (r. AD 249–251)	1
29. Trebonianus Gallus (r. AD 251–253)	1

Disposition: Leicestershire County Council Heritage Services hopes to acquire.

J LEWIS

---

483. Bath, Bath and North East Somerset: about 30,000 base-silver coins (PAS: GLO-40A9B6; Treasure: 2007 T677)

Date: Roman (deposited in c. AD 260s).

Discovery: Found by Cotswold Archaeology Ltd during excavations in advance of building work for the new Bath Spa in November 2007, and reported to Kurt Adams (Gloucestershire & Avon FLO).

Description: The find consists of a block of perhaps 130,000 base-silver coins from which 304 coins had become detached. The block remains intact for the present, and the detached coins listed here. The coins date from the early 3rd century to the AD 260s, the majority being base-silver *radiates*.

Central Empire:

1. ?Septimius Severus (r. AD 193–211)	1 *den*
2. Elagabalus (r. AD 218–222)	1 *den*
3–61. Gordian III (r. AD 238–244)	59 (including 3 *den*)
62–106. Philip I (r. AD 244–249)	45
107–109. Philip II	3
110–114. Otacilia Severa 5	
115–131. Decius (r. AD 249–251)	17
132–137. Herennia Etruscilla	6
138–142. Herennius Etruscus	5
143. Hostilian	1
144–160. Trebonianus Gallus (r. AD 251–253)	17
161–166. Volusian (r. AD 251–253)	6
167–169. Aemilian (r. AD 253)	3
170–190. Valerian I (r. AD 253–260)	21
191–193. Valerian II	3
194. Mariniana	1
195–197. Saloninus	3
198–216. Gallienus (r. AD 253–268)	19
217–224. Salonina (r. AD 253–268)	8

Gallic Empire:

225–226. Postumus (AD 260–268)	2
228–304. Uncertain	78

Disposition: The block of coins is currently at the British Museum, awaiting a final decision about conservation and publication. Roman Baths Museum, Bath hopes to acquire.

R REECE

---

484. Doncaster area, South Yorkshire: 15 base-silver *radiates* and a silver-gilt brooch (PAS: SWYOR-0AEF716; Treasure: 2007 T66)

Date: Roman (AD 265 (coin) and c. AD 1–50 (brooch)).

Discovery: Found while metal-detecting in January 2007, and reported to Peter Robinson (Doncaster Museum).

Description:

1. Gordian III (r. AD 238–244)	1
2. Philip I (r. AD 244–249)	1
-. Decius (r AD 249–251)	
3. Herennius Etruscus	1
4–5. Valerian (r. AD 253–260)	2
6–9. Gallienus (r. AD 253–260)	4
10–15. Postumus (r. AD 260–269)	6

(up to 3rd series; c. AD 263–265)

Brooch: A silver-gilt brooch of 'Birdlip' type. The flat narrow bow has a high single moulded rib; below the trumpet head are two moulded knops, and between these and the raised rib are a small horizontal projection and the broken remains of the projecting wing which characterises the type. There is a fracture in the centre of the bow. The triangular catch-plate has twelve perforations. There are traces of gilding in a number of places; the gilding survives particularly well on the bow. The pin and spring mechanism are missing. Length: 41.5mm. Width: 10.2mm.

Discussion: given the date of the coins, the brooch appears to have been kept for some years prior to burial, presumably because of its precious metal content. The Birdlip Type is not particularly common (Hattatt 1987: 38; Bayley and Butcher 2004: 149). **Disposition:** The brooch has been acquired by Doncaster Museum; the landowner donated their share. The coins have been returned to the finders.

R ABDY & R HOBBS

---

485. East Sussex (addenda): 1,030+ base-silver *radiates* (and fragments) (PAS: SUSS-6F6003; Treasure: 2006 T4)

Date: Roman (deposited in c. AD 268).
Discovery: Found during controlled excavation in March 2007 on the site of the original hoard, and reported to Liz Andrews-Wilson (Sussex FLO).
Description:

Central Empire

1–5. Caracalla (r. AD 211–217)	5
6–8. Julia Domna	3
9–16. Elagabalus (r. AD 218–222)	8
17. Julia Maesa	1
18. Balbinus (r. AD 238)	1
19. Pupienus (r. AD 238)	1
20–447. Gordian III (r. AD 238–244)	428
448–626. Philip I (r. AD 244–249)	179
627–650. Philip II Caesar	24
651–664. Philip II Augustus	14
665–701. Otacilia Severa	37
702–749. Decius (r. AD 249–251)	48
750–754. Herennius Caesar	5
755–757. Hostilian Caesar	3
758–774. Herennia Etruscilla	17
775. Divus Marcus Aurelius	1
776. Divus Severus Alexander	1
777–801. Trebonianus Gallus (r. AD 251–253)	25
802–822. Volusian	21
823–824. Aemilian (r. AD 253)	2
825. Cornelia Supera	1
826–846. Valerian I (r. AD 253–260)	21
847–875. Gallienus (r. AD 253–260)	29
876–891. Salonina	16
892–896. Valerian (r. AD 253–258) II	5
897. Saloninus (Caesar)	1
898. Irregular (Gordian III)	1

Gallic Empire

899–1025. Postumus (AD 260–269)	120 (+7*)
1026–1030+. Uncertain fragments	5+*

Discussion: The original find covered the same span of radiate-issuing emperors (Caracalla to Postumus, excluding the latter's debased issues of AD 268–269) and the total now stands at 2,893 coins (+ fragments). Also found with the addendum were some small pottery fragments, a copper-alloy tack and a heavily corroded iron fragment (for original find see *TAR* 2005/6, no. 1096). The coins were conserved by Pippa Pearce (British Museum).
Disposition: Bexhill Museum hopes to acquire at least a sample of the hoard.

R ABDY

---

486. Harrogate area, North Yorkshire: nine copper-alloy *radiates* (PAS YORYM-697A25; Treasure: 2007 T424)

Date: Roman (deposited in c. AD 274).
Discovery: Found sometime in 2004, allegedly at Plompton, near Harrogate, and reported to the Yorkshire Museum.
Description:

1. Gallienus (r. AD 260–268), m. Siscia (RIC: 575)	1
2. Postumus (r. AD 260–269), m. Principal (Cunetio: 2387/2391)	1
3. ?Victorinus (r. AD 269–271), m. I (Cunetio: 2534)	1
4–5. ?Tetricus I (r. AD 271–274), m. I (Normanby: 1473 & 1489)	2
6. ?Tetricus II (r. AD 271–274), m. I (Normanby: 1526 & 1533)	1
7. ?Tetricus I or II	1
8–9. Uncertain emperor	2

Discussion: The coins were deposited anonymously at the front desk of the Yorkshire Museum. The person depositing them said that they were addenda to the 'Plompton' Hoard. No such hoard is known and because the finder gave no contact details further research has not been possible. Sam Moorhead (National Finds Adviser) has catalogued the coins from descriptions provided.
Disposition: Yorkshire Museums Trust; not Treasure Trove.

L ANDREWS-WILSON & S MOORHEAD

---

487. Yarmouth, Isle of Wight (addenda): seven base-silver *radiates* (PAS IOW-936B93; Treasure: 2007 T152

Date: Roman (deposited in c. AD 274).
Discovery: Found by Alan Richardson on 28 February 2007, and reported to Frank Basford (Isle of Wight FLO). They are addenda to an earlier hoard that was declared Treasure in 2003 (2003 T57).
Description:
The entire hoard now probably comprises the following:

	Original hoard	Addenda
-. Gordian III (r. AD 238–244)	2	-
1. Valerian I (r. AD 253–260)	3	1
-. Mariniana	1	-
2. Gallienus (r. AD 260–268)	4	1
3–6. Postumus (r. AD 260–268)	19	4
-. Postumus or Victorinus	5	-
-. Victorinus (r. AD 269–271)	4	-
-. Claudius II (r. AD 268–270)	7	-
7. Tetricus I (r. AD 271–274)	2	1
	47	7

Total: 54

Discussion: Malcolm Lyne (numismatist) suggests that the baser coins of Gallienus and Tetricus I might be from the hoard, therefore giving a disposition date of AD 274 for the coins. One earlier Severan *denarius* and four later Constantinian/Valentinianic pieces were also found, but are almost certainly not from the hoard.

Disposition: Disclaimed; returned to finder.

F BASFORD, M LYNE & S MOORHEAD

---

488. Baschurch, Shropshire: 36 base-metal radiates (PAS: HESH-884BE4; Treasure: 2007 T665)

Date: Roman (deposited in c. AD 274).

Discovery: Found by Ian Collins and Paul Oakley while metal-detecting in September 2007, and reported to Peter Reavill (Herefordshire & Shropshire FLO).

Description and discussion: The identifiable coins are all of the Gallic Empire, ranging from AD 269 to 274.

1–2. Victorinus (r. AD 269–271), m. II	2
3–6. Tetricus I & II (r. AD 271–4), m. I	4
7–8. Tetricus I & II, m. II	2
9. Tetricus I & II, m. uncertain	1
10. Uncertain Gallic emperor	1
11–36. Uncertain emperor	24

Disposition: Disclaimed; returned to finder.

R ABDY

---

489. Storrington, West Sussex: 16 copper-alloy *radiates* (PAS: SUSS-BC6150; Treasure: 2007 T344)

Date: Roman (deposited in c. AD 275/285).

Discovery: Found by Anthony Gill while metal-detecting in June 2007, and reported to Liz Andrews-Wilson (Sussex FLO).

Description:

1. Gallienus (r. AD 260–268)	1
2. Claudius II (r. AD 268–270)	1
3–4. Victorinus (r. AD 269–271)	2
5–11. Tetricus I (r. AD 271–274)	6 + ?1
12–14. Tetricus II (r. AD 271–274)	2 + ?1
15. Gallic Empire uncertain	1
16. Barbarous Claudius II	1

Discussion: The latest official coin can be no later than AD 274. However, barbarous *radiates* were struck over a period of time from c. AD 275 to 285. Given the presence of only one barbarous coin, it might be plausible to suggest that the hoard was secluded closer to 275 than 285.

Disposition: Acquired by Storrington Museum; finder donated his share.

L ANDREWS-WILSON & S MOORHEAD

---

490. Ashbourne area, Derbyshire: two gold aurei (PAS: DENO-64DAE1 & 651C91; Treasure: 2007 T709)

Date: Roman (deposited in c. AD 293).

Discovery: Found by Derrick Fretwell during construction work in July 2007, and reported to Anja Rohde (Derbyshire & Nottinghamshire FLO).

Description: Two gold *aurei* of Carausius (r. AD 286–293).

1. Obv: VIRTVS CAR – AVSI. Ornately, cuirassed and helmeted bust, left; the helmet with an animal running left, possibly a 'big' cat. Rev: PAX – AVG. Pax standing left, holding branch in right hand and vertical sceptre in left. m. London, mm. -//-. Diameter: 20mm. Die axis: 12. Weight 4.65g.

2. Obv: IMP CARAVSIVS AVG. Laureate, draped and cuirassed, right. Rev: CONCORDIA – MILIT – VM (in exergue). Emperor standing right, clasping the hand of Concordia (*RIC*: 624; Huvelin 3–5), m. Rouen. Diameter: 19/21mm. Die axis: 6. Weight: 4.70g.

Discussion: Coin 1 is unpublished; it is the third London *aureus* of Carausius to bear a helmeted bust. The Ashbourne coins increase the corpus of known Carausian gold coins in the world from 23 to 25. A Roman soldier from this time might have expected an annual salary of 12 gold coins.

Disposition: Acquired by the British Museum (London coin) and Derby Museum and Art Gallery (Rouen coin) (Moorhead 2008, 397-9).

S MOORHEAD

SINGLE FINDS

---

491. Lutterworth, Leicestershire: gold *aureus* of Gordian III (PAS: LEIC-196037)

Date: Roman (AD 238).

Discovery: Found by Warren Gemmell while metal-detecting in May 2007, and recorded by Wendy Scott (Leicestershire & Rutland FLO).

Description: Gold *aureus* of Gordian III (r. AD 238–244). Obv: IOVI CONSERVATORI (AD 238), m. Rome, 1st Issue (Sear 8570; *RIC* IV: pt. 3, no. 8). Diameter: 19mm. Weight: 4.95 g.

Discussion: This is the first gold Roman coin recorded by the PAS in Leicestershire.

Disposition: Returned to finder.

W SCOTT

492. Pavenham, Bedfordshire: copper as of Philip I (PAS: BH-70C7D7)

Date: Roman (AD 244–249).

Discovery: Found by Mick Swannell while metal-detecting in October 2007, and recorded by Julian Watters (Bedfordshire & Hertfordshire FLO).

Description: Copper *as* of Philip I (r. AD 244–249). Obv: IMP M IVL PHILIPPVS AVG. Laureate and draped bust right. Rev: AEQVITAS AVGG, S C. Aequitas standing left holding scales and *cornucopiae*. m. Rome (*RIC* IV: pt 3, 166var). Diameter: 25mm. Weight: 8.49g.

Discussion: This reverse type is only recorded for *sestertii* in *RIC*, but the size, weight and obverse type suggest that it is an *as*.

Disposition: Returned to finder.

J WATTERS & S MOORHEAD

---

493. Crondall, Hampshire: copper-alloy 'Limesfalschung' as (PAS: SUR-EC7923)

Date: Roman (AD 244–249, or slightly later).

Discovery: Found by Mark Stonard while metal-detecting in around 1992, and recorded by David Williams (Surrey FLO) in 2007.

Description: Cast coin showing Otacilia Severa (wife of Philip I, r. AD 244–249) on the obverse, and Nero (r. AD 54–68) on the reverse. Diameter: 22.29mm. Weight: 4.89g.

Discussion: 'Limesfalschungen' are cast coins, found in the greatest numbers on the Rhine frontier. They were mostly made in the first half of the 3rd century. This is possibly the latest example found in Britain, the latest piece in a large group found at Caerleon (Wales) being for Gordian III (r. AD 238–244) (Boon 1965: 161–174).

Disposition: Returned to finder.

D WILLIAMS & S MOORHEAD

COINS OF CARAUSIUS (r. AD 286–293)

The following five coins were all struck by the emperor Carausius who ruled a breakaway empire in Britain and northern Gaul. Most of his coins were struck at London and an unknown British mint denoted by a 'C'. A few coins were issued at Rouen in Gaul. Carausius struck a large coinage in gold, silver and bronze, and there is an enormous number of varieties. The following coins underline how important it is to record detector finds; so far, there are around 1,100 coins of Carausius on the PAS database (see also 490).

---

494. Chichester area, West Sussex: copper-alloy *radiate* of Carausius (PAS: SUSS-39F9F8)

Date: Roman (c. AD 286–293).

Discovery: Found by Peter Sheffield while metal-detecting, and recorded by Laura Burnett (Sussex FLO); part of a large collection found between 1975 and 2007.

Description: Copper-alloy, possibly irregular (barbarous), *radiate* of Carausius (r. AD 286–293). Rev: Sol. m. RSR (London) (*RIC* V: pt. 2, 515 cf. no. 611). Diameter: 21.4mm. Weight: 2.7 g.

Discussion: The reverse legend on this example is more complete than that given in RIC and reads: ORIES [...] (P) NVSTAS +. The reporting of this coin has added to our knowledge of this coin type and demonstrates how even seemingly 'grotty' coins can be important.

Disposition: Returned to finder.

L BURNETT & S MOORHEAD

---

495. Shalfleet, Isle of Wight: copper-alloy *radiate* of Carausius (PAS: IOW-171BB7)

Date: Roman (c. AD 286–293).

Discovery: Found by Peter Peach while metal-detecting in 2007, and recorded by Frank Basford (Isle of Wight FLO).

Description: An incomplete copper-alloy *radiate* of Carausius. Obv: [I]MP CARAVSIVS A[VG]. Radiate bust, right. Rev: CO[NSERVAT?] AV. Sol standing left holding whip, in exergue: C (for m.'C'). Diameter: 22mm. Weight: 2.11g.

Discussion: This is apparently an unpublished coin. The two recorded CONSERVAT types of C Mint in RIC depict Hercules and Neptune (*RIC* V: pt 2, 482, nos. 212–214). There is, however, a Sol type on the ORIENS AVG issue which is similar (*RIC* V: 489, 293f). At the London mint there was a CONSERVAT AVG type with Sol (*RIC* V: 466, no. 29).

Disposition: Returned to finder.

F BASFORD & S MOORHEAD

---

496. Chedzoy, Somerset: copper-alloy *radiate* of Carausius (PAS: SOM-DF0782)

Date: Roman (c. AD 286–293).

Discovery: Discovered by Roy Beal while metal-detecting in 2007, and recorded by Naomi Payne (Somerset FLO).

Description: A copper-alloy *radiate* of Carausius (r. AD 286–293). Obv: IMP CARAVSIVS P F AVG. Radiate, draped and cuirassed, right. Reverse: P(A?) [X AVG?].
Pax standing left, holding transverse sceptre and branch. mm.F O//RSR, m. London. It is possibly an overstrike or is double-struck. Diameter: 22.8mm. Weight: 4.1g.

Discussion: This coin is apparently unpublished. The F O field letters confirm that the RSR coins were minted at London.

Disposition: Acquired by the British Museum.

N PAYNE & S MOORHEAD

497. Greywell, Hampshire: copper-alloy *radiate* of Carausius (PAS SUR-372B61)

Date: Roman (c. AD 286–293).
Discovery: Found by Chris Lacey before 2006, and recorded by David Williams (Surrey FLO) in 2007.
Description: Copper-alloy *radiate* of Carausius (r. AD 286–293). Obv: IMP CARAVSIVS AVG. Radiate bust right. Rev: blundered letters I I, reversed C, reversed F. Salus or Tutela standing left, holding *cornucopiae* and *patera* over altar (*RIC* V: pt 2, c.f. 666 & 684). mm. -//?R, m. Rouen. Diameter: 22.24mm. Weight: 3.54g.
Discussion: The mint at Rouen only operated for Carausius and these coins are rare.
Disposition: Returned to finder.

D WILLIAMS & S MOORHEAD

498. Hinton on the Green, Worcestershire: copper-alloy *radiate* of Carausius in the name of Diocletian (PAS WAW-747B03)

Date: Roman (c. AD 286–293).
Discovery: Found by Mr Hussey in February or March 2007 while metal-detecting, and recorded by Angie Bolton (Warwickshire & Worcestershire FLO).
Description: Copper-alloy *radiate* of Carausius (r. AD 286–293) struck in the name of Diocletian (r. AD 284–305). Obv: IMP C DIOCLETIANVS P F AVG, radiate, draped and cuirassed bust, right. Rev: PA AVGGG. Pax standing left, holding olive branch and transverse sceptre. mm. S P//MLXXI, m. London (RIC V: pt 2, no. 9var). Diameter: 24.55mm. Weight: 4.1g.
Discussion: Although this is a variant of *RIC* 9, there are three examples of this coin in the North West Suffolk Hoard (*TAR* 2005/6: no. 1112).
Disposition: Returned to finder.

A BOLTON & S MOORHEAD

4th century AD

There are four 4th-century hoards which comprise early *nummi* struck between c. AD 295 and 330, from Stanton area, Derbyshire (499), Barking, Suffolk (500), Flaxton, North Yorkshire (501) and St Paul with Malmesbury, Wiltshire (502). Many of these coins are scarce as single finds, but a rare London mint coin of Constantine I from Thoresby, Lincolnshire (511) and a new variety of a *nummus* of Crispus from Wood Enderby, Lincolnshire (512) have been found by chance and recorded as single finds, and are now in the British Museum. Another coin is a new variety that appears to conflate two types of Constantine I at the Arles mint, from Chipping Norton, Oxfordshire (513). Gold coins of this period are very rare as finds in Britain, but a *aureus* of Licinius I has been found near Salisbury, Wiltshire (510).

From the middle of the century comes a very large hoard of over 2,800 *nummi* of Magnentius and Decentius found in the Bridgnorth area, Shropshire (507), one of a class of hoards which were probably buried after the death of Magnentius in AD 353 and the outlawing of his coins by Constantius II in 354. A second example of a very rare silver *siliqua* of Jovian (r. AD 363–364) from Lyon has been found in the Chichester area, West Sussex (514), the other piece being found in the early 1990s.

There is one hoard of *nummi* of the House of Valentinian from the Newton Abbott area, Devon (508) which is the first hoard of its kind to be found west of Somerset. From this period there is also a gold *solidus* of Gratian found at Silverstone, Northamptonshire (518) and a rare *nummus* from the Trier mint, found at Bermondsey, Rotherhithe and Southwark, London (515). It is possible that a copper-alloy *nummus* of Procopius (r. AD 365–366) from West Wight, Isle of Wight (517) is the first coin of this emperor ever to be recorded in Britain. It came from the same site as a number of other 'eastern' mint coins, including the first British record for a VIRTVS AVGVSTI coin of Arcadius (519) - struck c. AD 395–401.

Two non-coin objects from Fulstow, Lincolnshire (516) are also recorded here, lead tablets with impressions from the obverses of coins of Valens (r. AD 364–378). It was initially thought that these might have been curse tablets, as the lead pieces are similar to curse tablets. However, it seems more likely that these were used to make cliché forgeries of silver *siliquae*, and they are the first objects of their type to be acquired by the British Museum.

HOARDS

499. Stanton area, Derbyshire: 62 copper-alloy *nummi* (PAS: DENO-4D6A35; Treasure: 2007 T570)

Date: Roman (deposited c. AD 305).
Discovery: Found by Adam Staples and Lisa Grace while metal-detecting in September and November 2007, and reported to Anja Rohde (Derbyshire & Nottinghamshire FLO).
Description: A small early *nummus* hoard containing coins dating from the introduction of the *nummus* (c. AD 294) to the end of the first Tetrarchy (c. AD 305).

1–9. m. London	9
10–47. m. Trier	38
48–53. m. Lyon	6
54–55. m. Ticinum	2
56–57. m. Aquileia	2
58. m. Cyzicus	1
59–62. m. Uncertain	4

Discussion: These large early *nummi* are more commonly found in hoards than as site-finds. The predominance of coins from Trier is to be expected.
Disposition: Derby Museum and Art Gallery hoped to acquire, but withdrew. The British Museum hopes to acquire coins 1 and 32.

R ABDY

---

500. Barking, Suffolk: 56 base-silver *nummi* (PAS: SF-2278D4; Treasure: 2007 T142)

Date: Roman (deposited in c. AD 313).
Discovery: Found by Suffolk County Council Archaeology Service during excavation in advance of quarry work in March 2007, and reported to Faye Minter (Suffolk FLO). The coins were located in a ditch beside a Roman road, in a tight group, possibly suggesting containment in a purse or bag.
Discussion: This small, early *nummus* hoard runs from the introduction of this coin type in the AD 290s up to AD 310–313 and displays the usual characteristics for a British find. The majority are from the local mints (London and Trier) with a decreasing presence from those further east. One (RIC Trier: 232b var) represents a minor type variant with Fortuna holding a *patera* and *cornucopia* rather than rudder and *cornucopia*. Another is a bust variety.
Disposition: To remain with the site archive, the Suffolk County Council Archaeological Store, Bury St Edmunds; the landowner donated his share.

R ABDY

---

501. Flaxton, North Yorkshire: 16 copper-alloy *nummi* (PAS YORYM-842863; Treasure: 2007 T176)

Date: Roman (deposited c. AD 324).
Discovery: Found while metal-detecting in March and April 2007, and reported to Beth Echtenacher (North & East Yorkshire FLO).
Description:

| | Early *nummi* | | Constantinian *nummi* | |
	309–13	313–7	318–24	Total
1–9. m. London	5	2	2	9
10. m. Trier	1	-	-	1
11–13. m. Lyon	1	1	1	3
14. m. Arles	-	1	-	1
15. m. Ostia	1	-	-	1
16. Irregular	-	-	1	1
Total	8	4	4	16

Discussion: This small, early *nummus* hoard has a small tail beyond the main run of pre-318 coins that is sometimes seen in such hoards that do not otherwise terminate c. AD 318. The condition of all the coins is similar so this hoard appears to have been a selective assemblage of older, larger *nummi*, alongside the odd contemporary piece from the AD 320s.
Disposition: Disclaimed; returned to finder.

R ABDY

---

502. St Paul with Malmesbury, Wiltshire (original and addenda): 37 (24 & 13) copper-alloy *nummi* and one copper-alloy *as* (PAS WILT-104653 & 284FB5; Treasure: 2007 T90 & T617)

Date: Roman (deposited in c. AD 325).
Description:

Date	Original	Addenda	Total
as			
1. (c. AD 228–231)	-	1	1
nummi			
2–4. (c. AD 302–305)	2	1	3
5–12. (c. AD 307–310)	8	-	8
13–23. (c. AD 310–313)	5	6	11
24–35. (c. AD 320–324)	7	5	12
36–37. Uncertain	2	-	2
Total	24	13	37

Discussion: The *as*, probably of Severus Alexander (r. AD 228–231), might not have been part of the hoard. However, its similar size to the early *nummi* might explain its presence.
Disposition: Acquired by Athelstan Museum; the finder and landowner donated their share.

D ALGAR

---

503. Catcote, County Durham (addenda): 11 copper-alloy *nummi* (PAS: NCL-637911; 2007 T314)

Date: Roman (deposited in c. AD 348).
Discovery: Found by Tees Archaeology during archaeological excavation in 2003, and reported to Rob Collins (North East FLO). The coins were excavated from a block of soil by conservators.
Description: All of the coins are *nummi* ranging from c. AD 321–c. 335.
1. Constantine II (AD 321), Rev: BEATA TRANQVILLITAS, m. Trier (*RIC* VII: 334).
2. Constantine II (AD 321–324), Rev: CAESARVM NOSTRORVM, m. Siscia (*RIC* VII: 182).
3. Constantine I (AD 323–324), Rev: SARMATIA DEVICTA, m. Lyon (*RIC* VII: 209).
4–5. Constantine II (AD 326), Rev: PROVIDENTIAE CAESS, m. Trier & Ticinum (*RIC* VII: 478 & 200).
6–7. Constantius II (AD 327–328 & 325–326), Rev: PROVIDENTIAE CAESS, m. Trier & Antioch (*RIC* VII: 506 & 66).
8. Constantine I (AD 332), Rev: GLORIA EXERCITVS (2 standards), m. Arles (*RIC* VII: 358).
9. Constantius II (AD 330–331), Rev: GLORIA EXERCITVS (2 standards), m. Trier (*RIC* VII: 525).
10–11. (AD 330–333), Rev: Wolf and Twins/VRBS ROMA, m. Trier (*RIC* VII: 522 & 547).
Discussion: For another *nummus* hoard from the same excavations, see *TAR* 2005/6, no.1121.
Disposition: To remain with the main site archive in Hartlepool Museum and Heritage Service.

R COLLINS

504. Aston Ingham, Herefordshire: 48 copper-alloy *nummi* (PAS: PAS-70D823; Treasure: 2007 T563)

Date: Roman (deposited in c. AD 335).
Discovery: Found by Mr D Sherratt and Mr D Hutton while metal-detecting in October 2006, and reported to Kurt Adams (Gloucestershire FLO).
Description: The coins date to c. AD 310–c. 335, during the reign of Constantine I (r. AD 306–337), but featuring several other rules with whom he briefly shared power.

	310–313	313–317	318–324	324–329	330–335	Total
1–9. m. London	4	3	1	1	–	9
10–25. m. Trier	7	2	3	4	–	16
26–29. m. Lyon	1	2	–	–	1	4
30–31. m. Siscia	–	–	2	–	–	2
32. m. Thessalonica	–	–	–	1	–	1
33–44. m. uncertain	3	2	3	3	1	12
45–48. Illegible	–	–	–	–	4	4
Total	15	9	9	9	6	48

Discussion: The findspot and similar types suggests these coins form addenda to the 1855 Aston Ingham Hoard, a hoard of around 2,000 coins ending in the reign of Constantine the Great, 37 of which are in the Gloucester City Museum (Robertson 2000: 1108).
Disposition: Herefordshire Museum and Art Gallery hopes to acquire.

R ABDY

505. Padstow, Cornwall: 27 copper-alloy *nummi* (PAS: CORN-84F996; Treasure: 2007 T576)

Date: Roman (deposited in c. AD 340).
Discovery: Found by Time Team and Wessex Archaeology in October 2007, during excavation of a site which had already produced Roman finds, in the backfill of a hollow which also held pottery and midden material, and reported to Anna Tyacke (Cornwall FLO).
Description: A mid-Constantinian *nummus* hoard with a large number (almost 45%) of barbarous copies of the coinage of the previous period (c. AD 330–335). There are, however, three rare issues for *nummus* hoards in Britain, VIRTVS AVGVSTI and 'Milvian Bridge' types, and a rare coin of Delmatius (nos. 43, 44 & 49).

	Sest	Gloria Exercitus (2)	Gloria Exercitus (1)	Irregular
1. m. Trier	-	1	-	-
2. m. Lyon	-	-	1	-
3–4. m. Rome	1	-	1	-
5. m. Contantinople	-	-	1	-
6–29. m. uncertain	-	1	9	12
Total	1	2	12	12

Disposition: Disclaimed; to remain with the main site archive at the Prideaux estate, Padstow.

R ABDY

506. Barbridge, Cheshire: 28 *nummi* and copper-alloy fragments (PAS LVPL-00DCE2; Treasure: 2007 T201)

Date: Roman (deposited in c. AD 351, or possibly AD 375).
Discovery: Found by Carl Thompson and Reg Baker while metal-detecting in April 2007, found over an area extending 60m, with 20 of the coins being within a distance of 5m of each other, and reported to Francis McIntosh (Cheshire, Greater Manchester & Merseyside FLO).
Description: Eleven of the coins are Constantinian *nummi* dating to the period c. AD 323–335; 16 date to the period after the coinage reform of AD 348, extending into the early 350s. The hoard might well have closed before the elevation of Decentius as Caesar in AD 351. The single Valentinianic *nummus* of the period 364–375 is probably a stray intruder which should not be associated with the hoard.

	323–329	330–335	348–350	350–351	[365–7]	Total
1. m. London	1	-	-	-	-	1
2–9. m. Trier	2	2	3	1	-	8
10–12. m. Lyon	-	-	2	1	-	3
13. m. Arles	-	-	-	1	-	1
14–15. m. other	2	-	-	-	-	2
16–21. m. unclear	-	4	-	1	1	6
22–8. m. imitations	-	-	4	3	-	7
Total	5	6	9	7	1	28

Disposition: Nantwich Museum hopes to acquire.

R ABDY

507. Bridgnorth area, Shropshire: hoard of over 2,800 coins of Magnentius and Decentius (PAS: HESH-881F86; Treasure 2007 T664)

Date: Roman (c. AD 350–c. 353).
Discovery: Found by Ian Botley while metal-detecting in 2007, and reported to Peter Reavill (Herefordshire & Shropshire FLO). The findspot was subsequently excavated by the FLO and finder.
Description: Detailed conservation and analysis is being undertaken by British Museum conservators and curators.
Discussion: The hoard consists of in excess of 2,800 bronze coins dating to the reign of emperors Magnentius (r. AD 350–353) and Decentius (r. AD 351–353). They were deposited in a large earthenware pottery vessel which had been inserted into a shallow gulley or ditch during the later Roman period. The pottery vessel is very friable (crumbly) and has considerable evidence of burning on the outer edges suggesting it had been used within a domestic setting, possibly for cooking or similar food preparation activities. Excavation of the findspot revealed evidence for the gulley, although detailed characterisation of it was not possible due to the nature of the small

excavation. It does, however, suggest a previously unknown late Roman site. Unfortunately it was impossible to understand where the hoard had been deposited in relation to the ditch as the area had been heavily disturbed by deep ploughing. The gulley was only identifiable in section suggesting that it had a sloping U-shaped profile. The deep ploughing for a potato crop had shattered the pottery vessel and spread the coins through the sub- and top-soil strata. The finder is to be congratulated on the careful plotting and speedy reporting of this hoard as it enabled the excavation to take place and vital depositional information recorded. In turn, this minimised the impact to the landowner and his farming activity.
Disposition: Shropshire County Museum Service hope to acquire.

P REAVILL

---

508. Newton Abbott area, Devon: 243 (193 & 50) *nummi* (Treasure: 2007 T209)

Date: Roman (deposited in c. AD 378).
Discovery: Found while metal-detecting in woodland (193 coins on 9 April 2007, and a further 50 on 7 May 2007), which were reported to Danielle Wotton (Devon FLO). The coins were found over an area of 10 x 20 feet with a concentration in the centre, suggesting that the hoard had been disturbed since seclusion.
Description: Of the 175 identifiable coins, the vast majority (165) date to the Valentinianic period of AD 364–378. Four coins are regular issues of the House of Constantine (AD 330–361) and 6 are copies struck in the period c. AD 350–364.

1–4. House of Constantine (c. AD 330–361)	4
5–10. Irregular coins (c. AD 350–364)	6
11–175. House of Valentinian (c. AD 364–378)	165
176–243. Uncertain	68

Discussion: Most of the coins were very poorly preserved, probably due to saturation in the soil. The general composition of the coins is consistent with other hoards of the period (Moorhead 1997: 406–407). This hoard is a considerable distance west of the normal region for Valentinianic bronze hoards (Somerset, Wiltshire and Gloucestershire).
Disposition: Royal Albert Memorial Museum, Exeter hopes to acquire.

S MOORHEAD

SINGLE FINDS

---

509. Cambridge, Cambridgeshire: copper-alloy *nummus* of Constantine I, commemorating Constantius I (PAS: CAM-7A36D7)

Date: Roman (c. AD 307–308).
Discovery: Found by Stephen Fordham while metal-detecting, and recorded by Philippa Walton (Cambridgeshire FLO).
Description: Copper-alloy *nummus* of Constantine I (r. AD 306–337) to commemorate his father, Constantius I (r. AD 296–307). Rev: MEMORIA FELIX, altar flanked by eagles. m. Trier (RIC VI: 789). Diameter: 29mm. Weight: 5.08g.
Discussion: Although not rare, these coins are not often found as single finds.
Disposition: Returned to finder.

P WALTON & S MOORHEAD

---

510. Salisbury area, Wiltshire: gold *aureus* of Licinius I (PAS: WILT-D86FB6)

Date: Roman (c. AD 313–July 315).
Discovery: Found by Martyn Quinn while metal-detecting in 2007, and recorded by Katie Hinds (Wiltshire FLO).
Description: Gold 1½ *solidus* (sometimes called a *Festaureus*) of Licinius I (r. AD 308–324). Rev: VBIQVE VICTORES (everywhere Victories). m. Trier (RIC VII: 163, no. 5). Diameter: 21mm. Weight: 5.32g.
Discussion: Three coins of this type are recorded of this type in RIC: in the British Museum, the Hunterian Museum (Glasgow) and the Ashmolean Museum (Oxford). The coin is struck from different dies to those used for the other known examples. Medallions (large coins or multiples) like this were struck for the emperor to distribute at special occasions. One coin of Constantius II (r. AD 337–361) actually shows the emperor in a chariot distributing largesse in the form of coins (RIC VIII: 518, no. 77).
Disposition: Returned to finder.

D ALGAR, K HINDS & S MOORHEAD

---

511. Thoresby, Lincolnshire: copper-alloy *nummus* of Constantine I (PAS: LIN-5AF4C4)

Date: Roman (c. AD 310–312).
Discovery: Found by Tom Redmayne while metal-detecting in 2007, and recorded by Adam Daubney (Lincolnshire FLO).
Description: Copper-alloy *nummus* of Constantine I (r. AD 306–337), CONCORD MILIT, m. London (*RIC* VI: no. 197). Diameter: 22mm.
Discussion: No example of this coin is known from Britain; the recorded example is in Vienna.
Disposition: The finder donated the coin to the British Museum.

A DAUBNEY & S MOORHEAD

512. Wood Enderby, Lincolnshire: copper-alloy *nummus* of Crispus (PAS: NCL-9B1082)

Date: Roman (AD 322).

Discovery: Found by Terry Peach while metal-detecting in September 2007, and recorded by Rob Collins (North East FLO).

Description: Copper-alloy *nummus* of Crispus (r. AD 317–326). Obv: IVL CRSIPVS NOB C. Cuirassed bust left, holding spear and shield. Rev: globe on altar, inscribed VOTIS XX; above, three stars. mm. probably -//PTR˅, m. Trier. Diameter: 18.49mm. Weight: 2g.

Discussion: The mintmark suggests this is an unpublished variety.

Disposition: Acquired by the British Museum.

R COLLINS & S MOORHEAD

513. Chipping Norton, Oxfordshire: copper-alloy *nummus* of Constantine (PAS: BERK-5AA8A2)

Date: Roman (c. AD 224–225).

Discovery: Found by Graham Cashmore while fieldwalking between 1978 and 2004, and recorded by Kate Sumnall (Oxfordshire & Berkshire FLO).

Description: Copper-alloy *nummus* of Constantine I (r. AD 306–337). Obv: CONSTANTINVS AVG. Laureate head, right. Rev: PROVIDENTIAE AVGG; camp-gate with four turrets; no star above. mm. -//T*AR, m. Arles. Diameter: 17.77mm. Weight: 2.06g.

Discussion: The PROVIDENTIAE AVGG types (e.g. *RIC* VII: 264) have only two turrets. The VIRTVS types (e.g. *RIC* VII: 291) have four. This coin apparently conflates the two types. Both types have a star above the gate; this coin has none.

Disposition: Returned to finder.

P LEVICK, K SUTTON & S MOORHEAD

514. Chichester area, West Sussex: silver *siliqua* of Jovian (PAS: SUSS-F74487)

Date: Roman (c. AD 363–364).

Discovery: Found by Aaron Bennett while metal-detecting in 2007, and recorded by Liz Andrews-Wilson (Sussex FLO).

Description: Silver *siliqua* of Jovian (r. AD 363–364). Obv: D N IOVIANVS P F AVG; pearl-diademed, draped and cuirassed, right. Rev: VOT V MVLT X in wreath. mm. -//LVG, m. Lyon (*RIC* VIII: 196 – not recorded). Diameter: 16.5mm. Weight 1.13g.

Discussion: This is only the second *siliqua* of Jovian recorded for the Lyon mint. The other example was found in the Whitwell Hoard (Rutland) between 1991 and 1993 and is now in the British Museum (*CHRB* X: 472, no. 40; BM 1992: 9.4.2). *RIC* VIII (196) suggested that such coins might exist, but recorded none. These two surviving specimens were struck from different dies. It is clear that the reverse was one engraved for use on coins of the previous emperor, Julian (r. AD 360–363, see *RIC* VIII: 195, no. 229), so Lyon quickly issued coins for Jovian when they heard from the Persian frontier that he was the new emperor, without engraving a new reverse type.

Disposition: Returned to finder.

L ANDREWS-WILSON & S MOORHEAD

515. Bermondsey, Rotherhithe and Southwark, London: copper-alloy *nummus* of Valens (PAS: LON-AD9CF4)

Date: Roman (c. AD 364–367).

Discovery: Found by Saul Odam while metal-detecting in April 2007, and recorded by Kate Sumnall (London FLO).

Description: Copper-alloy *nummus* of Valens (r. AD 364–378), GLORIA ROMANORVM Victory type. m. Trier (*LRBC* II: no. 106). Diameter: 17.17mm. Weight: 2.02g.

Discussion: This type was only struck at Trier, and only in small numbers. This is the first example recorded with the PAS.

Disposition: Returned to finder.

K SUMNALL & S MOORHEAD

516. Fulstow, Lincolnshire: two lead tablets with impressions of a coin of Valens (PAS: LIN-57F021 & 57B091)

Date: Roman (c. AD 364–378 or later).

Discovery: Found by Tom Redmayne while metal-detecting in January 2007, and recorded by Adam Daubney (Lincolnshire FLO).

Description: Two lead tablets which have both been drilled and folded. Both have the obverse impression (inverted) of a coin of Valens in the centre: D N VALEN – S P F AVG; pearl-diademed, draped and cuirassed, right. Dimensions: 92 x 60mm & 65 x 40mm. Weights: 56.04g & 6.1g.

Discussion: It is suggested that these were used by a forger to make silver cliché *siliquae*. Such a cliché coin of Valens was found in the Lakenheath (Palmer's Green, Suffolk) Hoard of 1983, now in the British Museum (BM 1983.6.33.9). Another interpretation is that these were curse tablets.

Disposition: Both tablets have been donated to the British Museum by the finder.

A DAUBNEY & S MOORHEAD

517. West Wight, Isle of Wight: copper-alloy *nummus* of Procopius (PAS: IOW-E6E981)

Date: Roman (c. AD 365–366).

Discovery: Found by Fred Cook in April 2007 while metal-detecting, and recorded by Frank Basford (Isle of Wight FLO).

Description: Copper-alloy *nummus* of Procopius (r. AD 365–366), probably from the mints of Constantinople or Cyzicus. Rev: REPARATIO FEL TEMP, emperor holding standard and shield (*RIC* IX: 240, *c.f.* 18–19). Diameter: 15mm. Weight: 1.75g.

Discussion: This was one of 35 single-finds (but not believed to be a hoard) found in an area 50 x 50m (see IOW-85AAB2 for general report). The group had an unprecedented number of eastern mint coins of the late Roman period. Coins of Procopius are extremely rare in Britain, this being the first recorded with the PAS. This obverse type was only struck at Constantinople and Cyzicus, the former being more prolific.
Disposition: Returned to finder.

F BASFORD & S MOORHEAD

---

518. Silverstone, Northamptonshire: gold *solidus* of Gratian (PAS: BUC-F59BB6)

Date: Roman (AD 378–383).
Discovery: Found while metal-detecting, and recorded by Ros Tyrrell (Buckinghamshire FLO).
Description: Gold *solidus* of Gratian (r. AD 367–383), CONCORDIA AVGGGI, Constantinopolis seated; mm. -//CONOB ('pure gold from Constantinople'), m. Constantinople (*RIC* IX: 45a). Diameter: 19.61mm. Weight: 4.48g.
Disposition: Returned to finder.

R TYRRELL

---

519. West Wight, Isle of Wight: copper-alloy *nummus* of Arcadius (PAS: IOW-E616B4)

Date: Roman (c. AD 395–401).
Discovery: Found by Justin Cavnor while metal-detecting in April 2007, and recorded by Frank Basford (Isle of Wight FLO).
Description: Copper-alloy *nummus* of Arcadius (r. AD 383–408), VIRTVS EXERCITI, Victory crowning emperor. m. unclear (*LRBC* II: 110, type 2). Diameter: 19mm. Weight: 2.07g.
Discussion: This is from the same group as 517; see IOW-85AAB2 for group details. This is apparently the first recorded find for this type in Britain. This coin was struck at an eastern mint and is extremely common on eastern Mediterranean sites but is rarely found west of Greece.
Disposition: Returned to finder.

F BASFORD & S MOORHEAD

5th century AD

The majority of the hoards from this period are late precious metal hoards, probably buried c. AD 402–430. Two include gold *solidi* from Saxmundham area, Suffolk (523) and Fareham, Hampshire (525) but most of the coins are silver *siliquae* which are often clipped. One of the hoards (522) was found in the same parish as the famous Mildenhall Hoard of silver plates and other finds. This coin hoard is a typical late clipped-*siliqua* hoard which contains coins that continued to be used during the early 5th century, probably after the island was cut off and no new issues were available (Moorhead 2008). Another addendum is to the equally famous Hoxne Hoard, also from Suffolk (526). The group from Whittington, Northumberland (527), from north of Hadrian's Wall, contains only the second recorded specimen from Britain of the eastern mint GLORIA ROMANORVM type of AD 406–408.

HOARDS

---

520. Hawkesbury, South Gloucestershire: one base-metal *radiate*, 41 *nummi*, a copper-alloy brooch fragment, a copper-alloy possible pendant, and a forger's mould (PAS: GLO-2AD8F2; Treasure: 2007 T566)

Date: Roman (c. AD 270–c. 402).
Discovery: Found by Tony Brown, Vic Francis, Nick Keeler, Robert Moyle, David Thorne and David Whailey while metal-detecting in September 2007, and reported to Kurt Adams (Gloucestershire & Avon FLO).
Description:

1. *Radiate* of the Gallic Empire (c. AD 260–275)	1
2. *Nummus* (c. AD 307–308)	1
3–7. *Nummi* (c. AD 318–329)	5
8–18. *Nummi* (c. AD 330–348)	11
19–32. Irregular and illegible (c. AD 330–348)	14
33–41. *Nummi* (c. AD 364–375)	9
42. *Nummus* (c. AD 388–402)	1

43. Coin forger's mould for a mid-Constantinian or Valentinianic *nummus*-sized coin, which might have been used in the production of a poor quality cast coin in the find (no. 18). Weight: 11.2g.
44. Brooch fragment from a copper-alloy Hod Hill Type hinged brooch of the 1st century AD (Bayley and Butcher 2004: 119).
45. A copper-alloy disc, elliptical in section, with a hole drilled near the edge which does not pass all the way through. It might be an unfinished weight or pendant.

Discussion: The coins probably represent finds lost over a period of time, although it is conceivable that the Constantinian period coins represent a small hoard.
Disposition: Not Treasure, returned to finder.

R ABDY & R HOBBS

521. Chichester area, West Sussex: a silver *miliarensis* and a silver *siliqua* (PAS: SUSS-68AA45 & 68D868; 2007 T719)

Date: Roman (c. AD 402).
Discovery: Found by Ken Mordle while metal-detecting in September 2007, and reported to Laura Burnett (Sussex FLO).
Description:
1. Part of a *miliarensis*, in two fragments, VIRTVS EXERCITVS Type of the House of Valentinian or Theodosius (c. AD 367–395).
2. *Siliqua*, VIRTVS ROMANORVM type, probably of the House of Theodosius (c. AD 388–402).
Disposition: Disclaimed; returned to finder.

S MOORHEAD

522. Mildenhall area, Suffolk (1st and 2nd addenda), Suffolk: 24 (x2) silver *siliquae* (PAS: SF-4BDF20; Treasure: 2007 T165)

Date: Roman (deposited in c. AD 402).
Discovery: Found by Jon Brown and Steve Foster while metal-detecting in 2002 and 2007, and reported to Faye Minter (Suffolk FLO).
Description: The coins range in date from AD 355 to 402 and have been clipped.

	Original hoard	First addenda	Second addenda	Total
1–4. AD 355–360	1	1	2	4
5–7. AD 364–367	-	1	2	3
8–14. AD 367–375	1	5	1	7
15–18. AD 375–378/9	1	1	2	4
19–28. AD 378/9–388	1	5	4	10
29–35. AD 388–395	1	1	5	7
36–53. AD 395–402	2	10	6	18
54–55. Irregular	-	-	2	2

Discussion: This is a typical late clipped-*siliqua* hoard. It contains coins which continued to be used during the early fifth century, probably after Britain was cut off from the rest of the Roman Empire and no new issues were available (c. AD 410) (Moorhead 2008: 38–43; for the original find, named the Worlington Treasure and acquired by Mildenhall District Museum, see *TAR* 2001, no. 201 – this report includes all the earlier coins as well).
Disposition: Acquired by Mildenhall District Museum.

F MINTER & R ABDY

523. Saxmundham area, Suffolk (addenda): three gold *solidi* and 58 silver clipped *siliquae* (PAS: SF-424843; Treasure: 2007 T514)

Date: Roman (deposited in c. AD 402).
Discovery: Found by David Cummings and Debbie Cook while metal-detecting in August 2007, and reported to Faye Minter (Suffolk FLO).
Description: All the silver coins (*siliquae*) were heavily clipped and only a few can be precisely identified:

Gold solidi

1. Gratian (AD 367–75), m. Milan (*RIC* IX: 5d)	1
2. Valentinian II (AD 388–95), m. Trier (*RIC* IX: 90)	1
3. Honorius (AD 395–402), m. Milan (*RIC* X: 1206)	1

Silver siliquae

4–9. Constantius II (AD 355–360), Julian Caesar (r. AD 355–360) and Julian Augustus (r. AD 360–363)	6
10–17. Valentinian I, Valens and Gratian (AD 367–375)	8
18. Valens, Gratian and Valentinian II (AD 375–378)	1
19–25. Gratian, Theodosius I, Valentinian II, Arcadius, Magnus Maximus and Flavius Victor (AD 378/9–388)	7
26–28. Theodosius I, Valentinian II, Eugenius and Arcadius (AD 388–395)	3
29–44. Honorius and Arcadius (AD 395–402)	16
45–62. Uncertain emperor (c. AD 355–402)	18

Discussion: This is a similar hoard to the previous entry from the Mildenhall area. Further addenda of one *solidus* and 59 *siliquae* will be in *TAR* 2008.
Disposition: Acquired by Colchester and Ipswich Museum Service.

R ABDY

524. Sible Hedingham, Essex: 19 silver coins and a silver toothpick fragment (Treasure: 2005 T371)

Date: Roman (deposited in c. AD 402).
Discovery: Found by Mr J Adkin and Mr P James while metal-detecting in September 2005.
Description:

1. Octavian (AD 29–27 BC)	1 *den*
2–4. Valentinian I, Valens and Gratian (AD 367–375), m. Trier,	3 *sil*
5–6. Valens, Gratian and Valentinian II (AD 375–378/9), m. Trier,	2 *sil*
7. Gratian, Theodosius I, Valentinian II, Arcadius, Magnus Maximus and Flavius Victor (AD 378/9–388), m. Trier,	1 *sil*
8. Theodosius I, Valentinian II, Eugenius and Arcadius (AD 388–395), m. Trier,	1 *sil*
9–16. Honorius and Arcadius (AD 395–402), m. Milan,	8 *sil*
17–19.	3 *sil**

20. Toilet implement fragment. Originally part of a late Roman double-ended type of implement with a comma-shaped 'toothpick' at one end, and an 'ear-scoop' at the other. Only part of the flat disc and comma-shaped point survive. The obverse is decorated with a Chi-Rho symbol, made by a series of punched chevrons. The reverse has similar impressed dots to form lines in an unclear design. It is possible that the fragment was deliberately cut (transforming it into a piece of hack-silver). Toilet implements with comma-shaped terminals are a well known late Roman type. The closest parallel is a complete implement from the Canterbury Hoard (Johns and Potter 1985: 326, no. 17), which also has a Chi-Rho symbol composed of punched dots.

Discussion: The *denarius* fragment is a more unusual find in this association. It dates to the early part of the reign of Octavian, later Augustus (r. 31 BC–AD 14), and could have been in regular circulation up until the early part of the 2nd century AD. However, occasional evidence from other finds of late Roman coins shows that such *denarii* sometimes survived into later periods – presumably kept for their silver content as the denomination would probably no longer have been familiar so long after the discontinuation of *denarius* production in the 3rd century AD.

Disposition: Acquired by Braintree District Museum; one finder donated his share.

R ABDY & R HOBBS

---

525. Fareham, Hampshire (2nd addenda): two gold solidi (PAS: HAMP-F6F384 & F71BD4; Treasure: 2007 T449)

Date: Roman (deposited in c. AD 406).
Discovery: Found by Michael Stevens while metal-detecting in August 2007, and reported to Rob Webley (Hampshire FLO).
Description: The two new coins are both gold *solidi*, making a total of 4 *solidi*.
Original find:
-. Honorius (AD 395–402), VICTORIA AVGGG. m. Milan (*RIC* X: 1206c)
First addendum:
-. Honorius (AD 402–403, 405–406), VICTORIA AVGGG. m. Ravenna (*RIC* X: 1287d)
Second addenda:
1. Honorius (AD 395–402), VICTORIA AVGGG. m. Milan (*RIC* X: 1206c)
2. Honorius (AD 402–3, 405–6), VICTORIA AVGGG. m. Ravenna (*RIC* X: 1287d)
Discussion: In the 5th century, four *solidi* appear to have represented a soldier's yearly subsistence (the original find, a single *solidus* purchased by Hampshire Museum Service, is recorded with the PAS as HAMP-F927E7; for the 1st addendum, also acquired by Hampshire Museum Service, see *TAR* 2005/6, no. 1140; HAMP-D43CA3).
Disposition: Hampshire Museums Service hopes to acquire.

R WEBLEY & R ABDY

---

526. Hoxne, Suffolk (addenda): nine silver *siliquae* and two *siliquae* fragments (PAS: SF-8AB7E8; Treasure: 2007 T604)

Date: Roman (deposited in c. AD 408).
Discovery: Found by Alan Smith while metal-detecting in October 2007, and reported to Faye Minter (Suffolk FLO).
Description:
1–2. Julian (AD 355–360), m. Lyon and uncertain
3–4. Arcadius (AD 388–395), m. Milan and uncertain
5–7. Arcadius (AD 395–402), m. Milan
8–9. Honorius (AD 395–402), m. Milan
10–11. Undiagnostic *siliquae* fragments
Discussion: This represents more *addenda* to the famous Hoxne Treasure (Guest 2005; for previous *addenda*, see *TAR* 2005/6, no. 1141).

Disposition: Acquired by the British Museum; finder and landowner donated their share.

R ABDY

---

527. Whittington, Northumberland: eight copper-alloy *nummi* (PAS: NCL-EE2655, EE7100, EEBF58, EEEB36, EF0D13, EF35F5, EF6DD1 & EF8E21)

Date: Roman (deposited in AD c. 318–c. 408).
Discovery: Found by Barry Seger while metal-detecting in May 2007, and reported to Rob Collins (North East FLO).
Description: Eight *nummi*, the earliest issued by Constantine (c. AD 318–319), and the latest issued by the House of Theodosius (c. AD 406–408).
1. Constantine I (AD 318), VICTORIAE LAETAE PRINC PERP, m. Siscia (*RIC* VII: 47–48)
2. Constantius II (AD 330–335), GLORIA EXERCITVS, m. ?Constantinople (*RIC* VII: 75)
3. Constans (AD 335–341), GLORIA EXERCITVS, m. Eastern
4. Constans (r. AD 333–350), FEL TEMP REPARATIO, falling horseman (irregular) (*RIC* VIII: as 191, no. 189)
5. Constans or Constantius II (AD 333–361), FEL TEMP REPARATIO, falling horseman (irregular) (*RIC* VIII: as 191, no. 189)
6. House of Valentinian (AD 364–378), SECVRITAS REI PVBLICAE, m. Arles (*LRBC*: 481–483)
7. Valentinian I (r. AD 364–375), SECVRITAS REI PVBLICAE, m. Arles (*LRBC*: 501)
8. House of Theodosius (c. 406–408), GLORIA ROMANORVM, m. Eastern (*RIC* X: 142ff).
Discussion: Because the coins are base metal, and because there are fewer than ten, this group does not constitute Treasure. The group is, however, very important, as it contains only the second example of a *Gloria Romanorum* coin of the three emperors of the House of Theodosius discovered thus far in Britain (528). This coin also dates the group to the early 5th century, and within one mile of Hadrian's Wall. The coin and the group are therefore important in terms of demonstrating 5th-century coin use in the frontier of Britain (the group is fully discussed in Collins 2008).
Disposition: Returned to finder.

R COLLINS & S MOORHEAD

Early Byzantine coins (c. AD 491–610)

The following are single finds of four early Byzantine coins dating to the period c. AD 491–c. 610. A significant number of Byzantine coins have been recorded with the PAS and have been the subject of several short articles (e.g. Moorhead 2008; Abdy and Williams 2006). The majority of the coins have come from the West Country and the south coast along to the Isle of Wight, a pattern mirrored by the finds of 5th- and 6th-century Byzantine pottery.

528. Single, Isle of Wight: gold *solidus* (contemporary copy) of Anastasius I (PAS: IOW-D7CB55)

Date: Early Medieval (c. AD 500–c. 580).
Discovery: Found by Gavin Leng while metal-detecting in April 2007, and recorded by Frank Basford (Isle of Wight FLO).
Description: Contemporary copy of a gold *solidus* of Anastasius I (r. AD 491–518).
Discussion: This coin was part of an Anglo-Saxon grave assemblage, see 158.
Disposition: Returned to finder.

F BASFORD & S MOORHEAD

529. Kings Stanley, Gloucestershire: copper-alloy *follis* of Justinian I (PAS: GLO-709856)

Date: Early Medieval (c. AD 527–537).
Discovery: Found by Raymond Williams while metal-detecting, and recorded by Kurt Adams (Gloucestershire FLO).
Description: Copper-alloy *follis* of Justinian I (r. AD 527–565) Obv: D N IVSTINIANVS P P AVG; pearl-diademed, draped & cuirassed right. Rev: Large M; above, cross; to left and right, star. mm. A//CON (*MIBE*: 83). Diameter: 31mm. Weight: 15.81g.
Discussion: Four other 6th-century *folles*, in poor condition, found in Devon, have also been recorded with the PAS (DEV-464726).
Disposition: Returned to finder.

K ADAMS & S MOORHEAD

530. Langport, Somerset: copper-alloy half-*follis* of Justinian I (PAS: SOM-3B55D0)

Date: Early Medieval (c. AD 550–c. 564).
Discovery: Found by Philip Pope during building work in 2004, and recorded by Naomi Payne (Somerset FLO) in 2007.
Description: Copper-alloy half-*follis* of Justinian I (r. AD 527–565) Obv: [D N IVSTINIANVS P P AVC] or similar; facing bust with cuirass and helmet, holding cross on globe and shield (in field right, cross). Rev: large K (above, ?cross); to right, unclear date numerals;

below, A (*MIBE*: Constantinople, 83). Diameter: 20.9mm. Weight: 5.5g.
Discussion: Because this coin was found in building work and has a sandy patina suggestive of a Mediterranean origin, it is quite likely that this is not an ancient loss.
Disposition: Returned to finder.

N PAYNE & S MOORHEAD

531. North Yorkshire: gold *solidus* of Phocas (PAS: NCL-6A6EF5)

Date: Early Medieval (c. AD 607–609).
Discovery: Found with a metal-detector around September 2007, and recorded by Rob Collins (North East FLO).
Description: Gold *solidus* of Phocas (r. AD 602–610). Obv: dN FOCAS PERP AVG; draped and cuirassed facing bust wearing crown and holding a *globus cruciger* in right hand. Rev: VICTORIA AVGYЄ; robed angel standing facing forward holding staff surmounted by christogram and a *globus cruciger*;. mm.-//CONOB (*MIB* II: 9). Diameter: 21mm.
Discussion: Although this is a surprising find, gold coins could move large distances in the Early Medieval period.
Disposition: Returned to finder.

R COLLINS & S MOORHEAD

Section editor and further research: Sam Moorhead.
Editor: Michael Lewis.

EARLY MEDIEVAL COINS
(c. 400–1066)

In 2007, finds of Early Medieval coins reported to the PAS and through the Treasure Act 1996 continued to further the understanding of the coinage circulating in pre-Conquest England and Wales. Seven hoards were recorded (217 & 532–537), a threefold increase on 2006, although fewer single finds were reported, a decrease of a third on 2006, with 235 records produced. This was surprising given the major increases seen for Medieval and Post-Medieval coin finds (see relevant sections below).

Hoards of this period are not common and the discovery of the 'Vale of York Hoard' (217), with 617 Late Anglo-Saxon coins, some of which are new types, contained with other precious metal objects in a silver-gilt cup, is of undoubted international importance, probably representing the most spectacular find of the year. The other Treasure finds are of a more everyday nature, probably mostly accidental purse losses, but this in itself is important as it illustrates that coinage was being carried regularly from an early date and that some form of monetary economy existed by the 8th century at least.

In comparison to the hoards, the single finds present a picture of more consistent coin use throughout the Early Medieval period, with coins from the 6th century onwards all recorded. A number of these provide evidence for Continental European links - such as the coins from Ware area, Hertfordshire (539) and Cawood, North Yorkshire (538) - and these are continually expanding the knowledge of the range of coins entering England, especially in the early Anglo-Saxon period. Some of the finds of English coinage have also proven very important for numismatic study, with a new coin type found for King Offa of Mercia, from Peckleton, Leicestershire (540) and a new moneyer for Ecgberht of Wessex, from Newport, Isle of Wight (543).

HOARDS

532. Bradford Peverell, Dorset: three Anglo-Saxon silver pennies
(PAS: DOR-B8A4A2, B8C382 & B8C682;
Treasure: 2007 T350)

Date: Early Medieval (c. 725).
Discovery: Found by Alan Maidment while metal-detecting in June 2007, and reported to Claire Pinder (Senior Archaeologist, Dorset County Council).
Description:
1. Penny (*sceat*), Series E, 'VICO' variety (c. 700–720), m. ?Frisia. Weight 1.18g.
2. Penny (*sceat*), Series E, variety E (c. 720–740), m. Frisia. Weight: 0.95g.

3. Penny (*sceat*), Series N-derived (c. 720–740) (*BMC* 58), m. ?southern England. Weight: 0.98g.
Discussion: All three of the coins date from the first half of the 8th century, coins 2 and 3 being of very similar date. Both have direct parallels found together in a hoard at Woodham Walter, Essex, dated to c. 725. Coin 1 is slightly earlier, but could easily still have remained in circulation alongside the other two.
Disposition: Dorset County Museum hopes to acquire.

G WILLIAMS

533. Harswell, East Yorkshire: eleven Anglo-Saxon base-silver/copper-alloy coins (PAS: YORYM-D5DFC2; Treasure: 2007 T311)

Date: Early Medieval (c. 840–c. 850).
Discovery: Found by Norman Smith while metal-detecting in June 2007, and reported to Beth Echtenacher (North & East Yorkshire FLO).
Description: Eleven base silver/copper-alloy coins, known as *stycas*, dating from the late 8th and 9th centuries. These were only minted in the kingdom of Northumbria.
1. Eanred (standard date r. 810–840; alternative date r. 810–c. 854), mn. Herred. Weight: 1g.
2. Æthelred II (standard date r. c. 840/1–844 & 844–849; alternative date r. c. 854–858 & c. 858–862), 1st reign, mn. Fordred. Weight: 0.92g.
3. Redwulf (standard date r. c. 844; alternative date r. c. 858), mn. possibly Wendleberht. Weight: 1.02g.
4. Æthelred II, 2nd reign (standard date r. c. 844–849; alternative date r. c. 858–862), mn. Eardwulf. Weight: 1.01g.
5. Æthelred II, 2nd reign (standard date r. c. 844–849; alternative date r. c. 858–862), mn. Eardwulf. Weight: 0.77g.
6. Æthelred II, 2nd reign (standard date r. c. 844–849; alternative date r. c. 858–862), mn. Monne. Weight: 0.81g.
7. Osberht (standard date r. 849–867; alternative date r. c. 862–867), mn. Winiberht. Weight: 1.01g.
8. Archbishop Eanbald II of York (standard date r. c. 796–c. 837; alternative date r. 796–c. 830), mn. Æthelweard. Weight: 0.81g.
9. Archbishop Wigmund of York (r. 837–854), mn. Æthelhelm. Weight: 0.92g.
10. Uncertain (c. 850), with blundered Eardwulf inscription. Weight: 1g.
11. Uncertain (c. 850), with blundered inscription. Weight: 0.74g.
Discussion: Coinage in Northumbria was not withdrawn from circulation when the reign changed, and the mixture of coins is typical for a hoard of the mid 9th century. All of the coins have very similar patination.
Disposition: East Riding Museum Service hopes to acquire.

G WILLIAMS

534. Alfriston area, East Sussex: two fused silver pennies (PAS: SUSS-C96E71; Treasure: 2007 T661)

Date: Early Medieval (c. 900–c. 1000).

Discovery: Found by Brian Standen while metal-detecting in September 2007, and reported to Laura Burnett (Sussex FLO).

Description: Two 10th-century silver pennies fused together with only the reverse of each visible and broken into two pieces. The two coins are bent inwards towards coin 2, and broken along the bend line. The break is modern. Only one is identifiable (coin 1), probably of Edward the Elder (r. 899–924). The combined weight is 3.03g, although it must be noted that the coins are slightly chipped in two places.

1. ?Edward the Elder (c. 899–c. 924), two line, *BMC*ii (HB1 E) (North: 649), Rev: VVLF/+ + +/ARD+, mn. Wulfheard. Diameter: 20.2mm.

2. Unidentified (? c. 899–c. 946), two line, *BMC*ii (HP1) (North: 649, 688/2 or 689), Rev: D(EO)RV/[...], mn. uncertain. Diameter: 20.7mm.

Discussion: The coins are solidly fused together although some air spaces remain between them. The distortion of the flan with small bubbles may suggest the coin has been burnt, presumably accidentally. This could have happened long after deposition but the fact the coins were in close proximity while being burnt may suggest they were held together in a purse or other container.

Disposition: Disclaimed; returned to finder.

L BURNETT & G WILLIAMS

535. Wymondham, Norfolk: five Anglo-Saxon silver pennies (PAS: NMS-C25257; Treasure: 2007 T685)

Date: Early Medieval (c. 900–c. 1000).

Discovery: Found while metal-detecting in November 2007, and reported to Erica Darch (Norfolk FLO).

Description: The coins, originally totalling at least five in number, had been stacked one on top of the other. At some point, the stack has fused together, probably as a result of exposure to heat. The stack contains at least four complete coins plus fragments, but only one legible face is visible. This is the reverse of a mid 10th-century coin carrying the moneyer's name HRODGAR as a circumscription around a small cross pattée.

Discussion: Circumscription reverses are used on various coin designs of the period, but the moneyer HRODGAR (Hrodgar/Hrothgar) of Norwich is recorded on coins of the Bust Crowned Type of both Eadmund (r. 939–946) and Eadred (r. 946–954). No die-duplicate has been traced, but the coin is a good match stylistically with recorded coins of both kings, and it is likely that the coin is of the same type, although the ruler is uncertain. There is no reason to doubt that the other coins are of the same period, although since there was a wide range of different coin types in circulation in the period, there could be other types represented here. Combined weight: 4.21g.

Disposition: Norwich Castle Museum hopes to acquire.

G WILLIAMS

536. Henley area, Oxfordshire: three fused Anglo-Saxon silver pennies (PAS: BERK-BC5CC2; Treasure: 2007 T432)

Date: Earl Medieval (980s).

Discovery: Found by Steven Venegas while metal-detecting in November 2007, and reported to Charlotte Burrill (Berkshire & Oxfordshire FLO).

Description: Three silver pennies fused together in exact alignment. Only one side of each of the two outer coins is visible, with nothing of the middle coin seen apart from the edge. Both of the outer coins show the obverse of the Second Hand Type of Æthelred II (r. 978–1016), issued in the 980s (North: 768). The third coin is likely to be of the same type, although it could plausibly be another issue from just before or after the Second Hand Type. With only the obverses visible, it is not possible to identify the mints and moneyers of the two outer coins and both are so badly damaged that it would be difficult, if not impossible, to match the dies with other examples. All three coins are slightly buckled, and one face is badly marked by striations, as if another coin or coins had at some point been fused to it, and subsequently levered off. The patination suggests that this did not take place recently. Both sides have the standard inscription of ÆÐELRÆD REX ANGLORVM (Æthelred, King of the English) around a diademed right-facing bust, with a sceptre in front of the bust. Combined weight: 3.23g.

Disposition: Oxfordshire Museums Service hopes to acquire.

G WILLIAMS

537. Arreton area, Isle of Wight: two Anglo-Saxon silver pennies (PAS: IOW-AEFBB1 & IOW-AFA8F1; Treasure: 2007 T273)

Date: Early Medieval (c. 997–c. 1003).

Discovery: Found by Dave Dent and Robin Mitchell while metal-detecting in May 2007, about 11m apart, and reported to Frank Basford (Isle of Wight FLO).

Description: Two silver pennies of Æthelred II (r. 978–1016), Long Cross Type (c. 997–c. 1003) (North: 774), mn. London.

1. Obv: ÆÐELRÆD REX ANGLO (N and G ligated), bare. Rev: +LYF/NIC/MOL/VND, mn. Lifinc, m. London. Diameter: 20mm. Weight: 1.67g. Same dies as British Museum 1959, 10-18, 6, same reverse die as *BMC*ii: 228, no. 255.

2. Obv: [Æ]ÐEL[RÆ]D REX ANGLO (N and G ligated). Rev. +SPE/TINC/MOL/VND, mn. Swetinc, m. London. Diameter: 20mm. Weight: 1.59g.

Disposition: Acquired by Isle of Wight Heritage Service.

F BASFORD & G WILLIAMS

SINGLE FINDS

538. Cawood, North Yorkshire: gold *tremissis* (PAS: SWYOR-B502C5)

Date: Early Medieval (c. 630–c. 650).

Discovery: Found by Wayne Dolan while metal-detecting in April 2007, and reported to Amy Cooper (South & West Yorkshire FLO).

Description: A 7th-century gold *tremissis*, minted in Dorestad (Netherlands). The obverse shows a bust, facing left, with the retrograde (anti-clockwise) inscription DORESTATE. The reverse has a central cross with two pellets above with the inscription RIMOALDVS MA, again retrograde, identifying the moneyer as Rimoaldus (see Zadoks-Josephus Jitta 1961: pl.1.3 for a very similar example). Dimensions: 12.7 x 1.3mm. Weight: 1.3g.

Discussion: Early coins from Dorestad are extremely rare in England, this being the first recorded by the PAS. Few others are known, and these come mostly from Norfolk with single outliers in Lincolnshire and North Yorkshire. All, however, are of the moneyer Madelinus, and this may be the first coin of Rimoaldus found in England. Both moneyers minted coins at Dorestad from c. 630 to c. 650, having previously worked at Maastricht (Netherlands). Madelinus coins are the most prolific and coins in his name continued to be minted at Dorestad after 650 (Grierson and Blackburn 1986: 137). The coin's importance is twofold, its rarity marking it out for special attention, and its location providing further evidence for the circulation of early gold coinage in England.

Disposition: Returned to finder.

J NAYLOR & A COOPER

539. Ware area, Hertfordshire: Merovingian silver *denier* (PAS: BH-86BC41)

Date: Early Medieval (c. 675–c. 750).

Discovery: Found by Kevin Easton while metal-detecting in February 2007, and recorded by Julian Watters (Hertfordshire & Bedfordshire FLO).

Description: A Merovingian silver *denier*, minted at Quentovic (now Étaples) by the moneyer Ela. Struck slightly off-centre. Obv: helmeted head facing right, the legend reads '+ELA....'. Rev: central cross surrounded by the legend 'VVICVS[]'. Dimensions: 12.1 x 1.4mm. Weight: 1.19g.

Discussion: The Merovingian dynasty lasted from the mid 5th to the mid 8th century and occupied the area roughly equivalent to that of ancient Gaul. Merovingian coinage is only found rarely in England, and this is most often gold *tremisses* rather than silver *deniers*.

Disposition: Returned to finder.

J WATTERS

540. Peckleton, Leicestershire: silver penny of Offa of Mercia (PAS: LEIC-94EB56; EMC 2007.0165)

Date: Early Medieval (c. 765–c. 792).

Discovery: Found by David Mann while metal-detecting in May 2007, and recorded by Wendy Scott (Leicestershire & Rutland FLO).

Description: A silver penny of King Offa (r. 757–796), minted by Almund. Obv: right-facing bust with the inscription 'OFFA REX MERCIOR' (Offa, King of Mercia). Rev: five small central pellets surrounded by four 'petals' arranged in a cross motif containing the moneyer's name, '+EALMVND' (Almund). Four raised bosses with beaded borders can be seen in the spaces between, each flanked by tow or three pellets. Dimensions: 17 x 0.75mm. Weight: 1.2g.

Discussion: This coin is a new type, combining the same reverse design as Chick 45 with an obverse design that has the same full legend and segmented inner circle as Chick 47, but with a different variety of bust. Unlike Chick 47, this bust features banded drapery similar to Chick 18, 23, 48, 67–71 and 126–129 (see Chick 2009).

Disposition: Returned to finder.

W SCOTT & R NAISMITH

541. Southwell area, Nottinghamshire: silver penny of Eadwald of East Anglia (PAS: DENO-CB8291)

Date: Early Medieval (c. 796–c. 798).

Discovery: Found by Bill French and Richard Northey while metal-detecting in August 2007, and reported to Anja Rohde (Derbyshire & Nottinghamshire FLO).

Description: A penny minted for King Eadwald (r. 796–798) by Botred. Obv: inscription reads 'EA+D +VVAL [ ] REX' (King Eadwald) in three lines. Rev: reads 'BOM[ ]ED' (most likely for Botred) within the arms of a tribrach, providing a variation on North: 432 and 433. Dimensions: 19.8 x 1.1mm. Weight: 1.2g.

Discussion: This is only the second coin known to record Botred as a moneyer for Eadwald, although the name is also known from coins of Offa (r. 757–796) and Coenred (r. 796–821). The other find was a small fragment, thus making the example from Southwell particularly important since it reveals the entire design, which is similar to the very earliest three-line pennies of King Coenwulf of Mercia struck at London in 796 to 797/8. These East Anglian coins of Botred should therefore probably be associated with the year or two immediately after the death of King Offa in July 796, perhaps before the development of some of the more distinctive features of Eadwald's coinage.

Disposition: Returned to finder.

R NAISMITH & A ROHDE

542. Ropley, Hampshire:
silver penny of Cuthred of Kent (PAS: SUR-013CA3)

Date: Earl Medieval (c. 802–c. 804).

Discovery: Found by Roger Courtman while metal-detecting in August 2007, and reported to David Williams (Surrey FLO).

Description: The coin is a 'non-portrait' type (North: 210.2) minted in Canterbury for King Cuthred (r. 798–807). The obverse shows a tribrach, each branch ending in an open circle at the outer edge of the coin dividing the inscription CVÐRED REX (King Cuthred). In the centre of the tribrach, three wedges form a 'propeller' with a pellet within each angle. The reverse also contains a central tribrach, with each branch bifurcating and both strands curving backwards on itself, again reaching the outer edge of the coin, dividing the inscription SIGEBERHT (Sigebeorht – the moneyer). Diameter: 18.61mm. Weight: 1.3g.

Discussion: Cuthred was installed on the Kentish throne by his brother, King Coenwulf of Mercia (r. 796–821), after a two-year revolt by the local population was suppressed. The region returned to direct Mercian control in 807. Finds of his coins are uncommon, this only the second Cuthred penny, and the first of its type, recorded by the PAS.

Disposition: Returned to finder.

J NAYLOR & D WILLIAMS

543. Newport, Isle of Wight: silver penny of Ecgberht of Wessex (PAS: IOW-05DF24)

Date: Early Medieval (c. 828–c. 839).

Discovery: Found by John Jerram while metal-detecting in September 2007, and recorded with Frank Basford (Isle of Wight FLO).

Description: A penny of King Ecgberht (r. 802–839), produced at the 'West Saxon' mint by the moneyer Weohthun. The obverse has the inscription +ECGBEORHT REX (King Ecgberht) around an irregular, central 'SAXON' monogram (North: 589). The reverse shows the inscription +PECHTHVN (Weohthun), for the moneyer, around a cross pattée. Diameter: 19.5mm. Weight: 1.3g.

Discussion: Finds of the 'SAXON' monogram types of Ecgberht are rare, and this is only one of nine Ecgberht pennies recorded by the PAS. The importance of the coin, however, lies in the fact that it adds a previously unknown moneyer to the issue. The name Weohthun is known from rare pennies minted for Ecgberht's predecessor King Beorhtric (r. 786–802) and it is possible, although uncertain, that this may be the same person. Another Weohthun penny was found near Shalfleet, Isle of Wight, in late 2007 by Roy Atkinson (PAS: IOW-7F79610).

Disposition: Returned to finder.

J NAYLOR & F BASFORD

544. Crawley, Hampshire: silver halfpenny of Eadred (PAS: HAMP-422CF4)

Date: Early Medieval (c. 946–c. 955).

Discovery: Found by Tim Chandler while metal-detecting in April 2007, and recorded with Rob Webley (Hampshire FLO).

Description: A halfpenny of King Eadred (r. 946–955) minted by the moneyer Martin (North: 722, HT1). The obverse reads +EADRED REX (King Eadred) around a central motif of a flower with twelve petals. The reverse gives the moneyer's name in two lines, MARTINN (Martin), divided by a line of three crosses, with a trefoil of pellets above and below the name. Dimensions: 14.8 x 0.45mm. Weight: 0.5g.

Discussion: Coins of Eadred are a rarity, this being only the third of his coins recorded by the PAS and the first find in Hampshire. Halfpennies were minted intermittently by kings from the later 9th century but are much less common finds than pennies. This example is firmly within the generally known distribution of Late Anglo-Saxon coinage, but its denomination adds to what is only a small corpus of coins.

Disposition: Returned to finder.

R WEBLEY

Section editor and further research: John Naylor
Editor: Michael Lewis

MEDIEVAL COINS (1066–1500)

In 2007, a significant increase was seen in the number of single finds reported to the PAS, up by around 50% on 2006 to 4,225 records. The number of Treasure cases remained about the same as the previous year, with hoards continuing to appear across the country. These provide new information on the circulation of coinage in Medieval England, including the use of foreign coinage at certain times, such as the finds from Myddle and Broughton, Shropshire (559) and Hitcham, Suffolk (562), and the large hoard from the Baschurch area, Shropshire (549) has added a significant new corpus of material from the Shrewsbury mint.

The recording of single finds has continued to increase rapidly and a very wide range of coins is being identified, from fine, high denomination gold issues, such as that from Ston Easton, Somerset (566), to low value farthings. Most of the coins found are typical English issues, although earlier post-Conquest coins - such as the coin of William I from Woking, Surrey (564) - remain relatively uncommon, and the range and distribution of foreign coinage continues to expand with more northern and western European coins found every year; examples include that from Brighstone, Isle of Wight (565) and the Hull area, East Yorkshire (567).

HOARDS

545. Bigby, North East Lincolnshire: nine silver pennies (PAS: NLM-145AF6; Treasure: 2007 T172)

Date: Medieval (c. 1207–1210).
Discovery: Found by John Turner while metal-detecting in March 2007, and reported to Lisa Staves (North Lincolnshire FLO).
Description: All of the coins belong to the English Short Cross coinage, Class V.
Vb1/Va2 (1204–1205)
1. Rev: +ARNAVD.ON.CA, mn. Arnaud, m. Canterbury. Weight: 1.32g.
2. Rev: +COLDWINE.ON.C, mn. Coldwine, m. uncertain. Weight: 1.32g.
Vb1 (1205)
3. Rev: +IOhAN.ON.[GI]P[E], mn. Iohan, m. Ipswich. Weight: 1.32g.
Vb2 (1205–1207)
4. Rev: +RICARD.B.ON.LV, mn. Ricard B, m. London (pierced or holed). Weight: 1.28g.
5. Rev: +RAVF.ON.WIN, mn. Rauf, m. Winchester. Weight: 1.37g.
Vb3 (c. 1206)
6. Rev: +GIFREI.ON.NOR, mn. Gifrei, m. Norwich. Weight: 1.32g.
Vc (c. 1207–c. 1210)
7. Rev: +ABEL.ON.LVNDE, mn. Abel, m. London. Weight: 1.38g.

8. Rev: +RAVF.ON[LV]DE, mn. Rauf, m. London. Weight: 1.39g.
9. Rev: +RICARD.ON.LVN, mn. Rauf, m. London (double struck). Weight: 1.3g.
Discussion: All of the coins were minted under King John (r. 1199–1216), who instituted a partial re-coinage in 1205 to remove clipped and poor quality coins from currency, although he did not change the general design. The coins do not appear to be significantly worn from use, and the fact there are no coins from classes VI onwards indicates deposition about 1207–1210.
Disposition: Acquired by North Lincolnshire Museum.

B J COOK

546. Dunton, Norfolk: three silver pennies (PAS: NMS-E8BBA3; Treasure: 2007 T275)

Date: Medieval (c. 1140–c. 1160).
Discovery: Found by Malcolm Higginbotham while metal-detecting in February 2007, and reported to Erica Darch (Norfolk FLO).
Description: Found in close proximity to each other, the three coins are all close in date. Two are of Stephen's (r. 1135–1154) first issue, known as the 'Watford' Type (c. 1136–1145, North: 873), the other an uncertain penny of similar date, probably one of North's uncertain Baronial issues (?North: 950).
1. Rev: GODRICV[...], mn. Godric, m. uncertain. Weight: 1.11g.
2. Rev: [...], mn. and m. uncertain. Weight: 1.21g.
3. Obv: ?[...]DTLVACX, ?Bust facing with sceptre. Rev: [..]A[..]:[...], Cross with annulet and pellet in each angle. Weight: 1.38g.
Disposition: British Museum hopes to acquire.

A B MARSDEN

547. Wellow, Bath and North East Somerset: sixteen silver pennies (PAS: SOM-BAA293; Treasure: 2007 T530)

Date: Medieval (late 1230s).
Discovery: Found by Geoffrey Pike and Philip Coombes while metal-detecting in September 2007, and reported to Naomi Payne (Somerset FLO).
Description: Fifteen of the coins belong to the English Short Cross coinage, the remaining coin being from the contemporary Scottish coinage, which mixed freely with the English coinage at this time and was produced to the same standards. This group consists of 11 full pennies and 5 cut halfpennies.
English Short Cross coins
Class I (c. 1180–c. 1189)
1. Ic (c. 1185–1189), mn. Raul, m. London. Weight: 1.32g.
Class III (c. 1189/90–c. 1194)
2. IIIab2 (c. 1190–1194), mn. Roberd, m. Canterbury Weight: 1.16g.
3. IIIab2, mn. Ricard, m. London. Weight: 1.39g.

Class V (c. 1204/5–c. 1209)

4. Cut halfpenny, Vb1 (1205), mn. ?Miles, m. Oxford. Weight: 0.65g.

5. Vb2 (1205–1207), mn. Hu(m)frei, m. Rochester. Weight: 1.48g.

6. Vc (1207–c. 1210), mn. Simon, m. Canterbury. Weight: 1.33g.

7. Cut halfpenny, V(?c), mn. Abel, m. London. Weight: 0.61g.

8. Vc, mn. Willelm B, mn. London. Weight: 1.35g.

Class VII (c. 1218–c. 1242)

9. Cut halfpenny, VIIa2 (1218-20), mn. Henri, m. Canterbury. Weight: 0.56g.

10. VIIb2 (c. 1229–1232), mn. Roger, m. Canterbury. Weight: 1.08g.

11. VIIb2, mn. Roger of R, m. Canterbury. Weight: 1.37g.

12. VIIb3 (c. 1232–1234), mn. Henri, m. Canterbury. Weight: 1.31g.

13. VIIb3, mn. Ioan Chic, m. Canterbury. Weight: 1.05g.

14. VIIb3, mn. Tomas, m. Canterbury. Weight: 1.49g.

15. Cut halfpenny, VIIb4 (c. 1234–1236), mn. Willem, mi Canterbury (double struck). Weight: 0.51g.

William I of Scotland (r. 1165–1214) or posthumous issue

16. Cut halfpenny, Short Cross Phase B (c. 1205–c. 1230), details illegible. Weight: 0.86g.

Discussion: The Wellow coins are mostly from the later classes of the Short Cross period, V–VII, but do not include any issues later than the mid 1230s, suggesting that they represent a single, small group of material taken from currency at about that time, probably around 1236 (the onset of class VIIc, the first issue not represented in the group).

Disposition: Acquired by Roman Baths Museum, Bath.

B J COOK

---

548. Corley, Warwickshire: 170 silver coins (PAS: WMID-2FAAC1; Treasure: 2007 T325 & T569)

Date: Medieval (c. 1260–1265).

Discovery: Found by David Wilcox while metal-detecting in September 2007, and reported to Duncan Slarke (Staffordshire & West Midlands FLO).

Description: The group consist of pennies or cut fractions of the English Long Cross coinage (1247–1279), or contemporary related coinages. Some of the coins survive in more than one fragment, but these are treated as single items for the purposes of this report. English Long Cross types are represented by 159 coins and seven from the accompanying Irish coinage of Henry III (r. 1216–1272); this coinage dates to c. 1251–1254. There are 92 full pennies, 70 cut halfpennies and four cut farthings. The face value of the group was 10 shillings and 8 pence.

English Long Cross coinage

Class 2 (1248)

2a

1. mn. Nicole, m. Winchester. Weight: 1.43g.

2b

2. Cut halfpenny, mn. Nicole, m. Canterbury. Weight: 0.65g.

3. Cut halfpenny, mn. Ieremie, m. York. Weight: 0.72g.

Class 3 (1248–1250)

3a

4. mn. Nicole, m. London. Weight: 1.33g.

5. Cut halfpenny, mn. Gefrei, m. Oxford. Weight: 0.66g.

6. Cut halfpenny, mn. Henri, m. uncertain. Weight: 0.71g.

3a or 3ab

7–8. Cut halfpennies (2007 T569), mn. uncertain, m. London. Weight: 0.65g.

3ab

9. Cut halfpenny (2007 T569), mn. uncertain, m. Bristol. Weight: 0.55g.

10. mn. Nicole, m. Canterbury. Weight: 1.41g.

11. Cut halfpenny, mn. Nicole, m. Canterbury. Weight: 0.72g.

12. mn. Lucas, m. Northampton. Weight: 1.31g.

13. Cut halfpenny (2007 T569), mn. uncertain, m. Northampton. Weight: 0.7g.

14. (2007 T569) mn. Henri, m. Oxford. Weight: 1.33g.

15. Cut halfpenny, mn. Willem, m. Oxford. Weight: 0.67g.

3b

16. Cut halfpenny, mn. Iacob, m. Bristol. Weight: 0.69g.

17. Cut halfpenny, mn. uncertain, m. Exeter. Weight: 0.69g.

18. mn. Lucas, m. Gloucester. Weight: 1.31g.

19. mn. Henri, m. London. Weight: 1.36g.

20–22. mn. Nicole, m. London. Weights: 1.47g, 1.45g & 1.36g.

23. Cut halfpenny, mn. uncertain, m. London. Weight: 0.57g.

24. mn. Philip, m. Northampton. Weight: 1.33g.

25–26. mn. Willem, m. Northampton. Weights: 1.38g & 1.26g.

27. Cut halfpenny, mn. Gefrei, m. Oxford. Weight: 0.59g.

28. mn. Lorenz, m. Shrewsbury. Weight: 1.45g.

29. mn. ?Lorenz, m. Shrewsbury. Weight: 1.32g.

30. mn. Peris, m. Shrewsbury. Weight: 1.35g.

31–32. mn. Willem, m. Wilton. Weights: 1.53g & 1.41g.

33. Cut halfpenny, mn. Huge, m. Winchester. Weight: 0.78g.

34. mn. Rener, m. York. Weight: 1.42g.

35. mn. Tomas, m. York. Weight: 1.45g.

36. Cut halfpenny, mn. Philip, m. uncertain. Weight: 0.68g.

37. Cut halfpenny (2007 T569), mn. Henri, m. uncertain. Weight: 0.61g.

3a–3b

38. Cut halfpenny, mn. Nicole, m. Canterbury. Weight: 0.69g.

39. Cut halfpenny (2007 T569), mn. uncertain, m. Lincoln. Weight: 0.6g.

40. Cut halfpenny, mn. Nicole, m. London. Weight: 0.65g.

41. Cut halfpenny, mn. uncertain, m. Northampton. Weight: 0.72g.

Possibly 3b

42. Cut halfpenny, mn. Nicole, m. London. Weight: 0.66g.

43. Cut halfpenny, mn. uncertain, m. Newcastle. Weight: 0.76g.

44. Cut halfpenny, mn. uncertain, m. Shrewsbury. Weight: 0.52g.

45. Cut halfpenny, mn. uncertain, m. Wilton. Weight: 0.66g.

46. Cut halfpenny, mn. Ion, m. uncertain. Weight: 0.7g.

47. Cut halfpenny (two fragments) (2007 T569), mn. uncertain, m. Wilton or Winchester. Weight: 0.69g.

3bc

48. mn. Ion, m. Lincoln. Weight: 1.41g.

49. mn. Huge, m. Winchester. Weight: 1.45g.

3c

50. (2007 T569) mn. Gilbert, m. Canterbury. Weight: 1.35g.

51. Cut halfpenny, mn. uncertain, m. Lincoln. Weight: 0.76g.

52. Cut halfpenny, mn. Roger, m. Gloucester. Weight: 0.69g.

53. (2007 T569) mn. Nicole, m. London. Weight: 1.33g.

54. mn. Nicole, m. London. Weight: 1.25g.

55. Cut halfpenny (2007 T569), mn. Ricard, m. London. Weight: 0.6g.

56. Cut halfpenny (2007 T569), mn. Rener, m. York. Weight: 0.52g.

3 (undefined)

57. Cut halfpenny (2007 T569), mn. Ierveis, m. Ilchester. Weight: 0.61g.

58. Cut halfpenny, mn. Willem, m. uncertain. Weight: 0.59g.

59. Cut halfpenny, mn. Henri, m. uncertain. Weight: 0.81g.

60–61. Cut halfpennies (2007 T569), mn. uncertain, m. Canterbury. Weights: 0.68g & 0.65g.

62. Cut halfpenny (2007 T569), mn. uncertain, m. Newcastle. Weights: 0.7g.

63. Cut halfpenny (2007 T569), mn. ?Ion, m. York. Weight: 0.64g.

64. Cut halfpenny, mn. and m. uncertain. Weight: 0.63g.

Class 5 (1251–1272)

5a2

65. mn. Willem, m. Canterbury. Weight: 1.43g.

66. mn. Ricard, m. London. Weight: 1.32g.

5a2 or 5a3

67. Cut halfpenny, mn. Gilebert, m. Canterbury. Weight: 0.77g.

68. Cut halfpenny, mn. Henri or Davi, m. London. Weight: 0.69g.

69–71. Cut halfpennies, mn. uncertain, m. London. Weights: 0.69g, 0.76g & 0.64g.

5a3

72. mn. Henri, m. London. Weight: 1.37g.

73. mn. Ricard, m. London. Weight: 1.34g.

5a

74. Cut farthing, mn. Nicole, m. uncertain. Weight: 0.3g.

5a–c

75. Cut halfpenny (2007 T569), mn. Johs/Johanes, m. Canterbury. Weight: 0.59g.

5b2

76–77. mn. Randulf, m. Bury St Edmunds. Weights: 1.47g & 1.38g.

78. mn Gilebert, m. Canterbury. Weight: 1.39g.

79. mn. Nicole, m. Canterbury. Weight: 1.43g.

80. (2007 T569) mn. Nicole, m. Canterbury. Weight: 1.43g.

81–82. mn. Nicole, m. Canterbury. Weights: 1.39g & 137g.

83. (2007 T569) mn. Nicole, m. Canterbury. Weight: 1.35g.

84. mn Willem, m. Canterbury. Weight: 1.39g.

85. (2007 T569) mn. Willem, m. Canterbury (fragment missing from coin). Weight: 1.25g.

86. mn. Willem, m. Canterbury. Weight: 1.23g.

87. Cut halfpenny (2007 T569), mn. uncertain, m. Canterbury. Weight: 0.62g.

88. mn. Henri, m. London. Weight: 1.42g.

89–90. mn. Nicole, m. London. Weights: 1.52g & 1.5g.

91. (2007 T569) mn. Nicole, m. London. Weight: 1.46g.

92. mn. Nicole, m. London. Weight: 1.37g.

93. Cut halfpenny, mn. Nicole, m. London. Weight: 0.75g.

94. Cut halfpenny, mn. uncertain, m. London. Weight: 0.82g.

5b or 5c

95. Cut halfpenny, mn. Iohs, m. Canterbury. Weight: 0.67g.

96. Cut halfpenny, mn. Henri, m. London. Weight: 0.76g.

97. mn. Ricard, m. London (double struck coin). Weight: 1.19g.

98–99. Cut halfpenny, mn. uncertain, m. London. Weights: 0.74g & 0.61g.

100. (2007 T569) Cut farthing, mn. uncertain, m. Canterbury. Weight: 0.38g.

101. (2007 T569) Cut halfpenny, mn. Nicole, m. uncertain. Weight: 0.58g.

5c

102. mn. Gilebert, m. Canterbury. Weight: 1.21g.

103. mn. Ion, m. Canterbury. Weight: 1.4g.

104. mn. Robert, m. Canterbury (coin is incomplete and in two fragments). Weight: 1.23g.

105. mn. Willem, m. Canterbury. Weight: 1.42g.

106. Cut halfpenny, mn. uncertain, m. Canterbury. Weight: 0.65g.

107. mn. Davi, m. London. Weight: 1.08g.

108. mn. Henri, m. London (double struck coin). Weight: 1.59g.

109. (2007 T569) mn. Henri, m. London. Weight: 1.45g.

110–111. mn. Henri, m. London. Weights: 1.45g & 1.31g.

112. Cut halfpenny, mn. Henri, m. London. Weight: 0.81g.

113. Cut halfpenny (2007 T569), mn. Henri, m. London. Weight: 0.73g.

114. mn. Iohs, m. London. Weight: 1.37g.

115–116. mn. Ricard, m. London. Weights: 1.38g (for both).

117. Cut halfpenny, mn. Ricard, m. London. Weight: 0.57g.

118. mn. Willem, m. London. Weight: 1.46g.

5f

119. mn. Willem, m. Canterbury. Weight: 1.38g.

5g

120. (2007 T569) mn. Alein, m. Canterbury (coin in two fragments). Weight: 1.41g.

121–122. mn. Gilebert, m. Canterbury (coin 121 is in three pieces). Weights: 1.39g & 1.31g.

123. mn. Iohs, m. Canterbury. Weights: 1.32g.

124.* (2007 T569) mn. Iohanes, m. Canterbury. Weight: 0.52g.

125. mn. Nicole, m. Canterbury. Weight: 1.31g.

126. mn. Robert, m. Canterbury. Weight: 1.48g.

127. (2007 T569) mn. Robert, m. Canterbury. Weight: 1.44g.

128–132. mn. Robert, m. Canterbury. Weights: 1.43g, 1.39g, 1.38g & 1.36g.

133. mn. Walter, m. Canterbury. Weight: 1.44g.

134. Cut halfpenny, mn. Walter, m. Canterbury. Weight: 0.67g.

135. mn. Willem, m. Canterbury (double struck coin). Weight: 1.48g.

136–137. mn. Willem, m. Canterbury. Weights: 1.46g & 1.36g.

138. mn. Henri, m. London. Weight: 1.51g.

139–140. mn. Renaud, m. London. Weight: 1.52g & 1.49g.

141. (2007 T569) mn. Renaud, m. London. Weight: 1.49g.

142. mn. Renaud, m. London (coin is in two fragments). Weight: 1.47g.

143–150. mn. Renaud, m. London. Weights: 1.45g, 1.44g (x2), 1.43g, 1.42g (x2), 1.38g & 1.37g.

151. (2007 T569) mn. Renaud, m. London. Weight: 1.36g.

152. mn. Renaud, m. London. Weight: 1.33g.

153–154.* (2007 T569) mn. Renaud, m. London. Weights: 1.33g & 1.17g.

155. Cut halfpenny, mn. Renaud, m. London. Weight: 0.6g.

156. Cut halfpenny, mn. Tomas, m. London. Weight: 0.63g.

157. Cut halfpenny, mn. uncertain, m. London. Weight: 0.77g.

158. (2007 T569) Cut halfpenny, mn. Nicole, m. uncertain. Weight: 0.68g.

159. Cut halfpenny, mn. Renaud, m. uncertain. Weight: 0.76g.

160. (2007 T569) Cut halfpenny, mn. Renaud, m. uncertain. Weight: 0.62g.

Class 5 (undefined)

161. (2007 T569) Cut halfpenny, mn. uncertain, m. Canterbury. Weight: 0.59g.

162. Cut farthing, mn. uncertain, m. Canterbury. Weight: 0.41g.

163. (2007 T569) Cut halfpenny, mn. Willem, m. uncertain. Weight: 0.69g.

Irish coinage of Henry III
(coinage dates to c. 1251–1254)

1a

164. Cut halfpenny, mn. Ricard, m. Dublin. Weight: 0.77g.

165. Cut halfpenny, mn. Davi, m. Dublin. Weight: 0.59g.

2a

166. mn. Davi, m. Dublin. Weight: 1.44g.

167. mn. Ricard, m. Dublin. Weight: 1.33g.

168. Cut halfpenny, mn. Ricard, m. Dublin. Weight: 0.81g.

2(?b)

169. (2007 T569) Cut halfpenny, mn. Davi, m. Dublin. Weight: 0.66g.

2d

170. Cut farthing, mn. uncertain, m. Dublin. Weight: 0.48g.

Discussion: This find contains coins of generally good weight, with classes ranging from 1 to 5g. The proportions are weighted towards the later Long Cross period and the cut fractions are disproportionately from the older period of the currency. It is highly likely, therefore, that this group represents a batch of material withdrawn from currency and deposited as a group during the issue of class 5g or shortly thereafter – probably in the early to mid 1260s. The presence of so many cut fractions (45% of the coins) is unusual, but not wholly unprecedented in the hoard record of the mid-13th century.

Disposition: Acquired by Warwickshire Museum.

B J COOK

---

549. Baschurch area, Shropshire: 190 silver pennies (PAS: HESH-A5B566; Treasure: 2007 T545)

Date: Medieval (c. 1265–1270).

Discovery: Found while metal-detecting in August 2007, and reported to Peter Reavill (Herefordshire & Shropshire FLO).

Description: All but one of the coins are official English silver pennies of King Henry III (r. 1216–1272), from the Long Cross coinage (issued 1247–1279). The remaining coin is a contemporary Scottish penny of King Alexander III (r. 1249–1286), which would have been struck to the same standards and would also have circulated in England during this period.

Class 3 (1248–1250)

3a

1. mn. ?Henri, m. London. Weight: 1.41g.

2–3. mn. Nicole, m. London. Weights: 1.36g & 1.34g.

4. Cut halfpenny, mn. Nicole, m. London. Weight: 0.68g.

5. mn. Ion, m. Gloucester. Weight: 1.23g.
6. mn. Nicole, m. uncertain. Weight: 1.24g.
7. mn. and m. uncertain. Weight: 1.4g.

3ab1
8. mn. Elis, m. Bristol. Weight: 1.44g (die duplicate in the British Museum).
9. mn. Ion, m. Exeter. Weight: 1.55g.
10. mn. Ierveis, m. Ilchester. Weight: 1.41g.
11. mn. Ion, m. Lincoln. Weight: 1.42g.
12. mn. Ricard, m. Lincoln. Weight: 1.47g.
13. mn. Walter, m. Lincoln. Weight: 1.2g.
14. mn. Willem, m. Northampton. Weight: 1.34g.
15–18. mn. Lorenz, m. Shrewsbury. Weights: 1.42g, 1.4g, 1.39g & 1.34g.
19–28. mn. Nicole, m. Shrewsbury. Weight: 1.49g, 1.47g, 1.45g, 1.43g, 1.37g (x2), 1.35g, 1.34g, 1.33g & 1.28g.
29. mn. Peris, m. Shrewsbury. Weight: 1.4g.
30–59. mn. Ricard, m. Shrewbury. Weights: 1.52g, 1.49g, 1.48g (x2), 1.46g (x4), 1.45g, 1.44g, 1.43g (x2), 1.42g (x2), 1.41g (x2), 1.4g, 1.39g (x2), 1.38g, 1.37g, 1.36g (x2), 1.35g, 1.34g (x2), 1.33g, 1.32g, 1.31g & 1.26g.
60. mn. Uncertain, m. Shrewbury. Weight: 1.48g.
61. mn. and m. uncertain. Weight: 1.0g.

3b
62. mn. Walter, m. Bristol. Weight: 1.49g.
63–64. mn. Nicole, m. Canterbury. Weights: 1.46g & 1.39g.
65. mn. Robert, m. Exeter. Weight: 1.46g.
66. mn. Ion, m. Lincoln. Weight: 1.41g.
67. mn. Henri, m. London. Weight: 1.41g.
68. mn. Nicole, m. London. Weight: 1.54g.
69. mn. Roger, m. Newcastle. Weight: 1.41g.
70. mn. Willem, m. Northampton. Weight: 1.33g.
71. mn. Huge, m. Norwich. Weight: 1.44g.
72–77. mn. Lorenz, m. Shrewsbury. Weights: 1.44g, 1.43g (x2), 1.39g, 1.34g & 1.37g.
78–121. mn. Nicole, m. Shrewsbury. Weight: 1.54g (x2), 1.51g (x3), 1.5g (x2), 1.48g, 1.46g, 1.45g, 1.44g (x2), 1.43g (x3), 1.42g, 1.41g (x3), 1.4g (x4), 1.39g (x2), 1.38g (x3), 1.37g, 1.36g (x5), 1.35g (x4), 1.35g, 1.28g, 1.26g, 1.25g, 1.2g & 0.94g.
122. mn. Peris, m. Shrewsbury. Weight: 1.26g.
122–136. mn. Ricard, m. Shrewsbury. Weight: 1.53g, 1.51g, 1.49g, 1.47g, 1.46g, 1.45g, 1.43g, 1.42g (x2), 1.39g, 1.37g, 1.36g, 1.35g & 1.34g.
137. mn. Nicole, m. uncertain. Weight: 1.35g.
138–140. mn. and m. uncertain. Weight: 1.42g, 1.5g & 0.77g.

3bc
141. mn. Nicole, m. Shrewsbury. Weight: 1.44g.

3c
142–143. mn. Henri, m. London. Weight: 1.36g & 1.35g.
144. mn. Nicole, m. London. Weight: 1.29g.
145. Cut halfpenny, mn. uncertain, m. Winchester. Weight: 0.7g.

Class 5 (1251–1272)
5a
146. mn. Ion, m. Bury St Edmunds. Weight: 1.43g.
5a2
147. mn. Henri, m. London. Weight: 1.33g.
148. Cut halfpenny, mn. ?Iohan, m. London. Weight: 0.6g.
149. mn. Ricard, m. London. Weight: 1.45g.
5b2
150. mn. Gilebert, m. Canterbury. Weight: 1.04g.
151. mn. Iohs, m. Canterbury. Weight: 1.35g.
152. mn. Ion, m. Canterbury. Weight: 1.48g.
153–155. mn. Nicole, m. Canterbury. Weights: 1.44g, 1.4g & 1.35g.
156. mn. Robert, m. Canterbury. Weight: 1.48g.
157–158. mn. Willem, m. Canterbury. Weights: 1.33g & 1.4g.
159–161. mn. Henri, m. London. Weights: 1.45g, 1.42g & 1.35g.
162–163. mn. Nicole, m. London. Weights: 1.45g & 1.44g.
164–165. mn. Ricard, m. London. Weights: 1.23g & 1.41g.
5c
166. mn. Nicole, m. Canterbury. Weight: 1.48g.
167. mn. Robert, m. Canterbury. Weight: 1.35g.
168. mn. Davi, m. London. Weight: 1.46g.
169–170. mn. Henri, m. London. Weights: 1.45g & 1.42g.
171. mn. Ricard, m. London. Weight: 1.45g.
172. mn. and m. uncertain. Weight: 1.41g.
5a–c
173. mn. Willem, m. Canterbury. Weight: 1.45g.
5b–c
174. mn. Iohs, m. Canterbury. Weight: 1.32g.
175. mn. Henri, m. London. Weight: 1.4g.
176. Cut halfpenny, mn. uncertain, m. London. Weight: 0.57g.
5g
177. mn. Iohanes, m. Canterbury. Weight: 1.39g.
178. mn. Walter, m. Canterbury. Weight: 1.38g.
179–180. mn. Willem, m. Canterbury. Weight: 1.46g & 1.38g.
181. mn. Henri, m. London. Weight: 1.43g.
182–184. mn. Renaud, m. London. Weight: 1.38g, 1.33g & 1.3g.
185. mn. Willem, m. London. Weight: 1.42g.
186. mn. Walter, m. uncertain. Weight: 1.06g.
Uncertain class
187. Cut halfpenny, mn. Nicole, m. uncertain. Weight: 0.8g.
188. mn. and m. uncertain. Weight: 1.5g.
189. mn. and m. uncertain. Weight: 1.28g.
Scottish coinage of Alexander III (First Coinage)
190. Type VII, mn. Alexander, m. Edinburgh. Weight: 1.41g.
191–193. mn. and m. uncertain. Weights: 0.86g, 0.36g & 0.21g.

Discussion: The latest coins present in the group belong to class 5g and were probably issued in the mid to late 1260s. The class 5g pennies present have a mean weight of 1.38g, and are in fact the least good portion of the material. The class 5 coins as a whole average 1.4g.

This is an unusual hoard. Nearly 58% of the coins in the find, 111 in all, originate at the local mint of Shrewsbury, active during 1249–1250 only and long-since closed by the date of issue of the latest coins in the group, those of class 5g. The Shrewsbury role in this hoard is massively disproportionate. The hoard does not seem to reflect the actual output of Shrewsbury, however. It lacks any coins of class 3c and it also does not represent the relative output of the four known moneyers named on the backs of the coins. It seems to be a batch acquired in unusual circumstances, and not taken from general currency. The unusually small proportion of class 5 coins in the hoard might suggest that the group could represent a carefully husbanded savings hoard occasionally augmented as and when this could be afforded.

Disposition: Shropshire County Museum Service hopes to acquire.

B J COOK

---

550. Deopham area, Norfolk: six silver pennies (PAS: EA4080; Treasure: 2007 T676)

Date: Medieval (deposited in the 1310s).
Discovery: Found by Mark Dover while metal-detecting in October 2007, and reported to Erica Darch (Norfolk FLO).
Description: Six silver pennies:
1. Irish (1279–1284), m. Waterford.
2. Class 10ab4 (c. 1303), m. London.
3. Class 10ab5 (c. 1303–1305), m. Canterbury.
4. Class 10cf1 (c. 1305–1306), m. London.
5. Class 10cf2 (c. 1306–1307), m. Bury.
Discussion: The group as found originally constituted six late 13th- to early 14th-century pennies. One was lost prior to handing in, although initial examination by the finder suggested it to be of a similar date to the others. The five surviving coins are all Edward I (r. 1272–1307) Long Cross pennies, one an Irish penny struck at Waterford. This shows signs of wear, the other four being in much better condition. All of these can be dated to a short period at the end of Edward's reign, from 1303 to 1307. The sharp condition of the four later coins makes it likely that the putative purse containing these coins was lost not long after this date, probably between c. 1310 and c. 1320.
Disposition: Norwich Castle Museum hopes to acquire.

A B MARSDEN

---

551. West Wratting, Cambridgeshire: 11 silver pennies (PAS: CAMHER-9B9C48; Treasure: 2007 T619)

Date: Medieval (deposited in the 1320s).
Discovery: Found by Ian and Susan James while metal-detecting in September and October 2007, and reported to Quinton Carroll (Historic Environment Team Manager, Cambridgeshire County Council).
Description: English issues of Edward I (r. 1272–1307) and Edward II (r. 1307–1327). There are 10 pennies, several of which are fragmentary, and one halfpenny.
1. Edwardian sterling imitation struck over a Namur sterling of Gui de Dampiene (Chalon 53; De May 69).
2. Class 5b (1289–1291), m. Canterbury. Weight: 1.25g (damaged).
3–5. Class 10cf2a (1306–1307), m. London. Weights: 1.2g, 1.27g & 1.37g.
6. Class 10cf2b (1306–1307), m. Canterbury. Weight: 1.34g.
7. Class 10cf2b (1306–1307), m. London. Weight: 1.24g (Mayfield lettering).
8. Class 10c3b1 (1307–1309), m. London. Weight: 1.09g (damaged).
9. Class 11b2 (late 1310–1314), m. London. Weight: 1.38g.
10. Class 14 (c. 1317–1320), m. Canterbury. Weight: 1.17g (damaged).
11. Halfpenny, Wither type 6 (c. 1292–1296), m. London. Weight: 0.63g.
Discussion: The latest coin present is of class 14, dated to c. 1317–1320.
Disposition: Fitzwilliam Museum, Cambridge, hopes to acquire.

B J COOK, M ALLEN & M PHILLIPS

---

552. Pinchbeck, Lincolnshire: eight medieval silver pennies and two silver halfpennies (PAS: LIN-C337E3, C32352, C31AD1, C30EF5, C30795, C300A3, C2E9D4, C2D313, C2A913, C291E6; Treasure: 2007 T252)

Date: Medieval (c. 1216–c. 1413).
Discovery: Found by Simon Loveley while metal-detecting in January 2007, and reported to Adam Daubney (Lincolnshire FLO).
Description: Eight hammered pennies and two cut halfpennies ranging in date from Henry III to Henry IV (1216–1413).
Henry II (r. 1154–1189)
1. Cut halfpenny, im. cross and crosslets (1158–1180), undefined type, mn. and m. uncertain.
Henry III (r. 1216–1272)
2. Short Cross, Class 7a (1217–1222). Rev: SIMON ON CANT, mn. Simon, m. Canterbury.
3. Short Cross, Class 8b (c. 1242–1247). Rev: NICOLE ON CANT, mn. Nicole, m. Canterbury.
4. Long Cross, Class 3ab (1248–1250). Rev: ROG/ER O/N G[ ], mn. Roger, m. Gloucester.

5. Long Cross, Class 5c (1251–1272). Rev: IOH'/SON/LVNDEN, mn. Iohan, m. London.

6. Cut halfpenny, Long Cross, Class 5 (1251–1272). Rev: WIL[LEM ON CANT]OR, mn. Willem, m. ?Canterbury.

Edward I (r. 1272–1307)

7. Class 1c (1279), m. London.

8. ?Class 9b (c. 1299–1300/1), m. York.

Edward III (r. 1327–1377)

9. Halfpenny, third coinage (1344–1351) (North: 1131), m. London.

Henry IV (r. 1399–1413)

10. Halfpenny, m. York.

Disposition: Not Treasure; returned to finder.

A DAUBNEY

---

553. Llanharry, Rhondda Cynon Taff: seven silver pennies (PAS: NMGW-9E0F60; Treasure: Wales 07.04)

Date: Medieval (deposited in the 1240s).

Discovery: Found by Michael Wareham whilst metal-detecting in February 2007, and reported to Mark Lodwick (Finds Co-ordinator, Wales).

Description: Six pennies and two cut halfpennies, of English Short Cross type:

1. cut halfpenny, Vb, mm. Iohan. Weight: 0.74g.
2. Vb2, mm. Hue, m. Canterbury. Weight: 1.37g.
3. cut halfpenny, Vc–VIc, mm. Walter, m. London. Weight: 0.73g.
4. VIIa, mm. Norman, m. Bury. Weight: 1.32g.
5. VIIa, mm. Terri, m. London. Weight: 1.24g.
6. VIIb, mm. Iohan (FR?), m. Canterbury. Weight: 1.55g.
7. VIIcA, mm. Nichole, m. London. Weight: 1.43g.
8. VIIc, mm. Nichole, m. London. Weight: 1.25g.

Discussion: A small scattered hoard, buried or lost in the 1240s.

Disposition: Disclaimed; returned to landowner and finder.

E M BESLY

---

554. Ysceifiog, Flintshire: three silver pennies (PAS: NMGW-9E40C5; Treasure: Wales 07.5)

Date: Medieval (c. 1310–c. 1315).

Discovery: Found by Peter Jones, the first while field walking in search of flints in July 2006, and two further coins found while metal-detecting between February and March 2007, and reported to Mark Lodwick (Finds Co-ordinator, Wales).

Description: Three pennies of Edward I–II (r. 1272–1327), and dated to c. 1307–14.

1. 10cf3, m. London. Weight: 1.23g.
2. 11a, m. London. Weight: 1.31g.
3. 11c, m. Canterbury. Weight: 1.21g.

Discussion: The coins are relatively unworn and original association likely.

Disposition: Acquired by Flintshire County Museums Service.

E M BESLY

---

555. Low Apley, Lincolnshire: 146 silver pennies (PAS: LIN-747367; Treasure: 2007 T229)

Date: Medieval (1317–1320).

Discovery: Found by John Blakely while metal-detecting in April 2007, and reported to Adam Daubney (Lincolnshire FLO).

Description: 146 silver pennies, with 143 issued by Edward I and Edward II; 139 are from English mints, and two are from Berwick-on-Tweed. The non-English coins comprise two contemporary Irish coins, two pennies issued by King Alexander III of Scotland and one continental sterling imitation of Count Arnold of Looz. Edward I (r. 1271–1307) and Edward II (r. 1307–1327)

Class 2 (1280)

1. 2b, m. Durham. Weight: 1.34g.

Class 3 (1280–1281)

2. 3c, m. Bristol. Weight: 1.22g.
3. 3c, m. Lincoln. Weight: 1.42g.
4. 3c, m. London. Weight: 1.39g.
5. 3c, m. York. Weight: 1.37g.
6. 3g, m. Canterbury. Weight: 1.34g.
7. 3g, m. Lincoln. Weight: 1.23g.
8–9. 3g, m. London. Weight: 1.36g & 1.32g.

Class 4 (1282–1289)

10. 4a1, m. London. Weight: 1.38g.
11. 4a4, m. Canterbury. Weight: 1.35g.
12–15. 4b, m. Canterbury. Weight: 1.43g, 1.39g, 1.38g & 1.25g.
16–18. 4b, m. London. Weight: 1.41g, 1.4g & 1.38g.
19. 4c, m. London. Weight: 1.37g.
20. 4d, m. Canterbury. Weight: 1.38g.
21. 4e/c, m. London. Weight: 1.41g.

Class 5 (1289–1291)

22. 5b, m. London. Weight: 1.42g.

Class 8 (1294–1299)

23. 8b, m. London. Weight: 1.37g.

Class 9 (c. 1299 to end 1300/early 1301)

24. 9a1, m. Canterbury. Weight: 1.13g (barred N; barred A on rev).
25. 9a2, m. London. Weight: 1.33g (star).
26. 9b1, m. Canterbury. Weight: 1.41g (star, unbarred Ns).
27. 9b1, m. Canterbury. Weight: 1.37g (no star, unbarred Ns).
28. 9b1, m. Canterbury. Weight: 1.38g (no star, pothook/unbarred Ns).
29. 9b1, m. Canterbury. Weight: 1.4g (star, pothook Ns).
30. 9b1, m. Kingston-upon-Hull. Weight: 1.38g (star, barred Ns).
31. 9b1, m. London. Weight: 1.39g (star, unbarred/pothooks).
32–33. 9b1, m. London. Weights: 1.4g & 1.35g (star, unbarred Ns).
34. 9b1, m. London. Weight: 1.34g (star, barred Ns).
35. 9b1, m. London. Weight: 1.35g (no star, barred Ns).
36. 9b1, m. London. Weight: 1.4g (no star, unbarred Ns).
37. 9b1, m. Newcastle. Weight: 1.38g (star, unbarred Ns).

38. 9b1, m. Newcastle. Weight: 1.17g
(no star, unbarred Ns).
39. 9b1, m. York. Weight: 1.28g (star, unbarred Ns).
40. 9b1, m. York. Weight: 1.42g (no star, unbarred Ns).
41–42. 9b2, m. Canterbury. Weights: 1.43g & 1.26g
(star, unbarred Ns).
43. 9b2, m. London. Weight: 1.38g
(star, unbarred/pothooks).
44–45. 9b2, m. London. Weights: 1.42g & 1.34g
(star, unbarred Ns).
Class 10 (early 1301 to late 1310)
10ab1 (early 1301)
46. 10ab1(b), m. London, Weight: 1.39g (pothooks).
47. 10ab1(b), m. Newcastle, Weight: 1.34g (barred N).
10ab2 (mid 1301 to early 1302)
48. 10ab2, m. London. Weight: 1.4g (unbarred).
49. 10ab2 m. London. Weight: 1.4g (pothooks).
10ab3 (c. early 1302 to c. early 1303)
50. 10ab3(a), m. Durham. Weight: 1.37g.
51. 10ab3(a), m. London. Weight: 1.4g
(flat S; unbarred Ns).
52. 10ab3(b), m. Canterbury. Weight: 1.3g.
10ab5 (c. mid 1303 to c. mid 1305)
53. 10ab5 (early type), m. Canterbury. Weight: 1.4g.
54. 10ab5 (late type), m. Canterbury. Weight: 1.33g.
55. 10ab5 (late type), m. Durham. Weight: 1.31g
(cross moline).
56–58. 10ab5 (late type), m. London. Weights: 1.44g,
1.43g & 1.41g.
10ab6 (c. mid 1305)
59. 10ab6, m. Canterbury. Weight: 1.44g.
60. 10ab6, m. London. Weight: 1.41g.
10cf1 (c. mid 1305 to c. mid 1306)
61. 10cf1, m. Canterbury. Weight: 1.42g.
62. 10cf1, m. Durham. Weight: 1.35g (cross moline).
63. 10cf1, m. London. Weight: 1.43g.
10cf2 (c. mid 1306 to c. mid 1307)
64–65. 10cf2(a), m. Canterbury. Weights: 1.44g & 1.2g.
66–67. 10cf2(a), m. Durham. Weights: 1.34g & 1.2g
(cross moline).
68. 10cf2(a), m. London. Weight: 1.42g.
69–73. 10cf2(a), m. London. Weights: 1.42g, 1.41g (x2),
1.4g & 1.37g (Mayfield lettering).
74. 10cf2(b), m. Bury St Edmunds. Weight: 1.39g.
75. 10cf2(b), m. Canterbury. Weight: 1.37g.
10cf3 (c. mid 1307 to c. early 1309)
76. 10cf3(a2), m. London, Weight: 1.39g.
77–81. 10cf3(a3), m. Canterbury. Weights: 1.44g (x2),
1.43g, 1.42g & 1.37g.
82. 10cf3(a3), m. Durham. Weight: 1.42g (cross moline).
83. 10cf3(a3), m. Durham. Weight: 1.39g
(cross illegible).
84. 10cf3(a3), m. London. Weight: 1.35g.
85–86. 10cf3(b1), m. Canterbury.
Weights: 1.44g & 1.35g.
87–94. 10cf3 (b1), m. London. Weights: 1.45g, 1.43g
(x2), 1.42g, 1.4g, 1.38g (x2) & 1.36g.
95–97. 10cf3(b2), m. London.
Weights: 1.45g, 1.37g & 1.18g.

10cf5 (c. mid 1309 to late 1310)
98. 10cf5(a1), m. Bury St Edmunds. Weight: 1.32g.
99. 10cf5(a1), m. London. Weight: 1.36g.
100. 10cf5(a1), m. London. Weight: 1.37g
(Obv: EDWARR).
101. 10cf5(a2), m. Canterbury. Weight: 1.39g.
102–103. 10cf5(a2), m. London.
Weights: 1.42g & 1.37g.
104. 10cf5(b), m. Canterbury. Weight: 1.4g.
105. 10cf5(b), m. Durham. Weight: 1.4g.
106. 10cf5(b), m. London. Weight: 1.42g.
Class 11 (c. late 1310 to c. 1314)
107. 11a1, m. London. Weight: 1.31g.
108. 11a2, m. Canterbury. Weight: 1.38g.
109–110. 11a2, m. London. Weights: 1.45g & 1.41g.
111. 11a3, m. Durham. Weight: 1.43g
(crozier end; Obv: TAS:).
112. 11b1, m. Canterbury. Weight: 1.39g.
113. 11b1, m. Durham. Weight: 1.52g (crozier end).
114. 11b2, m. Canterbury. Weight: 1.37g.
115. 11b2 m. Canterbury. Weight: 1.39g
(Obv: EDWARR).
116. 11b2, m. London. Weight: 1.43g.
117–119. 11b3, m. Canterbury.
Weights: 1.42g, 1.4g & 1.37g.
120. 11b3, m. Canterbury. Weight: 1.37g
(Obv: EDWARR).
121–122. 11b3, m. Durham. Weights: 1.45g & 1.3g
(crozier end).
123. 11b3, m. London. Weight: 1.34g.
124–125. 11b3 m. London. Weights: 1.44g & 1.41g
(Obv: EDWARR).
126. 11c, m. Bury St Edmunds. Weight: 1.44g.
127. 11c, m. Canterbury. Weight: 1.42g.
Class 13 (c. 1315 to c. 1317)
128. m. Durham. Weight: 1.42g (crozier end).
129. m. London. Weight: 1.44g.
Class 14 (c. 1317–1320)
130. m. Bury St Edmunds. Weight: 1.39g.
131–138. m. Canterbury. Weights: 1.46g, 1.44g, 1.42g,
1.4g (x3), 1.39g & 1.37g.
139. m. Durham. Weight: 1.41g (new E).
Coinage of Berwick-upon-Tweed
Class 4 (c. 1300–c. 1310)
140. 4b. Weight: 1.3g.
141. 4c. Weight: 1.29g.
Irish coinage of Edward I (r. 1272–1307)
Class 4 (c. 1297–1302)
142–143. 4a, m. Dublin. Weights: 1.46g & 1.44g.
King Alexander III of Scotland (r. 1249–1286)
Second coinage (c. 1280–1286)
144. Mc1. Weight: 1.38g (24 points on stars).
145. D1. Weight: 1.37g (26 points on stars).
Count Arnold of Looz (r. 1279–1323)
146. Sterling (Mayhew 1983: 76) Weight: 1.25g.
Discussion: The coinage of Edward I and Edward II
forms one continuous series from the coinage reform
of 1279 and just into the reign of Edward III, the coins

ranging from class 2 (1280) to class 14 (c. 1317–1320). The Irish coinage of Edward I and the contemporary Scottish coinage were struck to the same standards as the main English series and all circulated together within the British Isles in this period. Imitations of the English penny entered England in large numbers in the 1290s, but most were removed in a partial recoinage in c. 1300. However, examples in later hoards demonstrate that a number either survived this campaign or else entered English currency after that date. The coins found at Low Apley are mostly of very good weight, indicating a degree of selection and, also, there are no examples of the lesser denominations, halfpennies and farthings. The bulk of the coins present were issued after the partial recoinage of c. 1300, so the classes present do not evenly represent output across the Edwardian series.

Disposition: The Collection, Lincoln, had hoped to acquire but withdrew; returned to finder.

B J COOK

---

556. Astleys, Coventry, West Midlands: 38 silver pennies (PAS: NARC-0331C3; Treasure: 2007 T513)

Date: Medieval (deposited in the 1330s).
Discovery: Found by Northamptonshire Archaeology in July 2006 during excavation of a 13th- or 14th-century building; occupation on the site had continued into the 20th century. The coins were found stacked in the remains of a cylindrical wooden container concealed under the beaten-earth floor surface (Curteis 2008: 428-30). They were reported to Fi Hitchcock (Treasure Registrar) in 2007.
Description: 38 coins of Edward I to early Edward III (r. 1327–1377), including two contemporary Continental imitations. The overall date range is c. 1280–1335. The latest coin shows little wear indicating that the hoard was closed, and potentially deposited, in the early 1330s, which is supported by the lack of more common later coins.
Edward I (r. 1272–1307)
1–3. Class 2, m. London (x3).
4–10. Class 3, m. Bristol, Canterbury, Durham & London (x4).
11–12. Class 4, m. Canterbury & London.
13–14. Class 9, m. Bury & London.
Edward I–III (r. 1272–1377)
15–27. Class 10, m. Bury, Canterbury (x5) & London (x7).
28–30. Class 11, m. Canterbury (x2) & London.
31. Class 14, m. Canterbury.
32–34. Class 15, m. Bury, Canterbury & London.
Berwick mint (c. 1300–1312)
35. Class 4.
36. Class 5.
37–38. Continental sterlings (x2).
Discussion: The composition of the hoard is as expected from the evidence of contemporary hoarding, with a predominance of issues from Class 10, followed

by Class 3. The dominance of London, Canterbury and Durham is also not unexpected. The 38 pennies total a value of 3s.2d, and this was not an inconsequential amount at the time. The average daily pay of a labourer in the 1330s was 1 to 2d and 3 to 4d per day for a craftsmen, a pair of shoes cost 6d, while rent on a peasant's cottage was in the region of 5s year or 20s for a craftsmen's house (Dyer 1989: 175, 206–208).
Disposition: Acquired by Herbert Museum & Art Gallery, Coventry, with the main site archive; the landowner donated their share.

P MASON, I SODEN & M CURTEIS

---

557. Bonvilston, Vale of Glamorgan: two silver groats and a half groat (PAS: NMGW-9E6076; Treasure: Wales 07.03)

Date: Medieval (deposited in c. 1360).
Discovery: Found by Malcolm Pascoe and Steve Beverstock while metal-detecting between December 2006 and January 2007, and reported to Mark Lodwick (Finds Co-ordinator, Wales).
Description: two silver groats and a half groat of Edward III (r. 1327–77):
1. Groat, Series D/C, m. London. Weight: 4.52g.
2. Groat, Series F, m. London. Weight: 4.33g.
3. Halfgroat, Series E, m. York. Weight: 2.23g.
Disposition: Disclaimed; returned to the finders.

E M BESLY

---

558. Kirkby Stephen, Cumbria: 12 silver coins (PAS: LANCUM-F4A696; Treasure: 2007 T370)

Date: Medieval (deposited in the late 1360s).
Discovery: Found by Sharon Hastewell while metal-detecting in July 2007, and reported to Dot Boughton (Cumbria & Lancashire FLO).
Description: The group consists of one silver coin of Edward I and eleven of Edward III. The latest coins date to the period 1363–1369. The find consists of four groats, two halfgroats and six pennies.
Edward I (r. 1272–1307)
1. Penny, class 3b (1280–1281), m. Canterbury. Weight: 0.9g.
Edward III (r. 1327–1377), Fourth Coinage (1351–1377)
Pre-Treaty period (1351–1360)
2. Groat, Series E (1354–1355), m. York. Weight: 4.64g.
3. Groat, Series E (1354–1355), m. London. Weight: 4.56g.
4. Groat, Series Ga (1356–1361), m. London. Weight: 4.62g.
5. Groat, Series Gb (1356–1361), m. London. Weight: 4.53g.
6. Halfgroat, Series C (1351–1352), m. London. Weight: 2.22g.
7. Halfgroat, Series E (1354–1355), m. York. Weight: 2.31g.

8. Penny, Series Gg (1356–1361), m. Durham.
Weight: 1g.
Treaty Transitional Period (1361–1369)
9. Penny (N1229/1), m. Durham. Weight: 1.15g.
Treaty Period (1361–1369)
10–12. Penny, m. York (N1268) Weights: 1.13g, 1.11g
& 1.07g.
Discussion: Face value: 2s. 2d. The range and the
condition of coins are appropriate for the mid 14th
century. It is noticeable that the most recent coins are
from the northern mints of Durham and York, although
these were beginning to take the lead in the production
of pennies at this period anyway.
Disposition: Penrith Museum had hoped to acquire but
withdrew; returned to landowner.

B J COOK

---

559. Myddle and Broughton, Shropshire (addenda):
4 gold *doblas* (PAS: LVPL-E09DD8;
Treasure: 2007 T534)

Date: Medieval (deposited in the late 1360s–1370s).
Discovery: Found by Stanley Bulmer while metal-
detecting in September 2007, and reported to Frances
McIntosh (North West FLO).
Description: The coins are all gold *doblas* of King Pedro
I of Castile (Pedro the Cruel, r. 1350–1369). All the
coins were struck at the Seville mint, the main mint of
Castile. They are of good weight and are in generally
good condition, with slight indications of wear, so they
have seen some circulation.
Discussion: Finds of 14th-century gold coins are not
common in England. Documentary sources indicate
that foreign gold coins were regularly encountered until
about 1350, although these were generally Florentine
florins and French *écus*. The *doblas* can be considered
a very rare find. Perhaps finds of Pedro I should not be
surprising, since the sons of King Edward III
(r. 1327–1377) were heavily involved in Castilian
politics. The coins found at Myddle and Broughton
could well have been in the possession of a follower
of Edward, the Black Prince (1330–1376), who had
returned from the 1367 campaign to Castile. For
the original find of five coins acquired by the British
Museum, and for further discussion, see *TAR* 2005/6
no. 118.
Disposition: Acquired by Shropshire County
Museum Service.

B J COOK

---

560. Beulah Hill, Croydon, Greater London
(addenda): 12 gold and silver coins (PAS: LON-
5B20D4; 5B4B26; 5B52F7 ; 5B5AF7; 5B6003; 5B6603;
5B6B52; 5B70D4; 5B84C3; 5B8B28; 5B9254; 5B99C3;
Treasure: 2007 T173)

Date: Medieval (deposited in the late 14th century).
Discovery: Found by Joy Hulme while gardening in April
1953, but held back when the original 138-coin hoard
was reported and declared Treasure Trove at that time.
Found and reported to Fi Hitchcock (Treasure Registrar)
by Mr Hulme, while settling his late wife's estate.
Description: The group consists of one silver coin of
Edward I, six gold and four silver coins of Edward III, and
one silver coin of David II of Scotland. The latest coins
date to the period 1363–1369.
Edward I (r. 1272–1307)
1. Penny, 4b (1282–1289), m. Canterbury.
Weight: 1.05g.
Edward III (r. 1327–1377)
Fourth Coinage, Pre-Treaty period (1351–1361)
2. Gold noble, Series C (1351–1352). Weight: 7.69g.
3. Gold noble, Series E (1354–1355). Weight: 7.73g.
4. Gold noble, Series Gb/c (1356–1361). Weight: 7.71g.
5. Gold noble, Series Gd (1356–1361). Weight: 7.75g.
6. Groat, Series E/D (1354–1355), m. York.
Weight: 4.62g.
7. Groat, Series E (1354–1355), m. London.
Weight: 4.7g.
8. Groat, Series Gb/d (1356–1361), m. London.
Weight: 4.62g.
Fourth Coinage, Treaty period (1361–1369)
9. Gold quarter-noble, a/4. Weight: 1.92g.
10. Gold quarter-noble, b/1. Weight: 1.93g.
11. Halfgroat, f. Weight: 2.13g.
David II of Scotland (r. 1329–1371)
Second Coinage (1333–1367)
12. Groat, A (S.5094), m. Edinburgh. Weight: 4.67g.
Discussion: The Beulah Hill hoard as originally reported
consisted of 138 coins, including 14 of gold, with the
latest issues belonging to the period 1361–1369. The
recently declared coins are all of types also represented
in the older material, including the presence of
pennies of Edward I and a groat of David II of Scotland.
Although the new coins would not affect the dating
of the hoard, they are important because they
significantly alter its profile, by more than doubling the
quantity of gold coins present. The face value of the
original group was £3 15s. 10d., £2 of which was the
value of the 14 gold coins. The new group has a face
value of £1 11s. 7d., of which the gold coins comprised
£1 10s.
Disposition: Acquired by the Museum of London under
Treasure Trove, to join the original hoard.

B J COOK

561. Swindon area, Wiltshire: three silver coins (PAS: WILT-28BAF7; Treasure: 2007 T467)

Date: Medieval (deposited in about the 1460s).
Discovery: Found in August 2007 while metal-detecting topsoil removed by machine from within 1–2m of the excavated area of 2006 T369, and reported to Katie Hinds (Wiltshire FLO).
Description and discussion: The find consists of two pennies and a single halfgroat covering the period from Edward III to Henry VI (1st reign). These fall within the date range for the Swindon Hoard (2006 T369), with coins 2 and 3 in a similar bright condition to those from the previously declared hoard, indicating that these also belong together as a hoard, probably as part of 2006 T369 (see *TAR* 2005/6, no.1193).
Edward III (r. 1327–1377)
1. Penny, Pre-Treaty Series A (1351–1361)/Third 'florin' coinage (1344–1351) mule, m. Durham. Weight: 0.75g.
Henry VI (r. 1422–1461)
2. Penny, im. leaf-pellet (1445–1454), m. York (North: 1510). Weight: 0.76g.
3. Halfgroat, im. cross-pellet (1454–1460), m. London (North: 1519). Weight: 1.92g.
Disposition: Disclaimed, returned to finder.

D ALGER & K HINDS

562. Hitcham, Suffolk: Two silver double *patards* (PAS: SF-EAC074; Treasure: 2007 T715)

Date: Medieval (deposited in the late 1460s–1470s).
Discovery: Found by Gerry Fisk while metal-detecting in November 2007, and reported to Faye Minter (Suffolk FLO).
Description: The coins are both examples of the silver double *patard* (also known as the double plack) of Charles the Bold, Duke of Burgundy (r. 1467–1477), striking coins in his capacity as count of Flanders. Obv: +KAROLVS DEI GRA DVX B(VR)G COM FLA (Charles, by the Grace of God, Duke of Burgundy and Count of Flanders). Rev: SIT NOMEN DOMINI BENEDICTVM (Blessed be the name of the Lord).
Discussion: In 1469 a monetary convention between Duke Charles and King Edward IV (r. 1461–1470 and 1471–1483) made the former's coinage in the Low Countries legal tender in England. In practice, only the double *patard* established itself in currency, with a formal valuation equal to the silver groat. The currency of the double *patard* was reinforced by a series of English royal proclamations during the reigns of Henry VII (r. 1485–1509) and Henry VIII (r. 1509–1547), but its role was terminated by the onset of the Great Debasement in 1544 (in practice, there were probably few still in use by this date). However, in the late 15th century and first couple of decades of the 16th, double *patards* of Charles the Bold were a part of the English currency and feature regularly in hoards alongside English groats; they are also recovered as single finds. There have also been a few finds of small groups of double *patards* with no other coins.
Disposition: Moyse's Hall Museum, Bury St Edmunds, had hoped to acquire but withdrew; returned to finder.

B J COOK

563. East Lexham area, Norfolk: 11 silver groats (PAS: NMS-C277B7; Treasure: 2007 T484)

Date: Medieval (deposited in c. 1510–1520).
Discovery: Found by Roman Road Excavations during archaeological excavation over a period of four years concluding in August 2007, and reported to Erica Darch (Norfolk FLO).
Description and discussion: The eleven coins were discovered over a period of four years; the first two during excavations carried out at the site during 2004, the remaining nine in 2007, three during further excavations. Six of these were found while searching with a metal-detector. At this stage it was realised that all eleven coins constituted a dispersed hoard.
The groats vary widely in date from Edward III to Henry VII. The earliest coin is an Edward III Pre-Treaty issue (1351–1361), which is worn and quite heavily clipped. There are seven groats of Edward IV and three of Henry VII. The three latest coins, dating from 1490–1504, show some wear indicating they were in use for at least a few years before being withdrawn from circulation.
Edward III (r. 1327–1377)
1. Groat, Pre-Treaty series D, E, F or G (1352–1361), m. London.
Edward IV (r. 1461–1470 & 1471–1483)
2. Groat, series Va (1464–1465) (North: 1562).
3. Groat, series Vc (1464–1465) (North: 1567).
4. Groat, series VI (1465–1466) (North: 1569).
5–7. Groats, series VII (1466–1467) (North: 1570).
8. Groat, series XXI (1480–1483) (North: 1631).
Henry VII (r. 1485–1509)
9–11. Groats (1490–1504), m. London (North: 1705c).
Disposition: To remain with the site archive at Norwich Castle Museum; the landowner donated his share.

A MARSDEN

SINGLE FINDS

564. Woking, Surrey: cut halfpenny of William I (PAS: SUR-804085)

Date: Medieval (c. 1066–c. 1068).

Discovery: Found by Bob Stonard while metal-detecting, and recorded with David Williams (Surrey FLO).

Description: A cut halfpenny of William I's (r. 1066–1087) 'profile/cross fleury' type (North: 839). Obv: left-facing bust with a sceptre in front, with the inscription 'PILLE[MVS REX]' (King William). Rev: a cross fleury with the inscription 'E[]DRED O[N...]', possibly reading Eadred as the moneyer, but the mint is not shown on this half. Diameter: 18.53mm. Weight: 0.56g.

Discussion: William's coins continued the style of pre-Conquest coinage, citing the king's name on the obverse, and the moneyer and mint on the reverse, and are often found either as whole pennies or, as in this case, cut halfpennies. They are relatively rare finds, with just six recorded by the PAS in 2007, and this is only one of three coins of William I recorded in Surrey on the database.

Disposition: Returned to finder.

D WILLIAMS

565. Brighstone, Isle of Wight: silver Continental sterling penny imitation (PAS: IOW-E77922)

Date: Medieval (c. 1296–c. 1306).

Discovery: Found by Keith Stewart while metal-detecting in March 2007, and recorded with Frank Basford (Isle of Wight FLO).

Description: A complete but damaged imitation of an Edwardian sterling penny, known as a crockard, which has a chaplet of roses rather than a crown on the bust. It was issued at Cambrai (France), probably around 1297–1298, by Gui de Collemède, Bishop of Cambrai. Obv: a front-facing bust with a chaplet of three roses and the inscription '+GVIDO EPISCOPVS' (Bishop Guy). Rev: a long cross with the inscription 'CAM/ERA/CEN/SIS' (of Cambrai) (Mayhew: 99). Diameter: 19mm. Weight: 1.21g.

Discussion: The long cross pennies of Edwardian Type circulated across Continental Europe where they were also heavily imitated. These imitations are not uncommon finds and are known to have entered the country in high numbers until the prohibition on their use in 1299/1300 (Mayhew 1983: 59), and the coin here illustrates how the PAS is helping to further understanding of the circulation of foreign Medieval coinage in England and Wales.

Disposition: Returned to finder.

F BASFORD

566. Ston Easton, Somerset: gold noble of Edward III (r. 1322–1377) (PAS: SOM-BC8B83)

Date: Medieval (c. 1356–c. 1361).

Discovery: Found by Paul Clayton while metal-detecting in July 2007, and recorded with Naomi Payne (Somerset FLO).

Description: A gold noble of King Edward III's Pre-Treaty Series G. Obv: king standing and facing in a ship with the inscription 'EDWARD DEI GRA REX ANGL [Z] FRANC HYB' (Edward, by the grace of God, King of England, France and Ireland). Rev: a central floriated cross with lis at the end of each limb, a lion passant with crown above in each quadrant and the letter 'E' (for Edward) in the centre. The inscription reads 'IHC AVTEM TRANCIENS P MEDIUM ILLORVM IBAT' (But Jesus, passing through the midst of them, went His way).

Discussion: The gold noble was the highest denomination of coinage in Edward III's reign and are quite uncommon finds, this being the first from Somerset on the PAS database. It was minted in the pre-Treaty period, relating to the period immediately prior to the signing of the Treaty of Brétigny (8 May 1360), after which Edward renounced his claim to the French throne, King John II of France was released on ransom, and territories in France (held by the two kings) were ceded to one another.

Disposition: Returned to finder.

N PAYNE & J NAYLOR

567. Hull area, East Yorkshire: silver *Blanc guenar* of Charles VI of France (r. 1380–1422) (PAS: NLM-D883B5)

Date: Medieval (c. 1380–c. 1422).

Discovery: Found by Mike West while metal-detecting in August 2007, and recorded with Lisa Staves (North Lincolnshire FLO).

Description: A silver Blanc *guenar* of Charles VI of France (Duplessy: 377a). Obv: a central shield containing three fleur-de-lis and the inscription '+KAROLVS FRANCORV REX' (King Charles of France). Rev: a cross X with alternating crown of fleur-de-lis in each angle, and the inscription 'SIT nOME DnI BENEDICTV' (Blessed be the name of the Lord). Diameter: 28.3mm. Weight: 2.99g.

Discussion: The circulation of foreign coinage became increasingly controlled during the 14th and into the 15th centuries, initially as a reaction against Continental imitations of English sterling pennies. A petition to the House of Commons in 1423 against base silver 'Blankes' shows that foreign coinage remained a problem, and it is likely that coins such as this were included in this category (Cook 1999: 250–255, 263). It is the first *guenar* of Charles VI recorded by the PAS, and provides evidence that while foreign coin was reaching British shores, its survival was a far rarer occurrence.

Disposition: Returned to finder.

L STAVES & J NAYLOR

568. Ambrosden, Oxfordshire: gold quarter noble of Henry V (r. 1413–1422) (PAS: BUC-B21227)

Date: Medieval (c. 1413–c. 1422).

Discovery: Found by Dave Waxman while metal-detecting in April 2007, and recorded with Ros Tyrrell (Buckinghamshire FLO).

Description: A gold quarter noble of Henry V (North: 1384). Obv: a shield with the arms of England and France with a lis above, and the inscription '+HEnRIC DEI GRA' REX AnGL' (Henry by the Grace of God King of England). Rev: a floriated cross, with a central lis, and a lion passant within each angle and the inscription '+EXALTABITVR In GLORIA' (He shall be exalted in glory). Dimensions: 18.51 x 0.43mm. Weight: 1.71g.

Discussion: The gold coin issues of Henry V have been rare finds, with only eight so far recorded by the PAS, and so this example is a significant find. It is the first quarter noble to be found in Oxfordshire, and only the third recorded by the PAS.

Disposition: Returned to finder.

R TYRRELL

POST-MEDIEVAL COINS (1500 onwards)

The numbers of Post-Medieval coins recorded by the PAS and under the Treasure Act 2003 continues to increase year on year. In 2007, some 3,358 records were made of single finds dated between 1500 and 1800, an increase of over 50% on 2006. Treasure cases remained steady, mostly consisting of a handful of coins rather than anything more substantial, with the exception of 245 coins found in Rutland (577).
The recording of single finds includes a very wide range of material from diverse origins and reflects England's growing role in the world, and a range of connections on a truly global scale, including coins originating in India, such as that found at Laughton, Lincolnshire (584) and another from Bolivia, found at Exeter, Devon (582). Finds made in 2007 have ranged from rare, gold issues, such as that from Linstead Magna, Suffolk (579) to copper-alloy business tokens, including that from Ringmer, East Sussex (581).

HOARDS

569. Basingstoke area, Hampshire: three silver coins (PAS: HAMP-399633, 4A3752 & 4A6FC6; Treasure: 2007 T691)

Date: Post-Medieval (c. 1500–c. 1600).
Discovery: Found by Terry McAnish while metal-detecting in September 2007, and reported to Rob Webley (Hampshire FLO).
Description: A group of three silver coins, consisting of two examples of the silver double *patard* (also known as the double plack) of Duke Charles the Bold of Burgundy (r. 1467–1477), striking coins in his capacity as count of Flanders (no. 2) and duke of Brabant (no. 1). The remaining coin is a groat of the early period of Henry VII's reign (1485–1490), from the London mint.
Duke Charles the Bold of Burgundy (r. 1467–1477)
1. Double *patard* of Charles as Duke of Brabant. Weight: 2.99g.
2. Double *patard* of Charles as Count of Flanders. Weight: 2.91g.
Henry VII (r. 1485–1509)
3. Groat (?North: 1704), m. London. Weight: 2.89g.
Discussion: See comments for the Hitcham find (562).
Disposition: Acquired by Hampshire Museums Service; finder and landowner donated their share.

B J COOK & R WEBLEY

570. Preston area, Lancashire: 11 silver coins, including one Spanish real (PAS: LANCUM-141D42; Treasure: 2007 T241)

Date: Post-Medieval (early 1590s).
Discovery: Found by John Davies while metal-detecting in March 2007, and reported to Dot Boughton (Lancashire & Cumbria FLO).
Description: The group consists of ten silver coins of Elizabeth I and one silver real of the Spanish monarchs Ferdinand and Isabella (r. 1469–1504).
Elizabeth I (r. 1558–1603)
1. Sixpence (1568), im. coronet (1567–1570). Weight: 2.76g.
2. Sixpence (1572), im. ermine (1572–1573). Weight: 2.64g.
3. Sixpence (1575), im. eglantine (1574–1578). Weight: 2.92g.
4. Sixpence (1580), im. plain cross (1580–1581). Weight: 2.74g (in 3 fragments).
5. Groat, im. lis (1558–1560). Weight: 1.74g.
6. Groat, im. cross crosslet (1560–1561). Weight: 1.59g.
7. Groat, im. cross crosslet. Weight: 1.05g.
8. Threepence (1568), im. coronet. Weight: 1.44g.
9. Halfgroat, im. bell (1582/3–1583). Weight: 0.83g.
10. Halfgroat, im. crescent (1587–1589/90). Weight: 0.92g.
Ferdinand and Isabella of Spain (r. 1469–1504); coinage of 1597–1504
11. Real, m. Seville. Weight: 3.23g.
Discussion: The coins include a range of mid-level denominations from the Elizabethan period: four sixpences, three groats, one threepence and two halfgroats, amounting to a sum of 2 shillings and 7 pence. The latest coin dates to around 1590. The Spanish silver coin is much older, but coins of Ferdinand and Isabella do occur in late 16th- and early 17th-century English hoards and it is probable that they entered England perhaps from Scotland or Ireland, where they had formed a significant part of the currency.
Disposition: Harris Museum and Art Gallery, Preston, hopes to acquire.

B J COOK

571. Bures area, Essex: 13 silver coins (PAS: ESS-67D6B4; Treasure: 2007 T279)

Date: Post-Medieval (early 1590s).
Discovery: Found by Danny Reubins while metal-detecting in May 2007, and reported to Laura McLean (Essex FLO).
Description and discussion: The group consists of one coin of Mary I (r. 1553–1558) and twelve coins of Elizabeth I (r. 1558–1603), mostly shillings and sixpences, with just one threepence and a groat.
The face value of the group when deposited was 7s.9d.

Mary I (r. 1553–1558)
1. Groat, im. pomegranate. Weight: 1.64g.
Elizabeth I (r. 1558–1603)
2. Shilling, im. martlet (1560–1561). Weight: 5.75g.
3. Shilling, im. crescent (1587–1589/90). Weight: 6.33g.
4–5. Shillings (x2), im. woolpack (1594–1595/6).
Weights: 3.21g (reverse die has inverted As for V) &
6.13g.
6. Sixpence, im. pheon (1561). Weight: 2.79g.
7. Sixpence, im. lion or coronet (1567). Weight: 2.94g.
8. Sixpence, im. coronet (1567). Weight: 2.76g.
9. Sixpence, im. castle (1571). Weight: 2.71g.
10. Sixpence, im. eglantine (1575). Weight: 2.9g.
11. Sixpence, im. A (1587). Weight: 2.69g.
12. Sixpence, im. hand (1590 over 89). Weight: 2.69g.
13. Threepence, im. ermine (1573). Weight: 1.39g.
Disposition: Acquired by Braintree Museum; the
landowner donated their share.

B J COOK

---

572. West Tanfield, North Yorkshire: three fused six
pences (PAS: WMID-7D3DC2; Treasure: 2007 T703)

Date: Post-Medieval (1500–1700).
Discovery: Found by Patrick Dunne while metal-
detecting in September 2007, and reported to Duncan
Slarke (Staffordshire & West Midlands FLO).
Description and discussion: A group of three coins
which have become fused together, reportedly as
a result of stubble burn. The coins all appear to be
sixpences of Elizabeth I (r. 1558–1603), but the
condition of the visible faces does not currently permit
more precise identification. The finding of three coins
of the same denomination in such close proximity
allows a strong presumption that they were
deposited together.
Disposition: Disclaimed; returned to finder.

B J COOK

---

573. Nailstone, Leicestershire: four silver coins
(PAS: LEICS-CDED85, CDFC75, CE0C74, CE21A5;
Treasure: 2007 T366)

Date: Post-Medieval (c. 1600–c. 1700).
Discovery: Found by Mr G Betts while metal-
detecting in July 2007, and reported to Wendy Scott
(Leicestershire & Rutland FLO). The coins were found
separately over a period of three weeks, and may
constitute a purse loss.
Description: The four coins cover the period of
Elizabeth I and James I, and include English and Irish
issues, and three denominations, a sixpence, halfgroat
and two shillings.
Elizabeth I (r. 1558–1603)
1. Sixpence, im. coronet (1569). Weight: 2.04g.
James I (r. 1603–1625)
2. Halfgroat, First Coinage, im. thistle (1603–1604).
Weight: 1.12g.

3. Shilling, Irish, First Coinage, im. bell (1603–1604).
Weight: 4.14g.
4. Shilling, Irish, Second Coinage, im. ?rose
(1604–1607). Weight: 3.47g.
Discussion: Throughout the 17th century, until the
Great Re-coinage of 1694, the silver coins of Elizabeth
I continued to form a substantial element of the
English currency. James I's Irish coinage was struck to
a lighter weight standard than his English issues, and
Irish shillings were current in England at a reduced tariff
of ninepence and are found quite frequently in English
hoards. Thus the total value of the group in English
terms at the time of deposit was 2s 2d.
Disposition: Disclaimed; returned to finder.

B J COOK & W SCOTT

---

574. West Crewkerne, Somerset: ten silver coins
and an unassociated 19th-century silver bead
(PAS: SOM-8F7413; Treasure: 2007 T223)

Discovery: Found by Michael Charles while metal-
detecting in April 2007, and reported to Naomi Payne
(Somerset FLO).
Date: Deposited in the early 1640s (coins) and 19th
century (bead).
Description: A group of ten coins mostly originating in
the reign of Elizabeth I, with one earlier coin and two
Stuart coins.
Henry VII (r. 1485–1509)
1. Penny, Sovereign Type (c. 1489–1500) (Allen 3i),
m. York under Archbishop Thomas Rotherham.
Weight: 0.63g.
Elizabeth I (r. 1558–1603)
2. Sixpence, im. coronet (1567). Weight: 2.72g.
3. Groat, im. cross crosslet (1560–1561). Weight: 1.48g.
4. Halfgroat, im. uncertain (1558–1572). Weight: 0.56g
(damaged).
5. Halfgroat, im. A (1583–1584/5). Weight: 0.76g.
6. Halfgroat, im. tun (1591/2–1594). Weight: 0.98g.
7. Halfgroat, im. uncertain (1582–1603). Weight: 0.65g.
8. Penny, im. ?key (1595/6–1597/8). Weight: 0.38g.
James I (r. 1603–1625)
9. Shilling, Second or Third Coinage (1604–1625).
Weight: 2.98g†.
Charles I (r. 1625–1649)
10. Shilling, im. star (1640–1641). Weight: 5.87g.
11. A silver bead, with loop for suspension at one end.
It is machine-made and of recent manufacture.
Therefore it bears no relation to the coins reported
with it and cannot be associated with them.
Discussion: It seems reasonable to regard this group
of coins as representing one single deposit, dating to
the early 1640s. In the mid-17th century the currency
consisted overwhelmingly of issues of Elizabeth I,
James I and Charles I, with the older coins increasingly
worn and, in some cases, clipped, and this is reflected
in the coins here, although the low denominations
presumably mean that this particular group is a batch

of material intended for use in daily business rather than being selected for long-term saving and hoarding. The presence of an extremely clipped coin (no. 9) might also confirm this assessment.

The penny of Henry VII is, however, an odd addition. There are one or two 17th-century hoards which contain early Tudor material, presumably re-emerging into use after the termination of the Great Debasement in the mid-16th century, but this coin is very heavy for a penny in the 17th century, and may possibly have functioned more as a halfgroat. Counting it as a penny, the face value of the group as a whole was 3s.8d.

Disposition: Disclaimed; returned to finder.

B J COOK & D THORNTON

---

575. Ham and Stone, Gloucestershire: two silver pennies and a halfgroat with perforations (PAS: GLO-1002D2; Treasure: 2007 T384)

Date: Post-Medieval (deposited in the mid to late 1600s)
Discovery: Found by Mr A Brown while metal-detecting in May 2007, and reported to Kurt Adams (Gloucestershire & Avon FLO).
Description: Two silver pennies, one of Charles I and one of Charles II, and a halfgroat coin of the Commonwealth, all of which have been perforated. On both of the Charles' coins this is behind the bust, and through the top section of the reverse on the Commonwealth coin.
1. Charles I (r. 1625–1649), penny (c. 1632–1634) (North: 2268), 2 pellets. Weight: 0.62g (pierced).
2. Commonwealth (1649–1660), halfgroat (2 pence) (North: 2728). Weight: 0.81g (pierced).
3. Charles II (r. 1660–1685), penny (1660–1662) (North: 2774), hammered issue. Weight: 0.5g (pierced).
Discussion: It is possible the coins were pierced to check fineness.
Disposition: Acquired by Museum in the Park, Stroud.

B J COOK & K ADAMS

---

576. Welshpool, Powys: 40 silver coins and ceramic pot (PAS: NMGW-DDB267; Treasure: Wales 07.12)

Date: Post-Medieval (c. 1650–c. 1700).
Discovery: Found by Simon Stringer while metal-detecting in August 2007, and reported to PAS via Clwyd-Powys Archaeological Trust.
Description: Silver shillings and sixpences of Elizabeth I (r. 1558–1603; 6 shillings, 15 sixpences), James I (r. 1603–25; 6 shillings, 3 sixpences) and Charles I (r. 1625–49; 6 shillings, 4 sixpences), totalling 40 coins with a face value of £1 9s 0d; 18 of the coins were still within the remains of a small black-glazed pottery vessel.
Discussion: The latest coin is a sixpence of Charles I, privy-mark *Sceptre*, in use late 1646–January 1649. This

coin, like almost all others in the hoard, is heavily worn. This factor and the clipping of two James I shillings to their 'inner circles' suggest that the coins may have been deposited as late as the time of the Great Recoinage of 1696–7.

Disposition: Powysland Museum hopes to acquire.

E M BESLY

---

577. Rutland: 245 silver coins (PAS: LEICS-BDA7F1; Treasure: 2007 T139 & 2007 T240)

Date: Post-Medieval (deposited in the late 1680s).
Discovery: Found by Andy Tansley and Rob Coley while metal-detecting in March and May 2007, and reported to Wendy Scott (Leicestershire FLO).
Description: 245 silver coins ranging in date from Elizabeth I to James II, and including both lower and higher denominations.
Elizabeth I (r. 1558–1603)
Shillings:
1–2. (x2) im. cross crosslet (1560–1561). Weights: 5.65g & 4.56g†.
3. im. martlet (1560–1561). Weight: 5.25g.
4. im. escallop (1584/5–1587). Weight: 4.77g†.
5. im. crescent (1587–1589/90). Weight: 5.74g.
6. im. hand (1589/90–1591/2). Weight: 5.77g.
7–10. (x4) im. tun (1591/2–1594). Weights: 5.85g, 5.63g (in two pieces), 5.53g & 5.49g.
11. im. woolpack (1594–1595/6). Weight: 5.5g.
12–13. (x2) im. woolpack (1602–1603). Weights: 5.06g† & 4.41g†.
14. im. uncertain (1583–1603). Weight: 4.76g†.
15.* im. ?tun. Weight: 0.48g.
Sixpences:
16–17. (x2) im. pheon (1561). Weights: 2.53g & 2.52g.
18–20. (x3) im. pheon (1562).
Weights: 2.56g, 2.53g & 2.5g.
21. im. pheon (1564). Weight: 2.37g.
22. im. portcullis (1565). Weight: 2.32g.
23. im. uncertain (1566). Weight: 2.38g.
24–26. (x3) im. coronet (1567).
Weights: 2.66g, 2.51g & 2.45g.
27. (x2) im. coronet (1568). Weights: 2.47g & 2.08g.
28. im. ermine (1572). Weight: 2.69g.
29. im. acorn (1573). Weight: 2.47g.
30–31. (x2) im. eglantine (1575).
Weights: 2.77g & 2.59g.
32. im. eglantine (1576). Weight: 2.58g.
33–34. (x2) im. plain cross (1578).
Weights: 2.48g & 2.43g.
35–36. (x2) im. plain cross (1579).
Weights: 2.54g & 2.46g.
37. im. long cross (1580). Weight: 2.77g.
38–40. (x3) im. long cross (1581).
Weights: 2.88g, 2.68g & 2.65g.
41. im. bell (1582). Weight: 2.76g.
42–45. (x4) im. bell (1583). Weights: 2.54g, 2.53g, 2.38g & 2.35g.

46. im. crescent (1587). Weight: 2.43g.

47. im. hand (1590). Weight: 2.68g.

48–50. (x3) im. hand (1592).
Weights: 2.69g, 2.53g & 2.32g.

51. im. tun (1592). Weight: 2.3g.

52. im. tun (1593). Weight: 2.51g.

53. im. woolpack (1594): Weight: 2.71g.

54. im. key (1596). Weight: 2.56g.

55. im. cypher (1600). Weight: 2.47g.

56. im. 1 (1601).

57. im. 1 (1602). Weight: 2.77g.

58. im. 1 (1602). Weight: 2.68g.

James I (r. 1603–1625)
First Coinage (1603–1604)
Shillings:

59–63. (x5) 2nd bust, im. thistle. Weights: 5.71g, 5.69g,
5.53g, 4.88g & 4.42gt.

64–68. (x5) 2nd bust, im. lis (1604). Weights: 5.42g,
5.39g, 5.18g, 5.02g & 4.29gt.

69. 2nd bust, im. uncertain. Weight: 4.21gt.

Sixpences:

70–71. (x2) 2nd bust, im. thistle (1604).
Weights: 2.71g & 2.37g.

72. 2nd bust, im. uncertain (1604). Weight: 2.22gt.

73–74. (x2) 2nd bust, im. lis (1604).
Weights: 2.56g & 2.5g.

75. Uncertain bust (1603–1604). Weight: 2.65g.

Second Coinage (1604–1619)
Shillings:

76–77. (x2) 3rd bust, im. lis. Weights: 5.73g & 4.87gt.

78–81. (x4) 3rd bust, im. rose (1605–1606). Weights:
5.9g, 5.32g, 4.8gt & 4.58gt.

82. 3rd bust, im. uncertain. Weight: 4.52gt.

83–85. (x3) 4th bust, im. rose.
Weights: 5.66g, 5.56g & 4.85gt.

86–87. (x2) 4th bust, im. escallop (1606–1607).
Weights: 5.61g & 4.52gt.

88–89. (x2) im. grapes (1607). Weights: 5.6g & 4.21gt.

90. im. uncertain. Weight: 4.64gt.

91. 4th or 5th bust, im. coronet (1607–1609).
Weight: 5.16g.

92. 5th bust, im. coronet. Weight: 5.6g.

93. 5th bust, im. trefoil (1613). Weight: 4.76gt.

94–95. 5th bust, im. uncertain.
Weights: 4.58gt & 4.34gt.

Sixpences:

96. 4th bust, im. lis (1604). Weight: 2.39g.

97–99. (x3) 4th bust, im. rose (1605). Weights: 2.72g,
2.48g & 2.3g.

100. 4th bust (1605–1619). Weight: 2.43g.

Third Coinage (1619–1625)
Sixpences:

101. 6th bust, im. trefoil (1624). Weight: 2.68g.

Charles I (r. 1625–1649)
Tower mint
Shillings:

102. im. cross calvary (1625–1626) (North: 2216).
Weight: 5.07g.

103. im. plume (1630–1631) (North: 2221).
Weight: 4.19gt.

104. im. rose (1631–1632) (North: 2221).
Weight: 4.89gt.

105–107. (x3) im. harp (1632–1633) (North: 2223).
Weights: 5.82g, 5.64g & 4.39gt.

108–110. (x3) im portcullis (1633–1634) (North:
2223). Weights: 5.56g, 4.23gt & 4.17gt.

111–118. (x8) im. crown (1635–1636) (North: 2225).
Weights: 5.83g, 5.79g, 5.77g, 5.71g, 5.47g, 5.41g, 5.03g
& 4.43gt.

119–125. (x7) im. tun (1636-8) (North: 2225).
Weights: 5.87g, 5.8g, 5.76,g 5.63g, 5.31g, 5.19g &
4.28gt.

126. im. tun (small XII). Weight: 5.68g.

127–130. (x4) im. tun (North: 2229). Weights: 5.86g,
5.7g, 5.27g & 4.44gt.

131–138. (x8) im. anchor (1638–1639) (North: 2229).
Weights: 5.81g, 5.78g, 5.77g, 5.73g, 4.91g, 4.88gt,
4.54gt & 4.54gt.

139–140. (x2) im. triangle (1639–1640) (North: 2229).
Weights: 5.76g & 5.74g.

141–152. (x12) im. triangle (North: 2231). Weights:
5.9g, 5.77g (x2), 5.74g, 5.69g, 5.5g, 5.27g, 5.1g, 4.81g,
4.4gt, 4.28gt & 3.93gt.

153–166. (x14) im. star (1640–1641) (North: 2231).
Weights: 5.99g, 5.82g, 5.77g, 5.74g (x2), 5.65g, 5.64g,
5.63g (x2), 5.6g, 5.57g, 5.55g, 4.97gt, 2g (fragment).

167–188. (x22) triangle-in-circle (1641–1643) (North:
2231). Weights: 6.02g, 5.91g, 5.89g, 5.86g, 5.82g, 5.81g,
5.8g, 5.74g, 5.73g (x2), 5.71g, 5.68g, 5.67g (x2), 5.53g,
5.43g, 5.41g, 5.29g, 5.17g, 5.11g, 5.01g, 4.66gt.

189–193. (x5) im. (P) (1643–1644) (North: 2231).
Weights: 5.78g, 5.72g, 5.71g, 5.62g & 5.45g.

194–210. (x17) im. uncertain (North: 2231). Weights:
5.79g, 5.67g, 5.65g, 5.63g, 5.57g, 5.46g, 5.3g, 5.23g,
5.2g, 5.1g, 5g, 4.97gt, 4.96g, 4.76gt, 4.7gt, 4.37gt &
3.94gt.

211–212. im. eye (1645) (North: 2232).
Weights: 5.68g & 5.27g.

213–221. (x9) im. sun (1645–1646) (North: 2232).
Weights: 6.14g, 5.75g, 5.65g, 5.63g, 5.52g, 5.43g (x2),
5.24g & 5.21g.

222. Imitation, style of Group D. Weight: 3.92g.

Sixpences:

223. im. portcullis (North: 22401). Weight: 2.99g.

224. im. anchor (North: 22451). Weight: 2.72g.

225. im. triangle (North: 2246). Weight: 2.8g.

226. im. uncertain (North: 2246). Weight: 2.66g.

227. im. sceptre (1646–1649) (North: 2247).
Weight: 2.69g.

Charles II (r. 1660–1685)
Hammered Coinage (1660–1662)
Shillings:

228–230. (x3) im. crown (North: 2764). Weight: 5.71g,
4.97gt & 4.93gt.

Milled Coinage
Crown:
231. (1676). Weight: 29.18g.
Halfcrowns:
232–233. (x2) (1673). Weight: 15.07g & 14.48g.
234–235. (x2) (1676). Weights: 14.96 & 14.92g.
236. (1682). Weight: 14.96g.
237–238. (x2) (1683). Weights: 14.87g & 14.72g.
Shillings:
239. (1668). Weight: 5.81g.
240. (1672). Weight: 5.74g.
241. (1684). Weight: 5.79g.
James II (r. 1685–1688)
Shillings:
242–243. (1685). Weights: 6.12g & 5.84g.
244. (1685). Weight: 5.73g.
245. (1686). Weight: 6.09g.
Discussion: The coins in this group correspond to the contents of other hoards of the Stuart Restoration, being predominantly of the older hammered coinage of Elizabeth and the early Stuarts, but with some new mechanically made coins from the period 1662 onwards, this mostly consisting of higher denominations. The latest coin dates to 1686, and it might be tempting to associate the hoard with the turmoil of the period of the Glorious Revolution in 1688–1689, although this is by no means a certain conclusion.
Disposition: Rutland County Museum hopes to acquire.

W SCOTT & B J COOK

---

578. Ambleside, Cumbria: eight silver coins
(PAS: SWYOR-7ED5A2; Treasure: 2007 T722)

Date: Modern (deposited in around 1745).
Discovery: Found by Julian Szulc and Mark Taylor while metal-detecting in December 2007, and reported to Amy Cooper (South & West Yorkshire FLO).
Description: A group of eight coins ranging from Charles II to George II, with a face value of 11s.9d.
Charles II (r. 1660–1685)
1. Threepence (1684). Weight: 1.22g.
William III (r. 1689–1702)
2. Halfcrown (1696), m. London. Weight: 14.07g.
3. Halfcrown (1697), m. Exeter. Weight: 14.29g.
Anne (r. 1702–1714)
4. Halfcrown (1708), m. Edinburgh. Weight: 14.72g.
George I (r. 1714–1727)
5. Shilling (1723 SSC), m. London. Weight: 5.91g.
George II (r. 1727–1760)
6. Shilling (1739). Weight: 5.85g.
7–8. (x2) Shilling (1745 LIMA) m. London. Weight: 5.95g & 5.89g.
Disposition: Armitt Museum & Gallery, Ambleside, hoped to acquire, but withdrew; to be returned.

A COOPER

SINGLE FINDS

579. Linstead Magna, Suffolk: gold *ecu d'or au soleil de Bretagne* of Francis I of France
(PAS: WMID-FAFCF3)

Date: Post-Medieval (c. 1515–c. 1547).
Discovery: Found by Ross Evans while metal-detecting in October 2007, and recorded with Duncan Slarke (Staffordshire & West Midlands FLO).
Description: Gold *ecu d'or au soleil de Bretagne* of Francis I of France (r. 1515–1547) (Duplessy 789). Obv: a crowned shield containing three fleur-de-lis, with a sun above and to the left and right a crown and ermine, and the inscription 'FRANCISCVS D G (F)RANC[OR REX BRITANIE DVX]' (Francis, by the Grace of God King of France, Duke of Brittany). Rev: a cross of three strands, each arm ending in a fleur-de-lis, with a crowned 'F' in two opposing angles, a crowned ermine in the remaining two angles, and the inscription '[DEVS IN ADIVTOR]IVM MEVM INTEN[DE]' (O God, reach forth to my aid). Diameter: 24.6mm. Weight: 3.29g.
Discussion: This coin represents the first recorded 'stray' find of a Francis I gold coin in England, and is the first of its type from Suffolk. Kelleher (2007) has noted that only five Francis I gold coins have been recorded in total in England, all originating from hoards (one from Bearpark, County Durham, and four from Ely, Cambridgeshire). This example from Linstead Magna represents an important new find.
Disposition: Returned to finder.

D SLARKE

---

580. Great Yeldham, Essex: silver half *denga* of Ivan IV of Russia (PAS: ESS-B66F64)

Date: Medieval (c. 1533–c. 1547).
Discovery: Found by Kim Clarke while metal-detecting in January 2007, and recorded with Laura McLean (Essex FLO).
Description: A silver wire half *denga* of 'Great Prince' Ivan IV of Russia (r. 1533–1547), minted in Pskov in the period before he became Tsar (Kaim 1980: no. 1019). Obv: a horseman holding a sword pointing upwards. Rev: an inscription that reads '[K]HSb/[B]E[A]IИ/[I] BAH3/ΠCK' (Great Prince Ivan, Pskov). Dimensions: 10.94 x 14.24mm. Weight: 1.03g.
Discussion: Wire coins were made from thick silver wire cut to the correct weight and then struck, hence the slightly squashed, oval shape. Very few Russian coins have been recorded by the PAS, this being the first of Ivan IV and possibly the earliest Russian coin on the database.
Disposition: Returned to finder.

L MCLEAN & J NAYLOR

581. Ringmer, East Sussex: copper-alloy token of Joseph Easton of Boreham (PAS: SUSS-2864F4)

Date: Post-Medieval (1666).

Discovery: Found by William Piggott while metal-detecting in 2007, and recorded with Liz Andrews-Wilson (Sussex FLO).

Description: A copper-alloy local farthing trade token issued by Joseph Easton or Elston of Boreham (Boreham Street) in Wartling parish near Hailsham, East Sussex (Williamson 1891: 1162, no. 27 var.). Obv: the inscription reads '[IOSEPH] EASTON', around a design of the Mercers' Arms. Rev: the inscription reads 'BOREH[AM.IN.] SVSSEX around I.E. 1666'. Dimensions: 15.75 x 0.82mm. Weight: 0.8g.

Discussion: In the 17th century many traders and corporations issued tokens for use as small change to make up for the dearth of coins. Most had a fairly local distribution as they could only be exchanged within the area where the trader was known. This example is a variant on the published tyre for this issuer.

Disposition: Returned to finder.

L ANDREWS-WILSON

582. Exeter, Devon: silver eight *reales* of Charles II of Spain (PAS: DEV-AB49A5)

Date: Post-Medieval (1689).

Discovery: Found by Jeff Upsher while gardening in November 2007, and recorded with Danielle Wootton (Devon FLO).

Description: A silver eight *reales* cob coin of Charles II of Spain (r. 1661–1700), minted at Potosí (Bolivia). Obv: shows the symbols of Spain: a cross with a castle in the top left and bottom right, and a lion in the top right and bottom left. As is typical with these cob coins cut from silver bars, the coin is not well struck and little of the obverse inscription is visible, although the letters AROLV from CAROLVS (for Charles) can be seen. Rev: two pillars symbolising the Pillars of Hercules (Straits of Gibraltar), with waves below. The pillars intersect three lines of text which give details about date, mint and the assayer of the silver. The top line reads 'P 8 VR, P' giving the mintmark for Potosi; '8' the denomination of the coin, 8 *reales*; and 'VR' the initials of the assayer, who would check the quality of the silver. The middle line reads 'PLVS [VL]TRA', a Latin motto adopted by Charles I of Spain (Holy Roman Emperor Charles V) meaning 'Further Beyond' (representing Spain's expansion into the New World), and the bottom line: 'VR 89 P', repeats the mint and assayer, with two digits of the date between, in this case 1689. Dimensions and weight not recorded.

Discussion: The coin originates from the Potosí silver mines in Bolivia, the most important of Spain's New World mints. The cob coins were crudely made, cut into the correct weight from silver bars and stamped. They were often melted down once they reached Spain into better quality coinage. The 8 *reales* coins are more commonly known as 'pieces of eight'. The coin

was featured on BBC South West news and also has its own webpage for the 'Living Here West Exe Project', a website devoted to the area in which the coin was found.

Disposition: On loan to the Royal Albert Memorial Museum, Exeter.

D WOOTTON

583. Letcombe Regis, Oxfordshire: copper-alloy farthing of William III (PAS: SUR-1000F7)

Date: Post-Medieval (c. 1696).

Discovery: Found by Ian Laws while metal-detecting in September 2007, and recorded with David Williams (Surrey FLO) during a metal-detecting rally.

Description: A copper-alloy farthing, now very worn, of William III (r. 1688–1702). A right-facing bust is just visible on the obverse, and the reverse of the farthing, which appears to be dated 1696, has been over-stamped with a heart containing the letters I B and six pellets Diameter: 20.3mm. Weight: 4.07g

Discussion: The only known usage of 'I B' as a countermark is on a range of European copper coins supposedly countermarked for use in Barbados, probably in the late 17th or early 18th century, although one with a heart-shaped stamp is very unusual. The countermark on these coins seems to have been common enough in the Caribbean (they are known for Martinique, for example), but the assignment of countermarks is rarely very secure (Barrie Cook, *personal communication*).

Deposition: Returned to finder.

D WILLIAMS

584. Laughton, Lincolnshire: a copper-alloy *paisa* of Emperor Muhammad Akbar II (c. 1806–1837) of Gwalior State (India) (PAS: SWYOR-B55B81)

Date: Post-Medieval (c. 1796–c. 1825).

Discovery: Found by Roland Rodgerson while metal-detecting in July 2007, and reported to Amy Cooper (South & West Yorkshire FLO).

Description: A copper-alloy *paisa* of Gwalior State, India, Gwalior Fort mint, struck in the name of the Mughal emperor Muhammad Akbar II, during the reign of Maharaja Daulat Rao Scindia (r. 1796–1825). Details including the date are not seen due to the poor condition of the coin. Dimensions: 16.6 x 5.5mm. Weight: 8.6g.

Discussion: Indian coins are not uncommon finds in Britain, although this is one of only about 30 recorded by the PAS. It was, no doubt, brought back by people serving in the British Empire in India, rather than as a circulating medium.

Disposition: Returned to finder.

S BHANDARE & A COOPER

Section editor and further research: John Naylor
Editor: Michael Lewis

REFERENCES

Abdy, R and Williams, G, 2006, 'A catalogue of hoards and single finds from the British Isles, c. AD 410–675', in Cook, B and Williams, G (eds.), *Coinage and History in the North Sea World, c. 500–1250* (Brill, Leiden).

Åberg, N, 1923, *Die Goten und Langobarden in Italien*, Vilhelm Ekmans Universitetsfond, Uppsala 29 (Almqvist & Wiksells, Uppsala).

Åberg, N, 1926, *The Anglo-Saxons in England during the Early Centuries after the Invasion* (W Heffer and Sons, Cambridge and Uppsala).

Ager, B, forthcoming 2009, 'A preliminary note on the artefacts from the Vale of York hoard' in Abramson, T (ed.), *Studies in Early Medieval Coinage* 2 (Boydell, Woodbridge).

Alexander, J and Binski, P (eds.), 1987, *The Age of Chivalry: Art in Plantagenet England, 1200–1400* (Arts Council (exhibition catalogue), London).

Allason-Jones, L, 1986, 'An eagle mount from Carlisle', *Saalburg Jahrbuch* 42, 68–69.

Allen, C and Hopkins, D, 2000, 'Bronze Age accessory cups from Lincolnshire: Early Bronze Age pot?', *Proceedings of the Prehistoric Society* 66, 297–317.

Allen, D and Mays, M (eds.), 1995, *Catalogue of the Celtic Coins in the British Museum: Volume III Bronze Coins of Gaul* (British Museum, London).

Andrews-Wilson, L, forthcoming 2009, 'New evidence for Iron Age sword strap fasteners identified by the Portable Antiquities Scheme', in S Worrell, K Leahy, M Lewis and J Naylor (eds.), *A Decade of Discovery: proceedings of the Portable Antiquities Scheme Conference 2007*, British Archaeological Reports, British Series (John and Erica Hedges Ltd, Oxford).

Appels, A, and Laycock, S, 2007, *Roman Buckles & Military Fittings* (Greenlight Publishing, Witham).

Arnold, C J, 1982, *The Anglo-Saxon Cemeteries of the Isle of Wight* (British Museum, London).

Ashley, S J, Penn, K and Rogerson, A, 1990, 'Four continental objects of early Saxon date', *Norfolk Archaeology* 41, part I, 92–93.

Ashley, S, 2002, *Medieval Armorial Horse Furniture in Norfolk*, East Anglian Archaeology 101 (Norfolk Museums and Archaeology Service, Oxbow Books, Oxford).

Atkinson, R J C, 1951, 'List of skewer-pins and related types', in R J C Atkinson, C M Piggott and N K Sandars, *Excavations at Dorchester* (Ashmolean Museum, Oxford University, Oxford), 142–144.

Atkinson, R J C and Piggott, S, 1955, 'The Torrs chamfrein', *Archaeologia* 96, 197–235.

Avent, R and Evison, V I, 1982, 'Anglo-Saxon button brooches', *Archaeologia* 107, 77-124.

Bailey, S, 1994, 'Two copper-alloy cross-staff heads from Warwickshire', *Medieval Archaeology* 38, 171–173.

Barclay, C, 'Ugthorpe, Yorkshire', *Coin Hoards from Roman Britain* 11 (British Museum & Royal Numismatic Society, London), 121–124.

Bartlett, R, 1984, 'Two Late Saxon circular lead tanks from Willingham, Cambridgeshire' (unpublished).

Bartlett, R, 1985, 'A Roman tripod mount from Old Harlow, Essex', *Essex Journal* 20, 55–56.

Battiscombe, C F, 1956, *The Relics of Saint Cuthbert* (University Press, Oxford), 419–421, pl. 37, fig. 16.

Barrett, J C, Freeman, P W M and Woodward, A, 2000, *Cadbury Castle Somerset; The later prehistoric and early historic archaeology* (English Heritage, London).

Bayard, D *et al.*, 1986, *La Picardie, berceau de la France*: Clovis et les derniers Romains : 1500ème anniversaire de la bataille de Soissons, 486-1986, Association des conservateurs des collections publiques de Picardie, Direction des antiquités de Picardie, Réunion des musées nationaux S.l (Association des conservateurs des collections publiques de Picardie, Amiens).

Bayley, J, Drury, P, and Spencer, B, 1984, 'A Medieval mirror from Heybridge, Essex', *Antiquaries Journal* 64.2, 399–402.

Bayley, J and Butcher, S, 2004, *Roman Brooches in Britain: a technological and typological study based on the Richborough collection* (Society of Antiquaries of London, London).

Becker, K, 2000, *Eisenzeitliche Ringkopfnadeln in Großbritannien und Irland* (unpublished Magister thesis, University of Köln).

Bennett, J and Young, R, 1981, 'Some new and some forgotten stamped skillets, and the date of P. Cipius Polybius', *Britannia* 12, 37–44.

Biddle, M and Kjølbye-Biddle, B (2007) 'Winchester: from Venta to Winancaestir', in L Gilmour (ed.), *Pagans and Christians - from Antiquity to the Middle Ages. Papers in honour of Martin Henig, presented on the occasion of his 65th birthday*, British Archaeological Reports, International Series 1610 (Archeopress, Oxford), 189–214.

Biroli Stefanelli, L P, 1992, *L'oro dei Romani. Gioielli de età imperiale* (L' Erma di Bretschneider, Rome).

Bishop, M C, 1996, *Finds from Roman Aldborough, A catalogue of small finds from the Romano-British town of Isurium Brigantum*, Oxbow Monograph 65 (Oxbow, Oxford).

Bishop, M C, 1988, 'Cavalry equipment of the Roman army in the first century AD', in J Coulston (ed.), *Military Equipment and the Identity of Roman Soldiers: proceedings of the fourth Roman military equipment conference*, British Archaeological Reports, International Series 394 (British Archaeological Reports, Oxford).

Bishop, M C and Coulston, J C N, 2006 (2nd ed.), *Roman Military Equipment from the Punic Wars to the Fall of Rome* (Oxbow, Oxford).

Bjørn, A and Shetelig, H (ed.), 1940, 'Vikings antiquities in England', in Shetelig, H, *Viking Antiquities in Great Britain and Ireland* 4 (H Aschehoug & Co., Oslo).

Blackburn, M, 2006, 'Currency under the Vikings. Part 2: the two Scandinavian kingdoms of the Danelaw, c. 895-954', *British Numismatic Journal* 76, 204–226.

Blair, C, 2005, 'Surrey enamels reattributed 1', *Journal of the Antique Metalware Society* 13, 2–9.

Blair, C and Patterson, A, 2006, 'Surrey enamels reattributed 2', *Journal of the Antique Metalware Society* 14, 10–21.

Blunt, C E, 1974, 'The coinage of Athelstan, King of England 924–939', *British Numismatic Journal* 62, 35–158.

Bland, R F and Johns, C M, 1993, *The Hoxne Treasure, an illustrated introduction* (British Museum, London).

Böhme, H W, 1974, *Germanische Grabfunde des 4. bis 5. Jahrhunderts zwischen unterer Elbe und Loire* (C H Beck'sche Verlagsbuckhandlung, Munich).

Boon, G C, 1965, 'Light-weights and Limesfalsa', *Numismatic Chronicle*, 6th Series, V, 161–74.

Boon, G, 1974, *The Roman Town of Calleva* (David and Charles).

Boucher, S and Oggiano-Bitar, H, 1993, *Le Trésor des bronzes de Bavay* 29, no. 5 (Revue du Nord, Lille).

Boudet, R, 1988, 'Iberian type brooches', in B Cunliffe, *Mount Batten Plymouth; A prehistoric and Roman port*, Oxford University Committee for Archaeology Monograph 26 (Oxford University, Oxford, Oxford), 64.

Bradley, R, 1998, *The Passage of Arms: an archaeological analysis of prehistoric hoards and votive deposits* (Oxbow, Oxford).

Brailsford, J W, 1962, *Hod Hill Volume One, Antiquities from Hod Hill in the Durden Collection* (British Museum, London).

Brailsford, J W, 1964, *Guide to the Antiquities of Roman Britain* (British Museum, London).

Brailsford, J W, 1975, 'The Polden Hill hoard', *Proceedings of the Prehistoric Society* 41, 222–234.

Brenan, J, 1991, *Hanging Bowls and their Contexts: an archaeological survey of their socio economic significance from the fifth to seventh centuries AD*, British Archaeological Reports, British Series, 220 (Archaeopress, Oxford).

Briard, J, 1965, *Les Dépôts Bretons et l'Age du Bronze* (Atlantique, Rennes).

Briard, J, 1987, 'Dépôts de bronze, haches à douille, pré-monnaie et fausse monnai', in J Bousquet and P Naster (eds.), *Mélanges offerts au Docteur J.-B. Colbert de Beaulieu* (Le Léopard d'Or, Paris), 133–143.

Britton, D, 1963, 'Traditions of metalworking in the Later Neolithic and Early Bronze Age of Britain: part 1', *Proceedings of the Prehistoric Society* 29, 258–325.

Brown, P D C, 1973, 'Two Romano-British Bronze Terminals in the Ashmolean Museum, Oxford', *Antiquaries Journal* 53, 264–265.

Brown, M P, 2006, *The World of the Luttrell Psalter* (British Library, London).

Bruce-Mitford, R, 2005, *The Corpus of Late Celtic Hanging Bowls* (Oxford University Press, Oxford).

Bulleid, A and St George Grey, H, 1911, *The Glastonbury Lake Village; a full description of the excavations and the relics discovered 1892–1907*, vol. 1 (The Glastonbury Antiquarian Society, Glastonbury).

Burgess, C, Coombs, D and Davies, G, 1972, 'The Broadward Complex and barbed spearheads', in F Lynch and C Burgess (eds.), *Prehistoric Man in Wales and the West: essays in honour of Lily F Chitty* (Adams and Dart, Bath), 211–285.

Burgess, C B, 1979, 'A find from Boyton, Suffolk, and the end of the Bronze Age in Britain and Ireland', in C B Burgess and D G Coombs (eds.), *Bronze Age Hoards: some finds old and new*, British Archaeological Reports, British Series 67 (British Archaeological Reports, Oxford) 269–282.

Burnett, A and Gregory, T, 1988, 'Postick, Norfolk', *Coins Hoards from Roman Britain* 8 (British Museum, London), 33–36.

Bushe Fox, J P, 1949, *Fourth Report in the Excavations of the Roman Fort at Richborough, Kent*, Report Research Committee, Society Antiquaries of London 16 (Society of Antiquaries of London, Oxford).

Butcher, S, 2007, 'Part II: The Romano-British brooches and enamelled objects', in H E M Cool and D J P Mason (eds.), *Roman Piercebridge* (unpublished project design for English Heritage), 11–201.

Butler, J, 1963, 'Bronze Age connections across the north sea', *Palaeohistoria* 9, 1–289.

Butler, C, 2005, *Prehistoric Flintwork* (Tempus, Stroud).

Butler, J J and Steegstra, H, 2005–2006, 'Bronze age metal and amber in the Netherlands (III:2) catalogue of the socketed axes, Part C', *Palaeohistoria* 47–48, 207–240

Calkin, J B and Piggott, C M, 1939, 'An Iron Age habitation site at Langton Matravers', *Proceedings of the Dorset Natural History and Archaeological Society* 60, 66–72.

Calkin, J B, 1949, 'The Isle of Purbeck in the Iron Age', *Proceedings of the Dorset Natural History and Archaeological Society* 70, 29–59.

Campbell, J (ed.), 1982, *The Anglo-Saxons* (Phaidon, London).

Chapman, E, 2005, *A Catalogue of Roman Military Equipment in the National Museum of Wales*, British Archaeological Reports, British Series 388 (Archaeopress, Oxford).

Chick, D (ed. by M A S Blackburn and R Naismith), forthcoming 2009, *The Coinage of Offa and His Contemporaries*, British Numismatic Society Special Publications 6 (British Numismatic Society, London).

Clarke, G, 1979, *Pre-Roman and Roman Winchester Part II: the Roman cemetery at Lankhills,* Winchester Studies 3 (Clarendon, Oxford).

Coghlan, H H, 1970, *A Report upon the Hoard of Bronze Age Tools and Weapons from Yattendon, Near Newbury, Berkshire* (The Borough of Newbury Museum, Newbury).

Coleman-Smith, R and Pearson, T, 1988, *Excavations in the Donyatt Potteries* (Phillimore Chichester).

Collingwood, R G and Wright, R P, 1991, *Roman Inscriptions of Britain,* Vol. 2, Fascicule 3 (Sutton Publishing Ltd, Gloucester).

Collins, R, 2008, 'The latest Roman coin from Hadrian's Wall: a small Fifth-century purse group', *Britannia* 39, 256–261.

Collis, J, 1973, 'Burials with weapons in Iron Age Britain', *Germania* 51, 121–133.

Cook, B, 1999, 'Foreign coins in Medieval England', in L Traviani (ed.), *Local Coins, Foreign Coins: Italy and Europe 11th-15th centuries*, Collana di numismatica e scienze affini 2 (Società Numismatica Italiana, Milan), 231–284.

Cool, H E M, 1990, 'Roman metal hair pins from Southern Britain', *Archaeological Journal* 147, 148–82.

Corcoran, J P X P, 1952, 'Tankards and tankard handles of the British Early Iron Age', *Proceedings of the Prehistoric Society* 18, 85–102.

Corke, B, 2004, 'Excavations at Ringlemere 2004', *Friends of Canterbury Archaeological Trust Newsletter* 66, 11.

Cowgill, J, 1994, 'The lead vessel' in K Steedman (ed.), 'Excavation of a Saxon site at Riby Cross Roads, Lincolnshire', *Archaeological Journal* 151, 267-71.

Crummy, N, 1983, *The Roman small finds from excavations in Colchester, 1971-9*, Colchester Archaeological Report 2 (Colchester Archaeological Trust Ltd., Colchester).

Cunliffe, B, and Phillipson, D W, 1968, 'Excavations at Eldon's Seat, Encombe, Dorset', *Proceedings of the Prehistoric Society* 34, 191–237.

Cunliffe, B, and O'Connor, B, 1979, 'The Late Bronze Age Hoard from Danebury, Hants', in C Burgess and D Coombs (eds.) *Bronze Age Hoards: Some Finds Old and New*, British Archaeological Reports, British Series 67 (Archaeopress, Oxford), 235–245.

Curteis, M, 2008, 'A hoard of hammered silver coins from Coventry 2006', *Numismatic Chronicle* 168, 428–430.

Dalton, O M, 1912, *Catalogue of the Finger Rings. Early Christian, Byzantine, Teutonic, Medieval and Later, Franks Bequest* (British Museum, London).

Davies, D G, 1979, 'Hatfield Broad Oak Hoard, Essex, in C Burgess and D Coombs (eds.), *Bronze Age Hoards: some finds old and new*, British Archaeological Reports, British Series 67 (British Archaeological Reports, Oxford), 149–173.

Davis, M and Gwilt, A, 2008, 'Material, style and identity in first century AD metalwork', in D Garrow, C Gosden and J D Hill (eds.), *Rethinking Celtic Art* (Oxbow, Oxford), 146–185.

De Jersey, P, 1994, *Coinage in Iron Age Armorica*, OUCA Monograph 39 (Oxford University, Oxford).

Delestrée, L-P and Tache, M, 2002-7, *Nouvel Atlas des Monnaies Gauloises*, I-III (Éditions Commios, Saint Germain-en-Laye).

Dunning, G C, 1968, 'Medieval bronze tap handles from Lewes and Kirkstall Abbey', *Antiquaries Journal* 48, 310–311.

Dunning, G, 1934, 'The swan's-neck and ring-headed pins of the Early Iron Age in Britain, *Archaeological Journal* 91, 269–295.

Duplessy, J, 1989, *Les Monnais Français Royales: de Hughes Capet a Louis XVI (987-1793)* (Maison Platt, Paris).

Dyer, C 1989, *Standards of living in the later Middle Ages: social change in England c.1200-1520* (Cambridge University Press, Cambridge).

Eagles, B, 1986, 'Pagan Anglo-Saxon burials at West Overton', *Wiltshire Archaeology Magazine* 80, 103–119.

Egan, G and Pritchard, F, 1991, *Dress Accessories 1150–1450. Medieval Finds from Excavations in London* 3 (HMSO, London).

Egan, G, 1996, 'Some archaeological evidence for metalworking in London c. 1050 AD–c. 1700 AD', *Historical Metallurgy* 30.2, 83–94.

Egan, G, 1998, *The Medieval Household (Medieval Finds from Excavations in London 6)* (The Stationery Office, London).

Egan, G, 2001, 'Lead/tin alloy metalwork', in P Saunders (ed.), *Salisbury and South Wiltshire Medieval Catalogue* 3 (Salisbury and South Wiltshire Museum, Salisbury), 92–109.

Egan, G, 2005, *Material Culture in London in an Age of Transition: Tudor and Stuart Period Finds c. 1450–c. 1700 from Excavations at Riverside Sites in Southwark*, Museum of London Archaeological Service Monograph 19 (Museum of London, London).

Ehrenberg, M R, 1977, *Bronze Age Spearheads from Berkshire, Buckinghamshire and Oxfordshire*, British Archaeological Reports, British Series 34 (Archaeopress, Oxford).

Ehrenberg, M R, 1981, 'Inside socketed axes', *Antiquity* 55, 214–218.

Eluère, C, 1982, *Les Ors Prèhistoriques* (Picard, Paris).

Eluère, C, 1987, 'Celtic Gold Torcs', *Gold Bulletin* 20, 22–37.

Eogan, G. 1994, *The Accomplished Art: gold and gold-working in Britain and Ireland during the Bronze Age* (Oxbow, Oxford).

Evans, J, 1931, *English Posies and Posy Rings* (Oxford University Press, Oxford).

Evison, V I, 1967, 'The Dover ring-sword and other sword-rings and beads', *Archaeologia* 101, 63-103.

Feacham, R, 1991, 'Two quadrilobed harness-mounts from Hambleden, Buckinghamshire', *Antiquaries Journal* 71, 1–52.

Feugère, M, 1995, 'Les spatules à cire à manche figuré', in W Czysz, C-M Hüssen, H-P Kuhnen, C S Sommer and G W. (eds.), *Provinzialrömische Forschungen. Festchrift für Günter Ulbert zum 65 Geburtstag*, 321–328.

Forsyth, H and Egan, G, 2005, *Toys, Trifles and Trinkets: Base Metal Miniatures from London* (Museum of London, London).

Fowler, E, 1960, 'The origins and development of the penannular brooch in Europe', *Proceedings of the Prehistoric Society* 26, 149-77.

Fox Davies, A C, 1954, *A Complete Guide to Heraldry* (Nelson, London).

Fox, C, 1939, 'The non-socketed bronze sickles of Britain', *Archaeologica Cambrensis* 96, 136–162.

Gaimster, D., Hayward, M., Mitchell, D and Parker, K., 2002, 'Tudor Dress-Hooks: A New Class of Treasure Find in England', *Antiquaries Journal* 82, 157–196.

Geake, H, 1997, *The Use of Grave-Goods in Conversion-Period England, c. 600 - c. 850*. British Archaeological Reports, British Series 261 (John & Erica Hedges, Oxford).

Gingell, C, 1979, 'The bronze and iron hoard from Melksham and another Wiltshire find', in C Burgess and D Coombs (eds.), *Bronze Age Hoards: Some Finds Old and New*, British Archaeological Reports, British Series 67 (British Archaeological Reports, Oxford), 245–253.

Gurney, D, 2006, 'Archaeological Finds in Norfolk in 2005', Norfolk Archaeology 45, Pt1, 112–123.

Graham, A H., Hinton, D A and Peacock, D P S, 2002, 'The excavation of an Iron Age and Romano-British settlement in Quarry Field, south of Compact Farm, Worth Matravers, Dorset', in D A Hinton (ed.), *Purbeck Papers*, University of Southampton Department of Archaeology Monograph 4 (Oxbow, Oxford), 1–83.

Graham-Campbell, J, 1975, 'Bossed penannular brooches: a review of recent research', *Medieval Archaeology* 19, 33–47.

Graham-Campbell, J, 1980, *Viking Artefacts. A select catalogue* (British Museum, London).

Graham-Campbell, J, 1995, *The Viking-Age Gold and Silver of Scotland (AD 850–1100)* (National Museums of Scotland, Edinburgh).

Graham-Campbell, J, 2001, 'The northern hoards, from Cuerdale to Bossall/Flaxton', in N Higham and D H Hill (eds.), *Edward the Elder 899-924* (Routledge, London), 212–129.

Graham-Campbell, J, 2006, 'The rings', in S H Fuglesang and D M Wilson (eds.), *The Hoen Hoard: a Viking Gold Treasure of the Ninth Century* (Bardi Editore, Rome), 73–81.

Green, H S, 1980, *The Flint Arrowheads of the British Isles,* British Archaeological Reports, British Series 75 (British Archaeological Reports, Oxford).

Green, M, 1977, 'Theriomorphism, and the Role of Divine Animals in Romano-Celtic Art', in J Mumby and M Henig (eds.), *Roman Life and Art in Britain A celebration in honour of the eightieth birthday of Jocelyn Toynbee*, British Archaeological Reports, British Series 41 (ii) (British Archaeological Reports, Oxford), 297–325.

Green, M, 1996, 'Copper-alloy wheel models', in R J Williams, P J Hart and A T L.Williams (eds.), *Wavendon Gate A late Iron Age and Roman settlement in Milton Keynes*, The Buckinghamshire Archaeological Society Monograph Series No 10 , (Buckinghamshire Archaeological Society, Aylesbury), 113–116.

Greenwell, G and Brewis, W P, 1909, 'The origin, evolution and classification of the bronze spear-head in Great Britain and Ireland', *Archaeologia* 61, 439–472.

Grierson, P and Blackburn, M A S, 1986, *Medieval European Coinage 1: The early middle ages (5th – 10th centuries)* (Cambridge University Press, Cambridge).

Grimwade, A, 1990, *London Goldsmiths, 1697–1837* (Faber, London).

Gruel, K and Taccoen, A, 1992, 'Petit numéraire de billon émis Durant et après la conquête romaine dans l'Ouest de la Gaule' in M Mays (ed.), *Celtic Coinage: Britain and Beyond*, British Archaeological Reports, British Series 222 (Tempus Reparatum, Oxford), 165–188.

Guest, P S W, 2005, *The Late Roman Gold and Silver coins from the Hoxne Treasure* (British Museum, London)

Halfpenny, P and Beddoe, S, 1990, *Circus and Sport: English Earthenware Figures 1780–1840* (JB Speed Art Museum, Louisville).

Hårdh, B, 1976, *Wikingerzeitliche Depotfunde aus Südschweden* (Acta Archaeologica Lundensia, Bonn/Lund).

Hattatt, R, 1982, *Ancient and Romano-British brooches* (Dorset Publishing, Sherbourne).

Hattatt, R, 1987, *Brooches of Antiquity* (Oxbow, Oxford).

Hattatt, R, 2000, A Visual Catalogue of Richard Hattatt's Ancient Brooches (Oxbow, Oxford).

Hawkes, S C, and Dunning, G C, 1961, 'Soldiers and settlers in Britain, fourth to fifth century: with a catalogue of animal-ornamented buckles and related belt-fittings', *Medieval Archaeology* 5, 1–70

Hawkins, E, 1847, 'An account of coins and treasure found in Cuerdale', *Archaeological Journal* 4, 110-130, fig. 22.

Hawkins, E, 1885, *Medallic Illustrations of the History of Great Britain and Ireland, to the Death of King George II*, I (British Museum, London).

Henig, M, 1976, 'A Roman tripod-mount from the G. P. O. site, London', *Antiquaries Journal* 56, 248–249.

Henig, M, 1978, A *Corpus of Roman Engraved Gemstones from the British Sites*, British Archaeological Reports, British Series 8 (Archaeopress, Oxford).

Henig, M, 1984, *Religion in Roman Britain* (Batsford, London).

Henig, M and Leahy, K, 1986, 'A sceptre-head and two votive swords from Kirmington, Lincolnshire', *Antiquaries Journal* 66, 388–391.

Henig, M, 1987, 'An early Christian signet ring from the Roman villa at Moor Park', *Hertfordshire Archaeology* 9, 184–185

Henig, M, Scarisbrick, D and Fenton, J, 2003, *Finger rings* (Ashmolean Museum, Oxford).

Henig, M, 1990, *The Content Family Collection of Ancient Cameos* (Ashmolean Museum, Oxford).

Henig, M, Hassall, M and Bayley, J, 1993, 'Votive object: images and inscriptions. Figurines', in A Woodward and P Leach, *The Uley Shrines. Excavations of a Ritual Complex on West Hill, Uley, Gloucestershire: 1977–9*, English Heritage Archaeological Report 17 (English Heritage in association with British Museum Press, London).

Hills, C and Hurst, H, 1989, 'A Goth at Gloucester?', *Antiquaries Journal* 69, 154–158.

Holman, D, 2005, 'Iron Age coinage and settlement in Kent', *Britannia* 36, 1–54.

Howgego, C J, 1985, *Greek Imperial Countermarks* (Royal Numismatic Society, London).

Hughes, M J, 1972, 'A technical study of opaque red glass of the Iron Age in Britain', *Proceedings of the Prehistoric Society* 38, 98–107.

Hull, M R and Hawkes, C F C, 1987, *Corpus of Ancient Brooches in Britain; Pre-Roman Bow Brooches*, British Archaeological Reports, British Series 168 (BAR, Oxford).

Hume, I N, 1956, 'Ritual Burials on the Upchurch Marshes, *Archaeologia Cantiana* 70, 160–167.

Hutcheson, N C, 2004, *Later Iron Age Norfolk: metalwork, landscape and society*, British Archaeological Reports, British Series 361 (Archaeopress, Oxford).

Huth, C, 1997, *Westeuropäische Horte die Spätbronzezeit: Fundbild und Funktion* (R. Habelt in Komm, Regensburg).

Huth, C, 2000, 'Metal circulation, communication and traditions of craftsmanship in Late Bronze Age and Early Iron Age Europe', in C F E Pare (ed.), *Metals Make The World Go Round: the supply and circulation of metals in Bronze Age Europe* (Oxbow Books, Oxford), 176–193.

Huvelin, H, 1985, 'Classement et chronologie du monayage d'or de Carausius', *Revue Numismatique* 27, 107–119.

Jackson, C J, 1964, *English Goldsmiths and their Marks* (Dover, New York).

Jackson, R J P, 2005, 'Roman bound captives: symbols of slavery?', in N Crummy (ed.), *Image, Craft and the Classical World Essays in hour of Donald Bailey and Catherine Johns*, *Monographies instrumentum* 29 (éditions monique mergoil, Montagnac), 143–157.

Jope, E M, 2000, *Early Celtic Art in the British Isles* (Clarendon Press, Oxford).

Johansen, O S, 1973, Bossed penannular brooches. A systematization and study of their cultural affinities, *Acta Archaeologica* 44, 63-124.

Johns, C M, 1996, *The Jewellery of Roman Britain: Celtic and Classical Traditions* (University College London Press, London).

Johns, C M, 1997, The *Snettisham Roman Jeweller's Hoard* (British Museum Press, London).

Johns, C and Potter, T, 1983, *The Thetford Treasure: Roman Jewellery and Silver* (British Museum Press, London).

Johns, C and Potter, T, 1985, *The Canterbury Late Roman Treasure* (The Society of Antiquaries of London, London).

Kaim, R 1980, *Die Altrussiche Münzgeschichte und die Prägungen von 1350–1700, vol 2 1533–1700* (Hagen, R. Kain).

Kaufmann-Heinemann, A, 1998, *Götter und Lararien aus Augusta Raurica Herstellung, Fundzusammenhänge und sakrale Funktion figürlicher Bronzen in einer römischen Stadt*, Forschungen in Augst 26 (Römermuseum Augst, Augst).

Kelleher, R, 2007, 'Gold is the strength, the sinnewes of the world: continental gold and Tudor England', *British Numismatic Journal* 77, 210–225.

Keller, E, 1971, *Die spätrömishen Grabfunde in Südbayern,* Münchner Beiträge zur Vor- und Frühgeschichte 14 (Beck, München).

Kendrick, T D, 1938, 'An Anglo-Saxon cruet', *The Antiquaries Journal* 18, 377–381, pl. 74, no. 5.

Kent, J P C and Painter, K S, 1977, *Wealth of the Roman World Gold and Silver AD 300–700* (British Museum, London).

Kisch, B, 1965, *Scales and Weights: a historical outline* (Yale University Press, London).

Knowles, M and May, J, 1996, 'Catalogue of silver and copper alloy artifacts: votive objects', in J May, *Dragonby: report on excavations at an Iron Age and Romano-British settlement in North Lincolnshire,* vol. 1 (Oxbow, Oxford), 270–281.

Koch, A, 1998, *Bügelfibeln der Merowingerzeit im westlichen Frankenreich* (Habelt, Verlag des Romisch-Germanischen Zentralmuseums, Bonn).

Kotansky, R, 1994, *Greek Magical Amulets* (Opladen, Westdeutscher, Verlag).

La Tour, H, 1892, *Atlas des monnaies gauloises* (Claude Burgan / Maison Florange, Paris).

Lawson, A J, 1979, 'A Late Middle Bronze Age hoard from Hunstanton, Norfolk', in C Burgess and D Coombs (eds.), *Bronze Age Hoards: Some Finds Old and New*, British Archaeological Reports, 67 (British Archaeological Reports, Oxford), 42–92.

Lawson, A, 1999, 'The Bronze Age hoards of Hampshire', in A Harding (ed.) *Experiment and Design: archaeological studies in honour of John Coles* (Oxbow, Oxford), 94–108.

Leahy, K, 2003, *Anglo-Saxon Crafts* (Tempus, Stroud).

Leahy K, 2005, in Geake H, 'Portable Antiquities Scheme', *Medieval Archaeology* 49, 327–341.

Leins, I, 2007a, 'Coins in context: coinage and votive deposition in Iron Age south-east Leicestershire', *British Numismatic Journal* 77, 22–48.

Leins, I, 2007b, 'Beverley', *Numismatic Chronicle* 167, 244–245 nos. 8–9.

Lennartsson, M, 1999, 'Karolingische Metallarbeiten mit Pflanzenornamentik', *Offa* 54–55, 431–619 .

Lewis, M (2007) 'A New Date for Class A, Type 11a Stirrup Strap Mounts, and Some Observations on their Distribution', *Medieval Archaeology* 51, 178–184.

Lightbown, R W, 1992, *Medieval European Jewellery* (Victoria and Albert Museum, London).

Longworth, I H, 1967, 'Contracted mouth accessory cups', *British Museum Quarterly* 31, 111–122.

Lyne, M, 1999, 'Fourth century belt fittings from Richborough, *Spätrömische Militärausrüstung herausgegeben von Jürgen Oldenstein und Oliver Gupte*, Proceedings of the Eleventh International Roman Military Equipment Conference, Mainz, 1998, (Armatura Press, Braemar), 103–113.

Macdonald, P, 2007, *Llyn Cerrig Bach: a study of the copper alloy artefacts from the insular La Tène assemblage* (University of Wales Press, Cardiff).

MacGregor, M, 1962, 'The Early Iron Age metalwork hoard from Stanwick, N. R. Yorks', *Proceedings of the Prehistoric Society* 28, 17–57.

MacGregor, A, 1985, *Bone Antler, Ivory and Horn: the technology of skeletal materials since the Roman period* (Croom Helm, London).

MacGregor, A, 1987, *Antiquities from Europe and the Near East in the collection of the Lord McAlpine of West Green*, (Ashmolean Museum, Oxford)

MacGregor, A and Bolick, E, 1993, *A Summary Catalogue of the Anglo-Saxon Collections (Non Ferrous Metals)*: British Archaeological Reports, British Series 230 (Ashmolean Museum Publication, Oxford).

MacGregor, A, 2001, 'Objects of bone, antler and ivory', in P Saunders (ed.), *Salisbury and South Wiltshire Museum Medieval Catalogue* 3 (Salisbury and South Wiltshire Museum, Salisbury), 14–25.

MacGregor, M, 1976, *Early Celtic Art in North Britain*, Vol. 2 (Leicester University Press, Leicester).

Mackreth, D, 1985, 'Brooches from Roman Derby', *Derbyshire Archaeological Journal* 105, 281–314.

Mackreth, D, 1991, 'Brooches', in N Holbrook and P T Bidwell (eds.), *Roman Finds from Exeter*, Exeter Archaeological Reports 44 (University of Exeter Press, Exeter), 232–240.

Major, H, 1988, 'A late Iron Age linchpin in Saffron Walden Museum', *Essex, Archaeology and History* 18, 114.

Manning, W H, 1985, *Catalogue of the Romano-British Iron Tools, Fittings and Weapons in the British Museum* (British Museum, London), 63–66.

Maraszek R, 2006, *Spätbronzezeitliche Hortfundelandschaften in atlantischer und nordischer Metalltradition* (Landesamt fuër Denkmalpflege und Archaëologie Sachsen-Anhalt, Landesmuseum fuër Vorgeschichte, Halle (Saale)).

Marschak, B I, 1986, *Silberschätze des Orients. Metallkunst des 3.-13. Jahrhunderts und ihre Kontinuität* (E A Seemann, Leipzig).

Marshall, F H, 1907, *Catalogue of Finger-rings in the British Museum* (British Museum, London).

Marzinzik, S, 2006, 'Early Cross-Channel Contacts Revisited: The Anglo-Saxon cemetery at Ringlemere, East Kent', *Association française d'Archéologie mérovingienne, Bulletin de liaison* 30, 57–58.

Marzinzik S, 2007, 'Excavating an Anglo-Saxon Cemetery in Kent, *British Museum Friends Magazine* Spring/Summer 2007, 18.

Mawer, C F, 1995, *Evidence for Christianity in Roman Britain. The Small-Finds*, British Archaeological Report, British Series 243 (Tempus, Oxford).

May, J, 1971, 'An Iron Age spout from Kirmington, Lincolnshire', *Antiquaries Journal* 51, 253–259.

Mayhew, N, 1983, *Sterling Imitations of Edwardian Type*, Royal Numismatic Society special publication 14 (Royal Numismatic Society, London).

McNeil, R, 1973, 'A report on the Bronze Age hoard from Wick Park, Stogursey, Somerset', *Proceedings of the Somerset Archaeological and Natural History Society* 117, 47–63.

McPeake, J C and Moore, C N, 1978, 'A Bronze skillet-handle from Chester and other vessels from the British Isles', *Britannia* 9, 331–334.

Megaw, J. V. S, 1970, 'Cheshire Cat and Mickey Mouse: analysis, interpretation and the art of the La Tène Iron Age,' *Proceedings of the Prehistoric Society* 36, 261–279.

Menghin, W, 1983, *Das Schwert im Frühen Mittelalter* (K. Theiss, Stuttgart).

Menghin, W (ed.), 2007, *Merowingerzeit, Europa ohne Grenzen*. Catalogue: Pushkin Museum Moscow, State Hermitage St. Petersburg (Staatliche Museen zu Berlin & Edition Minerva, Berlin & Wolfratshausen).

Moorhead, T S N, 1997, 'All Cannings, Wiltshire', *CHRB* 10, 406–409.

Moorhead, T S N, 2001, *Roman Coin Finds from Wiltshire* (MPhil Thesis, University College London).

Moorhead, T S N, 2008, 'Two Carausian Aurei from Ashbourne, Derbyshire', *Numismatic Chronicle* 168, 397–399.

Moorhead, T S N, 2008, 'Numismatic enigmas', *Current Archaeology* 220 (July 2008), 38–43.

Murawski, P, 2003, *Benet's Artefacts of England and the United Kingdom* (Paul G Murawski, Cambridge).

Murdoch, T, 1991, *Treasures and Trinkets. Jewellery in London from pre-Roman times to the 1930s* (Museum of London, London).

Naylor, J (2007) 'The Circulation of Early-medieval European Coinage: a case study from Yorkshire, c. 650–c. 867', *Medieval Archaeology* 51, 41–61.

Needham, S P, Leese, M N, Hook, D R and Hughes, M J, 1988, 'Developments in the Early Bronze Age metallurgy of southern Britain, World Archaeology', *Archaeometallurgy* 20. 3, 383–402.

Needham, S P, 1990, *The Petters Late Bronze Age Metalwork: an analytical study of Thames Valley metalworking in its settlement context,* British Museum Occasional Paper 70 (British Museum, London).

Needham, S P, 1996, 'Chronology and periodisation in the British Bronze Age,' in K Randsborg (ed.), 'Absolute Chronology Archaeological Europe 2500–500 BC, Part II', *Acta Archaeologica* 67, 121–140.

Needham, S P, Bronk Ramsay, C, Coombs, D, Cartwright, C and Petitt, P, 1997, 'An independent chronology for British Bronze Age metalwork: the results of the Oxford Radiocarbon Accelerator Programme', *Archaeology Journal* 154, 55–107.

Needham, S, and Rohl, B, 1998, *The circulation of metal in the British Bronze Age : the application of lead isotope analysis* (British Museum, London).

Needham, S, Parfitt, K and Varndell, G, 2006, *The Ringlemere Cup: Precious Cups and the Beginning of the Channel Bronze Age.* British Museum Research Publication 163 (British Museum, London).

Needham, S, 2007, '800 BC: the great divide', in C Haselgrove and R Pope (eds.), *The Earlier Iron Age in Britain and the Near Continent* (Oxbow, Oxford), 39–63.

North, J J, 2000, *English Hammered Coinage Volume 1: Early Anglo-Saxon to Henry III c.600–1272* (Spink, London).

North, J J, 2000, *English Hammered Coinage Volume 2: Edward I to Charles II 1272–1662* (Spink, London).

Northover, J P, 1982, 'The exploration of the long-distance movement of bronze in Bronze and Early Iron Age Europe', *Bulletin of the Institute of Archaeology* 19, 45–72.

O'Connor, B, 1980, *Cross Channel Relations in the Later Bronze Age*, British Archaeological Reports, International Series S 91 (Archaeopress, Oxford).

O'Connor, B, 2007, 'Llyn Fawr metalwork in Britain: a review', in C Haselgrove and R Pope, *The Earlier Iron Age in Britain and the Near Continent* (Oxbow, Oxford) 64–79.

Olivier, A, 1996, 'Brooches of silver, copper-alloy and iron from Dragonby', in J May, *Dragonby Report on Excavations at an Iron Age and Romano-British Settlement in North Lincolnshire*, Oxbow Monograph 61 (Oxbow, Oxford), 231–264.

Oman, C, 1974, *British Rings 800–1914*, (Greenlight, Wiltham).

Painter, K and Sax, M, 1970, 'The British Museum collection of Roman head-stud brooches,' *British Museum Quarterly,* 34, 153–74 (British Museums Publications, London).

Palmer, N, 1980, 'A Beaker burial and medieval tenements in The Hamel', *Oxoniensia* 45, 124–134.

Papworth, J, 1961, *Ordinary of British Armorials* (Tabard Publications, London).

Parfitt, K and Brugmann, B, 1997, *The Anglo-Saxon Cemetery on Mill Hill, Deal, Kent, Society for Medieval Archaeology* 14 (Society for Medieval Archaeology, London).

Parfitt, K and Needham, S, 2005, 'More Important Discoveries at Ringlemere Farm', *Newsletter of the Kent Archaeological Society* 64, 13.

Payne, N, 2008, 'Finds reported to the Portable Antiquities Scheme in 2007', *Somerset Archaeology and Natural History* 151, 201–207.

Pearce, S, 1983, *The Bronze Age Metalwork of Southwestern Britain,* British Archaeological Reports, British Series 120 (Archaeopress, Oxford).

Pendleton, C, 1999, *Bronze Age Metalwork in Northern East Anglia*, British Archaeological Reports, British Series 279 (John and Erica Hedges, Oxford)

Penn, K, 2000, *Norwich Southern Bypass, Part II: The Anglo-Saxon Cemetery at Harford Farm, Caistor St. Edmund, East Anglian Archaeology* 92 (Norfolk Museums Service, Dereham).

Petersen, J, 1919, *De Norske Vikingesverd* (I kommission hos J. Dybwad, Oslo).

Pierce I, 2002, *Swords of the Viking Age* (Boydell, Bury St Edmunds).

Read, B, 1995, *History Beneath our Feet* (Anglia, Ipswich).

RIB = Roman Inscriptions in Britain (various authors and volumes)

Robinson, P, 1995. 'Miniature socketed bronze axes from Wiltshire', *Wiltshire Archaeological and Natural History Magazine* 88, 60–68.

Roberts, B, 2007, 'Adorning the living but not the dead: understanding ornaments in Britain c. 1400–1100 cal BC, *Proceedings of the Prehistoric Society* 73, 135–167.

Robertson, A S, 1975, *Birrens (Blatobulgium)* (T and A Constable, Edinburgh).

Robertson, A S, Hobbs, R and Buttrey T V (eds.), 2000, *An Inventory of Romano-British Coin Hoards*, Royal Numismatic Society Special Publication 20 (Royal Numismatic Society, London).

Roe, F E S, 1966, 'The battle-axe series in Britain', *Proceedings of the Prehistoric Society* 32, 199–245.

Roesdahl, E and Wilson, D M (eds.), 1992, *From Viking to Crusader. The Scandinavians and Europe 800-1200, Catalogue of the 22nd Council of Europe Exhibition* (Bohusläningens Boktryckeri AB, Uddevalla).

Rowlands, M, 1971, 'A group of incised decorated armrings and their significance for the Middle Bronze Age of southern Britain, in de G Sieveking (ed.), *Prehistoric and Roman Studies Commemorating the Opening of the Department of Prehistoric and Romano-British Antiquities* (British Museum, London).

Rowlands, M, 1976, *The Production and Distribution of Metalwork in the Middle Bronze Age in southern Britain*, British Archaeological Reports, British Series 31 (Archaeopress, Oxford).

Russel, A D, 1990, 'Two Beaker burials from Chilbolton, Hampshire', *Proceedings of the Prehistoric Society* 56, 153–172.

Saunders, P and E (eds.), 1991, *Salisbury and South Wiltshire Museum Medieval Catalogue, Part 1* (Salisbury & South Wiltshire Museum, Salisbury).

Savory, H, 1980, *Guide Catalogue of the Bronze Age Collections* (National Museum of Wales, Cardiff).

Savory, H, 1993, 'Strap hook', in K Blockley, F Asmore and P Ashmore (eds.), 'Excavations on the Roman fort at Abergavenny, Orchard site 1972–73', *Archaeological Journal* 150, 211–214.

Sear, D R., 2000-5, *Roman Coins and their values* (3 vols) (Spink, London).

Schmidt, P K and Burgess, C B, 1981, *The axes of Scotland and northern England* 9.7 (Prähistorische Bronzefunde, Müchen).

Sellye, I, 1939, *Les bronzes émaillés de la Pannonie Romaine* (Institut de numismatique et d'archeologie de l'universite Pierre, Budapest).

Sheehan, J, 1991-2, 'Coiled arm-rings – an Hiberno-Viking silver armring type', *Journal of Irish Archaeology* 6, 41–53.

Sheridan, A, 2007, 'The bone belt-hook from Bargrennan Pit 2', in V Cummings and C Fowler, *From Cairn to Cemetery: an archaeological investigation of the chambered cairns and Early Bronze Age mortuary deposits at Cairnderry and Bargrennan White Cairn, South-West Scotland*, British Archaeological Reports, British Series 434 (Archaeopress, Oxford), 112–115.

Sills, J, 2003, *Gaulish and Early British Gold Coinage* (Spink, London).

Skovmand, R, 1942, 'De danske Skattefund fra Vikingetiden og den ældste Middelalder indtil omkring 1150', *Aarbøger for Nordisk Oldkyndighed og Historie*, 1–275.

Smith, R A, 1909–11, 'On a Bronze Age hoard dredged from the Thames off Broadness', *Proceedings of the Society of Antiquities, London* 23, 160–171.

Smith, R A, 1925, *British Museum Guide to Early Iron Age Antiquities* (British Museum, London)

Speake, G, 1980, *Anglo-Saxon Animal Art and its Germanic Background* (Oxford University Press, Oxford).

Spencer, B, 1998, *Pilgrim Souvenirs and Secular Badges. Medieval Finds from Excavations in London 7* (The Stationery Office, London).

Spencer, P D, 2008, 'The Purbeck Hills Hoard', *The Searcher* 269, January 2008, 22–24.

Spink and Son, 1979, *The Ernest Brummer Collection. Vol. 1. Medieval and Renaissance Art* (Galerie Koller, Zürich).

Spratling, M, 1972, *Southern British Decorated Bronzes of the Late Pre-Roman Iron Age* (unpublished PhD thesis, University of London).

Stead, I M, 1979, *The Arras Culture* (Yorkshire Philosophical Society, York).

Stead, I.M, 1991, 'The Snettisham Treasure: excavations in 1990', *Antiquity* 65, 447–465.

Stead, I M, 1991, 'Many more Iron Age shields from Britain', *Antiquities Journal* 71, 1–35.

Stead, I M, 1998, *The Salisbury Hoard* (Tempus, Stroud).

Stenberger, M, 1947, *Die Schatzfunde Gotlands der Wikingerzeit,* Vol.2, (Hakan Ohlssons boktryckeri, Lund).

Strutt, J, 1801, *Sports and Pastimes of the People of England* (T Bensley for J White, London).

Sutton, K and Worrell, S (2007) 'Roman religious objects recorded by the Portable Antiquities Scheme in Oxfordshire and elsewhere,' in L Gilmour (ed.), *Pagans and Christians – from Antiquity to the Middle Ages. Papers in honour of Martin Henig*, British Archaeological Reports International Series 1610 (Archeopress, Oxford), 145-50.

Swan, V, 1984, *The Pottery Kilns of Roman Britain*, Royal Commission on Historical Monuments, Supplementary Series 5 (Stationery Office Books, London).

Swift, E, 2000, *Regionality in Dress Accessories in the late Roman West*, *Monographies Instrumentum* 11 (éditions monique merqoil, Montagnac).

TAR 2000 = Treasure Annual Report 2000 (DCMS, 2002).

TAR 2001 = Treasure Annual Report 2001 (DCMS, 2003).

TAR 2002 = Treasure Annual Report 2002 (DCMS, 2004).

TAR 2003 = Treasure Annual Report 2003 (DCMS, 2005).

TAR 2004 = Treasure Annual Report 2004 (DCMS, 2007).

TAR 2005/6 = Treasure Annual Report 2005/6 (British Museum, 2008).

Taylor, J, 1980, *Bronze Age Goldwork of the British Isles* (Cambridge University Press, Cambridge).

Thomas, R, 1989, 'The bronze to iron transition in Southern Britain', in M L Stig Sorensen and R Thomas (eds.), *The Bronze Age-Iron Age Transition in Europe*: 263–286, British Archaeological Reports, International Series, S 483 (Archaeopress, Oxford).

Thomas, G, 2003, *Late Saxon and Viking-Age strapends 750-1100: Part 1, Finds Research Group Datasheet* 32.

Thomas, G, 2004, *Late Saxon and Viking-Age strapends 750-1100: Part 2, Finds Research Group Datasheet* 33

Thomas, G, 2006, 'Reflections on a '9th-century' Northumbrian metalworking tradition: a silver hoard from Poppleton, North Yorkshire, *Medieval Archaeology* 50, 143-64.

Thompson, F H, 1954, 'A bronze spear-head from Donington on Bain, Lincolnshire', *Antiquaries Journal* 34, 238.

Thompson, F H, 1971, 'Some lost Roman bronzes from Lincoln', *Antiquaries Journal* 51, 100–103.

Thörle, S, 2001, 'Gleicharmige Bügelfibeln des frühen Mittelalters', *Universitätsforschungen zur prähistorischen Archäologie* 81.

Tomalin, D, 1989, 'A Roman symmetrical flanged bronze strainer found in Surrey and its counterparts in highland Britain', *Surrey Archaeology Collections* 79, 53–65.

Tomlin, R S O, 2008, 'Roman Britain in 2007 III: Inscriptions', *Britannia* 39, 369–389.

Toynbee, J, 1962, *Art in Roman Britain* (Phaidon, London).

VA = Van Arsdell, R D, 1989, *Celtic Coinage of Britain* (Spink, London).

Varley, W J, 1938, 'The Bleasdale Circle', *Antiquaries Journal* 18, 154–171.

Waddington, K E, 2007, 'The poetics of scale: miniature axes from Whitchurch', in V O Jorge and J Thomas (eds.), 'Overcoming the modern invention of material culture', *Journal of Iberian Archaeology* 9/10, 187–206.

Walters, B and Henig, M, 1988, 'Two busts from Littlecote', *Britannia* 19, 407–440

Wamers, E, 1991, 'Pyxides imaginatae. Zur Ikonographie und Funktion karolingischer Silberbecher', *Germania* 69, 97–152.

Ward Perkins, B, 1940, *Museum of London Medieval Catalogue* (HMSO, London).

Waugh, H and Goodburn, R, 1972, 'I. The non-ferrous objects', in S Frere, *Verulamium Excavations* 1, Reports of the Research Committee of the Society of Antiquaries of London, 28 (Society of Antiquaries of London, London).

Webster, G, 1990, 'Part of a Celtic linch-pin (from near Lapworth, Warks)', *Britannia* 21, 293–294.

Webster, L and Backhouse, J (eds.), 1991, *The Making of England: Anglo-Saxon Art and Culture AD 600 – 900* (British Museum, London).

Webster, L, 1995, 'The Iona Abbey ring bezel', in Graham-Campbell, J (ed.) *The Viking-Age Gold and Silver of Scotland (AD 850-110)* (National Museum of Scotland, Edinburgh), 49-51.

Wedlake, W J, 1958, *Excavations at Camerton, Somerset* (Camerton Excavation Club, Camerton).

Wheeler, R. E. M, and Wheeler, T. V, 1932, R*eport on the excavation of the prehistoric, Roman, and post-Roman site in Lydney Park, Gloucestershire* (Oxford University Press, Oxford)

Wild, J P, 1970, 'Button-and-loop fasteners in the Roman provinces', *Britannia* 1, 137–155.

Williams, D, 1997, *Late Saxon Stirrup Mounts*, Council for British Archaeology Research Report 111 (Council for British Archaeology, York)

Williams, D, 1997, *Stirrup Terminals*, Finds Research Group Datasheet 24.

Williams, G, *forthcoming* 2009, 'Monetary developments in the Northern Danelaw in the 920s, in the light of the Vale of York hoard' in Abramson, T (ed.), *Studies in Early Medieval Coinage* 2 (Boydell, Woodbridge).

Williams, G, *forthcoming*, 'The Coins from the Vale of York Viking Hoard: Preliminary Report', *British Numismatic Journal* 78.

Williams, R J, Hart, P J and Williams, A T L, 1996, *Wavendon Gate: a late Iron Age and Roman Settlement in Milton Keynes*, Buckinghamshire Archaeological Society Monograph Series 10 (Buckinghamshire Archaeological Society, Aylesbury).

Williamson, G C, 1891, *Trade Tokens Issued in the Seventeenth Century in England, Wales and Ireland by Corporations, Merchants, Tradesman, etc* (Elliot Stock, London).

Wilson, D M, 1960, 'The Fejø cup', *Acta Archaeologica* 31, 147-173, fig.15a-b.

Wilson, D M, 1964, *Anglo-Saxon Ornamental Metalwork 700-1100 in the British Museum. Catalogue of Antiquities of the Later Saxon Period*, Vol.1 (British Museum, London).

Woodward, P J, 1987, 'The excavation of an Iron Age and Romano-British settlement at Rope Lake Hole, Corfe Castle, Dorset', in N Sunter and P J Woodward (eds.), *Romano-British Industries in Purbeck, excavations at Norden by Nigel Sunter; excavations at Ower and Rope Lake Hole by Peter J Woodward*, Dorset Natural History and Archaeological Society, Monograph 6 (Dorset Natural History & Archaeological Society, Dorchester), 125–180.

Woodward, A, 2000, *British Barrows: a matter of life and death* (Tempus, Stroud).

Worrell, S, 2002, 'Recent Metalwork Discoveries in Hampshire', *Proceedings of the Hampshire Field Club and Archaeological Society* 57, 89–95.

Worrell, S, 2006, 'Roman Britain in 2005 II: finds reported under the Portable Antiquities Scheme', *Britannia* 37, 442–443.

Worrell, S, 2007a, 'Detecting the Later Iron Age: a view from the Portable Antiquities Scheme', in C Haselgrove and T Moore (eds.), *The Later Iron Age in Britain and Beyond* (Oxbow, Oxford), 371–388.

Worrell, S, 2007b, 'Roman Britain in 2006 II: finds reported under the Portable Antiquities Scheme', *Britannia* 38, 303–344.

Worrell, S, 2008, 'Roman Britain in 2007 II: finds reported under the Portable Antiquities Scheme', *Britannia* 39, 337–367.

Wymer, J J, 1987, 'A pair of bronze palstave moulds from Harling', *Norfolk Archaeology* 40, 122–126.

Zadoks-Josephus Jitta, A N, 1961, 'De Eerste Muntslag te Duurstede', *Jaarboek voor Munt-en Penningkunde* 48, 1–14.

Zadoks-Josephus Jitters, A N, Peters, W J T and van Es, W A, 1973, *Roman Bronze Statuettes from the Netherlands II. Statuettes Found South of the Limes*, Scripta Archaeologica Groningana 1 (J. B. Wolters; Groningen).

Zeiss, H, 1934, *Die Grabfunde aus dem spanischen Westgotenreich* (Walter de Gruyter & Co., Berlin/ Leipzig).

INDEXES

TABLE OF TREASURE CASES 2007

The following table lists all 2007 Treasure cases;
those mentioned in the catalogue have a cat. no.

Key to abbreviations:
TBA = To be acquired
A = Acquired
D = Disclaimed
DON = Donated (L = Landowner, F = Finder)
MW = Museum withdrew
NT = Not Treasure
NTT = Not Treasure Trove

BRONZE AGE

Cat. no.	Treasure no.	PAS no.	County	Parish	Description	Disposition	Acquiring Museum	Value
19	T388	SWYOR-C4F166	West Yorkshire	Stanbury	Copper-alloy funerary deposit	TBA	Bradford Museum	
24	T630	CORN-9155C2 & 90A647	Cornwall	Wadebridge	Copper-alloy palstaves	TBA	Royal Cornwall Museum	
31	T125	SUSS-15B261, 15DD86 & 15E741	East Sussex	Pett	Base-metal deposit	TBA	Hastings Museum	
32	T662	HAMP-2CB8E2 & 2CB8E2	Hampshire	Hambledon area	Base-metal group	A	Winchester Museums Service	£225
35	7.13	NMGW-99FED6	Wrexham	Burton	Gold bead and wire	TBA	National Museum Wales	
36	T510	NMGW-A93765	Wiltshire	Seagry	Gold bracelet fragment	TBA	Wiltshire Heritage Museum	
37	T118	BUC-9754C7	Buckinghamshire	Stone	Gold composite ring	A	Buckinghamshire County Museum	£800
38	T672	WAW-C0C0B3	Warwickshire	Ansley	Gold ribbon ornament	A	Warwickshire Museum	£60
39	T8	NMS-BE02A4	Norfolk	West Acre	Gold sheet strip fragment	TBA	Norwich Castle Museum	
40	7.23	NMGW-9AC224	Isle of Anglesey	Trearddur	Gold penannular ring	DON (L)	Oriel Ynys Mon, Llangefni	
41	T295	YORYM-954174	Wiltshire	East Knoyle	Base-metal hoard	A	Salisbury & South Wiltshire Museum	£600
44	T59	HAMP-4AA958	Hampshire	Fawley	Gold penannular ring	TBA	Hampshire Museums Service	
45	T475	NMS-EA2C32	Norfolk	Witchingham area	Gold penannular ring	DON (F)	Norwich Castle Museum	£130
46	T259	ESS-45C591	Essex	Theydon Mount	Gold penannular ring	A	Epping Forest District Museum	£100
47	T74	NARC-773944	Northamptonshire	Kettering area	Gold penannular ring	A	Northampton Museum	£450
51	T704	HAMP-4DE734, 4F1980, 4EB8B3, 4EA817, 4DE734 & 4F78E6	Hampshire	Amport area	Base-metal deposit	TBA	Hampshire Museums Service	
52	T497	ESS-259C45	Essex	Uttlesford District	Base-metal hoard	TBA	Saffron Walden Museum	
53	T555	NMS-1E6A46	Norfolk	Attleborough area	Base-metal deposit	A	Norwich Castle Museum	£220
54	T579	KENT-C2ABB7	Kent	Offham	Base-metal deposit	A	Maidstone Museum	£650
55	T580	KENT-C93982	Kent	Hoaden	Base-metal group	DON (F&L)	Dover Museum	
58	T490	IOW-FA17F8	Isle of Wight	West Wight	Gold penannular bracelet	MW	Isle of Wight Heritage Service	
60	T629	HAMP-2865F1	Dorset	Langton Matravers	Base-metal hoard	A	Dorset County Museum	£25,000
60	T640	HAMP-893364	Dorset	Langton Matravers	Base-metal hoard	A	Dorset County Museum	£17,500

Cat. no.	Treasure no.	PAS no.	County	Parish	Description	Disposition	Acquiring Museum	Value
	T17	DENO-DA8C26 DBE907, DC2B23, DC4C87,DC8D26	Derbyshire	Derby area	Base metal group	NT		
	T518	YORYM-CFEE95	East Yorkshire	Bolton	Bronze rapier fragments	NT		
	T429	IOW-BD19F8	Isle of Wight	near Shorwell	Gold bracelet fragment	D		
	T144	KENT-041F47	Kent	Cliffs End	Copper-alloy ingots	TBD		
	T526	SF-A6BE92	Suffolk	Great Finborough	Copper-alloy fragments	D		
	T206	SF-C98115	Suffolk	Halesworth area	Base-metal hoard	D		
	T615	WMID-AC2162	Warwickshire	Kenilworth	Bronze spearhead fragments	DON (F&L)	Warwickshire Museum	£40

IRON AGE

Cat. no.	Treasure no.	PAS no.	County	Parish	Description	Disposition	Acquiring Museum	Value
68	T104	NMS-D3BF38	Norfolk	Kings Lynn area	Electrum torc terminal	A	Norwich Castle Museum	£2,200
69	T119	NMS-C6DFC1	Norfolk	Norwich area	Gold torc fitting	A	Norwich Castle Museum	£1,000
75	T491	BH-B96102	Bedfordshire	Wilstead	Silver brooch fragment	DON (L)	Bedford Museum	£10
80	T589	NMS-248F38	Norfolk	Attleborough area	Copper-alloy/ iron linchpin elements	A	Norwich Castle Museum	£50
82	07.06	NMGW-9B2D52 & 9BEE04	Vale of Glamorgan	Cowbridge	Bronze terret and rein-ring	DON (L)	National Museum of Wales	£250
88	07.24	NMGW-9C0216	Gwent	Langstone, Newport	Bronze bowls, wine strainer and tankard	TBA	National Museum of Wales	
427	T608	BUC-6CFB85	Buckinghamshire	Little Horwood	Gold *staters*	A	Buckinghamshire County Museum	£800
428	T602	LIN-3400F2	Lincolnshire	Saxilby	Gold *staters*	A	British Museum (no. 4)	£1,200
429	T55	WILT-CDD3C6	Wiltshire	Urchfont	Silver units	TBA	Wiltshire Heritage Museum	
430	T624	KENT-049BF3	Kent	Westerham	Gold quarter *staters*	A	Maidstone Museum	£3,800
431	T660	YORYM-1EC684	East Yorkshire	Beverley	Gold *staters*	D		
432	T274	WAW-A89225 & A87636	Leicestershire	East Leicestershire	Silver units	TBA	Leicestershire County Council Museum Services	
433	T600	NCL-63DA22	East Yorkshire	North Dalton	Gold *staters* and silver unit	D		
434	T48	NCL-001A42	East Yorkshire	Driffield area	Gold *staters*	D		
435	T597	YORYM-1C8AA2	East Yorkshire	Driffield area	Gold *staters*	D		
	T247	KENT-0459F2	Kent	Cliffs End	Assemblage	TBD		
	T248	KENT-0464C2	Kent	Cliffs End	Assemblage	TBD		

Cat. no.	Treasure no.	PAS no.	County	Parish	Description	Disposition	Acquiring Museum	Value
	T124	LIN-338B36	Lincolnshire	Osbournby	Silver ingot	D		
	T122	LIN-337095	Lincolnshire	Osbournby	Gold band	D		
	T695		Norfolk	West Norfolk	Coin hoard	TBA	Norwich Castle Museum	

ROMAN

Cat. no.	Treasure no.	PAS no.	County	Parish	Description	Disposition	Acquiring Museum	Value
91	T140	CORN-929E07	Cornwall	St Buryan	Gold jewellery fragment	A	Royal Cornwall Museum	£100
92	T443	YORYM-CBED34	North Yorkshire	Snape with Thorpe	Gold jewellery component	A	British Museum	£30
93	T535	CAMHER-9B2FA5	Cambridgeshire	Ely	Silver finger-ring	A	Ely Museum	£80
96	T258	NCL-0061D8	Cumbria	Carlisle	Silver hair-pin fragment	A	Tullie House Museum & Art Gallery	£50
99	T438	SWYOR-6B2484	City of York	York area	Silver finger-ring	A	British Museum	£100
102	T187	YORYM-F9FB75	North Yorkshire	North Yorkshire area	Silver *ligula*	D		
106	T686	LVPL-035186	Cheshire	Hale	Silver brooch	A	National Museums Liverpool	£800
108 & 480	T391	NCL-D28051 & D488D8	County Durham	Seaton with Slingley	Silver brooch fragment and silver *denarius*	A	British Museum (brooch only)	£160
111	T41	WMID-3487F6	Leicestershire	Sheepy	Gold necklace fragment	TBA	Leicestershire County Council Heritage Services	
118	T411	CAMHER-995025	Cambridgeshire	Chesterton	Gold necklace componant	TBA	Peterborough Museum & Art Gallery	
119	T611	NLM-A74468	Lincolnshire	Roughton	Silver finger-ring fragment	D		
120	T357	BH-C3A8E7	Bedfordshire	Hockliffe	Silver finger-ring fragment	A	Luton Museum	£80
121	T437	LIN-1901F7	Lincolnshire	Well	Silver finger-ring fragment	DON (F&L)	The Collection, Lincoln	
122	T387	LVPL-E08676	Nottinghamshire	Gosford Farm	Silver finger-ring	TBA	Museum of Nottingham Life	
123	T587	SF-F82122	Suffolk	Wetheringsett	Gold finger-ring	D		
128	T386	ESS-455767	Essex	Bures area	Gold finger-ring	A	Braintree Museum	£750
131	T261	GLO-EF3774	Gloucestershire	North Nibley	Silver finger-ring	A	Museum in the Park, Stroud	£85
134	T112	WILT-6DF737	Wiltshire	Lacock	Silver finger-ring	A	British Museum	£100
135	T1	BERK-0B6771	Oxfordshire	South Oxfordshire	Gold foil amulet	TBA	British Museum	

Cat. no.	Treasure no.	PAS no.	County	Parish	Description	Disposition	Acquiring Museum	Value
136	T131	CAMHER-94FB77	Cambridgeshire	Godmanchester	Silver finger-ring	A	British Museum	£75
137	T335	YORYM-1CD342	North Yorkshire	Aldborough area	Gold finger-ring	TBA	British Museum	
138	T54	WILT-6D7DE7	Wiltshire	Lacock	Silver finger-ring	A	Wiltshire Heritage Museum	£145
146	T352	WAW-D04DD6	Warwickshire	Alcester	Silver spoon fragment	A	Warwickshire Museum	£40
148	T236	NMS-E7D6B7	Norfolk	Gunthorpe	Gold brooch	TBA	Norwich Castle Museum	£750
151	T590	WILT-773952	Wiltshire	Urchfont	Silver buckle	TBA	Wiltshire Heritage Museum	
153	T111	NCL-62C367	Northumberland	Vindolanda	Silver ingot	DON (L)	Vindolanda Trust	
459	T260	DENO-73ECB4	Nottinghamshire	Mansfield Woodhouse area	Silver *denarii* hoard	A	Mansfield Museum & Art Gallery	£840
461	T197	IOW-2CE096	Isle of Wight	Shorwell	Silver and copper-alloy coin hoard	D		
470	T315	LVPL-B8BD62, 8B6538 & EB9A86.	Cheshire	Whitchurch area	Silver *denarii*	D		
471	T377	SUSS-B27B77	West Sussex	Selsey area	Silver *denarii*	A	Chichester District Museum	£40
472	T106	SUSS-C3BB17	West Sussex	Petworth area	Silver *denarii* and pottery	TBA	Chichester District Museum	
473	T185	YORYM-109BE5	East Yorkshire	North Dalton	Silver *denarii*	A	East Riding Museums Service	£90
474	T198	NCL-62EF85	County Durham	Westgate area	Silver *denarii*	A	British Museum (1 coin)	£50
475	T667	HESH-887B04	Shropshire	Ellesmere	Copper-alloy *sestertii*	TBA	Shropshire County Museums Service	
476	T416	YORYM-743FA7	North Yorkshire	Ugthorpe	Silver *denarii*, silver fragments and copper-alloy brooch fragment	TBA	Whitby Museum	
477	T134		Devon	Kingskerswell	Silver *denarius*, bronze *sestertii* and copper-alloy fragments	NTT		
478	T220	NMS-D537C1	Norfolk	Postwick	Silver *denarii*	D		
479	T289	IOW-841278	Isle of Wight	Newchurch	Copper-alloy *sestertii* and fractions	D		
482	T312	NMGW-29BDC6; LEIC-215B27, 206F66, 213D57, 21A411 & 2228A4; WMID-909D93, D22C67 & D212F4	Leicestershire	Twycross	Silver *denarii* and *radiates*	TBA	Leicestershire County Council Heritage Services	
483	T677	GLO-40A9B6	Bath and North East Somerset	Bath	Base-silver coin hoard	TBA	Roman Baths Museum, Bath	
484	T66	SWYOR-AEF716	South Yorkshire	Doncaster area	Silver *radiates* and silver-gilt brooch	DON (L)	Doncaster Museum (brooch)	£50
486	T424	YORYM-697A25	North Yorkshire	Harrogate area	Copper-alloy *radiates*	NTT	Yorkshire Museums Trust	

Cat. no.	Treasure no.	PAS no.	County	Parish	Description	Disposition	Acquiring Museum	Value
487	T152	IOW-936B93	Isle of Wight	Yarmouth	Base-silver *radiates*	D		
488	T665	HESH-884BE4	Shropshire	Baschurch	Base-metal *radiates*	D		
489	T344	SUSS-BC6150	West Sussex	Storrington	Copper-alloy radiates	DON (F)	Storrington Museum	£50
490	T709	DENO-64DAE1 & 651C91	Derbyshire	Ashbourne area	Gold *aurei*	A	Derby Museum & Art Gallery and British Museum	£200,000
499	T570	DENO-4D6A35	Derbyshire	Stanton area	Copper-alloy *nummi*	TBA	British Museum (2 coins)	
500	T142	SF-2278D4	Suffolk	Barking	Base-silver *nummi*	DON (L)	Suffolk County Council Archaeology Store	
501	T176	YORYM-842863	North Yorkshire	Flaxton	Copper-alloy *nummi*	D		
502	T90	WILT-104653	Wiltshire	St Paul with Malmesbury	Copper-alloy *nummi*	DON (F&L)	Athelstan Museum	
502	T617	WILT-284FB5	Wiltshire	St Paul with Malmesbury	Copper-alloy *nummi* and *as*	DON (F&L)	Athelstan Museum	
503	T314	NCL-637911	County Durham	Catcote	Copper-alloy *nummi*	DON (L)	Hartlepool Museum and Heritage Service	
504	T563	PAS-70D823	Herefordshire	Aston Ingham	Copper-alloy *nummi*	TBA	Hereford Museum & Art Gallery	
505	T576	CORN-84F996	Cornwall	Padstow	Copper-alloy *nummi*	D	Prideaux Estate	
506	T201	LVPL-00DCE2	Cheshire	Barbridge	Copper-alloy *nummi* and fragments	TBA	Nantwich Museum	
507	T664	HESH-881F86	Shropshire	Bridgnorth area	Bronze coin hoard	TBA	Shropshire County Museum Service	
508	T209		Devon	Newton Abbot area	Copper-alloy *nummi*	TBA	Royal Albert Memorial Museum, Exeter	
520	T566	GLO-2AD8F2	South Gloucestershire	Hawkesbury	Base-metal *radiate*, *nummi* and objects	NT		
522	T165	SF-4BDF20	Suffolk	Mildenhall area	Silver *siliquae*	A	Mildenhall District Museum	£550
523	T514	SF-424843	Suffolk	Saxmundham area	Gold *solidi* and silver *siliquae*	A	Colchester & Ipswich Museum Service	£1,500
525	T449	HAMP-F6F384 & F71BD4	Hampshire	Fareham	Gold *solidi*	TBA	Hampshire Museums Service	
526	T604	SF-8AB7E8	Suffolk	Hoxne	Silver *siliquae*	DON (F&L)	British Museum	
	T466	BH-DE5443	Bedfordshire	Odell	Gold jewellery	D		
	T717	BERK-FED956	Buckinghamshire	Quarrrendon	Silver finger-ring	A	Buckinghamshire County Museum	£50
	T291	CAMHER-989D15	Cambridgeshire	Arbury Camp	Silver finger-ring fragment	D		
	T408	CAMHER-98C194	Cambridgeshire	Chesterton	Copper-alloy coins	NT		
	T409	PAS-594DC3	Cambridgeshire	Chesterton	Silver finger-ring	D		

Cat. no.	Treasure no.	PAS no.	County	Parish	Description	Disposition	Acquiring Museum	Value
	T82	BH-0F52A7	Cambridgeshire	Dry Drayton	Silver finger-ring fragment	D		
	T129	CAMHER-94CEE7	Cambridgeshire	Melborn	Silver umbonate stud	D		
	T620	CAMHER-9BCDF2	Cambridgeshire	West Wratting	Base-metal coin hoard	NT		
	T623	SWYOR-7ED5A2	Cumbria	Silloth area	Silver artefact	DON (F&L)	Senhouse Roman Museum	£35
	T99	SOMDOR-D9D227	Dorset	Stinsford	Copper-alloy strap-end	NT		
	T519	YORYM-CFDB11	East Yorkshire	Pocklington area	Silver finger-ring fragment	D		
	T153	LON-C2E168, C3FEC4, C40CA3, C41A24, C421E7 & C42D87	Greater London	Drapers' Garden	Gold and silver objects	TBA	East Riding Museums Service	
	T73	LON-FD56F7	Greater London	Tower Hamlets	Coin hoard	TBD		
	T719	SUSS-68D868 & 68AA45	Hampshire	Chichester area	Silver coins	D		
	T316	NMGW-261B34	Hampshire	Cole Henley	Silver finger-ring, incomplete	D		
	T22	BH-019D84	Hertfordshire	North Hertfordshire	Silver finger-ring	D		
	T550	BH-DE4385	Hertfordshire	St Ippolyts	Silver pendant	D		
	T225	IOW-85AAB2	Isle of Wight	Brighstone	Coin hoard	NT		
	T44	KENT-73F096	Kent	Offham	Gold finger-ring	D		
	T190	KENT-37A621	Kent	Ryarsh	Gold finger-ring	D		
	T253	LIN-33B105	Lincolnshire	Aswarby and Swarby	Silver finger-ring	D		
	T58	LIN-336194	Lincolnshire	Coningsby	Silver finger-ring	D		
	T478	LIN-3D76C2	Lincolnshire	East Barkwith	Silver finger-ring	D		
	T257	LIN-33C394	Lincolnshire	East Kirkby	Silver finger-ring	D		
	T123	LIN-337C26	Lincolnshire	Osbournby	Silver *intaglio* from a finger-ring	D		
	T461	NMS-E9CF81	Norfolk	Beeston with Bittering	Silver finger-ring fragment	D		
	T507	NMS-E9F975	Norfolk	Beeston with Bittering	Gold finger-ring	D		
	T269	NMS-2B7305	Norfolk	Foxley	Silver finger-ring	D		
	T103	NMS-D2D563	Norfolk	Sedgeford	Silver unidentified object fragment	D		
	T368	LVPL-E03C72	North Yorkshire	Fountains Abbey area	Silver finger-ring	MW	Harrogate Museum	
	T191	SWYOR-C43E55	North Yorkshire	Kellington	Silver finger-ring fragment	D		
	T21	YORYM-776F81	North Yorkshire	Littondale	Silver finger-ring	D		

Cat. no.	Treasure no.	PAS no.	County	Parish	Description	Disposition	Acquiring Museum	Value
	T557	DENO-CBB910	Northamptonshire	Islip	Silver finger-ring	TBA	Northampton Museum	
	T558	NARC-AE6AE2	Northamptonshire	Wilbarston	Silver finger-ring fragment	D		
	T547	LVPL-E0C814	Nottinghamshire	Weston	Silver finger-ring	DON (F&L)	Newark Museum	£55
	T541	BERK-CC1C60	Oxfordshire	East Hendred	Silver finger-ring fragment	D		
	T369	SF-06F3A2	Suffolk	Campsey Ash	Gold jewellery fragment	D		
	T588	SF-F7EF96	Suffolk	Stowmarket area	Silver finger-ring	D		
	T612	SF-F79045	Suffolk	Stowmarket area	Silver finger-ring	D		
	T228	WAW-792B78	Warwickshire	Wappenbury	Silver finger-ring fragment	D		
	T708	WILT-135C98	Wiltshire	North Newnton	Silver-gilt mount fragment	DON (F&L)		
	T231	WILT-4169C2	Wiltshire	Salisbury	Silver sheets	TBD		

EARLY MEDIEVAL

Cat. no.	Treasure no.	PAS no.	County	Parish	Description	Disposition	Acquiring Museum	Value
158	T203	IOW-244C13	Isle of Wight	West Wight	Gold, silver and base-metal assemblage	A	British Museum	£810
163	T552	NMS-1E5E68	Norfolk	Marham	Silver brooch fragment	A	Norwich Castle Museum	£120
164	T673	KENT-C37138	Kent	Worth	Gold coin pendant	TBA	British Museum	
166	T25	BH-4G0DEG	Hertfordshire	North Hertfordshire	Silver-gilt pyramid mount	MW	North Hertfordshire Museum	£600
167	T109	SOMDOR-D60932	Somerset	Chilton Trinity	Silver pin-head	A	Somerset County Museum	£100
168	T674	NMS-41D4B2	Norfolk	Fransham	Silver-gilt brooch fragment	TBA	Norwich Castle Museum	
169	T188	CAMHER-9583E3	Cambridgeshire	Weston Colville	Silver-gilt pyramid mount	TBA	Ely Museum	
170	T421	KENT-020610	Kent	Otford	Silver-gilt pin-head	DON (F&L)	Maidstone Museum	
171	T477	SF-9242E2	Suffolk	Diss area	Silver-gilt pyramid mount	A	Colchester & Ipswich Museums Service	£450
172	T502	KENT-F5A964	Kent	Ramsgate	Gold annular pendant	MW	British Museum	
174	T292	SF-DB2F43	Suffolk	Woodbridge area	Silver-gilt pommel fragment	DON (L)	Woodbridge Museum	£130
176	T9	NMS-BE3EB3	Norfolk	Mileham	Silver-gilt pommel	A	Norwich Castle Museum	£800
178	T78	DENO-633A60	Nottinghamshire	Tuxford area	Silver and glass setting	A	Bassetlaw Museum, Retford	£100

Cat. no.	Treasure no.	PAS no.	County	Parish	Description	Disposition	Acquiring Museum	Value
179	T149	ESS-458378	Essex	Chelmsford area	Gold and garnet setting	TBA	Chelmsford Museum	
180	T505	LIN-0FB775	Lincolnshire	Hatton	Gold gem-set setting	MW	British Museum	
181	T594	DENO-89E427	Nottinghamshire	Newark area	Gold and garnet cross-pendant	TBA	Newark Museum	
183	07.15	NMGW-9C0D76	Isle of Anglesey	Llanbedrgoch	Hack-silver and other finds	A	National Museum Wales	
184	T498	NCL-A09134	Redcar and Cleveland	Streethouse area	Gold and base-metal grave assemblage	TBA	Kirkleatham Museum	
185	T349	CAMHER-9C4BA8	Cambridgeshire	Ely	Gold and silver grave assemblage	TBD		
186	T245	SF-1E8422	Suffolk	North East Suffolk	Silver strap-end	A	British Museum	
187	T578	KENT-C30984	Kent	Denton with Wootton	Silver hooked-tag	A	Canterbury Museum	£40
188	T500	BERK-BB9E23	Gloucestershire	Coberley	Silver hooked-tag	TBA	Corinium Museum	
189	T464	NMS-412F26	Norfolk	North Tuddenham	Silver brooch fragment	A	British Museum	£80
190	T431	SOM-D90C24	Somerset	Long Sutton	Silver hooked-tag	TBA	Somerset County Museum	
191	T210	SF-E0A036	Suffolk	Woodbridge area	Silver pin	A	British Museum	£70
192	T265	HAMP-ECE595	Hampshire	Southampton area	Silver strap-end	D		
194	T281	SUSS-69F7E8	Hampshire	Crawley	Silver hooked-tag	A	Winchester Museums Service	£250
197	T186	YORYM-68FFE3	North Yorkshire	North Yorkshire	Hack-gold, hack-silver and other finds	TBA	British Museum	
198	T194	DENO-838F80	Derbyshire	Willington area	Silver mounts	NTT		
199	T528	SOM-65C991	Somerset	Milborne Port	Silver hooked-tag	TBA	Somerset County Museum	£150
200	T531	DOR-36DDA4	Dorset	Charminster	Silver hooked-tag	A	British Museum	£500
201	T536	CAMHER-9B5D02	Cambridgeshire	Weston Colville	Silver strap-end fragment	TBA	Fitzwilliam Museum, Cambridge	
202	T687		Norfolk	West Acre	Silver pin	A	Norwich Castle Museum	£150
203	T511	NMGW-A96F63	Herefordshire	Brampton Abbotts	Silver hooked-tag	TBA	Hereford Museum & Art Gallery	£90
204	T254	DENO-9A6C17	Nottinghamshire	Newark area	Gold finger-ring	TBA	Newark Museum	
206	T682	NLM-683755	North Lincolnshire	Roxby Cum Risby	Silver ingot fragment	DON (F)	North Lincolnshire Museum Service	£45
208	T445	YORYM-CB94B2	North Yorkshire	Snape with Thorpe	Hack-silver brooch fragment	A	British Museum	£25
209	T19	NCL-FEC824	North Yorkshire	Maunby	Gold ring	A	British Museum	£4,000

Cat. no.	Treasure no.	PAS no.	County	Parish	Description	Disposition	Acquiring Museum	Value
210	T180	YORYM-8F9D92	East Yorkshire	Grindale	Silver finger-ring	A	East Riding Museums Service	£200
211	T714	SF-E8A3A6	Suffolk	Ringshall	Silver ingot	MW	Moyse's Hall Museum, Bury St Edmunds	
212	T334	YORYM-32E6E6	North Yorkshire	Kirk Deighton area	Gold finger-ring	A	British Museum	£2,000
213	07.17	NMGW-9C2070	Powys	Talgarth	Silver ingot	TBA	Brecknock Museum	
216	T599	NCL-40E866	East Yorkshire	Bridlington area	Silver finger-ring	DON (L)	East Riding Museums Service	£400
217	T2	SWYOR-AECB53	North Yorkshire	Vale of York	Silver-gilt cup, hack-silver and coins	A	British Museum and Yorkshire Museums Trust	£1,082,800
224	T287	BH-E11856	Hertfordshire	Ware area	Silver-gilt coin pendant	DON (F)	Hertford Museum	£80
226	T653	SF-3465C7	Suffolk	Eye	Silver ?pendant	D		
532	T350	DOR-B8A4A2, B8C382 & B8C682	Dorset	Bradford Peverell	Silver pennies	TBA	Dorset County Museum	
533	T311	YORYM-D5DFC2	East Yorkshire	Harswell	Base-silver/copper-alloy coins	TBA	East Riding Museums Service	
534	T661	SUSS-C96E71	East Sussex	Alfriston area	Silver pennies	D		
535	T685	NMS-C25257	Norfolk	Wymondham	Silver pennies	TBA	Norwich Castle Museum	
536	T432	BERK-BC5CC2	Oxfordshire	Henley area	Silver pennies	TBA	Oxfordshire Museums Service	
537	T273	IOW-AEFBB1 & AFA8F1	Isle of Wight	Arreton area	Silver pennies	A	Isle of Wight Heritage Service	£400
	T297	BUC-C394C4	Bedfordshire	Stagsden	Silver ingot	A	Bedford Museum	£100
	T410	CAMHER-9917C5	Cambridgeshire	Chesterton	Brass fragment	NT		
	T622	LANCUM-389D97	Cumbria	Kirkby Stephen	Hacksilver	NT		
	T226	YORYM-30B2B5	East Yorkshire	Stamford Bridge area	Silver neckring fragment & unnasociated objects	A	East Riding Museums Service	£10
	T358	LON-BAF907	Greater London	Covent Garden	Assemblage	TBD		
	T200	BH-E0CBB3	Hertfordshire	East Hertfordshire area	Silver hooked-tag	DON (F)	Hertford Museum	£10
	T439	BH-DE4EC6	Hertfordshire	St Albans Districe	Silver hooked-tag	DON (F&L)	St Albans Museum	
	T146	KENT-043FC1	Kent	Cliffs End	Silver brooch	TBD		
	T147	KENT-044642	Kent	Cliffs End	Grave assemblage	TBD		
	T367	KENT-C80036	Kent	Meopham	Silver hooked-tag	DON (F&L)	Maidstone Museum	
	T489	KENT-048BC7	Kent	Springhead	Brooch, vessel and other objects	TBD		
	T422	KENT-A31134	Kent	Whitstable	Silver hooked-tag	D		
	T60	KENT-0887B6,	Kent	Wingham	Silver-gilt brooch fragments	NT		

Cat. no.	Treasure no.	PAS no.	County	Parish	Description	Disposition	Acquiring Museum	Value
	T193	DENO-CE6103	Leicestershire	Breedon on the Hill	Silver ingot	TBA	Leicestershire County Council Heritage Services	
	T57	LIN-334D17	Lincolnshire	Osbournby	Silver ingot	D		
	T235	NMS-E7BE60	Norfolk	Hindringham	Silver ingot	TBA	Norwich Castle Museum	
	T46	NLM-E96D16	North Lincolnshire	Scawby	Silver and iron knife handle	D		
	T38	NCL-A04B68	North Yorkshire	Borrowby	Silver ingot	D		
	T376	YORYM-CB6717	North Yorkshire	Burdale	Silver-gilt finger-rings	TBD		
	T184	YORYM-FA6027	North Yorkshire	Torksey	Silver droplet	D		
	T655	DENO-FD7452	Nottinghamshire	Newark area	Silver strap-end	DON (L)	Newark Museum	£120
	T242	SOMDOR-18D8F3	Somerset	Milborne Port	Silver strap-end	A	Somerset County Museum	£90
	T255	SF-1EFD68	Suffolk	Bury St Edmunds area	Silver hooked-tag	D		
	T720	SF-2A29B3	Suffolk	East of Colchester	Silver-gilt coin brooch	TBA	British Museum	
	T652	SF-3456A1	Suffolk	Eye	Gold fragment	D		
	T654	SF-33ACA8	Suffolk	Eye	Silver cosmetic implement	D		
	T221	SF-347272	Suffolk	Suffolk area	Silver ingot	NT		
	T692		Worcestershire	Wychavon	Silver strap-end	DON (F)	Leicestershire County Council Heritage Services	

MEDIEVAL

Cat. no.	Treasure no.	PAS no.	County	Parish	Description	Disposition	Acquiring Museum	Value
232	07.02	NMGW-9D92B2	Swansea	Port Eynon	Silver finger-ring	A	Swansea Museum	
233	T294	DENO-2C0235	Leicestershire	Long Whatton	Silver finger-ring	TBA	Leicestershire County Council Heritage Services	
234	07.19	NMGW-9D9A68	Vale of Glamorgan	Rhoose	Gold finger-ring	A	National Museum Wales	£1,500
236	T234	SF-89F2D6	Suffolk	Diss area	Gold finger-ring	A	Colchester & Ipswich Museum Service	£1,000
237	T561	YORYM-59F421	East Yorkshire	Beverley area	Gold finger-ring	DON (L)	East Riding Museums Service	
238	07.18	NMGW-9DC905	Vale of Glamorgan	Llanfair	Gold finger-ring	A	National Museum of Wales	£1,000
240	T296	DOR-B88E77	Dorset	Rampisham	Gold finger-ring	D		
246	T389	KENT-984E65	Kent	Boxley	Gold brooch	D		
247	T520	NMS-4180B3	Norfolk	South-east Norfolk	Silver-gilt pendant	A	Norwich Castle Museum	£250
248	T233	SF-89B470	Suffolk	Diss area	Gold finger-ring	A	Colchester & Ipswich Museum Service	£1,000
249	07.09	NMGW-9C2734	Swansea	Llanddewi	Silver brooch	TBA	Swansea Museum	

Cat. no.	Treasure no.	PAS no.	County	Parish	Description	Disposition	Acquiring Museum	Value
250	T62	NARC-7742D7	Bedfordshire	Lower Dean	Silver-gilt finger-ring	A	Bedford Museum	£100
251	T126	DOR-B80705	Dorset	Osmington	Silver-gilt pendant	A	British Museum	£2,000
252	T483	NMS-1E07E1	Norfolk	Langley with Hardley	Silver signet-ring	TBA	Norwich Castle Museum	
254	T175	BH-C5AF24	Essex	Theydon Garnon	Silver finger-ring	A	Epping Forest District Museum	£175
255	T493	KENT-299A33	Kent	Brookland	Silver-gilt finger-ring	TBA	Canterbury Museum	
258	T72	NMS-D26E35	Norfolk	Crimplesham	Silver-gilt brooch	DON (F&L)	Lynn Museum	£180
259	T264	HAMP-4D35C0	Hampshire	Winchester area	Silver bar-mount	DON (F&L)	Winchester Museums Service	
261	T34	NMS-BFE0C6	Norfolk	Leziate	Silver seal-matrix	A	Norwich Castle Museum	£750
263	T12	NMS-BEA416	Norfolk	Old Buckenham	Silver coin brooch/mount	DON (F&L)	Norwich Castle Museum	
264	T626	YORYM-60FCA5	East Yorkshire	Paull	Silver-gilt coin brooch	A	East Riding Museum	£170
267	T39	NCL-FFF137	North Yorkshire	Sealfield	Silver seal-matrix	A	Richmondshire Museum	£3,800
268	T465	BH-DE4686	Bedfordshire	Dunstable	Silver-gilt brooch	NTT		
273	T262	HAMP-C28BE4	Hampshire	Winchester area	Silver-gilt bar-mount	DON (F&L)	Winchester Museums Service	
274	T71	ESS-6EC685	Essex	Kelvedon	Silver-gilt brooch	A	Braintree Museum	£250
275	T137	ESS-288395	Essex	Finchingfield	Silver finger-ring	A	Braintree Museum	£250
276	T208	GLO-EF2CE8	Gloucestershire	South Glourcestershire	Silver-gilt brooch	A	Museum in the Park, Stroud	£60
277	T341	HAMP-8C1E11	Hampshire	Wonston	Silver scabbard chape	TBA	Winchester Museums Service	
278	T361	NCL-D1AF46	County Durham	Old Kirk Field area	Silver brooch	A	Hartlepool Museum & Heritage Service	£400
279	T684	NLM-FDB8B5	Lincolnshire	Binbrook	Silver brooch	D		
280	T501	KENT-2963F0	Kent	Brookland	Silver-gilt finger-ring	MW	Canterbury Museum	
281	T515	YORYM-763D18	North Yorkshire	Long Marston	Silver cross pendant	A	Harrogate Museum	£300
282	T212	NARC-774CD2	Northamptonshire	Walgrave	Silver scabbard chape	TBA	Northampton Museum	
283	T110	WILT-6F3276	Wiltshire	Wingfield	Silver finger-ring	A	Wiltshire Heritage Museum	£65
285	T339	SUR-D6C932	Surrey	West Clandon	Silver *piedfort*	A	British Museum	£1,800
286	T628	WMID-F4CF43	Staffordshire	Harlaston	Gold finger-ring	TBA	Potteries Museum & Art Gallery, Stoke	
290	T606	LVPL-0330D6	Cheshire	Winwick	Gold finger-ring	MW	Cheshire Museums Service	
291	T98	SOMDOR-D92905	Dorset	Charminster	Silver strap-end	D		

Cat. no.	Treasure no.	PAS no.	County	Parish	Description	Disposition	Acquiring Museum	Value
292	T300	DENO-D1A913	Derbyshire	South Wingfield	Gold finger-ring	TBA	Derby Museum & Art Gallery	
293	T598	YORYM-6CE0B1	North Yorkshire	Great Smeaton	Silver-gilt pendant	A	York Museums Trust	£300
294	T529	SOM-F52064	Wiltshire	Urchfont	Silver ivy-leaf pendant	DON (F&L)	Wiltshire Heritage Museum	
295	T174	NLM-688C74	North Lincolnshire	Bonby	Silver-gilt finger-ring	TBA	North Lincolnshire Museum	
296	T81	SWYOR-C4E534	West Yorkshire	Pontefract	Silver cross pendant	A	Wakefield Museum	£100
297	T37	NCL-FF8757	North Yorkshire	Aldbrough	Gold finger-ring	A	Harrogate Museum	£1,500
298	T232	SF-8A76E4	Suffolk	Diss area	Gold finger-ring	A	Colchester & Ipswich Museum Service	£1,900
299	T455	HAMP-E271F0	Hampshire	Hound	Silver mount	TBA	Hampshire Museums Service	
300	T512	NMGW-A8C737	Gloucestershire	Coberley	Silver-gilt finger-ring	A	Corinium Museum	£400
301	T671	LEIC-815FF6	Leicestershire	Thurlaston	Gold finger-ring	A	Leicestershire County Council Heritage Services	£500
302	07.08	NMGW-9DEB70	Vale of Glamorgan	Dinas Powys	Gold finger-ring	A	National Museum of Wales	£500
303	T486	BERK-BB15D7	West Berkshire	Swallowfield	Gold brooch	NT		
304	T179	YORYM-74B6A8	City of York	Naburn	Gold finger-ring	D		
307	T239	SUSS-BA4106	West Sussex	Stoughton area	Silver-gilt signet-ring	TBA	Chichester District Museum	
308	T632	KENT-C343E3	Kent	Lydd	Gold finger-ring	MW	Canterbury Museum	
309	T696	WILT-116095	Gloucestershire	Coberley	Silver-gilt fragment	A	Corinium Museum	£100
310	07.14	NMGW-9C3A27	Vale of Glamorgan	Penllyn	Silver brooch	A	National Museum of Wales	£80
311	T196	DOR-B85D80	Dorset	Cerne Abbas	Silver-gilt dress fitting	A	British Museum	£120
315	T204	LON-8809F7	Greater London	Tower Hamlets	Silver girdle terminal	D		
316	T224	BH-DE1292	Hertfordshire	Great Gaddesen	Gold rectangular mount	MW	Dacorum Heritage Trust, Berkhamsted	
317	T657	LANCUM-354065	Lancashire	Lancaster area	Silver crucifix pendant	MW	Lancaster City Museum	
318	T699	KENT-6D9885	Kent	Barham	Silver mount	A	Canterbury Museum	£220
321	07.07	NMGW-9E8024	Pembrokeshire	Kilgetty	Silver reliquary pendant	A	National Museum of Wales	£2,000
322	T533	WILT-BAB214	Hampshire	Vernhams Dean	Silver-gilt finger-ring	TBA	Hampshire Museums Service	
545	T172	NLM-145AF6	North East Lincolnshire	Bigby	Silver pennies	A	North Lincolnshire Museum	£550
546	T275	NMS-E8BBA3	Norfolk	Dunton	Silver pennies	TBA	British Museum	
547	T530	SOM-BAA293	Bath and North East Somerset	Wellow	Silver pennies	A	Roman Baths Museum, Bath	£750

Cat. no.	Treasure no.	PAS no.	County	Parish	Description	Disposition	Acquiring Museum	Value
548	T569	WMID-2FAAC1	Warwickshire	Corley	Silver coins	A	Warwickshire Museum	£300
548	T325	WMID-2FAAC1	Warwickshire	Corley	Silver coins	A	Warwickshire Museum	£1,250
549	T545	HESH-A5B566	Shropshire	Baschurch area	Silver pennies	TBA	Shropshire County Museum Service	
550	T676	NMS-EA4080	Norfolk	Deopham area	Silver pennies	TBA	Norwich Castle Museum	
551	T619	CAMHER-9B9C48	Cambridgeshire	West Wratting	Silver pennies	TBA	Fitzwilliam Museum, Cambridge	
552	T252	LIN-C337E3, C32352, C31AD1, C30EF5, C30795, C300A3, C2E9D4, C2D313, C2A913 & C291E6	Lincolnshire	Pinchbeck	Silver pennies and halfpennies	NT		
553	07.04	NMGW-9E0F60	Rhondda Cynon Taff	Llanharry	Silver pennies	D		
554	07.05	NMGW-9E40C5	Flintshire	Ysceifiog	Silver pennies	TBA	Flintshire County Museums Service	
555	T229	LIN-747367	Lincolnshire	Low Apley	Silver pennies	MW	The Collection, Lincoln	
556	T513	NARC-0331C3	West Midlands	Astleys	Silver pennies	DON (L)	Herbert Art Museum & Art Gallery	
557	07.03	NMGW-9E6076	Vale of Glamorgan	Bonvilston	Silver groats and half groat	D		
558	T370	LANCUM-F4A696	Cumbria	Kirkby Stephen	Silver coins	MW	Penrith Museum	£1,400
559	T534	LVPL-E09DD8	Shropshire	Myddle and Broughton	Gold *doblas*	A	Shropshire County Museum Service	£5,850
560	T173	LON-5B20D4, 5B4B26, 5B52F7, 5B5AF7, 5B6003, 5B6603, 5B6B52, 5B70D4, 5B84C3, 5B8B28, 5B9254 & 5B99C3	Greater London	Beulah Hill	Gold and silver coins	A	Museum of London	£7,500
561	T467	WILT-28BAF7	Wiltshire	Swindon area	Silver coins	D		
562	T715	SF-EAC074	Suffolk	Hitcham	Silver double *patards*	MW	Moyse's Hall Museum, Bury St Edmunds	
563	T484	NMS-C277B7	Norfolk	East Lexham area	Silver groats	DON (L)	Norwich Castle Museum	
	T288	BH-33F406	Bedfordshire	Bromham	Silver finger-ring fragment	D		
	T644	NARC-D3BF57	Bedfordshire	Hulcote	Silver finger-ring	D		
	T113	BUC-05CF54	Buckinghamshire	Fingest	Silver terminal	A	Buckinghamshire County Museum	£100
	T128	CAMHER-94A8F2	Cambridgeshire	Hemingford Grey	Silver-gilt finger-ring bezel	D		
	T621	CAMHER-9BE832	Cambridgeshire	West Wratting	Silver annular brooch	D		
	T249	CAMHER-961244	Cambridgeshire	Weston Colville	Gold finger-ring	D		

Cat. no.	Treasure no.	PAS no.	County	Parish	Description	Disposition	Acquiring Museum	Value
	T468	CAMHER-9B0D71	Cambridgeshire	Weston Colville	Silver spoon terminal	D		
	T202	LVPL-3F8372	Cheshire	Malpas	Silver brooch	D		
	T374	LVPL-714215	Cheshire	Cheshire	Gold finger-ring	TBA	Grosvenor Museum	
	T318	LANCUM-018C08	Cumbria	Kendal area	Silver finger-ring	D		
	T524	NLM-D2E0A1	Cumbria	Penrith	silver mount	TBA	Corinium Museum	
	T117		Devon	Pinhoe	Silver-gilt finger-ring	TBA	Royal Albert Memorial Museum	
	T669	DOR-9C0DE7	Dorset	Compton Abbas	Silver-gilt finger-ring	D		
	T277	DOR-16CDE5	Dorset	Minterne Magna	Silver-gilt annular brooch fragment	D		
	T49	SOMDOR-20FAC4	Dorset	Puddletown	Silver-gilt finger-ring	D		
	T351	DOR-B8D124	Dorset	West Stour	Silver buckle plate	D		
	T91	SOMDOR-B48C94	Dorset	Whitcombe	Silver jewellery fragment	D		
	T79	YORYM-409415	East Yorkshire	Melbourne Brooch	Silver annular brooch	D		
	T390	YORYM-6ABBA8	East Yorkshire	Thwing	Silver finger-ring	DON (F)	East Riding Museums Service	£30
	T343	SUSS-BC4C47	East Sussex	East Sussex area	Silver annular brooch	NT		
	T470	SUSS-029818	East Sussex	Firle	Silver buckle fragment	D		
	T586	SUSS-47EAE7	East Sussex	Near Hailsham	Silver annular brooch	D		
	T435	SUSS-EFEAB0	East Sussex	Southease	Silver brooch pin	D		
	T130	SUSS-45C5F1	East Sussex	Tarring Neville	Silver finger-ring	D		
	T136	ESS-6EB935	Essex	Mashbury	Silver-gilt finger-ring	D		
	T573	ESS-73A5D2	Essex	North of Colchester	Silver ring	D		
	T517	WILT-BA6BE7	Gloucestershire	Coberley	Silver finger-ring	TBA	Corinium Museum	
	T340	HAMP-62E216	Hampshire	Droxford	Silver finger-ring	D		
	T167	HAMP-71F6D4	Hampshire	Fawley	Silver-gilt finger-ring	TBA	Hampshire Museums Service	
	T342	HAMP-634840	Hampshire	Hound	Silver-gilt finger-ring fragments	D		
	T456	HAMP-E28057	Hampshire	Hound	Silver thimble	TBA	Hampshire Museums Service	
	T430	HAMP-D7D0B2	Hampshire	Hursley	Silver-gilt finger-ring	TBA	Winchester Museums Service	
	T166	HAMP-711114	Hampshire	Hurstborne Priors	Silver brooch	A	Hampshire Museums Service	£80
	T270	HAMP-6EC8B4	Hampshire	Littleton area	Gold finger-ring	MW	Winchester Museums Service	
	T698	BH-1D6502	Hertfordshire	Clothall	Silver buckle	D		

Cat. no.	Treasure no.	PAS no.	County	Parish	Description	Disposition	Acquiring Museum	Value
	T23	BH-5E12E1	Hertfordshire	North Hertfordshire	Silver-gilt brooch	A	North Hertfordshire Museum Service	£180
	T440	BH-DE5192	Hertfordshire	St Michael	Silver chape	DON (L)	St Albans Museum	£40
	T195	IOW-1C1362	Isle of Wight	Carisbrooke area	Silver terminal	D		
	T650	IOW-73CB12	Isle of Wight	Niton area	Silver-gilt pendant cross	A	Isle of Wight Heritage Service	£35
	T690	IOW-7608F4 & 75F6D5	Isle of Wight	Shalfleet area	Silver brooch pin	D		
	T460	IOW-BC99C0	Isle of Wight	Newport area	Gold finger-ring	A	Isle of Wight Heritage Service	£400
	T457	IOW-A52166	Isle of Wight	Shalfleet	Silver dress hook boss	D		
	T521	IOW-A4C3D0	Isle of Wight	Shalfleet	Silver-gilt spoon	D		
	T243	IOW-747B18	Isle of Wight	Shorwell	Silver brooch	D		
	T52	KENT-74B341	Kent	Lenham	Gold finger-ring	D		
	T45	KENT-743633	Kent	Northfleet	Silver mount/ plaque	D		
	T301	KENT-150E48	Kent	Romney Marsh area	Silver finger-ring	D		
	T227	LEIC-96C553	Leicestershire	Fenny Drayton area	Silver-gilt finger-ring	TBA	Leicestershire County Council Heritage Services	
	T355	LEIC-BD4C44	Leicestershire	Thurcaston and Cropston	Silver brooch fragment	D		
	T283	NLM-A3D054	Lincolnshire	Claxby	Gold finger-ring	D		
	T434	NLM-BF3250	Lincolnshire	Covenham	Silver coin brooch	A	The Collection, Lincoln	£180
	T199	LVPL-00B2B0	Lincolnshire	Normanby Le Wold	Silver brooch	D		
	T75	DENO-D58C44	Lincolnshire	Norton Disney	Silver-gilt mount	D		
	T485	LIN-33F681	Lincolnshire	Pinchbeck	Silver brooch	D		
	T102	NMS-D2A387	Norfolk	Aldeby	Silver annular brooch	D		
	T360	NMS-D2F3B0	Norfolk	Barton Bendish	Silver-gilt belt-mount	D		
	T462	NMS-E9DE96	Norfolk	Beeston with Bittering	Silver brooch fragment	D		
	T463	NMS-E9E9D3	Norfolk	Beeston with Bittering	Silver object	D		
	T10	NMS-BE6277	Norfolk	Fransham	Silver-gilt spoon handle fragment	D		
	T219	NMS-D51157	Norfolk	Great Dunham	Silver finger-ring fragment	D		
	T267	NMS-E860E6	Norfolk	Langley with Hardley	Silver sheet	D		
	T276	NMS-E8D072	Norfolk	Mattishall	Silver brooch	D		
	T508	NMS-4152E3	Norfolk	Raveningham	Gold finger-ring	D		
	T238	NMS-E829A0	Norfolk	Runcton Holme	Silver object	D		
	T216	NMS-D4C6D7	Norfolk	Surlingham	Silver cross	D		
	T688	NMS-D35995	Norfolk	Wereham	Gold finger-ring	D		

Cat. no.	Treasure no.	PAS no.	County	Parish	Description	Disposition	Acquiring Museum	Value
	T689	NMS-D38330	Norfolk	Wereham	Silver annular brooch fragment	D		
	T213	NMS-C73B06	Norfolk	West Acre	Silver brooch	D		
	T214	NMS-C70934	Norfolk	West Acre	Silver brooch	D		
	T215	NMSC72AC4	Norfolk	West Acre	Silver brooch	D		
	T347	NMS-E8E825	Norfolk	West Acre	Silver-gilt finger-ring	D		
	T554	NMS-D34A11	Norfolk	West Acre	Silver buckle fragment	D		
	T381	NMS-E9B392	Norfolk	Whinburgh and Westfield	Silver object	D		
	T474	NMS-EA0717	Norfolk	Witchingham area	Silver strap-end	D		
	T506	NLM-AA24E6	North Lincolnshire	Roxby cum Risby	Silver annular brooch	D		
	T171	NLM-A97266	North Lincolnshire	Scawby	Silver finger-ring fragment	D		
	T336	YORYM-32A614	North Yorkshire	Dunnington	Silver-gilt annular brooch fragment	D		
	T658	YORYM-1B6B74	North Yorkshire	Littlethorpe	Silver chape	D		
	T177	YORYM-761DC7	North Yorkshire	Naburn	Silver-gilt mount	D		
	T394	SWYOR-2D53D4; YORYM-6CA875	North Yorkshire	Saxton	Silver-gilt crucifix	MW	York Museums Trust	
	T441	YORYM-CE0B16	North Yorkshire	Snape with Thorpe	Silver coins	D		
	T694	DENO-D26395	North Yorkshire	Snape with Thorpe	Gold finger-ring	D		
	T70	SWYOR-BB82F6	North Yorkshire	Stapleton	Silver-gilt pendant	TBA	Richmondshire Museum	
	T610	NCL-642301	North Yorkshire	Thorpe Field	Silver strap-end	D		
	T084	SWYOR-F9BA40	North Yorkshire	Ulleskelf area	Silver finger-ring	D		
	T36	NCL-FF30C0	North Yorkshire	Wykeham	Silver annular brooch	D		
	T298	NARC-489CF7	Northamptonshire	Kislingbury	Silver finger-ring fragments	D		
	T133	NARC-775318	Northamptonshire	Rothersthorpe	Silver pendant	D		
	T170	NARC-775EE8	Northamptonshire	Rothersthorpe	Silver mount	D		
	T162	NCL-C5AF46	Northumberland	Bamburgh	Gold decorative fitting	TBD		
	T459	DENO-CBE013	Nottinghamshire	Kirklington	Silver finger-ring	MW	Newark Museum	£70
	T718	BERK-FF8C94	Oxfordshire	Drayton St Leonard	Gold finger-ring fragment	NT		
	T542	BERK-CC3D78	Oxfordshire	East Hendred	Silver-gilt mount	D		
	T546	WAW-B5A511	Oxfordshire	Wantage	Silver-gilt finger-ring	TBA	Oxfordshire Museums Service	
	T582	WAW-485713	Shropshire	Tong	Silver crucifix pendant	NTT		

Cat. no.	Treasure no.	PAS no.	County	Parish	Description	Disposition	Acquiring Museum	Value
	T584	WAW-461D73	Shropshire	Tong	Silver mount	NT		
	T585	SOM-4A6E31	Somerset	Wembdon	Silver annular brooch	A	Somerset County Museum	£80
	T68	SWYOR-C51917	South Yorkshire	Campsall	Gold finger-ring	D		
	T641	WMID-F14242	Staffordshire	Drayton Bassett	Silver annular brooch	D		
	T642	WMID-F46B62	Staffordshire	Lapley	Silver cross pendant	D		
	T326	WMID-46E157	Staffordshire	Swinfen and Packington	Silver annular brooch	D		
	T504		Suffolk	Bardwell	Silver scabbard chape	D		
	T63	SF-9EA4A1	Suffolk	Combs	Silver seal-matrix	D		
	T527	SF-3A5BC0	Suffolk	West Suffolk	Silver hooked-tag	TBA	Mildenhall and District Museum	
	T724	SF-EA7B62	Suffolk	Woodbridge area	Silver finger-ring fragment	D		
	T372	WAW-DD3BA5	Warwickshire	Alcester	Silver cosmetic implement	A	Warwickshire Museum	£90
	T609	NCL-646ED2	West Berkshire	Newbury area	Silver brooch	NT		
	T107	SUSS-45BB11	West Sussex	Houghton	Silver-gilt finger-ring	NTT		
	T364	SUSS-028791	West Sussex	Pulborough area	Silver-gilt finger-ring	TBA	Chichester District Museum	
	T716	WILT-AEB211	Wiltshire	Alton	Silver-gilt annular brooch	DON (F&L)	Wiltshire Heritage Museum	
	T53	WILT-296CB3	Wiltshire	Langley Burrell	Silver-gilt annular brooch	D		
	T282	WILT-EA65E4	Wiltshire	Laverstock	Silver seal finger-ring	DON (F&L)	Salisbury & South Wiltshire Museum	£100
	T56	WILT-6FAE14	Wiltshire	Stockton	Silver finger-ring fragment	D		
	T595	WILT-785EE2	Wiltshire	Urchfont	Silver-gilt finger-ring fragment	DON (F)	Wiltshire Heritage Museum	
	T596	WILT-88FF73	Wiltshire	Urchfont	Silver-gilt brooch pin	D		
	T3	WAW-87DFE5H	Worcestershire	Wychavon	Silver finger-ring	NT		

POST MEDIEVAL

Cat. no.	Treasure no.	PAS no.	County	Parish	Description	Disposition	Acquiring Museum	Value
326	T627	WMID-F4E937	Staffordshire	Harlaston	Silver coin brooch	D		
328	T26	BH-01C693	Cambridgeshire	Bluntisham	Silver-gilt hooked clasp	D		
329	T713	SF-E85546	Suffolk	Kelsale cum Carlton	Silver-gilt hooked clasp	A	Colchester & Ipswich Museum Service	£80
330	T211	BH-E15835	Hertfordshire	East Hertfordshire	Silver-gilt hooked clasp	DON (F&L)	Ware Museum	£100
331	T319	LANCUM-6E9692	Lancashire	Carnforth area	Silver hooked clasp	A	Lancashire County Museums	£180
332	07.22	NMGW-9F0C64	Monmouthshire	Wentlooge	Silver-gilt hooked clasp	TBA	Newport Art Gallery & Museum	
333	T182	YORYM-68E976	North Yorkshire	North Yorkshire	Silver-gilt cap hook	TBA	British Museum	£130
334	T89	WILT-6E7454	Wiltshire	Durnford	Silver-gilt dress pin	TBA	Salisbury & South Wiltshire Museum	
335	T192	DENO-D3CCD3	Derbyshire	Mercaston	Silver-gilt dress pin	A	Derby Museum & Art Gallery	£150
336	T306	NMS-2C2226	Norfolk	Emneth	Silver rumbler bell	A	Norwich Castle Museum	£30
337	T707	LEIC-757733	Leicestershire	Garthorpe	Silver whistle	D		
339	T544	HESH-A49557	Herefordshire	South Herefordshire	Silver vervel pendant	TBA	Hereford Museum & Art Gallery	
340	07.01	NMGW-B0C420	Vale of Glamorgan	Llancarfan	Silver-gilt dress-hook loop	TBA	National Museum of Wales	£20
341	T156	LVPL-00A457	Cheshire	Whitchurch area	Gold finger-ring	MW	Nantwich Museum	
342	T95	SUSS-70D736	East Sussex	Udimore	Silver seal-matrix	D		
343	T385	WMID-3DDE65	Staffordshire	Oulton	Gold finger-ring	D		
344	T120	NLM-BE8630	North Lincolnshire	Holme	Gold finger-ring	A	North Lincolnshire Museums Service	£475
345	T317	WILT-637426	Wiltshire	Winterbourne	Gold finger-ring	TBA	Salisbury & South Wiltshire Museum	
347	T679	NMS-1EB356	Norfolk	Foulsham	Silver vervel	A	Norwich Castle Museum	£1,750
348	T383	GLO-19A336	Gloucestershire	Newent	Silver-gilt finger-ring	DON (L)	Gloucester City Museum	£300
349	T489	BERK-BAB9D4	Oxfordshire	Swallowfield area	Gold finger-ring	TBA	Oxfordshire Museums Service	
350	T359	NMS-411415	Norfolk	Edgefield	Gold finger-ring	DON (L)	Norwich Castle Museum	£1,000
351	T207	WAW-CB51A1	Warwickshire	Wooton Wawen	Silver finger-ring	A	Warwickshire Museum	£350
352	T305	NMS-2C1204	Norfolk	Emneth	Silver vervel	A	Norwich Castle Museum	£600
360	T143	PAS-1917F7	Lincolnshire	Market Rasen	Gold finger-ring	D		
361	T516	WILT-BA3553	Wiltshire	Everleigh	Gold finger-ring	MW	Wiltshire Heritage Museum	£380
362	T5	GLO-EF2971	North Somerset	Kenn	Gold finger-ring	A	North Somerset Museum	£450

Cat. no.	Treasure no.	PAS no.	County	Parish	Description	Disposition	Acquiring Museum	Value
363	T333	GLO-195C52	Gloucestershire	Westbury-on-Severn	Gold finger-ring	MW	Dean Heritage Centre	£450
364	T163	SF-3A8B11	Cambridgeshire	Soham area	Gold finger-ring	A	Ely Museum	£900
365	T436	BUC-068008	Buckinghamshire	Buckingham	Gold finger-ring	A	Buckinghamshire County Museum	£150
366	07.16	NMGW-9F38B2	Vale of Glamorgan	Penllyn	Silver-gilt finger-ring	A	National Museum of Wales	£120
367	T307	NMS-2C5DA4	Norfolk	Emneth	Silver-gilt finger-ring	A	Norwich Castle Museum	£200
368	T42	WMID-345AB7	Staffordshire	Lapley, Stretton & Wheaton Aston	Silver bell	D		
369	T80	ESS-6EC030	Essex	Kelvedon	Silver thimble	DON (L)	Braintree Museum	£60
370	T487	BERK-B9F5A5	Oxfordshire	Wantage Down area	Silver seal-matrix	TBA	Oxfordshire Museums Service	
374	T404	BH-C54352	Hertfordshire	Shenley	Silver seal-matrix	A	Bushey Museum	£140
376	T86	NCL-C27BA0	County Durham	Coxhoe	Silver seal-matrix	DON (L)	Bowes Museum, Barnard Castle	£60
378	T345	SUSS-BC6F54	West Sussex	Oving	Silver spoon	D		
379	T15	ESS-6ECE34	Essex	Tendring area	Silver pendant	A	Colchester & Ipswich Museum Service	£80
380	T324	WMID-338537	Staffordshire	Drayton Bassett	Silver pendant	A	Potteries Museum & Art Gallery, Stoke	£80
382	T496	ESS-259730	Essex	East of Colchester	Silver locket fragment	A	Colchester & Ipswich Museum Service	£100
383	T33	NMS-BFBA71	Norfolk	Runhall	Silver pendant medallion	DON (L)	Norwich Castle Museum	£50
384	T522	HAMP-604ED1	Hampshire	Itchen Valley	Silver medal	A	Winchester Museums Service	£50
385	T217	NMS-2AD401	Norfolk	South Creake	Gold finger-ring	A	Lynn Museum	£500
386	07.21	NMGW-9F1A17	Powys	Old Radnor	Silver hawking whistle	TBA	Radnorshire Museum	
388	T451	SWYOR-B06054	North Yorkshire	Snape	Silver cockspur	D		
390	T403	HESH-1D4423	Herefordshire	Holmer	Silver seal-matrix	TBA	Hereford Museum & Art Gallery	
391	T453	HAMP-E23148	Hampshire	Droxford	Silver shoe buckle	TBA	Winchester Museums Service	
393	T525	LEIC-964413	Leicestershire	Thurlaston	Silver seal-matrix	MW	Leicestershire County Council Heritage Services	£200
395	T29	SUSS-356DB0	West Sussex	Boxgrove	Gold mourning ring	A	Chichester District Museum	£550
396	T77	LANCUM-362FE5	Lancashire	South-east Lancashire	Silver cufflinks	D		
398	T222	CORN-943711	Cornwall	Phillack	Silver bodkin	A	Royal Cornwall Museum	£100

Cat. no.	Treasure no.	PAS no.	County	Parish	Description	Disposition	Acquiring Museum	Value
399	T607	IOW-4074C3	Isle of Wight	Newport area	Silver shoe buckle	D		
401	07.11	NMGW-DDBBF5	Flintshire	Overton	Gold touch-piece	A	National Museum of Wales	£280
402	T16	BH-4B0E12	Bedfordshire	Kensworth	Gold mourning ring	A	Luton Museum	£150
403	T375	SWYOR-C542C8	Nottinghamshire	Hawton	Gold mourning ring	A	Newark Museum	£375
404	T678	SOM-574036	Somerset	West Crewkerne	Silver thimble	A	Somerset County Museum	£50
408	T116	LVPL-E05136	North Yorkshire	Buttercrame with Bossall	Gold mourning ring	MW	British Museum	
412	07.1	NMGW-9A96E6	Powys	Brecon	Silver finger-ring bezel	NT		
417	T643	CORN-FA0676	Cornwall	Padstow	Silver-gilt pendant	NT		
569	T691	HAMP-399633, 4A3752 & 4A6FC6	Hampshire	Basingstoke area	Silver coins	DON (F&L)	Hampshire Museums Service	
570	T241	LANCUM-141D42	Lancashire	Preston area	Silver coins	TBA	Harris Museum & Art Gallery, Preston	
571	T279	ESS-67D6B4	Essex	Bures area	Silver coins	DON (L)	Braintree Museum	£600
572	T703	WMID-7D3DC2	North Yorkshire	West Tanfield	Silver pennies	D		
573	T366	LEIC-CDED85, CDFC75, CE0C74 & CE21A5	Leicestershire	Nailstone	Silver coins	D		
574	T223	SOM-8F7413	Somerset	West Crewkerne	Silver coins and bead	D		
575	T384	GLO-1002D2	Gloucestershire	Ham and Stone	Silver pennies and a halfgroat	A	Museum in the Park, Stroud	£30
576	07.12	NMGW-DDB267	Powys	Welshpool	Silver coins and ceramic pot	TBA	Powysland Museum	
577	T139	LEIC-BDA7F1	Rutland	Rutland	Silver coins	TBA	Rutland County Museum	
577	T240	LEIC-BDA7F1	Rutland	Rutland	Silver coins	TBA	Rutland County Museum	
578	T722	SWYOR-7ED5A2	Cumbria	Ambleside	Silver coins	MW	Armitt Museum & Gallery, Ambleside	
	T593	BUC-08BCC5	Bedfordshire	Battlesden	Silver brooch or buckle	NT		
	T150	BH-339373	Bedfordshire	Colworth	Silver annular brooch	D		
	T392	BH-C5D398	Bedfordshire	Marston Moretaine	Silver-gilt dress-fitting	D		
	T393	BH-344CA1	Bedfordshire	Sharnbrook	Silver seal-matrix	NT		
	T605	BUC-093298	Bedfordshire	Stagsden	Silver button	D		
	T697	BH-1DB741	Bedfordshire	Stagsden	Silver dress-hook fragment	D		

Cat. no.	Treasure no.	PAS no.	County	Parish	Description	Disposition	Acquiring Museum	Value
	T543	BUC-699487	Buckinghamshire	Sherington	Silver button	TBA	Buckinghamshire County Museum	
	T591	BUC-9A0F76	Buckinghamshire	Sherington	Silver dress pin	TBA	Buckinghamshire County Museum	
	T592	BUC-087696	Buckinghamshire	Soulbury	Gold mourning ring	DON (F&L)	Buckinghamshire County Museum	£150
	T414	CAMHER-9A1344	Cambridgeshire	Chesterton	Silver spoon	TBA	Peterborough Museum & Art Gallery	
	T412	CAMHER-999AA1	Cambridgeshire	Chesterton	Gold accessory	NT		
	T415	CAMHER-9AB1F2	Cambridgeshire	Chesterton	Silver brooch	NT		
	T693	CAMHER-9C1383	Cambridgeshire	Ellington	Silver stud	NT		
	T160	CAMHER-953B95	Cambridgeshire	Harston	Silver thimble	D		
	T127	CAMHER-320272	Cambridgeshire	Hemingford Grey	Silver spoon terminal	D		
	T618	CAMHER-9B8011	Cambridgeshire	Leighton Bromswold area	Gold finger-ring	NT		
	T64	SF-9EEDD4	Cambridgeshire	Soham	Silver strap-mount	D		
	T420	CAMHER-9AF5A6	Cambridgeshire	St Ives	Silver dress pin	D		
	T418	CAMHER-9AC834	Cambridgeshire	West Wratting	Silver button	D		
	T419	CAMHER-9AE124	Cambridgeshire	West Wratting	Silver bell	D		
	T705	CAMHER-9C28E3	Cambridgeshire	Weston Colville	Silver finial	D		
	T417	CORN-A4B020	Cornwall	Phillack	Silver-gilt posy ring	D		
	T302	CORN-B31DC7	Cornwall	Tywadreath	Silver element	D		
	T523	NLM-D49976	Cumbria	Penrith	Silver cross	NT		
	T710	DENO-655D65	Derbyshire	Chesterfield area	Gold posy ring	NT		
	T169	SUSS-B7BA45	Devon	Coliford	Silver-gilt pin-head	TBA	Royal Albert Memorial Museum, Exeter	
	T47		Devon	Stoke Gabriel	Silver-gilt dress hook	NT		
	T670	DOR-9C4371	Dorset	Compton Abbas	Silver fragment	NT		
	T168	DOR-B83652	Dorset	Puddletown	Silver vervel	D		
	T299	DOR-4512B5	Dorset	Tarrant Hinton	Silver toothpick fragment	D		
	T400	YORYM-CAEC20	East Yorkshire	Everingham area	Silver spoon fragments	D		
	T560	YORYM-D01536	East Yorkshire	Pocklington	Silver dress pin	A	East Riding Museums Service	£50
	T97	SUSS-427C12	East Sussex	Chiddingly	Silver bodkin	D		
	T471	SUSS-02A804	East Sussex	Firle	Silver finger-ring	D		
	T96	SUSS-42CA96	East Sussex	Glynde	Silver thimble	D		

Cat. no.	Treasure no.	PAS no.	County	Parish	Description	Disposition	Acquiring Museum	Value
	T681	SUSS-ADCF71	East Sussex	Udimore	Silver bodkin fragment	D		
	T65	SUSS-5568D6	East Sussex	Willingdon and Jevington	Silver-gilt finger-ring incomplete	NT		
	T154	ESS-45AA66	Essex	East of Colchester	Gold finger-ring	NT		
	T631	ESS-74D144	Essex	Bulmer	Silver dress pin fragment	D		
	T250	ESS-B7F6A2	Essex	Colchester area	Silver hawking bell	D		
	T251	ESS-B77BB4	Essex	Colchester area	Silver hawking bell	D		
	T290	DENO-2C0235	Essex	Copford	Silver button	NT		
	T495	ESS-2592A7	Essex	East of Colchester	Silver cufflink element	TBA	Colchester & Ipswich Museum Service	
	T638	ESS-9A8C94	Essex	East of Colchester	Silver button	TBA	Colchester & Ipswich Museum Service	
	T7	ESS-286B04	Essex	East of Colchester	Silver-gilt dress fitting	D		
	T637	ESS-9A8337	Essex	East of Colchester'	Silver buckle	NT		
	T636	ESS-9A7BB7	Essex	Essex	Silver watch-chain fragment	NT		
	T401	ESS-4516A6	Essex	Great Waltham area	Silver cufflink	D		
	T668	ESS-9B89D3	Essex	Hatfield Broad Oak area	Silver cufflink	D		
	T138	ESS-289AA7	Essex	North East Essex	Silver bodkin	D		
	T537	ESS-CA9E84	Essex	North of Colchester	Silver button	D		
	T538	ESS-CAA3B6	Essex	North of Colchester	Silver dress pin fragment	D		
	T539	ESS-CAA883	Essex	North of Colchester	Silver dress pin	D		
	T571	ESS-739E76	Essex	North of Colchester	Silver dress pin	D		
	T564	GLO-407401	Gloucestershire	Coberley	Silver brooch	NT, but A	Corinium Museum	
	T18	GLO-3FD673	Gloucestershire	Dowdeswell	Gold posy ring	NT		
	T565	GLO-1B3252	Gloucestershire	Hartpury	Gold mourning ring	MW	British Museum	
	T28	LON-1BE182	Greater London	Addington	Silver shoe buckle	NT		
	T379	LON-DC3DA6	Greater London	City of London	Silver-gilt dress hook	D		
	T380	LON-DC6707	Greater London	City of London	Gold posy ring	NT		
	T365	LON-6D3145	Greater London	North London	Gold coin hoard	TBA	Hackney Museum	
	T157	LON-BC17A3	Greater London	Queenhithe	Silver button	D		
	T132	LON-822FB2	Greater London	St James' Clarkenwell	Copper-alloy earings	NT		
	T616	LON-0AEB16	Greater London	Wandsworth	Gold mourning ring	TBA	Wandsworth Museum	

Cat. no.	Treasure no.	PAS no.	County	Parish	Description	Disposition	Acquiring Museum	Value
	T454	HAMP-E24B93	Hampshire	Droxford	Silver spoon	NT		
	T332	HAMP-634830	Hampshire	Fawley	Silver thimble	D		
	T205	HAMP-5C0711	Hampshire	Houghton	Silver-gilt dress hook	DON (L)	Hampshire Museums Service	
	T50	HAMP-9A9D22	Hampshire	King's Somborne	Silver terminal element	NT		
	T263	HAMP-4C17A8	Hampshire	Winchester area	Silver bodkin fragment	D		
	T337	SUR-E9F217	Hampshire	Winchester area	Silver finger-ring fragments	NT		
	T286	BH-E031A2	Hertfordshire	Baldock area	Silver spoon	D		
	T24	BH-01EC33	Hertfordshire	North Hertfordshire	Silver vervel	D		
	T532	WILT-BA8DF2	Hertfordshire	St Albans	Silver strap fitting	D		
	T285	BH-E08757	Hertfordshire	St Ippolyts	Silver-gilt finger-ring fragment	D		
	T6	IOW-0AA2D4	Isle of Wight	Brighstone	Gold posy ring	NT		
	T51	IOW-872337	Isle of Wight	Brighstone	Silver containter	NT		
	T40	IOW-515B38	Isle of Wight	Brighstone area	Silver thimble	D		
	T574	IOW-461BE6	Isle of Wight	Calbourne	Gold posy ring	D		
	T509	IOW-87CDD1	Isle of Wight	Carisbrooke	Silver-gilt dress pin	D		
	T700	IOW-625E21	Isle of Wight	Carisbrooke area	Silver ferrule	D		
	T164	IOW-C69FA3	Isle of Wight	Gatcombe area	Gold ferrule	NT		
	T141	IOW-1358B6	Isle of Wight	Godshill area	Silver thimble	D		
	T354	IOW-CEE236	Isle of Wight	Ryde area	Base-metal ingot and ring	NT		
	T472	IOW-B65D91	Isle of Wight	Shorwell area	Silver whistle fragment	D		
	T362	IOW-B02D02	Isle of Wight	Yarmouth area	Silver thimble	D		
	T363	IOW-B09406	Isle of Wight	Yarmouth area	Silver thimble	D		
	T244	IOW-968201	Isle of Wight	Shalfleet	Gold posy ring	D		
	T482	KENT-E876B1	Kent	Bilsington	Silver dress pin	D		
	T494	KENT-29A9D4	Kent	Brookland	Silver-gilt finger-ring fragment	D		
	T614	KENT-C32FD7	Kent	Burmarsh	Silver brooch	NT		
	T378	KENT-D89CC4	Kent	Chiddingstone	Silver vervel	D		
	T145	KENT-043245	Kent	Cliffs End	Copper-alloy ingots	TBD		
	T425	KENT-E80D95	Kent	Cranbrook	Silver bracelet	NT		

Cat. no.	Treasure no.	PAS no.	County	Parish	Description	Disposition	Acquiring Museum	Value
	T426	KENT-E827A1	Kent	Cranbrook	Silver finger-ring	NT		
	T278	KENT-55BE42	Kent	East Kent	Gold fragment	NT		
	T577	KENT-C2F776	Kent	Old Romney	Silver pin	D		
	T481	KENT-E868B3	Kent	Old Romney	Silver finger-ring	NT		
	T61	KENT-4814E6	Kent	Ringwould with Kingsdown	Gold posy ring	NT		
	T246	KENT-47CCB1	Kent	Shepherdswell	Silver seal-matrix	D		
	T148	KENT-3790A8	Kent	Cliffe	Silver dress-hook	D		
	T480	LEIC-69A598	Leicestershire	Melton Mowbray	Silver cosmetic instrument	TBA	Leicestershire County Council Heritage Services	
	T562	LIN-76B104	Lincolnshire	Anderby	Gold finger-ring	D		
	T427	LIN-764E24	Lincolnshire	Boston	Gold posy ring	D		
	T625	LIN-343205	Lincolnshire	Fotherby	Silver scabbard chape	D		
	T284	LIN-33D707	Lincolnshire	Frampton	Gold posy ring	D		
	T398	PAS-2AD817	Lincolnshire	Gainsborough	Gold finger-ring	NT		
	T100	NLM-5185F2	Lincolnshire	Hemingby	Silver-gilt finger-ring fragment	D		
	T321	SWYOR-C55DF7	Lincolnshire	Legsby	Gold bracelet slide	NT		
	T603	LIN-341A61	Lincolnshire	Moulton	Gold finger-ring	D		
	T423	LIN-33E686	Lincolnshire	Pinchbeck	Silver-gilt dress-hook	D		
	T646	NLM-6D00D2	Lincolnshire	Tetney	Silver dress pin	D		
	T67	NLM-BEEF90	Lincolnshire	Wragby	Silver bodkin	D		
	T346	NMS-40F587	Norfolk	Ashill	Silver button	D		
	T11	NMS-BE8551	Norfolk	Cawston	Silver thimble	D		
	T32	NMS-BF9EF5	Norfolk	Congham	Silver-gilt pendant	D		
	T304	NMS-2BD2B0	Norfolk	Emneth	Silver button	D		
	T303	NMS-2B9B83	Norfolk	Emneth	Silver finger-ring	NT		
	T35	NMS-C03327	Norfolk	Fring	Gold finger-rings	NT		
	T30	NMS-BF0ED5	Norfolk	Horsham St Faith/ Newton St Faith	Silver pin	D		
	T31	NMS-BF33C5	Norfolk	Horsham St Faith/ Newton St Faith	Silver dress accessory fragments	D		
	T266	NMS-BF7224	Norfolk	Horsham St Faith/ Newton St Faith	Silver button	D		
	T309	NMS-E87756	Norfolk	Langley with Hardley	Silver thimble	D		

Cat. no.	Treasure no.	PAS no.	County	Parish	Description	Disposition	Acquiring Museum	Value
	T680	NMS-E88A33	Norfolk	Langley with Hardley	Silver thimble	D		
	T237	NMS-E81786	Norfolk	Lyng	Silver thimble	D		
	T20	NMS-BEBFD5	Norfolk	Mundford	Silver strap-end	D		
	T310	NMS-2C7951	Norfolk	Outwell	Silver button	D		
	T218	NMS-D4FA62	Norfolk	Postwick	Silver dress accessory	D		
	T268	NMS-E89E06	Norfolk	Rocklands	Silver thimble	D		
	T382	NMS-E97D03	Norfolk	Seething	Silver bodkin	D		
	T308	NMS-2C9E06	Norfolk	Shipdham	Gold posy ring	A	Norwich Castle Museum	£1,200
	T476	NMS-768695	Norfolk	Swannington area	Gold finger-ring	D		
	T348	NMS-E900F6	Norfolk	West Acre	Silver button	D		
	T553	NMS-D32AA5	Norfolk	West Acre	Silver bodkin fragment	D		
	T479	NMS-76E205	Norfolk	Wymondham	Silver button	D		
	T13	NLM-59BA03	North Lincolnshire	Crowle	Silver-gilt hooked-tag	D		
	T635	NLM-6871E2	North Lincolnshire	Hibaldstow	Silver annular brooch	A	North Lincolnshire Museums Service	£100
	T659	NLM-A99F53	North Lincolnshire	Saxby All Saints	Silver-gilt terminal	D		
	T135	LVPL-E06EE6	North Yorkshire	Buttercrambe	Silver button	D		
	T115	LVPL-3FF534	North Yorkshire	Buttercrame with Bossall	Silver cap hook	D		
	T405	SWYOR-417816	North Yorkshire	Cawood	Silver finger-ring	NT		
	T448	NCL-D3DA01	North Yorkshire	Dalton	Silver finger-ring	D		
	T567	SWYOR-B03DE1	North Yorkshire	Grimston	Silver object	NT		
	T92	SWYOR-AF34B2	North Yorkshire	North Milford	White metal object	NT		
	T93	SWYOR-32A8A7	North Yorkshire	Riccal	Silver mount	D		
	T656	LANCUM-DF9A36	North Yorkshire	Ripon	Silver dress hook	A	Harris Museum & Art Gallery	£100
	T396	SWYOR-2D7381	North Yorkshire	Saxton	Silver seal-matrix	NT		
	T397	SWYOR-2D60B1	North Yorkshire	Saxton	Silver cross-shaped pendant	NTT		
	T395	SWYOR-2D81D4	North Yorkshire	Saxton	Gold posy ring	NT		
	T442	YORYM-CC5C31	North Yorkshire	Snape with Thorpe	Silver fitting	D		
	T444	YORYM-CDC4D4	North Yorkshire	Snape with Thorpe	Gold finger-ring	NT		
	T69	SWYOR-EA9CB3	North Yorkshire	Stapleton	Silver-gilt object	NT		
	T633	SWYOR-B03852	North Yorkshire	Tadcaster area	Gold posy ring	D		
	T634	SWYOR-B03065	North Yorkshire	Tadcaster area	Gold posy ring	D		

Cat. no.	Treasure no.	PAS no.	County	Parish	Description	Disposition	Acquiring Museum	Value
	T189	BH-D703D3	North Yorkshire	North Yorkshire	Silver vervel	NT		
	T645	NARC-018EC7	Northamptonshire	Corby area	Silver-gilt ornamental ring	D		
	T556	NARC-5DC404	Northamptonshire	Islip	Silver scabbard chape	D		
	T428	NARC-773251	Northamptonshire	Kislingbury	Silver button or cufflink element	D		
	T161	NARC-7758C8 & BUC-23DC04	Northamptonshire	Northamptonshire area	Silver button	D		
	T101	NARC-775C94	Northamptonshire	Rothersthorpe	Silver button	D		
	T230	NARC-5DDC26	Northamptonshire	Northamptonshire	Base-metal finger-ring	NT		
	T447	NLM-D4E871	Nottinghamshire	Caunton	Silver finger-ring	NT		
	T613	LVPL-033E25	Nottinghamshire	Farndon	Silver-gilt dress fitting	DON (F&L)	Newark Museum	£25
	T4	DENO-08EE90	Nottinghamshire	Hawton	Gold posy ring	A	Newark Museum	£85
	T458	DENO-CBF274	Nottinghamshire	Kirklington	Gold pendant/ chain link	TBA	Newark Museum	
	T683	DENO-666812	Nottinghamshire	Radcliffe on Trent	Silver disc	NT		
	T433	BERK-0BB0E0	Oxfordshire	Asthal	Gold coin hoard	TBA	Asmolean Museum, Oxford	
	T568	BERK-5CDB60	Oxfordshire	Bampton	Gold posy ring	NT		
	T27	BERK-E563C0	Oxfordshire	Pyrton	Base-metal finger-ring	NT		
	T320	BERK-A7A604	Oxfordshire	Towersey	Silver coin	TBA	Oxfordshire Museums Service	
	T549	LEIC-CE9C04	Rutland	Brooke	Silver seal-die	DON (F&L)	Rutland County Museum	£100
	T503	LVPL-8CB955	Shropshire	Hengoed	Silver finger-ring	NT		
	T666	HESH-886844	Shropshire	Lilleshall area	Silver-gilt dress hook	D		
	T402	HESH-1998B5	Shropshire	Oswestry area	Silver finger-ring	D		
	T581	WAW-46EA23	Shropshire	Tong	Silver seal-matrix	NT		
	T583	WAW-48AAB3	Shropshire	Tong	Silver livery badge	NT		
	T158	SOMDOR-84A977	Somerset	Crewkerne	Silver button	NT		
	T121	SOMDOR-DA1AE6	Somerset	Greinton	Silver shoe buckle	NT		
	T159	SOMDOR-84D081	Somerset	Misterton	Silver seal-matrix	NT		
	T446	SOM-68B1D1	Somerset	Westonzoyland	Silver pendant	NT		
	T548	SOM-B5F3B3	Somerset	Whitelackington	Silver spoon fragment	D		
	T702	GLO-C03F43	South Gloucestershire	South Gloucestershire	Silver finger-ring	NT		
	T323	WMID-346695	Staffordshire	Blymhill & Weston-Under-Lizard	Gold band	NT		

Cat. no.	Treasure no.	PAS no.	County	Parish	Description	Disposition	Acquiring Museum	Value
	T331	WMID-47CE46	Staffordshire	Ilam	Silver plaque	NT		
	T43	WMID-962A51	Staffordshire	Leigh	Silver thimble	D		
	T327	WMID-1B6FD8	Staffordshire	Swynnerton	Silver thimble	D		
	T329	WMID-3472F1	Staffordshire	Staffordshire	Silver finger-ring fragment	NT		
	T322	WMID-479A04	Staffordshire	Waterhouses	Silver-gilt finger-ring	D		
	T256	SF-9CCB15	Suffolk	Bungay area	Silver-gilt hooked-tag	D		
	T473	SF-FFCFC6	Suffolk	Bury St Edmunds area	Silver bodkin	D		
	T280	SF-2B7792	Suffolk	Eye area	Silver cap hook	D		
	T723	SF-EBA136	Suffolk	Eye area	Silver mount	D		
	T712	SF-EB4B44	Suffolk	Eye area	Silver button	D		
	T293	SF-564705	Suffolk	Nettlestead	Silver-gilt dress accessory fragment	D		
	T373	SF-5FA926	Suffolk	Stowmarket area	Silver-gilt pin head	D		
	T151	SF-3B58A1	Suffolk	Wenhaston	Silver button	D		
	T711	SF-EA3EC6	Suffolk	Woodbridge area	Silver finger-ring fragment	D		
	T338	SUR-4DFA53	Surrey	Nutfield	Silver seal-matrix	NT		
	T87	SUR-747D4	Surrey	Wanborough	Silver cufflink element	NT		
	T328	WMID-1B5F45	Warwickshire	Lapworth	Silver thimble	NT		
	T601	SUSS-4DFD78	West Sussex	Clapham	Silver finger-ring	A	Worthing Museum	£600
	T469	SUSS-025B40	West Sussex	Eartham	Silver cufflinks	D		
	T88	SUR-3D6D97	West Sussex	Rusper	Silver buckle	NT		
	T450	SWYOR-B06827	West Yorkshire	Pontefract area	Gold stud	NT		
	T649	SWYOR-F52068	West Yorkshire	Wakefield	Silver-gilt mount	NT		
	T647	SWYOR-F4AAE1	West Yorkshire	Wakefield area	Gold posy ring	TBA	Wakefield Museum	
	T648	SWYOR-F4BDE7	West Yorkshire	Woolley	Silver bodkin fragment	TBA	Wakefield Museum	
	T492	WILT-ED9944	Wiltshire	East Wiltshire	Silver finger-ring	MW	Wiltshire Heritage Museum	
	T76	WILT-6FFA66	Wiltshire	Urchfont	Silver-gilt hooked-tag	TBA	Wiltshire Heritage Museum	
	T356	WILT-EB0D46	Wiltshire	Wroughton	Silver thimble	NT		
	T114	LVPL-8D0010	Wirral	Neston area	Yellow metal penannular bracelet	NT		
	T183	YORYM-2FB222	York	Dunnington	Silver vervel	D		
	T94	YORYM-83C284	York	Gate Helmsley	Silver-gilt belt mount	D		

UNDIAGNOSTIC

Cat. no.	Treasure no.	PAS no.	County	Parish	Description	Disposition	Acquiring Museum	Value
	T551	BH-DE3D16	Buckinghamshire	Stokenchurch	Gold fragment	NT		
	T407	SWYOR-313796	Cambridgeshire	Chesterton	Silver coiled object	NT		
	T413	CAMHER-99B6B5	Cambridgeshire	Chesterton	White metal fragment	NT		
	T108		Devon	Rousdon	Gold rod	NT		
	T313	NCL-635037	Durham	Bowes	White metal ingot	NT		
	T272	NCL-632933	East Yorkshire	Thwing	Gold fragment	NT		
	T178	YORYM-78ED24	East Yorkshire	Wilberfoss	Gold object	NT		
	T639	ESS-EDD307	Essex	Broxted	Gold finger-ring	NT		
	T499	ESS-25A227	Essex	East of Colchester	Silver ?bell fragment	NT		
	T83	BH-0F7032	Essex	Manuden	Silver strip	NT		
	T540	ESS-CAABF3	Essex	North of Colchester	Silver sleeve buttons	NT		
	T572	ESS-73A1F2	Essex	North of Colchester	Silver cufflink	NT		
	T575	ESS-73A9C0	Essex	North of Colchester	Gold bar fragment	D		
	T399	LON-031583	Greater London	City of London	Silver finger-ring	NT		
	T14	LON-933307	Greater London	Edgware	Silver rectangular mount	NT		
	T371	IOW-4B9CF7	Isle of Wight	Freshwater area	Metal fragment	NT		
	T701	KENT-6D84B5	Kent	Cliffe and Cliffe Woods	Silver figurine terminal	NT		
	T663	KENT-C361B1	Kent	Hagham	Gold bar	D		
	T155	KENT-2A9AD7	Kent	Shepherdswell	Gold penannular ring	NT		
	T559	YORYM-CFBBB7	Lincolnshire	Leasingham	Gold disc	D		
	T271	YORYM-77D9E6	North Yorkshire	Ainsbrook	Coins	NT		
	T452	SWYOR-B05B31	North Yorkshire	Green Hammerton	Gold finger-ring	NT		
	T675	YORYM-1B8376	North Yorkshire	Stanwick St John	White metal lump	NT		
	T706	SWYOR-E62C76	South Yorkshire	Doncaster area	Silver fragment	NT		
	T330	WMID-5A1E31	Staffordshire	Brewood	White metal droplet	NT		
	T651	SF-233CD7	Suffolk	Eye	Gold rod	NT		
	T85	SF-21B0D8	Suffolk	Mildenhall area	Silver object	NT		
	T353	WAW-D02AC6	Warwickshire	Alcester	Silver-gilt finger-ring fragment	NT		
	T105	LVPL-8CE002	Wirral	Ince Blundell	Silver finger-ring	NT		
	T181	YORYM-7E89F7	York	Dunnington	Silver-gilt finger-ring fragment	NT		

UPDATE ON 2005 AND 2006 TREASURE CASES

(finds for which details were not available at the time of publication of the *Treasure Annual Report* 2005/6)

TAR 2005/6 cat. no.	Findspot	Treasure number	Disposition	Value
9	Hinckley area	2006 T451	Leicester Museums Service	£300
23	Winchester area	2006 T635	Winchester College	£85
41	Ottery St Mary	2006 T36	Royal Albert Memorial Museum	£75
68	Keswick	2005 T409	Norwich Castle Museum	Landowner donated his share
107	North Cornwall	2006 T463	Royal Cornwall Museum	£175
113	Nether Wallop	2006 T166	Hampshire Museums Service withdrew	Returned to finder/landowner
187	Hockwold cum Wilton	2006 T362	Disclaimed	Returned to finder/landowner
189	Kington Langley	2005 T325	Wiltshire Heritage Museum withdrew interest	Returned to finder/landowner
226	Streethouse	2005 T540	Kirkleatham Museum	£5,520
	Streethouse	2006 T473	Kirkleatham Museum	£77,970
279	Farnborough area	2006 T330	Bromley Museums Service	£250, Landowner donated his share
315	Vernhams Dean	2006 T350	British Museum	£200
316	Wiltshire area	2006 T161	Salisbury & South Wiltshire Museum	Finder and landowner donated their share
577	Newent	2006 T140	Gloucester City Museum	£90
621	Weston Colville	2006 T134	Not Treasure	Returned to finder/landowner
647	Kingsbridge	2006 T646	Plymouth Museum	£100
648	Paignton	2006 T617	Royal Albert Memorial Museum	£55
818	Littlehempston	2006 T420	Royal Albert Memorial Museum	£1,000
1103	Leckford	2006 T194	Hampshire Museums Service	£350
1192	Brackley area	2005 T437	British Museum	£5,500 for 14 coins. Remainder returned to finder/landowner
1224	Boverton	05.10	National Museum Wales	£5,000
1227	Goldcliff	06.21	National Museum Wales	£700
1228	Llanbedr Duffryn Clwyd	06.11	National Museum Wales	£40
1229	Rhoose	05.14	National Museum Wales	£90
1234	Llancarfan	06.16	National Museum Wales	£250
1235	Llantwit Major	05.1	National Museum Wales	£800
1236	Penllyn	06.18	National Museum Wales	£60
1238	St Donats	05.3	National Museum Wales	£750
1242	Wenvoe	05.12	National Museum Wales	£100
1247	Trefeglwys	06.15	National Museum Wales	£30
1248	Cardiff Castle A	06.7	Archaeological Disclaim	Landowner donated his share
1249	Cardiff Castle B	06.8	Archaeological Disclaim	Landowner donated his share
1253	Llanbedrgoch	05.8	Archaeological Disclaim	Landowner donated his share
1255	Llanddona	05.13, 06.3	National Museum Wales withdrew	Returned to finder/landowner
1256	Llay	05.16	Wrexham Museum	£900
1257	Llantwit Major	06.19	National Museum Wales	£850
1260	Moneygran	Northern Ireland	Ulster Museum	£90

INDEX BY FINDSPOT

ENGLAND

Bath and North East Somerset
Bath, 483
Wellow, 547

Bedfordshire
Bedford area, 142, 230
Dunstable, 268
Eaton Bray, 26
Hockliffe, 120
Kensworth, 402
Lower Dean, 250
Pavenham, 492
Wilstead, 75

Berkshire
Swallowfield, 303

Buckinghamshire
Aston Clinton, 114
Brill, 306
Buckingham, 365
Chenies area, 144
Haversham, 161
Lane End area, 64
Little Horwood, 427
Little Kimble, 107
Longwick cum Ilmer, 439
Newton Blossomville, 457
Stone, 37
Wendover, 159

Cambridgeshire
Bluntisham, 328
Cambridge , 509
Chesterton, 118
Ely, 93, 185
Godmanchester, 136
Soham area, 364
West Wratting, 551
Weston Colville, 169, 201

Cheshire
Barbridge, 506
Churton by Aldford, 289
Goostrey, 468
Hale, 106
Marbury, 83
Northwich, 130
Plumley, 407
Weaverham, 9
Whitchurch area, 341, 470
Winwick, 290

Cornwall
Blisland, 30
Constantine, 71
Gwithian, 446
Lanivet, 463
Ludgvan, 266
Padstow, 417, 505
Paul, 13, 323
Phillack, 398
St Buryan, 91
St Minver, 104
Tywardreath, 56, 284
Wadebridge, 24

County Durham
Catcote, 503
Coxhoe, 376
Old Kirk Field area, 278
Seaton with Slingley, 108, 480
Westgate area, 474

Cumbria
Ambleside, 413, 578
Aspatria, 11
Broughton-in-Furness, 406
Carlisle, 96
Kendal, 25, 67
Kirkby Stephen, 558
Maryport, 132
Penrith, 424

Derbyshire
Ashbourne area, 490
Callow, 253
Mercaston, 335
South Wingfield, 292
Stanton area, 499
Willington area, 198

Devon
Bridestowe, 409
Exeter, 425, 582
Kingskerswell, 477
Newton Abbott area, 508
South Brent, 149
Thurlestone, 57

Dorset
Bradford Peverell, 532
Cerne Abbas, 311
Charminster, 200, 291
Chettle, 139, 324
Gussage All Saints, 346
Langton Matravers, 60
Maiden Newton area, 287
Osmington, 251
Rampisham, 240
South Perrott, 81

Tarrant Monkton, 453
Tarrant Rushton, 225
Wimborne Minster, 400

Essex
Beaumont area, 358
Bradfield, 288
Bures area, 128, 405, 571
Chelmsford area, 179
Colchester, East of, 382
Colchester, North of, 205
Elmstead, 314
Finchingfield, 275
Great Yeldham, 580
Kelvedon, 274, 369
Lavenham, 49
Little Laver, 219
Sible Hedingham, 524
Tendring area, 379
Theydon Garnon, 254
Theydon Mount, 46
Uttlesford District, 52
Wrabness, 2

Gloucestershire
Cherington, 133
Coberley, 188, 300, 309
Ham and Stone, 575
Highnam, 110
Kings Stanley, 529
Newent, 348
North Nibley, 131
Stanton Drew, 373
Westbury-on-Severn, 363

Gloucestershire, South
Hawkesbury, 520
Horton, 147
South Gloucestershire, 196, 227, 276

Greater London
Bermondsey, 515
Beulah Hill, 560
City of London, 7, 229, 371, 375, 422
Stepney, 126
Tower Hamlets, 315
Twickenham, 416

Greater Manchester
Atherton, 90

Hampshire
Amport area, 51
Andover, 125
Basingstoke area, 569
Binsted, 34
Breamore, 8
Broughton, 182

Crawley, 194, 544
Crondall, 493
Droxford, 391
Fareham, 525
Fawley, 44
Greywell, 116, 155, 497
Hambledon, 32
Hound, 299
Itchen Valley, 384
Micheldever, 443
Nether Wallop, 271
Ropley, 141, 397, 542
Southampton area, 192
Vernhams Dean, 322
Wherwell, 98, 245
Winchester area, 259, 273
Wonston, 277

Herefordshire
Aston Ingham, 504
Brampton Abbotts, 203
Holmer area, 390
Madley, 63
South Herefordshire, 339

Hertfordshire
East Hertfordshire, 330
Great Gaddesen, 316
Nash Mills, 387
North Hertfordshire, 166, 218, 442
Redbourn, 87
Ridge, 5
Shenley, 374
Ware area, 224, 539
Welwyn, 10
Wiggington, 481

Isle of Wight
Arreton area, 537
Brighstone, 565
Calbourne, 464
Calbourne area, 438
Carisbrooke, 175
Gatcombe area, 256
Isle of Wight, 454, 458
Newchurch, 479
Newchurch area, 456
Newport, 1, 543
Newport area, 399
Niton and Whitwell, 465
Ryde, 414
Shalfleet, 423, 495
Shorwell, 461
Single, 528
West Wight, 58, 158, 517, 519
Yarmouth, 487

Kent
Barham, 318
Boxley, 246
Brookland, 255, 280
Cliffe, 450
Denton with Wootton, 187
Eynsford, 89
Hoaden, 55
Lydd, 308
Offham, 54
Otford, 170
Ramsgate, 172
Ringlemere, 157
Sissinghurst, 437
Westerham, 430
Worth, 164

Lancashire
Carnforth area, 331
Fylde, 215
Gisburn, 105
Kirkham, 420
Lancaster area, 317
Preston area, 570
South-east Lancashire, 396

Leicestershire
East Leicestershire, 432
Frisby and Kirby, 177
Garthorpe, 337
Huncote and Leighfield, 127
Long Whatton, 233
Lutterworth, 491
Nailstone, 573
Narborough, 145
Peckleton, 540
Sheepy, 111
Thurlaston, 301, 393
Twycross, 482

Lincolnshire
Bardney, 20
Beckingham, 235
Belton and Manthorpe, 389
Binbrook, 173, 279
East Kirkby, 222
Fulstow, 516
Great Hale, 467
Hatton, 180
Irnham, 124
Laughton, 584
Low Apley, 555
Market Rasen, 360
Nettleton, 436
North Kesteven, 156
Osbournby, 440
Pinchbeck, 552
Ranby, 28

Roughton, 119
Saxilby, 428
Sleaford, 70
Thoresby, 511
Welbourn, 447
Well, 121
Wellingore, 426
Wood Enderby, 512
Wragby area, 265

Lincolnshire, North
Bonby, 295
Crowle, 357
Holme, 344
Roxby cum Risby, 65, 206
Scawby, 97

Lincolnshire, North East
Bigby, 545

Norfolk
Attleborough area, 53, 80
Crimplesham, 258
Deopham area, 550
Diss area, 171
Dunton, 546
East Lexham area, 563
Edgefield, 350
Emneth, 336, 352, 367
Foulsham, 347
Fransham, 168
Garveston, 23
Gunthorpe, 148
Hempnall, 33
King's Lynn area, 68
Langley with Hardley, 252
Leziate, 261
Marham, 163
Mileham, 176
Needham, 78
North Tuddenham, 189
Norwich area, 69
Old Buckenham, 263
Postwick, 478
Ringland, 15, 221
Runhall, 383
South Creake, 385
South-east Norfolk, 247
Stiffkey, 152
West Acre, 39, 202
Witchingham area, 45
Wymondham, 535

Northamptonshire
Corby area, 207
Kettering area, 47
Silverstone, 518
Walgrave, 282

Northumberland
Vindolanda, 153
Whittington, 527

Nottinghamshire
Annesley, 460
Clipstone, 74, 469
Collingham, 18
Gosford Farm, 122
Hawton, 403
Mansfield Woodhouse area, 143, 459
Newark area, 22,181, 204
Southwell area, 541
Treswell, 165
Tuxford area, 178
Worksop, 305

Oxfordshire
Ambrosden, 568
Chipping Norton, 513
Dorchester, 466
Henley area 536
Letcombe Regis, 583
South Oxfordshire, 135
Swallowfield area, 349
Wantage Down area, 370

Redcar and Cleveland
Streethouse area, 184

Rutland
Rutland area, 577

Shropshire
Alberbury with Cardeston area, 338
Atcham, 377
Baschurch, 488
Baschurch area, 549
Bridgnorth area, 507
Ellesmere, 475
Myddle and Broughton, 559
Shrewsbury area, 17
Telford area, 320
Whitchurch area, 195
Worfield area, 223

Somerset
Charlton Mackrell, 79
Chedzoy, 496
Chilton Trinity, 167
Langport, 530
Long Sutton, 190
Milborne Port, 199, 410
Ston Easton, 566
Tatworth and Forton, 6
West Crewkerne, 404, 574

Somerset, North
Kenn, 362
North Somerset, 272

Staffordshire
Blore with Swinscoe, 262
Drayton Bassett, 380
Harlaston, 286, 326
Hatherton, 85
Ilam, 48, 260, 353
Lapley, 368
Loggerheads, 29
Oulton, 343
Penkridge, 394

Suffolk
Barking, 500
Barrow, 327
Caple St Mary, 112
Cotton, 462
Diss area, 236, 248, 298
Eye, 226
Gedding, 117
Great Barton, 325
Hitcham, 562
Hoxne, 526
Kelsale cum Carlton, 329
Lavenham, 49
Linstead Magna, 579
Mildenhall, 12, 21
Mildenhall area, 522
North East Suffolk, 186
Ringshall, 211
Risby, 220
Saxmundham area, 523
Wetheringsett, 123
Wetheringsett cum Brockford, 269
Wickham Skeith, 140, 451
Woodbridge area, 174, 191

Surrey
Betchworth, 231
Bletchingley, 319
Camberley, 4
Guildford, 411
Leatherhead, 244
West Clandon, 285
Woking, 564

Sussex, East
Alfriston area, 534
Eastbourne area, 449
East Sussex, 485
Hurst Green, 419
Pett, 31
Plumpton, 214
Ringmer, 581
Udimore, 342
Willingdon and Jevington, 444

Sussex, West
Appledram, 59
Boxgrove, 395
Chichester area, 445, 448, 494, 514, 521
Findon area, 452
Middleton on Sea area, 239
Oving, 378
Petworth area, 472
Selsey area, 471
Shoreham by Sea, 455
Storrington, 489
Stoughton area, 307
Trotton with Chithurst, 43
West Sussex, 441

Warwickshire
Alcester, 146
Ansley, 38
Binton, 392
Corley, 548
Middleton, 103
Stoneleigh, 84
Warmington, 150
Weethley, 3
Wibtoft, 77
Wootton Wawen, 351

West Midlands
Astleys, 556

Wiltshire
Chiseldon, 355
Durnford, 334
East Knoyle, 41
Everleigh, 361
Heytesbury, 42
Kington St Michael, 241
Lacock, 134, 138
Landford, 418
Mildenhall, 50, 160, 381
Ogbourne St Andrew, 228
Salisbury area, 510
Seagry, 36
St Paul with Malmesbury, 502
Swindon area, 61, 561
Trowbridge area, 95
Urchfont, 151, 193, 294, 429
Wingfield, 283
Winterbourne, 345

Worcestershire
Hampton Lovett, 27
Hinton on the Green, 498
Inkberrow, 109
Rock, 242
Stoulton, 359
Wychavon, 73

York, City of
Naburn, 304
York area, 99

Yorkshire, East
Beverley, 431
Beverley area, 237
Bridlington area, 216
Burton Fleming, 86
Driffield, 72
Driffield area, 434, 435
East Yorkshire, 162
Grindale, 210
Harswell, 533
Hull area, 567
Lund, 313
North Dalton, 433, 473
Paull, 264
Pocklington, 94
Pocklington area, 356
South Cave, 115
Wressle, 257

Yorkshire, North
Aldbrough, 297
Aldbrough area, 137
Arncliffe, 270
Birkin, 14
Brearton, 372
Brompton, 113
Buttercrambe with Bossall, 408
Cawood, 538
Flaxton, 501
Great Smeaton, 293
Harrogate area, 486
Kirby Hill, 76
Kirk Deighton area, 212
Leyburn, 62
Long Marston, 281
Maunby, 209
Newby Wiske, 154
Newton Kyme cum Toulson, 101
North Yorkshire, 102, 197, 333, 531
Sealfield, 267
Snape, 388
Snape with Thorpe, 92, 208
Vale of York, 217
West Tanfield, 572
Ugthorpe, 476

Yorkshire, South
Doncaster area, 484

Yorkshire, West
Heptonstall, 16
Pontefract, 296
Stanbury, 19
Woolley, 415

WALES

Anglesey
Llanbedrgoch, 183
Trearddur, 40

Flintshire
Higher Kinnerton, 354
Overton, 401
Ysceifiog, 554

Gwent
Langstone, 88

Gwynedd
Duffryn Ardudwy, 421

Monmouthshire
Portskewett, 243
Wentlooge, 332

Pembrokeshire
Kilgetty, 321

Powys
Brecon, 412
Old Radnor, 386
Talgarth, 213
Welshpool, 576
Yscir, 129

Rhondda Cynon Taff
Llanharry, 100, 553

Swansea
Llanddewi, 249
Port Eynon, 232

Vale of Glamorgan
Bonvilston, 557
Cowbridge, 82
Dinas Powys, 302
Llancarfan, 340
Llanfair, 238
Penllyn, 66, 310, 312, 366
Rhoose, 234

Wrexham
Burton, 35

INDEX BY ACQUIRING MUSEUM

Athelstan Museum, Malmesbury, 502

Bassetlaw Museum, Retford, 178

Bedford Museum, 75, 250

Bexhill Museum, 485

Bowes Museum, Barnard Castle, 376

Bradford Museums, 19

Braintree Museum, 128, 274, 275, 369, 524, 571

Brecknock Museum, 213

Bristol City Museum and Art Gallery, 196, 227

British Museum, 92, 99, 108, 134, 135, 136, 137, 157, 158, 164, 186, 189, 191, 197, 200, 208, 209, 212, 217*, 251, 285, 311, 333, 428, 444, 447, 455, 464, 474, 480, 490*, 496, 499, 511, 512, 516, 526, 546

Buckinghamshire County Museum, 37, 365, 427

Bushey Museum, 374

Canterbury Museum, 187, 255, 318

Chelmsford Museum, 179

Chichester District Museum, 307, 395, 471, 472

Colchester and Ipswich Museums Service, 112, 171, 205, 236, 248, 298, 314, 329, 358, 379, 382, 523

The Collection, Lincoln, 121

Corinium Museum, Cirencester, 188, 300, 309

Derby Museum and Art Gallery, 292, 335, 490*

Doncaster Museum, 484

Dorset County Museum, 60, 532

Dover Museum, 55

East Riding Museums Service, 210, 216, 237, 264, 473, 533

Ely Museum, 93, 169, 364

Epping Forest District Museum, 46, 254

Fitzwilliam Museum, Cambridge, 201, 551

Flintshire County Museums Service, 554

Gloucester City Museum, 348

Guildford Museum, 231, 244

Hampshire Museums Service, 44, 51, 125, 299, 322, 397, 525, 569

Harris Museum and Art Gallery, Preston, 570

Harrogate Museum, 281, 297

Hartlepool Museum and Heritage Service, 278, 503

Hastings Museum, 31

Herbert Museum and Art Gallery, Coventry, 556

Hereford Museum and Art Gallery, 203, 339, 390, 504

Hertford Museum, 224

Isle of Wight Heritage Service, 537

Kirkleatham Museum, 184

Lancashire County Museums Service, 331

Leicestershire County Council Heritage Services, 111, 233, 301, 432, 482

Luton Museum, 120, 402

Lynn Museum, 258, 385

Maidstone Museum, 54, 170, 430

Mansfield Museum and Art Gallery, 459

Mildenhall District Museum, 522

Museum of London, 375, 560

Museum of Nottingham Life, 122

Nantwich Museum, 506

National Museum Wales, 35, 66, 82, 88, 183, 234, 238, 302, 310, 312, 321, 340, 366, 401

National Museums Liverpool, 106

Newark Museum, 181, 204, 403

Newport Art Gallery and Museum, 332

Northampton Museum, 47, 282

North Lincolnshire Museums Service, 206, 295, 344, 545

North Somerset Museum, 362

Norwich Castle Museum, 39, 45, 53, 68, 69, 80, 148, 163, 164, 168, 176, 202, 247, 252, 261, 263, 336, 347, 350, 352, 367, 383, 535, 550, 563

Oriel Ynys Môn, Llangefni, 40

Oxfordshire County Museums Service, 349, 370, 536

Peterborough Museum and Art Gallery, 118

Potteries Museum and Art Gallery, Stoke, 286, 380

Powysland Museum, 576

Radnorshire Museum, Llandrindod Wells, 386

Richmondshire Museum, 267

Roman Baths Museum, Bath, 483, 547

Royal Albert Memorial Museum, Exeter, 508, 582

Royal Institution of Cornwall, 56, 71, 446, 463

Royal Cornwall Museum, Truro, 24, 91, 266, 398

Rutland County Museum, 577

Saffron Walden Museum, 52

Salisbury and South Wiltshire Museum, 41, 334, 345

Shropshire County Museums Service, 195, 475, 507, 549, 559

Somerset County Museum, 167, 190, 199, 404

Storrington Museum, 489

Stroud, Museum in the Park, 131, 276, 575

Swansea Museum, 232, 249

Tullie House Museum and Art Gallery, Carlisle, 96

Vindolanda Trust, 153

Wakefield Museum, 296

Ware Museum, 330

Warwickshire Museum, 38, 84, 146, 351, 548

Whitby Museum, 476

Wiltshire Heritage Museum, 36, 138, 151, 283, 294, 429

Winchester Museums Service, 32, 194, 259, 273, 277, 384, 391

Woodbridge Museum, 174

Yorkshire Museums Trust, 113, 217*, 293, 486

Museums withdrawing from the acquisition of catalogued Items

Armitt Museum and Art Gallery, Ambleside, 578

The British Museum, 172, 180, 408

Canterbury Museum, 280, 308

Cheshire Museums Service, 290

Dacorum Heritage Trust, 316

Dean Heritage Centre, 363

Derby Museum and Art Gallery, 499

Isle of Wight Heritage Service, 58

Lancaster City Museum, 317

Leicestershire County Council Museums Service, 393

Moyse's Hall Museum, 211, 562

Nantwich Museum, 341

North Hertfordshire Museums Service, 166

Norwich Castle Museum, 189

Penrith Museum, 558

The Collection, Lincoln, 555

Wiltshire Heritage Museum, 361

York Museum Trust, 209

Other museums acquiring Treasure cases reported in 2007 (but not catalogued in report)

The Ashmolean Museum, Oxford

Grosvenor Museum, Chester

Hackney Museum

Mildenhall and District Museum

St Albans Museum

Worthing Museum

*Joint Acquisition

RECORDING FINDS

All finds recorded by the Portable Antiquities Scheme (PAS) are entered onto its database – www.findsdatabase.org.uk. The aim is to make as much of this data as possible available for research and education, while protecting finders' details and archaeological sites from damage. Although the full data is made available for archaeological and research purposes, the public database does not provide finders' details or precise findspot information.

The PAS website and finds database

During 2007, the PAS's web technology was put under pressure by the database supplier, Oxford ArchDigital (OAD), being sent into receivership and some hardware problems with the servers. However, all management of the PAS's ICT has now been taken over by Dan Pett (ICT Adviser) and steps were implemented for the revamp of the website which will be delivered in late 2009.

Even with these problems, the recording of objects has continued apace. There has also been an improvement in both the quality of records and images produced by the staff and volunteers who record.

Table 1. Average number of visitors, visits, page requests and user hits on the PAS website and finds database 2004 to 2007.

Year	Unique visitors	Number of visits	Pages	Average pages viewed per visit
2004	84,174	289,595	4,847,892	16
2005	152,711	555,289	9,639,621	18
2006	247,103	720,369	15,469,127	21
2007	165,120	295,567	3,710,381	13

There have been new developments to the PAS website, perhaps most importantly by the incorporation of Oxford University's Celtic Coin Index (www.finds.org.uk/CCI) which has over 37,000 Celtic coins from England and Wales (and a few from Continental Europe). This site features many of the elements that will appear in the PAS's redesigned database, including Google mapping, data downloads and a more intuitive user interface. Developments outlined in last year's PAS Annual Report have proved to be popular, with the Roman coin guide now accounting for 15% of visitors to the main website. The PAS website has been first on search engine ranking for 'Roman coins' for the entire period of the report, and the statistical analysis provided on staff profile pages now provides a snapshot of activity within the counties. The numismatic overhaul has allowed in-depth analysis of Roman coin discoveries from England and Wales, which is now tied to the coin guide and is aiding the research of the PhD being conducted by Philippa Walton (Institute of Archaeology, University College, London). As the PAS staff speak to more researchers, the database is adapting to their research needs and is becoming more accessible.

Experimentation with www.flickr.com has also proved to be popular, with images licensed under a Creative Commons licence. This has driven usage of PAS images on third party websites and increased the PAS's penetration into external resources. Some personal websites now display lists of the owner's discoveries via the use of RSS, e.g. www.ourpasthistory.com run by Corinne Mills. It is hoped that more individuals and organisations will start to do this over the next few years.

Objects recorded by quantity

66,311 archaeological objects were recorded on the PAS database in 2007 (this does not include 11,295 finds from Norfolk, recorded before 2007, which were uploaded in 2007); Table 2a shows objects recorded by geographical area and Table 2b shows objects recorded by recording area. The most productive 'geographic' areas were Suffolk (9,451), Lincolnshire (3,895), and Wales (3,796), while the most productive 'recording' areas were Suffolk (11,066), Sussex (5,020), and Wales (3,863). Many factors influence the numbers of finds recorded, including archaeology, land use and traditions of liaison with finders; Katherine Robbins (Southampton University) has begun work on an AHRC funded PhD to examine such factors influencing PAS data.

The PAS's Finds Liaison Officers (FLOs) record finds found anywhere in England or Wales. People may find objects away from where they live, but in most cases finders prefer to record finds locally. This is highlighted by the fact that the Surrey FLO, for example, recorded at least 465 non-Surrey finds in 2007.

Table 2a: Objects recorded by geographical area in 2007

County	Records	Finds recorded	
Avon	97	329	
Bedfordshire	605	608	
Berkshire	150	360	
Buckinghamshire & Milton Keynes	1,712	1,920	
Cambridgeshire	1,062	1,607	
Cheshire	323	328	
Cornwall	345	346	
Cumbria	442	710	
Derbyshire	207	301	
Devon	253	499	
Dorset	739	879	
Durham	35	242	
Essex	1,026	2,562	
Gloucestershire	324	2,036	
Greater London	582	623	
Greater Manchester	24	26	
Hampshire	1,591	1,844	
Herefordshire	175	180	
Hertfordshire	1,717	1,756	
Isle of Wight	962	1,163	
Kent	888	970	
Lancashire	329	445	
Leicestershire	961	2,891	
Lincolnshire	2,205	3,895	
Merseyside	72	72	
Norfolk [3]	2,391	2,431	
North Lincolnshire	620	625	
Northamptonshire	680	1,271	
Northumberland	178	287	
Nottinghamshire	753	781	
Oxfordshire	1,116	1,706	
Rutland	113	389	
Shropshire	414	2,771	
Somerset	972	1,621	
Staffordshire	214	280	
Suffolk	3,467	9,451	
Surrey	807	943	
Sussex, East	1,746	1,988	
Sussex, West	1,473	2,961	
Teesside	26	37	
Tyne and Wear	5	5	
Warwickshire	1,003	2,029	
West Midlands	10	10	
Wales	391	3,796	
Wiltshire	1,547	2,220	
Worcestershire	302	400	
Yorkshire, East	765	981	
Yorkshire, North	1,421	1,738	
Yorkshire, South	259	294	
Yorkshire, West	184	195	
Other	432	509	
Total	38,115	66,311	

[3] A further 11,261 records of 11,295 old finds from Norfolk were uploaded to the PAS database in 2007.

Table 2b: Objects recorded by recording area in 2007

	Posts	Months	Records	Finds recorded	
Bedfordshire & Hertfordshire	1	12	2,002	2,043	
Berkshire & Oxfordshire	1	12	1,102	1,863	
Buckinghamshire	1	12	1,968	2,172	
Cambridgeshire	1	10	815	1,205	
Cheshire, Gtr Manchester & Merseyside	1	10	599	614	
Cornwall	0.5	12	355	356	
Derbyshire & Nottinghamshire	1	12	1,136	1,296	
Devon	1	12	283	504	
Essex	1	7	1,089	1,202	
Gloucestershire & Avon	1	12	406	3,273	
Hampshire	1	12	1,284	1,583	
Herefordshire & Shropshire	1	12	496	2,855	
Isle of Wight	0.3	12	955	1,152	
Kent	1	12	822	893	
Lancashire & Cumbria	1	12	1,004	1,387	
Leicestershire & Rutland	1	12	1,019	3,215	
Lincolnshire	1	12	1,408	3,056	
London	0.5	12	491	534	
Norfolk [4]	1.5	12	2,681	2,722	
Northamptonshire	1	12	707	1,389	
North East	1	12	447	670	
North Lincolnshire	1	12	826	831	
Somerset & Dorset	1.8	12	1,753	2,468	
Staffordshire & West Midlands	1	11	431	522	
Suffolk	1.5	12	3,524	11,066	
Surrey	0.5	12	1,250	1,408	
Sussex (East & West)	1	12	3,323	5,020	
Warwickshire & Worcestershire	1	12	1,218	1,410	
Wiltshire	1	12	1,555	2,328	
Yorkshire (North & East) [5]	1.5	12	1,747	2,385	
Yorkshire (South & West)	1	12	960	1,026	
Wales	1	12	459	3,863	
Total			**38,115**	**66,311**	

[4] A further 11,261 records of 11,295 old finds from Norfolk were uploaded to the PAS database in 2007.

[5] The full-time FLO post was vacant from 31 March until 1 October 2007.

Table 2c shows the monthly average of objects recorded in 2006 and 2007 by recording area. The most productive areas in 2007 were Suffolk (922), Sussex (418), and Wales (322). Various factors explain these regional variations. It should be noted that finds recording is only one aspect of an FLO's work, albeit a very important one.

Table 2c: Monthly average of objects recorded in 2006 and 2007 by recording area

	Posts	Average 2006	Average 2007	
Bedfordshire & Hertfordshire	1	120	170	
Berkshire & Oxfordshire	1	164	155	
Buckinghamshire	1	113	181	
Cambridgeshire	1	185	121	
Cheshire, Gtr Manchester & Merseyside	1	27	51	
Cornwall	0.5	31	30	
Derbyshire & Nottinghamshire	1	103	108	
Devon	1	23	42	
Essex	1	155	172	
Gloucestershire & Avon	1	160	273	
Hampshire	1	124	132	
Herefordshire & Shropshire	1	57	238	
Isle of Wight	0.3	73	96	
Kent	1	104	74	
Lancashire & Cumbria	1	61	116	
Leicestershire & Rutland	1	106	268	
Lincolnshire	1	229	255	
London	0.5	81	45	
Norfolk	1.5	229	227	
Northamptonshire	1	53	116	
North East	1	41	56	
North Lincolnshire	1	81	69	
Somerset & Dorset	1.8	201	206	
Staffordshire & West Midlands	1	108	47	
Suffolk	1.5	681	922	
Surrey	0.5	102	117	
Sussex (East & West)	1	475	418	
Warwickshire & Worcestershire	1	128	118	
Wiltshire	1	164	194	
Yorkshire (North & East)	1.5	160	199	
Yorkshire (South & West)	1	53	86	
Wales	1	494	322	

Table 2d shows that the eastern and southern parts of England, and therefore closest to the Continent, are the most productive. In order of productivity these are the East (18,238 finds), South East & London (14,625), and the East Midlands (9,787).

Table 2d: Objects recorded by region in 2007

Region	Records	Finds recorded	
North West	1,603	2,001	
North East	447	670	
Yorkshire & Humber	2,707	3,411	
West Midlands	2,145	4,787	
East Midlands	5,096	9,787	
East	10,111	18,238	
South West	4,352	8,929	
South East & London	11,195	14,625	
Wales	459	3,863	
total	38,115	33,311	

Objects recorded by class

Table 3 shows the number of objects recorded by class (where known). In contrast to 2006, coins account for the highest percentage of finds recorded (37.95%) followed by metal objects (30.6%), but there are notable regional variations. For example, a higher than average percentage of coins were recorded in the East (54.81%) and the East Midlands (45.48%) but considerably less in Wales (3.97%), the North West (13.82%), and the West Midlands (16.86%). The West Midlands (52.99%), North West (50.55%), and Yorkshire & the Humber (50.07%) recorded a substantially higher than average percentage of metal objects, whereas those in Wales (5.81%) and the East (17.49%) were lowest. It is important to note that these relationships between the percentages of objects recorded by region do not reflect the quantity of objects recorded; for example while metal objects in the East only account for 17.49% of the finds recorded by class, the total number of metal finds (4,334) is greater than all regions, apart from the South East & London (6,197) and the East Midlands (4,418). An above average percentage of finds of worked stone were recorded in Wales (89.9%) and the South West (27.54%), in contrast to the North West (1.79%) and North East (1.24%). A higher than average percentage of pottery finds were recorded in the North East (38.87%) and North West (32.18%), whereas that in the East Midlands (4.55%) and Wales (0.16%) was relatively low.

Table 3: Objects recorded by class (where known) in 2007 – percentage shown in brackets (%)

	FLOs	Metal objects		Coins		Worked stone		Pottery		Other		Total
North West	2	790	(50.55)	216	(13.82)	28	(1.79)	503	(32.18)	26	(1.66)	1,563
North East	1	212	(37.46)	119	(21.02)	7	(1.24)	220	(38.87)	8	(1.41)	566
Yorkshire & the Humber	3	1,919	(50.07)	1,082	(28.23)	280	(7.3)	408	(10.64)	144	(3.76)	3,833
West Midlands	3	3,014	(52.99)	959	(16.86)	1,079	(18.97)	465	(8.17)	171	(3.01)	5,688
East Midlands	5	4,418	(43.59)	4,610	(45.48)	547	(5.39)	461	(4.55)	100	(0.99)	10,136
East [6]	7	4,334	(17.49)	13,585	(54.81)	592	(2.39)	5,367	(21.66)	905	(3.65)	24,783
South West	6	2,475	(24.76)	2,614	(26.15)	2,752	(27.54)	2,092	(20.93)	62	(0.62)	9,995
South East & London	8	6,197	(37.11)	5,907	(35.38)	1,746	(10.46)	2,710	(16.23)	137	(0.82)	16,697
Wales	1	221	(5.81)	151	(3.97)	3,417	(89.9)	6	(0.16)	6	(0.16)	3,801
Total	36	23,580	(30.6)	29,243	(37.95)	10,448	(13.56)	12,232	(15.87)	1,559	(2.02)	77,062

[6] This table includes full Norfolk data (see footnote 4).

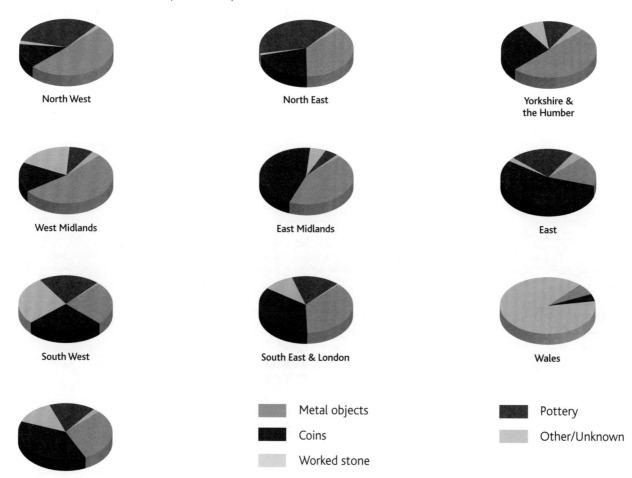

North West

North East

Yorkshire & the Humber

West Midlands

East Midlands

East

South West

South East & London

Wales

Total

Metal objects	Pottery
Coins	Other/Unknown
Worked stone	

Objects recorded by period

Table 4 shows the number of objects recorded by period (where known). As in 2006, Roman finds account for the highest percentage for any period (43%), followed by Medieval (19.92%) and then Stone Age (15.84%). Although the FLOs aim to record all finds over 300 years old, they will be more selective in recording more recent finds. This said, it is interesting that 13.52% of finds recorded in 2007 were post-Medieval or Modern.

There are regional differences. The percentage of Stone Age finds recorded in Wales (89.88%) and the South West (26.52%) were above average, while those in the East Midlands (4.99%), East (4.38%) and North East (0.53%) are comparatively low. A substantially higher than average percentage of Bronze Age finds was recorded in the North East (13.35%), whereas it was low in Yorkshire & the Humber (0.59%) and Wales (0.55%). Higher than average percentages of Iron Age material was recovered in the East (3.82%) and Yorkshire & the Humber (2.69%), with lower numbers in the West Midlands (0.78%) and Wales (0.18%). Roman finds accounted for an above average percentage in the West Midlands (55.04%), the East (54.02%), and the East Midlands (54.04%), but were very low in Wales (3.14%), as might be expected. An above average percentage of Early Medieval finds was recorded in the North West (16.96%), but again low in Wales (0.13%). The percentage of Medieval finds was higher than average in the North East (44.66%), and again in Wales was low (2.85%). The averages of post-Medieval finds recorded were highest in the North West (21.90%), the South East & London (18.77%), and Yorkshire & the Humber (18.59%), but were lowest in the North East (5.16%) and Wales (3.24%). An above average percentage of Modern finds was recorded in the North West (3.85%), but percentages were low in Wales (0.03%), the East (0.01%), and the North East (0%).

Table 4: Objects recorded by period (where known) in 2007 – percentage shown in brackets (%)

	Stone Age	Bronze Age	Iron Age	Roman	Early Medieval	Medieval	Post-Medieval	Modern	Total
North West	135 (8.67)	16 (1.03)	15 (0.97)	441 (28.32)	264 (16.96)	285 (18.3)	341 (21.9)	60 (3.85)	1,557
North East	3 (0.53)	75 (13.35)	6 (1.07)	184 (32.74)	14 (2.49)	251 (44.66)	29 (5.16)	0 (0)	562
Yorkshire & the Humber	265 (7.07)	22 (0.59)	101 (2.69)	1,103 (29.42)	346 (9.23)	1,194 (31.85)	697 (18.59)	21 (0.56)	3,749
West Midlands	1,068 (19.37)	219 (3.97)	43 (0.78)	3,034 (55.04)	109 (1.98)	664 (12.04)	374 (6.78)	2 (0.04)	5,513
East Midlands	500 (4.99)	302 (3.01)	163 (1.63)	5,416 (54.04)	380 (3.79)	2,004 (19.99)	1,205 (12.02)	53 (0.53)	1,0023
East [7]	1,089 (4.38)	210 (0.84)	950 (3.82)	13,407 (54.02)	690 (2.78)	5,448 (21.95)	3,028 (12.2)	3 (0.01)	24,825
South West	2,623 (26.52)	205 (2.07)	187 (1.89)	3,878 (39.2)	118 (1.19)	1,417 (14.32)	1,438 (14.54)	27 (0.27)	9,893
South East & London	3,001 (18.27)	401 (2.44)	299 (1.82)	5,250 (31.96)	496 (3.02)	3,831 (23.33)	3,082 (18.77)	64 (0.39)	16,424
Wales	3,409 (89.88)	21 (0.55)	7 (0.18)	119 (3.14)	5 (0.13)	108 (2.85)	123 (3.24)	1 (0.03)	3,793
Total	12,093 (15.84)	1,471 (1.93)	1,771 (2.32)	32,832 (43)	2,422 (3.17)	15,202 (19.92)	10,317 (13.52)	231 (0.3)	76,129

[7] This table includes full Norfolk data (see footnote 4).

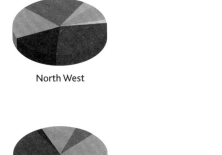

North West

North East

Yorkshire & the Humber

West Midlands

East Midlands

East

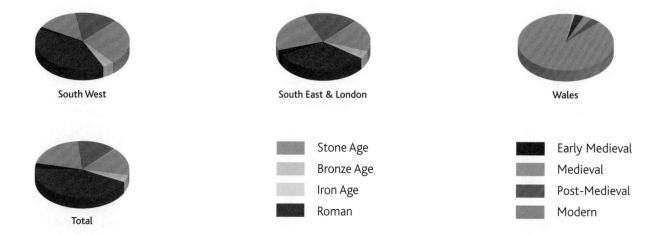

	Stone Age		Early Medieval
	Bronze Age		Medieval
	Iron Age		Post-Medieval
	Roman		Modern

South West   South East & London   Wales   Total

Findspot precision

Finders are asked to provide at least a six-figure National Grid Reference (NGR) – accurate to 100m^2 – for findspots of finds recorded with the PAS. Table 5b shows that in 2007 90% of finds recorded with the PAS were recorded to at least a six-figure NGR. Almost 50% of all finds were recorded to an eight-figure NGR (10m^2). Increasing numbers of finders are using handheld Global Positioning Systems (GPS) devices to ensure the better recording of findspots in the field, following advice set out in the *Code of Practice for Responsible Metal-Detecting in England and Wales*.

Table 5a shows that there are regional differences in findspot precision. The areas that achieved the greatest proportion of finds recorded to a six-figure NGR were Bedfordshire & Hertfordshire (99.41%), Cornwall (99.13%), and Suffolk (99.03%), while the lowest were Wales (4.23%), North Lincolnshire (75.36%), and Derbyshire & Nottinghamshire (77.82%). The areas that recorded the highest proportion of finds to an eight-figure NGR were Norfolk (97.04%), Isle of Wight (94.32%), and Herefordshire & Shropshire (76.82%), but these percentages were lowest in Wales (2.37%), Staffordshire & the West Midlands (9.28%), and Cheshire, Greater Manchester & Merseyside (14.32%).

Table 5a: Findspot precision by recording area 2007

	Findspots	No NGR	4 figure	6 figure	8 figure	10 figure	12 figure
Bedfordshire & Hertfordshire	2,364	10	4	1,593	552	192	13
Berkshire & Oxfordshire	2,066	45	45	1,043	754	178	1
Buckinghamshire	1,920	21	65	605	1,152	77	0
Cambridgeshire	1,607	137	2	1,038	397	33	0
Cheshire, Gtr Manchester & Merseyside	426	9	60	296	58	3	0
Cornwall	346	2	1	109	184	50	0
Derbyshire & Nottinghamshire	1,082	191	49	613	140	84	5
Devon	499	61	10	145	280	2	1
Essex	2,562	43	32	1,968	240	279	0
Gloucestershire & Avon	2,365	86	49	1,090	1,088	52	0
Hampshire	1,844	87	53	930	633	141	0
Herefordshire & Shropshire	2,951	223	40	421	231	2,035	1
Isle of Wight	1,163	16	0	50	20	1,077	0
Kent	970	84	3	481	269	132	1
Lancashire & Cumbria	1,155	86	1	584	320	142	22
Leicestershire & Rutland	3,280	33	1	1,492	1,633	121	0
Lincolnshire	3,895	214	311	1299	790	1281	0
London	623	27	1	209	40	341	5
Norfolk	13,726	177	72	157	3,480	9,839	1
Northamptonshire	1271	99	4	757	196	201	14
North East	571	74	2	242	243	10	0
North Lincolnshire	625	106	48	380	40	51	0
Somerset & Dorset	2,500	103	23	1,742	581	51	0
Staffordshire & West Midlands	290	41	5	217	14	13	0
Suffolk	9,451	61	31	5,628	2,853	859	19
Surrey	943	3	49	639	155	97	0
Sussex (East & West)	4,949	50	100	2,676	967	1,154	2
Warwickshire & Worcestershire	2,429	165	118	1072	684	390	0
Wiltshire	2,220	317	82	1,295	458	68	0
Yorkshire (North & East)	2,719	129	5	1,784	522	276	3
Yorkshire (South & West)	499	25	4	377	59	34	0
Wales	3,806	3,059	586	71	55	35	0
Totals	**77,117**	**5,784**	**1,856**	**31,003**	**19,088**	**19,298**	**88**

Table 5a: Findspot precision by recording area 2007 (cont.)

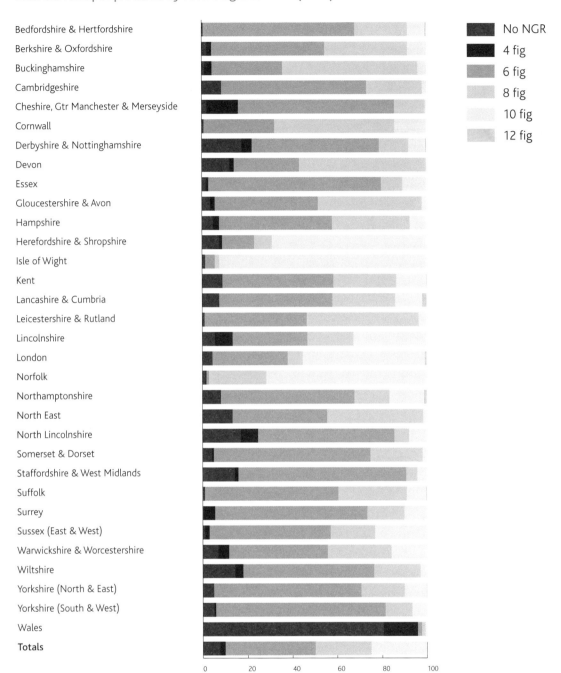

Bedfordshire & Hertfordshire
Berkshire & Oxfordshire
Buckinghamshire
Cambridgeshire
Cheshire, Gtr Manchester & Merseyside
Cornwall
Derbyshire & Nottinghamshire
Devon
Essex
Gloucestershire & Avon
Hampshire
Herefordshire & Shropshire
Isle of Wight
Kent
Lancashire & Cumbria
Leicestershire & Rutland
Lincolnshire
London
Norfolk
Northamptonshire
North East
North Lincolnshire
Somerset & Dorset
Staffordshire & West Midlands
Suffolk
Surrey
Sussex (East & West)
Warwickshire & Worcestershire
Wiltshire
Yorkshire (North & East)
Yorkshire (South & West)
Wales
Totals

Legend:
- No NGR
- 4 fig
- 6 fig
- 8 fig
- 10 fig
- 12 fig

Table 5b: Change in findspot precision since 1997; percentage of findspots with at least a 6-figure NGR

Year	Average (%)
1997–1999	56
1999–2000	60
2000–2001	68
2001–2003	70
2003–2004	73
2004–2005	75
2005–2006	86
2006	90
2007	90

Finders

Table 6a shows that 6,870 individuals offered finds for recording with the PAS in 2007, an increase on the 2006 figure (6,126). Of these, 63.83% were metal-detectorists, but more than a third were other types of finders.

Table 6a: Number of individuals offering finds for recording in 2007

	Metal-detectorists	Others	Total
Bedfordshire & Hertfordshire	293	75	368
Berkshire & Oxfordshire	135	45	180
Buckinghamshire	295	13	308
Cambridgeshire	40	150	190
Cheshire, Gtr Manchester & Merseyside	150	80	230
Cornwall	50	50	100
Derbyshire & Nottinghamshire	99	25	124
Devon	49	200	249
Essex	116	21	137
Gloucestershire & Avon	63	26	89
Hampshire	60	29	89
Herefordshire & Shropshire	164	287	451
Isle of Wight	80	15	95
Kent	320	105	425
Lancashire & Cumbria	103	98	201
Leicestershire & Rutland	71	47	118
Lincolnshire	161	17	178
London	71	183	254
Norfolk	230	60	290
Northamptonshire	61	57	118
North East	350	150	500
North Lincolnshire	67	5	72
Somerset & Dorset	84	126	210
Staffordshire & West Midlands	90	5	95
Suffolk	170	10	180
Surrey	45	20	65
Sussex (East & West)	190	80	270
Warwickshire & Worcestershire	41	54	95
Wiltshire	100	246	346
Yorkshire (North & East)	195	65	260
Yorkshire (South & West)	129	96	225
Wales	256	102	358
Total	**4,328**	**2,542**	**6,870**

The FLOs continue to make regular visits to metal-detecting clubs; the proactive nature of the PAS ensures finders continue to record finds with the PAS. Table 6b shows that of the 170 metal-detecting clubs known to exist, the FLOs have contact with 161 of them on a regular basis. Although it is apparent that most metal-detecting clubs welcome the FLO, a small minority (9) do not.

There are at least 6,543 members in the known metal-detecting clubs. This does not include 'independent' detectorists (not members of clubs), who also record with the PAS; it has been estimated that 1,320 independents are known to the FLOs. Some detectorists are members of more than one club (and hence the duplication of numbers in this table is likely), some members of clubs no longer actively detect, and others do not search for archaeological material (i.e. they detect on beaches).

Table 6b: Metal-detecting clubs and FLO contact [8]

	No. of clubs (membership)	No. in regular contact with FLO (membership)
Bedfordshire & Hertfordshire	5 (290)	4 (270)
Berkshire & Oxfordshire	3 (210)	3 (210)
Buckinghamshire	4 (75)	4 (75)
Cambridgeshire	2 (55)	2 (55)
Cheshire, Gtr Manchester & Merseyside	8 (427)	8 (427)
Cornwall	3 (95)	3 (95)
Derbyshire & Nottinghamshire	7 (270)	7 (270)
Devon	5 (150+)	4 (150+)
Essex	7 (357)	6 (307)
Gloucestershire & Avon	6 (175)	6 (175)
Hampshire	3 (80)	3 (80)
Herefordshire & Shropshire	4 (85)	3 (70)
Isle of Wight	3 (120)	3 (120)
Kent	12 (376)	12 (376)
Lancashire & Cumbria	5 (275)	5 (275)
Leicestershire & Rutland	4 (135)	3 (95)
Lincolnshire	4 (110)	4 (110)
London	4 (178)	4 (178)
Norfolk	5 (205)	5 (205)
Northamptonshire	5 (253)	4 (233)
North East	13 (281)	11 (256)
North Lincolnshire	2 (85)	2 (85)
Somerset & Dorset	4 (150)	4 (150)
Staffordshire & West Midlands	6 (353)	6 (353)
Suffolk	2 (230)	2 (230)
Surrey	6 (180)	6 (180)
Sussex (East & West)	8 (191)	8 (191)
Warwickshire & Worcestershire	3 (72)	3 (72)
Wiltshire	5 (118)	5 (118)
Yorkshire (North & East)	4 (155)	4 (155)
Yorkshire (South & West)	8 (252)	7 (237)
Wales	10 (555+)	10 (555+)
Total	170 (6,543+)	161 (6,358+)

[8] This chart shows metal-detecting clubs by FLO area, and it should be noted that some FLOs visit clubs outside their area. It also excludes online clubs that do not meet and metal-detecting groups (such as the Weekend Wanderers) which organise outings for detectorists who are both members of other clubs as well as independents. The membership of the Weekend Wanderers is estimated to be about 650, of which about one third belong to other clubs, *personal communication* Peter Welch.

How do metal-detecting clubs in England and Wales facilitate the recording work of the PAS?

In April 2008, Eleni Vomvyla (an MA student at the Institute of Archaeology, University College, London), undertook a survey of how metal-detecting clubs in England and Wales facilitate the recording work of the FLOs. She obtained data on 153 clubs in England and Wales (vacancies in some FLO areas made a comprehensive survey impossible) of which nine did not welcome FLO visits. The survey showed that 79% of clubs welcomed the FLO at any of their meetings – normally monthly. Besides 'club members' it was estimated that 1,320 'independent' detectorists were also in contact with the FLOs.

In general, club chairmen (67%) appeared to have an enthusiastic attitude towards finds recording, and only 7% were perceived to have a negative attitude.

It was discovered that most FLOs (68%) prefer to borrow finds for recording, returning them to finders at the next meeting. However, a significant minority (16%) recorded finds during the club meeting. In general FLOs can make a better record of a find if they borrow it for a time to study in good light with reference books to hand.

According to the survey metal-detecting clubs seem to facilitate recording in a number of different ways. 73% of clubs announce the attendance of the FLO, proactively encouraging members to record finds; 54% also provide the FLO with an area to record and examine finds. A minority of clubs (10%) have a Club Finds Recording Officer to help the FLO record finds.

The survey showed that the number of members making finds available for recording varies. In 27% of clubs it is estimated that more than three-quarters of the membership make finds available for recording. In just less than half of all clubs (49%), more than half of all members offer finds for recording. It should be noted that some clubs' members might not search for archaeological finds, or even be active detector users.

It is believed that 65% of detectorists who record finds with the PAS are selective in the finds they record, choosing those they think are most important; 25% show all the finds they find. 25% record finds to an eight-figure NGR (10m^2) or better, while the majority (42%) record to a six-figure NGR (100m^2).

Disappointingly, relatively few club detectorists use handheld GPS devices to record finds in the field. In 50% of clubs no finders use GPS, and in only 12% of clubs more than 10% of finders use GPS to record findspots. Likewise, in most clubs (38%) less than 5% of finders have made a record of the NGR (such as on the finds-bag) when they present the find for recording – so this has to be done retrospectively; the normal manner is for the FLO to ask the finder to indicate the findspot on a map. However, to obtain the greatest findspot precision it is best practice that finders should record the find in the field (preferably using GPS) and make a note of this with the find – such as bagging finds individually and recording the findspot on the finds-bag.

The survey also shows that the club chairman's attitude towards finds recording has an impact upon the number of members recording finds and findspot precision. In clubs believed to have an enthusiastic chairman, 35% of clubs had more than three-quarters of members recorded finds, which contrasts with 22% of (a minority of) clubs where the chairman is believed to be negative toward finds recording. Similarly, in clubs where the chairman was pro finds recording, 31% of finds are recorded to a eight-figure NGR, which contrasts to 9% in clubs that have a chairman negative towards finds recording.

The frequency of FLO visits to club meetings also appears to have a positive correlation on the number of members recording finds. Of clubs that received monthly FLO visits, 48% of them have more than three-quarters of members making finds available for recording, which contrasts with 33% of clubs visited bi-monthly. Likewise, in clubs visited by the FLO on a monthly basis the findspot precision was greater; 34% of finds were recorded to at least an eight-figure NGR in clubs visited every month, compared with 27% in those visited bi-monthly. Where the FLOs attended less regularly, only 11% of club members recorded to an eight-figure NGR. It is important to note that FLOs tend not to regularly visit clubs were finders are less receptive to finds recording.

The presence of a Club Recording Officer impacts on the number of club members recording finds; in 42% of clubs that have a Club Recording Officer more than three-quarters of members record finds, which contrasts with 22% of clubs without Club Recording Officers.

In conclusion, while it is apparent that most detectorists welcome the FLO and have a positive attitude towards finds recording, most detecting clubs are passive in as much as they do relatively little to encourage finds recording – though most do at least announce the FLO is present to record finds. In order to improve finds recording it would be best practice for more finders to record locational information in the field. The recording work of the FLO at the club could be supported by providing space for the recording of finds and helping with the identification and recording of finds at the club.

Method of discovery

Table 7 shows that almost 85% of finds recorded in 2007 were found by metal-detectorists. Of these, almost 4% were non-metallic finds (such as pottery and worked stone) spotted by finders while metal-detecting; the FLOs are keen to record such finds as they can provide important archaeological information. The next highest are field-walked finds, accounting for almost 11% of finds recorded by the PAS.

The regional trend broadly reflects the national one, but there are differences. The proportion of metal-detected finds was higher than average in the East Midlands (93.31%), Wales (88.21%), and the East (86.9%), and significantly lower than average in the North East (31.42%) and the South West (53.25%). Interestingly in the North East 35.24% of finds were chance finds found while metal-detecting, which is significantly higher than the national average. Field-walked finds were proportionally above average in the South West (24.2%), the West Midlands (19.68%), and the North West (17.84%), and lowest in the North East (1.56%) and the East Midlands (0.54%). Other chance finds were proportionally highest in the North East (27.78%), while finds discovered through controlled archaeological investigation were proportionally highest in the North East (2.26%), and those discovered through building or agricultural work were most significant in the South West (2.83%).

Table 7: Method of discovery (where known) in 2007 – percentage in brackets (%)

	Metal-detecting	Chance find while metal-detecting	Field-walking	Other chance find/gardening	Controlled archaeological investigation	Building/ agricultural work	Total
North West	1,239 (79.78)	4 (0.26)	277 (17.84)	33 (2.12)	0 (0)	0 (0)	1,553
North East	181 (31.42)	203 (35.24)	9 (1.56)	160 (27.78)	13 (2.26)	10 (1.74)	576
Yorkshire & Humber	3,161 (82.51)	268 (6.99)	187 (4.88)	157 (4.1)	52 (1.36)	6 (0.16)	3,831
West Midlands	4,124 (72.61)	319 (5.62)	1,118 (19.68)	82 (1.44)	1 (0.02)	36 (0.63)	5,680
East Midlands	9,455 (93.31)	428 (4.22)	55 (0.54)	178 (1.76)	4 (0.04)	13 (0.13)	10,133
East [9]	21,523 (86.9)	0 (0)	2,554 (10.31)	676 (2.73)	13 (0.05)	1 (0.01)	24,767
South West	5,318 (53.25)	999 (10)	2,417 (24.2)	918 (9.19)	53 (0.53)	283 (2.83)	9,988
South East & London	13,628 (81.86)	801 (4.81)	1,317 (7.91)	873 (5.24)	17 (0.1)	13 (0.08)	16,649
Wales	3,352 (88.21)	1 (0.03)	431 (11.34)	13 (0.34)	0 (0)	3 (0.08)	3,800
Total	61,981 (80.51)	3,023 (3.93)	8,365 (10.87)	3,090 (4.02)	153 (0.2)	365 (0.47)	76,977

[9] This table includes full Norfolk data (see footnote 4).

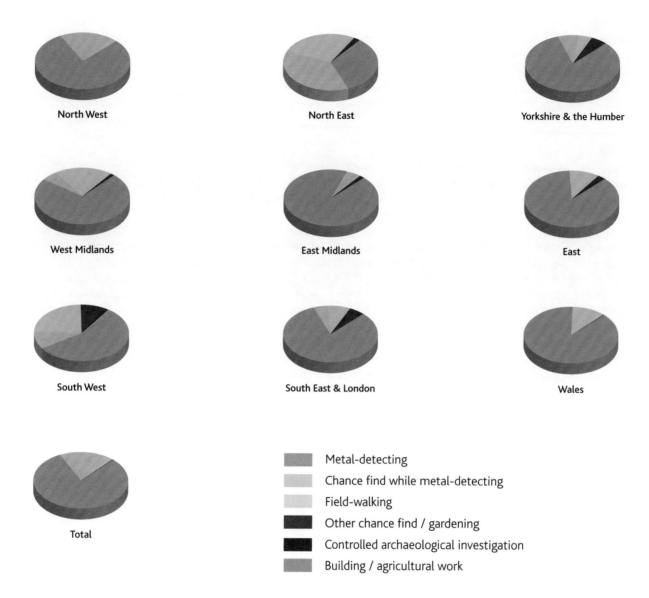

North West

North East

Yorkshire & the Humber

West Midlands

East Midlands

East

South West

South East & London

Wales

Total

Metal-detecting

Chance find while metal-detecting

Field-walking

Other chance find / gardening

Controlled archaeological investigation

Building / agricultural work

Date of discovery

Table 8 shows that almost 54% of finds recorded in 2007 were also found that year, and that almost 79% of finds recorded were found in the past three years. It is mostly the case that more recent finds will have the most precise findspot information, although the FLOs are enthusiastic to record all finds, whenever they were found, with good findspot data.

Table 8: Date of discovery in 2007 (where known) [10]

Date of discovery	Finds	Percentage of total	
Before 1980	1,121	1.76	▮
1980–9	816	1.28	▮
1990–9	5,340	8.4	▬
2000	589	0.93	▮
2001	155	0.24	▏
2002	807	1.27	▮
2003	2,218	3.49	▬
2004	2,521	3.97	▬
2005	3,964	6.24	▬
2006	12,012	18.9	▬▬
2007	34,016	53.52	▬▬▬▬
Total	63,559		

[10] This table includes full Norfolk data (see footnote 4).

Land use

As in previous years, the majority of finds recorded by the PAS is recovered from cultivated land (91.73%), where they are vulnerable to agricultural damage and natural and artificial corrosion processes.

Table 9: Land use of findspots in 2007 (where known)

Land use	Finds	Percentage of total	
Cultivated land	49,568	91.73	▬▬▬▬▬
Grass and heathland	1,013	1.87	|
Woodland	454	0.84	|
Coastland	333	0.62	|
Open fresh water	584	1.08	|
Wetland	4	0.01	
Other	2,080	3.85	▮
Total	**54,036**		

Treasure

Under the Treasure Act 1996 finders have a legal obligation to report all finds of potential Treasure.[11] The process allows a national or local museum to acquire such finds for public benefit. If this happens a reward is paid, which is normally shared equally between the finder and landowner. The reward is fixed at the full market value of the finds, determined by the Secretary of State on the advice of an independent panel of experts known as the Treasure Valuation Committee (TVC).

Number of Treasure cases and geographic distribution

The number of Treasure cases reported in 2007 continues to increase (Table 10a), from 665 in 2006 to 747 in 2007; this is a 272% increase on the first full year of the Act (1998). To a great extent this increase in the reporting of Treasure reflects wider understanding on the part of finders of their obligations under the Act, through the education and outreach work of the PAS and its FLOs.

Table 10a: Number of Treasure cases reported 1988–2007 (England, Wales & Northern Ireland)

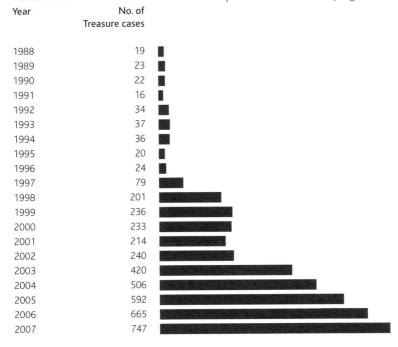

Year	No. of Treasure cases
1988	19
1989	23
1990	22
1991	16
1992	34
1993	37
1994	36
1995	20
1996	24
1997	79
1998	201
1999	236
2000	233
2001	214
2002	240
2003	420
2004	506
2005	592
2006	665
2007	747

Table 10b illustrates in detail the geographic distribution in Treasure cases. Here it can be seen that reporting in 2007 is highest in Norfolk (77 cases), followed by North Yorkshire (56) and Kent (42), whereas several areas have only a handful (or no) cases reported. This broadly reflects the pattern of cases reported since 1997 where reporting was highest in Norfolk (607), followed by Suffolk (326) and then Kent (279). It is interesting that in 2007 a significant number of cases for North Yorkshire were reported, which is a reverse of the trend of previous years. Reporting of Treasure in 2007 was significantly lower in Wales (24 cases) and Northern Ireland (0) compared with England (723); Wales has only a single full-time PAS post (though recording work is sub-contracted to the Welsh Archaeological Trusts) and Northern Ireland is not covered by the Scheme.

[11] For a full definition see the leaflet *Advice for Finders of Archaeological Objects, Including Treasure*. See also www.finds.org.uk/treasure

Table 10b: Summary of all Treasure cases 1997–2007 by county

	1997 (1)	1997 (2)	1998	1999	2000	2001	2002	2003	2004	2005	2006	2007	Total
Bath & NE Somerset	-	-	1	-	-	-	-	-	-	-	2	3	-
Bedfordshire	-	1	2	3	1	2	3	2	6	7	8	15	50
Berkshire & Reading	1	-	7	-	-	2	1	-	3	4	2	2	22
Bristol	-	-	-	-	1	-	-	-	-	-	-	-	1
Buckinghamshire & Milton Keynes	1	-	2	5	2	2	1	10	8	14	13	9	67
Cambridgeshire & Peterborough	-	3	2	2	5	4	3	6	2	12	22	34	95
Cheshire & Merseyside	-	1	3	1	3	3	5	6	3	4	1	9	39
Cornwall	-	-	-	1	1	1	1	-	3	4	3	7	21
Coventry	-	-	-	-	-	-	-	-	-	-	-	2	2
Cumbria	-	-	-	-	1	-	4	-	1	2	3	8	19
Derbyshire	-	1	3	-	1	1	-	3	5	9	3	7	33
Devon	-	-	5	4	5	1	2	8	6	15	10	6	62
Dorset	-	3	5	9	3	6	8	15	9	10	16	17	101
Durham	-	-	1	-	-	-	1	2	-	1	1	4	10
Essex	2		8	8	8	8	9	19	25	44	44	36	211
Gloucestershire	-	2	2	6	3	2	2	2	10	12	15	12	68
Gloucestershire, South	-	1	2	-	-	-	-	1	1	3	5	2	15
Hampshire	-	1	5	10	10	11	10	18	27	30	33	30	185
Herefordshire	-	1	-	-	-	-	-	-	2	2	5	4	14
Hertfordshire	-	1	5	5	5	4	3	3	12	4	14	16	72
Isle of Wight	-	-	3	-	1	-	3	9	15	21	19	30	101
Kent	1	1	12	18	18	12	11	36	40	49	39	42	279
Lancashire	-	1	-	1	-	1	-	3	6	3	3	4	22
Leicestershire & Rutland	-	1	4	2	2	5	-	6	4	6	14	15	59
Lincolnshire	2		8	9	13	13	16	29	18	27	26	34	195
Lincolnshire, North	-	2	2	1	1	1	1	5	6	4	3	9	35
London, Greater	-	1	3	2	1	1	1	5	2	5	6	14	41
Manchester, Greater	-	-	-	-	-	-	-	-	2	2	1	-	5
Norfolk	5	8	40	49	43	43	46	58	78	84	76	77	607
Northamptonshire	-	1	1	3	6	-	1	8	3	8	12	12	55
Northumberland	-	-	-	1	-	-	2	1	1	6	2	2	15
Nottinghamshire	-	3	2	4	4	3	3	6	6	13	4	14	62
Oxfordshire	1	1	2	1	3	4	5	4	7	10	14	12	64
Shropshire	-	-	-	5	2	1	3	3	7	8	9	12	50
Somerset	-	-	3	4	3	4	6	4	12	16	13	12	77
Somerset, North	-	1	-	-	-	-	1	1	-	3	1	1	8
Staffordshire	-	2	3	1	2	2	2	2	11	14	2	15	56
Suffolk	2	6	18	15	32	23	30	47	37	27	48	41	326

	1997 (1)	1997 (2)	1998	1999	2000	2001	2002	2003	2004	2005	2006	2007	Total
Surrey	-	-	3	7	1	3	3	7	3	5	13	3	48
Sussex, East	1	-	1	1	1	1	1	6	23	21	13	13	82
Sussex, West	1	-	2	1	3		2	6	16	7	16	11	65
Teesside, Redcar & Cleveland	-	-	-	-	-	-	1	-	-	1	2	3	7
Tyne and Wear	-	-	-	-	-	-	-	1	-	-	-	-	1
Warwickshire	1	1	4	8	10	9	8	8	6	8	21	9	93
West Midlands	-	-	2	2	-	-	-	-	-	-	-	-	4
Wiltshire & Swindon	1	5	9	10	4	7	9	8	11	18	18	25	125
Worcestershire	-	-	2	3	-	1	-	4	1	2	4	1	18
York, City of	-	-	2	-	3	1	3	2	4	2	6	4	27
Yorkshire, East	-	2	3	7	6	10	7	16	16	6	18	19	110
Yorkshire, North	3	3	9	8	12	5	6	18	24	18	31	56	193
Yorkshire, South	-	-	-	4	1	5	1	1	3	4	6	4	29
Yorkshire, West	-	-	1	1	-	-	1	2	-	1	1	5	12
Unknown	-	-	-	-	-	-	-	-	-	1	3	2	6
England	22	54	191	223	221	202	226	401	485	577	642	723	3967
Bridgend	-	-	-	-	-	-	-	-	-	1	-	-	1
Carmarthenshire	-	-	-	-	2	-	-	3	1	-	2	-	8
Denbighshire	-	-	-	1	-	-	-	-	1	-	1	-	3
Ceredigion	-	-	1	-	-	-	-	1	-	-	-	-	2
Flintshire	-	-	-	-	1	-	-	1	1	-	-	1	4
Gwynedd	-	-	-	1	-	-	-	-	-	-	-	1	2
Isle of Anglesey	-	2	2	2	1	3	3	6	3	2	1	2	27
Monmouthshire	-	-	4	1	2	-	1	6	3	1	6	-	24
Neath, Port Talbot	-	-	-	1	-	-	-	-	-	-	-	-	1
Newport	-	-	-	1	-	-	1	1	-	-	2	2	7
Pembrokeshire	-	-	1	2	2	1	1	2	-	-	-	2	11
Powys	-	-	1	1	1	1	1	-	1	1	2	4	13
Rhondda Cynon Taf	-	-	-	-	-	-	-	1	1	-	-	-	2
Swansea	-	-	-	2	1	-	3	1	-	-	-	2	9
The Vale of Glamorgan	-	1	-	-	2	3	2	4	7	8	8	9	44
Wrexham	-	-	-	-	-	-	1	-	1	1	1	1	5
Wales	-	3	9	12	12	8	13	19	19	14	23	24	156
County Antrim	-	-	-	-	-	1	-	-	-	-	-	-	1
County Armagh	-	-	1	-	-	1	-	-	1	-	-	-	3
County Down	-	-	-	1	-	1	1	-	-	-	-	-	3
County Londonderry	-	-	-	-	-	1	-	-	-	1	-	-	2
County Tyrone	-	-	-	-	-	-	-	-	1	-	-	-	1
Northern Ireland	-	-	1	1	-	4	1	-	2	1	-	-	10
Total	22	57	201	236	233	214	240	420	506	592	665	747	4133

Analysis of Treasure finds

Table 11a provides a snapshot of the outcome of Treasure cases according to their period and type. This shows that of the cases reported in 2007, 35.61% (266) have been (or are in the process of being) acquired by a museum, 4.95% (37) have been donated, 40.30% (301) have been disclaimed and returned to finder/landowner, 16.73% (125) were deemed not to be Treasure, and 2.41% (18) are still to be determined. Combined with the number of cases where at least one party has donated their share of a potential *ex gratia* reward, over 40% of cases from 2007 are due to end up in museum collections.

The number of Treasure finds acquired by chronological period varies and differs between the categories of objects and coins. For example in 2007, museums acquired 66.67% (20) of Bronze Age objects and 52.78% (38) of Early Medieval objects, which compares - perhaps unsurprisingly - with 36.46% (66) Medieval objects and 29.38% (62) of Post Medieval objects. The pattern for coins cases differs. Proportionally highest were Early Medieval (87.5% - 7 cases) and Post Medieval (72.73% - 8) cases, whereas Medieval (45.45% - 10) and Roman (48.71% - 19) were proportionally lowest.

Table 11a: Analysis of 2007 Treasure finds by period and category

Objects	Acquired	Donated	Disclaimed	Not Treasure	To be determined	Total
Bronze Age	20	2	4	2	2	30
Iron Age	4	1	2	-	2	9
Roman	25	4	33	2	3	67
Early Medieval	38	8	14	8	4	72
Medieval	66	10	91	10	4	181
Post-Medieval	62	7	125	16	1	211
18th-20th Centuries	-	-	3	55	-	58
Undiagnostic	-	-	3	24	-	27
Total Object Cases	**215**	**32**	**275**	**117**	**16**	**655**

Coins	Acquired	Donated	Disclaimed	Not Treasure	To be determined	Total
Bronze Age	-	-	-	-	-	0
Iron Age	6	-	4	-	-	10
Roman	19	3	10	6	1	39
Early Medieval	7	-	1	-	-	8
Medieval	10	2	8	1	1	22
Post-Medieval	8	-	3	-	-	11
18th-20th Centuries	1	-	-	-	-	1
Undiagnostic	-	-	-	1	-	1
Total Coin Cases	**51**	**5**	**26**	**8**	**2**	**92**
Grand Total - All Finds	**266**	**37**	**301**	**125**	**18**	**747**

Table 11b gives the method of discovery of finds reported Treasure in 2007. As in previous years (*TAR* 2005-6, 8), metal-detecting accounts for the vast majority of Treasure cases; the slight drop of 0.76% is insignificant.

Archaeological finds made up a slightly higher proportion of cases in this year than in the last two, rising 0.2%, but the largest gain came from those finds reported by buyers or inheritors. Together they accounted for five Treasure cases (0.7% of the total), whilst only three such cases were reported in all of 2005 and 2006. One factor which contributed to this increase was the British Museum's monitoring of eBay for listings of potentially unreported treasure finds (see below). Several Treasure cases were a direct result of the British Museum contacting sellers and making them aware of the Treasure Act and their legal obligations.

Table 11b: Method of discovery for 2007 Treasure finds.

	# of finds	%	
Metal detecting	690	92.4%	████████████████
Archaeological find	33	4.4%	▋
Chance find	19	2.5%	▊
Reported by buyer	3	0.4%	|
Inherited	2	0.3%	|
Total	747	100.0%	

Treasure reporting by FLO area

Although Treasure cases account for a relatively small proportion of archaeological finds found by the public in England and Wales, the FLOs play an increasingly important role in the effective operation of the Treasure Act, advising finders of their legal obligations, providing advice on the process and writing reports on Treasure finds. Through this work it is clear the FLOs have a significant impact on the reporting of Treasure. Table 12 shows that since 2003, when the PAS was expanded to the whole of England and Wales, there has been an average increase of 193.68% in the reporting of Treasure. The most significant increases have been in the Isle of Wight (1,506.84% and Sussex (964%); both areas had an FLO for the first time in 2003. The only area to have a decrease is Northern Ireland (-51.72%), which is not covered by the PAS.

Table 12: Treasure reporting: 1997 to 2003 and since 2003

	Treasure cases 1997–2002	Average per year 1997–2002	Treasure cases 2003–7	Average per year 2003–7	Average increase (%)
Bedfordshire & Hertfordshire	35	5.83	87	17.4	198.46%
Berkshire & Oxfordshire	28	4.67	58	11.6	148.39%
Buckinghamshire	13	2.17	54	10.8	397.70%
Cambridgeshire	19	3.17	78	15.6	392.11%
Cheshire, Gtr Manchester & Merseyside	16	2.67	28	5.6	109.74%
Cornwall	4	0.67	17	3.4	407.46%
Derbyshire & Nottinghamshire	25	4.17	70	14	235.73%
Devon	17	2.83	45	9	218.02%
Essex	43	7.17	168	33.6	368.62%
Gloucestershire & Avon	24	4	71	14.2	255.00%
Hampshire	47	7.83	138	27.6	252.49%
Herefordshire & Shropshire	12	2	52	10.4	420.00%
Isle of Wight	7	1.17	94	18.8	1,506.84%
Kent	73	12.17	207	41.4	240.18%
Lancashire & Cumbria	8	1.33	33	6.6	396.24%
Leicestershire & Rutland	14	2.33	45	9	286.2%
Lincolnshire	61	10.17	134	26.8	163.52%
London	9	1.5	32	6.4	326.67%
Norfolk	234	39	376	75.2	92.82%
Northamptonshire	12	2	43	8.6	330.00%
North East	6	1	27	5.4	440.00%
North Lincolnshire	8	1.3	27	5.4	315.38%
Somerset & Dorset	54	9	124	24.8	175.56%
Staffordshire & West Midlands	16	2.67	46	9.2	244.57%
Suffolk	126	21	201	40.2	91.43%
Surrey	17	2.83	31	6.2	119.08%
Sussex	15	2.5	133	26.6	964.00%
Warwickshire & Worcestershire	47	7.83	64	12.8	63.47%
Wiltshire	45	7.5	81	16.2	116.00%
Yorkshire (North & East)	92	15.33	241	48.2	314.42%
Yorkshire (South & West)	14	2.33	27	5.4	131.76%
Wales	57	9.5	109	21.8	129.47%
Northern Ireland	7	1.16	3	0.6	-51.72%
Other	0	0	5	1	-
Total	1,205	200.83	2,949	589.8	193.68%

Table 12 (cont.): Treasure reporting: 1997 to 2003 and since 2003

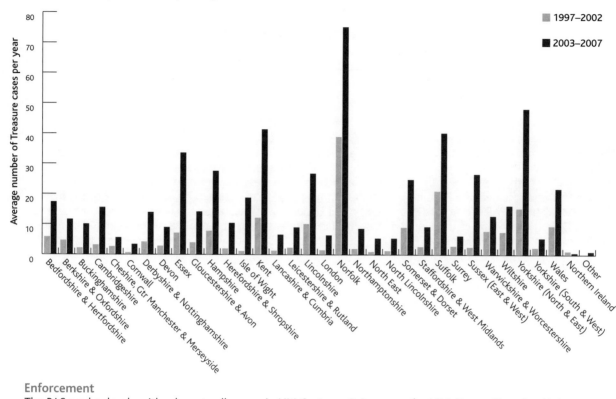

Enforcement

The PAS works closely with relevant colleagues in HM Customs & Revenue, the MLA Export Licensing Unit, as well as the Metropolitan Police Service's Art & Antiques Unit.

Since February 2007 Michael Lewis (Deputy Head of PAS) has been seconded two days a month to the Metropolitan Police's Art & Antiquities Unit as an ArtBeat Special Police Constable. To date he has been involved in several high profile cases and operations regarding archaeological finds.

The British Museum's Department of Portable Antiquities and Treasure continues to monitor eBay for items of potential Treasure, and question vendors of such finds. In 2007 intelligence on 144 cases was passed to the Metropolitan Police's Art & Antiques Unit. Since September 2007 the Department has also been an expert adviser on the Export Licensing of detector finds, and in 2007 approved 312 licences, of which more than 85% are for export outside the European Union.

The Department has also been working with the Association of Chief Police Officers (ACPO) in the hope of developing guidance for local police forces on how to tackle heritage crime, such as illicit metal-detecting. Also relevant to this work is the English Heritage funded Oxford Archaeology project to assess the extent of nighthawking in the UK, which presented its results in February 2009 (see www.helm.org.uk/nighthawking). This report makes the following recommendations:

- Provide clear guidance to the police, Crown Prosecution Service and Magistrates on the impact of nighthawking, how to combat it, levels of evidence and possible penalties.
- Provide more information for landowners on identifying nighthawking and what do if they encounter it.
- Develop better ways to understand the extent of nighthawking, and establish and promote a central database of reported incidents (PAS believes this intelligence must be shared with the police).
- Publicise the positive effects of responsible metal-detecting and the negative effects of nighthawking.
- Ensure the PAS is fully funded, so that links between archaeologists and metal-detectorists are further strengthened.
- Integrate metal-detecting into the archaeological process, including development control briefs.
- Implement changes recently introduced in Europe which increase the obligation on sellers of antiquities to provide provenances and establish legal title, and urge eBay to introduce more stringent monitoring of antiquities with a UK origin offered for sale on their website.

Consequently, English Heritage will be working with others, including the PAS, to take these recommendations forward.

Editors: Michael Lewis and Ian Richardson (Treasure)
Statistics: Dan Pett

CENTRAL UNIT

Department of Portable Antiquities and Treasure
British Museum, London WC1B 3DG
+44 (0)20 7323 8611/8618
PAS: info@finds.org.uk
Treasure: treasure@britishmuseum.org

Head of Portable Antiquities and Treasure
Roger Bland
+44 (0)20 7323 8611
rbland@britishmuseum.org

Deputy Head of Portable Antiquities and Treasure
Michael Lewis
+44 (0)20 7323 8611
mlewis@britishmuseum.org

Resources Manager
Claire Costin
+44 (0)20 7323 8618
ccostin@britishmuseum.org

ICT Adviser
Daniel Pett
+44 (0)20 7323 8618
dpett@britishmuseum.org

Treasure Registrar
Ian Richardson
+44 (0)20 7323 8243
irichardson@britishmuseum.org

Assistant Treasure Registrars
Andrew Basham (post-inquest)
+44 (0)20 7323 8509
abasham@britishmuseum.org

Caroline Barton (pre-inquest)
+44 (0)20 7323 8243
cbarton@britishmuseum.org

Caroline Lyons (post-inquest)
+44 (0)20 7323 8509
clyons@britishmuseum.org

Hilary Orange (archaeological cases)
+44 (0)20 7323 8546
horange@britishmuseum.org

Janina Parol (post-inquest)
+44 (0)20 7323 8509
jparol@britishmuseum.org

CONTACTS AND ORGANISATIONS

NATIONAL FINDS ADVISERS

Prehistoric & Roman Artefacts
Sally Worrell
+44 (0)20 7679 4730
s.worrell@ucl.ac.uk

Iron Age & Roman Coins
Sam Moorhead
+44 (0)20 7323 8432
smoorhead@britishmuseum.org

Medieval Artefacts
Helen Geake
+44 (0)1223 333323
hg260@cam.ac.uk

Later Medieval & Post-Medieval Artefacts
Geoff Egan
+44 (0)20 7566 9333
gegan@britishmuseum.org
gegan@museumoflondon.org.uk

Medieval & Post-Medieval Coins
John Naylor
+44 (0)1865 278065
john.naylor@ashmus.ox.ac.uk

Metals & Metalworking
Kevin Leahy
+44 (0)1652 658261
leahy.pas@btinternet.com

FINDS LIAISON OFFICERS

England

Berkshire (East)
To be filled

Bedfordshire & Hertfordshire
Julian Watters
+44 (0)1727 751826
julian.watters@stalbans.gov.uk

Buckinghamshire
Ros Tyrrell
+44 (0)1296 624519
rtyrrell@buckscc.gov.uk

Cambridgeshire
Elizabeth Gill
+44 (0)1223 717573
+44 (0)1733 343329
elizabeth.gill@cambridgeshire.gov.uk
lizzie.gill@peterborough.gov.uk

Cheshire, Greater Manchester & Merseyside
Vanessa Oakden
+44 (0)151 478 4259
vanessa.oakden@liverpoolmuseums.org.uk

Cornwall
Anna Tyacke
+44 (0)1872 272205 ext.219
annatyacke@btinternet.com
anna.tyacke@royalcornwallmuseum.org.uk

Derbyshire & Nottinghamshire
Rachel Atherton & to be filled
+44 (0)1332 641906
rachel.atherton@derby.gov.uk

Devon
Danielle Wootton
+44 (0)1392 665983/858
danielle.wootton@exeter.gov.uk

Dorset
Ciorstaidh Hayward Trevarthen
+44 (0)1305 228254
c.h.trevarthen@dorsetcc.gov.uk

Essex
Laura McLean
+44 (0)1206 506961
laura.mclean@colchester.gov.uk

Gloucestershire & Avon
Kurt Adams
+44 (0)117 922 2613/3571
+44 (0)1452 425705
kurt.adams@bristol.gov.uk

Hampshire
Rob Webley
+44 (0)1962 848558
rwebley@winchester.gov.uk

Herefordshire & Shropshire
Peter Reavill
+44 (0)1584 813641
peter.reavill@shropshire.gov.uk

Isle of Wight
Frank Basford
+44 (0)1983 823810
frank.basford@iow.gov.uk

Kent
Jennifer Jackson
+44 (0)1622 221544
jennifer.jackson@kent.gov.uk

Lancashire & Cumbria
Dot Boughton & Stuart Noon
+44 (0)1772 532175
+44 (0)1228 618760
dot.boughton@mus.lancashire.gov.uk
dotb@carlisle.gov.uk
stuart.noon@mus.lancashire.gov.uk
stuartn@carlisle.gov.uk

Leicestershire & Rutland
Wendy Scott
+44 (0)116 305 8325
wendy.scott@leics.gov.uk

Lincolnshire
Adam Daubney
+44 (0)1522 552361
adam.daubney@lincolnshire.gov.uk

London
Kate Sumnall
+44 (0)20 7814 5733
ksumnall@museumoflondon.org.uk

Norfolk
Erica Darch & Hazel White
+44 (0)1362 869289
erica.darch@norfolk.gov.uk
hazel.white@norfolk.gov.uk

Northamptonshire
Julie Cassidy
+44 (0)1604 237249
jucassidy@northamptonshire.gov.uk

North East
Robert Collins & Frances McIntosh
+44 (0)191 222 5076
+44 (0)191 370 8843
robert.collins@ncl.ac.uk
frances.mcintosh@durham.gov.uk

North Lincolnshire
Martin Foreman
+44 (0)1724 843533
martin.foreman@northlincs.gov.uk

Oxfordshire & West Berkshire
Anni Byard
+44 (0)1865 300557
+44 (0)7827 822617
+44 (0)1635 519534
Anni.Byard@oxfordshire.gov.uk

Somerset
Anna Booth
+44 (0)1823 362855
albooth@somerset.gov.uk

Staffordshire & West Midlands
Duncan Slarke
+44 (0)121 303 4636
+44 (0)1782 232323
duncan_slarke@birmingham.gov.uk_

Suffolk
Andrew Brown, Jane Carr & Faye Minter,
+44 (0)1284 352449
andrew.brown@et.suffolkcc.gov.uk
jane.carr@et.suffolkcc.gov.uk
faye.minter@et.suffolkcc.gov.uk

Donna Wreathall (Illustrator)
+44 (0)1284 352449
donna.wreathall@et.suffolkcc.gov.uk

Surrey
David Williams
+44 (0)1737 247296
+44 (0)1483 518771
+44 (0)7968 832740
david.williams@surreycc.gov.uk

Sussex
Laura Burnett
+44 (0)1273 405731
flo@sussexpast.co.uk

Warwickshire & Worcestershire
Angie Bolton & Tom Brindle
+44 (0)1905 721130
abolton@worcester.gov.uk
tbrindle@worcester.gov.uk

Wiltshire
Katie Hinds
+44 (0)1722 332151
+44 (0)1793 466556
+44 (0) 01380 727369
katiehinds@salisburymuseum.org.uk

Yorkshire (North & East)
Liz Andrews-Wilson
+44 (0)1904 687668
liz.andrews-wilson@ymt.org.uk

Yorkshire (South & West)
Amy Cooper
+44 (0)1924 305359
acooper@wyjs.org.uk

Wales

Finds Co-ordinator Wales
Mark Lodwick
+44 (0)2920 573226
mark.lodwick@nmgw.ac.uk

North Wales
Sarah Pevely
+44 (0)1745 353814
sarah.pevely@denbighshire.gov.uk

Cambria-Dyfed Archaeological Trust
Richard Jones & Marian Page
+44 (0)1558 823121
cambria@acadat.com
richardj@cambria.org.uk
marion@cambria.org.uk

Clwyd-Powys Archaeological Trust
Jeff Spencer & Chris Martin
+44 (0)1938 553670
trust@cpat.org.uk
jeff@cpat.org.uk
chrismartin@cpat.org.uk

Glamorgan-Gwent Archaeological Trust
Steve Sell
+44 (0)1792 655208
curatorial@ggat.org.uk

Gwynedd Archaeological Trust
Nina Steele
+44 (0)1248 352535
nsteele@heneb.co.uk

ORGANISATIONS
**The following are national and/or local partners
in the Portable Antiquities Scheme**

Amgueddfa Cymru – National Museum Wales
Ashmolean Museum (Oxford)
Association of Local Government Archaeological Officers
Bedfordshire County Council
Birmingham Museum & Art Gallery
(Birmingham City Council)
Borough Council of Wellingborough
Bradford Museums Galleries and Heritage
Brewhouse Yard Museum of Nottingham Life
(Nottingham City Council)
Bristol City Museum (Bristol City Council)
British Museum
Buckinghamshire County Museum
Calderdale Museum and Gallery Service
Cambria Archaeology
Cambridgeshire County Council
Cheshire Museums Service

City & Council Museum, Lincoln
City of Plymouth Museums & Art Gallery
Clywd Powys Archaeological Trust
Colchester & Ipswich Museum Service
Corby Borough Council
Cornwall County Council
Cornwall Historic Environment Service
Council for British Archaeology
Council of Museums in Wales
Country Business & Landowners Association
Dartmoor National Park Authority
Daventry District Council
Department for Culture, Media and Sport
Derby Museum & Art Gallery
Derbyshire County Council
Devon County Council
Doncaster Museum & Art Gallery
Dorset County Council
Durham County Council
East Northamptonshire Council
East Sussex County Council
English Heritage
Essex County Council
Exmoor National Park Authority
Fitzwilliam Museum (Cambridge)
Glamorgan Gwent Archaeological Trust
Gloucestershire County Council
Gwynedd Archaeological Trust
Hampshire County Museums Service
Hampshire County Planning Department
Hereford Museum & Art Gallery
(Hereford Heritage Services)
Hull & East Riding Museum
Institute of Archaeology, University College London
Isle of Wight Heritage Service
Jewry Wall Museum
Kent County Council
Kirklees Museums & Galleries
Kettering Borough Council
Lancashire County Museum Service
Leeds Museums & Galleries
Leicestershire County Council
Lincolnshire County Council
Manchester Museum
Milton Keynes Council
Museums, Libraries and Archives Council (MLA)
Museum of Antiquities
(University of Newcastle-upon-Tyne)
Museum of Barnstaple & North Devon
Museum of London
Museum of Reading
Museums Resource Centre, Standlake
Museums Sheffield
National Council for Metal Detecting
National Farmers Union
National Museums Liverpool
New Forest National Park Authority
Norfolk Museums & Galleries

Northampton Borough Council
Northamptonshire County Council
North Lincolnshire Museum (North Lincolnshire Council)
Nottinghamshire County Council
Oxfordshire County Council
Peterborough Museum
Potteries Museum & Art Gallery, Stoke-on-Trent
Reading Borough Council
Rotherham Museums Service
Roman Museum of Verulamium
Royal Albert Memorial Museum (Exeter County Council)
Royal Commission on the Ancient and Historical
Monuments of Wales
Royal Institution of Cornwall
Salisbury & South Wiltshire Museum
Shrewsbury Museum Service
Shropshire County Museum Service
Society of Museum Archaeologists
Somerset County Museums Service
(Somerset County Council)
Southampton City Museums
South Northamptonshire Council
South Yorkshire Archaeology Service
Suffolk County Council
Surrey Archaeological Society
Surrey County Council
Sussex Archaeological Society
Swindon Museum & Art Gallery
Torbay Council
Tullie House Museum & Art Gallery, Carlisle
University of Cambridge
Wakefield Museums Service
Warwickshire Museum
West Berkshire Council
West Midlands Archaeological Collections Research Unit
West Midlands Regional Museum Council
West Sussex County Council
West Yorkshire Archaeology Advisory Service
Wiltshire Archaeological & Natural History Society
Wiltshire County Council
Winchester Museums Service
Worcester City Museums
Worcestershire County Museum
York Archaeological Trust
York Museums Trust

ACKNOWLEDGEMENTS

Many people have been involved with the production of this report.

Contributors are listed against the appropriate entries in the catalogue of PAS and Treasure finds. Other people involved with the discovery, reporting and reporting and/or research of finds are listed within the text, unless they have requested otherwise or such information was not available; we apologise if anyone has been accidentally omitted. Editors of the various sections of the report are listed at the end of the relevant sections.

Several people in the British Museum's Marketing department have worked on the design and production of this report, in particular Kirsti Gardner, Ann Lumley, Sonia D'Orsi and Andrew Shore. Caroline Barton, Janina Parol and Ian Richardson of the Museum's Department of Portable Antiquities & Treasure worked on photo editing the images and other aspects of the report. Zoe Brady and Emma Traherne (Institute of Archaeology, University College, London) also worked as volunteers on the report.

Michael Lewis

ILLUSTRATIONS

England

Artefacts

Stone Age	292
Bronze Age	298
Iron Age	314
Roman	322
Early Medieval	342
Medieval	362
Post-Medieval	389

Coins

Iron Age	414
Roman	419
Early Medieval	425
Medieval	426
Post-Medieval	430

Note: All objects are illustrated at approximately life-size unless otherwise stated.

1. Newport, Isle of Wight: flint handaxe. Half life-size.

2. Wrabness, Essex: flint tranchet adze. Half life-size.

3. Weethley, Warwickshire: perforated stone pebble. Half life-size.

4. Camberley, Surrey: perforated stone implement

5. Ridge, Hertfordshire: collection of five flint blade cores.

6. Tatworth and Forton, Somerset: flint implement.

7. City of London: polished stone axehead. Half life-size.

8. Breamore, Hampshire: polished flint axehead. Half life-size.

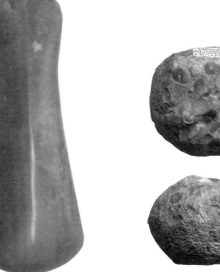

9. Weaverham, Cheshire: flint adze. Half life-size.

10. Welwyn, Hertfordshire: puddingstone grain rubber or hammerstone. Half life-size.

11. Aspatria, Cumbria: rough-out for a stone axe.
Quarter life-size.

12. Mildenhall, Suffolk: flint axehead. Half life-size.

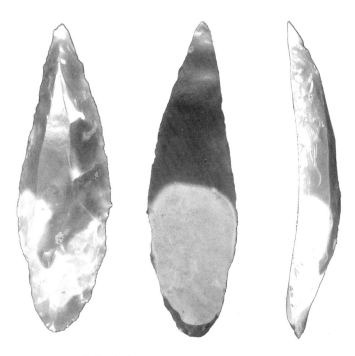

13. Paul, Cornwall: flint knife.

14. Birkin, North Yorkshire: flint arrowhead.

15. Ringland, Norfolk: flint arrowhead.

19. Stanbury, West Yorkshire: urn in situ.

16. Heptonstall, West Yorkshire: wooden
weaving paddle. Quarter life-size.

17. Shrewsbury area, Shropshire: copper-alloy flat axe.
Half life-size.

18. Collingham, Nottinghamshire: copper-alloy miniature flat axe.

20. Bardney, Lincolnshire: copper-alloy flat axe.

22. Newark area, Nottinghamshire: copper-alloy spearhead. Half life-size.

21. Mildenhall, Suffolk: copper-alloy axe-chisel.

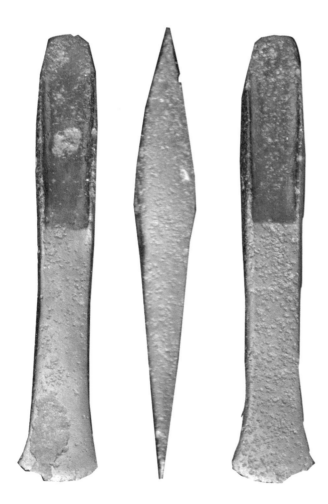

23. Garveston, Norfolk: copper-alloy chisel.

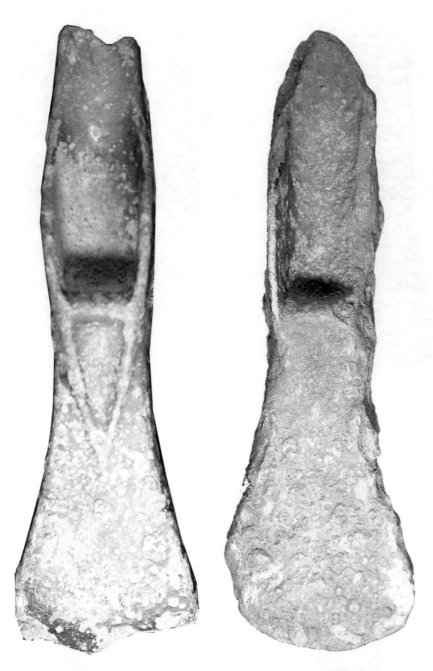

24. Wadebridge, Cornwall: copper-alloy palstave axes.

25. Kendal, Cumbria: copper-alloy rapier fragment.

26. Eaton Bray, Bedfordshire: copper-alloy knife.

27. Hampton Lovett, Worcestershire:
copper-alloy tanged chisel.

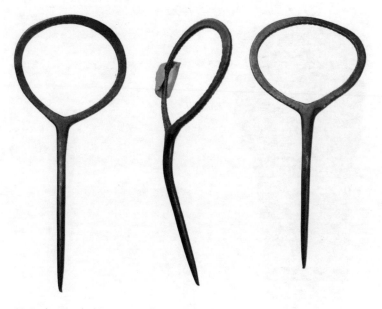

28. Ranby, Lincolnshire: copper-alloy quoit-headed pin.
Half life-size.

30. Blisland, Cornwall: copper-alloy palstave axe
blade fragment.

29. Loggerheads, Staffordshire: copper-alloy palstave axe.
Half life-size.

31. Pett, East Sussex: copper-alloy palstave axes. Half life-size.

32. Hambledon, Hampshire: copper-alloy palstave axe and
socketed hammer. Half life-size.

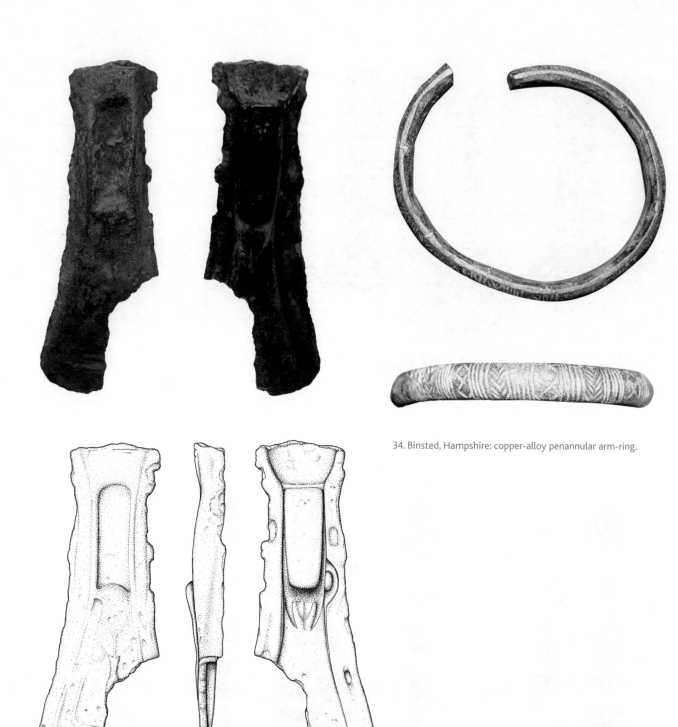

34. Binsted, Hampshire: copper-alloy penannular arm-ring.

33. Hempnall, Norfolk: copper-alloy palstave axe mould. Half life-size.
Illustration: Donna Wreathall.

35. Burton, Wrexham: gold bead and wire.

38. Ansley, Warwickshire: gold ribbon ornament. Twice life-size.

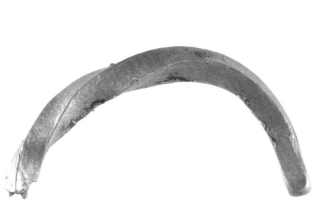

36. Seagry, Wiltshire: gold penannular bracelet fragment. Twice life-size.

39. West Acre, Norfolk: gold sheet strip fragment.

37. Stone, Buckinghamshire: gold composite ring. Twice life-size.

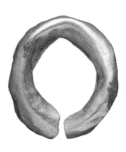

40. Trearddur, Isle of Anglesey: gold penannular ring. Twice life-size.

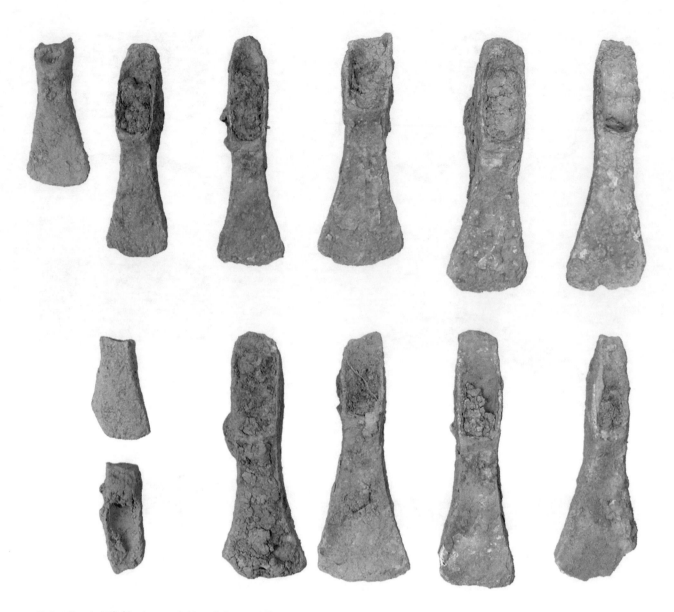

41. East Knoyle, Wiltshire: base-metal hoard of copper-alloy palstave axes. Half life-size.

42. Heytesbury, Wiltshire: copper-alloy palstave axe.
Half life-size.

45. Witchingham area, Norfolk: gold
penannular ring. Twice life-size.

43. Trotton with Chithurst, West Sussex:
copper-alloy hammer. Half life-size.

46. Theydon Mount, Essex:
gold penannular ring. Twice life-size.

44. Fawley, Hampshire: gold penannular ring.
Twice life-size.

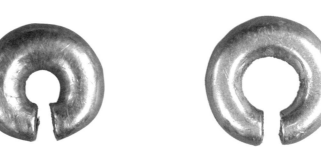

47. Kettering area, Northamptonshire:
gold penannular ring. Twice life-size.

48. Ilam, Staffordshire: copper-alloy socketed axehead. Half life-size.

49. Lavenham, Suffolk: copper-alloy harness fitting

50. Mildenhall, Wiltshire: copper-alloy model for socketed axehead.

51. Amport area, Hampshire: group of copper-alloy palstave and socketed axes. Half life-size.

52. Uttlesford District, Essex: base metal hoard of socketed axes and
metalworking fragments. Half life-size.

53. Attleborough area, Norfolk: group of a copper-alloy socketed axe and metalworking fragments.
Half life-size.

54. Offham, Kent: group of copper-alloy socketed axes and other metalwork fragments. Half life-size.

55. Hoaden, Kent: group of copper-alloy axes and other metal-working fragments. Half life-size.

56. Tywardreath, Cornwall: copper-alloy socketed axehead. Half life-size.

57. Thurlestone, Devon: copper-alloy spearhead.

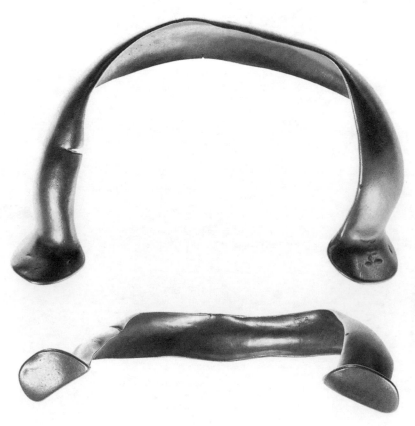

58. West Wight, Isle of Wight: gold penannular bracelet.

59. Appledram, West Sussex: copper-alloy spearhead.

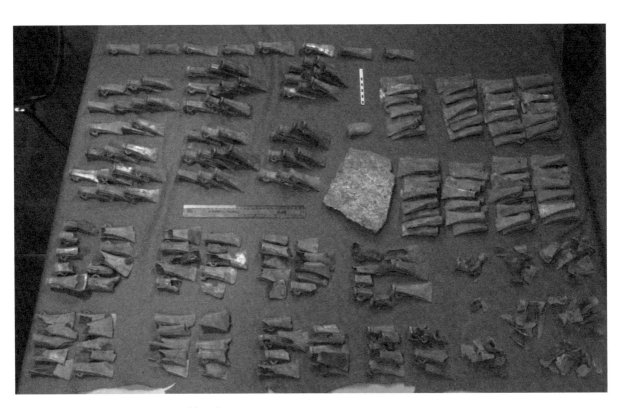

60. Langton Matravers, Dorset: base-metal hoard.

61. Swindon area, Wiltshire: copper-alloy 'moustache-like' object.

62. Leyburn, North Yorkshire: copper-alloy pin.

63. Madley, Herefordshire: copper-alloy brooch.

64. Lane End area, Buckinghamshire: copper-alloy brooch.

65. Roxby cum Risby, North Lincolnshire: copper-alloy brooch. Twice life-size.

66. Penllyn, Vale of Glamorgan: copper-alloy terret.

67. Kendal, Cumbria: copper-alloy terret.

69. Norwich area, Norfolk: gold torc fitting.

68. King's Lynn area, Norfolk: electrum torc terminal.
Twice life-size.

70. Sleaford, Lincolnshire: copper-alloy possible miniature shield

73. Wychavon, Worcestershire: copper-alloy possible miniature wheel.

71. Constantine, Cornwall: copper-alloy baldric ring.

72. Driffield, East Yorkshire: copper-alloy amulet.

74. Clipstone, Nottinghamshire: copper-alloy and iron linchpin. Not life-size.

75. Wilstead, Bedfordshire: silver brooch fragment.

78. Needham, Norfolk: copper-alloy possible drinking horn terminal.

76. Kirby Hill, North Yorkshire: copper-alloy enamelled terret.

77. Wibtoft, Warwickshire: enamelled copper-alloy and iron linchpin terminal.

79. Charlton Mackrell, Somerset: copper-alloy toggle. Twice life-size.

81. South Perrott, Dorset: copper-alloy brooch.

80. Attleborough area, Norfolk: copper-alloy and iron linchpin elements.

82. Cowbridge, Vale of Glamorgan: copper-alloy terret and rein-ring. Half life-size.

83. Marbury, Cheshire: copper-alloy fob.

84. Stoneleigh, Warwickshire: copper-alloy harness mount.

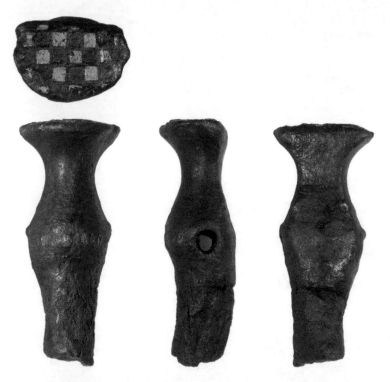

85. Hatherton, Staffordshire: copper-alloy and iron linchpin.

86. Burton Fleming, East Yorkshire: copper-alloy mount.

87. Redbourn, Hertfordshire: copper-alloy horse harness strap-mount.

88. Langstone, Newport: copper-alloy bowls, wine strainer and tankard. Quarter life-size.

89. Eynsford, Kent: copper-alloy pan-handle.

90. Atherton, Greater Manchester: copper-alloy brooch.

91. St Buryan, Cornwall: gold jewellery fragment.
Twice life-size.

92. Snape with Thorpe, North Yorkshire: gold jewellery
component. Twice life-size.

93. Ely, Cambridgeshire: silver finger-ring. Twice life-size.

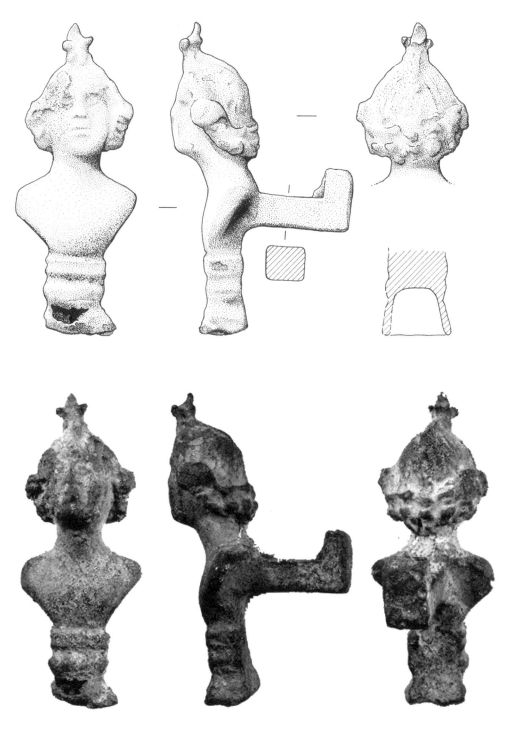

94. Pocklington, East Yorkshire: copper-alloy tripod mount.
Illustration: Dom Andrews.

95. Trowbridge area, Wiltshire: copper-alloy knife terminal.

96. Carlisle, Cumbria: silver hair-pin fragment. Twice life-size.

97. Scawby, North Lincolnshire: copper-alloy pan-handle.
Half life-size.

98. Wherwell, Hampshire: copper-alloy crocodile figurine.

99. York area: silver finger-ring. Twice life-size.

100. Llanharry, Rhondda Cynon Taff: copper-alloy wax spatula handle.

101. Newton Kyme cum Toulson, North Yorkshire: copper-alloy figurine of Cautopates.

102. North Yorkshire area: silver *ligula*.

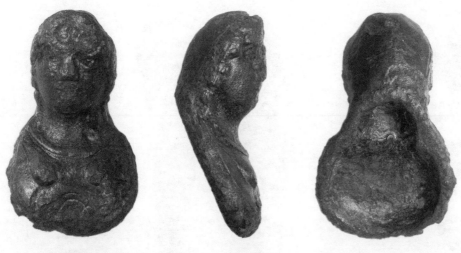

103. Middleton, Warwickshire: copper-alloy bust.

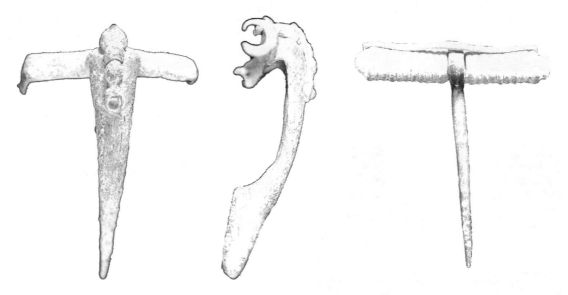

104. St Minver, Cornwall: copper-alloy brooch.

105. Gisburn, Lancashire: copper-alloy brooch.

106. Hale, Cheshire: silver brooch.

107. Little Kimble, Buckinghamshire: copper-alloy brooch.
Twice life-size.

108. Seaton with Slingley,
County Durham: silver brooch fragment.

109. Inkberrow, Worcestershire: copper-alloy brooch.

110. Highnam, Gloucestershire: copper-alloy brooch.

111. Sheepy, Leicestershire: gold necklace fragment. Twice life-size.

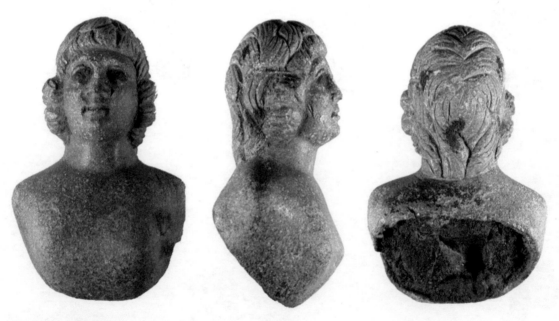

112. Capel St Mary, Suffolk: copper-alloy bust.

113. Brompton, North Yorkshire: copper-alloy military diploma.
Half life-size.

114. Aston Clinton, Buckinghamshire:
copper-alloy fastener.

115. South Cave, East Yorkshire: copper-alloy
button-and-loop fastener.

116. Greywell, Hampshire: copper-alloy brooches.

117. Gedding, Suffolk: copper-alloy brooch.

118. Chesterton, Cambridgeshire: gold necklace component. Twice life-size.

121. Well, Lincolnshire: silver finger-ring fragment. Twice life-size.

119. Roughton, Lincolnshire: silver finger-ring fragment. Twice life-size.

122. Gosford Farm, Nottinghamshire: silver ring. Twice life-size.

120. Hockliffe, Bedfordshire: silver finger-ring fragment.

123. Wetheringsett, Suffolk: gold finger-ring.

124. Irnham, Lincolnshire: copper-alloy knife handle.

125. Andover, Hampshire: copper-alloy figurine. Twice life-size.

126. Stepney, London: mosaic fragments. Half life-size.

127. Huncote and Leighfield, Leicestershire: greyware kiln bars.

128. Bures area, Essex: gold finger-ring. Twice life-size.

129. Yscir, Powys: copper-alloy military horse harness fitting.

130. Northwich, Cheshire: copper-alloy brooch.

131. North Nibley, Gloucestershire: silver finger-ring.

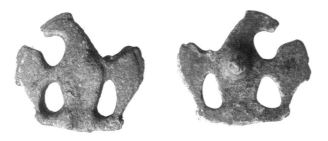

132. Maryport, Cumbria: copper-alloy mount.

133. Cherington, Gloucestershire: limestone tombstone fragment.
Quarter life-size.

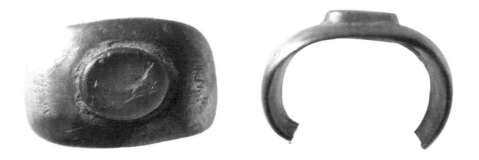

134. Lacock, Wiltshire: silver finger-ring with intaglio. Twice life-size.

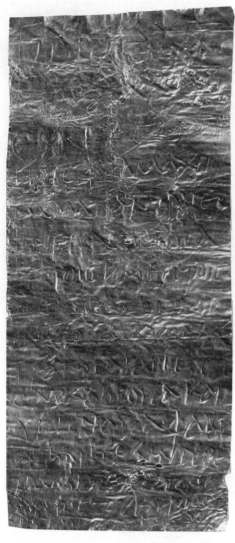

135. South Oxfordshire: gold foil amulet. Twice life-size.

136. Godmanchester, Cambridgeshire: silver finger-ring with intaglio. Twice life-size.

137. Aldborough area, North Yorkshire: gold finger-ring. Twice life-size.

138. Lacock, Wiltshire: silver finger-ring.

139. Chettle, Dorset: iron hipposandal.

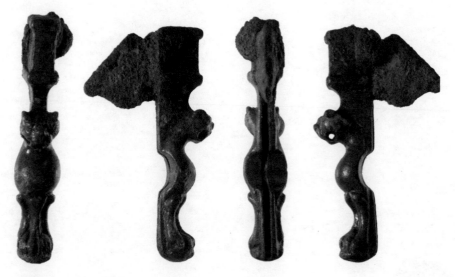

140. Wickham Skeith, Suffolk: copper-alloy
folding knife handle.

141. Ropley, Hampshire: copper-alloy folding
knife handle.

142. Bedford area, Bedfordshire: copper-alloy mount.

143. Mansfield Woodhouse area, Nottinghamshire: lead amulet.
Twice life-size.

144. Chenies area, Buckinghamshire: copper-alloy dog figurine.

145. Narborough, Leicestershire: copper-alloy seal-ring. Twice life-size.
Illustration: David Williams.

146. Alcester, Warwickshire: silver spoon fragment.
Twice life-size.

148. Gunthorpe, Norfolk: gold brooch.
Twice life-size.

147. Horton, south Gloucestershire: copper-alloy buckle.

149. South Brent, Devon: copper-alloy brooch. Twice life-size.

150. Warmington, Warwickshire: copper-alloy buckle plate.

151. Urchfont, Wiltshire: silver buckle.
Twice life-size.

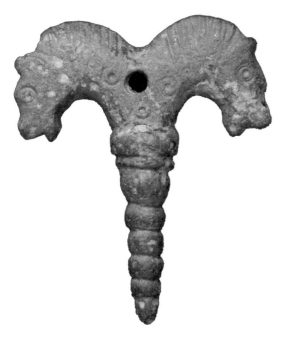

152. Stiffkey, Norfolk: copper-alloy pendant. Twice life-size.

153. Vindolanda, Northumberland: silver ingot.

154. Newby Wiske, North Yorkshire: copper-alloy brooch.

155. Greywell, Hampshire: copper-alloy sword scabbard chape.

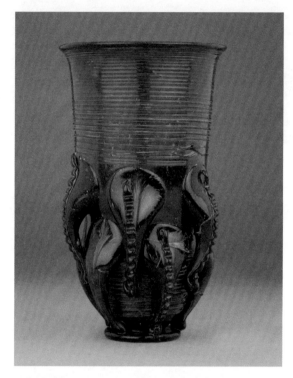

156. North Kesteven, Lincolnshire: copper-alloy brooch.

157. Ringlemere, Kent: glass claw beaker. Not life-size.

158. West Wight, Isle of Wight: gold Gallic imitative *solidus* in the name of Anastasius I. Twice life-size.

159. Wendover, Buckinghamshire: gilded
copper-alloy brooch.

160. Mildenhall, Wiltshire: copper-alloy bowl with iron handle.
Quarter life-size.

161. Haversham, Buckinghamshire: copper-alloy belt mount.
Twice life-size.

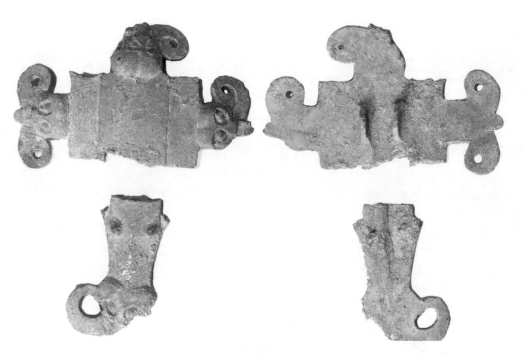

162. East Yorkshire: lead-alloy brooch.

163. Marham, Norfolk: silver
brooch fragment. Twice life-size.

164. Worth, Kent: gold coin pendant.
Twice life-size.

165. Treswell, Nottinghamshire: gilt copper-alloy brooch. Half life-size.

166. North Hertfordshire: silver-gilt pyramidal mount. Twice life-size.

167. Chilton Trinity, Somerset: silver pin-head. Twice life-size.

168. Fransham, Norfolk: silver-gilt fragment, probably from a brooch. Twice life-size.

169. Weston Colville,
Cambridgeshire: silver-gilt
pyramidal mount. Twice life-size.

172. Ramsgate, Kent: gold annular pendant. Twice life-size.

170. Otford, Kent: silver-gilt pin-head.
Twice life-size.

173. Binbrook, Lincolnshire: copper-alloy hanging bowl mount.

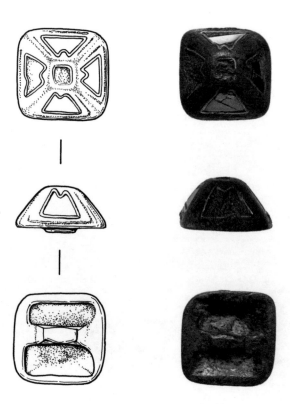

171. Diss area, Norfolk silver-gilt pyramidal sword mount.
Twice life-size.

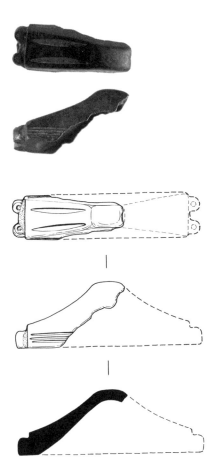

174. Woodbridge area, Suffolk: silver-gilt sword pommel fragment. Illustration: Donna Wreathall.

175. Carisbrooke, Isle of Wight: copper-alloy *Pressblech* die. Twice life-size.

176. Mileham, Norfolk: silver-gilt sword pommel cap. Twice life-size.

177. Frisby and Kirby, Leicestershire: copper-alloy mount.
Twice life-size.

178. Tuxford area, Nottinghamshire: silver and glass setting.
Twice life-size.

179. Chelmsford area, Essex: gold and garnet cloisonné setting.
Twice life-size.

180. Hatton, Lincolnshire: gold gem-set setting.
Twice life-size.

181. Newark area, Nottinghamshire: gold and garnet cross-pendant.

182. Broughton, Hampshire: copper-alloy hanging-bowl escutcheon.

184. Streethouse area, Redcar and Cleveland: gold pendant and gold and glass beads.

183. Llanbedrgoch, Anglesey: hack-silver.

185. Ely, Cambridgeshire: glass palm cup and gold pendants.
Various sizes.

186. North East Suffolk: silver strap-end. Twice life-size.

187. Denton with Wootton, Kent: silver hooked-tag. Twice life-size.

189. North Tuddenham, Norfolk: silver brooch fragment. Twice life-size.

188. Coberley, Gloucestershire: silver hooked-tag. Twice life-size.

190. Long Sutton, Somerset: silver hooked-tag. Twice life-size.

191. Woodbridge area, Suffolk: silver polyhedral pin.
Twice life-size.

194. Crawley, Hampshire: silver hooked-tag. Twice life-size.

192. Southampton area, Hampshire: silver strap-end.
Twice life-size.

195. Whitchurch area, Shropshire: copper-alloy mount.

193. Urchfont, Wiltshire: copper-alloy mount from a hanging bowl.

352 | EARLY MEDIEVAL

196. South Gloucestershire: copper-alloy
strap-end. Twice life-size.

199. Milborne Port, Somerset: silver hooked-tag.
Twice life-size.

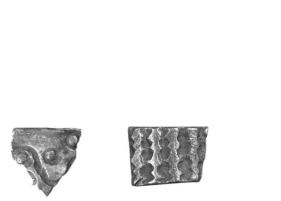

197. North Yorkshire area: hack-silver. Twice life-size.

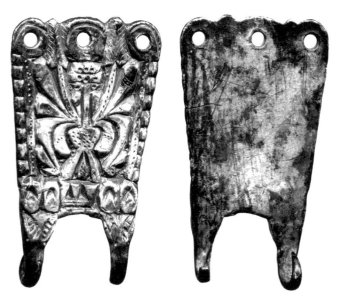

200. Charminster, Dorset: silver hooked-tag.
Twice life-size.

198. Willington area, Derbyshire: silver mount. Twice life-size.

201. Weston Colville, Cambridgeshire: silver strap-end fragment. Twice life-size.

204. Newark area, Nottinghamshire: gold finger-ring. Twice life-size.

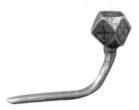

202. West Acre, Norfolk: silver pin.

203. Brampton Abbotts, Herefordshire: silver hooked-tag. Twice life-size.

205. North of Colchester, Essex: copper-alloy strap-end. Twice life-size.

206. Roxby cum Risby, North Lincolnshire: silver ingot fragment. Twice life-size.

207. Corby area, Northamptonshire: lead vat or tank. Quarter life-size.

208. Snape with Thorpe, North Yorkshire: hack-silver brooch fragment. Twice life-size.

211. Ringshall, Suffolk: silver ingot. Twice life-size.

209. Maunby, North Yorkshire: gold ring. Twice life-size.

210. Grindale, East Yorkshire: silver finger-ring. Twice life-size.

212. Kirk Deighton area, North Yorkshire:
gold finger-ring. Twice life-size.

213. Talgarth, Powys: silver ingot. Twice life-size.

214. Plumpton, East Sussex: copper-alloy brooch. Twice life-size.

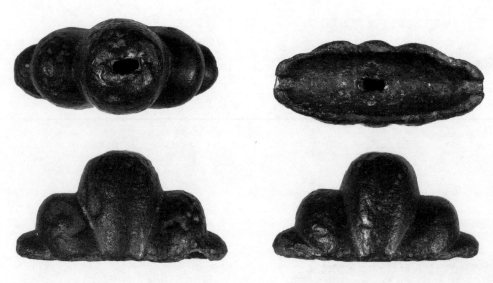

215. Fylde, Lancashire: copper-alloy sword pommel cap.

216. Bridlington, East Yorkshire: silver finger-ring.
Twice life-size.

217. Vale of York, North Yorkshire: silver-gilt cup, gold arm-ring, hack silver and coins. Not life-size.

218. North Hertfordshire: copper-alloy knife chape.

219. Little Laver, Essex: copper-alloy strap-end.

220. Risby, Suffolk: copper-alloy possible upper sword-guard.

221. Ringland, Norfolk: copper-alloy staff terminal.

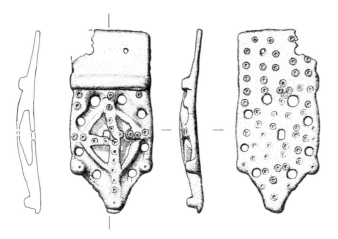

222. East Kirkby, Lincolnshire: copper-alloy strap-end.

223. Worfield area, Shropshire: copper-alloy buckle and plate.

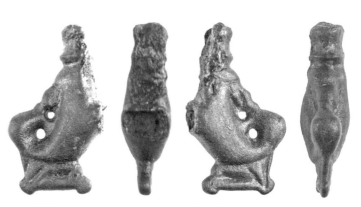

225. Tarrant Rushton, Dorset: copper-alloy stirrup terminal.

224. Ware area, Hertfordshire: gilded silver coin-pendant.
Not life-size.

226. Eye, Suffolk: silver probable pendant. Twice life-size.

227. South Gloucestershire: copper-alloy buckle with integral plate.

228. Ogbourne St Andrew, Wiltshire: copper-alloy probable strap union or junction.

229. City of London: bone counter.

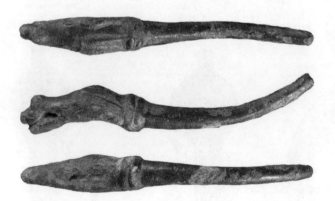

230. Bedford area, Bedfordshire: copper-alloy possible tool handle.

231. Betchworth, Surrey: gilded copper-alloy buckle plate.
Twice life-size.

35. Beckingham, Lincolnshire: bone chess piece.

232. Port Eynon, Gower, Swansea: silver finger-ring.
Twice life-size.

233. Long Whatton, Leicestershire: silver finger-ring.
Twice life-size.

234. Rhoose, Vale of Glamorgan: gold finger-ring.
Twice life-size.

236. Diss area, Suffolk: gold finger-ring.
Twice life-size.

237. Beverley area, East Yorkshire: gold finger-ring. Twice life-size.

240. Rampisham, Dorset: gold finger-ring. Twice life-size.

238. Llanfair, Vale of Glamorgan: gold finger-ring. Twice life-size.

241. Kington St Michael, Wiltshire: gilded copper-alloy enamel panel from a processional cross.

239. Middleton on Sea area, West Sussex: copper-alloy heraldic horse harness pendant. Twice life-size.

242. Rock, Worcestershire: lead papal *bulla* of Celestine III.

243. Portskewett, Monmouthshire: copper-alloy figurine of Christ. Twice life-size.

244. Leatherhead, Surrey: lead seal matrix. Twice life-size.

245. Wherwell, Hampshire: copper-alloy zoomorphic annular brooch.

248. Diss area, Suffolk: gold finger-ring.
Twice life-size.

246. Boxley, Kent: gold oval brooch.
Three times life-size.

249. Llanddewi, Gower, Swansea: silver
brooch. Twice life-size.

247. South-east Norfolk: silver-gilt pendant cross.
Twice life-size.

252. Langley with Hardley, Norfolk: silver signet ring. Twice life-size.

250. Lower Dean, Bedfordshire: inscribed silver-gilt finger-ring. Twice life-size.

251. Osmington, Dorset: silver-gilt pendant with intaglio. Twice life-size.

253. Callow, Derbyshire: copper-alloy tap-housing with spout. Half life-size.

254. Theydon Garnon, Essex: silver finger-ring.
Twice life-size.

255. Brookland, Kent: silver-gilt finger-ring.
Twice life-size.

256. Gatcombe area, Isle of Wight: pilgrim's lead *ampulla*.

257. Wressle, East Yorkshire: mirror case.

258. Crimplesham, Norfolk: silver-gilt brooch.
Twice life-size.

259. Winchester area, Hampshire: silver bar-mount.
Twice life-size.

260. Ilam, Staffordshire: copper-alloy oval buckle. Twice life-size.

261. Leziate, Norfolk: silver seal matrix. Twice life-size.

262. Blore with Swinscoe, Staffordshire: copper/lead-alloy
sword pommel.

263. Old Buckenham, Norfolk: silver coin-brooch or mount.
Twice life-size.

264. Paull, East Yorkshire: gilded coin brooch. Twice life-size.

265. Wragby area, Lincolnshire: lead/tin pilgrim badge.

267. Sealfield, North Yorkshire: silver seal matrix. Twice life-size.

266. Ludgvan, Cornwall: copper-alloy (possible) weight.

268. Dunstable, Bedfordshire: silver-gilt brooch in the form of a finger-ring.
Twice life-size.

269. Wetheringsett cum Brockford, Suffolk: copper-alloy sword pommel.
Not actual size.

270. Arncliffe, North Yorkshire: copper-alloy pyx lid.
Not actual size.

271. Nether Wallop, Hampshire: copper-alloy seal matrix. Twice life-size.

274. Kelvedon, Essex: silver-gilt oval brooch. Twice life-size.

275. Finchingfield, Essex: inscribed silver finger-ring. Twice life-size.

272. North Somerset: copper-alloy annular brooch. Twice life-size.

273. Winchester area, Hampshire: silver-gilt bar-mount. Twice life-size.

276. South Gloucestershire area: silver-gilt brooch.
Twice life-size.

277. Wonston, Hampshire: silver scabbard chape.
Twice life-size.

278. Old Kirk Field area, Hartlepool, County Durham: inscribed silver brooch.
Twice life-size.

279. Binbrook, Lincolnshire: inscribed silver brooch.
Twice life-size.

280. Brookland, Kent: silver-gilt finger-ring.
Twice life-size.

281. Long Marston, North Yorkshire: silver pendant-cross.
Twice life-size.

282. Walgrave, Northamptonshire: silver
scabbard chape. Twice life-size.

283. Wingfield, Wiltshire: unfinished silver finger-ring.
Twice life-size.

284. Tywardreath, Cornwall: lead papal *bulla*.

285. West Clandon, Surrey: silver *piedfort*. Not actual size.

286. Harlaston, Staffordshire: inscribed gold finger-ring.
Twice life-size.

287. Maiden Newton area, Dorset: copper-alloy strap-end.
Twice life-size.

289. Churton by Aldford, Cheshire: copper-alloy harness pendant.

288. Bradfield, Essex: copper-alloy buckle frame.

290. Winwick, Cheshire: gold finger-ring.
Twice life-size.

291. Charminster, Dorset: engraved silver
strap-end. Twice life-size.

292. South Wingfield, Derbyshire:
gold finger-ring. Twice life-size.

293. Great Smeaton, North Yorkshire: silver-gilt pendant reliquary.
Twice life-size.

294. Urchfont, Wiltshire: silver ivy-leaf pendant.
Twice life-size.

295. Bonby, North Lincolnshire: silver-gilt finger-ring.
Twice life-size.

298. Diss area, Suffolk: gold finger-ring.
Twice life-size.

296. Pontefract, West Yorkshire: silver cross-pendant.
Twice life-size.

297. Aldbrough, North Yorkshire: gold finger-ring.
Twice life-size.

299. Hound, Hampshire: silver mount.
Twice life-size.

300. Coberley, Gloucestershire: silver-gilt finger-ring.
Twice life-size.

301. Thurlaston, Leicestershire: gold finger-ring.
Twice life-size.

302. Dinas Powys, Vale of Glamorgan: gold finger-ring.
Twice life-size.

303. Swallowfield, West Berkshire: gold brooch.

304. Naburn, City of York: gold finger-ring. Twice life-size.

305. Worksop, Nottinghamshire: copper-alloy fertility badge.

306. Brill, Buckinghamshire: lead-alloy (possible) ink holder.

307. Stoughton area, West Sussex:
silver-gilt signet ring. Twice life-size.

308. Lydd, Kent: gold finger-ring. Twice life-size.

311. Cerne Abbas, Dorset: silver-gilt dress fitting.
Twice life-size.

309. Coberley, Gloucestershire: silver-gilt fragment in the form
of a human arm.

312. Penllyn, Vale of Glamorgan: lead *ampulla*.

310. Penllyn, Vale of Glamorgan: silver brooch. Twice life-size.

313. Lund, East Yorkshire: copper-alloy pilgrim badge.
Twice life-size.

314. Elmstead, Essex: copper-alloy devotional badge depicting the Crucifixion.
Twice life-size.

315. Tower Hamlets, London: silver girdle terminal.

316. Great Gaddesen, Hertfordshire: gold rectangular mount.
Twice life-size.

317. Lancaster area, Lancashire: silver crucifix pendant.
Twice life-size.

318. Barham, Kent: engraved silver mount. Twice life size.

319. Bletchingley, Surrey: copper-alloy harness boss. Not life-size.

320. Telford area, Shropshire: copper-alloy purse bar.

321. Kilgetty, Pembrokeshire: silver-gilt pendant.
Twice life-size.

322. Vernhams Dean, Hampshire: silver-gilt finger-ring.
Twice life-size.

323. Paul, Cornwall: copper-alloy signet finger-ring.
Twice life-size.

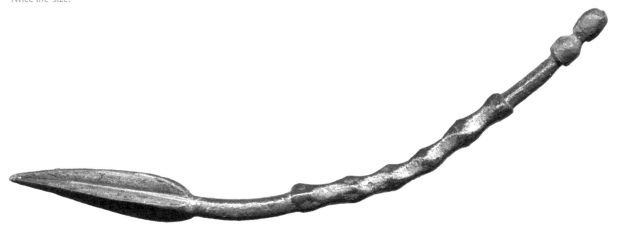

324. Chettle, Dorset: copper-alloy pen.
Twice life-size.

325. Great Barton, Suffolk: copper-alloy bell with heraldic arms.

326. Harlaston, Staffordshire: silver coin brooch.

327. Barrow, Suffolk: lead pilgrim badge. Twice life-size.

331. Carnforth area, Lancashire: silver hooked clasp.

328. Bluntisham, Cambridgeshire: silver trefoil hooked clasp. Twice life-size.

332. Wentlooge, Monmouthshire: silver-gilt hooked-clasp. Twice life-size.

329. Kelsale cum Carlton, Suffolk: silver-gilt circular hooked clasp. Twice life-size.

333. North Yorkshire: silver-gilt cap hook. Twice life-size.

330. East Hertfordshire: silver-gilt hooked clasp. Twice life-size.

334. Durnford, Wiltshire: silver-gilt dress-pin.

335. Mercaston, Derbyshire: silver-
gilt dress-pin.

339. South Herefordshire: enamelled silver armorial (possible)
vervel pendant. Twice life-size.

336. Emneth, Norfolk: silver rumbler bell. Twice life-size.

337. Garthorpe, Leicestershire: silver 'bosun's' whistle.
Not actual size.

340. Llancarfan, Vale of Glamorgan: silver-gilt dress-hook loop.
Not actual size.

338. Alberbury with Cardeston area, Shropshire: lead-
alloy bird-feed or water container. Size?

341. Whitchurch area, Cheshire:
gold finger-ring. Not actual size.

342. Udimore, East Sussex: silver seal matrix.
Twice life-size.

343. Oulton, Staffordshire: gold finger-ring.
Not actual size.

344. Holme, North Lincolnshire: gold finger-ring.
Twice life-size.

345. Winterbourne, Wiltshire: gold finger-ring.
Twice life-size.

346. Gussage All Saints, Dorset: copper-alloy knife-handle terminal.
Twice life-size.

347. Foulsham, Norfolk: silver shield-shaped vervel.
Twice life-size.

348. Newent, Gloucestershire: silver-gilt finger-ring.
Twice life-size.

349. Swallowfield area, Oxfordshire: gold finger-ring.
Twice life-size.

350. Edgefield, Norfolk: gold finger-ring.
Twice life-size.

353. Ilam, Staffordshire: copper-alloy manilla.

351. Wootton Wawen, Warwickshire: silver decade
finger-ring. Not actual size.

352. Emneth, Norfolk: silver hawking vervel.
Not actual size.

354. Higher Kinnerton, Flintshire: lead toy figurine.

355. Chiseldon, Wiltshire: lead toy figurine. Twice life-size.

356. Pocklington area, East Yorkshire: lead toy figurine.

357. Crowle, North Lincolnshire: copper-alloy toy multiple cauldron.

358. Beaumont area, Essex: copper-alloy socketed candlestick.

359. Stoulton, Worcestershire: lead cloth seal.
Twice life-size.

362. Kenn, North Somerset: gold finger-ring.
Twice life-size.

360. Market Rasen, Lincolnshire: gold finger-ring.
Twice life-size.

363. Westbury-on-Severn, Gloucestershire: gold finger-ring.
Twice life-size.

361. Everleigh, Wiltshire: gold finger-ring. Twice life-size.

364. Soham area, Cambridgeshire: gold finger-ring.
Twice life-size.

368. Lapley, Stretton and Wheaton Aston,
Staffordshire: silver bell. Not actual size.

365. Buckingham, Buckinghamshire: gold finger-ring.
Twice life-size.

369. Kelvedon, Essex: inscribed silver thimble. Twice life-size.

366. Penllyn, Vale of Glamorgan: silver-gilt finger ring.
Twice life-size.

367. Emneth, Norfolk: silver-gilt finger-ring. Twice life-size.

370. Wantage Down area, Oxfordshire: inscribed silver seal matrix.
Twice life-size.

371. City of London, London: iron knife. Twice life-size.

372. Brearton, North Yorkshire: copper-alloy ring with four seal matrices .

373. Stanton Drew, Gloucestershire: copper-alloy quadruple seal matrix.

375. City of London: stone musket ball mould.

374. Shenley, Hertfordshire: silver seal matrix. Twice life-size.

376. Coxhoe, County Durham: silver seal matrix. Not actual size.

377. Atcham, Shropshire: ceramic vessel. Quarter life-size.

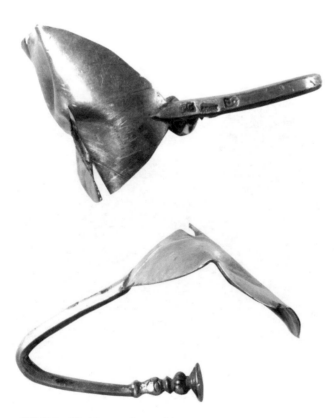

378. Oving, West Sussex: silver seal-top spoon.

379. Tendring area, Essex: silver pendant of Charles I.
Twice life-size.

382. East of Colchester, Essex: silver locket fragment.
Twice life-size.

380. Drayton Bassett, Staffordshire: silver pendant of Charles I.
Twice life-size.

381. Mildenhall, Wiltshire: copper-alloy enamelled buckle.
Twice life-size.

383. Runhall, Norfolk: silver pendant medallion. Twice life-size.

384. Itchen Valley, Hampshire: silver medal of Charles II.
Twice life-size.

386. Old Radnor, Powys: silver hawking whistle.
Twice life-size.

385. South Creake, Norfolk: gold finger-ring.
Twice life-size.

387. Nash Mills, Hertfordshire: lead cloth seal.

388. Snape, North Yorkshire: silver (possible) cockspur. Not life-size.

389. Belton and Manthorpe, Lincolnshire: lead hornbook. Twice life-size.

390. Holmer area, Herefordshire: silver seal matrix. Twice life-size.

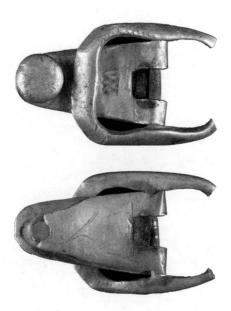

391. Droxford, Hampshire: silver shoe buckle.
Twice life-size.

393. Thurlaston, Leicestershire: silver double-sided seal matrix.
Twice life-size.

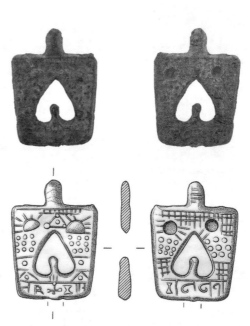

394. Penkridge, Staffordshire: lead, possible hornbook handle.
Illustration: Jane Goddard.

392. Binton, Warwickshire: copper-alloy spoon.
Half life-size.

395. Boxgrove, West Sussex: gold mourning ring.
Not life-size.

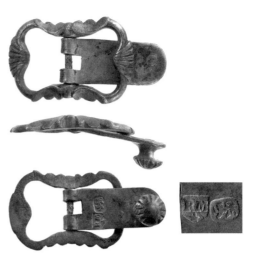

399. Newport area, Isle of Wight: silver shoe buckle.
Twice life-size.

396. South-east Lancashire: silver cufflinks. Twice life-size.

397. Ropley, Hampshire: silver double-sided seal matrix.
Twice life-size.

400. Wimborne Minster, Dorset: glass bottle.

398. Phillack, Cornwall: silver bodkin.

401. Overton, Flintshire: gold touch-piece of James II. Not life-size.

402. Kensworth, Bedfordshire: gold mourning ring. Not life-size.

403. Hawton, Nottinghamshire: gold mourning ring. Not life-size.

404. West Crewkerne, Somerset: silver thimble. Twice life-size.

405. Bures area, Essex: copper-alloy pipe tamper.

406. Broughton-in-Furness, Cumbria: gilt copper-alloy seal matrix.

407. Plumley, Cheshire: lead owl figurine.

408. Buttercrambe with Bossall, North Yorkshire: gold mourning ring.
Not life-size.

409. Bridestowe, Devon: ceramic jug. Half life-size.

410. Milborne Port, Somerset: gold and *niello* mourning ring.
Twice life-size.

411. Guildford, Surrey: copper-alloy clog clasp.
Twice life-size.

412. Brecon, Powys: silver finger-ring bezel with intaglio. Twice life-size.

413. Ambleside, Cumbria: copper-alloy pipe tamper.

414. Ryde, Isle of Wight: lead pugilist figurine.

416. Twickenham, London: leather shoe.
Not actual size.

415. Woolley, West Yorkshire: iron sword.
One tenth life-size.

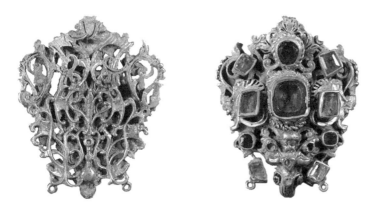

417. Padstow, Cornwall: silver-gilt jewelled pendant.

418. Landford, Wiltshire: gold fob-seal matrix. Twice life-size.

419. Hurst Green, East Sussex: lead/tin toy milk churn.

421. Duffryn Ardudwy, Gwynedd: silver finger-ring.
Twice life-size.

422. City of London: stone scarab.

420. Kirkham, Lancashire: copper-alloy pet coffin.

423. Shalfleet, Isle of Wight: lead gaming piece.

424. Penrith, Cumbria: ceramic gaming piece. Twice life-size.

425. Exeter, Devon: tin ration container. Half life-size.

426. Wellingore, Lincolnshire: white-metal German military tag.
Twice life-size.

427. Little Horwood (addenda), Buckinghamshire: two gold *staters*. Twice life-size.

429. Urchfont, Wiltshire: two silver units. Twice life-size.

430. Westerham (3rd addenda), Kent: gold quarter *staters*. Twice life-size.

428. Saxilby, Lincolnshire: four gold *staters*.

431. Beverley (addenda), East Yorkshire: North-Eastern (Corieltavian) gold *staters*.

433. North Dalton, East Yorkshire (1st addenda): four North-Eastern (Corieltavian) coins.

432. East Leicestershire (1st addenda): two silver units. Twice life-size.

437. Sissinghurst, Kent: Gallo-Belgic
gold *stater*.

434. Driffield area (addenda), East Yorkshire:
three North-Eastern (Corieltavian) gold *staters*.

438. Calbourne area, Isle of Wight: Gallo-Belgic gold *stater*.
Twice life-size.

435. Driffield area (addenda), East Yorkshire:
two North-Eastern (Corieltavian) gold *staters*.

436 Nettleton, Lincolnshire: Carthaginian
copper-alloy unit. Twice life-size.

439. Longwick cum Ilmer, Buckinghamshire:
Gaulish copper-alloy *potin*.

444. Willingdon and Jevington, East Sussex: Gallo-Belgic gold
quarter *stater*. Twice life-size.

440. Osbournby, Lincolnshire: copper-alloy *potin*.

445. Chichester area, West Sussex: Gallo-Belgic gold *stater*.
Twice life-size.

441. Stopham, West Sussex: silver unit of Eastern Gaul.
Twice life-size.

446. Gwithian, Cornwall: Armorican
base-silver *stater*.

442. North Hertfordshire: contemporary
copy (gold-plated *stater)* of Addedomaros.

447. Welbourn, Lincolnshire: North-Eastern
(Corieltavian) gold quarter *stater*.

443. Micheldever, Hampshire:
copper-alloy *potin*.

448. Chichester area, West Sussex:
copper-alloy unit.

449. Eastbourne area, East Sussex: Southern (Atrebatic) silver unit. Twice life-size.

454. Isle of Wight: Armorican silver fractional unit. Twice life-size.

450. Cliffe, Kent: Kentish (Cantii) silver unit. Twice life-size.

455. Shoreham by Sea, West Sussex: silver unit of Tincomarus.

451. Wickham Skeith, Suffolk: Kentish (Cantii) copper-alloy unit.

456. Newchurch area, Isle of Wight: Southern (Atrebatic) gold *stater* of Tincomarus.

452. Findon area, West Sussex: South Western (Durotrigan) silver half unit.

457. Newton Blossomville, Buckinghamshire: Eastern (Trinovantian) gold *stater* of Andoco.

453. Tarrant Monkton, Dorset: South Western uninscribed silver *stater*.

458. Isle of Wight: Southern silver unit inscribed CRAB. Twice life-size.

No's 459-461 no image.

462. Cotton, Suffolk: Republican silver
denarius of Lepidus.

463. Lanivet, Cornwall: Republican
silver *denarius* of Mark Antony.

464. Calbourne, Isle of Wight:
silver *denarius* of Augustus.

465. Niton and Whitwell, Isle of Wight:
copper *as* of Augustus or Tiberius.

466. Dorchester, Oxfordshire: copper
quadrans of Claudius.

467. Great Hale, Lincolnshire:
silver *denarius* of Galba.

468. Goostrey, Cheshire: copper-alloy *quadrans*.

469. Clipstone, Nottinghamshire: silver *drachm*
of King Nahapana.

470. Whitchurch area, Cheshire:
three silver *denarii*.

No's 471, 474–480, 482–488 no image.

472. Petworth area, West Sussex: 103 silver *denarii* and associated pottery. Not life-size.

473. North Dalton, East Yorkshire: three silver *denarii*.

489. Storrington, West Sussex: 16 copper-alloy *radiates*.

481. Wiggington, Hertfordshire: copper-alloy *dupondius* of Trajan.

490. Ashbourne area, Derbyshire: two gold *aurei* of Carausius.

491. Lutterworth, Leicestershire:
gold *aureus* of Gordian III.

496. Chedzoy, Somerset:
copper-alloy *radiate* of Carausius.

492. Pavenham, Bedfordshire:
copper *as* of Philip I.

497. Greywell, Hampshire:
copper-alloy *radiate* of Carausius.

493. Crondall, Hampshire:
copper-alloy 'Limesfalschung' *as*.

498. Hinton on the Green, Worcestershire: copper-alloy
radiate of Carausius in the name of Diocletian.

494. Chichester area, West Sussex:
copper-alloy *radiate* of Carausius.

499. Stanton area, Derbyshire: copper-alloy *nummi*.

495. Shalfleet, Isle of Wight:
copper-alloy *radiate* of Carausius.

No. 501, 503–508 no image.

500. Barking, Suffolk: base-silver *nummi* hoard in situ.

502. St Paul with Malmesbury, Wiltshire:
37 copper-alloy *nummi* and one copper-alloy *as*.

509. Cambridge, Cambridgeshire: copper-alloy *nummus* of
Constantine I, commemorating Constantius I.

510. Salisbury area, Wiltshire: gold *aureus* of Licinius I.

511. Thoresby, Lincolnshire:
copper-alloy *nummus* of Constantine I.

512. Wood Enderby, Lincolnshire:
copper-alloy *nummus* of Crispus.

513. Chipping Norton, Oxfordshire:
copper-alloy *nummus* of Constantine.

516. Fulstow, Lincolnshire: two lead tablets with
impressions of a coin of Valens.

514. Chichester area, West Sussex:
silver *siliqua* of Jovian. Twice life-size.

515. Bermondsey, Rotherhithe and Southwark,
London: copper-alloy *nummus* of Valens.

517. West Wight, Isle of Wight: copper-alloy
nummus of Procopius.

No's 520–522, 524 & 526 no image.

518. Silverstone, Northamptonshire:
gold *solidus* of Gratian.

519. West Wight, Isle of Wight:
copper-alloy *nummus* of Arcadius.

523. Saxmundham area, Suffolk: two gold *solidi*.

525. Fareham, Hampshire: two gold *solidi*.

527. Whittington, Northumberland:
nummus of Gloria Romanorum, 3
emperor type.

528. Single, Isle of Wight: gold *solidus*
(contemporary copy) of Anastasius I.

529. Kings Stanley, Gloucestershire:
copper-alloy *follis* of Justinian I.

530. Langport, Somerset: copper-alloy
half-follis of Justinian I.

531. North Yorkshire: gold *solidus* of Phocas.

532. Bradford Peverell, Dorset: three Anglo-Saxon silver pennies. Twice life-size.

534. Alfriston area, East Sussex: two fused silver pennies.

535. Wymondham, Norfolk: five fused Anglo-Saxon silver pennies.

536. Henley area, Oxfordshire: three fused Anglo-Saxon silver pennies.

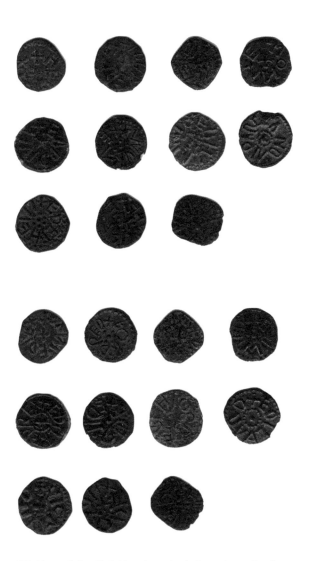

537. Arreton area, Isle of Wight: two Anglo-Saxon silver pennies of Æthelred II.

538. Cawood, North Yorkshire: gold *tremissis*. Twice life-size.

533. Harswell, East Yorkshire: eleven Anglo-Saxon base-silver/copper-alloy coins.

No. 546 no image.

539. Ware area, Hertfordshire: Merovingian silver *denier*. Twice life-size.

540. Peckleton, Leicestershire: silver penny of Offa of Mercia.

541. Southwell area, Nottinghamshire: silver penny of Eadwald of East Anglia.

542. Ropley, Hampshire: silver penny of Cuthred of Kent.

543. Newport, Isle of Wight: silver penny of Ecgberht of Wessex.

544. Crawley, Hampshire: silver halfpenny of Eadred.

545. Bigby, North East Lincolnshire: nine silver pennies of John.

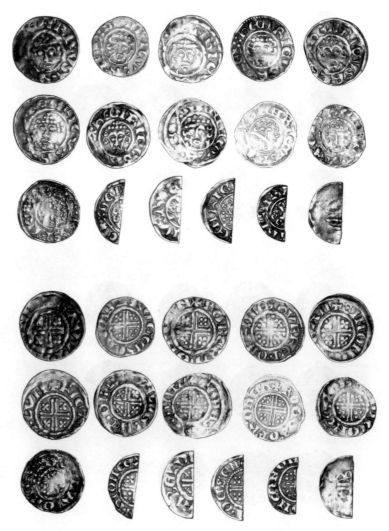

547. Wellow, Bath and North East Somerset: sixteen silver pennies.

548. Corley, Warwickshire: silver coin hoard
(selection).

No's 549, 551–553 & 557 no image.

550. Deopham area, Norfolk: silver penny hoard.

554. Ysceifiog, Flintshire: three silver pennies
of Edward I–II.

556. Astleys, Coventry, West Midlands: silver penny hoard
(selection).

555. Low Apley, Lincolnshire: 146 silver pennies.
Not life-size.

558. Kirkby Stephen, Cumbria: silver half groat of
Edward III.

No's 561, 563 no image.

559. Myddle and Broughton, Shropshire (addenda): gold *dobla* of Pedro I of Castile.

562. Hitcham, Suffolk: Two silver double *patards*.

564. Woking, Surrey: cut halfpenny of William I.

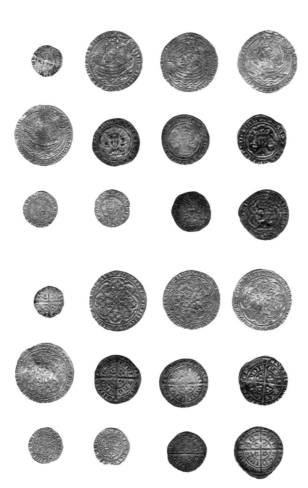

565. Brighstone, Isle of Wight: silver Continental sterling penny imitation.

560. Beulah Hill, Croydon, Greater London (addenda): 12 gold and silver coins. Not life-size.

No. 570 no image.

566. Ston Easton, Somerset: gold noble of Edward III.

567. Hull area, East Yorkshire: silver Blanc *guenar* of
Charles VI of France.

569. Basingstoke area, Hampshire: three silver coins.

568. Ambrosden, Oxfordshire:
gold quarter noble of Henry V.

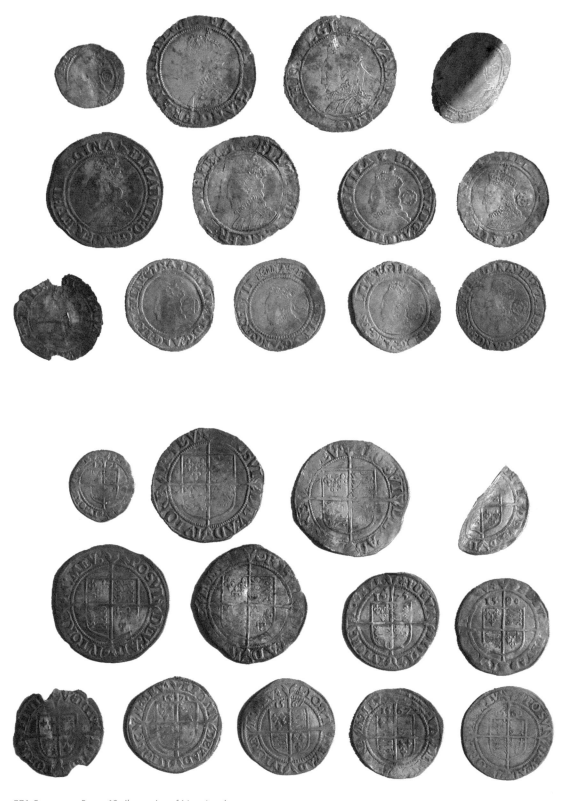

571. Bures area, Essex: 13 silver coins of Mary I and
Elizabeth I.

572. West Tanfield, North Yorkshire: three fused sixpences.

573. Nailstone, Leicestershire: four silver coins of Elizabeth I and James I.

574. West Crewkerne, Somerset: ten silver coins. Not life-size.

No. 578 no image.

579. Linstead Magna, Suffolk: gold *ecu d'or au soleil de Bretagne* of Francis I of France.

575. Ham and Stone, Gloucestershire: two silver pennies and a halfgroat with perforations. Twice life-size.

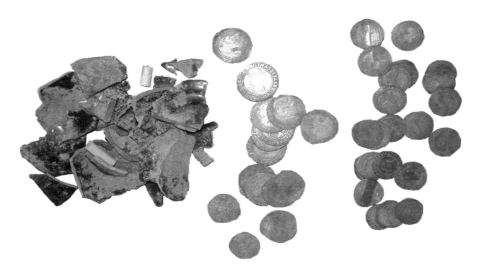

576. Welshpool, Powys: 40 silver coins and ceramic pot. Not life-size.

577. Rutland: 245 silver coins. Not life-size.

580. Great Yeldham, Essex: silver half *denga* of Ivan IV of Russia. Twice life-size.

581. Ringmer, East Sussex: copper-alloy token of Joseph Easton of Boreham.

582. Exeter, Devon: silver eight *reales* of Charles II of Spain.

583. Letcombe Regis, Oxfordshire: copper-alloy farthing of William III.

584. Laughton, Lincolnshire: a copper-alloy *paisa* of Emperor Muhammad Akbar II.